F
341
.H28

Harris, William Charles

The day of the carpet-
bagger

DATE DUE			

D1453074

The Day of the Carpetbagger

The Day of the
Carpetbagger

Republican Reconstruction
in Mississippi

WILLIAM C. HARRIS

Louisiana State University Press
Baton Rouge and London

Copyright © 1979 by Louisiana State University Press
All rights reserved
Manufactured in the United States of America
Designer: Albert Crochet
Typeface: VIP Caledonia
Typesetter: G & S Typesetters, Inc., Austin, Texas
Printer and Binder: Thomson-Shore, Inc.

LIBRARY OF CONGRESS CATALOGING IN PUBLICATION DATA

Harris, William Charles, 1933–
    The day of the carpetbagger: Republican Reconstruction in Mississippi.

    Continues the author's Presidential Reconstruction in Mississippi.
    Bibliography: p.
    Includes index.
    1. Reconstruction—Mississippi.   2.   Mississippi—Politics and government—
1865–1950.   I.   Title.
F341.H28   976.2'06   78–18779
ISBN 0–8071–0366–7

To my wife
Betty Glenn Harris

Contents

Illustrations

Following page 96

Map

Preface

A century has passed since carpetbag Governor Adelbert Ames, facing impeachment charges, resigned his office and fled north, marking the end of Republican Reconstruction in Mississippi. Even before Ames and his counterparts in other southern states gave up the fight for a new political order in the post-Civil War South, the baleful legend of Reconstruction was unfolding and by the twentieth century would become ingrained in the American as well as the southern consciousness. Indeed, no period in American history has been subjected to anything approaching the defamation that the Reconstruction era has suffered.

During the past three or more decades a steadily increasing corps of revisionist historians have labored zealously to correct the traditional interpretation of Reconstruction. Nevertheless, the impact of their work has been little felt outside the historical profession. To be sure, the Reconstruction myth that black participation in politics was a mistake has been debunked. This change, however, came about because of the force of mid-twentieth-century events and owed little to the scholarly reevaluation of the role of blacks in Reconstruction affairs. The legend that Reconstruction was a dark and regrettable episode in southern history remains a part of the common lore.

In spite of the persistence of the Reconstruction myth—indeed, because of it—the work of studying and revising the story of the Republican era needs to continue. Perhaps the influence of a continuing stream of revisionist books and articles will eventually have the desired effect, and Reconstruction will lose its popular image as a sordid aberration of the American past. This book, though not always in agreement with recent revisionist historians, attempts to contribute in a small way to the emergence of such an awareness.

The book is a comprehensive account of Reconstruction in one southern state, Mississippi, and it is designed to reveal in a reasonably full measure the impact of military reconstruction and Repub-

lican civil rule on the people of the state. Mississippi, a state in
which blacks constituted a majority of the population and which experienced military and Republican control for almost nine years
(1867–1876), offers an excellent setting for an in-depth examination
of the so-called Radical period of Reconstruction. In writing about
postwar Mississippi, I am competing with the works of two able
predecessors, James W. Garner, a traditional historian of Reconstruction, and Vernon Lane Wharton, a revisionist whose book
focuses on black Mississippians from 1865 to 1890. It is my hope
that the use of additional sources and the perspective of time have
permitted me to build successfully on their fine accounts.

Although the framework for the study is political, an examination
of contemporary sources reveals that the minds of most Mississippians, both black and white, were not preoccupied with the politics
of Reconstruction, however significant or exciting the political
campaigns might have been. Problems of recovery and adjustment
from the devastating effects of the Civil War lingered into the
1870s and caused Mississippians to give high priority to domestic
concerns and the compelling need to regain their livelihoods. Their
response to political developments during Reconstruction frequently was conditioned by their overwhelming concern for economic rehabilitation and local social stability. Therefore, the perceptions that people had of events and affairs were a powerful force
in Mississippi Reconstruction. In describing these perceptions and
relating them to postwar issues and developments, I have tried to
do justice to all elements and participants in the Reconstruction
story.

I have not attempted a detailed account of the social and cultural
history of blacks in postwar Mississippi, since Professor Wharton
has dealt with these topics in his study. Instead, I have sought to
weave black activities into the general story of Reconstruction in
the state. I hope that I have contributed a few new insights into the
history of the black struggle to achieve a meaningful freedom during Reconstruction.

An explanation regarding the use of the word "Radical" is perhaps in order. In this book the word is not used in a pejorative
sense, although it was normally employed loosely and derisively by
conservative opponents to describe the ultra Republicans. Most

Radicals ignored the epithet and referred to themselves simply as Republicans. The meaning of the word actually changed with time. "Radical" in 1867–1868 generally meant a Mississippi Republican who favored equal political rights for blacks coupled with the disfranchisement or political proscription of a large number of former Confederates. After black suffrage was firmly established and proscription was relegated to the dustbin by President U. S. Grant, "Radical" usually referred to Republicans who favored advanced rights, or so-called "social equality," for blacks. The word also was used to describe those persons who favored an active federal presence in the state to protect the Republican order from conservative threats and violence and who frequently appeared indifferent to the need for attracting a large number of whites to the party. By 1873 the epithet "Radical" was attached to members of the Adelbert Ames faction of the Republican party, whatever their political ideology (or lack of one) might be.

Numerous individuals and several institutions have aided in the preparation of this book. I am sincerely thankful for the assistance and encouragement that my friends and colleagues first at Millsaps College and later at North Carolina State University have given. Ross H. Moore and Frank M. Laney of Millsaps College especially encouraged me during my early work on the subject. For several years the late Stuart Noblin was a constant source of comfort and good cheer, and Joseph P. Hobbs rendered encouragement during the final months of writing. Burton F. Beers and Donald M. Scott have read portions of the manuscript and have offered very useful suggestions. The work was also assisted by research grants from Millsaps College and the American Association of State and Local History. In addition, the National Endowment for the Humanities generously provided me with a year's grant-in-aid to further the study, and North Carolina State University gave me a semester's leave of absence at a critical time in the writing of the book and also provided assistance in its publication.

Librarians, archivists, and custodians of collections have rendered valuable aid to this study. A word of thanks is due to the staffs of the Mississippi Department of Archives and History, the Southern Historical Collection of the University of North Carolina Library, Chapel Hill, the Manuscript Division of the Duke University Library, the North Carolina State University Library, the Department of Archives of Louisiana State University, Baton Rouge, the Rutherford B. Hayes Memorial Library, Fremont, Ohio, the National Archives and its Atlanta branch, and the manuscript and newspaper divisions of the Library of Congress. I also desire to thank Kathryn Park and Betty Wooldridge for assisting in the research and Kathryn Hardee, Donna Holtsclaw, and Suzanne Gool for typing the manuscript. I am much indebted to Mary Jane Di Piero of the Louisiana State University Press for providing able and generous assistance in the final preparation of the book for publication.

I wish especially to express my deep gratitude to Thomas B. Alexander of the University of Missouri, Columbia, who for many years has inspired my work on Reconstruction and has given advice and assistance on numerous occasions. I can never repay the debt that I owe this outstanding mentor and scholar. Finally, I want to express my thanks to my wife Betty and our children Nelson and Frances for assisting me in innumerable ways in the preparation of the book. It is an old cliche, but true in my case: I could hardly have completed the task without their support.

The Day of the Carpetbagger

Mississippi in 1873

1

The Institution of
Military Rule

The Civil War had been over for almost two years when on March 26, 1867, General Edward Otho Cresap Ord climbed the bluffs at Vicksburg and assumed military control of Mississippi and Arkansas. He came to Vicksburg as the instrument of Congress to enforce "peace and good order . . . until loyalty and republican State governments" could be established in the two states under his authority. As provided for in the congressional reconstruction acts of March 2 and 23, Ord, along with the other district commanders in the South, was specifically directed "to protect all persons in their rights of persons and property, to suppress insurrection, disorder, and violence, and to punish, or cause to be punished all disturbers of the public peace and criminals."[1] At his discretion Ord could retain the civil officials who had been elected under President Andrew Johnson's plan of reconstruction, provided they did not interfere with the congressional program that the general had been sent to set in motion. In this regard Ord was to register a new electorate, which would include all black male adults but exclude certain Confederates. Once this process was completed the general had the responsibility for holding elections in Mississippi and Arkansas for delegates to state conventions that would frame constitutions guaranteeing Negro political equality. The eligible voters of either state, however, could refuse to cooperate by simply voting down the convention, whereupon the state would remain under military rule. But if the voters approved the calling of the convention, ratified its work in a separate election, and obtained the approval of Congress, military supervision would be lifted and the state would be restored to full equality in the Union.[2]

Like that of the other district commanders in the South, Ord's

1. *U.S. Statutes at Large*, XIV, 428–29; XV, 2–4.
2. The congressional program also required that before the state could be restored to the Union the new legislature must meet and ratify the Fourteenth Amendment. No state, however, could be readmitted until the amendment had been approved by the necessary three fourths of all of the legislatures.

1

military career had not trained him for the complexities and subtle-
ties of governing a civilian population; his difficulties were compounded by the uniqueness of the reconstruction experience and
of military intervention in civil affairs in the history of the republic. Born in Cumberland, Maryland, in 1818, and raised in the
national capital, Ord attended the United States Military Academy,
graduating in 1839. As a regular army officer, he participated in the
war with Mexico and later served on the Indian frontier. When the
Civil War began, he was appointed brigadier general of volunteers
and placed in a command near Washington. Elevated to major
general in 1862 and transferred to the Army of the Tennessee, he
became one of General Ulysses S. Grant's most effective lieuten-
ants. After the surrender he was placed in charge of Federal troops
in Arkansas, where he was performing dull military routines when
Congress gained control of reconstruction policy. Upon the recommendation of Grant, President Johnson appointed him to command the Fourth Military District.[3]

Ord brought to his new assignment a soldier's strong sense of
duty, a military virtue tempered in his case by a firm belief in the
American tradition of civil dominance over the military and the
danger of armed intervention in the political process. He had made
few political statements during his career, but one, made in 1866 to
General William Tecumseh Sherman, indicated an early opposition to Negro suffrage. He wrote Sherman that the rising agitation
over black suffrage would sooner jeopardize than ensure Union or
Republican control of the national government, since the soldiers,
whose support was necessary to the party's success in the North,
would "vote almost to a man against such a proceeding."[4] Nevertheless, when Ord assumed command of the Fourth Military District in 1867, he was determined to carry out his duties with a strict
regard for the reconstruction acts, which included the imposition
of black political equality in the "rebel" states. Except for congressional enactments, which were of a general nature, Ord was practically autonomous in directing affairs in his district, although he
could be removed by the dispirited President Johnson. The gen-

3. *Dictionary of American Biography*, XIV, 48.
4. Howard K. Beale, *The Critical Year: A Study of Andrew Johnson and Reconstruction*
(New York, 1930), 180.

eral made it clear from the beginning, however, that he would not exercise his authority in an arbitrary or despotic manner, preferring instead that the civil officials elected under presidential reconstruction continue to perform the regular functions of government.[5] The acts of the Republican Congress did not require the military to serve a peculiarly political purpose, and Ord fully intended that his command should not be tainted with the charge of partisanship in the implementation of the reconstruction program.

Economic and social conditions in Mississippi in early 1867 seemingly conspired with Congress for the acceptance of its reconstruction plan by the old citizens and for the success of General Ord's mission in the state. Whites had become demoralized by the state's failure to be restored to the Union and, after the Republican triumph in the congressional elections of 1866, were increasingly apprehensive about their fate if they continued to oppose congressional reconstruction. Mississippians had known little peace since before the war, and many now realized that President Johnson's obstructionist tactics had misled them on national reconstruction objectives. The indecision on reconstruction policy compounded the difficulties of combatting internal strife and averting even more serious conflict in the future. Accentuating the problems confronted by white Mississippians as presidential reconstruction gave way to the congressional program was the deplorable status of the postwar economy of the state, which after a brief revival in early 1866 had taken a new turn downward with the failure of the cotton and grain crops in the fall.[6]

Hard times prevailed throughout the state, but conditions were especially severe in east Mississippi where the small corn and cotton crops had failed almost completely. Local and northern hu-

---

5. General Order 1, March 26, 1867, in Records of the War Department, United States Army Command, Fourth Military District, Orders, 1867–70, Record Group 98, National Archives, on microfilm in the Mississippi Department of Archives and History, Jackson, hereinafter cited as Records of the Fourth Military District; Percy L. Rainwater (ed.), "The Autobiography of Benjamin Grubb Humphreys, August 26, 1808–December 20, 1882," *Mississippi Valley Historical Review*, XXI (September, 1934), 249.

6. William C. Harris, *Presidential Reconstruction in Mississippi* (Baton Rouge, 1967), 180–81, 237–39; George Mortimer to [?], August 8, 1867, in Mármaduke Shannon and Mrs. William O. Crutcher Family Papers, Mississippi Department of Archives and History; Jonathan Tarbell, a northern settler in central Mississippi, to the New York *Times*, April 29, 1867.

manitarian efforts alleviated some of the critical suffering in the area, but the basic economic problem, as reflected in the insuperable indebtedness of the people, remained.[7] Even people who held money or possessed assets that could be used as collateral for loans refused to release their hard-earned and valuable cash or to extend credit to those who wanted to plant again in the spring. This loss of confidence in the future also found expression in the financial condition of the Johnsonian state government. The state auditor of public accounts lamented on the eve of military rule that Mississippi warrants (*i.e.* promissory notes of the state) were being hawked in the streets of Jackson at a large discount, and he therefore refused to receive any more of them from sheriffs in payment of taxes for fear state finances would completely collapse. His insistence that county officials pay their taxes in specie or greenbacks was ignored; as a result funds in the state treasury declined to a point in 1867 that brought the administration of the state to a virtual standstill.[8]

The end of reconstruction strife and the restoration of the state to the Union on the terms of the dominant party in the North now appeared to many Mississippi leaders to be necessary before economic recovery could occur and social order could be restored. The uncertainties of political reconstruction, Ethelbert Barksdale, the influential editor of the Jackson *Clarion*, pointed out, "presses as a mountain of lead upon the energies [of the people], paralyzing energy, destroying confidence, over-throwing credit and forbidding emigration."[9] Furthermore, many leading Mississippians feared that unless the old citizens cooperated with Congress and accepted the principle of Negro suffrage a more radical settlement, including the confiscation of property, would be imposed. Prominent men like Amos R. Johnston, James Lusk Alcorn, and former governors Albert Gallatin Brown and John J. Pettus filled the columns of state newspapers with assertions that "domestic radical-

7. Harris, *Presidential Reconstruction in Mississippi*, 164–65; New York *Times*, April 21, 1867. The pervasiveness of economic depression and financial embarrassment during this period is vividly described in letters between lawyer L. P. Reynolds of northeast Mississippi and his hard-pressed clients. L. P. Reynolds Papers, Mississippi Department of Archives and History.

8. Thomas J. Swann to Marmaduke Shannon, January 15, 1867, in Shannon-Crutcher Papers; Jackson *Clarion*, February 15, 1867.

9. Jackson *Clarion*, March 16, 1867. See also the Vicksburg *Herald*, March 14, 1867.

ism" would not result from the extension of the ballot to Negroes if "good and patriotic men" acquiesced in the reconstruction acts and convinced blacks that they were sympathetic to their interests.[10] State Supreme Court Justice Henry T. Ellett declared, "it is not the negroes we have to fear, but unprincipled white men who will seek to use them for selfish and wicked ends." The control of the Negro vote by outside political adventurers could be avoided, Barksdale insisted, if conservatives in good faith accepted the reconstruction settlement and acted quickly to win the confidence of their former slaves.[11]

Conservative spokesmen also assured white Mississippians that the deployment of federal troops (which probably never exceeded 2,100 men and officers) under the reconstruction laws should be no cause for alarm. The troops, Barksdale declared, should be "regarded by our people as a police force, to be brought into requisition in order to compel obedience to laws which are indispensable to the safety of their lives and property. And their presence need not be regarded with distrust or disfavor while our political affairs remain in a state of uncertainty and almost of anarchy." General Ord, in fact, would merit the gratitude of the people if he used the army to stamp out lawlessness, as called for by the reconstruction acts.[12] Ord's inoffensive record in the South since the surrender suggested to some Mississippians that he would respect their rights and would not use his authority in a tyrannical manner.[13]

In the spring of 1867 the white masses seemed disposed to follow the advice of their old leaders and cooperate with Congress in its plan of reconstruction. Even Mississippi Unionists reported a grass-roots change in sentiment toward the Republican settlement. Federal Judge Robert A. Hill, a persistent Unionist during the war, wrote Senator John Sherman: "I believe that a majority of the white population are now prepared to accept in good faith the proposed terms, with the exception of Gov [William Lewis] Sharkey,

10. Jackson *Clarion*, March 9, 16, 1867; Meridian *Semi-Weekly Gazette*, March 16, 20, May 1, 1867; Vicksburg *Herald*, March 9, 14, 1867; Natchez *Weekly Democrat*, March 19, April 9, 1867. A more detailed account of the changing white position on reconstruction in early 1867 appears in Harris, *Presidential Reconstruction in Mississippi*, 236–42.
11. Jackson *Clarion*, March 9, April 25 (quote), June 11, 1867.
12. *Ibid.*, May 11, 1867.
13. Columbus (Miss.) *Southern Sentinel*, March 26, 1867.

and a few other prominent old Whigs." Sharkey and his supporters rejected any compromise with Republican reconstruction on the ground that the whole proceedings were unconstitutional. Friends of Congress also reported that a second group, consisting mainly of young hotspurs, opposed the reconstruction program because it lacked a congressional guarantee that no other requirements would be made of the southern people. Agreeing that such an assurance should be given, Unionists claimed that once it was written into the reconstruction laws the day of the demagogue and disunionist in Mississippi would be ended. [14]

General Ord's early policies were designed to encourage the development of moderate white sentiment toward the reconstruction acts. After establishing his headquarters at Vicksburg, he visited Governor Benjamin Grubb Humphreys in Jackson and requested that the elected officials continue in office and carry on the normal administration of the state. Ord admitted that he might be forced to intervene on occasion, but his intention was to give civil officials every opportunity to manage affairs and enforce the old laws of the state, except where these laws specifically conflicted with acts of Congress. Humphreys, a weather-beaten hero of the Lost Cause who had served the cause of union until the moment of Mississippi's act of secession, promised the general that he would cooperate. Nevertheless, it was soon clear that local officials were confused regarding their status, many having suspended the functions of their offices when the reconstruction measures were enacted. A belief existed in some areas of the state that the military acts had made all civil laws invalid, including tax measures and those providing for the faithful observance of contracts. [15] To counter the disintegration of local governments and to end the confusion regarding the responsibilities of civil officers under Ord's supervision, Governor Humphreys on April 6 issued a proclamation pointing out that until replaced the existing administration in the state was recognized by both Congress and the district commander. Therefore, he announced, local officials would be held to a

14. Robert A. Hill to John Sherman, July 3, 1867, in John Sherman Papers, Manuscript Division, Library of Congress. See also A. H. Arthur to Joseph Holt, March 14, 1867, in Joseph Holt Papers, Manuscript Division, Library of Congress.

15. Rainwater (ed.), "Autobiography of Humphreys," 299; General Order 2, March 26, 1867, in Records of the Fourth Military District; William F. Wallace to law firm of Reynolds, Boone, and Reynolds, March 10, 1867, in Reynolds Papers.

"strict accountability for the performance of their duties in carrying out the provisions of the laws, for the maintenance of the civil Government, and for the full and ample protection of all classes of inhabitants of the State, both white and black, in all of their rights of person, property, liberty and religion." He also called on the people to obey all laws, to sustain the civil officers in their efforts to maintain peace, order, and security, and to acquiesce in military reconstruction. "Military power may become intolerable only when it is placed in the hands of the vicious and unjust, which, happily, is not the case in Mississippi," Humphreys declared.[16]

Although the civil authorities proved ineffective in dealing with the pressing financial and social problems facing the state, Ord followed the wishes of the old citizenry by retaining in office almost all of the Johnsonian officials. The first dismissals did not occur until late summer, and altogether the commander removed few officials and none on the state level.[17] He did, however, fill a number of local vacancies, approximately seventy in all, with "loyal" men, although these were not necessarily individuals who could take the ironclad oath—that is, swear that they had never given any aid or comfort to the Confederacy. One of these appointees was Benjamin T. Montgomery, a successful black planter and former plantation manager for Joseph and Jefferson Davis. Montgomery's appointment as justice of the peace for Davis Bend on the Mississippi River made him the first Negro to hold public office in Mississippi. Ord later decreed that blacks could serve as clerks and judges of election and as delegates to the state constitutional convention.[18] Friends of the Negro and the infant Republican party in the state, however, found little comfort in Ord's patronage policies, and soon they were clamoring for his removal

16. Humphreys' proclamation may be found in the Vicksburg *Herald*, April 11, 1867, and the Meridian *Semi-Weekly Gazette*, April 10, 1867.

17. Jackson *Weekly Clarion*, September 4, 1867; James W. Garner, *Reconstruction in Mississippi* (Gloucester, Mass., 1964), 164. A number of men whom Ord retained in office were former Confederate soldiers who had been elected to their positions in the fall election of 1865. E. A. Duncan to B. F. Whittemore, April 5, 1869, in Petitions for the Removal of the Legal and Political Disabilities Imposed by the Fourteenth Amendment: Mississippi, in Legislative Records, Record Group 233, National Archives, hereinafter cited as Fourteenth Amendment Relief Papers, Mississippi.

18. *Appleton's Annual Cyclopaedia and Register of Important Events* (15 vols.; New York, 1861–75), 1867, pp. 515–16; Jackson *Weekly Clarion*, September 19, 1867. The *Clarion* in the same issue reported that Montgomery "possesses the confidence and respect of the white people."

from command, claiming that he had ignored loyal men in his appointments to office.[19]

From the beginning the success of congressional reconstruction in Mississippi depended upon the suppression of the spirit of lawlessness that prevailed there. Republican critics attributed the insecurity in Mississippi society to a continuation of the spirit of rebellion which tolerated assaults by incorrigible men upon defenseless freedmen and Unionists. Such an environment, they believed, had bred a general disrespect for the law and for republican government, and this condition was reflected in the fact that the courts were unwilling or unable to deal with the problem.[20] Only the military, Republicans reasoned, could put down the lawless elements in the population and make the state safe for the political changes envisioned by the reconstruction laws.

Actually, this explanation for the violence and lawlessness in Mississippi was only partly correct. Mississippi, as well as other southern states, had long suffered from an overemphasis on the Bowie knife, the pistol, or any other convenient weapon to settle delicate points at issue between antagonists. The celebrated code duello did not shape this syndrome of violence, but was, rather, a mature manifestation of the general unruly condition of society. The origins of the syndrome, especially in the interior, were in the boisterous and strongly individualistic frontier society of the not-too-distant past, whose tradition of an eye for an eye and a tooth for a tooth lingered into the postwar era.

Late antebellum authorities had been reasonably successful in establishing social stability as frontier conditions receded in most areas of the state. But when Mississippi became a battlefield in 1862, interior regions reverted to near primitive conditions, characterized by the collapse of the usual processes of law and justice. After the surrender officials in the Johnsonian government were able to suppress only the more extreme manifestations of lawlessness, such as brigandage, whereas the continued impoverishment

19. Edward J. Castello to R. C. Schenck, December 17, 1867, in Papers of the United States House of Representatives' Select Committee on Reconstruction, 40th and 41st Congress, Dealing Primarily with Conditions in the Former States of the Confederacy: Mississippi, Legislative Records, Record Group 233, National Archives, hereinafter cited as Papers on Conditions in Mississippi; Charles W. Clarke to John Covode, August 31, 1867, in John Covode Papers, Manuscript Division, Library of Congress.

20. William C. Harris, "The Creed of the Carpetbaggers: The Case of Mississippi," *Journal of Southern History*, XL (May, 1974), 203, 209.

of the people worked against the restoration of civil order and made more certain an increase in vagabondage and crime.[21]

The presence of the Negro accentuated the ready resort to violence in Mississippi society. The slave institution had conditioned many whites to react violently to infractions of the master-slave relationship and to black demonstrations of disrespect toward any white person. Only in the plantation districts did the results of the war and emancipation force a significant change in the white response to black assertiveness. Living on agricultural units where labor was at a premium, planters generally adjusted to the fact that a violent white response to black violations of racial mores would undermine their efforts to retain free Negro workers. Furthermore, the breakdown of authority in the state had increased the feeling of insecurity that planters and other whites felt in the plantation districts where blacks were a distinct majority of the population. The fear of disorders or "black outrages" caused most whites in these districts to pause before reacting aggressively to Negro transgressions against established racial practices. But in the nonplantation districts, where the white population was clearly predominant, yeoman whites had few reasons to restrain their disposition to violence when they came into conflict with blacks.[22] As a result they continued into Reconstruction the antebellum practice of using force to settle issues with Negroes, despite the attempts of the Freedmen's Bureau in 1865 to obtain the cooperation of civil authorities for the suppression of such outrages. Blacks also contributed, although perhaps less than their share, to the violence and disrespect for the law that afflicted Mississippi. Their acts of violence were usually directed against each other, whereas their crimes against whites were normally limited to petty thievery.[23]

21. Harris, *Presidential Reconstruction in Mississippi*, 4–6, 36, 68–69.

22. Report of Alvan C. Gillem, assistant commissioner of the Freedmen's Bureau in Mississippi, for October, 1867, in Records of the Bureau of Refugees, Freedmen, and Abandoned Lands, Record Group 105, Microcopy Roll 50, National Archives, hereinafter cited as Freedmen's Bureau Records with microcopy roll number included. When the manuscript records are used, "Mississippi" will replace the roll number.

23. For statements of the tendency of many blacks toward petty thievery, see report of James Biddle, December 9, 1867, in Freedmen's Bureau Records, Mississippi, and report of General Gillem, December, 1867, in Jackson *Clarion*, December 29, 1867. Most issues of state newspapers soon after the war carried numerous accounts of robberies, assaults, and brutal murders, but very few reports of rape; these accounts also provide evidence of the biracial nature of crime in Mississippi.

This was the social situation that General Ord faced when he assumed command in 1867. With instructions from Congress to suppress "all disturbers of the public peace and criminals," Ord immediately asked General-in-Chief Grant in Washington for additional troops, especially cavalry units, to track down lawbreakers. He complained to Grant that the one regiment assigned to him was not even sufficient to restore order and security in one third of the counties; furthermore, none of the companies in the command was mounted. While waiting for Grant's action, he dispatched the available units to key towns in the interior, which were generally situated along lines of communication. These forces were encamped in or near the towns in military "posts," and they were usually commanded by a major or captain who reported directly to Ord's headquarters at Vicksburg. By the fall of 1867 Ord had established fifteen posts in Mississippi, which were garrisoned by 2,073 troops, including two companies of cavalry that Grant sent him in May. Troop strength in the state dropped slightly below this level in 1868, and six posts were abandoned. In 1869, the last year of military rule, the number of soldiers in Mississippi was reduced to fewer than one thousand.[24]

When Ord took command in Mississippi, the Freedmen's Bureau seemed in its death throes, having fallen victim to President Johnson's obstructionist policies. In early 1867 only eleven of the sixty counties were staffed by bureau agents. In order to coordinate the efforts of federal forces in his district, Ord assumed control of the bureau and increased its responsibilities as well as its staff of military officers.[25] The bureau thus gained a new lease on life in Mississippi, which would continue as long as Ord commanded in the state.

General Ord did not wait for the arrival of additional military units before singling out horse thieves for special treatment. In a general order of May 16 he directed post commanders to assume complete jurisdiction over horse stealing, which in some areas of the state was "materially destructive of the interests of the honest,

24. *Senate Executive Documents*, 40th Cong., 1st Sess., No. 14, p. 136. A chart of troop strength in Mississippi and other southern states during Reconstruction is found in James E. Sefton, *The United States Army and Reconstruction, 1865–1877* (Baton Rouge, 1967), Appendix B.

25. General Order 4, April 13, 1867, in Records of the Fourth Military District.

respectable property-owners." Accused horse thieves, even those arrested by civil authorities, were to be tried by military commissions and speedily sentenced when found guilty. In the same order Ord asked the people of the state to cooperate fully with the military authorities in bringing these criminals to justice. He admonished citizens to provide information on the suspicious activities of persons in their communities and to serve as guides for military units when they came seeking the hiding places of outlaws. Punishment for horse thieves was to be severe. Ord requested and received permission from the War Department to send them to Dry Tortugas, an inhospitable military prison off the coast of Florida.[26] Nevertheless, of the thirty-two men (of both races) convicted by military commissions for stealing horses and mules, only six, all of whom were white, were sentenced to Dry Tortugas to serve terms ranging from two to seven years; the remainder received accommodations in the state penitentiary. Long in need of security for their draft animals, responsible whites of the state praised Ord's war on horse thieves. Soon the wholesome effect of the commander's harsh policy was evident, and by late fall this kind of theft had largely been suppressed.[27]

Ord also acted forcibly to check the resort to violence in personal disputes that by 1867 had assumed epidemic proportions in some parts of the state. On September 9 he directed both civil and military officers to take strong measures to prevent the bearing of firearms by citizens, and this action was followed by orders prohibiting the carrying of any type of concealed weapon and banning the assembling of armed men. Violators of these directives were to be tried by military commissions.[28] The general court-martial records for the Fourth Military District, however, contain no evidence that citizens were tried for carrying concealed weapons or for assembling with arms. In creating commissions to try offenders Ord acted in cases where doubt existed that justice could be obtained. Except for the establishment of military commissions to deal with horse thieves, martial justice was restricted to cases in-

26. General Order 9, May 16, 1867, *ibid.*
27. Report of James Biddle, December 9, 1867, in Freedmen's Bureau Records, Mississippi; Jackson *Clarion*, May 21, 1867.
28. General Order 28, September 9, 1867, in Records of the Fourth Military District.

volving white assaults on freedmen, voter registrars, and Union men. So thorough were Ord's efforts in this regard that at one time he reported thirty-five civilians in the guard house awaiting military trial on assault charges.[29] By the end of the year, however, the need for military trials had declined considerably, and few civilians faced judgment at the hands of army officers during the remaining two years of military rule.

A revealing account of military arrest, confinement, and trial by a commission of army officers was left by Dr. Anthony Foster of Panola County, who was charged with the murder of a Unionist. Foster recorded his experience in a diary which he began on the day he was arrested in October, 1867, and continued until his acquittal by a military commission on January 7, 1868. Arrested originally by civilian authorities, Foster was taken from their hands by an agent of the Freedmen's Bureau and sent to Grenada to await the action of General Ord. At Grenada Foster was placed in the custody of another officer of the Freedmen's Bureau, who permitted him unlimited visiting privileges while in confinement.[30] Here he was notified of the birth of a son, whom he defiantly named Robert E. Lee Foster.

Meanwhile, Ord directed that Foster be held for military trial and sent to Vicksburg for safekeeping until a commission could be formed. Upon his arrival in Vicksburg and after a friendly interview with General Alvan C. Gillem, Ord's chief lieutenant in Mississippi, Foster was placed in a cell less than five feet in width. After several days of a bland diet consisting mainly of bread and "something intended for coffee," Foster was blessed with a stroke of good fortune. The celebrated and generous William H. McCardle of Vicksburg was arrested by the military and put in an adjacent cell. Using his connections with both his friends in town and his jailors, McCardle began supplying the suffering Foster with such delicacies as apples, oranges, fried chicken, ham, good coffee, and "superb wine."[31]

Although he admitted that he was treated well by his soldier-

29. Edward O. C. Ord to Zachariah Chandler, September 16, 1867, in Zachariah Chandler Papers, Manuscript Division, Library of Congress.
30. Entries for October 6, 10, 1867, in Anthony Foster Diary, Mississippi Department of Archives and History.
31. Entries for November 1–6, 10, 18, 1867, *ibid.*

jailors, Foster was embittered by the "high-handed assumption of power which wrested my case from the civil authorities and put my life and freedom at the risk of Military Commissions." As for congressional reconstruction, he had the utmost contempt: "If radical fanaticism directs and controls the affairs of the nation much longer, the consequences must be ruinous to the nation. The freedom of the negro was not only a great wrong, but a most stupendous blunder. No wonder God did not suffer the author of this outrage [Lincoln] to live." The doctor made a distinction between the "low-flung scoundrels" from the North "who, dressed in a little brief authority, have done and are yet doing all they can to persecute and crush the Southern people," and his keepers, whom he "found as perfect gentlemen and as true men" as anybody. He even included the district commander in the latter category, and regarded himself "as fortunate in having such a gentleman as Gen. Ord placed over me."[32]

On December 13 Foster was transferred to Holly Springs where he was to be tried by a military commission. During the trial he was permitted to leave the jail to visit and eat with his family at the residence of his attorney, Harvey W. Walter, the Whig candidate for governor in 1859. As the trial progressed, he became confident that he would be acquitted, since "there is not one particle or word of testimony going to show that I am guilty as charged." Nevertheless, he would have felt safer had his fate been decided in a civil court and by a jury. After a two-week trial the military commission found him "not guilty," and, as if to apologize for the trouble the army had caused him, Major John Power, the post commander and a member of the commission, invited Foster to his home where "a demijohn of fine liquor went the rounds" in celebration of the event.[33] Yankee justice was not without its virtues.

Despite military intervention in certain types of cases, jurisdiction in most criminal matters, including violations of the controversial state vagrancy law, remained with the civil courts. Although these courts met irregularly and not at all in some areas, they still

32. Entries for November 27, December 1, 9, 13, 30, 1867, *ibid.*

33. Entries for December 13, 23, 26, 27, 1867, January 4, 7, 1868, *ibid.* Ironically, Foster later became a Republican, supporting the James Lusk Alcorn faction of the party. Petition of Foster for removal of Fourteenth Amendment disabilities, n.d., in Fourteenth Amendment Relief Papers, Mississippi.

conducted the bulk of the judicial business of the state.[34] Actually, few people were touched by military rule, and some who lived in remote communities and did not venture far from home may not have seen a bluecoat during the entire period of military reconstruction.

In localities occupied by military units everyday relations between the old citizens and the troops were rarely marred by hostile acts or even discourtesies. Because of the general feeling of insecurity that prevailed in the state, a contingent of white soldiers was frequently a welcomed addition to a community.[35] Despite their recent enmity, enlisted men especially and even many officers in these units sympathized with members of their own race in the face of a possible political revolution that might establish black supremacy in the state. Local whites, who quickly perceived the prevalence of anti-Negro sentiment among the troops, normally disassociated the army from the obnoxious congressional policies that it was there to enforce. Then, too, Ord and his officers had taken careful steps to ensure the protection of the fundamental rights of the people against arrogant and unruly soldiers.[36] The post commander at Meridian went so far in his desire to shield local citizens from improper behavior on the part of his men that he prohibited the sale of alcoholic beverages to army personnel. And in Holly Springs, an officer was arrested by his superior for permitting his men to insult civilians who were in military custody.[37]

Several officers achieved a degree of social acceptance that was remarkable in view of their purposes in Mississippi. General Gil-

34. Circular 23, December 14, 1867, in Records of the Fourth Military District. The business of the military courts did not primarily involve civilians but was mainly concerned with the discipline of troops. Also, soldiers found no immunity from the regular courts. On at least two occasions they were tried and sentenced to prison by local courts. Jackson *Clarion*, May 19, 29, 1867.

35. For accounts of the good rapport between troops and the local citizenry, see Ethan A. Allen to President Johnson, May 17, 1867, in Andrew Johnson Papers, on microfilm in Manuscript Division, Library of Congress; entries for January 7, 8, 1868, in Foster Diary; the Natchez *Weekly Democrat*, April 6, 1868; and the Jackson *Clarion*, May 6, 1868. There were no black soldiers stationed in Mississippi during military reconstruction.

36. For reports on the excellent condition of military discipline, see Report of Inspector General D. B. Sacket, May 1, 1867, in Records of the Office of the Inspector General of the Army, Record Group 159, National Archives; the Meridian *Semi-Weekly Gazette*, September 4, 1867; and the Vicksburg *Herald*, December 14, 1868.

37. Meridian *Semi-Weekly Gazette*, July 7, 1867; Jackson *Clarion*, January 10, 1868.

lem, the handsome East Tennessean, was probably the most popular man to wear the blue uniform in the state during the Reconstruction era, although he reportedly had "no love for rebels" and occasionally acted in a manner that drew the ire of the old citizens.[38] General Galusha Pennypacker was popular in north Mississippi and often entertained former Confederate officers in his home. Lieutenant Colonel James Biddle, who commanded two companies of troops in southwest Mississippi and also served as the district supervisor for the Freedmen's Bureau, found life quite pleasant in the sedate and cultivated river town of Natchez. Although forced by circumstances to live briefly in a former slave cabin near the military camp, Biddle and his wife were immediately accepted in Natchez society after he upheld the position of a Unionist judge in a quarrel with local Radicals. While the colonel enthusiastically entered his birds in the popular cockfights of the river town, his young wife in the company of local gentry followed the foxhounds and visited in the lovely mansions overlooking the Mississippi River. When Biddle was transferred from Natchez, he and his wife were escorted to the steamboat by the city's brass band and at the wharf a large number of people were present to bid them farewell.[39]

In Vicksburg the post band was in great demand to play for both public and private functions. It was not unusual for Federal soldiers to pay court to and wed southern belles, and one officer of the Freedmen's Bureau married the widow of a Confederate soldier.[40]

Ord and his successors in command permitted to a remarkable extent freedom of speech and press, a tolerance that often included forbearance in the face of hostile criticism of the reconstruction

38. Jackson *Clarion*, April 4, 1868. For evidence of Gillem's popularity see William L. Sharkey to President Johnson, November 7, 1868, and Hill to Johnson, November 6, 1868, both in Johnson Papers. Gillem even had admirers among Republicans. After the general had left the state, carpetbagger George F. Brown claimed that peace and stability had been restored mainly because of Gillem's "elevated statesmanship." George F. Brown to Johnson, November 7, 1868, and Elza Jeffords to Johnson, November 7, 1868, both in Johnson Papers. Radical Republicans were not so fond of Gillem or his men. Negro Henry Mayson wrote in 1869 that "Gillem's Democrats in Blue" were "tramping the life-blood out of Loyalists." Mayson to T. L. Tullock, March 12, 1869, in Papers on Conditions in Mississippi.

39. Natchez *Weekly Democrat*, April 6, 1868; Ellen McGowan Biddle, *Reminiscences of a Soldier's Wife* (Philadelphia, 1907), 28, 30, 34–36, 41; Jackson *Clarion*, May 6, 1868.

40. Vicksburg *Herald*, September 9, 1868; entry for October 28, 1867, in Foster Diary.

laws and military authority. The general demonstrated his good faith toward conservative editors when he court-martialed an army officer in Arkansas for destroying an inflammatory press and upbraided the man's commanding officer for claiming that military officers in the district were the masters of the people.[41] But his patience wore thin with vituperative editors close to home.

In Vicksburg, the site of Ord's headquarters, editorial tilting had broken out between William H. McCardle of the conservative *Times* on one side and Joshua S. Morris and James Dugan of the *Republican* on the other. Ord found McCardle's editorials especially offensive, since the impetuous editor directed some of his venom at the reconstruction laws and at military authorities, including the commanding general. McCardle, whose contribution to the Confederate cause somehow had been obscured until after the fighting had ended, was of a small corps of former Whig journalists who showered Mississippi during Reconstruction with sharp editorial darts aimed at those who carried out or acquiesced in the congressional settlement for the South. This elite group included McCardle, Dr. J. S. Davis of the Iuka *Gazette*, Edward M. Yerger of various Vicksburg and Jackson newspapers, Arthur J. Frantz of the Brandon *Republican*, and Alexander G. Horn of the Meridian *Mercury*. In a biting editorial of November 6, 1867, entitled "The Scoundrelism of Satraps," McCardle referred to the district commanders in the South, Ord included, as "infamous, cowardly, and abandoned villains, who, instead of wearing shoulder straps and ruling millions of people, should have their heads shaved, their ears cropped, their foreheads branded, and their precious persons lodged in a penitentiary."[42] This editorial, along with other outbursts by the foolhardy McCardle, resulted on November 8 in his arrest and confinement by order of General Ord. He was charged with impeding reconstruction, libeling individuals, and disturbing the public peace by inciting people to riot and even insurrection.[43]

Ord did not anticipate the loud outburst of criticism that followed his action. When he was vilified even by many in the state

41. Sefton, *United States Army and Reconstruction*, 151–52; Jackson *Clarion*, June 16, October 24, 1867.

42. As reported in Charles Fairman, *Reconstruction and Reunion, 1864–88*, Vol. VI of *History of the Supreme Court of the United States* (11 vols.; New York, 1971–), 416.

43. *Ex parte McCardle*, 6 Wallace 320 (1867).

who had been consistent defenders of his policies, he sought to demonstrate his impartiality in policing editorial excesses by ordering a similar fate for the scalawag Morris and the carpetbagger Dugan, both of whom were charged with "disturbing the public peace by publishing and uttering libelous assaults" upon McCardle. An old murder charge was revived to add to Morris' misfortunes.[44]

Meanwhile, McCardle had taken his case to the federal courts. On November 12, 1867, through his distinguished battery of lawyers which included former Provisional Governor William Lewis Sharkey and former United States Senator Walker Brooke, McCardle petitioned the United States Circuit Court for a writ of habeas corpus, contending that his arrest contravened the decision in the Milligan case (1866). The writ was issued, asking General Gillem, who held custody of the fire-eating editor, to show cause for imprisonment. Not only did Gillem give the reasons for the arrest and confinement, he also surrendered McCardle to the jurisdiction of the court.[45] McCardle was now given a hearing before Federal Judge Robert A. Hill, a mild-mannered and respected Unionist from the hills of northeast Mississippi, who privately had expressed strong approval of the congressional policy toward the South.[46] The judge decided that the McCardle case transcended normal judicial matters, involving the broad question of the legality of the reconstruction laws. In his view the military acts were constitutional and Ord was within his authority when he arrested McCardle and held him for trial by military commission. Hill therefore remanded the editor to the custody of General Gillem in Vicksburg.[47] Immediately, McCardle's lawyers appealed to the United States Supreme Court for a writ of habeas corpus, and just as quickly Gillem released him on bail without restrictions on his editorial activities.[48]

The printer's ink on his last issue of the *Times* had hardly dried

44. Special Order 198, December 5, 1867, in Records of the United States Army Command, Fourth Military District, Civil Affairs, Special Orders, 1867, Record Group 94, National Archives.

45. *Ex parte McCardle*, 6 Wallace 320 (1867).

46. Hill to John Sherman, July 3, 1867, in John Sherman Papers.

47. *Ibid.* Judge Hill's decision in full may be found in the Meridian *Semi-Weekly Gazette*, November 27, 1867.

48. Jackson *Clarion*, December 5, 1867.

when McCardle returned to his desk, pending the disposition of his case by the Supreme Court, and resumed writing denunciatory commentaries on military reconstruction. The tone of his farewell salute to Ord upon the general's reassignment to the Indian frontier in late 1867 was typical of McCardle's journalism. "Poor old Ord," the irrepressible editor wrote. "The best excuse that can be trumped up for his insolence and tyranny·is his utter want of brains."[49] Actually, the general, after his initial mistake of ordering McCardle's arrest, had shown remarkably good sense in cooperating with the federal tribunals in the case, even to the point of issuing a general order to members of his command that they should obey all writs of habeas corpus issued by United States courts.[50]

McCardle's elation at the removal of Ord from command soon turned to despair because of developments in Washington regarding his case. Congress, aroused by the possibility that the Supreme Court might declare the heart of its reconstruction program unconstitutional if it heard the McCardle case, passed an act depriving the court of jurisdiction in appeals from lower federal courts where the writ of habeas corpus was involved. The court meekly accepted the congressional verdict and returned McCardle to the military authorities "for want of jurisdiction."[51] But rather than contribute any further to McCardle's move toward martyrdom, General Gillem, Ord's successor and a protégé of President Johnson, quietly dropped the charges against him and also those against the Republican editors, Morris and Dugan. Ironically, Morris, who later served as the first Republican attorney general of the state, spent more time in military confinement than his Bourbon rival, but the glory of arbitrary imprisonment at the hands of a "military despot" was to be McCardle's sole prize.

An important part of General Ord's mission was the protection of black rights. He envisaged the revived Freedmen's Bureau as the main instrument for ensuring fair treatment for blacks in their everyday relations with whites. The importance with which Ord

49. Vicksburg *Times*, January 4, 5, 1867.
50. General Order 40, December 12, 1867, in Records of the Fourth Military District.
51. *Ex parte McCardle*, 7 Wallace 515 (1868). For a provocative discussion of the McCardle case in the context of the power struggle in Washington regarding reconstruction, see Stanley I. Kutler, "*Ex parte McCardle*: Judicial Impotency? The Supreme Court and Reconstruction Reconsidered," *American Historical Review*, LXXII (April, 1967), 835–51.

viewed the bureau was demonstrated when he increased the authority of the assistant commissioners for Mississippi and Arkansas and at the same time appointed them as his chief military subordinates in their states. In Mississippi, Assistant Commissioner Gillem, despite political ties with Johnson that predated Reconstruction, acted with energy in 1867 to make the bureau into a reasonably effective agency for the suppression of white assaults on blacks and to assist the former slaves in their economic relations with planters and merchants.[52] This east Tennessee general appointed special bureau officers to investigate the rash of black accusations against whites that came to his attention during the early months of military reconstruction. Most of the allegations dealt with planter-labor relations or with minor infractions of the rights of blacks, which were settled without recourse to military trials. But in those instances where the charges were serious and Gillem had reason to doubt that justice would be done by the regular courts, he forwarded the investigating officer's report to Ord with the recommendation that a military commission be formed to try the case.[53]

Nevertheless, in 1867 only four whites were brought before army courts on charges of assaulting blacks. All were convicted, and one, whose victim died, was sentenced to ten years in the state penitentiary, the harshest penalty meted out by a military commission in Mississippi Reconstruction. The effect of these trials, along with numerous instances of bureau intervention that stopped short of formal action, was dramatic. By the fall of 1867 Gillem could report to his superiors that complaints of violence against Negroes had virtually ceased.[54]

52. Gillem had been appointed assistant commissioner of the Freedmen's Bureau in Mississippi one month before the passage of the first reconstruction law.

53. James Biddle to J. W. Sunderland, October 8, 1867, in Freedmen's Bureau Records, Mississippi; reports of Gillem for October and November, 1867, Microcopy Roll 50, and Gillem to Oliver O. Howard, April 8, 1868, Microcopy Roll 54, all in Freedmen's Bureau Records; Clifton L. Ganus, Jr., "The Freedmen's Bureau in Mississippi" (Ph.D. dissertation, Tulane University, 1953), 296.

54. Report of Gillem for October, 1867, in Freedmen's Bureau Records, Microcopy Roll 50. In 1868 two military courts appointed by Gillem convicted four whites of assaults on blacks. *General Court Martial Orders from the Headquarters, Fourth Military District, 1868* (Vicksburg, 1869). Two of these men were soon released from army confinement on a writ of habeas corpus issued by Judge Hill who earlier had denied a similar petition from McCardle. The ground for their release was that the military commission that tried them had imposed punishment violating the state criminal code. Vicksburg *Herald*, November 6, 7, 1868.

The intervention of the army and the Freedmen's Bureau extended into all aspects of race relations and the affairs of blacks. Although several features of the harsh Black Code of 1865 were retained, Ord directed his officers to take action to ensure that these laws were enforced without discrimination against Negroes. On June 27, 1867, he declared null and void the state poll tax on adult male blacks that had been levied during presidential reconstruction to support the "Freedmen's Pauper Fund."[55] Gillem followed up this directive with instructions for local officials to provide for the care of impoverished and disabled blacks out of the regular state and county appropriations. No requirement, however, was made that the county poor houses should be racially integrated. On a limited scale, Gillem revived the early bureau practice of issuing rations to destitute blacks, but most of these provisions went to impoverished patients in the bureau hospitals of the state. By mid-1868 only two hundred blacks who could demonstrate their "absolute incapacity" received government rations on a regular basis.[56]

Ord and Gillem also revived early bureau programs designed to provide medical aid for Negroes and to improve health conditions in the black ghettoes of the larger towns. Several small, primitive hospitals and dispensaries for freedmen had been established in 1865, but these facilities were either closed or permitted to languish after only a few months of operation. When Ord assumed command of the state in 1867, he directed Gillem in his capacity as assistant commissioner of the Freedmen's Bureau to establish hospitals and other medical facilities to care for blacks. Gillem acted immediately to revitalize the hospitals at Lauderdale (near Meridian), Vicksburg, and Natchez and to open dispensaries at Jackson, Vicksburg, and Grenada to provide medicine for blacks who were treated at home. General Gillem and his officers, who contracted with local physicians to serve the medical needs of Negroes, increased the capacity of the hospitals to almost five hun-

55. Ord to Zachariah Chandler, September 16, 1867, in Zachariah Chandler Papers; report of Gillem for quarter ending March 31, 1868, in Freedmen's Bureau Records, Microcopy Roll 54; General Order 15, June 27, 1867, in Records of the Fourth Military District.

56. Report of Gillem for April, 1867; H. R. Williams to Gillem, May 19, 1867, Microcopy Roll 47; report of Gillem for quarter ending September 30, 1868, Microcopy Roll 59, all in Freedmen's Bureau Records.

dred beds by early 1868, and during the first quarter of the new year 1,207 patients received treatment in these institutions. The failure, however, of the federal government to provide adequate funds to sustain the bureau's promising medical program resulted by October, 1868, in the closure of all of the facilities except the hospital at Vicksburg.[57]

Concern for the freedmen's health caused General Ord to adopt an extreme plan of disease prevention, which if enforced to its fullest extent by unsympathetic officers would have violated the basic freedom of blacks. Fearing a sudden outbreak of cholera in the black community (which later occurred in the river counties), Ord on May 1, 1867, instructed his subordinates to prevent nonresidents from congregating in towns and, in communities where federal officers were available, to provide for sanitary inspections of "all rooms and buildings occupied by freedmen." Where unhealthy conditions were found, immediate steps were to be taken to ensure that the occupants police the premises. In addition, where overcrowding existed and conditions were beyond immediate improvement, camps were to be established under the supervision of military officers for the "surplus inhabitants." Ord also directed that Freedmen's Bureau officials, military officers, and local doctors pool their resources and cooperate in an effort to improve sanitary and health conditions among blacks, with the bureau providing supplies that could not otherwise be obtained.[58]

There is no evidence that compulsory camps were actually established for blacks. Most post commanders instead insisted on the strict enforcement of sanitary rules to prevent disease, and where they found vagrants in towns they sent them to the country. These measures, however, did not avert a summer outbreak of cholera, which caused great suffering and death among both town and plantation blacks.[59]

Both Ord and Gillem believed that the Negro's main problem in

57. Report of Gillem for quarter ending March 31, 1868, Microcopy Roll 54, and report of Gillem for quarter ending September 30, 1868, Microcopy Roll 59, both in Freedmen's Bureau Records.

58. General Order 9, May 1, 1867, in Records of the Fourth Military District.

59. Meridian *Semi-Weekly Gazette*, May 22, 1867; Jackson *Weekly Clarion*, September 26, 1867; entry for July 29, 1867, in Susan Sillers Darden Diary, Mississippi Department of Archives and History. On some plantations in the river district almost 50 percent of the black population died in the cholera epidemic. Ganus, "Freedmen's Bureau in Mississippi," 169.

freedom was economic and financial, and their policies from the beginning revealed this concern. Fearing at first that blacks might desert the fields at inopportune times to attend political rallies, Ord soon after assuming command instructed his officers to disabuse the freedmen of the notion that the congressional extension of political rights to them would appreciably improve their condition in society. The district commander plainly announced:

> The most important duty devolving upon freedmen in their new condition is that of providing by their own labor for the support of themselves and families. They now have a common interest in the general prosperity. This prosperity does not depend so much on how men vote, as upon how well each member of society labors and keeps his contracts. Freedmen are therefore urged not to neglect their business to engage in political discussion, but continue to comply with their contracts and provide for themselves and families, for unless they do so, a famine may come and they will have no food. When the time comes for them to have their names entered in the books of voters, . . . the general commanding will send them word through proper United States or county officers.[60]

Nevertheless, by the fall it had become clear to Ord that the real threat to the economic success of blacks was not their propensity for political discussion, but rather the disposition of planters to deal unfairly with them in the yearly crop settlements. From throughout the state black complaints of mistreatment and outright fraud at the hands of planters and merchants flooded the headquarters of Ord and Gillem, even before the cotton-picking season had begun. Hard pressed to pay their debts in a shrinking cotton market, many planters dismissed their wage laborers on a pretense after the "lay-by" of the cotton crop in midsummer. Sharecroppers, who constituted the bulk of the black laboring force, discovered after they had brought in the crop in the fall that they were no better off than the wage earners. Many planters and merchants, who had extended credit and provisions to the sharecroppers during the year, began seizing the tenants' share of the

60. General Order 5, April 15, 1867, in Records of the Fourth Military District. Ord had formed his opinion on black needs in Reconstruction as a result of his military experience in Arkansas after the war, which included a brief tenure as assistant commissioner of the Freedmen's Bureau for that state. For Gillem's opinion regarding Reconstruction priorities for blacks, see his report for October, 1867, in Freedmen's Bureau Records, Microcopy Roll 50.

crop (or in some cases expelling tenants from the land before the cotton was picked) on the grounds that because they held a first lien on the crop they were simply protecting their rights and interests.[61]

Ord viewed the situation in a different light, and beginning in August he acted to force planters to observe their contractual obligations to the freedmen. He directed the Freedmen's Bureau to investigate all allegations of fraud brought against planters, including those related to the crop of 1866, and in cases in which the complaints seemed valid the offenders were to be arraigned before military commissions. In instances of dispute over the possession of the crop, or any portion of it, bureau officers were instructed to prevent the movement of the cotton to market until a just settlement had been made. Ord provided for the creation of three-member boards of arbitration to hear and render decisions in each case of conflict over the cotton crop. He directed that the boards consist of one referee selected by the landowner or merchant, one by the laborer, and the third by the other two board members.[62] He later extended the jurisdiction of the boards of arbitration to include conflicts between laborers and furnishing merchants. In these disputes Ord directed that "the claims of the laborer will be the first satisfied. This is deemed necessary to afford proper encouragement to free labor."[63]

Anticipating planter criticism of his action, Ord sought to soothe ruffled feathers by announcing that "only a low class of men" were guilty of defrauding their tenants, and the vast majority of landowners had no reason to fear military intervention in their affairs. He claimed that instead of compounding the labor difficulties experienced by planters his policy would go far toward restoring labor stability in the state, since the work morale of black tenants would be bolstered by the knowledge that they would not be cheated out of a just return for their efforts.[64]

The results of Ord's labor policies were encouraging at first.

61. Gillem to Howard, August 5, 1867, Microcopy Roll 47, and report of Gillem for October, 1867, Microcopy Roll 50, both in Freedmen's Bureau Records.
62. General Order 19, August 13, 1867, in Records of the Fourth Military District.
63. Circular of October 23, 1867, circular 22, November 30, 1867, and circular 24, December 16, 1867, all in *ibid.*
64. General Order 19, August 13, 1867, *ibid.*

During the fall, boards of arbitration and officers of the Freed-men's Bureau adjudicated hundreds of disputes over cotton and wages, almost five hundred cases being decided in October alone.[65] Even many planters grudgingly admitted that military intervention in plantation affairs tended to give blacks confidence and restore a degree of labor stability during an otherwise difficult period for Mississippi agriculture. Conservative newspapers carried very few complaints regarding the activities of labor referees, and in the eastern part of the state, an area that would later be plagued by Ku Klux Klan terror, a bureau officer reported that the boards of arbitration "have worked well and [have] been of great service to many of the whites as well as to the colored people."[66]

Nevertheless, the labor referee system had a brief existence. When the crop of 1867 fell far short of expectations and poverty once again raised its ugly head, General Gillem, who had by then replaced Ord, abolished the boards of arbitration and returned planter-labor disputes to the regular courts.[67] Gillem, who increasingly came to sympathize with white planters and merchants as social and economic conditions seemingly reached crisis proportions during the winter of 1867–1868, concluded that the summary settlement of disputes over cotton and compensation for tenants uniformly and unjustly injured the planter's interest and critically delayed the restoration of the state's economy. In most cases, Gillem pointed out, planters had furnished laborers with provisions, which they had gone into debt to secure either from outside wholesalers or from local merchants; when planters could not collect from their tenants because of military interference, they were unable to meet their obligations, much less to realize a profit from the cotton crop. "Instances have occurred where the planters have entirely abandoned the crop to the laborers, losing their time, the use of their animals and implements and the supplies advanced," Gillem reported. "Cases have been brought to my attention of planting where not only the entire crop has been turned over to the laborers to satisfy their claims, but also the mules and implements

65. Report of Gillem for October, 1867, Microcopy Roll 50, and report of Gillem for quarter ending March 31, 1868, Microcopy Roll 54, both in Freedmen's Bureau Records.

66. John D. Moore to Merritt Barber, January 31, 1868, in Freedmen's Bureau Records, Mississippi.

67. General Order 6, January 27, 1868, in Records of the Fourth Military District.

used in its production. The result of this condition of affairs is the almost universal determination of planters to abandon the culture of cotton, and even if they wished to prosecute it another year, it would, I apprehend, be impossible for them to procure further advance of the necessary supplies from any merchant."[68] The termination of the boards of arbitration would go far, Gillem believed, to restore planter and merchant confidence in the agricultural future of the state. As a result landowners and merchants would come forward to make arrangements with laborers for the new year, and the "tumult of anarchy" that the conservative press had predicted would be avoided.

General Ord's intervention in economic matters was not restricted to the protection of blacks in labor contracts. His first—and most popular—action to counter economic distress in the Fourth Military District was his order of June 12, 1867, imposing a moratorium until January 1, 1868, on forced sales of property.[69] Prior to this the dockets of the civil courts had groaned with foreclosure petitions. The elected officials, most of whom were credit-conscious, old-line Whigs, had done nothing to prevent the mass sacrifice of property for debts and taxes, fearing that such action would further tarnish the financial reputation of Mississippi, which had suffered since the state's repudiation of the Planters' and Union Bank bonds during the 1840s. The district commander's decree was designed to give relief to hard-pressed debtors until the federal bankruptcy law of 1867 became effective and until the year's cotton crop was harvested.

In the same order Ord directed his subordinates to seek out and destroy illicit whiskey distilleries (*i.e.*, those that neither had a license to operate nor paid the federal tax on whiskey). All whiskey confiscated in these operations was to be sold to legitimate dealers and the proceeds divided among the poor of the county where it was seized. By this action, Ord sought to conserve for the tables of the poor the scarce supply of grains in the region. In addition, he used this campaign against moonshiners to point out the more

68. Gillem's comments on the workings of Ord's labor policies are contained in his special report of December 10, 1867, dated three weeks before he assumed command of the Fourth Military District. The report may be found in *Appleton's Annual Cyclopaedia*, 1867, p. 518, and in the Jackson *Clarion*, December 29, 1867.

69. General Order 12, June 12, 1867, in Records of the Fourth Military District.

direct relationship of hard liquor to impoverishment. "Poverty increases where whiskey abounds," he succinctly observed, suggesting that if southerners curbed their consumption of alcohol their economic problems would be reduced. The old citizenry generally did not find Ord's policy toward moonshiners offensive, since, as the Jackson *Clarion* remarked, obviously with tongue in cheek, "We do not think that [it] is applicable to many cases in Mississippi."[70]

When social and economic conditions did not improve in late 1867, Ord became a convert to the conservative crusade for white immigration as a partial solution to the state's economic difficulties. He requested from county officials information and statistics on a variety of items, which he planned to compile and publish for the benefit of prospective immigrants.[71] This information, however, was never collected, and a unified state effort to secure immigrants did not develop until after military reconstruction.

By December a winter of social unrest appeared to be closing in on Mississippi mainly as a consequence of the disastrous crop failure. Gillem reported to Ord that the production of cotton for the year "has not exceeded half of what was regarded as an average crop, and that has commanded but one-half of the previous year, thus reducing the proceeds to one-fourth of what was anticipated by the planter and freedman as the proceeds of the year's labor." As a result, Gillem informed his superior, "thousands are without labor, and must subsist; consequently depredation [on livestock] is the rule and honesty is the exception" among blacks.[72]

The political excitement generated by the impending "Black and Tan" Convention and the spread of rumors that at Christmas Negroes would finally receive their forty acres of land heightened the feeling of crisis that prevailed in the state in late 1867. Gillem excitedly informed Ord that he feared an outbreak of racial violence in the plantation counties unless measures were taken immediately to aid blacks in distress and to maintain order. "I receive almost daily petitions and memorials asserting the existence of organized companies of freedmen, and asking the presence of troops, and al-

70. Jackson *Clarion*, June 16, 1867.
71. Form letter of instructions from Ord to county civil officials, November 21, 1867, in Records of the Fourth Military District; Columbus *Southern Sentinel*, November 22, 1867.
72. As reported in the Jackson *Clarion*, December 29, 1867.

though I am satisfied that these presentations are generally the result of fear and exaggerated rumors, yet the existence of such organizations in some sections of the State is certain." The bureau, Gillem said, was doing all in its power to prevent a racial clash. "Commanders of troops and agents of the Bureau have been instructed to urge upon the freedmen the absolute necessity of abstaining from armed demonstrations. They will be protected in all their rights, but they must not seek redress by force of violence."[73]

The most unsettling reports came from Lauderdale County where Union Leagues were organized into military companies and reportedly were planning to invade Meridian and the neighboring town of Marion. The purpose of the rumored invasion was not to seize or demand lands but to secure by force the food and clothing that merchants were unwilling to extend to blacks on credit. Apparently a group of militant blacks in the leagues actually plotted such an assault, but moderate counsel prevailed after R. C. Merryman, a white Republican organizer from Virginia who, according to his own statement, had been offered the command of the invasion force, revealed the plans of the radicals. This disclosure was followed by the military arrest of several Negroes suspected of plotting insurrection.[74]

Distressed by the Meridian incident and by reports of mounting racial tension in the plantation counties, Ord wired General Grant on December 7 that unless outside federal aid was extended to the destitute "a war of races" would erupt in the state. In the river counties, he informed Grant, little corn had been produced during the past two years, and the cotton crop of 1867 had not made expenses for either planters or sharecroppers. Planters were reluctant to employ freedmen for the new year, and blacks were reciprocating by rejecting the contracts that were offered. Negroes, reported Ord, "have spent the results of this year's work—are in large numbers armed and plundering for food. Owners are leaving the country for safety—and there is reason to fear a war of races if

73. *Ibid.* In southwest Mississippi, an area of perennial racial conflict, the former commander of the state militia blamed the heightened tensions of the winter on both ragtag secessionists and black troublemakers. Oscar J. E. Stuart to O. G. Greene, Ord's adjutant, December 20, 1867, in John B. S. Dimitry Papers, Duke University Library, Durham.

74. Meridian *Semi-Weekly Gazette*, December 4, 7, 1867. At the same time a march on Columbus by local blacks was dispersed peacefully by federal troops. *Hinds County Gazette* (Raymond, Miss.), December 6, 1867.

the blacks are not fed. From all sides appeals reach me for troops to protect the whites. . . . An appropriation of half a million to repair levees from Tunica to Vicksburg by blacks might avert this disaster. There is no time to lose."[75]

At the same time Ord dispatched Gillem to Washington to plead the necessity of federal aid for Mississippi. Gillem conferred with President Johnson, General Grant, and Commissioner Oliver Otis Howard of the Freedmen's Bureau.[76] Grant was not persuaded that a crisis existed, and a few days later in a presentation to the Johnson cabinet he criticized Ord for exaggerating the threat of racial disorders in Mississippi. Overlooking Gillem's role in creating the near hysteria at Fourth Military District headquarters, Grant called for Ord's removal, a recommendation that Johnson approved on December 27.[77]

Only Commissioner Howard was impressed by the seriousness of conditions in the state. Although he had limited financial means to support a large-scale relief program, Howard authorized Gillem as head of the bureau in Mississippi "to adopt such a system of aid . . . as the condition of affairs in the State might demand." The only qualification that Howard attached to this authorization, according to Gillem, was that government provisions must be extended through the planters and not given directly to tenants. When Gillem returned to Mississippi, he instructed subordinates to make "a rigid inspection of the entire State" to determine if the need for government rations still existed. Never as favorable as Ord to a policy of federal aid for the poor, Gillem, now in command of the military district, concluded from the reports of his officers that the necessity for assistance had passed and the cause of labor stability would be best served if he dropped the whole subject.[78]

75. Ord to Ulysses S. Grant, December 7, 1867, in Records of the United States Army Commands, Fourth Military District, Civil Affairs, Letters Sent, 1867, Record Group 98, National Archives.

76. Jackson *Clarion*, December 29, 1867; *Hinds County Gazette*, January 3, 1868; report of Gillem for quarter ending March 31, 1868, in Freedmen's Bureau Records, Microcopy Roll 54.

77. Entries for December 24, 27, 1867, in Orville H. Browning, *The Diary of Orville Hickman Browning* (2 vols.; Springfield, 1933), II, 170–71; Natchez *Weekly Democrat*, January 6, 1868.

78. Report of Gillem for quarter ending March 31, 1868, in Freedmen's Bureau Records, Microcopy Roll 54.

While awaiting the response of Washington to his request for
material aid and prior to his replacement as district commander,
Ord took steps to prevent the expected outbreaks of violence.
Somewhat uncharacteristically, Ord gave civil authorities the main
responsibility for initiating action to prevent racial violence, although military officers were directed to arrest and hold for trial
incendiaries and persons who incited the freedmen "to illegal and
seditious acts." Civil authorities were to call on the army for assistance only after they had tried and failed to control local disturbances. Ord authorized the issuance of a proclamation by Governor
Humphreys warning disorderly persons that civil officials would
have the full support of the military in suppressing violent clashes.
Humphreys acted immediately: on December 9 he issued a proclamation directed at both whites and blacks, though its tone indicated that the governor obviously intended the message to be mainly
for Negroes.[79] He plainly told blacks that an insurrection to seize
property would end in bitter failure and a setback for the cause of
Negro freedom. Conspiracies against the peace of the state would
be discovered early, and the first clash of arms "will signalize the
destruction of your cherished hopes and the ruin of your race." On
the other hand if they remained peaceful and continued in their
occupations they would be protected in all of their "rights, privileges, liberty and property." The governor advised blacks that
their "only security and hope of prosperity [was] in honest and
virtuous peace."

At the same time Governor Humphreys admonished whites to
respect the rights of blacks. "As you prize constitutional liberty for
yourselves, so you must accord to the black race the full measure of
their rights, privileges, and liberties secured to them by the Constitution and laws of the land," he told fellow whites. "You cannot
live with them in peace and prosperity as wrongdoers. You must
deal justly in all your transactions and contracts with them, and in
no case undertake to redress wrongs, except in the mode authorized by law." The governor, moreover, directed officials to enforce faithfully "the laws without bias or partiality towards either

79. Ord's authorization and Humphrey's proclamation may be found in circular 23, December 14, 1867, in Records of the Fourth Military District, and in the January, 1868,
issues of the Jackson *Clarion*.

race, and should resistance be made to legal process too formidable to be suppressed by the ordinary course of law, prompt assistance will be afforded by the United States military authorities."

Mississippi blacks and their white Republican allies could find no redeeming features in Governor Humphreys' proclamation. Negroes meeting at Columbus to denounce the governor's prejudicial action resolved that "the proposition to 'seize lands' is so absurd to our minds that we hardly know how to treat it." They recommended that members of their race throughout the state hurriedly call similar meetings to protest the proclamation.[80] Although only a few meetings were held, so strong was the reaction to the proclamation that Ord felt the need to explain his part in the affair to indignant Negroes. He pleaded that he had "never apprehended such foolish and illegal acts as a seizure by violence of the property of others by intelligent colored men; such acts, if contemplated, would be committed by the ignorant and evil ones." The actions of the authorities in the matter, Ord weakly insisted, "were intended as a warning to such men (white or black)."[81]

The Republican-dominated constitutional convention that met in Jackson in January, 1868, took up the proclamation issue and appointed a committee to determine if there had been any truth in the reports that blacks plotted insurrection. This committee, consisting of six Republicans, found no evidence of such plans; conversely, it reported that Mississippi freedmen were "true and loyal to the country, and patient and submissive even when the victim of cruel and oppressive wrongs." The committee admitted, however, that neither the military authorities nor the governor had made available the documents that pertained to the insurrection scare.[82] The matter continued to be a sore point with blacks, and in

---

80. Black leader John Hinton to Governor Humphreys, December 21, 1867, in Governors' Correspondence, Record Group 27, Vol. 68, Mississippi Department of Archives and History, hereinafter cited as Governors' Correspondence. The Columbus blacks declared that their race wanted no part of violence: "We want peace and reconciliation with the whites, and as for believing that we would be the victors in such a conflict, we cannot in reason believe such an absurdity, with numbers, intellect, wealth, and, in fact, everything against us." Vicksburg *Times,* January 7, 1868.

81. Ord's assistant adjutant general to [?] Thomas, December 30, 1868, in Records of the United States Army Commands, Fourth Military District, Civil Affairs, Letters Sent.

82. *Journal of the Proceedings in the Constitutional Convention of the State of Mississippi, 1868* (Jackson, 1871), 396–97.

subsequent political campaigns Republicans used it to good effect to rally blacks to their standard.

Gillem, who succeeded Ord as district commander on January 9, 1868, while continuing as assistant commissioner of the bureau, believed that racial tension could be eased only after planters and laborers had made agreements for the new planting season. Blacks at first refused to enter labor contracts for 1868, not so much because they expected to receive their mythical forty acres, as many reports indicated, but because the compensation that planters were willing to offer then was considerably less than that promised (although not necessarily received) in 1867.[83] In addition, the bitter feeling that they had been shortchanged in the fall crop settlements caused many to hesitate to contract for the new year. Planters on the other hand blamed their failures on the inefficiency of Negro labor and its high price in 1867. During the winter numerous meetings were held in which planters resolved to reduce substantially the freedman's wages or share of the crop in the 1868 contracts. The result was an impasse in negotiations between planters and blacks which extended into the new year and became critical as the time for planting approached.[84]

Many blacks were so discouraged that they left the state. The Aberdeen *Examiner* reported, "Not a train passes up the Mobile and Ohio Railroad but bears many of them to Tennessee and Alabama, while we learn that they are leaving the counties on the Mississippi river by every steamer passing up to Missouri, Illinois and other of the States of the great West." The decrease in the black population of Monroe County (Aberdeen) alone was reported to have been between three and four hundred.[85] The Washington

83. *Ibid.*, pp. 225–26; *Appleton's Annual Cyclopaedia*, 1867, p. 518; Jackson *Clarion*, February 22, 1868; George W. Corliss to Barber, January 31, 1868, in Freedmen's Bureau Records, Mississippi. Not all planters reneged on their promises to their black tenants when the crop failed in 1867. Some planters continued to sustain their tenants even after their own credit with merchants was depleted and they were experiencing severe difficulty in making ends meet. Entry for August 6, 1867, in Darden Diary; William Shields to Barber, January 31, 1868, in Freedmen's Bureau Records, Mississippi.

84. Jackson *Clarion*, December 5, 19, 1867, January 7, 1868; Natchez *Tri-Weekly Courier*, January 8, 1868; entries for December 28, 1867, and January 1, 1868, in Darden Diary; report of Gillem for quarter ending March 31, 1868, in Freedmen's Bureau Records, Microcopy Roll 54.

85. As reported in the Natchez *Weekly Democrat*, February 3, 1868. See also Jackson *Clarion*, February 13, 1868.

National Intelligencer claimed that a large group of Mississippi blacks, who had not received the wages they desired, had petitioned Congress to provide the means for them to go to Africa.[86] Most plans to leave the state never materialized; nonetheless, in 1868 for the only time during Reconstruction a large number of Mississippi blacks felt a strong impulse to seek opportunities elsewhere. Ironically, black disillusionment and the desire to shake off the dust of Mississippi—caused mainly by the economic dislocation of the winter—was most intense at a time when black political expectations were the highest, after the election of 1867 and the convening of the constitutional convention of 1868 that promised to make secure black political equality in the state.

In order to break the deadlock between planters and laborers, Gillem in January, 1868, directed bureau officers "to use every means in their power to procure situations for laborers on the best terms." Federal authorities refrained, however, from forcing freedmen to make contracts, as they had done in 1866 and as some planters expected them to do in 1868; instead bureau agents, following Gillem's instructions, sought out opportunities for blacks and encouraged them to accept only promising employment.[87] Nevertheless, the need for work became so crucial to most Negroes as the planting season approached that they spurned the good offices of bureau agents and made contracts that represented pretty much what the planters had initially offered. Whereas wage hands in the 1867 contracts had received as high as eighteen dollars a month in the river counties and ten to fifteen dollars elsewhere, their compensation for 1868 rarely exceeded ten dollars a month, and in nonplantation districts it dropped to as low as four.[88] Many black sharecroppers, however, secured almost complete independence from the supervision of the landowner, a status that had eluded them in 1867, the first year in which sharecropping was practiced on a large scale. But the new freedom from planter control proved a mixed

86. Jackson *Clarion*, February 22, 1868.

87. Gillem's directive may be found in the *Journal of the Constitutional Convention of 1868*, pp. 225–26.

88. *Ibid.*, 224; report of bureau agent Allen P. Huggins, April 30, 1868, report of George S. Smith, February 10, 1868, report of J. D. Webster, May 1, 1868, all in Freedmen's Bureau Records, Mississippi; report of Gillem for quarter ending March 31, 1868, in Freedmen's Bureau Records, Microcopy Roll 54.

blessing for most blacks. Sharecroppers under this arrangement were required to furnish all of their farm equipment and mules as well as to make arrangements with local merchants for the necessities of life. Inexperienced in farm management and unable to obtain adequate credit, many black sharecroppers, who in the beginning of the year saw an opportunity to gain their independence from planter control, soon found themselves mired in a hopeless situation. All too frequently in early 1868 they were without the means to secure or feed a mule, if they had one; many blacks were thus forced to plant their crops with hoes and live in want, even while their representatives met at the state capitol to make them the political equals of whites in Mississippi.[89]

89. Report of Gillem for quarter ending March 31, 1868, in Freedmen's Bureau Records, Microcopy Roll 54; L. H. Thistle to Elizabeth Calcote, March 25, 1868, in Dimitry Papers.

2

Interregnum

The military regime in Mississippi combatted crime, initiated action to protect the fundamental rights of blacks, intervened in planter-labor disputes, demonstrated a concern for the health and education of freedmen, and set in motion the plan of political reconstruction imposed by Congress. Nevertheless, military authorities, who controlled affairs from March, 1867, to March, 1870, failed to provide the kind of positive leadership in the administration of the more traditional functions of state and local government demanded during this critical period of postwar adjustment and uncertainty.[1] Although possessing broad authority to act, General Ord and his successors in command did not believe that their responsibilities under the reconstruction laws would be served by an active policy of intervening in the civil administration of the state. In order to avoid military abuses the district commanders maintained a close supervision over the post commanders who dealt directly with the people and with local officials. These officers were expected to be as unobtrusive as possible in exercising their authority and were discouraged, though not prohibited, from interfering with the regular administration of the state. Except when ordered to do so, post commanders rarely risked the displeasure of the district commander by dabbling in civil matters.

To some extent the military was wise in shunning interference in matters that required legislative policy decisions and in refusing to take action on issues that might be overturned with the restoration of civil control. Moreover, the intricacies of postwar problems called for the formulation and implementation of policies that were beyond the competence of professional army officers. But in maintaining an aloofness from most of the mundane affairs of government and thereby contributing to the confusion regarding the au-

1. An account of the implementation of political reconstruction will follow this chapter. See Chap. 10 herein for a discussion of the role of the Freedmen's Bureau in the education of black youths. The period of military reconstruction was longer in Mississippi, Texas, and Virginia than in the other affected southern states. Although military control ended in 1868 in most of the states, it lingered until 1870 in Mississippi, Texas, and Virginia.

thority of the holdover civil administration, the military rulers, as time would soon prove, were condemning the state to all of the stifling effects of an interregnum.

During military reconstruction a number of public matters needed the immediate and careful attention of public authorities. The state institutions—the insane asylum, the penitentiary, the deaf and blind asylum, the public hospitals at Natchez and Vicksburg, and the university at Oxford—languished in a deplorable condition after years of neglect. The financial structure of the state tottered on the edge of ruin, and the legal-judicial system needed to be revitalized and reformed to conform to postwar realities. In addition, public direction for essential internal improvements and the material development of the state, including the extension of railroad lines, the construction of a durable levee to protect inundated Delta lands, and the development of the promising Gulf Coast and piney woods, was urgently required. The legislature, the normal instrument for giving life to such programs, adjourned one month before Ord's arrival in Mississippi and was not permitted to meet again during the three-year period of military reconstruction. Officials in the holdover government, although directed by Governor Humphreys to remain in their positions until relieved, were demoralized and confused about their responsibilities under army supervision. In most cases they thought of themselves as caretakers without authority to plan or carry out policies, no matter how pressing or desirable these might be.[2] While the firm hand of General Ord was in control, even though he refused to intervene directly in most matters, the dual government showed few signs of weakness or inefficiency; however, under General Gillem in 1868 and General Adelbert Ames in 1869 the descent toward paralysis became rapid. "The evil is terrible," Giles M. Hillyer, the venerable Union-Whig editor of the Vicksburg *Times*, declared in 1869. "We are without law, without courts, without officers of justice; the whole county judicial system of the State is paralyzed; the whole municipal system is stopped."[3]

The most obvious shoals upon which the dual military-civil gov-

2. For a clear indication of such an attitude, see Oscar J. E. Stuart to O. G. Greene, December 20, 1867, in Dimitry Papers. See also the Jackson *Clarion*, July 15, 1869, the *Hinds County Gazette*, July 7, 1869, and R. B. Mayes to John Tyler, March 22, 1869, in Dimitry Papers.

3. Vicksburg *Times*, April 6, 1869.

ernment floundered were financial. The ambiguous nature of authority, particularly in interior areas of the state where authority was never taken very seriously anyway, made it extremely difficult for officials to collect the tax revenue necessary to operate the state and local governments. In many cases sympathetic sheriffs, who doubled as tax collectors in the counties, simply refused to put pressure on citizens to meet the levies. Public indifference, if not hostility, toward taxes was accentuated by the economic hardships of the period. The refusal to pay taxes, however, resulted in the continued depreciation of warrants, which had been issued in anticipation of a steady flow of revenue into the state and county treasuries. If not checked, the decline in the value of the warrants could soon lead to financial disaster.

Appeals by the state auditor to the military commanders for a show of authority to force the payment and collection of taxes under the laws of the state produced inadequate results. By late 1867 an estimated one fourth to one third of the people of the state were avoiding the payment of all taxes levied against them; others were only meeting part of their tax obligations.[4] The situation became so bad that State Treasurer John H. Echols reported in mid-1868 that when he received a few dollars from tax collectors he immediately distributed the money to warrant holders "who are so plentiful and anxious that they swarm in and about my office at all times; and I can say without fear of contradiction that their attendance has been so continuous that I have never opened a remittance without witnesses from one to twenty persons." Echols complained that he did not even have the funds to purchase stationery for the constitutional convention of 1868.[5]

Speculation in depreciated state and county warrants became an

4. Thomas J. Swann to J. B. Randolph, April 28, 1868, and Swann to Homer C. Powers, in Letterbook of the Auditor of the State of Mississippi for 1868, Mississippi Department of Archives and History; *Hinds County Gazette*, November 8, 1867. The correspondence of the state auditor during this period only rarely alludes to the existence of military authority in Mississippi. On matters of finance, tax assessment, collection of taxes, sale of lands for taxes and their redemption, civil officials, although imperfectly and hesitantly, followed the acts of the legislature of 1865–67. The only exception to this policy was a directive issued by Gillem regarding the collection of the tax levied by the 1868 constitutional convention. Thomas J. Swann to J. M. Lewis, April 30, 1868, and Swann to Robert Williams, April 23, 1868, in Auditor's Letterbook.

5. John H. Echols to Adelbert Ames, July 21, 1868, in Governors' Correspondence, Vol. 69; New York *Tribune*, January 16, 1868.

inviting field for financially shrewd individuals and for unscrupulous officials who participated in schemes to defraud the public in the exchange of currency for warrants. Manipulation of the local warrant market was developed to a fine art in Vicksburg, where carpetbag chief Charles E. Furlong and his cronies began defrauding the taxpayers soon after the military commander appointed him sheriff. His corrupt manipulation of the warrant-currency exchange continued until the reform movement of the early 1870s ran him out of office.[6]

Sharp reductions in state expenditures for public services in 1869 somewhat improved the status of warrants as military rule gave way to civil authority. The amount of outstanding state warrants had been reduced from $778,632 in 1868 to $287,993 in March, 1870, when the Alcorn administration took office. Nevertheless, by 1870 warrants were being sold for as little as sixty cents on the dollar with little immediate hope that their value would rise.[7] County finances were in no better shape; for example, in Hinds County (Jackson), formerly one of the wealthiest counties in the state, local warrants on the eve of Republican control were being hawked for sixty cents on the dollar, the same rate that state warrants could command.[8]

The most obvious sufferers from the impecunious financial condition of the government and the ambiguity of administrative authority during the military phase of reconstruction were the public institutions. Nowhere was the situation more critical than in the penitentiary at Jackson. Partially destroyed during the war and with increased demands placed upon it as a result of the dramatic social changes that followed emancipation and Confederate defeat, the state penitentiary had proved such a drain on the treasury during presidential reconstruction that the Humphreys administration

6. See the Vicksburg *Herald*, October 6, 1868, and Henry B. Whitfield to the Stewart and Hamilton Company of Jackson, March 21, 1868, in Henry B. Whitfield and Company Papers, Mississippi Department of Archives and History.

7. State treasurer's report for 1868, in Jackson *Weekly Clarion*, June 3, 1869; *Appleton's Annual Cyclopaedia*, 1870, p. 514; *Journal of the Senate of the State of Mississippi [1870]* (Jackson, 1870), Appendix, 109; *Annual Message of Governor Jas. L. Alcorn to the Mississippi Legislature, Session of 1871* (Jackson, 1871), 45.

8. Clay Sharkey, "Misrule in Mississippi," essay in Clay Sharkey Papers, Mississippi Department of Archives and History. One traveler in central Mississippi in 1868 found only one county that had a manageable debt. Jackson *Clarion*, May 12, 1868.

in 1867 introduced the system of convict leasing.[9] This arrangement provided for the farming out of prisoners to a private contractor who agreed to assume responsibility for the convicts in exchange for their labor. Although the lease on the penitentiary later
became a prize that planters and businessmen eagerly sought,
Governor Humphreys met with failure in his early efforts to obtain
a long-term contract for the prisoners, and he soon found himself
in a critical bind to maintain the institution. By late 1867 the legislative appropriation for the prison had been spent, leaving penitentiary officials without money to purchase supplies and pay the
guards. Humphreys met with General Ord and informed him that
unless the military assumed direction of the penitentiary he would
soon be forced either to starve the inmates or grant a general par-
don. The governor made it clear that he preferred military control
to the alternatives; however, for the record, in case he was later
called to account for his actions, Humphreys requested that if Ord
agreed to take charge of the prison he do so by a show of military
force. The general promised his cooperation, and in a few days a
squad of soldiers "seized" control of the penitentiary, much to the
relief of Humphreys and other state officials.[10]

Army control of the prison, however, brought little improvement in conditions for the 263 inmates. Ord could get no financial
support from the War Department for the prison, and the lieutenant in command of the largely civilian staff (which included the
former superintendent) passed the problem back to Humphreys
and asked him for money to keep the institution in operation. In his
request to the governor, the officer somberly described the situation in the prison. "I am compelled to state," he declared, "that
one half of the inmates have and are at present wearing the under-
clothing they have had on for six and seven months, and the same
being ragged and full of holes. I doubt if there is a more destitute
institution of the kind in the United States." He further reported
that he could find no useful employment for the prisoners, and he

9. Jackson *Clarion*, November 3, 1866, January 29, 1867.
10. Humphreys recalls this episode in a letter to a special committee of the legislature
investigating the convict lease system (January 22, 1880, in Governors' Correspondence,
Vol. 69). The policy of leasing prisoners to private contractors was adopted in all southern
states during Reconstruction, and it had been attempted in Alabama and Kentucky before
the Civil War.

was forced to keep them in their unsanitary cells most of the time. Disturbed by this report, Humphreys in an act of doubtful legality authorized the issuance of a small number of state warrants to meet the emergency and provide bare subsistence until a new lessee could be found for the penitentiary.[11]

Meanwhile, state and military authorities, working together, provided crude industrial equipment for the prisoners and employed them in producing boots, shoes, mattresses, cordwood, and furniture. In addition, penitentiary officials put a few prisoners to work as blacksmiths and wheelwrights. Competition with local private enterprise flared when the military superintendent of the prison placed an advertisement in Jackson newspapers declaring that convict goods and services could be obtained at "20 per cent. less than charged elsewhere." Their material interests challenged by the production of the prison, local artisans and businessmen organized the Jackson Mechanics' Association to counter the threat.[12] They breathed a sigh of relief in November, 1868, when Edmund Richardson, a prominent Jackson merchant and planter, obtained the lease to the penitentiary. But it was not until 1870 that the majority of the inmates were removed from the prison walls and from competition with local enterprise and put to work on Richardson's plantations in the Delta.[13]

During the military period the state insane asylum at Jackson experienced some of the same problems as the penitentiary, with the

11. Report of Edward T. Wallace to Governor Benjamin G. Humphreys, March 31, 1868 (quote); John R. Haynes to Humphreys, May 27, 1868, both in Governors' Correspondence, Vol. 69. The dual governing arrangement was carried into the penitentiary. Lieutenant Wallace described his role as "Military Superintendent" of the prison, though the civilian superintendent was permitted to continue in office. Conditions in county jails were also deplorable; in the small Vicksburg jail, for example, some eighty prisoners faced the winter of 1868–69 without proper facilities. Many convicts in this jail were awaiting transfer to the overcrowded state penitentiary, some of whom had languished in confinement for a year while awaiting vacancies in the state institution. Vicksburg *Herald*, October 1, 1868.

12. Advertisement in the Jackson *Clarion*, May 12, 1868. The mechanics secured local bipartisan support for their cause. Thomas J. Wharton, a prominent secession Democrat of the capital, and Edward Stafford, carpetbag editor of the Republican Jackson *Pilot*, were the main movers in the formation of the Mechanics' Association. Stafford, who was elected president of the organization, believed that convicts should be put to work in enterprises that did not compete with town artisans or laborers—meaning, they should be leased out to cotton planters.

13. Report of Penitentiary Committee to Governor James Lusk Alcorn, in Governors' Correspondence, Vol. 72.

difference that the district commanders demonstrated a greater concern for the plight of asylum patients than they did for prison inmates. When Superintendent A. B. Cabaniss first complained to the military in late 1867 that appropriated funds had been spent and he would have to send the patients home unless he received outside assistance, General Ord extended emergency aid to keep the institution in operation. One month later General Gillem again scraped the military barrel to aid the asylum. To provide more long-term assistance, Gillem, upon the urging of civil officials, took the unorthodox action of directing the state auditor simply to issue warrants, unsupported by tax levies, to sustain the institution.[14] These measures, however, proved insufficient. As a result, Gillem, in his capacity as assistant commissioner of the Freedmen's Bureau, assumed control of the asylum and administered it until the summer of 1868, when the institution was returned to civil management. While under federal control, a Negro ward was added and twenty-five black mental patients from the bureau hospitals at Vicksburg and Lauderdale were admitted. Gillem reported to Commissioner Howard that the policy of limited racial integration in the asylum was accomplished without difficulty.[15]

Small state hospitals at Vicksburg and Natchez, which ministered mainly to the old and infirm but also served a handful of mentally disturbed people, were neglected by both military and civil authorities. Local citizens provided adequate support to keep the doors of these institutions open until the state government was revived and resumed responsibility for them in 1870. When the Freedmen's Bureau closed its hospital at Vicksburg in 1869 and turned over its one hundred patients to the state hospital there, General Adelbert Ames extended army funds to cover the expense of the new additions.[16]

The University of Mississippi at Oxford, which had a precarious existence before the war, made little progress during Reconstruc-

14. Jackson *Clarion*, December 5, 1867, January 19, 24, 1868; Vicksburg *Herald*, August 30, 1868.

15. Ganus, "Freedmen's Bureau in Mississippi," 172; report of Gillem for quarter ending March 31, 1868, Microcopy Roll 54, and report of Gillem for quarter ending June 30, 1868, Microcopy Roll 59, both in Freedmen's Bureau Records.

16. Report of E. Swift of the state hospital in Vicksburg, March 30, 1870, in Governors' Correspondence, Vol. 72.

tion. The condition of the institution was especially bleak during the period of military rule. With inadequate facilities and a small and underpaid faculty, the university could accommodate fewer than three hundred students at this time. When legislative appropriations and income from a state lottery, chartered in February, 1867, were exhausted in 1868, Ames directed that a sufficient amount of warrants be issued to keep the doors of the university open until civil government was restored.[17] Even so, most students, hard pressed to make ends meet, found it extremely difficult to remain in school. In 1867 one half of those who were registered for classes were unable to pay for their meals and were forced to secure food from home. Like soldiers in the field, which many of them had been, they prepared their messes on the school grounds and camped out under the stars.[18]

Military authorities, including Ames who by 1869 had become a partisan Republican, showed no interest in the academic life of the university at Oxford, even though the faculty included such prominent secessionists as Lucius Q. C. Lamar. The absence of legislative authority and the disinterestedness of the dual administrators of the state prevented Mississippi during the late 1860s from claiming its share of the donation of federal lands for the university, which had been authorized by the land-grant-college act of 1862 and the supplementary law of 1866. Not until 1871 was provision made by the state for the conversion of this valuable asset to interest-bearing bonds and the application of the revenue to university needs.[19]

The indomitable university, nevertheless, survived the hard times of the early postwar period. By the end of 1869, even without adequate state support, the institution was showing clear signs of revival. Buildings had been repaired during the year and the optimistic board of trustees directed President John N. Waddel to reform the curriculum along the lines of those of the best national

17. James A. Cabaniss, *A History of the University of Mississippi* (Oxford, 1949), 80; Jackson *Clarion*, August 29, 1867 (advertisement), May 19, 1868.

18. *Appleton's Annual Cyclopaedia*, 1867, p. 520.

19. *Laws of the State of Mississippi, 1871* (Jackson, 1871), 704–706. To be eligible under the terms of the land-grant-college act, the states were required either to establish schools of agricultural and mechanical arts or to set up departments in existing universities that would teach these subjects. Mississippi chose the latter and less expensive course during Reconstruction.

universities. Curriculum reform, however, did not become a reality until the state had been restored to the Union.[20]

The material development of Mississippi, after several years of stagnation, was quite as dependent on a strong and dynamic state government as were the public institutions. No material interest required more attention and more enlightened leadership during Reconstruction than the reclamation and development of the Yazoo-Mississippi Basin or Delta. An imperfect levee to protect the rich Delta lands from the spring ravages of the swollen Mississippi River had been completed on the eve of the Civil War, only to be neglected and washed away during the conflict. The legislature of 1865 established a board of levee commissioners for the counties most susceptible to the overflows and levied a tax on cotton and land to finance the restoration of the levees. The commissioners immediately encountered difficulties in marketing their bonds because of a delinquent debt of $1,500,000 that had been accumulated by the antebellum levee district. To settle the debt and thereby restore the confidence of capitalists in levee improvements, the 1867 legislature created the Liquidating Levee Board and placed an additional, though not very large, tax on landowners in the district. Insolvent as a result of the war and the agricultural difficulties that followed it, many Delta planters could not meet these levies, which were in addition to the regular state and county taxes. The result was a mass forfeiture of alluvial properties to the state and to the two levee boards.[21]

Nevertheless, the loss of title to their lands was not an unmitigated disaster for Delta planters. The state and levee authorities could not find purchasers who were willing to risk paying delinquent taxes on property that carried an imperfect title and might never be theirs. Furthermore, potential buyers, whether outsiders or local residents, were leery of investing their money in planting in the water-ravished and labor-uncertain lowlands. Consequently, impecunious planters continued to live on and work lands that were technically in the possession of public officials. Since state-

20. Alexander M. Clayton to Charles Clark, August 4, 1869, in Charles Clark Papers, Mississippi Department of Archives and History; Jackson *Clarion*, September 23, 1869; Jackson *Weekly Pilot*, December 24, 1870.

21. For a fuller treatment of levee developments immediately after the war, see Harris, *Presidential Reconstruction in Mississippi*, Chap. X.

held lands could not be taxed, planters on these tracts had a definite advantage over their neighbors who still owned their own lands and were subject to state and levee board exactions. The effect of this situation on levee construction and the development of the rich lowlands was devastating.[22] Lacking an adequate source of revenue, levee authorities became entangled in a web of debt which postponed for many years the construction of a durable system of embankments to protect the Delta country. In addition, the futile attempts to finance the reclamation of the bottom country created an incredibly confused pattern of land tenure in the Delta which became worse during the 1870s.

Military authorities, possessing only a limited knowledge of complex Delta problems, refused to intervene and take vigorous action to reform the situation before irreparable damage was done to the economic development of the area. During the three years of military reconstruction the obsolete rules and procedures governing the levee district remained unchanged. Although unsuccessful, General Ord did join Mississippians and New York cotton interests in urging Congress to assume responsibility for the construction of a durable levee from Memphis to Vicksburg.[23] Without representatives in Congress to lobby for a practical and uniform plan of federal aid, local efforts to secure national assistance became obscured by speculative and fanciful ventures that had all the earmarks of the land-grabbing schemes that plagued such states as Louisiana and Florida during Reconstruction. One highly dubious plan that secured the support of a number of prominent Mississippians and was eventually considered by Congress called for the construction of an elevated railroad along the four-hundred-mile winding route of the river from Memphis to the mouth of the Yazoo River above Vicksburg that, when completed, would serve

22. John W. Wade, "Lands of the Liquidating Levee Board Through Litigation and Legislation," *Publications of the Mississippi Historical Society*, IX (1906), 289, 298.

23. Thomas J. Swann to J. Boatman, April 22, 1868, in Auditor's Letterbook; Jackson *Clarion*, December 19, 1867, January 10, 1868; New York *Times*, April 14, 29, October 25, 1867; James Lusk Alcorn, *Views of the Honorable J. L. Alcorn on the Political Situation of Mississippi* (Friar's Point, Miss., 1867), 4–5. The New York *Times* was especially active in seeking federal aid for the protection of Mississippi Valley lands. "No single measure," the editor averred on October 25, 1867, "so directly affects [the South's] industry and wealth as this of levee improvement." Not mentioned by the editor were the benefits that would accrue to New York merchants and shippers with the reclamation of the rich cotton lands.

also as a levee protecting the bottom lands from overflow. Not incidentally, the promoters of the scheme asked for a federal grant of twenty thousand acres of land for each mile of the route. Carpetbag editor Edward Stafford of the influential Jackson *Pilot* endorsed the plan, but when he was replaced as editor by scalawag Matthew B. Hewson, the newspaper denounced the scheme as "one of the wildest projects that ever challenged the investment of capital."[24] This cynical proposition, paralleled by a similar levee swindle in Louisiana that actually was launched much to the delight of the ring of speculators who promoted it, discredited for a time all efforts to secure national assistance for the reclamation of the Mississippi bottoms.[25]

The confusion regarding authority during the military period contributed to the financial embarrassment of the regular levee commissioners and the Liquidating Levee Board. The sheriff-tax collectors were reluctant to collect the exactions of the levee authorities even when planters were able to pay, evidently believing that the law creating the Liquidating Levee Board and levying taxes to retire the old debt was either invalid because of the imposition of military rule or would soon be voided by the district commander. Of the Delta sheriffs who served during the military phase of reconstruction only William A. Alcorn of Tallahatchie County collected and paid taxes into the treasury of the liquidating board.[26]

The regular board fared little better financially; but under the energetic leadership of board president Samuel G. French, who when appointed in 1868 had found the treasury empty, a makeshift levee was constructed by the summer of 1869, protecting most of the Delta lands from minor floods. Contributing to this surprising, though ephemeral, success was the use of inexpensive convict labor, which French secured from General Gillem and sustained for a time at his own expense. As the work progressed and revenue began to flow into the levee district treasury, French, a former

24. Jackson *Clarion*, March 9, 1868; Vicksburg *Herald*, November 26, 1868; Jackson *Weekly Pilot*, June 11, 1870.

25. Joe Gray Taylor, *Louisiana Reconstructed, 1863–1877* (Baton Rouge, 1974), 193–96; Jackson *Weekly Pilot*, May 28, June 4, 11, 1870.

26. *Journal of the House of Representatives of the State of Mississippi, 1872* (Jackson, 1872), Appendix, 915; Jackson *Pilot*, May 2, 1871.

Confederate major general, was able to market bonds in the North at a reasonably favorable rate. His achievements, however, were not appreciated by General Ames when he assumed command in the state. The young New Englander summarily removed French and the other commissioners because they could not take the iron-clad oath.[27] The new levee proved inadequate against major floods, and the Ames appointees to the board were incapable of dealing with the difficult problems involved in reclaiming the alluvial bottoms.[28] Until the levee debts could be settled and protection against overflows provided, the exploitation of the fertile Delta remained on dead center.

Although lacking the rich agricultural resources of the Delta, the piney woods, consisting of much of the vast region between the Pearl River and the Alabama border in southern Mississippi, offered a virtually virgin area for economic development and diversification during the Reconstruction era. The area's most earnest promoter was John F. H. Claiborne, the prominent historian who was also a moderately successful landowner near Pass Christian on the Gulf Coast. With only a slight suggestion of the promoter's enthusiasm for the piney woods, Claiborne in an essay vividly described the land and the possibilities for its material development:

> The soil of this region is generally thin, interspersed with small tracts of fertile land. Grass of the coarse, rank species peculiar to pine woods, grows luxuriantly, and upon it the cattle feast and fatten. In winter they find a rich pasturage in the cane and reedbrakes, and in marshes and ravines, and the long moss that hangs from the drooping limbs of

27. Samuel G. French to William T. Sherman, June 8, 9, 1869, in William Tecumseh Sherman Papers, Manuscript Division, Library of Congress; construction account, beginning with the organization of the board of levee commissioners to May 10, 1869, in Report of the Levee Commissioners, 1871–75, Series N, Vol. XVIII, Mississippi Department of Archives and History; Vicksburg *Times*, April 30, 1869. Ames could have avoided applying the ironclad requirement in the case of the levee commissioners; in fact, the Grant administration suggested that he reappoint French and his associates, but Ames refused to do so. Horace Porter to Ames, May 17, 1869, in Ulysses S. Grant Papers, Manuscript Division, Library of Congress.

28. Report of the board of levee commissioners for 1870 in the *Journal of the Senate of the State of Mississippi, 1871* (Jackson, 1871), Appendix, 480–95. The Ames board over-issued bonds to the amount of $188,000 in order to complete the levee, trusting that the first legislature under civil rule would approve the amount and make provision for its payment. The obligation was eventually assumed by the state, but only after a clash had occurred between Governor Alcorn and the legislature on the method to be used to redeem the bonds. *Senate Journal, 1871*, Appendix, 482, 498.

the swamp and live oaks. Horses, cattle, mules and sheep may be bred with profit, and without stable or grain. But the great source of wealth for this section must ultimately be the trade in lumber. It is thickly planted with a vast forest of yellow pine; on low lands with pitch pine; on lower and water lands with meadow pine—all valuable for sawing. Then on the water-courses there are large bodies of white oak, water oak, hickory or gum, of many varieties and of gigantic proportions. The swamps are studded with juniper, cedar and cypress. Finer, straighter, loftier trees than these forests can show, are nowhere found. For a hundred and fifty miles on a stretch, one may traverse these ancient woods, and see them as they stood for countless years, untouched by the hand of man, scathed only by lightning or the hurricane.[29]

Their appetite for profits whetted by such descriptions, lumbermen immediately after the war erected "peckerwood" sawmills along the two north-south trunk lines that led to New Orleans and Mobile and also established larger mills near the mouths of the rivers that flowed into the Mississippi Sound. But the development of the lumber industry in the piney woods, as well as other economic activities in the area, was limited by inadequate port facilities on the coast and by the lack of feeder railroad lines traversing the interior. Furthermore, the long-heralded proposal to build a railroad from some point in central or northern Mississippi to the undeveloped deep-water harbor near Ship Island had not received the state assistance necessary to get the project moving. The completion of such a road would not have produced the miraculous economic development of the region that its two generations of promoters anticipated, but it would have gone far toward opening a large area to future growth. The period immediately after the war, when old economic patterns were shattered and enthusiasm was strong for new directions in state growth, was crucial to the development of the southern coast. The absence of a continuous and effective government in the state capital after the war, however, retarded local efforts along these lines. State encouragement and aid were essential to the success of ambitious projects that would

29. This description may be found in Richard Griggs (comp.), *Guide to Mississippi* (Jackson, 1874), 12. See also other postwar sketches by Claiborne of the new Mississippi frontier in *Report of Mississippi State Board of Centennial Managers, Including Historical Address of Gen. A. M. West, and Letter from Hon. J. F. H. Claiborne, Descriptive of the Pine Region of Mississippi* (Jackson, 1877), 28–38, and John F. H. Claiborne, *The Pine District of Mississippi* (N.p., 1881).

serve as foundations for future economic progress in south Mississippi.

A major need that received only fleeting attention from public officials in Jackson was the improvement of the harbor at the mouth of the Pascagoula River, the center of the promising lumber industry along the coast. The legislature of 1867, dominated by old-line Whigs who traditionally had supported public improvements of this kind, was anxious to aid the work at Pascagoula. But lacking funds, the legislature instead placed in private hands the task of improving the harbor. A charter was granted to James O. Noyes of New Orleans to deepen the channel at the mouth of the Pascagoula so that ocean-going vessels could navigate the river and drop anchor near the sawmills. When the work was finished, Noyes could collect tolls on ships using the river. Completed in May, 1868, the Noyes channel was a severe disappointment to Pascagoula promoters, since it could only be used by light-draft vessels and since the improvements were obviously temporary in nature. Gulf Coast entrepreneurs again looked to Jackson for assistance but were met with indifference from the provisional state government. Turning to the federal government in Washington, they soon discovered that they had little chance for success until the state had been restored to the Union and had representatives in Congress who could plead for harbor improvement funds.[30]

The most ambitious and popular undertaking to develop the piney woods and the Mississippi coast was the antebellum scheme for a railroad from the heartland of the state, through the central piney woods, and on to deep water near Ship Island. Beginning with the conception of the plan in 1850 and continuing until its promoters became disillusioned with the project during the 1880s, public discussions of the merits of the Ship Island scheme were marked by hyperbole and a naïve faith that its early completion would produce a commercial revolution in south Mississippi.[31] Proposals for this road took many forms, and almost all of them

30. James Ossaze to Humphreys, May 26, 1868, in Governors' Correspondence, Vol. 69; Pascagoula (Miss.) *Star*, February 1, 28, 1874.

31. For examples of the enthusiasm of Mississippians for the Ship Island road, see the *Journal of the House of Representatives of the State of Mississippi, 1858* (Jackson, 1858), Appendix, 4–18; the Jackson *Weekly Mississippian*, February 17, 1858; and the Forest (Miss.) *Register*, June 30, 1869.

represented peculiarly local interests. From the beginning the inability of these interests to agree on a route for the road and a plan for financing it worked against the success of the scheme, and the political confusion accompanying military reconstruction resulted in the temporary abandonment of efforts to build the railroad.

Hardly noticed by Mississippians of the interior was the beginning of construction in March, 1869, of the New Orleans and Mobile Railroad.[32] Chartered before military reconstruction but given no state financial aid, this road when completed in 1870 would connect the Mississippi Gulf Coast by railroad with the outside world, making available important new commercial opportunities for the area.

Despite the lack of state leadership for economic development during this period, Mississippians were alive to all kinds of railroad schemes. To many people railroad development offered a means for curing their severe economic ills. Promoters of railroad enterprises had hoped to obtain state aid, but since the legislature could not meet to authorize assistance and army authorities refused to sanction such projects, they were forced to turn to local governments for financing. Money was tight at first, but in 1869, when a brief financial rally occurred as a result of the relatively successful cotton crop of the previous fall, communities and counties became quite receptive to railroad appeals. Military authorities permitted local elections to be held (as provided for by the laws of the state) to allow voters to decide whether or not they wanted to subscribe to the stock or bonds of the companies. In most cases voters approved the requests for aid, and in some counties the people committed themselves to a tax of more than $200,000 toward the construction of pet railroads.[33] Because of a lack of overall surveillance, several of the railroad elections were conducted under questionable circumstances. On one occasion a town board of aldermen without legal authority approved a $100,000 subscription to the bonds of a shaky railroad company.[34] Only roads, however, that had been in-

32. Jackson *Weekly Clarion*, March 18, 1869.

33. *Ibid.*, April 1, 22, May 27, 1869; Jackson *Weekly Pilot*, December 25, 1869; *Hinds County Gazette*, April 28, 1869; Vicksburg *Times*, March 18, 1869.

34. Affidavit of Joel Abney, president of the Calhoun County Board of Supervisors, September 1, 1873, in Papers Relating to Railroads in Mississippi, File N-19, Mississippi Department of Archives and History. Ironically, the railroad of Nathan Bedford Forrest,

corporated prior to military control could seek public financial assistance, and such promising enterprises as the Yazoo Valley Railroad through the heart of the Delta and the Natchez and Jackson Railroad were forced to wait for civil rule before securing charters and becoming eligible for aid. Even so, the roads that had received local pledges of support before the 1870 reconstruction of the state found that these were often empty promises, since tax revenues were not forthcoming to meet the subscriptions.[35] Furthermore, sums of money far in excess of what local governments could provide were needed to complete most of the proposed railroads.

The impatience of railroad enthusiasts to get on with the work of construction caused many of them to desire a quick political reconstruction of the state, despite the probable Republican character of the new administration. The success of the railroad projects, they realized, depended on the restoration of a civil government that could act on petitions for charters and on requests for material aid to build the lines.[36]

Although maintaining a proper military aloofness on projects for the economic development of Mississippi, General Ames, alone of the army commanders, intervened against the established railroads to force them to honor their obligations to the state. He did not hesitate to draw swords with the New Orleans, Jackson, and Great Northern Railroad when reports reached him that a scheme was afoot to defraud the public of $346,000 that the road owed the state from the 1856 loan of the Chickasaw School Fund.[37] Three other interstate railroad companies had also received antebellum loans

---

one of the most villainous of Confederate generals in the eyes of northerners, was the chief beneficiary of army looseness in local subscription matters. Minutes of the Board of Aldermen of the City of Aberdeen, passed in reference to the Selma, Marion, and Memphis Railroad Company, November 7, 1868, *ibid.*

35. See the Natchez *Weekly Democrat*, December 16, 1869, and the Vicksburg *Times*, March 18, 1869.

36. E. W. Smith to Henry Musgrove, June 27, 1873, in Railroad Papers; *Hinds County Gazette*, December 22, 1869.

37. John D. Freeman, *Petition of the New Orleans, Jackson and G. N. Railroad Company to the Governor and Legislature of Mississippi* (Jackson, 1870), 6, 9–10. Not all railroad managers were as wise as the officers of the Vicksburg and Meridian Railroad in cultivating the goodwill of the military rulers. In an action designed to obtain General Gillem's support for the railroad, they secured his election to the company's board of directors. Jackson *Clarion*, May 5, 1868.

from this fund, and after the war all had refused to recognize the debt, claiming that the money had been invested in Confederate and state securities which were worthless at the end of the war. The state government during presidential reconstruction had sought a settlement with the companies; but proceedings were snarled when military reconstruction was imposed in 1867.[38] Then, in the spring of 1869 Ames received information, allegedly from "parties" seeking the control of the New Orleans road, that a scheme had been hatched to pay off the company's obligations to the state with notes and bonds of highly questionable value, including Union and Planters' Bank bonds, issues which had been repudiated by the state during the 1840s. Actually, the New Orleans railroad had earlier rejected the English bondholders' scheme, to be implemented by Mississippi agents, which entailed selling Union bonds at a large discount to officials of the road, who in turn were to use the discredited bonds to meet the railroad's debt to the state. But Ames, misinformed of the New Orleans company's true intentions regarding the scheme, threatened to seize the railroad. A hurried conference with officers of the company, however, resulted in Ames agreeing to postpone action against the road. Meanwhile, he directed all four of the railroads that were in arrears to the Chickasaw Fund to make arrangements with state officials to pay off both the principal and interest of the debt. To ensure that the companies complied, suits were initiated in the state courts to recover the money.[39] Before settlements could be reached, military reconstruction was superseded by a civil government headed by James Lusk Alcorn, and the new regime inherited the vexatious Chickasaw issue.

Military rulers rarely interfered with the routine administration of the local governments. On occasion and usually in response to

38. White and Chambers, railroad attorneys, to Humphreys, June 9, 1866, in Governors' Correspondence, Vol. 66. Immediately after the war a special legislative committee fixed the total railroad indebtedness to the Chickasaw Fund at $813,083. *Journal of the Senate of the State of Mississippi, October, November, and December, 1865* (Jackson, 1866), Appendix, 31.

39. Freeman, *Petition of New Orleans Railroad*, 9–10, 28–31; Ames to Benjamin F. Butler, December 18, 1869, in Benjamin F. Butler Papers, Manuscript Division, Library of Congress; Ames to Absalom M. West, 1869, in Governors' Correspondence, Vol. 69. Ames at the time of the proceedings against the railroad companies was acting in the dual

local petitions for changes in municipal tax ordinances the district commanders intervened by simply decreeing the desired revisions.[40] But they refused to impose general tax reforms, despite the unprogressive nature of the assessment and revenue laws of 1865. Blacks especially felt oppressed by the workings of tax laws that included a two dollar levy on each bale of cotton grown in the state but at the same time provided for only a small tax on the real estate of planters. In addition, the one dollar poll tax on blacks ostensibly to support the "Freedmen's Pauper Fund," which Ord had declared null and void in 1867, was quietly revived in 1868 by some local officials.[41]

As military reconstruction progressed, army commanders felt less and less compunction about intervening to remove old officers and appoint new ones. Ord made few changes in the Johnsonian officialdom in the state, but as vacancies occurred and the incompetence of many of the holdover officers became apparent, military authorities found it desirable to make numerous changes. The ironclad oath was not regularly applied to officeholders until early 1869, although from the beginning of military reconstruction an ill-defined test of "loyalty" had been required of all new appointees. Until General Ames assumed command in 1869 the military rulers gave a liberal interpretation to the meaning of loyalty; as a result they selected a number of old citizens for public office. Gillem, who served as district commander for more than a year, particularly favored prominent Union Whigs, as opposed to embittered loyalists, for positions in the civil administration. He demonstrated this preference when he selected two from this group to serve on the state supreme court. Republicans, who desired to use the weapon of patronage to promote the interests of their party in Mississippi, found Gillem's appointments a bitter pill to swallow.[42] One an-

---

capacity of military commander and provisional governor. As military commander in Mississippi, he threatened to seize the New Orleans road; as provisional governor he sought civil redress against the railroad companies.

40. Corinth (Miss.) *Weekly News*, August 15, 1868; Vicksburg *Herald*, August 25, December 8, 1868.

41. Thomas W. Stringer and George Paine to the Committee on Reconstruction, n.d., in Papers on Conditions in Mississippi; U. Ozanne to Butler, March 24, 1869, in Butler Papers; Natchez *Weekly Democrat*, September 28, 1868.

42. Irvin McDowell to Ulysses S. Grant, June 15, 1868, in Johnson Papers; Vicksburg *Times*, February 26, March 11, 18, 1868; Jackson *Weekly Clarion*, April 8, 1869.

guished Republican organizer charged that in assuming office Gillem's new officeholders "had to have the oath greased to make it go down easy."[43] Many of his appointees, however, eventually affiliated with the party of the new order.

To fill positions at the local level, General Gillem frequently turned to nonpartisan northerners, who in most cases had come to the state as officers in the army. Most of these appointees proved highly competent in civil affairs, and, indeed, they managed to establish a significant degree of rapport with local whites. Gillem took a special interest in the affairs of turbulent Vicksburg, the largest town in the state, where on three occasions he was called on to make appointments to the office of mayor. All three of his appointees were moderate and mature northerners who had served in the Union army. Dr. E. A. Duncan, the most popular of the three, was a former member of Gillem's staff and had a local reputation as a humorist and a poet. He carried out a series of reforms, initiated by his predecessor, former Colonel E. F. Brown, which temporarily checked the flagrant disregard for the law and the "disgusting scenes of licensed debauchery" (gambling) that afflicted the river town. Duncan did not rule by military fiat; instead he conducted affairs in conformity with the town's charter and ordinances and with the assistance of the civil administration, which included a council consisting partly of former Confederate soldiers.[44] The tenure of Gillem's benevolent mayors, however, was short-lived. When complete civil authority was restored under Republican auspices, Vicksburg came under the debasing influence of Sheriff Charles E. Furlong, a true adventurer from the North who had gained control of the Union Leagues of Warren County for his own shady purposes.

Only in Jackson did General Gillem dip into the active military rolls to fill the office of mayor. Virtually burned to the ground during the war, the state capital had been rapidly rebuilt, but its unpainted stores, shops, and homes presented a threadbare and

43. Ozanne to Butler, March 24, 1869, in Butler Papers.

44. E. A. Duncan to B. F. Whittemore, April 5, 1869, in Fourteenth Amendment Relief Papers, Mississippi; Vicksburg *Herald*, September 22, November 1, 6, December 2, 1868. Mayor Duncan was also active in charity movements in Vicksburg, and when he left the state to receive medical treatment in the East the Democratic Vicksburg *Herald* lamented his departure.

gloomy appearance to visitors during Reconstruction. Residents were forced to pay heavy taxes, but because of the need to retire an old debt they received in exchange only meager municipal services and few material improvements. During military reconstruction the town's indebtedness prevented officials from raising sufficient funds to install a much-needed and relatively inexpensive system of gas lighting. Without proper lighting crime flourished in the economically depressed capital. Finally, in 1868, after a racial affray at a Negro ball which was triggered by three intoxicated white soldiers from the local post, General Gillem intervened, removed the inept Johnsonian mayor, and appointed Major Thomas H. Norton, a native of Virginia, to the position. Although Norton retained his commission in the army, he continued the civil administration of the town, permitting the old board of aldermen to function as before. Norton's record as mayor was not as distinguished as that of Gillem's Vicksburg appointees, but even those whites hostile to the arbitrary character of congressional reconstruction did not complain of his administration. He was succeeded in 1869 by Major Joseph G. Crane, another popular army officer, who soon died at the hands of the unstable Edward M. Yerger.[45]

Whether from the ranks of the old citizens or transplanted northerners in the state, appointments by the military commanders were not always judicious. Contributing to the failure of these officials was the fact that many of them, like the Johnsonian holdovers, considered themselves merely caretaker administrators. Only a few, however, abused their offices for personal or political advantages. Nevertheless, a definite trend toward incompetence and partisanship in office developed during the last months of military reconstruction when General Ames, in pursuance of instructions from Congress, dismissed more than two thousand local and state officers who could not take the ironclad oath, replacing them with so-called "loyal men."[46] Then, in the political contest of 1869, Ames intervened on the side of the regular Republicans in the state against an insurgent conservative faction of the party and in

45. Jackson *Clarion*, April 13, 14, 29, May 5, 1868. Not only did Norton retain his army rank, but he continued to perform his military duties at the Jackson post. See pp. 58–61, for a discussion of the Crane murder and the trial of Yerger.

46. Jackson *Weekly Clarion*, May 13, 1869; undated list of appointments by Governor Ames, in Governors' Correspondence, Vol. 69, Miscellaneous Folder.

the process narrowed the qualifications for officeholding to include only those members who were loyal to the party. He thus removed from office several prominent northern Republicans, including State Supreme Court Justice Elza Jeffords and Secretary of State Alexander Warner, who supported congressional reconstruction but were aligned with the wrong wing of the party.[47] In making appointments to office Ames took pride in the Radical Republican boast that he "recognized loyalty and ignored rebellion as no other officer who has commanded the state since the war."[48]

Ames's patronage policies opened wide the door of opportunity for adventurers and scamps claiming unstinting loyalty to the Union and professing an abiding faith in Republican principles. Most of these soldiers of fortune, of both northern and southern origins, were already in the state, but when it became known that there were numerous offices to be filled by only the most loyal, a migration into Mississippi of undesirable adventurers from New Orleans and Memphis reportedly occurred. "Mississippi has become the Mecca of our 'played-out' carpetbaggers," the Memphis *Avalanche* claimed. "The air of that noble old State is vocal with the 'tramp, tramp' of the seedy professionals whose occupation in Memphis, like that of broken-hearted Othello, is gone."[49]

In several counties informants faithfully reported the disloyal activities of conservative officeholders, and even of some early Ames appointees. These "spies" were often able to secure the swift removal of those whom they labeled disloyal, whether Democratic or Republican. For example, the two leading northerners in the county adjacent to Memphis, both of whom had invested heavily

47. For a clear statement of Ames's narrow definition of loyalty and his almost paranoid attitude toward "rebel democrats" and those northerners who "are the tools by which the democracy propose to deceive the world," see Ames to General Sherman, August 17, 1869, in William T. Sherman Papers.

48. Ames to John Eaton, September 13, 1869, in John Eaton Papers, University of Tennessee Library, Knoxville.

49. As reported in the *Hinds County Gazette*, October 6, 1869. For accounts of recent arrivals from New Orleans and elsewhere who immediately received appointments from Ames, see the *Hinds County Gazette*, July 7, 1869, and the Jackson *Weekly Clarion*, June 24, July 15, September 16, 1869. Not all of the Ames appointees were incompetent, partisan, or unscrupulous. Probate Judge D. N. Walker—a stranger in Natchez when appointed by Ames—received the approbation of local conservatives because, as the Natchez *Weekly Democrat* (December 14, 1870) testified, his conduct on the bench was "pure, untrammelled by politics and unwarped by prejudice."

in cotton planting soon after the war, were removed from influential local offices, because, as they said, they refused to contribute to the Radical Republican campaign fund.[50] They were replaced by self-proclaimed Radicals. Ames appointed William Kellogg, a former Republican congressman from Illinois and an old associate of Lincoln, as a circuit judge in central Mississippi, but dismissed him from office when he announced his support of the aberrant Republican faction in the state. Kellogg was superseded by a newcomer from New Orleans who, according to the testimony of black witnesses, early arranged for the companionship of a Negro mistress.[51] In Rankin County, across the Pearl River from the state capital, the sheriff and probate judge, both northern recipients of the commanding general's patronage, were arrested for fraud and bribery soon after assuming office. The carpetbag editor of the Jackson *Pilot* frankly admitted that he could not find "an excuse for, or an extenuating circumstance surrounding these men's acts. And the people of Rankin feel justly outraged at this bold, bare-faced attempt to rob the county of thousands of dollars."[52] Despite the criticism, Ames retained both men in office while they awaited trial, which brought the public administration of the county to a standstill. The general's embarrassment was complete when the two men escaped from jail and fled to parts unknown rather than face trial and probable conviction at the hands of a biracial jury.[53]

Ames was far more discriminating in his appointment of Negroes to office than he was of whites. Although he saw the need to protect them in their basic civil rights, as set forth in the Civil Rights Act of 1866, the Fourteenth Amendment, and the reconstruction laws of 1867, Ames at this time was skeptical of the qualifications of blacks for office. Nevertheless, as military governor he established the pattern for Negro officeholding when he selected blacks to serve as town aldermen, justices of the peace, constables, and in

50. Hernando (Miss.) *Weekly Press*, June 10, July 1, September 23, 1869; Jackson *Weekly Clarion*, June 10, 1869.

51. Vicksburg *Times*, May 12, 1869; Jackson *Weekly Clarion*, October 13, 1869; statement of Harriet Cook, January 13, 1870; statement of Melinda Townsend, January 13, 1870; William Price to James Lusk Alcorn, January 14, 1870, all in Governors' Correspondence, Vol. 72.

52. As reported in the Jackson *Weekly Clarion*, August 19, 1869.

53. *Ibid.*, September 2, 9, November 4, 1869.

other minor offices. He appointed no blacks to significant judicial posts or to state offices.[54]

The young general's most significant contribution to the cause of Negro equality in Mississippi was his order of April 27, 1869, that "all persons, without respect to race, color or previous condition of servitude, who possess the qualifications prescribed by . . . the Revised Code of 1857, shall be competent jurors."[55] Surprisingly, prominent whites refrained from criticizing Ames's jury order. Ethelbert Barksdale of the Jackson *Clarion*, the leading conservative newspaper in the state, dismissed its significance with the gratuitous remark: "In this matter, as in others, the freedman, feeling his incapacity and want of information, will gladly profit by the experience and yield to the influence of the superior intelligence of the white citizen."[56] George W. Harper, the crusty Union-Whig editor of the *Hinds County Gazette* who prided himself on maintaining a consistent opposition to radicalism in every form, demonstrated some flexibility in accepting the jury directive. His rationale for it, however, was a labored affair and belied his approval of Negro rights in court. Harper averred that the presence of blacks on juries would relieve yeoman whites for more important farm chores, since it would reduce their courtroom responsibilities by one half. With a dash of sarcasm he added: The jury order "is something gained by the poor oppressed whites, and we feel mightily like calling a public meeting of the white people of Hinds for the purpose of passing resolutions of thanks to Gen. Ames for his continued disposition to relieve them to his utmost from the many burthens which have been imposed on them in the past. Our colored citizens have no right to complain of Gen. Ames for this Order. While they are in the full enjoyment of all the privileges and blessings of 'the best government the world ever saw,' they must expect to bear some share of its burthens."[57] Even George L. Potter, the early leader of the antireconstructionists, though opposing the jury policy advised white Mississippians to acquiesce in the order and aid the Negro in understanding his new duty.[58]

The lack of public opposition to such a radical innovation as plac-

54. Ames to Butler, April 30, 1869, in Butler Papers.
55. General Order 32, April 27, 1869, in Records of the Fourth Military District.
56. Jackson *Weekly Clarion*, April 29, 1869.
57. *Hinds County Gazette*, May 12, 1869.
58. Jackson *Weekly Clarion*, June 3, 1869.

ing blacks in the jury box was probably dictated by an early belief
that Ames, like his predecessor, General Gillem, could be flattered
into supporting the conservative cause, or at least could be neutral-
ized in the forthcoming political struggle between conservatives
and Republicans for control of the state. His unobtrusive management of affairs as provisional governor, prior to his elevation to
the command of the district, had received the approbation of all
elements of the white community.[59] But conservatives failed to
turn the young general's head, even though, as Ames later claimed,
they "were only too eager to offer the highest honors in the state
to me, would I sell myself to them."[60] When Ames in 1869 showed
his strong preference for Republicans in office and directed his subordinates to ignore writs of habeas corpus issued by any court,
conservatives quickly turned against him. The Jackson *Clarion*,
which had an early reason to doubt the general's statesmanship
since he had issued an order depriving the newspaper of its state
printing contract, was soon castigating Ames as a "weak, malignant
and selfish dictator" who was determined to subvert the remaining
liberties of the people.[61]

Departing from the military's nonpartisan stance in Mississippi
reconstruction, General Ames's decision to cast his lot with the
Republican party and assist it in gaining control of the state was not
a sudden one. Since arriving in 1868, Ames had viewed with alarm
the failure of Mississippi whites to accept the results of the Civil
War as expressed in the congressional or Republican plan of
reconstruction. By the summer of 1869 his transformation into a
Republican activist was complete. Now viewing his purpose in the
state as a "Mission with a large M,"[62] Ames explained to William
Tecumseh Sherman, the skeptical general-in-chief of the army,
the reason for his decision to take sides in the local political struggle. He wrote:

> The contest [in Mississippi] is not between two established parties, as
> they are elsewhere, but between loyal men and a class of men who are
> disloyal—a class who are opposed to the principles which are generally

59. Hazlehurst (Miss.) *Copiahan*, March 13, 1869; *Hinds County Gazette*, March 17,
1869; Jackson *Weekly Clarion*, March 11, 1869.
60. Ames to General Sherman, August 17, 1869, in William T. Sherman Papers.
61. Jackson *Weekly Clarion*, August 12, September 29, 1869.
62. Ames to the historian James W. Garner, January 17, 1900, in James W. Garner
Papers, Mississippi Department of Archives and History.

conceded should prevail among us. I honestly believe that the success
of the men who took this state from the union will establish a reign of
terror which will cause many of the white Union men, especially
northern men, to leave the state at once. I am convinced that among
the masses the animosity to the "Yankee," northern or southern, is as
strong now as it has ever been—defeat will make their lives and property highly insecure. . . . The number of murders and outrages
taking place in this state at the present time is startling, nor are they
the usual events of ordinary times. They are Ku-Klux outrages mainly
based on political enmity and hatred. . . . It is my duty to protect all.
It can not be done by putting this state into the hands of ex-rebels. The
war still exists in a very important phase here.[63]

At this time in his Mississippi career Ames felt no special responsibility for the helpless freedmen, although he expressed the fear
that unless blacks were made secure in their political rights they
"will by threats and actual violence be reduced to a condition bordering on serfdom."

Thus, even though Ames identified his mission in Mississippi
with politics and associated the disrespect for law and rights in the
state with the spirit of rebellion, fundamentally his attitude
resulted from a sensitivity, or perhaps more accurately a revulsion,
to the harshness of the semideveloped and impoverished society that he found there. The state's benighted society contrasted
sharply with the well-ordered, literate, and highly developed
community life he had known in his native New England. Ames, as
well as other carpetbaggers, found Mississippians sadly lacking in
moral principles and in respect for human rights and dignity.[64]

The deficiencies in Mississippi society were poignantly brought
home to Ames on June 8, 1869, when Major Joseph G. Crane, the
provisional mayor of Jackson, was brutally murdered by Edward
M. Yerger. The act occurred in front of the state capitol before
numerous witnesses after Yerger, the mentally unsound scion of a
distinguished Mississippi family, accosted Crane and violently
denounced him for placing Yerger's piano on the auction block in
order to satisfy back taxes. His design was obviously to provoke a
fight, but when Crane turned the other cheek, the hot-headed

63. Ames to General Sherman, August 17, 1869, in William T. Sherman Papers.
64. For this view of Mississippi society by a number of carpetbaggers, see Harris,
"Creed of the Carpetbaggers," 202–204.

southerner drew a "thug-knife" and fatally stabbed the major.[65]

Outraged by the murder, Ames immediately ordered the military arrest and confinement of Yerger. A civilian coroner's jury of inquest was soon held, and it ruled, as everyone already knew, that Crane had met his death at the hands of Yerger. Local citizens appeared genuinely horrified by the murder, and reports that emanated from the Jackson press pictured Crane, the tall, mild-mannered and chivalrous son of a former Ohio congressman, as a popular figure in town. Even the carpetbag editor of the Jackson *Pilot* acknowledged in his columns the people's outrage at the assassination and asked that northerners not condemn Mississippi whites for the senseless act of the enraged and disreputable Yerger.[66]

Two days after the Crane murder a hurriedly formed military commission convened to try Yerger. For four weeks and until the United States Supreme Court recognized Yerger's plea for a writ of habeas corpus, the trial occupied the attention of both the local and the national press. It is clear from the comprehensive reports of the proceedings that, although the officers admitted having preconceived notions about the defendant's guilt, they were determined to give him a fair and lengthy hearing.

The published testimony of prominent Mississippians, including John K. Yerger, an uncle, regarding Yerger's character and personality provides strong evidence that the accused man suffered from what twentieth-century psychiatrists would describe as paranoia. For example, one influential acquaintance of "Prince Edward" testified that Yerger had earlier assaulted a stranger simply because he believed that the man planned to assassinate him. In addition, a few days before the Crane tragedy, another witness recalled, Yerger became enraged at Ethelbert Barksdale because, as he told his friends, the *Clarion* editor was plotting his death in order to prevent his rise to political prominence in the state.[67]

65. For extensive testimony on the murder see W. S. M. Wilkinson, *Trial of E. M. Yerger Before a Military Commission for the Killing of Bv't-Col. Joseph G. Crane, at Jackson, Miss., June 8th, 1869* (Jackson, 1869). A brief account of the murder may be found in the New York *Times*, June 16, 1869.

66. Jackson *Weekly Clarion*, June 17, 1869; New York *Times*, June 16, 1869; George Moorman to General Sherman, June 12, 1869, in William T. Sherman Papers; Biddle, *Reminiscences of a Soldier's Wife*, 48–50.

67. Jackson *Weekly Clarion*, July 1, 8, 15, 1869; Wilkinson, *Trial of E. M. Yerger*, 28, 32–33, 36–37.

Yerger's paranoid tendencies, exacerbated by excessive drinking, seem to have been of late origin, but he had long held illusions of military and political grandeur. Despite his ambitions, he somehow managed to avoid military service during most of the Civil War, preferring the safety of Union lines after west Mississippi fell to Grant to taking his chances with the conscription officers in the interior of the state. He regained his courage near the end of the war when, as editor of an impoverished Jackson newspaper, he "went into ecstasies" over the murder of Lincoln and extolled John Wilkes Booth as "greater than Brutus."[68] His intrepidity knew no bounds by the 1868 impeachment of President Johnson. Yerger urged Johnson to take up arms rather than submit to impeachment proceedings, and he generously offered to raise thirty thousand men in thirty days to defend the president and the Constitution.[69]

When the military trial began, Yerger's lawyers, including his distinguished Uncle William, unsuccessfully sought a writ of habeas corpus from the Circuit Court of the United States for the Southern District of Mississippi. They then appealed to the Supreme Court, and in a remarkable reversal of its ruling in the McCardle case, the court accepted the plaintiff's argument and released Yerger to civil custody.[70] The constitutional significance of the Yerger decision was immense, since the Supreme Court after two years of subservience to Congress in reconstruction matters reasserted its judicial powers and checked the exercise of arbitrary military authority in the South. However, except for Mississippi, Texas, and Virginia, congressional reconstruction had ended and the necessity for military intervention in southern judicial proceedings had diminished considerably.

While still in military confinement, Yerger conspired with several of his jailors to escape. But before he could make his flight,

---

68. "Rebel Recruits for the Copperhead Cause, Being a Historical Account of the Past Activities and the Present Political Positions of Horatio Seymour and F. P. Blair, Jr., and the Delegates to the New York Convention Who Nominated Them," in William E. Chandler Papers, Manuscript Division, Library of Congress; Moorman to General Sherman, June 12, 1869, in William T. Sherman Papers. Yerger's stormy career began in college, when he was expelled for whipping the insubordinate slave of the brother of the college president. Franklin A. Montgomery, *Reminiscences of a Mississippian in Peace and War* (Cincinnati, 1901), 276–77.

69. Edward M. Yerger to President Johnson, March 25, 1868, in Johnson Papers.

70. *Ex parte Yerger*, 8 Wallace 75 (1869).

the scheme was uncovered by the post commander, and ten soldiers were arrested for their part in the plot. Later, when in the hands of the civil authorities, "Prince Edward" did escape from jail, only to return voluntarily after a week of hunting and fishing.[71] Yerger had scarcely finished cleaning his cell when Chief Justice Thomas C. Shackleford, a prominent Unionist who had been appointed to the position by General Gillem, released him on bail. State Republicans reacted with indignation to Shackleford's action, and calls for his impeachment rang in the halls of the capitol where the newly elected legislature was meeting. The chief justice was saved from impeachment by the installation of a new state judiciary, appointed by Governor Alcorn.[72]

The irrepressible Yerger never came to trial. When the issue of prosecuting him came before the local circuit court, his attorneys successfully argued for dismissal on a plea of double jeopardy—the first peril consisting of the abortive proceedings before the military commission. His ambitions for glory checked by the Republican ascendancy in Mississippi, Yerger moved to Maryland where he became editor of the Baltimore *Evening Journal* and ran unsuccessfully for Congress in 1872. When he died in Baltimore in 1875, his death was hardly noticed in Mississippi.[73]

In addition to Ames and the regular Republicans in the state, a number of northerners in Mississippi, like Alexander Warner, who had flirted with the conservative wing of the Republican party (and some even with old Democrats) were appalled by the Crane murder and the failure to bring Yerger to justice. Many carpetbaggers attributed this failure to the spirit of rebellion that they believed still existed in the state. Coming on the eve of the important campaign of 1869, when two Republican tickets were in the field, the episode played a significant role in uniting the discordant elements in the party behind the regular ticket headed by Alcorn and contributed to its landslide victory at the polls. The Yerger case also influenced dominant Republicans in the North to take a harder position on reconstruction developments in the South. Spe-

71. Jackson *Weekly Clarion*, September 23, 1869, March 17, 1870; Jackson *Weekly Pilot*, March 19, 1870.

72. Jackson *Weekly Pilot*, April 23, April 30, 1870.

73. Fairman, *Reconstruction and Reunion*, 590; Montgomery, *Reminiscences*, 277; Natchez *Weekly Democrat*, October 2, 1872; Jackson *Weekly Clarion*, April 28, 1875.

cifically, it resulted in the temporary triumph of the Radicals in Grant's cabinet, led by Secretary of Treasury George S. Boutwell, and the defeat of the moderate effort to remove General Ames from command and have the conservative faction recognized as the legitimate Republican party in Mississippi.[74]

Actually, the Yerger imbroglio was only an extreme manifestation of the unsettled social conditions that had existed in Mississippi since the early part of the war. General Ord's stern measures against the lawless had temporarily checked crime and disorder in the state, but when his firm hand was removed, the descent toward anarchy continued. Nevertheless, most Mississippians fervently desired an end to the violence and general lawlessness that prevailed in many communities, if for no other reason than the soothing political effect in the North that a restoration of good order in the state would have. The Jackson *Clarion* warned Mississippi whites that "nothing more delights the ultra Radical demagogues than reports of violence and resistance to constituted authority in the State" which could be used to convince moderate and apathetic northerners of the necessity for more extreme reconstruction measures. "In view of the consequences of violence, either open or concealed, direct or indirect, he is not [a] patriot nor true friend of his people, who resorts to it," the editor declared. "A few deeds of this character have been recorded in our State during the past year, but they are few indeed compared to the records of crime in other States."[75] Weekly reports of violence and crime in the columns of the *Clarion* and other newspapers at the time, however, belied this smug conclusion.

Ames's policy of removing conservative judges and law officers and replacing them with untested (and often incompetent) newcomers compounded the difficulties of maintaining peace and good order in the state. When removals were made, the offices frequently remained vacant for several weeks while Ames searched for a politically reliable replacement. A critic of the Ames regime estimated that at one time during the summer of 1869 from one

74. This conclusion is based mainly on the northern press's outraged reaction to reports of the Crane murder. The incident was soon followed by the ascendancy of Boutwell in the Grant cabinet and the administration's stiffening position on reconstruction affairs in the southern states.

75. Jackson *Weekly Clarion*, April 8, 1869.

half to two thirds of the public offices in Mississippi were vacant.[76] In some cases Ames removed intrepid officers who were waging a vigorous and relatively successful campaign against desperadoes. By 1869 a number of harassed outlaws were seeking legitimacy in the eyes of local whites by posing as members of the Ku Klux Klan and robbing from alleged Radicals and their sympathizers. One opponent of these self-styled defenders of white supremacy was Circuit Judge Alexander M. Clayton, a member of both the state's secession convention and the Confederate Congress. Elected to office under presidential reconstruction, Clayton was making significant progress in suppressing masked desperadoes in his district when Ames removed him from office in 1869.[77] Josiah A. P. Campbell was another Johnsonian circuit judge who was waging a relentless war on lawbreakers, including whites who perpetrated brutal outrages on blacks, when Ames discovered his secessionist background (as well as his antebellum service as speaker of the state house of representatives) and summarily dismissed him from office.[78]

A reduction in the strength of the occupation forces also increased the difficulty of suppressing lawbreakers during the latter part of military reconstruction in Mississippi. From an October, 1867, high of 2,073 men stationed at fifteen posts, the number of troops in the state was reduced to 716 at six posts by October, 1869, lessening the fear of criminals that they would be apprehended and dealt with severely. When caught by military

76. *Ibid.*, June 3, July 15, 1869; Vicksburg *Times*, April 6, 1869. Once apprehended, lawbreakers were almost impossible to keep in the state's dilapidated jails. A. R. Howe to Ames, December 25, 1869, in Governors' Correspondence, Vol. 69.

77. A brief account of the judge's war against masked men may be found in General Gillem's endorsement of Clayton's petition to Congress for the removal of his political disabilities (February 15, 1869, in Fourteenth Amendment Relief Papers, Mississippi). Clayton was an early supporter of the Fifteenth Amendment, "although an ardent Southern man from birth, education and principle." A. M. Clayton to George E. Harris, March 8, 1870, and petition of Thomas Maddox, *et al.* to the Congress on behalf of A. M. Clayton, March 17, 1868, both in Fourteenth Amendment Relief Papers, Mississippi. For evidence of the criminal element's association with the Klan, see W. C. McGowan to Ames, September 3, 1869, and C. Rodney Taylor to O. H. Crandall, September 17, 1869, both in Governors' Correspondence, Vol. 69.

78. "Autobiography of J. A. P. Campbell" (MS in Josiah A. P. Campbell Papers, Southern Historical Collection, University of North Carolina Library, Chapel Hill); J. A. P. Campbell to George S. Boutwell, February 9, 1869, in Fourteenth Amendment Relief Papers, Mississippi.

forces, accused criminals, in contrast to their fate at the hands of General Ord, were almost always turned over to the civil courts for trial.[79] By 1869 the use of military commissions to try law violators had been abandoned except for the most flagrant violations, such as the murder of Mayor Crane of Jackson.

In essence, military reconstruction provided Mississippi with no sense of direction toward solving the massive social and economic problems confronting the people after the war. Even in matters which it was preeminently qualified to handle, such as the reestablishment of order, the United States army, with a limited number of troops available, acted in a piecemeal and inconsistent fashion. The result was failure in an important aspect of reconstruction.

An aloof Congress was probably more to blame than the district commanders for this condition of affairs. Experienced public men in Congress were in a far better position than narrowly trained army officers to formulate a comprehensive reconstruction plan for the southern states and to insist on its proper implementation. Such reforms, to be reasonably effective, did not call for the often-mentioned confiscation of rebel estates and their division among the freedmen. In fact a confiscation program of this kind, if it could have marshaled the approval of the necessary two-thirds majority in Congress for passage over President Johnson's veto, would have increased the complexities and difficulties of restoring the economic and social fabric of Mississippi and clearly would have made unlikely the development of a strong corps of white Republicans in the state. A feasible policy of land reform could have been based on a substantial congressional appropriation to provide blacks with the means to purchase property, even at a premium rate, from demoralized and financially distressed planters. In addition, Congress could have directed that the numerous tracts of tax-forfeited land held by state authorities be distributed to blacks, with the federal government assuming the financial burden for redeeming the property. The amount of these state-controlled lands exceeded two million acres by the end of military reconstruction, or approx-

---

79. *House Executive Documents*, 41st Cong., 2nd Sess., No. 1, Pt. II, pp. 160–61; Jackson *Weekly Clarion*, December 16, 1869; William Carter to Ames, October 28, 1869, in Governors' Correspondence, Vol. 69. The army's judge advocate general visited Mississippi during the summer of 1869 and reported an unusual amount of lawlessness there. Jackson *Weekly Clarion*, August 5, 1869.

imately one tenth of the land area of Mississippi. To ensure the proper enforcement of such a program, if it had been enacted, and to protect blacks in their relationships with whites until substantial economic freedom had been achieved, Congress could have wisely extended the life of the Freedmen's Bureau for several years and increased its authority, as well as its appropriations. With a vigorous and ongoing assist from the federal government—and a free ballot to provide political clout—blacks might very well have made a promising beginning during Reconstruction toward independent farming, although no agrarian utopia for them was likely because of their inexperience as managers and because of the chronically depressed status of southern agriculture after the war. Such federal support for black landholding, however, was not in the congressional cards, even though in retrospect national financial assistance to aspiring Negro property holders does not appear to have been a very radical step for a government that could impose a potentially revolutionary political settlement on ten southern states and could create an extralegal agency like the Freedmen's Bureau to oversee, albeit temporarily, the black adjustment to freedom.

The general economic recovery of Mississippi might have been significantly advanced had Congress sent along with its military commanders liberal financial support for such important projects as the reclamation of the Delta (a program of aid that various commercial interests in the Northeast favored), the extension of well-conceived railroad lines into the interior—especially into the dense piney woods of southern Mississippi—and the development of small harbors along the Mississippi coast. Coming so soon after the bitter Civil War, however, the extension of aid for internal improvements in the South generally and Mississippi specifically was not politically possible in the North. More realistically, the policy makers in Washington might have provided the district commanders with a contingent fund for civil purposes instead of limiting them to their military budgets and the meager amount of money that the Freedmen's Bureau received in the state.[80] A

80. In March, 1867, Congress appropriated only $500,000 to support the army in all of the southern states. This sum of money was so insignificant that even the obstructionist President Johnson approved of the appropriation. *House Executive Documents*, 40th Cong., 1st Sess., No. 14, p. 1.

generous appropriation for civil affairs could have gone far during military reconstruction toward restoring the vitality of the war-shattered public institutions in Mississippi. The insane asylum, the penitentiary, the state university, the two small state hospitals, and the modest public school systems that had emerged in the principal towns before the war could have benefited substantially from the infusion of even a modicum of federal aid. Instead, these institutions languished during military reconstruction, and the delay in providing for their rehabilitation compounded the difficulties of administering the institutions when civil rule was restored in 1870.

As revisionist historians of Reconstruction have frequently pointed out, the purpose of Congress in its reconstruction policy was a narrowly political one, a point that was not missed by most of the military commanders in the South. Their main task as instruments of congressional designs was to prepare the ground for a new political order in their districts. Army commanders were to register a new electorate, including black males and excluding certain former Confederates, provide for the election of constitutional conventions, and oversee the elections to ratify the new constitutions, which would be held simultaneously with the contests for offices in the new governments. The district commanders in carrying out these responsibilities were expected to maintain a proper military aloofness from party politics, while at the same time imposing political conditions that would facilitate the organization of a new and potentially revolutionary party in the South. General Ord, the first commander in the Fourth Military District, seemed better qualified by temperament than most available generals to implement the reconstruction program without becoming directly involved in the emotional and controversial political contests that would accompany it. The fateful responsibility for working out the details of the congressional plan and setting the stage for the ascendancy of a new political order in Mississippi was in the hands of this middle-aged professional soldier.

3

The Process of
Reconstruction

A few days after his arrival in Mississippi General Ord began preparations for the registration of a new electorate based on the reconstruction laws of March 2 and 23. Working independently of the other district commanders and without specific instructions from Congress on some important points, the general selected a board of four officers, headed by the invaluable Gillem, to devise a comprehensive plan for the registration of all eligible persons. Ord directed the board to divide the state into convenient registration districts and to recommend to him three "loyal men" as registrars for each district. As Ord told General Grant, he desired to choose two of the three members of the local boards of registration from the ranks of former Union soldiers who had settled in the state, and the third from the Unionist class. But finding this impossible for all areas of his command, he instructed the state board simply to recommend for each district three men who could take the ironclad oath regardless of their place of origin.[1]

Ord's headquarters at Vicksburg during April and May was the scene of frenetic activity as the general and his officers created registration districts (which for the sake of convenience followed county lines), selected registrars, and issued detailed instructions regarding the procedure for voter enrollment. Ord deliberately sought registrars who were not vindictive Unionists or Republican party organizers, hoping thereby to avoid the taint of partisanship in his implementation of the reconstruction acts.[2] His selection of nonpartisan registrars was not always possible, and in some counties he was forced to appoint embittered Unionists who were determined to exclude as many former secessionists as possible from the voter rolls. Illustrative of this class of Unionists was John M. Dickerson, an itinerant and impoverished lawyer who had re-

1. *Senate Executive Documents*, 40th Cong., 1st Sess., No. 14, pp. 136, 147–48.
2. Newspaper clipping of a letter from John F. H. Claiborne to the editor of the Handsboro *Democrat*, August 10, 1869, in John F. H. Claiborne Papers, Southern Historical Collection, University of North Carolina Library, Chapel Hill; Meridian *Semi-Weekly Gazette*, July 4, 1867.

turned to central Mississippi after the war hissing his scorn at former Confederates and plotting their political oblivion. A local critic of Dickerson described him as a "mean, miserable carrion crow" who was "despised and forsaken socially and politically."[3] Another vindictive registrar was Abel Alderson, whose persistent unionism during the war was suspect, yet who, in 1865, suggested to President Johnson that a few leading "rebels" should be hanged, beginning with Jefferson Davis.[4] Alderson feared that unless a thorough reconstruction occurred, Mississippi, "the chief of rebel sinners, [would] go back into the hands of those whose garments are still red with the blood of union victims."[5]

In most of the populous counties, however, Ord found a sufficient number of moderate and competent loyal men to select for the task of registering the new electorate. Some of them were proud and independent Whig planters who, secretly in most cases, had retained their loyalty to the federal government during the war. Not all Unionists, however, were willing to become agents of a reconstruction program that enfranchised the former slaves and made possible the political radicalization of the state.

Nevertheless, Unionists of the planter class in accepting commissions as registrars provided some comfort to troubled whites who feared the revolutionary implications of Negro suffrage. These planter-registrars saw no particular need to seek out blacks and instruct them in their right to vote under the reconstruction laws. Thomas Shackleford, as an example of this type of registrar, was a member of a prominent planter-lawyer family of Madison County and would be appointed chief justice of the state supreme court in 1868. Shackleford had been forced to flee the state during the early part of the war because of his Union sentiments, only to return and assist General Sherman's army in its sweep through Madison County in 1864.[6] Another Ord registrar appointee from

3. J. B. Covington to William N. Whitehurst, May 10, 1869, in William N. Whitehurst Papers, Mississippi Department of Archives and History. A list of Ord's appointees as registrar, along with his orders to each local board, may be found in *Senate Executive Documents*, 40th Cong., 1st Sess., No. 14, pp. 148–91.

4. Abel Alderson to President Johnson, December 3, 1865, in Johnson Papers; Jackson *Clarion*, April 18, 1868.

5. Alderson to Joseph Holt, July 18, 1869, in Holt Papers.

6. Thomas Shackleford to President Johnson, June 4, 1865, in Johnson Papers; Charles E. Furlong to William T. Sherman, March 6, 1868, in Fourteenth Amendment Relief Papers, Mississippi.

the planter class was Ephraim G. Peyton, an elderly Unionist of Copiah County and a "high toned, genial gentleman of Virginia ancestry" who was elevated to the state supreme court in 1868. Two years later he succeeded Shackleford as chief justice, serving in that position until the end of the Republican era.[7] Despite an early conservatism during Reconstruction, Peyton warmed to the idea of black suffrage, and in the constitutional convention of 1868 he actively participated as a Republican delegate.

The most prominent Ord appointee as registrar was John F. H. Claiborne, a former United States congressman, an influential Democratic editor before the war, and a historian of some distinction in the Mississippi Valley. During the war Claiborne served as a spy for the Union along the Gulf Coast, and soon after the surrender he expressed to President Johnson his belief that the disastrous spirit of rebellion would be revived if a harsh reconstruction settlement was not imposed on the South. But when the reconstruction acts of 1867 were passed, he publicly cautioned moderation and attempted to persuade his old friends to cooperate with Congress, gain the confidence of the new black voters, and control postwar affairs.[8]

Despite the presence of some prominent Unionists as enrolling officials, northerners who had settled in the state, beginning with Grant's campaign in the Mississippi Valley, constituted the most numerous group on the local boards of registrars. Of the 183 registrars appointed by General Ord more than one hundred were former Union soldiers.[9] Most of these northerners were young men who, like their compatriots who went west, had come to the state in search of economic opportunity. Some of the less resolute newcomers abandoned their dreams of riches after the cotton crop failure of 1866 and returned home to inveigh against the inhospita-

7. Oscar J. E. Stuart to J. A. Mitchell, September, 1875, in Oscar J. E. Stuart Papers, Mississippi Department of Archives and History; Dunbar Rowland, *Courts, Judges, and Lawyers of Mississippi, 1798–1935* (Jackson, 1935), 97. Albert Gallatin Brown, pride of the antebellum Democratic party, had studied law under Peyton.

8. Claiborne to President Johnson, May 1, 1865, in Johnson Papers; newspaper clipping of a letter from Claiborne to the editor of the Handsboro *Democrat*, August 10, 1869, in Claiborne Papers, University of North Carolina Library. For Claiborne's activities as a Civil War spy for the federal forces in the area, see Herbert H. Lang, "J. F. H. Claiborne at 'Laurel Wood' Plantation, 1853–1870," *Journal of Mississippi History*, XVIII (February, 1956), 11–14.

9. Alvan C. Gillem to Oliver O. Howard, July 25, 1867, in Freedmen's Bureau Records, Microcopy Roll 47.

ble South. But a large number remained, all the wiser now regarding the necessity for patience and proper management in their business affairs.[10]

Where possible, Ord passed over enlisted veterans of the Union army and selected former officers as registrars. A comparison of the names of these officials with identifiable northerners in Mississippi indicates that he was generally successful in his purpose of appointing newcomers who were not politically active. A relatively large number of moderate and even conservative northerners who had invested heavily in the state and who had found favor with local whites accepted appointments. Some had been induced by white conservatives to seek the position for fear that Radicals would be chosen if "good men" were not selected.[11] At least four of Ord's northern registrars were later active in the opposition to the Republican party in the state, but most of these officials never became involved in political affairs, except to vote in the elections.

On the other hand some of the newcomers appointed by Ord entered Republican politics as a result of their service as registrars and the contacts they had made while enrolling black voters. To these politically minded northerners the success of the Republican party and its reconstruction policies offered the only hope for the preservation of the fruits of Union victory in the South. Of course, some who became involved in politics at this time were not oblivious to the opportunities for quick personal advancement contained in the congressional plan enfranchising blacks and temporarily disfranchising many former Confederates.[12] Jonathan Tarbell, Charles W. Clarke, Albert R. Howe, Charles E. Furlong, Alexander Warner, and Archie C. Fisk were all former Federal officers who after serving as registrars became Republican leaders in the state. Only a few, like scalawag Alston Mygatt of Vicksburg, were already engaged in the work of organizing blacks into Union Leagues and Republican clubs when Ord tapped them for service as registrars.[13] The vast majority of these officials, of both southern and northern backgrounds, lacked political ability or ambition, and,

10. Harris, *Presidential Reconstruction in Mississippi*, 169–72.
11. Meridian *Semi-Weekly Gazette*, May 18, 1867; Vicksburg *Herald*, April 26, 1867; Jackson *Weekly Clarion*, May 10, 1867.
12. For a detailed account of northern motivation in Mississippi Reconstruction, see Harris, "Creed of the Carpetbaggers," 199–224.
13. Vicksburg *Herald*, April 26, 1867.

having performed the task of enrolling the new electorate, they returned to the obscurity they had previously known.

When the selection of registrars was completed, Ord issued detailed instructions regarding the procedure for voter enrollment. He directed that the three-member local boards divide their districts into precincts, notify the people by handbills when and where they would appear in each precinct, and place their orders at his headquarters for registration forms. Their sojourn in each community was to be long enough to permit a full registration of qualified voters.[14] As set forth in the reconstruction laws, all male adults of both races could register except those whites who had "been disfranchised for participation in any rebellion or civil war against the United States," or who, having held a civil office, had later engaged in insurrection or given aid and comfort to the enemies of the Union.[15] Actually, few had been disfranchised before the passage of the reconstruction acts; only those former Confederates, like Robert Toombs of Georgia, who had defiantly refused amnesty from President Johnson were on the excluded list. Therefore, in reality, the disfranchisement clause in the reconstruction laws applied only to antebellum officeholders who subsequently had supported the Confederacy. But the military acts were vague as to the specific executive and judicial offices that were included in the prohibition.

Pending the decision of Attorney General Henry Stanbery on the matter, Ord directed his registrars to exclude anyone about whom there was any doubt of eligibility. The general, however, expressed the belief that Stanbery would give a liberal interpretation to the franchise provision of the reconstruction acts, which would permit many of the doubtful class to enroll before the completion of the registration.[16] On May 24 Stanbery issued his opinion, through the medium of the press, and, as Ord had predicted, he excluded from the meaning of the disfranchisement clause persons who had held minor offices, such as town officials and county road commissioners.[17] Ord on June 10 gave new instructions to

14. Circular 1, May 13, 1867, in Records of the Fourth Military District.
15. *U. S. Statutes at Large*, XV, 2–4.
16. Circular 1, May 13, 1867, in Records of the Fourth Military District.
17. Sefton, *United States Army and Reconstruction*, 131–32. Stanbery's opinion, as approved by the cabinet, may be found in *House Executive Documents*, 40th Cong., 1st Sess., No. 34, pp. 1–8.

the local boards which in essence followed Stanbery's opinion, although President Johnson did not announce it as an official policy until June 20. The district commander departed slightly from the Stanbery decision by including in the disfranchised class mayors who possessed judicial powers. Nevertheless, in the liberal spirit of the Johnsonian interpretation Ord directed his officers to enroll everyone who insisted on registering; registrars were, however, to make a note of doubtful cases and report these to his headquarters for investigation by a military commission. In all such cases the applicants were to be warned before they took the registration oath of the serious penalty for perjury.[18]

Ord soon discovered that Stanbery's opinion was not considered binding by dominant Republicans in Congress nor was his liberality in applying it in the Fourth Military District appreciated by General-in-Chief Grant. Already aligned with Congress in its struggle with Johnson over the implementation of the reconstruction laws, Grant wrote the district commander that he completely disagreed with Ord's view that local boards should register all applicants who were willing to take the oath.[19] Each board, Grant declared, should "see so far as it lies in [its] power, that no unauthorized person is allowed to register. To secure this end registers should be allowed to administer oaths and examine witnesses." The general-in-chief admitted, however, that his interpretation was only advisory, since the district commanders, in the absence of congressional clarification, were a law unto themselves in the matter.[20] Instead of acting on Grant's strong advice, Ord waited for further instructions from Congress, which came with the passage of the third reconstruction act on July 19. This law affirmed Grant's position and gave the local boards sweeping authority to reject voter applicants of doubtful eligibility. In addition, registrars were directed to apply a strict interpretation to the provisions in the March reconstruction laws disfranchising former civil officers; they were to exclude from voting all persons who had held

18. Circular 3, June 10, 1867, in Records of the Fourth Military District. This circular also may be found in *Senate Executive Documents*, 40th Cong., 1st Sess., No. 14, pp. 141–42.

19. Martin E. Mantell, *Johnson, Grant, and the Politics of Reconstruction* (New York, 1973), 2–4.

20. *Senate Executive Documents*, 40th Cong., 1st Sess., No. 14, p. 143.

any office created by state law and had later supported the rebellion.[21] Upon receipt of a copy of the July act Ord directed his boards to be regulated by it and to revise their voter lists in order to conform strictly to the law's provisions.[22]

Meanwhile, by every form of mid-nineteenth century transportation, including row boats and wagons, registrars were traversing the state and performing the tedious but often gratifying work of enrolling the new electorate. Henry W. Warren, a young graduate of Yale University who came to Mississippi in 1866 and settled in Leake County as a small planter, has left a vivid account of the activities of one board of registration as it rode the circuit of backcountry precincts during the summer of 1867. His partners were Walter C. Brewer, a seventy-year-old Unionist who could hardly write his name, and David Larr, a former Federal soldier. Warren wrote of the experience:

> We travelled over the County, in the discharge of our official duties, in a lumber wagon drawn by two mules, and Mr. Brewer furnished the mules and drove and cared for them. He was an expert in this line. We were all of us personae non gratae to most of the former slave holders of the County who either didn't acquiesce in the plan of reconstruction or were not eligible to register, and this class would not board us while tarrying at the places designated for carrying on registration. As we did not care to board with the "poor whites," so-called, or the negroes, we boarded ourselves, Mr. Brewer acting in the capacity of cook and man of all work. He could fry bacon in a frying pan and bake corn dodgers in a skillet, and what more could we ask him to do?
>
> David Larr was made secretary of the Board, and was a good one. He was a jolly young fellow who could adapt himself to all sorts of adverse circumstances, as can most ex-soldiers. It was my duty as chairman of the Board to explain the law to applicants for registration, and to administer the prescribed oath, assisting incidentally in every way possible in making the rough places smooth for both whites and blacks, thus unwittingly "casting bread upon the water."

Warren recalled that a large number of poor whites registered, many of whom were illiterate, and almost all of the Negro men in the county stepped forward eagerly to claim their new privilege.

21. *U. S. Statutes at Large*, XV, 14–16. This law applied to a large number of officers, including such minor officials as county ranger and cotton weigher.
22. Circular 11, August 6, 1867, in Records of the Fourth Military District.

For many blacks "registration was their newly acquired badge of citizenship."[23]

The work of registration proceeded smoothly and with a high degree of efficiency. Problems, however, did develop. The difficulty of ascertaining the correct ages of black youths who sought to register was a constant problem for the enrolling officers.[24] One army officer appointed to inspect the procedure reported that many who had no idea of their age but probably had not attained the required twenty-one years for voting might have been induced to register by "evil disposed persons." How extensive this practice was is impossible to determine; conservatives, as might be expected, loudly charged that hundreds, if not thousands, were illegally registered in order to increase Radical voting strength in the state.[25]

Surprisingly, in view of the revolutionary implications of Negro suffrage, few incidents of outright intimidation or violence occurred during the three-month period of registration. The absence of such activity was due mainly to General Ord's decision to act immediately against any effort to obstruct the process. When an impetuous white yeoman of east Mississippi tongue-lashed members of the board of registration in his county and denounced black suffrage as "a God-damned humbug," Ord dispatched him to Dry Tortugas, the federal prison off the Florida coast, for a ninety-day period of reflection.[26] Coming at a time when he was waging a relentless war on horse thieves, this arbitrary action by Ord had a wholesome effect on the subsequent course of voter registration in Mississippi.

A more serious threat to the success of the new registration

23. Henry W. Warren, *Reminiscences of a Mississippi Carpetbagger* (Holden, Mass., 1914), 9, 23, 34–35. Warren later served as speaker of the Mississippi House of Representatives.

24. Ord ruled that all males twenty-one years of age who had resided in the state for one year (later changed to nine months) and who were not disqualified by the reconstruction laws or for criminal actions could register to vote. Circular 6, June 24, 1867, in Records of the Fourth Military District.

25. *House Miscellaneous Documents*, 40th Cong., 3rd Sess., No. 53, p. 116; Jackson *Clarion*, May 20, 1868. The Natchez *Weekly Democrat*, October 11, 1871, claimed that during the four years beginning with the 1867 registration there was never a time "when there were not at least five hundred negroes under twenty-one years of age registered as voters after being urged to commit perjury by the white Radical leaders."

26. General Court Martial Order 10, Headquarters, Fourth Military District, August 24, 1867, in Johnson Papers.

was the deception that some whites employed to persuade blacks to keep a safe distance between themselves and the enrolling officials. Mischievous whites frequently advised Negroes that the purpose of the enrollment was to secure members of their race for foreign military service, probably in Mexico. Such fabrications actually were believed by many Negroes, especially in interior regions where they still lacked adequately informed leadership and effective organization. In Oktibbeha County terrified blacks even fled to the woods to escape the registrar's snare after a report swept the Negro community that they were marked for conscription into the army. Another subterfuge to keep freedmen from registering was the often repeated tale that the boards sought their names in order to draw up new tax lists. Most whites, however, did not engage in these beguiling games with blacks. Indeed, the influential Ethelbert Barksdale of the Jackson *Clarion* called for the suppression of such deception, warning fellow conservatives that a policy of deceit would not defeat the work of reconstruction but could very well result in tightening the screws of congressional despotism in Mississippi.[27]

When reports reached Ord of white tricks to discourage blacks from registering, he bristled with indignation. He immediately ordered agents of the Freedmen's Bureau to visit the plantations and black communities in their area to inform the freedmen of the true object of the registration. He also directed registrars to make a special effort to explain the meaning of the right to vote to blacks when they appeared to take the registration oath. Moreover, Ord instructed his officials to advise blacks that if they were "interfered with, threatened, or deprived of any advantage, place or hire, on account of their registering or showing a wish to register . . . it is their duty to report such interference or deprivation" in order that the military may deal with the offenders.[28] Lest this directive be construed as encouragement for political activity by his subordinates or by his registrars, Ord reminded them of the government's policy against officials participating directly in politics. Ord's intervention to ensure a full and untrammeled registration

27. Jackson *Clarion*, June 26, 1867; General Order 16, June 29, 1867, in Records of the Fourth Military District.
28. *House Executive Documents*, 40th Cong., 2nd Sess., No. 342, pp. 134–35.

of voters again checked an attempt to subvert the reconstruction laws. By late July his headquarters could report that incidents of intimidation and subterfuge, including economic coercion, were rare and no longer a threat to the registration canvass.[29]

When the registration books were closed in the fall, the revolutionary implications of congressional reconstruction in Mississippi were obvious. Blacks emerged from the registration the preponderant political element in the state. Only time would tell whether or not they could be marshaled into a political force dedicated to the cause of making drastic changes in the state's economic and social structure. Of a total enrollment of 137,561 voters, 79,176 were black, compared to only 58,385 white registrants.[30] Constituting a majority in thirty-four of the sixty-one counties in the state, the Negro electorate represented 57 percent of the total enrollment. (In 1870 blacks constituted 54 percent of the population of the state.)

Actually, members of both races turned out in impressive numbers to register; in fact, approximately 80 percent of the eligible voting population put their names on the rolls before the fall election. Despite the reluctance of many whites to participate in what they considered a revolutionary proceeding, the overwhelming majority of those who were qualified sought out Ord's registrars in response to the appeal of conservative leaders for them to register even if they did not plan to vote in the election.[31] Interestingly, the disfranchisement of certain former Confederates by the reconstruction laws was not a significant obstacle to a large white enrollment. Fewer than 2,500 Mississippians were disqualified

29. Circular 9, July 29, 1867, in Records of the Fourth Military District; Gillem to Howard, July 25, 1867, in Freedmen's Bureau Records, Microcopy Roll 47.
30. Voter Registration and Report, in Records of the United States Army Commands, Fourth Military District, Civil Affairs, 1867–69, Record Group 98, National Archives. The above figures include the supplementary registration completed on the eve of the fall election. They exceed by thirty thousand the number of voters reported by Garner in his *Reconstruction in Mississippi*, 175, and by Vernon Lane Wharton, *The Negro in Mississippi, 1865–1890* (Chapel Hill, 1947), 146. These historians used only the figures that were compiled by Ord after the initial registration and before the revision. An additional revision was held during the spring of 1868, in time for the ratification election on the Republican constitution. As a result of this revision the number of voters increased to 86,973 blacks and 68,587 whites ("Statistics of Registration," in section containing General Orders, 1869, Records of the Fourth Military District).
31. F. R. Cope to John Covode, August 28, 1867, in Covode Papers; Columbus *Southern Sentinel*, October 22, 1867; Meridian *Semi-Weekly Gazette*, August 10, 1867.

from voting by these acts.[32] Of greater importance in reducing
the size of the white registration was the fact that twenty-seven
thousand Confederates, most of whom would have been eligible
to cast ballots in Reconstruction elections, did not return from
the war.

While General Ord and his officials were energetically preparing
the new registration, political activity and excitement was sweeping Mississippi as the state prepared for its first biracial election.
Scheduled for November 5, the election would determine whether
or not the voters desired to advance to the second step of political
reconstruction—the meeting of a convention to frame a new state
constitution that would recognize Negro suffrage and civil rights.
In the same election delegates were to be selected for the proposed
convention. If the new electorate failed to approve the calling
of the convention, the process of reconstruction would be stymied,
and the state would remain under military rule.

Congress not only expected the voters to approve the meeting
of the southern constitutional conventions, it also anticipated that
a majority of the delegates elected to them, especially in those
states containing a near majority or more of black voters, would
be "loyal" men, *i.e.* Republicans. The reconstruction acts, however, did not require the success of a particular political group,
the Republican party included, to make the process valid and to
secure the restoration of a state to the Union. Under these laws
a conservative or anti-Republican party could legitimately gain
control of the constitutional convention of a state. In theory, Congress would approve the product of a conservative-dominated convention, provided black suffrage and rights were guaranteed in the
new state constitution. Long accustomed to making legalistic distinctions, many southern leaders in early 1867 did not miss the
point that under the congressional plan they might yet control
the course of events in their states.

In Mississippi, as well as in other southern states with a pre-

32. The number of former Confederates disfranchised by congressional reconstruction
has been almost invariably exaggerated. The conclusion that fewer than 2,500 Mississippians
were disqualified from voting at this time is based on a compilation of persons disabled
later by the Fourteenth Amendment, which included the same prohibitions for officeholding
as the reconstruction acts did for voting under military rule. These figures may be found in
the *Senate Journal, 1871*, Appendix, 1126–27.

ponderance of black voters, the success of such a scheme depended on the willingness of a large number of rank-and-file whites
to sublimate their racial prejudices, drop their opposition to black
rights, including suffrage, and cooperate with Congress in its plan
of reconstruction. In view of the traditional attitudes of Mississippi whites toward blacks, a political conversion of this kind was
highly unlikely in 1867.

The stakes, however, were too high for many of the old citizens
to permit Mississippi to fall by default to "alien adventurers" who,
as one prominent editor insisted, were intent upon "the utter ruin
of our people and the complete destruction of our interests and
section."[33] Trained in the school of emotional sectional politics
but sobered by its tragic results, an impressive number of antebellum leaders stepped forward to promote a policy of cooperation
with Congress in order to save the state from Radical domination.
One of these leaders, Judge James W. Robb of Jackson, in an
open letter that appeared in many conservative newspapers put
the case plainly to white Mississippians.[34] Writing in June, he argued that unless whites acted before the end of the summer to
win control of the black voters these Negroes would "be organized
under the lead of men sent here from the North. They will be
banded together in the advocacy of social equality, the confiscation of estates, the further disfranchisement of rebels and animat-
ed by the same malice that actuates the radical party in Congress."
Whites, Robb declared, must win the confidence of the Negro
by discarding racial prejudices, providing the black man with all
of the privileges and rights of freedom, and endowing him with
a system of public schools for his children. As a guarantee that
blacks would be content in their labor arrangements with planters,
he advocated the passage of laws, once reconstruction was completed, that would ensure a speedy remedy for laborers seeking
payment of wages from delinquent employers. But one privilege
Robb would not extend immediately to emerging blacks: he would
not permit them to serve on juries until they acquired property
or became educated. Robb held up the spectre of "an exterminat-
ing war of races" if whites rejected cooperation with Congress in
its program of reconstruction.

33. *Hinds County Gazette*, November 29, 1867.
34. Robb's letter may be found in the Jackson *Clarion*, June 11, 1867.

Cooperationists like Robb exhibited a shrewd comprehension of the national forces and events that had produced the reconstruction acts. The editor of the Ripley *Advertiser* typified the emerging sense of realism regarding reconstruction when he wrote:

> No sane or intelligent man can for a moment doubt that the question of negro suffrage has ceased to be an open one. In the election of the Fortieth Congress that question was submitted to the northern people, who alone control the politics of the new nation created by the war, and was by an overwhelming majority determined in favor of the negro. It was imposed upon us as a punishment for rejecting with scorn the Constitutional Amendment, and Congress will enforce the verdict. Neither is the question of reconstruction an open one. The time has come when the Republican party must reconstruct the Southern States in some form. It is imperatively demanded by the necessities of the country, and the only question is what proportion of the so-called rebel element shall be allowed to participate.[35]

The editor drew a distinction between the moderate Republicans of the John Sherman stripe in Congress, who at the time controlled the reconstruction process, and the Stevens-Sumner Radicals who were bent upon a policy of reducing former Confederates to second-class citizenship and confiscating their lands. By cooperating with the moderate-conceived program of reconstruction, the editor declared, Mississippians could contribute to the defeat of Radical schemes in Congress.

Former secession Democrats, after a period of political eclipse in the state, were especially active in the cooperation movement. But former Whig leaders, who had been the chief beneficiaries of reconstruction under President Johnson, were not missing in the effort to persuade the white masses to accept the congressional settlement. Union Whigs like Judge Robb, John W. C. Watson, and William Yerger consorted in the campaign with such prominent secessionists as Albert Gallatin Brown, John J. McRae, and Ethelbert Barksdale. On the other hand Whig patriarchs William Lewis Sharkey and George L. Potter refused support to a movement that acquiesced in the "tyranny" of congressional reconstruction and whose leadership included Brown and Barksdale, the principal chiefs of the "Jackson Clique" Democracy. Led by James

---

35. As reported in *ibid.*, July 7, 1867. See also similar comments by the editor of the Lexington *Advertiser*, July 4, 1867, and by Albert Gallatin Brown, August 29, 1867, both in *ibid.*

Lusk Alcorn, another group of Union Whigs not only abhorred an alignment with secession Democrats but rejected the policy of the cooperationists because it did not go far enough in accepting the need for major political reform in Mississippi. Furthermore, the Alcorn Whigs doubted that the Democratic leopard could change its spots and honor the terms that Congress had imposed on the state.[36] Although most of them did not step forward to join the Republican party at this time, Alcorn Whigs were nonetheless moving inexorably in that direction—and some like Alcorn himself would eventually emerge as leaders in the party.

The inability of the cooperationists to rally the old-line Whig leadership to the movement was a serious blow to their hopes for success. Since the end of the war and the collapse of the Democratic party, whites of the state had looked to the Whigs for guidance on reconstruction matters. But the confusion in old-line Whig councils over cooperation with Congress doomed to failure in 1867 any effort to rally the white masses to a policy of acquiescence in the reconstruction laws. Given the endemic nature of anti-Negro feeling among yeoman whites in Mississippi, only the Whig leadership's unified and vigorous support for cooperation could perhaps have persuaded the white masses of the expediency of accepting in good faith the congressional terms, muffling their opposition to black rights, and participating in the fall election.

This obstacle to success was not apparent in the beginning of the cooperationist campaign. Cooperationists in the spring and summer of 1867 made a determined effort to organize a moderate biracial coalition and seize control of reconstruction in the state. With encouragement from twenty-three newspapers, they held meetings throughout Mississippi, especially in counties with large Negro populations.[37] Emphasizing the need for harmony between

36. Alcorn, *Views on the Political Situation*; Jackson *Clarion*, September 19, 1867; Meridian *Semi-Weekly Gazette*, May 18, 1867.

37. The number of newspapers supporting the cooperationist policy is given in the Jackson *Clarion*, May 17, 1867. For elaborate statements of the reconstruction positions of some prominent Mississippians from both old parties, see *ibid.*, June 11 (Robb, Whig), June 22 (Yerger, Whig), September 5 (Watson, Whig), 1867; Meridian *Semi-Weekly Gazette*, March 16 (Johnston, Whig), March 20 (Wiley P. Harris, Democrat), July 25 (McRae, Democrat), August 21 (Brown, Democrat), 1867; William L. Sharkey, (Whig) to Stuart, August 8, 1867, in Dimitry Papers.

the races, cooperation spokesmen at these gatherings appealed to
blacks to accept the leadership of the old master class and asked
whites to recognize in good faith Negro rights as guaranteed by
the reconstruction laws. The first racially mixed rally occurred
in Oktibbeha County only a few days after the passage of the
first military bill, followed by a large meeting of both races at
Columbus, which the press of the town referred to as "the most
novel one ever witnessed." [38] The Columbus rally served as a model for subsequent local gatherings sponsored by reconstructionists.
In this meeting, black and white leaders made lengthy speeches,
and biracial committees drafted impressive resolutions and recommended an organizational framework for the local reconstruction
movement, which received the quick approval of the assembled
masses. Denying that Mississippi whites had ever been unfriendly
to Negroes, the resolutions of the Columbus meeting averred that
"politically the white and black men of the South occupy the same
position under the laws, [and] their interests are identical." The
local reconstruction association promised to advance the cause of
equal political and civil rights for blacks and to promote the establishment of public schools for both races. [39]

A resort to deception, however, was not missing from the cooperationist appeal. William S. Barry, an antebellum Democratic
congressman, made a special effort in his remarks to blacks at
the Columbus meeting to connect the local Republican party,
which only that morning had organized in the county, with a secessionist plot to regain power. Barry failed to mention, however,
that he had been the leading disunionist in the county and had
served as president of the convention that took Mississippi out
of the Union in 1861.

Moderate spokesmen were quick to hail the work of the Columbus meeting and call for similar rallies throughout the state. The
former secession editor of the Meridian *Gazette* expressed the
view of many cooperationists when he declared that the platform
drawn up by the Columbus meeting "is the true one to restore
our State to her proper place and save the people from such tyrany

---

38. Meridian *Semi-Weekly Gazette*, April 10, 20, 1867; Columbus *Southern Sentinel*,
April 23, 1867; Jackson *Clarion*, April 24, 1867.
39. Jackson *Clarion*, April 24, 1867.

[*sic*] as is now felt in Missouri and Tennessee. . . . We believe the career of the Radicals will end with the reconstruction of the South and the admission of our representatives" to Congress. Other local meetings followed the Columbus one, and by May the *Gazette* could report, though with obvious exaggeration, that so strong was the reconstruction movement in east Mississippi that "every man heretofore prominent, whether as secessionist or Union[ist]," favored the cooperationist policy.[40] If planters were not imperious in instructing Negroes in their political responsibilities, Barksdale of the Jackson *Clarion* declared, it would be an easy task for cooperationists "to convince the new voters that there is a medium ground which they may occupy between the Impracticables on the one hand and [the] Radicals on the other."[41]

Other reports seemed to support the sanguine expectations of these editors. In sedate and aristocratic Natchez, the black leader Burrell Foley addressed a large biracial meeting and urged the Negroes in attendance to unite with southern moderates. The Negro bishop of the African Methodist Episcopal Church in Mississippi gave similar advice to his flock at an integrated rally on the grounds of the state capitol. Even in Meridian, the raw and predominantly white trading center of east Mississippi, mixed meetings were held, and a number of whites, by invitation, attended a festival in a local black church.[42] This spirit of racial goodwill and political cooperation was climaxed by a large Fourth of July rally at Terry, a small community a few miles below Jackson on the New Orleans, Jackson, and Great Northern Railroad. The mixed gathering, augmented by "a very numerous company of blacks" who arrived by train from the capital, listened to the conciliatory oratory of representatives of all of the important political elements in the state. Walker Brooke of Vicksburg, a former United States senator, and James W. Robb represented the Union-Whig persuasion, Albert Gallatin Brown the former southern fire-

40. Meridian *Semi-Weekly Gazette*, April 20, May 1, 1867. See also an optimistic account of this movement in the New York *Times*, May 18, 1867.
41. Jackson *Clarion*, May 9, 1867. An authoritarian approach by planters in the political instruction of the freedmen, Barksdale warned, would arouse their resentment and awaken their suspicion that something was amiss. *Ibid.*, May 17, 1867.
42. *Ibid.*, April 30, May 22, July 6, 1867; Meridian *Semi-Weekly Gazette*, May 1, 13, July 4, 1867; Natchez *Weekly Democrat*, April 18, 23, 1867.

eaters, and Thomas Palmer the persistent Unionists. Even the northern element participated in the rally, with former Union Captain Hiram T. Fisher coming from Jackson to provide encouragement for the movement. The only incident to mar the festivities at Terry was the obstreperous conduct of an inebriated obstructionist, though federal soldiers, who had been requested to be on hand, quickly removed the troublemaker. [43]

A few weeks later, in one of the last integrated rallies before the ambitious cooperation movement floundered on the rocks of white opposition and Republican success in appealing to blacks, former Governor Brown declared that he was "not only willing but anxious to instruct" the freedman in the "ABCs of his politics." As to the Negro's desire for land, Brown thought it a commendable ambition, and there was land for all; the black man, however, should demonstrate first that he could earn his provisions, then he could secure title to a farm. [44]

By late summer it was obvious to the cooperationists that their plan for winning the black vote had failed. Everywhere former slaves were flocking to Republican rallies, joining Republican clubs, and, in the black counties, marching to Union League meetings. Nevertheless, cooperationists refused to abandon their effort to form a moderate reconstruction party—one that now would have to depend almost entirely on the votes of whites. They recognized, however, that such a party, without substantial black support at the polls, could not dominate any future reconstruction government. But if white cooperationists organized thoroughly and participated fully in the reconstruction elections, they might still serve as a strong force for stability and virtue in state and local affairs. Cooperationists denounced as foolish the emerging conservative strategy of inaction, or "masterly inactivity," in the forthcoming fall contest, since such a course would result in the election of an unfettered majority of Radical delegates to the state

43. Meridian *Semi-Weekly Gazette*, July 14, 1867. Walker Brooke later became a leader of those opposing cooperation with Congress. So vociferous was the growing white criticism of the mixed rallies that Barksdale through the columns of the Jackson *Clarion* (July 6, 1867) felt impelled to reassure finicky Mississippians that the meetings "were marked by strict decorum and a due regard for social usages which have heretofore prevailed in our State."

44. Meridian *Semi-Weekly Gazette*, August 21, 1867.

constitutional convention. Wiley P. Harris, a leading cooperationist and a former Democratic congressman, expressed this position
when he wrote: "Self-preservation, the integrity of Government,
and the safety of civil society here, demand that we should en-
deavor to obtain as much influence for virtue and intelligence in
the Convention, the Legislative body, and in the administration
of the Government as possible. . . . Whites ought not to put
themselves in a position in which they could do nothing in favor
of order and good government; [certainly] a course of inaction
would result in committing our local government to the most ignorant and depraved class of the people."[45]

To organize for the coming campaign, a group of cooperationists,
mainly from Hinds County, met on the capitol grounds on September 23 and announced the formation of "the Reconstruction party
of Mississippi." As a matter of policy, the convention attempted
to balance membership on its committees and governing body
between old-line Whigs and Democrats, a practice that would be
followed in subsequent anti-Republican conventions during the
Reconstruction era. The leading spirits in the meeting were Democrats Harris, Barksdale, and Thomas J. Wharton, and Union Whigs
William Yerger and Thomas Palmer. Yerger presided over the
convention and was selected as the first permanent chairman of the
new party. The convention resolved "that while we feel that the
Congressional plan of Reconstruction is impolitic and oppressive . . . there is no escape from the necessity of reorganizing our
State government under the control of the present Congress.
Firmly believing that a rejection of this plan will lead to accumulated oppressions to our people and the infliction of disabilities exceeding those already provided, we do earnestly advise the people
of Mississippi without regard to old party distinctions to vote for
a Convention and for the best available delegates to constitute
said body."[46] Lest there be doubters, the platform adopted by
the convention made it clear that the Reconstruction party was
"a distinctive political organization, having no association or connection with the extremists of the Republican party." Still, some

45. As reported in the Jackson *Clarion*, August 29, 1867.
46. The platform and resolutions of the Reconstruction party may be found in the Jackson *Weekly Clarion*, September 24, 1867, and the Natchez *Weekly Democrat*, October 7,
1867.

of its planks had a Republican ring to them. The cooperationist convention, like the Republicans, expressed itself in favor of "efficient systems of public schools for all classes of our people," the encouragement of northern and European immigration to Mississippi, the extension of outside capital "with its powerful agencies in rebuilding our natural resources," and the protection of labor "in its right to adequate reward." Finally, the party platform manifested a spirit of sympathy for and understanding toward the freedmen. "We wish them to be prosperous and happy in their present condition of freedom, and shall oppose all legislation discriminating against them."

By the time of the Reconstruction party's convention, however, it was already apparent that the cooperationist effort to win the support of the white masses was faltering. Whites, after the initial shock of the military reconstruction acts had worn off, became increasingly hostile to the policy of cooperating with those whose object, they believed, was to rivet upon the South "the vilest and most corrupt despotism which has disgraced the annals of history."[47] White emotions were aroused by the sight of Negroes attending political rallies, and the radical tendencies of the state Republican convention, occurring two weeks before the meeting of the Reconstruction party, strengthened white determination to take no part in the fall election. Since they expected the Radicals to win anyway, the white masses saw no point in voting; participation in the election would tend to legitimize the congressional program of reconstruction and degrade Mississippi further in the eyes of the world. Moreover, if whites boycotted the election, the Mississippi constitutional convention, along with those in other southern states, would be so overwhelmingly Radical (and perhaps black as well) that northern voters would react in disgust and in the next national election would mandate the end of congressional reconstruction.

Unable in the fall to obtain speakers to stump the state for the Reconstruction party, Barksdale and a few like-minded editors made a strong attempt through the columns of their newspapers to check the mushrooming white resistance to the cooperationist policy. Barksdale pleaded with whites to "consult their true inter-

47. The quote is from the Vicksburg *Herald*, September 4, 1868.

ests by accepting the terms offered" by Congress and to avoid being misled into an injudicious course because of their outrage at "the agrarian doctrines which were preached by the levellers in the late Republican convention." The hour was not too late, Barksdale claimed, for conservatives to win the support of the blacks and defeat the Republican adventurers' plans to radicalize the new political element. "We have not believed that there would be any separate and distinct organization of the negro voters on an exclusively caste basis, unless a pretext for such an organization should be furnished by the consolidation of the whites into a separate party with a view to deprive the former of the privilege conferred upon them by Congress." As to the contention of the "Impracticables" that Radical reconstruction would be overturned as a result of the national election of 1868, Barksdale realistically observed: "[My] opinion is very decided that if the Democracy should succeed in overthrowing the present dominant party in the next Presidential election, it will be through the influence of issues more potent than the negro suffrage question," specifically the question of the national debt and its payment. Southerners should not be deluded into believing that rescue by northern conservatives from congressional tyranny was in the cards, at least before southern action was required under the reconstruction laws. From a material standpoint, Barksdale argued, the success of the Reconstruction party was crucial. The investment of northern capital, an immediate increase in white immigration into the state, and the early restoration of prosperity for Mississippians depended on the emergence of a strong moderate force in reconstruction affairs—a force that would give confidence to economic interests in the future stability of the state.[48]

The efforts of Barksdale and his associates, however, proved fruitless except in a handful of counties where influential Reconstructionists campaigned vigorously and won election as delegates to the constitutional convention.[49] By the time of the fall election the overwhelming majority of whites supported the uncompromising Constitutional Union party and its policy of "masterly inactivity."

48. Jackson *Clarion*, September 25, October 5, 8, 9, 30, 1867.
49. *Ibid.*, October 29, 1867; Meridian *Semi-Weekly Gazette*, October 29, 1867.

The Constitutional Union party emerged rapidly during the summer of 1867 to provide direction for the growing white resistance to congressional reconstruction. The guiding spirit behind the party was George L. Potter, a Union Whig and one of the most influential conservatives in the state during the early Reconstruction period. Born in New Haven, Connecticut, and trained in law at Yale University, Potter came to Mississippi in 1835 and settled in Natchez. He practiced law there until 1840, when he moved to Jackson. By 1861 he had achieved first rank among the lawyers of Mississippi, a state where the legal profession without regard to politics constituted a virtual priesthood. Potter demonstrated little ambition for public office, and the fact that he supported the Union cause, at least until the secession of the state, made unlikely a successful political career for him in antebellum Mississippi even if he had desired one. But after the war, when Mississippians turned to old-line Whigs for leadership, Potter came forward to lead the more conservative elements in the state. As a delegate to the Johnson reconstruction convention of 1865, he arraigned the federal government for freeing the slaves of nonparticipants in the war. Then, during the fall political campaign he led the forces opposed to Negro testimony in court, and in 1866 he was one of the state organizers of the National Union (Johnson) party. In all of these movements he was on the losing side.[50]

To Potter, as well as to other Union-Whig conservatives like William L. Sharkey and Amos R. Johnston, the Constitution had come to have a near sacred meaning, personifying much that was stable and meaningful in a world threatened with chaos. According to these conservative Whigs, the restoration of the Constitution to its "pristine vigor" offered the only hope for the reconstruction of a Union of comity and strength—one that could check the disrespect for legitimate authority that had become prevalent in the nation as a result of the bitter civil war. Radicalism of both the antislavery and the secessionist varieties had violated the spirit, if not the letter, of the Constitution and destroyed the Union in 1860–1861, conservative Whigs believed, and deadly extremism

50. James D. Lynch, *The Bench and Bar of Mississippi* (New York, 1881), 445; Harris, *Presidential Reconstruction in Mississippi,* 49, 51, 53, 107, 230.

of a similar type was at work in 1867 in the congressional plan
of reconstruction, poisoning the efforts of men of good will to
reunite the nation and reestablish constitutional supremacy. For
most southerners after the war the Constitution was the sole symbol of national unity and virtue; it thus seemed logical to Potter
Whigs that a program of reconstruction, designed to achieve a
true reconciliation of the sections, should build on this base and
satisfy former Confederates that this emblem of a common past
would not be further violated. Antipathy toward black rights—
perhaps as much a class matter as a racial one for these Whigs—
obviously contributed to their insistence that the Constitution remain inviolate in face of congressional designs after the war. Union
Whigs before the war had found solace in the Constitution, albeit
without a strong states' rights tinge, when southern fire-eaters
pushed for disunion in order to maintain white racial integrity.
Ironically, during Reconstruction these original Unionists became
as dogmatic and inflexible in their defense of constitutional rights
as had their Democratic opponents during the late antebellum
period. This understanding of the Union-Whig mind is necessary
for a comprehension not only of the reasons why most Whigs during Reconstruction rejected Republican overtures but also why
many of them demonstrated a strong reluctance to cooperate with
their old Democratic antagonists in a campaign to defeat radicalism
in the state. Only in the stirring contests of 1868 and 1875 would
a united front of conservatives, including the surviving leadership
of both antebellum parties, be achieved in Mississippi.

Unable to commandeer what was left of the old political structures in the state, Potter and his associates during the summer
simply announced the creation of a new party, named appropriate-
ly after the Constitutional Union party of 1860 which ran John Bell
for the presidency on a platform of Union and sectional conciliation. Potter announced that the purpose of the party was to unite
"citizens in defense of constitutional government. It is not a partizan organization, but is, and was intended to be, an association
upon the common platform of the Constitution to defeat Radicalism and to secure the practical supremacy of the Constitution."[51]

From the stump and in the newspapers the founders of the

51. Natchez *Tri-Weekly Courier*, February 3, 1868.

Constitutional Union party launched a vigorous campaign to counter the early cooperationist advantage and win the support of the
white masses for their strategy of "masterly inactivity" in the fall
election. The reasoning behind this strategy was simple: the reconstruction act of March 23, 1867, required the participation of
a *majority* of the registered voters to make the election valid;
therefore, according to the Potterites, if whites registered but
failed to vote in the election a majority would not be obtained
and the Radical convention would not be held. As a result, military
rule under General Ord, which was preferable to a Radical ascendancy and the vitiation of the Constitution, would continue until
pressure in the North demanded the repeal of the reconstruction
laws. Indeed, Potter and his followers believed that the success
of their strategy would discredit the Republican party in the North
and contribute to an early end of its dominance in the nation.
"By remaining from the polls," Edward M. Yerger declared, "we
can earnestly exert all our influence to convince [northerners] of
the wickedness of the scheme of reconstruction and in this manner
may effectually defeat the object of the mongrels."[52]

Political developments in the North during the early autumn
gave a dramatic boost to the Potterite strategy in Mississippi. In
October Democrats won victories in Pennsylvania and Ohio, and
a Negro suffrage amendment was defeated in the Buckeye state.
A worse fate seemed to await Republicans in the November elections. Preferring to believe that the Republican decline was caused
by its unwise reconstruction policy, the Meridian *Gazette* exclaimed gleefully after hearing the results of the early elections:
"The reaction seems to be extending from one end of the land
to the other, and the signs now are that the politics of the country
will be completely revolutionized before Christmas."[53] David C.
Glenn, a secessionist leader in the crisis of 1860–1861 but a cooperationist in early 1867, wrote his old friend L. Q. C. Lamar that
a recent trip to the North had cured him of the heresy of aiding
in the work of congressional reconstruction, and he had come

52. Meridian *Semi-Weekly Gazette*, August 10, October 29, 1867; Vicksburg *Herald*,
October 15 (quote), 19, 1867; Jackson *Weekly Clarion*, September 5, 24, 1867.
53. Meridian *Semi-Weekly Gazette*, October 12, 1867. For the influence of the 1867
northern elections on Mississippi politics, see James Lusk Alcorn, *Address of J. L. Alcorn
to the People of Mississippi* (Friar's Point, Miss., 1869), 5.

home "utterly unreconstructed." He added, "I think I saw signs of the downfall of Radicalism North, and in twelve months I think the South can breathe again."[54] Glenn's analysis of the course of northern politics received wide publicity in the Constitutional Union press, and, coming from a former Democratic leader, went far to neutralize among old Democrats the submission advice of party patriarchs Brown, Barksdale, and McRae.[55]

To prepare further for the fall campaign, Potter and a group of friends met in Jackson in September, formulated a declaration of principles for the Constitutional Union party, and issued a call for a state convention of the new party. The declaration flatly rejected the policy of granting suffrage to blacks, since "their own interests, no less than those of the white population, require their exclusion from the ballot-box." The declaration also placed the party on record as favoring "a rigid economy" in government in order to keep taxes at a low level and sustain the credit of state and local governments.[56] True to its Whiggish antecedents, the new party's declaration of principles avoided any reference to the national Democratic party, despite the fact that much of its success depended upon Democratic victories in the North.

Attendance at the state Constitutional Union convention, which convened on October 15, disappointed its sponsors. Fewer than a dozen counties sent delegations, a weak showing that was blamed on rumors of the spread of yellow fever in some areas of the state and also on the brief period available for organizing local meetings before the convention met.[57] Even so, the party had no trouble obtaining the support of the white masses, and by the

54. David C. Glenn to Lucius Q. C. Lamar, September 22, 1867, in Lucius Q. C. Lamar and Edward Mayes Papers, Mississippi Department of Archives and History.

55. Meridian *Semi-Weekly Gazette*, October 12, 1867. Prior to this time Potterites had warned Mississippians of the perfidy of Democratic politicians who urged cooperation with Congress in its plan of reconstruction. "The old journeymen politicians who led [Mississippians] into secession," Arthur J. Frantz of the Brandon *Republican* wrote, "cannot lead them back into the Union at the expense of their honor. They made them believe in 1860 that they should sacrifice life and property rather than live under Yankee rule, but they cannot make them believe that they ought to sacrifice every principle of manhood and honor to get back." As reported in *ibid.*, May 1, 1867. See also the comments of Edward M. Yerger in *ibid.*, July 4, 1867, and George W. Harper in the *Hinds County Gazette*, June 28, 1867.

56. Jackson *Weekly Clarion*, September 24, 1867.

57. *Ibid.*, October 16, 1867; Vicksburg *Herald*, October 17, 1867. Presiding over the state convention was Union Whig Walker Brooke. Potter's chief assistant in the party was David Shelton, a Union Whig from Rankin County.

November election the old citizenry was almost solid in its support for the policy of "masterly inactivity."

The most spectacular political development to occur in Mississippi, as well as in other southern states during military reconstruction, was the organization and meteoric rise of the Republican party. Protected by the military, friends of Congress and Negro rights during the spring and summer of 1867 formed secret Union Leagues and Republican clubs to organize the black masses and a scattering of sympathetic whites into a phalanx of Republican voters. The leadership in this movement came from three sources —transplanted northerners, Mississippi Unionists, a number of whom were "to the manor born," and black leaders who were already on the scene providing religious and educational instruction to the recently freed members of their race.

The most energetic of the Republican organizers were the transplanted northerners, or carpetbaggers, who in almost all cases had come to the state, for a variety of reasons, before the passage of the reconstruction laws. After the war the plantation districts and neighboring commercial centers were flooded with northerners, many of whom were former Union soldiers who had campaigned in the state. Most of these northerners came seeking their big chance through commercial and planting enterprises rather than through political activity. They were especially reluctant to become involved in Republican politics, either because of their fear of ostracism from white society or their aversion to the advanced doctrine of Negro rights that the Stevens-Sumner wing of the party advocated. Indeed, the politically active carpetbag class in Mississippi was never very numerous, probably at no time exceeding two hundred men and never including the majority of newcomers from above the Ohio.[58] Those who did join in the work of or-

58. This figure is based on an identification of 156 northern settlers who participated in Republican politics in the state. Many obscure carpetbaggers were identified by comparing newspaper lists of membership in the Mississippi chapters of the Grand Army of the Republic with accounts of participants in local Republican meetings. (The assumption is that individuals who associated with this veterans' organization were of northern origin.) Some carpetbaggers perhaps have eluded discovery. It is reasonable to conclude, however, that almost all the local functionaries of this class, in addition to more prominent ones, have been identified, since the two leading state Republican newspapers of the period, the Jackson *Pilot* and Vicksburg *Times and Republican*, both owned and edited by carpetbaggers, often carried the proceedings of local party meetings and sometimes referred to an individual's

ganizing the Republican party in the state appeared motivated primarily by a desire to protect the fruits of Union victory—*i.e.* bona fide freedom for blacks and an end to the spirit of rebellion (as they perceived its existence) in the South. Under President Johnson's plan of reconstruction the results of the war seemed to these newcomers to be in serious jeopardy. The triumph of Congress in the reconstruction struggle, however, offered new hope for concerned northerners in Mississippi. Consequently, many of them abandoned their reluctance to engage in politics and began the work of organizing black voters. Nevertheless, the more hesitant ones entered the Republican sanctuary through the cooperationist antechamber. Future notables in the party like Beroth B. Eggleston, Hiram T. Fisher, Albert R. Howe, and Henry W. Barry became Republicans only after a flirtation with conservatives in the Reconstruction party. When this movement faltered during the summer, they abandoned it and joined the Republican party.

In contrast to the northerners who came south for economic reasons, a number of officials in the Freedmen's Bureau and teachers who had been sent to Mississippi by missionary and benevolent associations became early and enthusiastic supporters of congressional reconstruction. Moved by the exhilarating idealism of Union, freedom, and equality that had swept the North during the last decade and daily witnessing the violation of these principles in the South, this group of northerners expressed a deep concern for the rights of blacks in postwar Mississippi, along with the common northern fear that the spirit of rebellion was still rampant in the state. Many bureau officers and teachers, like Superintendent of Education Henry R. Pease and young Charles W. Clarke, both of whom would become leading Republicans, seemed genuinely to believe that a new political orientation in the state, based on universal male suffrage, free labor, tolerance of opinions, and free public schools would benefit all classes and would make Mississippi the equal of the most progressive states in the North.[59] Because of General Ord's order prohibiting federal officials from engaging in politics, those bureau agents who sought political careers were forced first to resign their offices, or commissions, with

---

place of origin. Mississippi's conservative press also provided information leading to the positive identification of many carpetbaggers.

59. Harris, "Creed of the Carpetbaggers," 199–224 *passim*.

the government. Since these carpetbaggers had been working with the freedmen, they had the inside track on gaining the political confidence of the new electorate, a status that virtually ensured their rapid rise to positions of influence in the state's Republican party.

Despite the high idealism of a number of early carpetbaggers, the desire for political power and office was not entirely absent in the decision of these newcomers to become active Republicans. The heady anticipation of instant political influence obviously appealed to many of the carpetbag class. The subsequent Reconstruction careers of such prominent Republicans as Adelbert Ames, Henry R. Pease, Ridgley C. Powers, and G. Wiley Wells attest to the frequent intermingling of political ambition and wartime idealism in the motivation of the carpetbagger in Mississippi. Although impossible to determine precisely, the mixture of these motives differed with each northerner. Only a few carpetbaggers, however, were outright adventurers. The most notorious of these was Charles E. Furlong of Vicksburg who, after posing as a conservative for business reasons, organized the Union Leagues in Warren County into a pliant and corrupt political machine.

Scalawags, or antebellum citizens who affiliated with the Republican party after the war, generally viewed Reconstruction opportunities (or responsibilities) in a different light from most carpetbaggers. Usually lacking the idealistic commitment of their carpetbag associates to Negro rights and freedom, most scalawags found in the Republican party a counterweight to the restoration to power of myopic secessionists and a hope for progress in the future. Mainly of the Unionist class before the war, most of them at first resented the intrusion of the Negro question into the purpose of the war and into the reconstruction settlement. But their outrage at the prospect of a "Johnson style" rebel revival caused many of this group to swallow their opposition to Negro suffrage as a matter of policy and affiliate with the Republican party.[60] As long as the Republican program of reconstruction remained moderate, stopping short of economic and social equality for blacks and the disfranchisement of the white masses, these Unionists

60. B. F. Moore to Sharkey, July 28, 1865, in Governors' Correspondence, Vol. 61; statement of Unionist Wilson F. Dillon, in Frank W. Klingberg, *The Southern Claims Commission* (Berkeley, 1955), 108; speech of Unionist James Elliott as reported in the Jackson *Clarion*, February 13, 1868; statement of Unionist Joseph W. Field, in Jackson *Clarion*, May 20, 1869.

could be content in the Republican fold. In fact, the more they thought about the alternative to black suffrage under Republican aegis—*i.e.* the restoration of Brown-Barksdale Democrats to power—the less distasteful Negro political equality became. Black voters, Union Republicans realized, could be controlled by "loyal" whites and used to maintain a truly Union government in power without any real threat to white supremacy or to the prospects of economic recovery by the state.

As time would prove, an impressive number of scalawags, whatever their motivation in the beginning, accepted in good faith the Republican principle of black political equality and worked consistently during Reconstruction for its practical implementation. Few Republicans, North or South, could match the radicalism of Robert Worth Flournoy, a humane former slaveholder and Union Democrat of Pontotoc County who frequently during Reconstruction urged the state Republican leadership to go beyond political rights for blacks and end discrimination against them in public places and in the schools.[61] Joshua S. Morris, a Union Whig of Claiborne County, was another early scalawag who would in time demonstrate a courageous support for black rights. As attorney general in 1873 he brought to trial and successfully prosecuted a violator of a recently passed state law prohibiting racial discrimination in public places. In his arguments before the state supreme court, Morris declared that the war had elevated the former slaves "to a plane of absolute legal equality with the hitherto dominant class." Blacks "have been invited, and have accepted the invitation, to enter the race of life as competitors with the white man for the goal of a higher and nobler civilization," he announced.[62] Despite the examples of Flournoy, Morris, and a few others, most scalawags were of the James Lusk Alcorn persuasion and tried hard throughout Reconstruction to avoid identification with the Radical wing of the Republican party. Only by keeping the party on a moderate political course, they believed, could the new order build a bridge to the larger white community, which in turn would ensure Republican success in the state.

Usually neglected in the story of the rise of the Republican

61. William C. Harris, "A Reconsideration of the Mississippi Scalawag," *Journal of Mississippi History*, XXXII (February, 1970), 11–13.
62. *George Donnell* v. *State of Mississippi*, 48 Miss. 661 (1873).

party in the South was the yeoman work of black leaders in welding the politically unsophisticated of their race into a solid bloc of voters. In Mississippi there were a number of black missionaries from the North and the border states who quickly became involved in Republican politics after the passage of the reconstruction laws. The most outstanding of these preacher-politicians was James Lynch, a brilliant young orator who arrived in Mississippi in early 1867 to serve as bishop of the northern Methodist church for the state.[63] Thomas W. Stringer, Lynch's chief rival in the black community, also came to Mississippi in the migration of Negro ministers southward, serving as the general superintendent of missions and presiding elder for the African Methodist Church before becoming involved in the organization of blacks into Union Leagues and Republican clubs.[64] Although not as influential in politics as Lynch and Stringer, Hiram Rhoades Revels, a northern Methodist missionary in the Natchez area, spent as much time in 1867 instructing blacks in Republican doctrine as he did in instructing them in the tenets of his church.[65] Indeed, the merger of religious zeal and Republican enthusiasm was pervasive in the work of early black politicians in Mississippi. Politician-missionary Jeremiah M. P. Williams of Natchez made this connection when he declared to a group of black followers: "The Republican party has been the grand instrument in the hands of God to give my countrymen, my people, our race, liberty, the right to vote, sit on juries, to hold office, and to enjoy the privileges of free education. . . . On the ministers of the gospel a great responsibility rests. They are to guide the people like the prophets of Israel when the surrounding nations threatened their destruction."[66]

The native Negro community also contributed men of temerity and organizational skill to the work of organizing the Republican party throughout the countryside. Although generally not as well educated as the black emissaries from the North, men like Charles Caldwell, a Clinton blacksmith during slavery; Merriman Howard,

63. William C. Harris, "James Lynch: Black Leader in Southern Reconstruction," *Historian*, XXXIV (November, 1971), 41–44.

64. Wharton, *The Negro in Mississippi*, 149.

65. Annie L. Pierson, biographical sketch of Hiram R. Revels, in Hiram R. Revels Folder, Subject File Collection, Mississippi Department of Archives and History.

66. As reported in the Natchez *Weekly Democrat*, April 19, 1871. See also a similar declaration by Doctor (his first name) Stites, a Negro leader in the Delta, reported in the Jackson *Pilot*, February 23, 1871.

a former house servant for a Jefferson County family; J. Aaron Moore, a Meridian blacksmith and minister; Henry Mayson, a Jackson barber; Robert Gleed, a Columbus merchant who was reportedly worth $15,000 in 1872; and Emanuel Handy, a native of Copiah County who had served in the Union army during the war, rendered valuable service in arousing blacks to political activity in 1867–1868.[67] But soon recognized as the most capable of the homegrown black leaders was John R. Lynch, a mulatto youth twenty years old in 1867 and a photographer in Natchez. By 1873 Lynch had served as speaker of the state house of representatives, had been elected to Congress, and had ousted from control the powerful carpetbag clique that since 1867 had dominated Adams County politics. The importance of homegrown black leaders in rallying blacks to the Republican standard during the early Reconstruction period can hardly be exaggerated.

Since the end of the war local black leaders had been waiting for an opportunity to organize the masses of their race for political purposes. Aroused in late 1865 by the anti-Negro policies of the Johnsonian government in the state, Henry Mayson and a group of freedmen in the Jackson-Vicksburg area held a meeting in September to protest the system of "warranteeism" for blacks that was replacing slavery in Mississippi.[68] This meeting led to an October conference and a call for a statewide convention of local Negro leaders to organize an "equal rights league" for the protection and advancement of freedmen rights. Although at the time the fundamental freedom of blacks was at issue, the October consultation meeting went further in its protest; it advanced the radical proposition "that the elective franchise is the lawful right of the colored as well as the white native born citizens."[69] There is no record, however, that the proposed state convention was held or that blacks continued their efforts to organize, until the advent of military rule in 1867.

In 1867 a flurry of organizational activity greeted the coming of spring which occurred simultaneously with the arrival of federal

67. Montgomery, *Reminiscences*, 275; Washington *New National Era*, February 22, 1872, March 6, 1873.

68. New York *Tribune*, October 10, 1865.

69. Vicksburg *Journal*, November 5, 1865. Wharton in *The Negro in Mississippi*, 140, reports that a mass black meeting was held at Vicksburg in June, 1865, and the assemblage,

James Lusk Alcorn, scalawag

Adelbert Ames, carpetbagger

Ethelbert Barksdale, conservative

Albert Gallatin Brown, conservative

Alvan C. Gillem, military commander

John R. Lynch, black leader

William H. McCardle, conservative

George C. McKee, carpetbagger

Edward O. C. Ord, military commander

Ridgley C. Powers, carpetbagger

Hiram R. Revels, black leader

G. Wiley Wells, carpetbagger

The *Natchez*, though the loser in the famous 1870 race with the *Robert E. Lee*, was the most

troops to protect the state's new political element. At first the greatest effort to organize the Republican party was made in the predominantly black river counties where potential members and local leaders were numerous. In mid-April a disturbed Natchez editor reported that Radical organizers were at work in several communities and were laboring "with that rapidity of action which usually characterizes the movements of revolutionary organizations." Already arrangements had been completed for the establishment of Republican journals in Meridian and Vicksburg, and plans were afoot to place newspaper organs in other important towns of the state.[70]

An important instrument for enrolling freedmen in the Republican party was the celebrated Union or Loyal League, a secret, oath-bound association that had originated in the North during the war. The league appeared to many Republican politicos in the South as the perfect means for systematically organizing politically inexperienced and timid freedmen into a phalanx of devoted followers. A secret society of this kind supposedly appealed to the freedman's affinity for nocturnal meetings and mystery, to his gregarious tendencies, and, most significantly, to his need for security in numbers and discipline to overcome his fear in challenging the tradition of white political supremacy. Although the local leagues provided some social opportunities for blacks, the main purpose of the organization was admittedly a political one, with each member swearing to support only Union men (Republicans) for public office. In Mississippi, as elsewhere, the local unit was known as a council, and it assembled frequently, usually twice a week during the heyday of the Union League. In these ostensibly secret sessions speakers extolled fidelity to the Union and to the party of Lincoln; Republican catechisms were repeated; and new members were initiated into the league. Leaders in the community councils

---

under the influence of a white northern soldier, drew up a resolution appealing to Congress to enfranchise the freedmen. "Redeemer" John S. McNeily's "War and Reconstruction in Mississippi, 1863–1890," *Publications of the Mississippi Historical Society, Centenary Series,* II (1918), 275–76, is Wharton's source for this information. McNeily was probably thinking of the October meeting and was evidently incorrect concerning the role of the northern soldier even in that meeting.

70. R. J. Mosely and Company to William H. Seward, April 1, 1867, and Philip Henson to Edward McPherson, April 25, 1867, both in Edward McPherson Papers, Manuscript Division, Library of Congress; Natchez *Weekly Democrat,* April 15, 16, 1867; Vicksburg *Herald,* April 24, 1867; Columbus *Southern Sentinel,* April 23, 1867.

met periodically in a grand council of the county leagues to discuss common problems and to decide on candidates to support for
the local Republican nominations.[71]

The extreme secrecy and martial character of Union League
meetings has often been exaggerated. Clandestine rallies in the
swamps or deep woods of Mississippi were rare until the rise
of the Ku Klux Klan threat in the eastern counties in 1870–1871.
Meetings were normally held in drab black churches or in the
homes of prominent league members, and such sessions probably
lacked the elaborate rituals associated with the leagues. Blacks
did not usually come armed to the meetings, but where their
leadership was weak and insecure military demonstrations were
very much in evidence. Displays of martial might not only inflamed whites but also encouraged intimidating power struggles
within the Union League itself. In addition, as conservatives
charged, armed zealots coerced some reluctant blacks into joining
the league. In at least one county, Lauderdale (Meridian), strong-
arm methods were used to maintain for a time the despotic control
of a white adventurer, R. C. Merryman, over local Negroes. After
several months of his high-handed conduct, a revolt led by white
Republicans of the county, with the support of black dissidents,
overthrew Merryman's dominance of the league. Interestingly,
this adventurer was not of northern origin, nor was he an embittered Unionist; he was a native of Virginia who reputedly had
ridden with Jeb Stuart during the war.[72]

Warren County (Vicksburg) was especially plagued by the demagogic control of the local Union Leagues, although unlike in Lauderdale strong-arm methods were rarely practiced by those in
charge. Union Leagues had hardly been established in the county
when a bitter conflict erupted between a cabal of white northerners who controlled the grand council of the leagues and the white
nonleague Republicans, also mainly northerners but with a few
scalawags. In the ensuing struggle the party lost much of its idealistic reforming zeal. By 1869 both the Union League and the Re-

71. Vicksburg *Weekly Republican*, March 3, 1868; Meridian *Semi-Weekly Gazette*,
August 7, 1867.

72. Meridian *Semi-Weekly Gazette*, October 19, 29, December 4, 1867; Meridian
Chronicle, January 22, March 10, 1868; Jackson *Clarion*, January 14, 1868.

publican party in the county had come under the domination of Furlong, a former colonel in Sherman's army.[73]

Furlong came to Vicksburg before the end of the war and formed a partnership with a local merchant. Until 1868 the antebellum citizenry of the town found him to be a conservative and sensible northerner, whereas Republicans viewed him as "one of the most virulent Democrats and anti-blackman advocates" in Vicksburg.[74] His conversion to the Republican party occurred after the imposition of military rule and his appointment as sheriff by General Gillem. Seeing an opportunity to extend his lease on power in the county, Furlong "ingratiated himself into the favor of the unenlightened class," as a Republican opponent put it, and in their eyes he could do no wrong. With a ratio of five blacks to one white at the polls, Republicans in Warren County, who were primarily interested in local power and little concerned about the strength of the state party, could afford the luxury of divisions in their ranks, as long as the loyalty of most Negroes was retained. Controlling the county's Union Leagues, Furlong spurned the efforts of moderate northerners to build a strong white Republican party, even though the county had a relatively large Union-Whig concentration that might have been amenable to Republican advances; instead he established a courthouse "ring" to rule in the interests of a few local officeholders and friends. By 1871 the political odor from Vicksburg was so strong that Governor Alcorn took the unusual step of intervening and removing Furlong as sheriff. This action, with the decline of black enthusiasm for the Union League, loosened the carpetbagger's hold on county affairs. Although Furlong was reelected to his old office in the fall election of 1871, he saw the handwriting on the wall as Negro leaders like Thomas W. Cardozo and Peter Crosby rose to challenge his authority. Furlong now threw in his lot with the reform wing of the Republican party in Vicksburg, and in 1873 he proudly campaigned as an "Alcorn Republican." Assisted by conservative votes, he won a seat in the state senate, and from its rostrum he delivered

73. Vicksburg *Weekly Republican*, June 16, 23, 30, 1868; Vicksburg *Times and Republican*, September 14, October 3, 6, 1871; A. H. Arthur to Holt, February 7, 1870, in Holt Papers.

74. Natchez *Tri-Weekly Democrat*, May 7, 1867; Vicksburg *Times and Republican*, September 14, 1871.

one of the most scurrilous attacks made on the unfortunate Ames administration.[75] This performance raised him from carpetbag to hero status among white conservatives and ensured that he could remain in the state as a respected citizen after "redemption."

Despite the disreputable examples of the Warren and Lauderdale organizations, Union Leagues in Mississippi were not the all-pervasive and omnipotent instruments of Radical control described by hostile contemporaries and often by historians. For one reason, some Republican organizers, familiar with the intolerance that characterized the secret Know-Nothing movement of the 1850s, shunned the Union League device for rallying blacks to the party standard. In the hands of unprincipled men, some leading Republicans realized, a mysterious organization of this kind could be easily used for baleful purposes. Furthermore, the prevalence of the Union League could encourage the local development of the clandestine Ku Klux Klan, which at the time was spreading its tentacles out of Tennessee into other southern states. Republican critics of the organization saw no real need for the secrecy and the martial paraphernalia of the league, since federal troops, they believed, would be available to protect blacks who openly joined the regular Republican clubs, which as political associations were less repugnant to conservative whites. Both black leader James Lynch and Radical scalawag Flournoy, two of the leading party organizers in the state, opposed the formation of blacks into Union Leagues, and their opposition was an important reason for the relatively limited development of the society in Mississippi.[76]

Ironically, the Union League was strongest in the heavily black river counties where the necessity for Republican militancy was least. Conversely, it was weakest in the predominantly white counties where a disciplined and active organization was most needed to protect and advance Negro rights. Contributing to the relative insignificance of the Union League in many areas of the state was the fact that the local units lacked effective central direc-

75. Vicksburg *Times and Republican*, September 14, 27, October 6, 8, 1871; Charles E. Furlong, *Origin of the Outrages at Vicksburg: Speech of Hon. Chas. E. Furlong, Senator from Warren County, in the Senate of Mississippi, December 18, 1874* (Vicksburg, 1874).

76. Jackson *Weekly Clarion*, September 28, 1867; Meridian *Semi-Weekly Gazette*, October 16, 1867; Jackson *Weekly Pilot*, February 12, 1870; *House Reports*, 42nd Cong., 2nd Sess., No. 22, p. 6.

tion. A shadowy and weak state council existed to provide some semblance of statewide unity for the league, but it was independent of the state Republican executive committee and was viewed with suspicion by several members of the Republican hierarchy. Nevertheless, the presidency of the state Union League during its entire history was held by one of Mississippi's leading Radicals, the scalawag Alston Mygatt.

Mygatt, a native of New York and a graduate of Hamilton College in that state, came to Mississippi in 1837 for reasons of health and went into business at Vicksburg.[77] Since college days, when he was a classmate of Gerrit Smith, the famous abolitionist, Mygatt had held antislavery views, but in antebellum Mississippi he was forced to keep his beliefs to himself. When the state seceded and war occurred, he chose to remain in Vicksburg, although his loyalty to the Union was well known. After Grant captured the town in 1863, Mygatt worked successfully for the state's early restoration to the Union. A combination of Unionist zeal and antislavery fervor impelled him not only to become an early postwar convert to the Republican party but also to become an outspoken Radical. To him the Union victory in the Civil War had destroyed the twin relics of barbarism in America, slavery and secession; a new day was dawning for the Western world and for the dignity of man.[78]

Mygatt, like a few other Radical Republicans in Mississippi who viewed their presence there as a mission, found an important source of inspiration in the authoritarian and rigid Old Testament, which revealed to him that God would not permit the faithful of the new political order to fail. In a speech before the constitutional convention of 1868, which he temporarily chaired, Mygatt, a tall, bent man in his late fifties, reminded the Republican delegates of their sacred responsibility to erect an edifice of freedom and equal rights in heathen Mississippi that would withstand the forces of rebellion and sin. He exclaimed:

> Our enemies predicted a failure. And shall we fail? Not all the powers of an apostate President, with all his official sympathisers, and

77. A sketch of Mygatt appears in the Washington *New National Era*, February 13, 1873.

78. The loss of several thousand dollars' worth of property as a consequence of an incendiary's attack on his store in Vicksburg in early 1867 did not deter Mygatt from his purpose of organizing Union Leagues in Warren County. Vicksburg *Herald*, February 27, 1867; Vicksburg *Times and Republican*, June 17, 1873.

the power of a hostile press, and the bitter opponents of reconstruction shall cause us to fail. But if we descend to wicked compromises, time-serving expedients, then we shall fail, and our work shall perish. If [however] we plant on the firm basis of truth and justice to all, irrespective of race or color, the gates of hell shall not prevail against us. God in His Providence, will not permit us to fail. The over-ruling Providence, as a cloudy, firery [*sic*] pillar, that brought us through the Red Sea, passed the thunders of Mount Sinai into the political wilderness, shall guide us before the glad shouts of our loyal hosts, the walls of rebellion shall fall, and their giant leaders, with their train of mourners over the "lost cause," shall flee away. The Great Jehovah who rules on high and directs the affairs of men—who sets up and casts down whom He will, and whose blazing eyes penetrates the universe . . . will hold us responsible for this our solemn trust.[79]

Thus, in the person of Alston Mygatt democratic idealism and biblical moralism merged to form one prototype of the Radical Republican in southern Reconstruction—the intense and uncompromising crusader for right and justice, associated with God and Union. Mygatt, like others of this small class of Republicans, was unsuited by temperament for postwar political leadership, and he was particularly ill prepared for the difficult task of managing the state organization of the Union League.

Only rarely after the Union League became identified with blacks were efforts made to bring yeoman whites into the society. Stigmatized as "associations composed mostly of negroes and controlled by the refuse of Northern penitentiaries," these instruments of Republican political control and "prolific breeders of social disorder" had little chance for success among the race-conscious white farmers of the interior. Only in one county was a white Loyal League established after the imposition of congressional reconstruction, and in this case its leaders found it expedient to exclude blacks.[80]

A more effective and less controversial method for enlisting both blacks and whites into the party of Union was through the regular Republican organizations in local communities. Open and more broadly based than the Union Leagues, Republican clubs and

---

79. *Journal of the Constitutional Convention of 1868*, pp. 4–5.
80. C. F. Condrey to President Johnson, August 21, 1867, in Johnson Papers; Warren, *Reminiscences of a Carpetbagger*, 44.

county conventions usually made an effort to have all three party elements—carpetbaggers, scalawags, and blacks—represented in the organization and business of the local party. The fact that most whites found the Republican clubs less threatening than the secretive Union Leagues made it easier for sympathetic whites to associate with the party. Consequently, in all sections of Mississippi antebellum citizens could be found, even though in small numbers in most counties, who were willing to participate in the formation of the local Republican party.

The establishment of local Republican parties usually began when a few supporters of congressional reconstruction met informally and issued a call for an organizational meeting. The invitation was directed at all friends of Negro rights and Union in the community, or, where the black population was small, in the county. The first order of business in these meetings was to appoint committees on resolutions and organization, which almost invariably included members of both races. While the committees were preparing their reports, the assembled crowd listened to grandiloquent speeches by local organizers and by outside "dignitaries" like state Republican leaders James Lynch and Henry R. Pease who visited numerous counties in 1867 for the purpose of encouraging organizational work. (Few county Republican organizations were as fortunate as the one in Yazoo County where fifteen transplanted northerners, working harmoniously and without outside assistance, in a few months formed three thousand blacks into a solid bloc of Republican voters.[81]) The resolutions adopted by the Republican meetings were stronger in their support of Negro rights and education and in their denunciation of the past misdeeds of the state Democratic party than those adopted by the Brown-Barksdale cooperationists.[82]

Even before the local organizations had been perfected, plans were made for the formation of a state Republican party. On July 2, 1867, a group of rising Republicans, primarily from the river counties, met at Vicksburg, adopted a temporary platform for the party, and issued a call for counties to send delegates to a convention to

81. Charles W. Clarke to Covode, August 31, 1867, in Covode Papers.
82. For accounts of early organizational meetings of local Republicans, see the Columbus *Southern Sentinel*, April 23, 1867, and the Natchez *Democrat*, April 6, 16, 1867.

be convened at Jackson on September 10.[83] Chosen in many cases in an informal fashion and without the sanction of county conventions, an assortment of delegates attended the first state Republican convention to be held in Mississippi. Approximately one third of the delegates were blacks, the leader of whom was the moderate James Lynch.[84] The white members of the convention represented a fairly broad spectrum of Mississippi society. Officials of the Freedmen's Bureau, political adventurers, northern planters, southern Unionists, and former Confederates all rubbed elbows. Some of the delegates were identified as Radicals, such as scalawags Flournoy and Mygatt and carpetbagger Pease; others, like former Union generals Jonathan Tarbell, J. A. Maltby, and George C. McKee, were viewed as moderates. A handful of delegates, led by Confederate Whig Richard Cooper, pursued a conservative course in the convention.

The delegates, after selecting Mygatt to preside, launched into a vigorous debate on the platform for the state Republican party. Lines were quickly drawn between Radicals and "agrarians" on one side and moderates and conservatives on the other. "Osawatomie" Flournoy, "a wretched renegade from his own record and race," as the antagonistic Jackson *Clarion* described him, declared for the political proscription of all persons who had supported the rebellion. Then, citing the wrongs that blacks had experienced in slavery, he called for a strong plank in the party platform guaranteeing the protection of all the rights of Negroes in the state and the education of their children. A more incendiary speech than Flournoy's was delivered by Matthew T. Newsom, a black Methodist minister from Claiborne County, who proposed that the delegates go beyond mere political rights for his race and commit the party to the confiscation of Confederate estates and their distribution to the landless freedmen.[85]

83. Jackson *Weekly Clarion*, September 19, 1867.
84. Garner, *Reconstruction in Mississippi*, 180. Although blacks constituted a minority, the convention approved the motion of scalawag Joshua S. Morris that in the appointment of committees "an equal number of white and colored delegates be selected as far as practicable and convenient." Jackson *Weekly Clarion*, September 19, 1867.
85. The only known extant account of the Republican convention proceedings is in the Jackson *Weekly Clarion*, September 19, 26, 1867. Ethelbert Barksdale expressed shock at Newsom's proposal and suggested that if the Negro minister kept talking about dividing Mississippi lands he might soon be presented with "a snug landed possession—small but comfortable and compact—three by six feet." *Ibid.*, September 19, 1867.

Moderate and conservative delegates, fearing that the adoption of a radical platform would destroy all hopes for a broadly based party in the state, reacted sharply to Flournoy's and Newsom's proposals. Moderates, however, could agree with the Radicals on the need for a strong declaration regarding Negro rights and education. But they adamantly opposed the confiscation and division of rebel lands and the exclusion of Confederates from either the franchise or from public office. Moderate Republicans hoped especially to attract to the party cooperationists of the Albert Gallatin Brown and James W. Robb following, most of whom had supported the Confederate cause and would be irretrievably alienated from the new order by a Republican policy of property confiscation or political proscription.[86] Furthermore, these moderates argued, Congress required no such harsh settlement for former Confederates. The Radical proposal in the convention, they pointed out, far exceeded the temporary disabilities imposed by the reconstruction laws.

In order to prevent an early split in the party, the Republican convention adopted a compromise plank on the political status of former Confederates. The convention pronounced in favor of extending the "ballot to every man not disfranchised for crimes, including treason."[87] The reservation regarding treason left the door open for the political proscription of large numbers of whites, if the Radicals were to win control of the constitutional convention that would be voted on in the fall election. In the minds of many Unionists and Radicals, "treason" involved any action in support of the Confederacy, a definition that would include most white Mississippians.

Moderate Republicans were not satisfied with the convention platform, but in the interest of party unity they indicated a willingness to wait and see what action the constitutional convention would take on the issue of proscription. Conservative Republican delegates, however, refused to accept a platform that appeared to commit Republicans to a radical program if their party should gain control of the state. The selection of Abel Alderson, a rancor-

86. Letter from carpetbagger Jonathan Tarbell to Richard Cooper, *ibid.*, September 26, 1867.
87. The Republican platform may be found in the Meridian *Chronicle*, January 22, 1868. Inexplicably, the platform ignored the question of Confederate eligibility for office.

ous Unionist of Jefferson County, as president of the state organization seemed to confirm conservative fears that the party had been taken over by the Radicals. Thus, the handful of conservative delegates, most of whom were obscure Union Whigs, renounced the Republican party and returned home to inveigh against the radicalization of Mississippi politics. The belief that radicalism had gained control of the Republican organization dashed the hopes moderates had that a substantial number of cooperationists would soon affiliate with the party of the new order. In fact, the adoption of the halfway Radical platform contributed to the failure of the cooperationist movement (or the Reconstruction party) and the overwhelming success of the Constitutional Union party in winning the support of the white masses in the fall election.[88]

Although the military forces in Mississippi provided protection for the activities of the new party, General Ord antagonized Republican organizers by refusing to use his authority directly to advance the party's interests. Intense Republicans came increasingly to view the general as a stooge of President Johnson, who had appointed him to command the district. Ord's order prohibiting officials of the government, including officers of the Freedmen's Bureau, from participating in reconstruction politics, his refusal to take public printing from "rebel" journals and give it to struggling "loyal" sheets, and his slowness in replacing Johnsonian officials with Union men convinced state Republican leaders that the district commander was determined to defeat the intention of Congress in the reconstruction laws.[89] Carpetbagger Charles W. Clarke expressed the growing Republican discontent with the Ord regime when he wrote Congressman John Covode in August, 1867. "The North is paying a vast amount of money to reconstruct this country," he declared, "and it is truly to be regretted that their agts are not allowed to urge the people to reorganize and become loyal to the govt. Yet this is the state of affairs in Miss. with a Copperhead Genl. commanding, a Rebel Governor & rebels filling every office in the state, and with papers sustained by the Govt

88. Jackson *Weekly Clarion*, September 19, 1867; Jackson *Clarion*, January 7, 1868; Meridian *Semi-Weekly Gazette*, September 25, 1867.

89. Several of the young, struggling Republican newspapers depended upon public printing for their survival, and when Ord refused to cooperate some of these journals failed. Mosely and Company to William H. Seward, April 17, 1867, James Dugan to Edward McPherson, October 29, 1867, both in McPherson Papers.

patronage to denounce reconstruction and a loyal Congress."[90] Indeed, Clarke claimed, this state of affairs had encouraged a revival of the rebel spirit in Mississippi, reinforced by Johnson's recent removal of Secretary of War Edwin M. Stanton and General Philip Sheridan, commander of the Fifth Military District, both of whom were supporters of a thorough reconstruction policy for the South. Only the impeachment and removal of Johnson, followed by the reassignment of General Ord to a purely military command, could make possible the reconstruction of the state on a truly loyal basis, Clarke asserted.

Ord dismissed Republican charges against his policies with the tart comment that the army had no connection with politics, and he could not see how his orders interfered with the organization of any political party in the state. Nevertheless, rising criticism from national Republicans and the failure of the moderate cooperationist party to win the support of Mississippi whites caused Ord during the late summer to reevaluate his posture of neutrality and to tilt his authority slightly in favor of the Republicans.[91] The general's new policy became evident in his preparations for the fall election. He selected a handful of Negroes as election judges, announced that blacks could serve as delegates to the convention, and apportioned the state for the purpose of electing convention delegates on the basis of total population, instead of following the apportionment used for the convention of 1865 which skewed the division of seats in favor of the white counties. These actions for the first time brought Ord under attack from the conservatives.[92]

90. Clarke to Covode, August 31, 1867, in Covode Papers. Radical organizers Edward J. Castello and William H. Gibbs also claimed that unless changes were made at the highest levels in the execution of congressional reconstruction, the Republican experiment in Mississippi would fail. Castello to R. C. Schenck, December 17, 1867, in Papers on Conditions in Mississippi; Wiliam H. Gibbs to Elihu B. Washburne, September 30, 1867, in Elihu B. Washburne Papers, Manuscript Division, Library of Congress. Gibbs even blamed the reticent Grant for the deterioration of reconstruction affairs in the South. "The doubtful position of Genl Grant," he wrote Washburne, "has served to embolden [the unreconstructed] to hope that he would uphold the President against Congress." Actually, Grant had already demonstrated that his sympathies lay with Congress. Mantell, *Johnson, Grant, and Reconstruction*, 2–4.

91. Meridian *Semi-Weekly Gazette*, June 9, 1867; Edward O. C. Ord to Zachariah Chandler, September 16, 1867, in Zachariah Chandler Papers.

92. General Order 31, September 26, 1867, in Records of the Fourth Military District; Jackson *Clarion*, October 2, 1867; *Appleton's Annual Cyclopaedia*, 1867, pp. 515–16; Natchez *Weekly Democrat*, October 7, 1867. Many of Ord's election officials had served as registrars; to qualify, all of these officers had to be able to take the ironclad oath.

Ord also issued detailed instructions to election officials to ensure against intimidation, fraud, or inaccuracy in the counting of the ballots, and he dispersed military units into the interior with orders to suppress any disturbance that might occur. Saloons were ordered closed on days when political meetings were held in towns and also at the time of the election. In addition, to relieve tension in the crowded towns on election day, where evidently Ord believed violence was most likely to occur, he directed that the balloting continue for two days, November 5 and 6, with one day set aside for whites and the other for blacks.[93]

Ord's thorough preparations diffused the political tension in the state and the election passed quietly. But for four weeks after the polls had closed Mississippians were kept in suspense regarding the outcome, while officials tabulated, checked, and forwarded the returns to the commander's headquarters. For a time conservative hopes soared when it appeared that a majority of the total registration of 137,561 required by Congress to make the election valid had not been cast.[94] This prospect was based on unofficial returns from several counties indicating that qualified whites en masse had stayed away from the polls in support of the Potter plan of "masterly inactivity." Of the 355 eligible white voters in Meridian, only 16 voted, according to one source. In Chickasaw County, where more than 1,900 whites were registered, 23 reportedly went to the polls; in Vicksburg 8 whites voted, causing William H. McCardle to scurry about town in a vain attempt to get the names of these "interesting sneaks." Only in counties where prominent cooperationists sought election as delegates to the constitutional convention did whites turn out in large numbers. A Republican source later estimated that of the 58,385 whites who were registered in the state only 12,000 participated in the election.[95]

On December 5 General Ord shattered the illusions of conservatives that the convention would not be held. He announced that the necessary majority of registered voters had been polled in the

93. Ord listed the thirteen towns affected by his decree in Circular 18, October 2, 1867, in the Jackson *Clarion*, October 8, 1867.

94. As late as November 29 an unofficial compilation of returns in the Jackson *Clarion* showed that convention supporters were still 14,000 votes short of the necessary majority; however, several counties had not reported.

95. Meridian *Semi-Weekly Gazette*, November 12, 19, 23, 1867; Jackson *Clarion*, November 13, 1867; Forest *Register*, November 27, 1869.

election and, furthermore, that the referendum on the convention had passed by a resounding vote. Ord called for the convention to convene at the capitol on January 7. A few days later, after an investigation of alleged election irregularities, he released the final returns and gave the names of the delegates who had been elected. He reported that 69,739 had voted in favor of the convention under the terms outlined by Congress, whereas only 6,277 were opposed.[96] Although the precise number of Republicans elected as delegates was unknown until after the convention met and the party caucus was held (the distinction between Republican and cooperationist, or Reconstructionist, had been blurred in several counties during the campaign), it was clear that the party of the new order had captured a substantial majority of the seats in the convention.

The trauma of defeat for whites was heightened by the ominous fact that the freedmen had turned out in large numbers in most counties and had cast their ballots solidly for the convention and for Republican candidates. Of the 79,176 black registrants, 63,800 had voted in the election and had cast their ballots in favor of the convention, according to an informed estimate.[97] This meant also that approximately 6,000 whites, whether as Republicans or Reconstructionists, had voted in support of the convention. Neither conservative Reconstructionists nor Potterites had expected blacks to respond, at least this soon after obtaining the ballot, with any such degree of support to the appeals of Republican leaders. Even James Lynch had expressed a fear during the campaign that members of his race would follow the lead of Republican politicians in several counties who under pressure were "selling out to the conservatives."[98] Because of this threat to the party, numerous Republican organizers, like Lynch, Flournoy, and Pease on the state level, worked all the more assiduously, and with success, to achieve a bloc Negro vote in the election.

The magnitude of black participation in the election and its support of the Republican party strongly suggests that the party would

96. General Order 37, December 5, 1867, and General Order 42, December 16, 1867, both in Records of the Fourth Military District.

97. This estimate may be found in the Forest *Register*, November 27, 1869. It is clear that some blacks voted for friendly cooperation candidates, but after the election whites overlooked this fact.

98. James Lynch to John Eaton, October 9, 1867, in Eaton Papers.

have won a majority of convention seats even if whites had almost unanimously given their support to the Reconstruction party. Ethelbert Barksdale, in subsequent issues of the Jackson *Clarion*, never tired of chiding members of his race for their failure to back the cooperationists and vote in the election, the result of which, he claimed, had been to open the gates for the "Black Republican anarchists" to impose their "iniquitous scheme of Africanization" upon the state.[99] Nevertheless, judging from a comparison of the registration figures by race and county with the size of the county delegations, which were based on total population, Republicans could have reasonably expected to win sixty-five of the one hundred seats in the constitutional convention even if whites had voted at the same rate as blacks and for cooperation candidates. White inaction, however, did permit the Republicans to win such an overwhelming majority of seats that they could proceed with the task of framing a constitution without regard to the sensitivities of the conservative masses and the old leadership of the state.

The severe economic and social conditions that had settled upon the land since the war made the political events of the time even more foreboding for the white masses. As the winter of 1867–1868 approached, these conditions became critical. Planter-labor conflicts and black restiveness, accompanied by threats of racial disorders which Generals Ord and Gillem and Governor Humphreys had been quick to react to in late 1867, were only symptoms of a calamitous economic situation that pervaded the state and affected all classes. Although labor difficulties and the destructive forces of nature—weather, caterpillars, inundation—contributed, the fundamental reason for the crisis was the sharp decline in the 1867 price of cotton and the people's failure to produce an adequate supply of grain or meat to sustain them through the winter. In a sobering editorial, Barksdale aptly described the situation as it developed in the fall:

> Our impoverished people, staggering under the weight of debt contracted before the war, which left them without resources, have paid in many instances as high as twenty-five per cent for credit with which to carry on their farming business during the present season, besides,

99. Professor Garner follows the Barksdale view when he says that the Republicans won the election solely because whites permitted it to go by default. Garner, *Reconstruction in Mississippi*, 181.

mortgaging their crops and what little property they had saved from the general wreck. They had calculated, at least, upon prices some what approximating the rates that ruled the last season; but now, after struggling against the ills of inefficient labor, of excessive rains at one time, drought at another, and of destroying insects, they are brought to face the appalling calamity of price reduced below one half of the quotations of the past season.[100]

Mississippians in all sections of the state faced a bleak future. Even during the latter part of the war, observers reported, conditions had never been as bad as they were during the winter of 1867–1868. People in the interior had earlier felt the heavy hand of destitution, but now deprivation had spread to the river counties where adequate provisions of bread and meat were no longer available as they had been in the past.[101] In normally prosperous Hinds County, George W. Harper reported that society had been leveled to a state of poverty by the economic crisis of 1867. He indicated that property retained little or no value in the county, money had virtually disappeared from circulation, and debtors en masse refused to meet their obligations. In north Mississippi, where county officials insisted on enforcing the laws against debtors who failed to meet their payments, land was sold for as low as five cents an acre and usually from twenty-five to thirty-three cents to meet the overdue obligations. At this time almost all of the business in the courts involved debtor-creditor litigation, with creditors frequently reversing their role in other suits and forlornly assuming the position of debtors. Members of the once-favored legal fraternity discovered that the proliferation of debtor cases was no godsend for them; clients simply could not pay their fees, and consequently many lawyers in desperation abandoned the profession.[102]

Because of the hard times of 1867–1868, not only did a large

100. Jackson *Clarion*, October 8, 1867. See also the Forest *Register*, January 29, 1868; and Gillem's report of December 10, 1867, on economic and social conditions in Mississippi, in *Appleton's Annual Cyclopaedia*, 1867, p. 518.

101. Whitehurst to W. B. Norman, March 28, 1870, in Whitehurst Papers; Mrs. John C. Burrus to her son, September 24, 1867, in John W. Burrus Papers, Mississippi Department of Archives and History; Columbus *Southern Sentinel*, December 31, 1867; New York *Tribune*, January 10, 16, 1868; report of Gillem for quarter ending March 31, 1868, in Freedmen's Bureau Records, Microcopy Roll 54.

102. *Hinds County Gazette*, December 6, 1867, February 7, 1868; Natchez *Weekly Democrat*, March 9, 1868; Stuart to his niece, February 14, 1868, in Dimitry Papers; entry for March 3, 1868, in Samuel A. Agnew Diary, Southern Historical Collection, University of North Carolina Library, Chapel Hill; folders for 1867–68 in Reynolds Papers.

amount of land change hands to satisfy debts but also thousands of acres were forfeited to the state for delinquent taxes.[103] Unable to meet their obligations, numerous planters, some out of fear of the violent consequences that abject poverty might have on Negro laborers, abandoned their fertile lands, leaving the blacks to shift for themselves. A veritable "Texas fever" struck Mississippi, but despite a great deal of talk about going to Texas, or elsewhere, very few people had the means to set out on such a venturesome undertaking.[104] The times would be more propitious in 1869 for migration to the west. This impetus to leave the Deep South, unlike in 1865 when hundreds of Confederates sought political asylum in foreign lands, was mainly motivated by economic reasons rather than being an attempt to escape the clutches of radicalism—although, to be sure, restless Mississippians did not expect the impending Republican political order to improve their economic chances in the state.

Some observers feared that thousands would starve to death before the first vegetables appeared in the spring. One observer lamented, surely with exaggeration, that two thirds of the population of Mississippi faced starvation unless outside aid could be obtained. The outside assistance did not come, but Mississippians survived with few cases of actual starvation.[105] The social milieu of both races placed great stress upon cooperation within the extended family; this often forgotten virtue of societies where family ties and interpersonal relations are strong, as in Mississippi during Reconstruction, averted a major disaster in early 1868.

In their despair and often in bitterness white Mississippians found convenient scapegoats for their misfortunes. Cotton received some blame, but mainly they lashed out at Congress and local Rad-

103. *Senate Journal [1870]*, Appendix, 108; Natchez *Weekly Democrat*, March 9, 1868.

104. Entry for January 24, 1868, in Diary-Journal of Flavellus G. Nicholson, Mississippi Department of Archives and History; report of Gillem for quarter ending March 31, 1868, in Freedmen's Bureau Records, Microcopy Roll 54; entry for April 20, 1868, in Agnew Diary; Hamet Pinson to [?], February 1, 1868, in Hamet Pinson Family Papers, Louisiana State University Archives, Baton Rouge; Robert J. W. Matthews to Robert L. Matthews, May 23, 1868, in James E. and Samuel Matthews Papers, Mississippi Department of Archives and History.

105. Ord to Grant, December 7, 1867, in Records of the United States Army Command, Fourth Military District; Jackson *Clarion*, January 18, 1868; *Hinds County Gazette*, February 7, 1868; report of Gillem for quarter ending June 30, 1868, in Freedmen's Bureau Records, Microcopy Roll 59.

icals for setting in motion a political revolution that had produced sweeping and disastrous consequences for their society.[106] Mississippians, the "unhappy victims of Congressional cruelty," Harper asserted, "must become pensioners upon national charity or perish from starvation." After the fall election and the triumph of the Republicans, Barksdale, no longer inclined toward cooperation with Congress in its program of reconstruction, nor interested in explaining the recession in economic terms, attributed the hard times to "the utter insecurity of all values, resulting from the agrarian ideas and revolutionary schemes of the Radical majority" in the state. The instability of agricultural labor, according to Barksdale and other conservatives, resulted directly from the propagation of these ideas among the ignorant and gullible freedmen who preferred to wait for manna from heaven than to go to work.[107]

The worst was yet to come, according to the conservative version of events. The expected promulgation and imposition of a radical constitution by "a base assembly of blackguards," conservatives wailed, would seal the fate of Mississippi, permanently impoverishing the people and producing "the terrible tumult of social anarchy." Now more defiant than ever, white journalists declared that the masses of their race "will scorn and spit" upon the work of "the great polecat reconstruction convention" that was scheduled to meet in January.[108] Even normally moderate editors, shaken by the ominous developments of the fall and winter, joined with McCardle and other vituperative journalists to denounce passionately the triumphant forces of the new order. In this vein the usually mild-mannered editor of the Natchez *Democrat* characterized the constitutional convention as "the illegitimate offspring of

106. Samuel Matthews to John H. Matthews, September 19, 1867, in Matthews Papers; Vicksburg *Herald*, May 12, 1868; entry for January 24, 1868, in Nicholson Diary-Journal.

107. *Hinds County Gazette*, February 7, 1868; Jackson *Clarion*, March 17, 1868. No doubt the reluctance of black laborers to pick the 1867 crop or to contract for the new year—caused to a great extent by their belief that they had been cheated out of promised compensation for past work—aggravated the economic situation. Labor instability, however, was mainly a product of the collapse of the cotton market and other distressing economic developments of 1867–68 rather than the agitation and promises of Republican politicians or officials of the Freedmen's Bureau. Some Republican organizers, in fact, made a special effort to get reluctant blacks to return to work. Entries for December 28, 1867, and January 1, 1868, in Darden Diary; Gillem's report of December 10, 1867, in *Appleton's Annual Cyclopaedia*, 1867, p. 518.

108. The quotes are from the *Hinds County Gazette*, February 7, 1868.

negro supremacy, begotten of vindictive malevolence, conceived in treachery, to be brought forth in revolution, nurtured by confiscation and plunder, upheld by military despotism, and perpetuated (if perpetuated it shall be) by the wholesale disfranchisement of every white man who had the humanity to detest or the moral courage to denounce and resist the execution of the infamous reconstruction schemes."[109] Thus, the work of the constitutional convention of 1868 was prejudged and rejected from the beginning by fearful and aroused whites—an attitude of defiance that would not subside during the critical months ahead.

109. Natchez *Weekly Democrat*, January 13, 1868. See also the Vicksburg *Times*, January 7, 1868, and the Natchez *Tri-Weekly Courier*, January 31, 1868.

4

The Framework of the
New Order

In an atmosphere charged with tension and forebodings, the constitutional convention opened its sessions in the capitol on a cold January 7, 1868, almost simultaneously with assemblages of the same kind in other southern states. In spite of the assumptions and fears of the old citizenry, the delegates to the convention were not the wild-eyed, power-hungry radicals pictured in Reconstruction lore. Nevertheless, on occasion during the four-month session the shrill rhetoric of several delegates, frequently prompted by conservative animadversions, seemed to justify white distress. The overwhelming majority of the Republicans involved were inexperienced reformers, not fanatical or dangerous revolutionaries. Ninety-six of the ninety-seven delegates have been identified as to political affiliation; of these seventy-nine were Republicans and only seventeen were conservatives.[1] Eighteen blacks held seats, only one of whom affiliated with the conservative faction. Of the twenty-three carpetbaggers who sat in the body, nineteen had served in the Federal army during the war, fourteen as officers. With forty-one delegates, southern white Republicans comprised the most numerous element in the convention.

More significant, however, than the geographic origins of the delegates were the political variations present in the Republican camp. Of the Republican delegates of both races, only thirteen, as indicated by their actions and statements prior to and during the convention, could be classified as true Radicals, that is, men who desired unequivocally to disfranchise former Confederates, provide strict guarantees for black rights, and use the convention to establish a solidly Republican foundation in the state. Eighteen Republicans pursued decidedly moderate objectives, and eight of their colleagues often aligned with them on important issues, espe-

1. Three of the one hundred delegates who were elected did not serve in the convention. Republican members included R. C. Merryman, who was elected as a Republican but switched to the Democratic party during the convention.

cially during the early sessions. In these three white groups were the most influential members of the convention; the other forty Republican delegates, particularly during the first two months, approached major convention issues in an uncertain and vacillating manner. These members eluded identification as either Radicals or moderates, although they ultimately followed the Radical leadership in its policy of excluding many former Confederates from the political life of the state.

Aside from their political behavior, and at the risk of misconstruing the motives and character of members of the convention, it appears that only ten delegates could be classified as adventurers who were primarily cynical seekers of power and influence.[2] Six of these political jobbers were identified with the stalwart Radical faction; the other four, including William T. Combash, the only Negro associated with this group, preferred to shift their support from one faction to another as the situation demanded. The most notorious of these adventurers was R. C. Merryman of Meridian, who, when not inebriated, spent most of his time in the convention consorting with the conservative delegates.

Whether idealist or adventurer, or a little of both, the Radical Republicans were the most determined and aggressive members of the constitutional convention of 1868. The faction consisted of ten carpetbaggers, two antebellum white citizens of the state (Alston Mygatt and Abel Alderson), and one Negro (Matthew T. Newsom). Probably the most active carpetbag Radical in the convention was Edward J. Castello, the "wheel-horse" of the Natchez Republican party. Castello, a prewar resident of Missouri, had served in the Federal army, attaining the rank of major, and after the war he had received an appointment as a deputy sheriff in St. Louis. When he left Missouri to come to Mississippi in 1867, the St. Louis *Times* claimed that he had absconded with several thousand dollars in public funds.[3] This charge may have merely reflected the kind of partisan slander, designed to discredit a political opponent, that

2. This conclusion is based on a study of the backgrounds and subsequent careers of the delegates. Admittedly the conclusion is tenuous, since information on most of the delegates is sketchy.

3. As reported in the Meridian *Semi-Weekly Gazette*, October 9, 1867.

characterized newspaper reporting in the nineteenth century. Nevertheless, Castello's subsequent career in Mississippi, in which he abandoned the Radical cause to become a conservative after losing his influence in the Natchez Republican party, suggests that he was not strongly motivated by idealism in his participation in Reconstruction politics. Evidence also exists that before his conversion to the Republican party and the cause of Negro rights in 1867 Castello had expressed a stout opposition to black equality.[4]

Another leading Radical delegate whose political behavior seems to have been influenced mainly by a desire for quick personal advancement was Henry W. Barry of Holmes County. A native of upstate New York, in 1859 at the age of eighteen Barry moved to Kentucky. For two years he served as the principal of an academy at Locust Grove, Kentucky, and when the war began he entered the Union army as a private. He rose rapidly in the army, and during the latter part of the war, having attained the rank of colonel, he organized the first regiment of Negro troops raised in Kentucky. By the end of the war he had been brevetted a major general for meritorious service.[5] After the surrender and before coming to Mississippi as an agent of the Freedmen's Bureau, Barry studied law at the Columbia Law College, now George Washington University.[6] In the constitutional convention of 1868 he exulted in his radicalism. "The purity of our cause," he exclaimed before that body, "is measured by the opposition it excites."[7] Subsequently, however, as a member of Congress, he associated radicalism on the suffrage issue more with a practical politics than with a concern for the protection of black rights. "The colored vote of the South," Barry told fellow congressmen in 1871, "was necessary to balance the rebel vote and to prevent that section of our common country from falling into hands hostile to our Union."[8] According to carpetbagger Henry R. Pease, Barry "succeeded by his cunning and

4. Natchez *Weekly Democrat*, May 25, 1868.

5. Jackson *Pilot*, September 3, 1870, April 15, 1871. For a Republican newspaper's account of Barry's perfidy, see the Columbus *Press*, July 12, 1872.

6. *Journal of the Constitutional Convention of 1868*, p. 151.

7. Jackson *Clarion*, January 17, 1868.

8. *Speech of Hon. Henry W. Barry, of Mississippi, Delivered in the House of Repres., April 5, 1871, on the Ku Klux Democracy* (N.p., 1871), 1–2.

shrewdness in holding a controlling influence over several prominent men in the party," thereby early damaging the reputation of
the party in the state.[9]

John R. Parsons of Hinds County was another Radical carpetbagger whose motivation in Reconstruction politics was far from
pure. A graduate of Yale University and a veteran of four years of
service in the Federal army, Parsons came to Mississippi after the
war and commenced making "a mean article of soda water, which
he sold to the negroes." He soon entered politics and assisted in
the organization of blacks into the local Republican party. Socially
ostracized by local whites, he turned to drink and allegedly to co-
habitation with a black woman in Jackson. Parsons' influence declined after the constitutional convention, and in March, 1869, his
body was found in a creek near Jackson. Some Radicals charged
foul play, but the local military surgeon ruled that he had died
accidentally.[10]

Few Radicals in Mississippi were as continuously influential or as
enigmatic as William H. Gibbs of Wilkinson County. A smiling,
jovial carpetbagger from Illinois, Gibbs disarmed conservative critics to such an extent that they reversed their early opinion of him
as "that lovely disciple of villainy and niggerism, that tallow-faced
beauty from Wilkinson" who was an advanced proscriptionist in the
constitutional convention. Soon after settling in the state, however,
he privately expressed nothing but contempt for the former Confederates whom he met. "They are as bitter & malignant to day as
they were in 1861," he declared, "and nothing but the decisive
action of Congress upholding Union men in their rights and assisting them to establish and secure their rights by Constitutional enactments will save them."[11]

Gibbs remained a stalwart Republican throughout Reconstruction, serving in 1868–1869 as chairman of the Radical Committee
of Five which unsuccessfully sought to have Congress impose the
constitution of 1868 upon the state after it was rejected at the polls.

9. Henry R. Pease to Oliver O. Howard, October 14, 1868, and Samuel E. Day to
Howard, August 7, 1867, both in Freedmen's Bureau Records, Microcopy Roll 59.
10. *Hinds County Gazette*, March 17, 24, 1869; Jackson *Weekly Clarion*, March 18,
April 18, 1869.
11. Jackson *Pilot*, March 12, 1870; Vicksburg *Times*, January 21, 1868; William H. Gibbs
to Elihu B. Washburne, September 30, 1867, in Washburne Papers.

His early extremist predilections, however, were soon forgotten; as a member of the Mississippi senate from 1870 to 1874 and then as state auditor of public accounts Gibbs demonstrated real administrative ability, which, along with his good humor and tact toward opponents, made him acceptable to all but the most rabid anti-Republicans. When the "redemption" of the state occurred in 1875–1876, only Gibbs and two other Republicans managed to survive the purge of Radical state officials. The Gibbs story, however, had an unhappy ending. Impeccable in office during Reconstruction, years later Gibbs was convicted by a federal jury of embezzling funds while serving as postmaster of Jackson and was sentenced to five years in prison.[12]

Most of the Radical Republicans in the constitutional convention of 1868 made no effort to court white favor or placate white fears. None was more intense in his radicalism or more alienated from white society than Albert T. Morgan of Yazoo County. A farm boy from Wisconsin, Morgan came to Mississippi in 1865 after serving for four years as an officer in the Federal army. Like other Union soldiers, he hoped to succeed at cotton planting in the rich Mississippi bottoms. Morgan and his brother Charles leased a Yazoo River plantation of nine hundred acres from its impoverished southern owner. With little knowledge of cotton cultivation and its marketing system, the Morgans' farming operations failed in 1866, but Charles's wise management of a sawmill forestalled their financial collapse and made possible their continuance in the county. In the beginning the brothers received the full benefit of southern hospitality; however, when they provided the means for the establishment of a Negro school in the community, white friendliness toward them turned to hostility. As a young man of twenty-three when he came to the state, Albert T. Morgan had never participated in politics, except to vote in 1864, and his initial inclination in Mississippi was to avoid the cauldron of Reconstruction affairs. Nevertheless, like many fellow northerners in the state, from the beginning he was in sympathy with the national Republican resolve to protect the fruits of the war—namely, the restoration of the southern states on a clearly loyal basis and the protection of the

12. Gibbs was soon pardoned, and he returned to Jackson to live his remaining years. New York *Times*, August 18, 1909.

fundamental rights of blacks. Morgan was opposed at first to the Radical policy of extending suffrage to blacks without some qualifications; by 1867 he had dropped all reservations on the matter. Years later, in his memoirs, he explained the reasons for his conversion to the cause of political equality for the black man. Morgan wrote: "After only two years' contact with him I was able to answer the question—the ballot for the negro, or not for him—not only for myself, but also for the country; for, I said, any means that will enable us to live here in peace, and enjoy the fruits of our toil, can but be helpful and good for the whole country. Therefore, with the call for this election [in 1867], there came to Charles and myself a hope of succor through the power of the ballot, backed as it was by the power of the nation."[13]

Even though the Morgans survived the economic crisis of 1866, they failed in 1867 and their prosperous sawmill was seized and sold because of an alleged failure to pay the rent on the plantation, which the landowner conveniently discovered after Albert was elected as a Republican delegate to the constitutional convention of 1868. His early radicalism, as he implies in his memoirs, was partly inspired by such mistreatment at the hands of his white neighbors. In Morgan's mind, white discourtesies and misconduct toward northerners and the freedmen in his community clearly demonstrated that the ungodly spirit of rebellion still lived in the bosoms of Mississippians. As a leader in the "Black and Tan" Convention and in the first Republican legislature, Morgan warmed to the need for black equality. His identification with radicalism became complete when in 1870 he married a mulatto schoolmistress from New York, much to the dismay of most white Republicans in the state. With the possible exception of Flournoy and Ames, no white Republican was able to gain and retain the confidence of Mississippi blacks as did this tall carpetbagger from Yazoo County.

Less controversial than Morgan but no less ardent in the cause of radicalism in 1868 was Charles W. Clarke, a young idealist from Ohio who had come to the state as an official in the Freedmen's Bureau. Born in Vermont in 1840, Clarke moved with his family to Ohio several years before the war. He taught school prior to

13. Albert T. Morgan, *Yazoo; or on the Picket Line of Freedom in the South* (Washington, D.C. 1884), 17, 26, 83, 105–107, 130 (quote).

entering Western Reserve Eclectic Institute, where James A. Garfield served as president. When the war began, young Clarke entered the army in Garfield's command and participated in several important campaigns, including the siege of Vicksburg. Retaining his commission with the rank of captain, Clarke after the surrender served in the Freedmen's Bureau at Natchez, Meridian, and finally Yazoo City. He remained in the Delta after leaving the bureau, and, like Morgan, sought his fortune as a planter. Clarke was farming in Yazoo County and helping to organize blacks into Union Leagues and Republican clubs when he was elected as a delegate to the constitutional convention. Later he moved to Washington County where he became a pillar of the party in that large Delta county.

Like his chief, Garfield, Clarke was especially interested in educational and moral reform in the South, which in theory would be extended to both races. In an uncharitable moment, he expressed the belief that "if the money sent [through the Freedmen's Bureau] to feed these indolent, lazy whites, who will not support themselves by honest labor, had been sent to reorganize and enlighten the ignorant and assist in establishing a loyal govt much more would have resulted."[14] Despite his desire to eliminate ignorance among whites, Clarke's efforts in Mississippi were designed primarily for the benefit of unfortunate blacks. He early established a freedmen's school on his plantation and built a church for blacks in Yazoo City; in addition, he was instrumental in the organization of several schools and churches in rural communities of the county. Then, in the convention of 1868 Clarke wrote the education article for the constitution, and as a member of the legislature of 1870 he assisted in shaping the organic law for the public school system.[15]

The moderate wing of the Republican party was not as well represented in the constitutional convention as was the Radical faction. Influential moderate carpetbaggers like Jonathan Tarbell of Scott County, George F. Brown of Warren, Elza Jeffords of Issaquena, Alexander Warner of Madison, Ridgley C. Powers of Noxubee, and Edward Stafford, editor of the newly established Jackson *Pilot*,

14. Charles W. Clarke to John Covode, August 31, 1867, in Covode Papers.
15. *Ibid.*; Vicksburg *Weekly Republican*, June 9, 1868; Jackson *Weekly Pilot*, May 7, 1870.

had not sought election to the convention. In addition, James Lynch and Robert Gleed, both moderate black leaders, were absent from the convention, as were moderate scalawags James Lusk Alcorn, Green C. Chandler, and William M. Hancock of the piney woods, Jefferson Wofford of Tishomingo County, and Joseph Bennett of Rankin, all of whom would play important roles in future Reconstruction affairs. A few of the moderate Republicans in the convention were men of intelligence and some political capacity, but they were no match for the aggressive Radical delegates whose following among Republican members grew as the session became long and the debates heated.[16]

The leading moderate Republican among the northerners in the convention was George C. McKee of Vicksburg. Indeed, few carpetbaggers during Reconstruction proved more consistent or more active in the advocacy of moderation and conciliation than McKee. A native of Illinois, McKee was educated at Knox College in that state and became a practicing attorney at Centralia in 1858. His professional career was interrupted by the call to arms in 1861. He entered the army as a private, but was soon elected captain of his company. His meritorious service at Shiloh, Vicksburg, and Yazoo City earned him rapid promotions, culminating in his appointment as a brigadier general in 1864. In 1863 he was given a brief respite from the hazards and barbarisms of war when he was assigned as provost marshal of Natchez. In this picturesque and sedate setting on the banks of the Mississippi, he found congenial the company of a large number of friendly Unionists. When he returned for a visit later in the year, his southern friends gave him an enthusiastic reception.[17] This pleasant wartime experience in Natchez was an important reason for McKee's decision to settle in the area after the surrender. But economic opportunities were not good in Natchez, his first choice as a home; the town for several years had experienced financial doldrums because of the shift of agricultural production and commerce away from southwestern Mississippi to the more fertile lands of the interior and the Delta. McKee saw in

16. Of the Radical Republicans in the state, only Flournoy and Pease were conspicuously absent from the convention.

17. "Biographical Sketches of Mississippians: George C. McKee" (MS in William H. McCardle Papers, Mississippi Department of Archives and History); Natchez *Courier*, October 6, November 6, 1863.

Vicksburg, Natchez' sister town to the north, the center for a booming cotton trade after the war and an important link in an east-west railroad extending into Texas and perhaps even across the Great Plains. Consequently, when he left the army in 1865, he nailed up his shingle in Vicksburg and also purchased a cotton plantation in Madison County, north of Jackson. In 1867 the Republican party of Warren County was formed in his office, but he was never privy to the activities of the powerful Union Leagues of the county, though he received their support for election to Congress in 1869.[18] As a member of the House of Representatives, McKee persistently worked for legislation to rebuild the levees and improve the Yazoo River, to refund the cotton tax of 1865–1868, and to remove the political disabilities imposed on southerners by the Fourteenth Amendment. Associated with the moderate scalawag Alcorn, on the House floor McKee attacked carpetbaggers of the Adelbert Ames type who, he claimed, sought only political advantage in the South without any intention of identifying with the interests of the people. As for his own place in Mississippi, this moderate carpetbagger declared with a degree of oratorical flourish: "All that I have is in Mississippi. My property and my interests are there. There my hopes of the future are centered. I rejoice in her rejoicings and sympathize in her sorrows. In the happy and prosperous days which I think and hope are coming to Mississippi in the not far distant future, under the auspices of peace and order, I shall claim my share of her gladness and her prosperity; and if, which [may] God avert, sorrow and disaster should come to Mississippi, though with bowed head and sorrowing heart, yet will I not shrink from bearing her cross."[19] After Reconstruction McKee, as he had promised, remained in Mississippi, bearing the humiliation of the failure of the new political order that he had helped launch.

The well-educated Albert R. Howe of Panola County was another young moderate northerner of some influence in the constitutional convention. A native of Massachusetts and an honors' graduate of Yale University, Howe settled in Panola County in

18. "Biographical Sketch of McKee," in McCardle Papers; Vicksburg *Times and Republican*, June 16, 1872, March 3, 1873.
19. *Speech of Hon. Geo. C. McKee of Miss., Delivered in the House of Repres., April 3, 1871, on Enforcement of Fourteenth Amendment* (N.p., 1871), 7.

1865 after serving as a junior officer in the Federal army. Along with his brother, William W. Howe, he purchased a large plantation strategically located near the Mississippi and Tennessee Railroad, and, unlike most recent arrivals in the state, he prospered. Possessing the rare combination of a deep humanitarian concern for their black laborers and a shrewdness in business matters, the Howe brothers expanded their agricultural interests during the early Reconstruction period, and when Ames visited them in 1871 he found 250 blacks living and working on their estate of 2,400 acres. Conservative opponents of the Howes admitted years later that the brothers "were unusually affable and pleasant, and had a special tact in making themselves agreeable among the Democrats in the county in a social way."[20]

But in their devotion to the Republican principles of equal rights and education for blacks and in their advancement of the local party, the Howe brothers were unyielding. Although a moderate in the constitutional convention, Albert, the more politically active of the brothers, soon identified with the Radical wing of his party, serving as a floor leader in the legislative sessions of 1871 and 1872. A tall, slender man, who dressed in fine style, "always wearing a long, black frock coat [that was] closely buttoned,"[21] Howe represented the best of Mississippi society during Reconstruction. His election to Congress in 1872 is evidence that Radicals did not fail to appreciate and advance their ablest and finest men to high public positions.

At least fourteen of the eighteen clearly moderate Republicans in the Black and Tan Convention of 1868 were antebellum residents of Mississippi.[22] The most active and probably the most influential of these scalawags was Joseph W. Field, an intrepid and outspoken Unionist of Columbus. Known as "a very rabid

20. Blanche Butler Ames (comp.), *Chronicles from the Nineteenth Century: Family Letters of Blanche Butler and Adelbert Ames* (2 vols.; Clinton, Mass., 1957), I, 320; John W. Kyle, "Reconstruction in Panola County," *Publications of the Mississippi Historical Society*, XIII (1913), 38–40; Washington (D.C.) *New National Era*, March 27, 1873.

21. Washington (D.C.) *New National Era*, March 27, 1873; Jackson *State Leader*, January 1, 1872. Another prominent moderate of northern antecedents in the constitutional convention was Henry Musgrove, whose later performance as state auditor was outstanding.

22. The prewar residency of two of the eighteen moderate Republicans has not been identified. There were no black delegates associated with this faction, although the maverick Republican William T. Combash often voted with the moderates and the conservatives (Democrats) in the convention.

Radical" at home despite his moderation or even conservatism on some issues, Field expressed more profoundly than most southern Unionists his reluctance to interpret the results of the war as a mandate for the immediate enfranchisement of the blacks. As a matter of policy, however, he accepted a limited franchise for them. The war, according to Field, had been fought to preserve the Union, to extinguish the doctrine of extreme states' rights, and to destroy the slave institution. These having been accomplished, he believed that a "liberal reconstruction" policy was essential to bring about an end to sectional strife and the restoration of the national spirit that had long been the great hope of the Western world.[23] Radicals who claimed that a generation of southerners should be punished for the rebellion and their society levelled badly misconstrued the fundamental cause of the war, Field insisted. The reason for the conflict was indeed slavery; but, he averred, southerners of the mid-nineteenth century were unfortunately placed at a time in history when "the extension of knowledge . . . caused the civilized world to realize that slavery gave too much authority to the portion of the community which held them; also it was discovered to be inconsistent with the natural equality of men." Field's definition of slavery extended beyond the limited American one to include serfdom, peonage, and other remnants of feudalism in the Western world. Driven by international forces, southerners, Field believed, were innocent bystanders, if not victims, in the Atlantic struggle to free men. "The parties who have been antagonistic in the strife . . . were brought into collision by the conflict going on throughout the world between the party of progress, against that of conservative inaction, so far as the extension of liberty and equality [was] concerned." Once liberty for all had been won—and by implication a theoretical condition of equality by birth achieved—Field believed that there would no longer be any need for conflict between the two forces. The triumph of the party of progress was now virtually complete in this country.

Most white southerners of the postwar period, by virtue of hav-

23. Field's views may be found in a speech before the constitutional convention, as reported in the Jackson *Clarion*, February 13, 1868, and in a letter to the editor of the Columbus *Index*, copied in *ibid.*, May 20, 1869. See also his testimony before the Joint Committee on Reconstruction in *House Miscellaneous Documents*, 40th Congress, 3rd Session, No. 53, pp. 49–51.

ing lived for many years in a static society, according to Field, were a little slow in measuring up to the spirit of the age. They would, however, soon join "all true Republicans to promote every rational improvement [for blacks] and impose their influence to arrest the rash spirit of political innovation that would commit the present and future interest of a great and growing nation to the control and government of individuals possessing none of the moral, religious, pecuniary, educational, or other qualifications essential to future progress in Christian civilization." Field never rejected the settlement for the South offered by the Fourteenth Amendment, sponsored by moderate Republicans, or the principle of limited black suffrage, but he was more fearful than many moderates in his party, such as McKee and Howe, of the revolutionary course that congressional reconstruction might take in the hands of demagogues selected by ignorant voters. His death in October, 1869, removed from the Mississippi scene one of the most respected Republicans in the state and the predecessor of Alcorn as leading spokesman for the moderate wing of the party.[24]

Probably no delegate was as prominent in his community as Jason Niles, a soft-spoken Republican from Attala County, who because of sickness arrived three months late to attend the convention. Niles, a leader of the Union party in his county in 1851 and again in 1860, illustrates the shift that several delegates made from support of the conservative Reconstruction party in 1867 to affiliation with the Republican party by the spring of 1868. He early supported reconstruction under the military acts of 1867 and reluctantly agreed to run in the fall election as a cooperationist candidate for the convention. After his brief service in the convention, he signed the new instrument of government; then in the June election he ran for a seat in the legislature as a Republican, although at the time he made known his opposition to the more extreme features of the constitution. Niles, who preferred to study the works of the giants of British literature than to participate in politics, continued to support the Republican party and in 1872 was elected to Congress without opposition.[25]

24. Friar's Point (Miss.) *Weekly Delta*, October 13, 1869.
25. Clipping from the Kosciusko *Chronicle*, 1869, in Jason Niles Scrapbook, Vol. XLI, Southern Historical Collection, University of North Carolina Library, Chapel Hill.

In addition to Field and Niles, there were other moderate scalawags in the convention who were respected men in their communities. These included the Unionist George Stovall of Carroll County, a Negrophobe, Dr. Horatio N. Ballard of DeSoto, a native of Massachusetts but an old resident of Mississippi who desired the establishment of a New England style of society in his adopted state,[26] Robert J. Alcorn of Yallobusha, a cousin of James Lusk Alcorn, Colonel William G. Vaughn of Lafayette, the commander of the famed Nineteenth Mississippi Regiment during the war, and Andrew S. Dowd of Coahoma who later served as president of the state senate.

Like the moderate scalawags, the seventeen conservative or anti-Republican delegates in the convention (including one former Union officer) in most cases had earlier professed the need for Mississippians to cooperate with Congress in its plan of reconstruction. But unlike the moderates, when the convention met they announced their intention to resist all efforts by the Republicans to promulgate a constitution that would include unrestricted black suffrage and other rights for Negroes. The leader of the conservative forces in the convention was John W. C. Watson, a Union Whig who had served in the Confederate senate. In a lengthy speech before the convention Watson posed the spectre of revolution if the delegates implemented the congressional plan calling for unqualified black suffrage.[27] Under such an arrangement, he argued, blacks, who constituted a clear majority of the voting population of Mississippi, would dominate the legislature and impose heavy taxes upon property, which in turn would stagnate the economy and destroy "all the great interests of society." Watson declared that "by a tax on property, which the colored population would not feel, a most expensive system of common schools, or even collegiate education, enuring almost exclusively to the benefit of the colored race, might be established." A black-dominated government might also "set on foot a general system of internal

26. Ballard believed, as he expressed to George S. Boutwell of his native state, that the establishment of a universal system of elementary education, accompanied by the reestablishment of law and order, would make possible "a condition of things like that you enjoy now and which I once enjoyed in my native Massachusetts." Horatio N. Ballard to George S. Boutwell, February 13, 1869, in Papers on Conditions in Mississippi.

27. Watson's speech is found in the Jackson *Clarion*, March 20, 1868.

improvements at a most ruinous cost to property holders" for the purpose of increasing the demand for labor and thereby obtaining higher wages for Negro workers.

Nevertheless, Watson, who during the antebellum period had operated "Sunday schools" for the education of his and neighboring slaves, insisted that blacks should be protected in all of their legal rights as citizens and should be provided with educational opportunities. "It is to the interests of the State that they be intelligent," he announced, and whites "will find their own interests advanced in the progress of the colored population of the State in education, morals, industry, and wealth."

The extent of the conservative faction's concession to blacks in the constitutional convention was contained in a proposal known as "a guaranty of rights and privileges" for the freedmen. The plan called for provisions in the constitution that would guarantee blacks equal protection under the laws of the state, but would stop short of suffrage and the privilege of sitting in the jury box. Conservatives also proposed the creation of a system of separate schools for the races.[28] In addition, the conservative "guaranty" included an economic feature designed to appeal to the large body of black laborers in the state. Conservatives would add to the constitution a section giving laborers first lien on the property of landowners for wages owed to them. Under the inequitable lien law of January, 1867, passed by the Johnsonian legislature during its closing days, the interests of merchants and planters were protected at the expense of the laborer. But by 1868 Mississippi conservatives were willing to make a major concession to blacks on this issue, in order, they hoped, to head off the implementation of the feared revolutionary objectives of the Radicals and also to pacify disgruntled black workers who thought they had been cheated in their dealings with planters in 1867. The entire guaranty of rights and privileges, however, was summarily rejected by the Republican majority in the convention. By the time the proposal was advanced, Republicans had agreed on a political program for Mississippi and were in no mood to accept any part of a conservative settlement, however appealing some of its features might be.

28. Jackson *Clarion*, March 11, 1868.

In view of Republican differences on such important issues as black rights and the political proscription of former Confederates, it was unlikely that the convention would give substance to conservative fears by imposing a truly radical political settlement on the state. When the convention convened in January, Radical success seemed remote. Although the stalwart Republican Mygatt was selected on the first day as temporary chairman of the assembly, a reputedly moderate carpetbagger, Beroth B. Eggleston, was chosen as its permanent president. Eggleston, whose prominence in Mississippi politics was meteoric even by Reconstruction standards, came to the state in late 1865 after a distinguished Civil War career in which he rose from private to brigadier general and served as military commander of Atlanta after its fall in 1864. A native of upstate New York, Eggleston was a merchant-farmer in Ohio when in 1861 he answered the call to fight for the Union. In postwar Mississippi, after a brief apprenticeship in cotton planting as an overseer on a northern-owned estate, Eggleston invested his money in a plantation near Columbus, and he was engaged in harvesting his crop when he attended a meeting of the local Reconstruction party at Columbus in the fall of 1867. Moderate in their political orientation, the Columbus Reconstructionists selected Eggleston to head their ticket of delegates to the constitutional convention.[29] Even though Eggleston did not have the support of the local "agrarian Radicals," his record as a Federal brigadier during the war had sufficient appeal among the Negroes of the black-belt county to secure his easy election to the convention.

Eggleston's selection as president of the constitutional convention reflected the desire of the Republican majority, at least in the beginning, to follow a middle road and avoid the pitfalls of radicalism. Even the Radical delegates supported Eggleston's candidacy, since the alternative appeared to be the election of Watson, the popular nominee of the seventeen conservatives and the more moderate Republicans in the convention. Moderate Republican delegates in agreeing to support Watson for president hoped to form an anti-Radical coalition in the convention that would make few changes in the fundamental law of the state, going no further

29. Vicksburg *Herald*, September 17, 1868; Vicksburg *Weekly Herald*, May 19, 1868; Jackson *Clarion*, October 22, 1867.

in the direction of imposing black rights and Confederate disabilities than the reconstruction laws required. As a former Confederate senator (despite his Union-Whig background) and an opponent of black suffrage, Watson's support among the Republican delegates was limited. In Eggleston the Republicans had a candidate who could appeal to all elements of the party, including some moderates. As a result, by a vote of fifty-three to thirty-three Eggleston easily defeated Watson for the presidency of the convention.[30]

The former Federal brigadier had scarcely grasped the speaker's gavel when he showed his preference for the Radicals by appointing them to chair most of the committees that would write the first drafts of the various articles of the constitution. To head these committees, Eggleston selected eleven Radicals and only four moderates. Nine of his appointees were fellow carpetbaggers (two of whom, however, were aligned with the moderate Republicans) and six were scalawags. He chose the partisan and impetuous Mygatt to preside over the work of the important committees on the bill of rights and the franchise. To ensure Radical dominance of the latter committee, Eggleston stacked it with such prominent Radicals as Castello and Morgan, in addition to Mygatt. Ignored in the appointment of committee chairmen were able moderate Republicans like Robert J. Alcorn, Ballard, Field, and James L. Herbert, as well as representatives of both the black and conservative delegations in the convention.

The sudden conversion of Eggleston to the cause of radicalism (or at least a half-way station between Radical and moderate positions) owed a great deal to the torrent of abuse showered on the convention by the conservative press during the winter of 1867–1868. Alienated by the intemperance of these "rebel sheets," Eggleston evidently saw the wisdom of cooperating with the Radicals after he arrived in Jackson to take his seat in the convention. His resentment toward the old citizens was complete when the Democratic press began prefixing his name with the epithet "Buzzard." In spite of his identification with the Radical wing and an altercation with Charles H. Townsend, a conservative northern delegate, on the capitol grounds, Eggleston secured and

30. *Journal of the Constitutional Convention of 1868*, p. 7.

maintained rapport with all factions in the convention. Only a little effusive praise shows through in Henry W. Warren's description of the former brigadier as "an excellent presiding officer, deliberate, impartial, judicial, [who] at all times kept the Convention well in hand."[31]

The vituperations of the conservative press also affected other Republicans and slowly undermined the cause of moderation in the convention. In their hell-bent desire to denigrate the assemblage, extremist, or Bourbon, editors like McCardle seemed to compete with each other for first prize in an undeclared contest to determine who could describe the convention in the most ludicrous terms. McCardle carried daily in his Vicksburg newspaper the minutes of the convention under the heading, "Ord's Nigger Convention." He referred to the convention as "a lovely assemblage—such a one as was never brought together in Mississippi, and we pray God that such another will never again pollute the Hall where in other days the brightest and best of our State were wont to meet." In Brandon northern-born A. J. Frantz, McCardle's chief rival for the most slanderous editor prize, casually labeled the assembly the "Polecat Convention" and reserved his most poisonous darts for specific targets, namely the Republican delegates and their newspaper organ, the Vicksburg *Republican*.[32] He described this journal, which actually expressed more moderate sentiments than the Radicals in the convention, as a "filthy, slimy, stinking, negro-equality, negro-loving, white-man-hating, hate-engendering organ of perjured scoundrels."[33] Even the influential and mild-mannered Giles M. Hillyer of the Natchez *Courier* turned his attention to penning epithets of the Republican-dominated assembly, alternating his references to it as a "collection of wild and imported animals," "the Jackson monstrosity," and "the Black and Tan Menagerie."[34] Although usually more responsible in his attacks, Barksdale through the columns of the Jackson *Clarion* nonetheless sought to maintain his reputation as Missis-

31. Warren, *Reminiscences of a Carpetbagger*, 36.
32. Vicksburg *Times*, January 7, 9, 11, 17, 18, 25, 1868; R. H. Henry, *Editors I Have Known Since the Civil War* (New Orleans, 1922), 32.
33. This quote may be found in the Vicksburg *Weekly Republican*, March 3, 1868. There are no extant issues of Frantz's newspaper for this period of Reconstruction.
34. Natchez *Tri-Weekly Courier*, January 10, 13, 31, 1868.

sippi's leading conservative editor and the most vigorous foe of the "mongrelization" of the state. Dismissing the purpose of the convention as a scheme to put its "Jacobin" members in office, Barksdale declared that the delegates "have no constituency outside of the ignorant black rabble whom they are seeking to convert into convenient tools for the promotion of their own selfish ends."[35]

The obstructionist tactics of the conservatives in the convention further impelled moderate and uncommitted Republicans to take the side of Radical delegates on important issues. Furthermore, the rebirth of the state Democratic party while the convention was in session convinced many Republican delegates that the fruits of the war and the purposes of congressional reconstruction were in serious jeopardy in Mississippi. The cause of Union and bona fide black freedom could only be preserved by a radical settlement that would guarantee Negro rights, including unrestricted black suffrage, and disfranchise certain Confederates. As an ultimate provocation, Jefferson Davis, the archenemy himself, appeared in Jackson in early February as the guest of Governor Humphreys and walked the streets of the town in full view of the infuriated Republican members of the convention. The force of these events and the climate of opinion existing in Mississippi at the time worked inexorably to destroy the early spirit of moderation and caution among the Republican delegates. Nevertheless, the Radical triumph was never complete, and differences among the delegates continued to plague the Radical effort to impose an extreme political settlement on the state.

Despite a growing feeling of bitterness and alienation among the Republican delegates, the convention proceeded in a reasonably orderly and businesslike fashion to promulgate a new constitution for Mississippi. Few incidents marred the proceedings in the hall of representatives at the capitol, and these were usually in the form of verbal clashes in which tempers flared momentarily and subsided short of physical violence.[36] These clashes were not

35. Jackson *Weekly Clarion*, January 14, 1868.
36. The most notable exception to the relatively peaceful convention proceedings was a melee that occurred in the capitol grounds with Eggleston, Morgan, and Townsend

always between Republicans and conservatives but frequently involved disputes between members of the Radical faction. As in all deliberative bodies, debate on the floor was often of a rambling and trivial nature. Conservative delegates frequently responded to the Republican leadership's insistence that they be heard by ridiculing the work of the convention. The brevity of the daily sessions, usually from four to six hours in length with a long recess at noon, left the appearance, which the conservative press gleefully exploited, that the purpose of the delegates was to extend the life of the convention in order to collect per diem.

The main business of the convention, however, was done in the hotel and boardinghouse rooms of the delegates. Here the committees met and carefully prepared the various articles of the constitution.[37] Then they reported to the floor of the convention where each section was considered, along with amendments from the floor. The articles were either approved by the convention or returned to the committee for restudy and revision. Actually, the full convention made few significant changes in the drafts recommended by the committees. In less than a month after the session convened, most of the committees had completed their work and submitted reports to the convention for consideration.

While the measures were being ironed out in the committee rooms, debate broke out on the floor on several issues that had no direct relationship to the framing of a new constitution. The first issue involved the question of aid for the victims of the economic crisis that had gripped the state during the winter of 1867–1868. The debate took two forms: a call for immediate assistance for the large numbers of impoverished people in the state, particularly blacks in the river counties, and a proposal that General

---

as the principal combatants. Professor Garner cites this incident as evidence that the bitterness in the convention "became so great that personal altercations and fights were of common occurrence." Garner, *Reconstruction in Mississippi*, 201n. This conclusion cannot be substantiated by the evidence.

37. *Journal of the Constitutional Convention of 1868*, p. 37. The fact that the committees assumed the initiative in preparing the provisions of the constitution did not prevent the introduction of various proposals and resolutions on the convention floor. Often of an unrealistic character, since they were introduced primarily for public consumption or for personal gratification, these measures were normally tabled or referred to the appropriate committee.

Gillem issue an order staying the collection of debts until conditions had improved.

Radicals in the convention assumed the lead in calling for direct material assistance to the destitute. A committee on destitution, headed by the Radical scalawag Abel Alderson, reported "an alarming state of destitution among the laboring classes," concluding that no fewer than thirty thousand people were suffering from want of the necessities of life. Basing his information on discussions with Republican delegates in the convention, Alderson asserted that only eleven counties in the state were free from distress. His committee proposed, in the form of a resolution to be implemented by the district commander, that the convention authorize the immediate creation of a public works program for unemployed persons, to be administered by county officials and financed by the much-abused state poll tax that had been initially levied by the legislature of 1865. Public roads were to receive the main attention under the Alderson plan, but local officials were also to find other worthwhile projects for the jobless. Those individuals enrolled in the program would receive as much as four dollars per day in wages. Meanwhile, they were to seek private employment, and their eligibility for public assistance would immediately cease when they found work.

Several moderate Republican delegates, joined by conservatives, strongly objected to such a radical scheme of relief for the destitute, preferring a plan introduced by George Stovall that would delay the payment of debts until economic conditions improved and also would prohibit the sale of property for delinquent taxes. In supporting the Stovall resolution, several former Whigs in the convention, including Stovall himself, abandoned their life-long opposition to repudiation on the ground that under the economic circumstances of 1868 debtor relief, as Joseph W. Field put it, constituted "a National, State, and social necessity, paramount to all law."

Ten white Radicals and eleven of the eighteen blacks in the convention vigorously opposed the Stovall measure. They argued that the proposal would confuse the issue of relief and forestall action by General Gillem on the Alderson plan, which, more than the moderate scheme, would provide assistance for struggling blacks. Despite the heated debate on what form relief should take, both the Stovall and the Alderson resolutions received the approval of the convention and were sent to the district commander for implementation.[38]

It was soon clear, however, that the Tennessee-born Gillem did not view the problems of economic distress in the same light as did the majority in the convention. He rejected both the Alderson and Stovall proposals. The general, who had the authority to disallow ordinances and resolutions of the constitutional convention, based his decision on "a careful investigation" of the claims of widespread poverty existing in the state, and he concluded that the convention had exaggerated the extent of suffering in Mississippi. Like many of his conservative contemporaries, Gillem conceived of poverty and suffering strictly in terms of unemployment. Without denying that times were hard, Gillem testily informed the convention that jobs could be obtained by all needing employment, and he announced that he had directed officers of the Freedmen's Bureau "to use every means in their power to procure situations for laborers on the best terms, and at points as convenient to their stations as possible." Gillem pointed out that even as he penned this message to the convention five hundred laborers could find employment through the auspices of the bureau agent in Vicksburg. As for incapacitated adults and orphaned children, they could be cared for in the hospitals and asylums of the state. In declining an order staying the collection of debts, as his predecessor had done, Gillem expressed the belief that most indebtedness in the state was the result of the war, and he wondered why debtors during the three years since the surrender had not availed themselves of the opportunities to pay their creditors.

In minimizing the existence of poverty and suffering in the state, Gillem ignored the report of the bureau supervisor in the central Delta area, though he appended it to his message to the convention on the issue. This official reported that approximately one half of the twelve to thirteen thousand blacks in Washington County faced destitution because they could not be employed for the coming year. "In the vicinity of Greenville," he grimly informed

38. *Journal of the Constitutional Convention of 1868*, pp. 68–70, 85–86, 157–58, 402–403. For other debtor relief proposals see pp. 15, 31, 43–44, 55, 58, 145.

Gillem, "I found several families, numbering in all some sixty or seventy persons, houseless, and with only sufficient food to keep them for two or three days at the farthest. They have been recently turned out of the cabins they occupied last year, without means of any description. There are a great many similar cases throughout the county." To provide temporary relief for those persons facing starvation, he had purchased and distributed corn and meat; but this afforded no permanent solution to the problem of destitution in the Delta or to the effects of the reduction in pay which for many laborers exceeded two thirds of their 1867 wages. In order to avoid a deluge of supplicants for immediate assistance, Gillem directed that those sufferers who applied for rations would "be considered as placing themselves at the disposal of the Assistant Commissioner, to be sent to such places as employment can be procured for them."[39]

Although failing to secure Gillem's cooperation, Republicans in the constitutional convention continued their agitation for debtor relief. On the eve of adjournment the convention ordered that five hundred copies of scalawag James Weir's summation of the "loyal element's" position on relief for oppressed debtors be printed and distributed, admittedly "for the benefit of the Republican party, as a campaign document."[40]

The district commander also refused to cooperate with the convention on other matters—a contravention that contributed to the growing feeling of alienation and defiance on the part of the Republican delegates. Early during the session the cautious Gillem rejected a comprehensive tax ordinance drawn up by the convention to defray its expenses, including per diem payments for the delegates. At the same time he refused to recognize the corps of agents selected by the Republican majority to collect these and other taxes. Gillem objected to the tax ordinance on the grounds that the convention had interpreted too liberally its authority (contained in the March 23, 1867, supplementary act of Congress) to tax property for its support. He disapproved of the convention-appointed revenue agents because such functionaries were "unknown to the laws of the State" and independent of the regular

39. *Ibid.*, 174–75, 223–26.
40. *Ibid.*, 569.

civil officers. Indeed, Gillem complained, they were given unlimited authority in the proposed ordinance to assess and collect
whatever taxes they desired. The general directed the delegates
to prepare a new revenue measure, one that would meet his
reservations.[41]

Despite some Radical sentiment in the convention to defy Gillem
and appeal over his head to General Grant and Congress, most
Republican delegates swallowed their pride and agreed to a tax
ordinance that the district commander would accept. Included in
the second ordinance, however, was a levy of 0.5 percent on railroad property, which, delegates estimated, would raise fifty thousand dollars for the convention. Reacting immediately, railroad
officials appealed to Gillem to invalidate this section of the revenue
measure. They claimed that the duty on the roads violated their
charter rights. The general submitted the question to the state
auditor and the attorney general in the holdover administration,
and both of them agreed with the railroad managers that the property of the roads should be exempt from all state taxes. Gillem
accepted the opinion and issued orders for officials to cease collecting the levy on the railroads.[42] Immediately another storm
of protest erupted in the convention, and on this occasion moderate scalawags joined in the hue and cry against Gillem, denouncing
his action in exempting such "a large, powerful and oppressive
monopoly" from taxation. Carpetbaggers in the convention, however, seemed to lack the vehemence of their scalawag allies in
the affair; furthermore, their objections, when expressed, were
directed more toward the district commander's exercise of arbitrary military power than to any protection that he had given to
powerful railroad corporations. These protests were futile, however. The general's will prevailed.[43]

The result of the district commander's checkmating policies was
to discredit the efforts of the constitutional convention to raise
the money necessary to pay its expenses. In addition, Gillem's

41. *House Executive Documents*, 40th Cong., 3rd Sess., No. 1, Pt. I, pp. 586–87, 621–
23.
42. *Ibid.*, 634–35, 641–42; Jackson *Clarion*, February 14, 27, 1868; *Journal of the
Constitutional Convention of 1868*, pp. 215–21, 313, 705–707.
43. *Journal of the Constitutional Convention of 1868*, pp. 688; Jackson *Clarion*, February 28, 1868.

obstinate course led to the emergence of a conservative organization in Vicksburg which announced its determination to resist paying the convention taxes. Although protest meetings were held in other communities, no statewide association was formed. Holdover sheriffs nonetheless showed an unusual reluctance to collect the convention levies. So derelict were many of these officers that only $87,000 had been collected by May 13, 1868, a few days before the adjournment of the convention, and nineteen of the sixty sheriffs in the state had failed to make revenue reports, despite proddings by Gillem.[44] The Republican majority in the convention fully expected to have as much as $300,000 in the state treasury by the time of adjournment to cover the warrants issued under its authority. A much lower sum, $130,886 in state notes, was actually paid out to meet expenses, but because of the uncertainty regarding Gillem's position on the collection of taxes to redeem them, these obligations fluctuated between forty and sixty cents on the dollar. Not only did this mean that the cost of the "Black and Tan" Convention was much less than outraged Mississippi conservatives claimed (not more than $160,000 in greenbacks, according to black delegate Thomas W. Stringer), but also the controversial per diem expense of ten dollars for each delegate was in effect reduced to as little as four in greenbacks. By the same token, the printing expenses of the convention were much less than the $60,000 paid out in warrants for the work.[45]

Republican delegates also clashed with Gillem when they sought to conduct an investigation of events leading to Governor Humphreys' proclamation of December 9, 1867. This edict, as previously described, warned blacks against participating in a rumored insurrection to seize lands. When the convention sought to examine the reports to the military regarding the episode, Gillem denied them access to the files, claiming that the documents on the insurrection threat "partake of a confidential nature" and could not be divulged. Radicals in the convention also found cause to criticize Gillem's administration of the Freedmen's Bureau, espe-

44. *Journal of the Constitutional Convention of 1868*, pp. 190, 428–29, 514, 678–79, 713; Vicksburg *Times*, February 4, 7, 1868; Jackson *Clarion*, February 5, 12, 1868.

45. Thomas W. Stringer and George Paine, to the Joint Committee on Reconstruction, n.d., in Papers on Conditions in Mississippi; *Journal of the Constitutional Convention of 1868*, pp. 494, 569; *Senate Journal [1870]*, Appendix, 108.

cially denouncing his policy of having vagrant blacks arrested in districts where work was available. In effect, Republicans charged, the general's uncooperative policies had confounded the work of the convention, had thwarted their efforts to organize a strong party in time for the election on the new constitution, and had given encouragement to reactionary forces in the state.[46]

On January 20 carpetbagger Edward J. Castello introduced in the convention an ultraradical proposal to govern suffrage, jury service, and officeholding under the new constitution. This plan made unquestioned loyalty to the Union during the war the necessary test for voting, holding office, serving on juries, and even teaching in the public schools and colleges. Everyone seeking these privileges would have to take an oath affirming his past loyalty and also indicating that he accepted "the civil and political equality of all men, and [agreed] not to attempt to deprive any person or persons on account of race or color, or previous condition, of any political, religious or civil rights."[47] Except for persons who served in the United States army after their misadventure in rebellion, there was no procedure in the plan for the removal of disabilities. Modeled after the proscriptive features in the constitution of Castello's native Missouri, the proposal would bar from public life almost the entire white population of Mississippi, including such prominent Republicans as Flournoy, Morris, and Alcorn.

The opposition press immediately seized upon the Castello proposal as the undiluted Radical program for Mississippi, fully expecting it to be accepted by the convention. The plan, the Jackson *Clarion* exclaimed, "will unite the whole white population of the State because it is a complete negro domination scheme."[48] Although an outcry from conservatives to any Radical proposal could be anticipated, it is clear that Castello's measure went far beyond the desires of the majority of the Republicans in the convention

46. *Journal of the Constitutional Convention of 1868*, pp. 59, 396–400; *House Miscellaneous Documents*, 40th Cong., 3rd Sess., No. 53, pp. 35, 265; Henry Mayson to T. L. Tullock, March 12, 1869; Jonathan Tarbell to John A. Bingham, January 26, 1869, both in Papers on Conditions in Mississippi.

47. The Castello proposal is in the *Journal of the Constitutional Convention of 1868*, pp. 63–68.

48. Jackson *Clarion*, January 23, 1868.

and was even too extreme for several Radicals. Submitted to the all-Radical Committee on the Franchise, of which Castello was a member, the measure soon gave way to a milder proposal for the disfranchisement of former Confederates. The new plan, probably drawn up by Mygatt, the Radical chairman of the committee and its only scalawag member, was reported to the convention floor on March 4. This measure would temporarily disfranchise only those persons who were disqualified by the proposed Fourteenth Amendment and the reconstruction laws of 1867—*i.e.*, former officeholders who had earlier taken an oath to defend the Constitution of the United States and had violated that oath by participating in the rebellion.[49] Under this arrangement, only two or three thousand whites would be disfranchised, and they could regain their voting privileges by a two-thirds vote of the legislature. For purposes of holding office, however, only persons who could take the ironclad oath of past loyalty were eligible, at least until July 4, 1876, when the requirement would be dropped.

A few days later carpetbagger Albert T. Morgan, who because of illness had missed the meetings of the franchise committee, submitted a minority report providing a more stringent settlement for the old citizens than the Mygatt plan. Even so, the features of this proposal were less harsh than the Castello scheme. Morgan would impose the same suffrage disabilities as Mygatt but with the important addition that all persons registering to vote must affirm their support for the political and civil equality of all men. As for officeholding, Morgan followed Mygatt's recommendation that the ironclad oath be required of state officials; however, the Yazoo County carpetbagger proposed no procedure for the subsequent repeal of this requirement, a condition that would permanently bar former Confederates and their sympathizers from office.[50] This latter omission became crucial for many uncommitted Republican delegates and a few Radicals, including the influential Mygatt, who

49. For the Mygatt report, see the *Journal of the Constitutional Convention of 1868*, pp. 295–96.

50. *Ibid.*, 312–13, 322–23. Mygatt, unlike Morgan, would require the ironclad oath of county officials as well as state officeholders. Neither of these reports made recommendations regarding qualifications for jurors. In fact, the completed constitution was silent on this question, and the matter was left to the legislature.

opposed a policy of permanently excluding the Confederate masses from office.

Delegates did not wait for the beginning of the formal debate on the franchise reports to express their opinions on the question of the political proscription of former rebels. At frequent intervals individuals took to the floor to argue their position on what became the most provocative issue before the convention. The inability of Republicans, and even Radicals for that matter, to agree on proscription and the related question of general suffrage and office-holding qualifications made inevitable heated exchanges that on occasion produced challenges for a more violent form of confrontation. The vociferousness with which Mississippi conservatives attacked the various proscriptive proposals and the general climate of defiance in the state increased the determination of Radical Republicans to secure the passage of a clause that at least for a time would exclude former Confederates from public life. Whether they supported a policy of permanent Confederate proscription or one that would only apply temporarily, as contained in the Mygatt plan, most Radicals presumed that relatively few whites would support the Republican party in the near future regardless of the political settlement adopted by the convention. Instead, they put their faith in the preponderance of black voters in Mississippi and in their own ability to keep these new voters united behind the Republican party. A few Radicals like Mygatt believed, despite the pervasiveness of anti-Republican belligerency at the time of the convention, that a strong biracial party could still be developed in the state, though only after a "loyal" government, free of former rebels, was established and had demonstrated to the old citizens the blessings of the new order. Then the proscriptive clauses could be lifted and the door opened for all whites to affiliate with the Republican party.[51]

On the other hand, avowed moderate Republicans in the convention insisted that the inclusion of a proscriptive clause in the constitution would destroy all hope of attracting a large body of whites

51. For the positions of several Republicans on the proscription issue, see the Jackson *Clarion*, February 22, 28, March 11, 21, 1868, and the *Journal of the Constitutional Convention of 1868*, pp. 385, 394, 409, 484.

to the party. Moderates pointed out that already in the predominantly white border states the Republican party faced oblivion because of its association with the wartime proscription of rebels and copperheads. The Republican party, moderates insisted, could not long survive in the state without a solid base of support among the stronger and more intelligent race.

The scalawag editor of the Meridian *Chronicle*, the Republican newspaper organ of predominantly white east Mississippi, especially promoted the need for a strong white party and implored the constitutional convention to be lenient with former rebels. The disfranchisement of Confederates, this editor prophesied, "will entail upon the Republican party in the State a humiliation from which it will never recover." Furthermore, he declared, such a policy "is contrary to the spirit of the Republican party," since it seeks "to elevate one class above the other politically. . . . The rebels have all along accused the Republican party of thrusting Negro domination upon the South. This charge we have denied, and we will still deny it in name of the Republican party; but this wholesale disfranchisement [threat] smacks loudly of such a policy."[52] The effect on the party and the reconstruction settlement would be immediate, he said; the constitution, which in other ways would be an enlightened and progressive document, would surely fail at ratification. On the floor of the convention carpetbagger George C. McKee expressed a similar view, and he was joined by other moderate Republicans. McKee argued that the convention in its policy toward fallen Confederates should go no further than the acts of Congress which did not require that the new state constitutions disfranchise rebels.[53]

A liberal policy toward former Confederates, however, was undermined to some extent by the insistence of a handful of moderate Republicans that not only should there be no disfranchisement of rebels but certain restrictions should be placed on the general exercise of the ballot—restrictions obviously aimed at the uneducated and propertyless freedmen. Former Union Whig James L.

52. Meridian *Chronicle*, April 21 (quote), 28, May 16, June 2, 1868. The influential Vicksburg *Weekly Republican* also opposed a proscriptive policy toward former Confederates. See issues of April 7, May 12, 1868.
53. Jackson *Clarion*, March 21, 1868.

Herbert advocated an educational qualification for voting.[54] Fellow moderate Joseph W. Field offered an interesting and elaborate formula that would prohibit the dispossessed from participating in the selection of state senators. He partly agreed with the Radicals that the ballot for former Confederates should be extended only to those persons "who will give evidence of devotion to a perpetual union and the elevation of the newly made colored citizens." But in the elitist Whig tradition, the soundness of which was reinforced in the minds of Union Whigs like Field by their observation of the calamitous behavior of the white masses in the secession crisis, this Columbus Republican advanced a dual system for the exercise of the voting privilege.

> In the election of members of the [state] Senate, I am decidedly in favor of a property qualification, for both white and black. This will have the effect [of securing] the controlling power of the State, and retain[ing] it, in the hands of the better portion of both classes, thus giving security to the present civilization of both. . . . To consign all power to the majority of ignorant and vicious citizens will sooner or later eventuate in common ruin. On the other hand, to refuse to grant a voice in the affairs of the general government to a large portion of the citizens in perpetuity will breed such perpetual discord and dissatisfaction as to result in the same unhappy consequences.[55]

Nevertheless, only in the election of members of the state senate would Field place restrictions on the exercise of the ballot.

The efforts of Herbert and Field to limit the suffrage privilege, along with the more blatant conservative attempts to checkmate Negro suffrage entirely, not only produced a strong reaction among Radicals in the convention but persuaded uncommitted and some moderate Republicans to take a stand in favor of universal black suffrage and at least a temporary disfranchisement of certain classes of whites. State Supreme Court Justice Ephraim G. Peyton, a Union Whig of Copiah County who as a delegate had not previously associated with the Radical faction and was believed to be a moderate on reconstruction issues, vigorously denounced the movement to restrict the ballot, except as it applied to former secessionists.

54. *Ibid.*, February 22, 1868.
55. Field's comments during the convention are reported in *ibid.*, February 13, 1868. See also his proposal regarding the oath to be taken by all prospective voters. *Journal of the Constitutional Convention of 1868*, pp. 54–55.

If limitations were placed on suffrage, Peyton told the convention, the state and local governments would soon be in the hands of hostile whites who would make sure that blacks could not vote or hold any other rights. Peyton agreed with conservatives that the freedmen were generally ignorant and unsophisticated in political matters, but this condition, he said, was due to a lack of educational opportunity in slavery which could be quickly overcome; indeed, since emancipation Negroes had made rapid strides toward responsible citizenship through training received in schools sponsored by the Freedmen's Bureau. Peyton labeled as absurd the charge that the black majority would rule Mississippi if the franchise privilege was not restricted. Even though Negroes would have a majority at the polls under the Radical program, he felt certain there would be no disposition on their part or on that of their leaders to dominate state affairs. By implication, white loyalists would control the black electorate. Finally—and this seems to be the key to the Copiah Unionist's attachment to universal black suffrage—Negro enfranchisement would serve as a safeguard against the restoration of rebels to power. Already, and specifically with the recent reorganization of the state Democratic party, Peyton saw signs of rebels arousing themselves from their political slumbers and conspiring to regain their seats of authority in the state. Blacks, the aristocratic Peyton averred, would make far better citizens and voters than secessionists and demagogues of the Barksdale and McCardle class.[56]

On March 19 the constitutional convention began formal consideration of the franchise article. Immediately, and before the moderates could marshal their forces, Morgan's radical proposal on the proscription of Confederates was substituted for the more liberal Mygatt plan contained in the report of the Committee on the Franchise. But because many Republican delegates soon had second thoughts regarding the Morgan proposal, further consideration of the matter was postponed until an effort could be made to reconcile the conflicting views of the majority.[57] Even supporters of the harsh proscription scheme hesitated, since they realized that

56. Jackson *Clarion*, February 28, 1868.
57. *Journal of the Constitutional Convention of 1868*, pp. 381–84, 394, 409–410.

a premature vote that failed to achieve a majority for proscription might permanently dash their hopes for success. It was clear that most Republicans favored some form of political proscription of Mississippi rebels, but many were reluctant to approve the unreasonable and vindictive clause in the Morgan substitute requiring voters to admit the political and civil equality of all men. They also disapproved of the proposed section forever disqualifying from office all persons who in any manner had supported the Confederate cause.[58]

Meanwhile, moderate Republicans labored feverishly to head off an agreement on proscription between the Radicals and the reservationists. Scalawag Stovall, who preferred the political association of white secessionists to that of black Republicans, employed the tactic of ridicule in an attempt to sway confused colleagues against the equality affirmation in the Morgan substitute. While the franchise question simmered and debate on other issues occupied the floor, Stovall called for the inclusion of an equality provision in routine proposals that had no relation to personal rights. Stovall's tactic failed to persuade many of the uncommitted Republican delegates to vote against the Morgan proposal. Most Republicans who supported Morgan's substitute evidently recognized the bull-against-the-comet character of the equality proviso; however, they lined up behind it mainly to prevent conservatives from obtaining a sense of satisfaction at its defeat.[59]

The first victory for the Morgan Radicals came on April 16 when they were able to push through the convention their stringent plan on officeholding. With several moderate Republicans absent from the session and Mygatt along with his handful of devotees temporarily won over to their point of view, these Radicals revived the franchise article, shut off debate on section five dealing with the eligibility of officeholders, and called for a vote on it, in the face of a frantic effort by northern conservative Charles H. Townsend to offer a substitute for the Morgan measure. Forty-four delegates

---

58. For indications at this time of reservations voiced by Republicans other than moderates on proscription, see *ibid.*, 385, 394, 409, 495.

59. *Ibid.*, 384, 393. Even Union League organizer John R. Parsons ridiculed the equality affirmation in the registration oath. However, like other Radicals, he voted for it.

answered in favor of the section; twenty-five opposed it.[60] An analysis of this crucial roll-call vote reveals that almost all of the uncommitted and usually silent Republicans in the convention went with the ultra Radicals. Only three Radical delegates opposed the action of the majority, and they were joined in their opposition by twelve moderate Republicans and ten conservatives. Of the fifteen black delegates voting on the issue, only one indicated opposition. Carpetbaggers in the convention also were strong in support of the proscriptive section, with sixteen of them voting for it and only five against. No such clear-cut alignment appeared among the scalawags. Eight of them expressed approval of the Radical-sponsored section and six indicated opposition; however, of the ten scalawags who did not participate in the roll call, seven were associated with the moderate cause.

With the floor of the convention in turmoil following the approval of the proscriptive section, a motion to reconsider the action was defeated by a voice vote. The obstreperous Townsend, the new hero of the conservative faith, leaped to his feet and demanded a roll-call vote. President Eggleston coolly rejected the demand, whereupon Townsend in uncomplimentary terms denounced Eggleston for his autocratic management of the convention. Carpetbagger Henry W. Barry immediately came to the president's defense, and in the shouting match that followed he questioned Townsend's claims to being classified as a gentleman. The former Federal captain wasted no time in inviting the young Radical to settle the new issue outside of the convention hall. When Barry, who consistently upheld his aversion to southern violence, rejected the invitation, Morgan agreed to take his place and follow Townsend to the capitol grounds. After some sparring between the two Reconstruction warriors, they were joined in the melee by Eggleston and other Radicals. Townsend quickly lost his underdog status when "a mob of disorderly and riotous persons" entered the fray against the carpetbaggers. The now one-sided fight was soon halted by Jackson constables. For his efforts in defense of Confederates' rights Townsend was expelled from the

60. One of the forty-four members voting for the section was Townsend, who did so in order that, under parliamentary rules, he could immediately move for a reconsideration of the action. The roll-call vote is found in *ibid.*, 519.

convention, a measure taken just before he submitted his resignation. Eggleston, who had already been nominated as the Republican candidate for governor, was tried for assault, pleaded guilty, and was fined ten dollars.[61] Unruffled, the former military commander of Atlanta continued as convention president.

Conservative delegates did not await Republican action on the remainder of the franchise article before resigning from the convention. Eleven delegates, including two moderate Republicans, left immediately after the vote on section five, and the next day they were followed by two other members.[62] Yet the disruptive and ominous events surrounding the passage of the officeholding section had sobered several of the more perspicacious Republicans, and they pressed successfully for an amendment to section five that would exempt army privates from the provision that permanently disqualified all Confederates from public office. With the log jam broken, the convention by a vote of thirty-seven to thirteen immediately passed the complete franchise article. As in the original vote on section five, most scalawags refused to commit themselves to a proscription policy; sixteen of this class did not vote, and of the eight who participated in the roll call on the franchise article, four voted against it.[63]

The provision on suffrage, in addition to enfranchising black males as required by Congress, disfranchised all persons who had been temporarily prohibited from voting by the reconstruction laws of 1867; however, those antebellum officials affected by the disqualification, numbering no more than 2,500, could be relieved from the disability by a future legislature. The clause requiring a prospective voter to "admit the political and civil equality of all men, so help me God," was a far more significant weapon

61. *Ibid.*, 519, 527; Jackson *Clarion*, April 16, 17, 1868; Vicksburg *Weekly Republican*, May 19, 1868.

62. *Journal of the Constitutional Convention of 1868*, pp. 520–21, 544. Actually, the total number of members resigning was fourteen, but one delegate later applied for readmission to the convention, claiming that his name had been erroneously placed on the list of bolters. *Ibid.*, 570.

63. *Ibid.*, 543. Only two conservatives remained in the convention to cast their votes on the franchise article. Stephen Johnson, the convention's only Negro conservative, voted against the article, whereas John Elliott, a conservative Unionist of the northeast Mississippi hill country who had no love for either rebels or Republicans, joined the Radicals on this issue and voted for the political proscription of his Confederate neighbors.

of disfranchisement than was the voting prohibition against former officeholders.[64] Few conservatives, given the climate of racial and political opinion in the state during Reconstruction, would subscribe to an oath that they found demeaning and vindictive. In effect, then, if the constitution were ratified, this requirement would cause the bulk of the white masses of the state to voluntarily disfranchise themselves.

The nature of the conservative reaction to the convention's passage of the illiberal clauses was predictable. With a horrendous vision of impending doom, Barksdale of the Jackson *Clarion* called out to white Mississippians, "To Your Tents, Oh Israel!" He characterized the Radical settlement for former Confederates as "the most sweeping, the most infamous, the most vindictive measure of proscription which has yet been passed by, or introduced into, any of the Military Conventions."[65] Barksdale's harsh appraisal was echoed in the anti-Republican press of the state, as editors indignantly predicted that ignorance, venality, and disorder would reign in Mississippi if the constitution that contained this diabolical feature was ratified. At first even the Republican journals, without exception, admitted the foolhardiness of the delegates in framing the proscriptive clauses. Republican editors, however, soon abandoned their criticism of the convention and joined in the campaign to secure the ratification of the constitution, with the proscriptive features included. These illiberal clauses in the proposed constitution provided Democrats like Barksdale with the perfect issue to use in uniting whites behind a militant campaign to strike down the Radical Goliath and regain conservative ascendancy in the state. Even those Union Whigs like George L. Potter who had not yet been lured into the Democratic party, would find it difficult to resist the *Clarion's* call and would march as one with their antagonists of a simpler and less foreboding era.

Actually, radicalism in the so-called Black and Tan Convention began and ended with the proscriptive suffrage and officeholding provisions. But the debate on the education article in the constitution raised fears among conservatives that a mixed school system would be imposed on the state by the "Jacobin" delegates.

64. The franchise article, as approved, may be found in the *Journal of the Constitutional Convention of 1868*, pp. 732–33.
65. Jackson *Clarion*, April 16, 1868.

The cornerstone of the Republican program of reform in Mississippi, as well in other southern states, public education received considerable attention in the committee rooms and on the convention floor. Little heed was paid to the question of mixed schools —an issue that was then convulsing Louisiana and South Carolina —until the decisive defeat of an amendment to the education article, introduced by the moderate scalawag George Stovall, requiring separate schools for the races. The vote on the Stovall amendment caused conservatives to conclude immediately that the Radicals were determined to impose a mixed system of schools upon the state, and the outcry was heard throughout Mississippi that the "mongrel convention" intended to bring about "social equality" and the amalgamation of the races. Not to be outdone this time by his Bourbon competitors, Barksdale led the editorial charge against the Radical "scheme of plunder and miscegenation, designed . . . to supercede the laws of our civilization with the horrible creed of the Black and Tan socialists, in the name of 'Public Education.'" Whites would never attend such schools, he declared, yet they would be forced to pay the taxes for a system of education benefiting blacks only. Disclaiming any opposition to the principle of Negro education, Barksdale protested against a system that "will impose a burthen on the white population, and then cheat them of its benefits."[66]

Radical Republicans in the convention expressed surprise at the outrage produced by the defeat of the Stovall amendment. They pointed out that the proposed article on education did not provide for mixed schools, nor had the Radical-dominated Committee on Public Education recommended such an arrangement. Stovall's injection of the issue into the debate on the school article was inflammatory and unnecessary, they insisted. Furthermore, the racial composition of individual schools was not a matter for the constitutional convention to decide; this was a question for the new legislature, which, several Radicals predicted, would make explicit a policy of separate schools for the races.[67]

66. *Journal of the Constitutional Convention of 1868*, pp. 148–50, 316–17; Vicksburg *Weekly Republican*, April 7, 1868; Meridian *Chronicle*, March 27, 1868; Jackson *Clarion*, March 11, 21, 1868.

67. Jackson *Clarion*, March 21, May 5, 1868; Vicksburg *Weekly Republican*, April 7, 1868.

The Radicals, however, failed to mention that the main reason for the defeat of the Stovall segregation proviso was the opposition of black delegates to it. The seventeen black Republicans in the convention, although realizing that an explicit statement in the constitution requiring mixed schools would undermine the public school system at its inception, nonetheless insisted that the question be left open for future consideration by the legislature. In fact, the black delegates threatened rebellion against the white Republican leadership if it permitted the adoption of the Stovall proviso requiring segregated schools. When the vote was taken, white Radicals and even some moderate Republicans like Field, fearing the political effects of black independence, joined the Negro bloc in rejecting the amendment.[68]

Nevertheless, white fears that a system of integrated schools would be imposed on Mississippians were soon largely allayed. Most troubled minds were soothed by assurances from influential Republicans, including black leader James Lynch, that if the party gained control of the state government it would not press for mixed schools.[69] When the ratification contest began in earnest, conservatives, except for an occasional demur from the pen of Barksdale and a more vigorous protest by Bourbon editors like McCardle, ceased their attacks on the public school article in the proposed constitution. By this time it was clear to most Democratic leaders that many of their white constituents supported a comprehensive system of common schools, insisting only that the races be separated in the classrooms. Furthermore, the Democratic hierarchy had embarked on a campaign to persuade blacks to support the conservative ticket in the forthcoming election; if they expected to be successful they could not oppose the education article in the constitution, which blacks strongly favored.[70]

The article on education as approved by the convention provided the framework for the public school system of Mississippi that has endured to the present day. Modeled primarily after mid-

68. Vicksburg *Weekly Republican*, April 7, 1868; Jackson *Clarion*, April 13, May 5, 1868; *Journal of the Constitutional Convention of 1868*, pp. 316–17, 508. Of the black delegates, only the unstable William T. Combash voted in favor of the Stovall amendment.

69. Vicksburg *Weekly Republican*, April 7, May 26, 1868.

70. See, for example, the Forest *Register*, April 1, 1868, and the address of state Democratic chairman John D. Freeman in the Jackson *Clarion*, April 28, 1868.

western systems but also with strong roots in the Mississippi past, the article gave explicit direction to future legislatures in establishing and maintaining free public schools in the state.[71] Expressing the belief that "the stability of a Republican form of government depends mainly upon the intelligence and virtue of the people," the framers of the article instructed the first legislature elected under the constitution to provide for "a uniform system of free public schools, by taxation or otherwise, for all children between the ages of five and twenty-one years." A state common school fund was to be established, supported by revenues from the sale of state lands, including those forfeited by citizens for failure to pay taxes, from fines collected from violators of state laws, and from license fees. In addition, the legislature could levy "a poll tax not to exceed two dollars a head, in aid of the school fund, and for no other purpose." Missing from the article was any mention of the authority that county and town governments would have in raising money for the support of the schools.

To administer the school system, the framers created the office of state superintendent of public education, which would be filled by popular election every four years. The superintendent was to join with the secretary of state and the attorney general to form a state board of education with general supervisory powers and with the authority to appoint county school superintendents. A future legislature, however, might provide for the election of the county superintendents.

Except for the provisions on the franchise and on public education, the articles in the constitution of 1868 were adopted in a generally routine fashion with little comment from outside of the convention. Although a number of innovative provisions were advanced by various members from the floor, few received the convention's approval. A majority of the delegates, including some moderate Republicans and conservatives, preferred to follow the

71. The school article, as approved, may be found in the *Journal of the Constitutional Convention of 1868*, pp. 733–34. Later, the carpetbagger editor of the *Mississippi Educational Journal*, I (March, 1871), 55–62, affirmed the antebellum influence in the establishment of the postwar public school system. For a brief account of the earlier efforts to create a system of free schools in the state, see George D. Humphrey, "Public Education for Whites in Mississippi," *Journal of Mississippi History*, III (January, 1941), 26–27, and chapter 10 herein.

committee reports in framing the various sections of the constitution. And these recommendations were hardly radical, much less revolutionary. Even the potentially explosive question of individual rights received a fairly dispassionate and methodical treatment. Nevertheless, a brief flurry of debate erupted, threatening the tranquility of the late sessions of the convention, when black members and several white Radicals attempted to write into the bill of rights specific clauses guaranteeing equal rights for Negroes in public accommodations and in such state institutions as the insane asylum, the state hospitals, and the University of Mississippi. Calm was restored after the majority agreed to two ambiguous provisions that satisfied few delegates but delayed consideration of the issue until reconstruction had been achieved. The first measure provided that no public funds "shall be appropriated for charitable or other public institution in this State, making any distinction among the citizens." The public school system, however, was specifically exempted from this provision. The second measure declared that "the right of all citizens to travel upon public conveyances shall not be infringed upon, nor in any manner abridged in the State." Except for these clauses the traditional bill of rights underwent few changes at the hands of the Republican framers.[72] An effort by friends of Negro rights to include a clause guaranteeing equal treatment for blacks in public places of entertainment failed by four votes. Black delegates voted unanimously for the amendment, but because only eighteen white Republicans supported them this effort to obtain advanced rights for Mississippi Negroes was doomed to defeat.[73]

Radical Republican delegates held no monopoly on the sponsorship of progressive, nonracial measures in the new constitution. Most of these innovations were included in the general recom-

72. *Journal of the Constitutional Convention of 1868*, pp. 156, 720–22.
73. *Ibid.*, 47, 256, 722. Despite its poor record in providing for advanced rights for blacks, the convention defeated formidable efforts to incorporate into the bill of rights two provisions of the notorious Black Code of 1865. One was a measure introduced by George Stovall that would have imposed a mandatory five-year sentence on anyone convicted of intermarriage with the other race. The vote to table the proposal barely passed, with only two black delegates voting against it. *Ibid.*, 199, 211–12. The other proposal would have provided for the restoration, with constitutional sanction, of the Black Code system of apprenticeship for helpless minors. *Ibid.*, 242–43.

mendations made by the various committees and usually were approved without a roll-call vote. A review of the sketchy minutes in the journal and the few recorded roll-call votes on issues other than political proscription and race indicates that moderate Republicans like scalawags Field, Stovall, and even the conservative Dr. William M. Compton played important roles in the formulation and quick passage of these provisions. For example, a measure protecting the property rights of women in marriage, a progressive innovation often cited approvingly by historians and attributed to the Radicals, actually received its strongest support from moderates in the convention; indeed, Radical Republicans, including black delegates, were seriously divided on this issue.[74] Broadly based support in the convention allowed the delegates to strike hard at the practice of dueling, which although illegal since the antebellum period had flourished in a crude and brutal form since Lee's surrender. Hoping finally to end the practice, the convention provided for disqualifying from voting or officeholding all persons who in any way participated in dueling. A section also sought to ban the lottery games that had become popular in the Mississippi Valley after the war, as impecunious southerners sought to recover their broken fortunes. As a result of this constitutional prohibition, Mississippi during the next two decades escaped the kind of chicanery and political corruption that prevailed in Louisiana where a powerful lottery held sway.[75]

Reflecting the general unpopularity after the war of the state's repudiation of the antebellum Planters' and Union Bank bonds, the framers of the 1868 constitution inserted a clause that forbade the state from pledging or loaning its credit "in aid of any person, association, or corporation." The state also was prohibited from becoming a stockholder in any corporation, although the antebellum financial interest of the state in the New Orleans, Jackson, and Great Northern and the Mississippi Central railroads could be retained. In restricting state aid to private enterprise, the Republican delegates were not motivated by any desire to uphold the principle of laissez-faire. Their main concern was to limit state

74. *Ibid.*, 345.
75. *Ibid.*, 722, 739.

involvement in speculative schemes then afoot in the South that were ostensibly designed to revive and expand the economic life of the area but in reality were advanced for selfish reasons. Nevertheless, the delegates did not prohibit altogether public assistance to corporations. Nothing in the new constitution, for example, prevented the state government from extending subsidies to railroads or other enterprises, nor did it prohibit the donation of state lands to private corporations. And as would later become clear, another potentially serious violation of the public welfare was the provision that by a two-thirds vote of its electorate any county or town might loan its credit to a private corporation.[76] The local desire for internal improvements, properly cultivated by promoters, would frequently overcome the restraining principle supposedly contained in the two-thirds requirement authorizing the community's participation in these projects.

The Republican-dominated convention demonstrated a degree of sensitivity to the peculiar economic problems experienced by postwar Mississippians. In addition to its unsuccessful efforts to obtain immediate assistance for the destitute through General Gillem, the delegates reversed the negative policy toward debtor relief developed by the Whig government during presidential reconstruction. In a sweeping declaration, they empowered the first legislature under the new constitution to "pass relief, stay, injunction, insolvent, and homestead laws, and . . . any and every act deemed necessary for the relief of debtors, subject only to the restrictions imposed by the Constitution of the United States." To provide guidance and assistance to the depressed agricultural interest, the delegates created the office of commissioner of immigration and agriculture. Furthermore, they instructed the first legislature to organize a board of public works. Although the duties of this board were not prescribed, by implication, since this section was the only one appearing under the article entitled "internal improvements," the agency would provide state direction for the clearing of rivers and harbors where federal aid could not be obtained.[77] Excluded from the jurisdiction of this board were the railroads and the Delta levees.

76. *Ibid.*, 737–38.
77. *Ibid.*, 735, 739.

In their efforts to provide a framework for the economic rehabilitation of Mississippi, delegates to the constitutional convention
did not neglect the interests of the small and dispossessed farmers
of the state. An important section in the constitution, which departed drastically from prewar practices, provided that "Taxation
shall be equal and uniform throughout the State. All property shall
be taxed in proportion to its value, to be ascertained as directed
by law." The convention also directed that tax-forfeited lands must
not be disposed of in tracts of more than 160 acres.[78] This provision was designed to secure a broad distribution of the thousands
of acres of property that had been sold for taxes.

A few important, and on the whole undemocratic, changes were
made in the structure of the state government. The governor's
term was extended from two to four years, but more significantly,
he received the power to appoint all judges in the state above
the rank of justice of the peace. Motivated mainly by partisan
considerations, Radical Republicans by means of an appointive
judiciary hoped to control the courts in white conservative districts. With a statewide majority of Republican voters, the party
could expect to elect the governor, and in turn he would fill the
judicial positions with loyal Republicans. Several moderate Republicans protested, since this method of selecting the judiciary reversed the principle of the popular election of judges contained
in the Jacksonian constitution of 1832. Along with the convention's
conservatives they attempted to retain the old system, but the
Radical leadership, backed by the solid vote of the black delegation and a majority of the white Republican members, easily defeated the move.[79]

The issue of the appointive judiciary simmered throughout Reconstruction, until the conservatives came to power in 1876 and
were able to appoint their own members to the bench. But the
arrangement of 1868 was not without its defenders among the
antebellum leaders of the state. Jehu A. Orr of Columbus, a distinguished lawyer and jurist, asserted that the section in the con-

78. *Ibid.*, 392, 739.
79. *Ibid.*, 166–67, 434–45, 727, 729–30. The governor also received the authority to
appoint all militia officers. Under the old system only the upper echelon of the militia
was selected by the governor; lower ranking officers were elected by the men.

stitution making judges appointive demonstrated the true conservatism of the framers. Writing four years after the events of 1868, Orr, a secession Democrat in 1861 and a former member of both the United States and Confederate congresses who subsequently affiliated with the Republican party, believed that the convention's action in restoring to the governor·the power to appoint the judiciary was long overdue. "An elective judiciary is the abomination of the age," he declared.

> In 1832 the demagogues carried the day, and the wild democracy degraded the courts by exposing them to the dependence—partisan dependence [of the people]. Deeply as this was regretted by the wise and the good from that day to 1868 neither the Democratic nor Whig parties ever had the courage to make an effort to restore a conservative judiciary to the State. *Vox Populi, Vox Dei,* was the sentiment that degraded the public policy of each of these old parties on this question. The honor was saved to that much hated and much abused convention of 1868 to march with a heroic grandeur and sublime moral courage, to the music of true conservatism and in defiance of the clamor of demagogues, restore to the State an independent judiciary— of which she had been robbed for nearly forty years.[80]

Other changes in the apparatus of government received little attention, either inside or outside of the convention. Without fanfare the office of lieutenant governor was added to the state hierarchy, and this official was empowered to serve as chief executive not only upon the death of the governor but also when the latter was absent from the state or disabled by a lengthy illness. The convention abolished the cumbersome system of probate courts and restored the more efficient and presumably less expensive chancery arrangement to handle routine judicial business at the local level. Except for making the lieutenant governor the presiding officer of the senate, the framers made no important alteration in the structure of the legislature. The formula for apportioning membership in the legislature, however, underwent change: representation would now be based upon the number of qualified voters in a county or district instead of on the number of white inhabitants, as the old method provided. The constitution directed

80. Jehu A. Orr to Ridgley C. Powers, December 29, 1872, in Governors' Correspondence, Vol. 80.

that an enumeration of registered voters should be made every ten years, beginning in 1870, and this count was to serve as the basis for apportionment during the decade.[81]

Until the apportionment plan could be implemented, the constitutional convention provided for a division of the seats in the legislature, which gave the Radicals some political advantage in the situation. The assignment of seats in the lower house conformed to General Ord's equitable apportionment of the constitutional convention; the division for the senate, however, was obviously designed to ensure a majority of black voters in several districts. For example, the convention placed Rankin and Simpson counties, with their racially well-balanced electorates in the same senatorial district with overwhelmingly black Hinds County and gave this district two senators instead of the usual one.[82] The river county of Claiborne, with a large Negro vote, was joined with racially balanced Copiah County to form a senatorial district. The same arrangement was made for heavily black Jefferson County and white Franklin County. Even moderate Republicans found a degree of gerrymandering desirable to ensure the success of their party in the forthcoming elections to the state senate.

The constitutional convention adjourned on May 18, after a session of more than four months. Before leaving for home to participate in the ratification campaign that was already gaining momentum, the Republican delegates put through the convention one of their most audacious measures. Hurling defiance at the authority of General Gillem, whom Congress had given the sole responsibility for conducting the ratification election, the delegates created a committee with extensive powers to oversee the whole procedure, including the issuance of a proclamation to authenticate the results of the election. If the constitution were rejected, the Committee of Five, as it was known, could reconvene the convention—a procedure that had no basis in the reconstruction acts. President Eggleston selected three Radicals and two moderate Republicans to this committee, designating as chairman the Radical William H. Gibbs. Ignoring the presumed authority of the convention over

81. *Journal of the Constitutional Convention of 1868*, pp. 726, 728.
82. This apportionment may be found in *ibid.*, 736–37.

the election, Gillem nonetheless indicated to the Committee of Five that he would permit its observers to be present at the polls and at the counting of the votes.[83]

When the hour of adjournment arrived, Eggleston, who already had been designated as the Republican nominee for governor, charged the delegates to work vigorously for the ratification of the constitution and to "stimulate and encourage your people to renewed efforts in the cause of equal rights. . . . Of our success, I feel confident, if we each do our part, and remember that the eyes of the people not only of the United States but of the whole world are upon us."[84]

Thus ended the so-called Black and Tan Convention of 1868. Had it possessed the will the convention might have given Mississippi a truly radical constitution, but only on the matter of the political proscription of many former Confederates did the latent spirit of radicalism raise its head. Although alienated by the abusive attacks of conservative editors and the hostility of the white community, dominant white Republicans in the convention were fundamentally too similar to the old citizens in their racial and political attitudes to frame a radical constitution for the state. Certainly neither the Republican majority nor even the Radical vanguard had any thought of democratic leveling. The Republican delegates, whether moderate or Radical, had as their dominant objective reforms that would expurgate the profane and retrogressive spirit of rebellion and would also vitalize republican institutions in Mississippi, including the principles of freedom, tolerance, and Union. Even the concepts of Negro suffrage and mass education were advanced more to achieve this purpose, along with the omnipresent partisan purpose—to win political control of the state—than to advance the cause of democracy in the state and in the South.

If black suffrage, which had been required by Congress, is excluded from consideration, the constitutional convention of 1868 actually restricted democratic practices in Mississippi, reversing the egalitarian direction set by the constitution of 1832—a direction that made Mississippi, according to a careful scholar of prewar

83. *Ibid.*, 586, 587–88, 597–98, 745–46.
84. *Ibid.*, 719–20.

southern political institutions, the most democratic state in the South during the late antebellum period.[85] Not only were thousands of whites to be disfranchised and barred from office by the proposed constitution of 1868, but judges and local militia officers were now to be appointed by the governor. Furthermore, permanent legislative apportionment was to be based on the number of registered voters, not on the population, and the convention's temporary division of seats in the legislature, by following the eastern practice of gerrymandering, could very well establish a precedent for the maldistribution of legislative places.

This analysis does not intend to suggest that the constitution was not a progressive document. Indeed it was; but historians have exaggerated the democratic purposes and achievement of the framers. In addition to the extension of suffrage to blacks, the article on public education, provisions protecting the fundamental civil rights of blacks (however ambiguous on advanced rights for the race), and the clause requiring that taxation be equitable, with property paying its just share, were all progressive measures.

Not surprisingly, conservatives would admit no virtue in the constitution or the purposes of its framers. To the vast majority of Mississippi whites the provisions for the massive enfranchisement of blacks and the massive disfranchisement of former Confederates stamped the document as radical and as one that would revolutionize the state if ratified. As a result the old citizens entered the ratification campaign with a fierce determination to defeat the constitution and overcome "the Mongrel despotism which the carpet-bag aliens and their African confederates are seeking to foist upon the people."[86]

85. Ralph A. Wooster, *The People in Power: Courthouse and Statehouse in the Lower South 1850–1860* (Knoxville, 1969), 21.
86. Jackson *Clarion*, May 19, 1868.

5

The Crucible of the New Order:
The Campaign of 1868

The opponents of Republican reconstruction did not even wait for the "Black and Tan" Convention to assemble in January, 1868, before launching efforts to organize Mississippians into a conservative coalition to defeat the constitution. The visionary policy of "masterly inactivity," inspired by George L. Potter's Constitutional Union party, was abandoned in the wreck of the fall 1867 election. Nevertheless, Potter and his associates hoped to change the party's strategy and once again lead the crusade against the "mongrels." With this in mind, they called a meeting of the Constitutional Union party to be held at Jackson on January 15.[1] Representatives from only twenty counties responded, and in order to present a broader front to the people, the delegates—who were mostly former Whigs—agreed to invite members of the press convention, then in session in Jackson, to join them. These newspapermen eagerly accepted the invitation and poured into the meeting hall.[2] Much to the dismay of the Potter stalwarts, who had long been adversaries of the party of secession, the new element quickly subverted the meeting and hoisted the tattered banner of the state Democratic party. The main instigators of the take-over were the Barksdale "submissionists" of 1867 and the McCardle extremists or Bourbons, the leading factions in the influential Mississippi press association. Although opponents in 1867, they now agreed on reconstruction policy. Potter bitterly protested the insurgents' violation of good manners, charging that once inside the meeting hall they arrogantly "did not stop at advising but proceeded to action, as if the Constitutional Union party were defunct and its members all transferred into Democrats."[3]

Despite Potter's opposition, however, victory for the Barksdale-

1. Meridian *Semi-Weekly Gazette*, December 14, 1867; George L. Potter to William N. Whitehurst, December 31, 1867, in Whitehurst Papers; *Hinds County Gazette*, January 3, 1868.

2. New Orleans *Picayune*, January 18, 1868.

3. Natchez *Tri-Weekly Courier*, February 3, 1868.

McCardle coalition occurred on the first day when the convention by a slim majority adopted a committee report endorsing the principles of the national Democratic party and assuming its name. In an effort to placate Potter followers the convention selected Amos R. Johnston, a prominent Union Whig and Potterite, as permanent chairman of the body.[4] The success of the insurgents inspired the gleeful McCardle to publish an "obituary" for the Constitutional Union party, concluding in his customary style that the failure of the movement "has served to teach self-constituted leaders of the people that their influence is not great because they think it is."[5]

In spite of his smugness, McCardle was correct in claiming that the Constitutional Union party could not command sufficient support for its continuance. Potterites had no national organization, and without such a base the party could never have much strength. Few politicians could be expected to develop enthusiasm for a purely local party that could not command public patronage. On the other hand a successful national Democratic party could provide sustenance for affiliated local organizations and, moreover, constituted the only force in the North that might yet reverse the federal government's reconstruction policy. Indeed, the prospect for redemption under Democratic auspices appeared promising in early 1868. The political fortunes of the national party were on the upswing after its victories in the fall elections, and under its leadership opposition to Republican reconstruction and Negro suffrage appeared to be growing by leaps and bounds in the North, providing renewed hope for southern conservatives in their struggle to escape Radical domination.

The old Democratic leaders in the state—men whose antebellum politics had been narrowly sectional—viewed southern salvation in 1867–1868 in a more national perspective, despite their anti-Republican bias, than did Potter stalwarts of Whig antecedents, who traditionally had prided themselves on a broad approach to critical issues but were now unable to grasp the national significance of their problems. As a part of their plan to win northern support, former secession leaders like Barksdale and Albert

4. New York *Times*, January 16, 1868; Vicksburg *Times*, January 17, 1868; New Orleans *Picayune*, January 18, 1868.
5. Vicksburg *Times*, January 17, 1868.

Gallatin Brown eschewed sectional recriminations in 1867–1868, indicating instead a strong desire to restore close ties with northerners, to promote the large-scale extension of eastern capital, and to entice Yankee settlers to the area.[6] These Mississippi spokesmen, who had become practitioners of the art of realpolitik since the tragic failure of their separatist policies, felt that the issues of reconstruction and Negro suffrage ought to be debated on the high plane of national interest, involving the vital concerns of northerners as well as southerners. Specifically, this meant that northern sympathy for race and kin and for constitutional legitimacy should be carefully and persistently cultivated by southern conservatives. The imposition of black suffrage and Radical rule in the South should be presented as a crime against American civilization itself, a crime that would eventually affect northern society. As Barksdale expressed it: "The cause of civil liberty and constitutional freedom is the same in every portion of the country; and the act that establishes negro government in the South establishes a negro balance of power in the Federal government. The blow that paralyzes the industry of the South falls upon the manufacturing interests of the East and upon the producing classes of the West."[7]

Barksdale and associates therefore recognized the latent racism in the North and the self-interest of important commercial groups there, specifically those that sought to reenter the provisions and cotton trades in the lower South. They consequently expected sympathetic northerners, despite the persistence of wartime hatreds, soon to assert themselves through the auspices of the Democratic party and rescue Mississippi and the South from the impending Radical supremacy. Southerners could "rely upon the intelligence, patriotism and magnanimity of the Northern people" to check the diabolical schemes of social and political revolution that the Republican Congress had set in motion, Barksdale confidently declared. By the time of the national elections in the fall, these conservatives predicted, the northern reaction to radicalism would be complete and Democrats would sweep the Republicans from power in Wash-

6. See the Jackson *Clarion*, February 28, March 30, April 8, May 6, 1868; the Meridian *Semi-Weekly Gazette*, August 21, 1867; and the Vicksburg *Herald*, August 29, September 2, October 15, 1868.

7. Jackson *Clarion*, March 17 (quote), May 6, 11, 1868.

ington, thereby ending the Radical program for the South and restoring the region's natural leaders to power.[8]

Since Republicans constituted a majority at the polls in Mississippi, white unity in the forthcoming election on the Black and Tan constitution was of the greatest essence to the conservative cause. The national redemption from congressional "tyranny," according to the Democratic timetable, could not possibly occur until after Mississippi had voted on the question of ratifying the work of the constitutional convention. If conservatives did not unite in the election, the Radical constitution would be imposed upon the state regardless of what occurred in the national contests of the fall. But although most conservatives realized that white unity was crucial, divisiveness reared its head immediately after the Democrats captured control of the Constitutional Union convention in January. Potter and his chief lieutenant, David W. Shelton, stalked out of the meeting, declaring that they would have no part of the new anti-Radical party. In a scathing denunciation of what they described as a Democratic conspiracy to regain its lost influence in Mississippi, the two charged that the coup had been masterminded by politicos who in 1867 had "belonged to that imposing executive committee of the Conservative Reconstruction party—the little party that lived in Jackson."[9]

The legend of a "Jackson clique" of Democrats, presided over by Barksdale and Brown and leading the state into rebellion, was a vivid memory for many Whigs, and they were quick to be aroused to indignation by charges that the cabal had been revived.[10] A Potterite and Union Whig of north Mississippi later recalled his chagrin at the Democratic coup, since, as he wrote, in 1867–1868 the

8. *Ibid.*, February 28, 1868; Natchez *Weekly Democrat*, January 13, July 20, August 3, 1868. James Lynch, the indefatigable Negro leader in the state, asserted at this time that white Mississippians would now be reconciled to congressional reconstruction and the new order had they not been incited to opposition by northern Democratic successes in the fall, 1867, elections and by the anti-Republican harangues of the party's leadership in the North. "The Democratic organs of the worst type are the educators of public sentiment in Mississippi"—specifically the LaCrosse *Democrat*, the Philadelphia *Age*, and the New York *World*—Lynch declared. His comments appear in the New York *Tribune*, January 16, 1868.

9. Natchez *Tri-Weekly Courier*, February 3, 1868.

10. Actually, the Constitutional Union party was vulnerable to the same charge, since the movement had begun in Jackson and several of its leaders, including Potter and Shelton, were residents of that town.

Constitutional Union party "bid fair to be a party of the people, but secession Democrats who [had] ruined the state could not rest content until they [had] ruined our party also. The editor of the Clarion led the onslaught." He admitted, however, that the Democrats had persuaded most of the Potterites to support "a party we detested, on the plea that in that way only could Mississippi be brought into the Union on a sound basis. We succumbed, for we wanted Union and peace."[11]

After the convention prominent secessionists like Brown, fearing a white reaction to the sudden Democratic revival, wisely took back seats and permitted others to lead the anti-Radical movement. Old Democrats also feared that if they were too conspicuous in the new party many Whigs might be persuaded to cast their lots with the Republicans. Partly as a result of Democratic self-denial, former Whig leaders, with the exception of Potter diehards and a few like Alcorn who affiliated with the Republican party, sublimated their traditional political prejudices and joined in the crusade to rally whites under the Democratic banner. Some of these new Democrats undertook the task of convincing rank-and-file devotees of Henry Clay that they would not be struck dead by a bolt of lightning if they temporarily called themselves "Democrats" and consorted with old secessionists. Former United States Senator Walker Brooke, who had supported the Potter movement in 1867, reminded fellow Whigs that "it is the Democratic party that is now fighting our battles to the North, or that can fight them with any prospect of success. . . . It is and ever has been a States' Right party, and we can now appreciate the excellence of its creed."[12] Giles M. Hillyer, the influential Whig editor of the Natchez *Courier*, would not go so far as to pay homage to the

11. "Union Whig" to the Friar's Point *Weekly Delta*, April 28, 1869. For the tortured explanations of some Whigs who supported the decision in the convention, see the Jackson *Clarion*, January 30, February 5, 1868. In the latter issue, one Whig correspondent declared that although the Democratic party in the past had "practiced enormities," these had been far exceeded "by the bold, impudent and devilish machinations of the Republican party." Now only the Democratic party could save the country, and the writer called on Whigs to lay aside their prejudices toward that party and join "the army of Liberty." Then, after Republican despotism had been crushed at the ballot box, Whigs, this writer said, would "be free to support such new issues as may be presented."

12. Walker Brooke to Edward M. Yerger, January 4, 1868, in Vicksburg *Times*, February 5, 1868.

states' rights creed of his antebellum adversaries, but he insisted that former Whigs, adrift without a party organization, must accept fellowship with the national Democratic party and agree to be called Democrats if a white man's government was to be preserved in Mississippi and radicalism defeated in Washington. Prominent Union Whigs like Governor Humphreys, William T. Martin of Natchez, Amos R. Johnston of Jackson, and Sylvanus Evans, the leading Whig of east Mississippi, also gave early encouragement to the movement for the union of whites in the Democratic party.[13]

Whigs indeed had little cause to feel slighted in the state and local organization of the revived Democratic party. In several politically significant counties they actually assumed the initiative in the formation of Democratic associations.[14] In Adams County (Natchez), where Whigs were traditionally strong, Martin, who claimed to have been the last man in the state to canvass for the Union during the secession crisis but who later served in the Confederate army as a major general, dominated the Democratic movement from its inception. The only bona fide Democrat Martin brought into the counsels of the local party was Paul A. Botto, the able editor of the Natchez *Democrat*. Whigs also clearly provided the county leadership for the Democratic organizations in Warren (Vicksburg) and Noxubee in east Mississippi. In many county associations a deliberate effort was made to divide party responsibilities equally among old Democrats and Whigs, usually reserving for a prestigious Union Whig the position of president. Even in some counties where Whigs were few in number, such as Lee County in northeast Mississippi, they were given equal status with Democrats in the new organizations.[15]

The same distribution policy was employed in the selection of

13. Natchez *Tri-Weekly Courier*, January 8, 13, 1868; Jackson *Clarion*, January 11, 18, 1868; Vicksburg *Times*, January 11, 1868.

14. These findings are based on an examination of the extant proceedings of several local Democratic meetings, recorded in the Vicksburg *Times*, February 9, 1868, the Natchez *Tri-Weekly Courier*, January 31, 1868, the Jackson *Clarion*, February 5, 12, 18, 20, 22, 1868, the *Hinds County Gazette*, February 14, 1868, and in Julia Kendel, "Reconstruction in Lafayette County," *Publications of the Mississippi Historical Society*, XIII (1913), 250.

15. Only in one county, Madison, is there evidence that Whigs were missing from the new Democratic leadership; however, the most prominent Douglas or Union Democrat in the county was involved in the first meeting of the local association.

officers for the state party organization and for delegates to the national Democratic convention of 1868. Such an arrangement was necessary not only to secure the support of rank-and-file Whigs, who had constituted about 40 percent of the antebellum electorate, but also to cultivate the support of Douglas or Union Democrats and postwar independents. These political elements were generally opposed to the resuscitation of a fire-eating Democracy and looked to the Union-Whig leadership for assurances that the new Democratic party was conservative and would exclude "the chiefs of sinners" from its leadership. In fact, antisecessionist sentiment so threatened white political unity in Mississippi in 1868 that Barksdale, himself one of the leading sinners of 1860–1861, made a special plea that secession Democrats not be left out of the state convention scheduled for late February.[16] Thus it appears that although Barksdale Democrats were the prime movers in the January, 1868, coup d'etat that destroyed the Whig-dominated Constitutional Union party, the new Democratic party replacing it —actually an anti-Radical coalition of whites rather than a restoration of the antebellum organization—soon found itself to a remarkable extent in the hands of former Whigs. These old-line Whigs were more broadly representative of postwar Whiggery in Mississippi than Potter and his uncompromising followers who had lost control of the conservative movement.

In an atmosphere electrified by the meeting of the "Black and Tan" Convention nearby, state Democrats convened at Jackson on February 19 to map plans for the thorough organization of whites in the ratification campaign. The Democratic convention brought together for the first time since the war most of the surviving giants of the old antebellum parties. Noticeably missing, for different reasons, were Democrats Jefferson Davis and Lucius Q. C. Lamar and Whigs William L. Sharkey and Potter.[17] Answering the roll call were such important past Democratic leaders as Brown, who as governor for two terms and a former member of both the United

16. Jackson *Clarion*, February 19, 20, 21, 1868.
17. Actually, Jefferson Davis, who had recently been released from federal confinement, was in Jackson a few days before the Democratic convention met, but evidently he did not comment on the course of southern reconstruction. A list of the delegates to the convention may be found in the Vicksburg *Times*, February 21, 1868. No effort is made to give the numerous sources used to extract the background information on these leaders.

States and Confederate senates, had been more consistently influential in Mississippi affairs than any other politician, including Davis; Barksdale, the state's most prominent editor, celebrated as both the Warwick of Mississippi politics and the "war-horse of secession Democracy" and having served as chairman of the state's delegation to the ill-fated Charleston convention in 1860 and representative to the Confederate Congress; Otho R. Singleton of Canton, who had served for several terms in the United States Congress and later in the Confederate one; John D. Freeman of Jackson, a former congressman and state attorney general; Wiley P. Harris, another former member of Congress, "the unchallenged leader of the state bar," a states' rights advocate, and a delegate to the 1861 Montgomery convention that formed the Confederacy— though he nonetheless opposed secession as late as 1860 and worked as early as 1864 for the restoration of the state to the Union; Thomas J. Wharton of Jackson, the state attorney general during the war and one of the most influential Democrats in Mississippi; and Winfield Scott Featherston of Holly Springs, an antebellum congressman and popular Confederate general. Also included in this distinguished group were two prominent Douglas Democrats, William L. Hemingway of Carroll County, who at the time of the February meeting was also serving as a conservative delegate in the constitutional convention, and George Washington Brooke of Rankin County. Except for Brooke, all of these Democrats later played important roles in the so-called redemption of the state from Republican rule.

Heading the list of outstanding Union Whigs in the convention was John W. C. Watson of Holly Springs, a former Confederate senator, leader of the conservative faction in the constitutional convention, and one of the most influential men in the state during the early Reconstruction period. Present also was Amos R. Johnston, the brilliant lawyer who was to campaign as vigorously and as consistently against radicalism during Reconstruction as he had against the antebellum secessionists. Another outstanding Whig lawyer in the convention was William Yerger, a justice on the state supreme court during the 1850s and a persistent Unionist during the war who met secretly with General Sherman in 1864 in a premature effort to secure the reconstruction of the state. A reluctant politician, Yerger had exercised considerable behind-the-scenes influence during presidential reconstruction.[18]

Although not as well known in the state as several of his convention colleagues, Horatio F. Simrall of Warren and Wilkinson counties possessed one of the best legal minds in the Mississippi Valley. A native of Kentucky, Simrall had begun his career as a member of the legislature of that state, and before moving to Mississippi in 1861 he had occupied a chair of law at the University of Louisville and had also been selected to the Confederate "council" for Kentucky. After the war he led the dominant Whig faction in the Mississippi legislature that drew up the Black Code. He also served as a delegate to the ill-fated National Union or Johnson convention that met in Philadelphia in 1866. The following year Simrall supported the cooperationist movement, but in reaction to the radicalization of the constitutional convention he announced in early 1868 his support for the reorganization of the state Democratic party. Despite the emotionalism surrounding Reconstruction issues, he retained his sense of perspective and moderation regarding postwar affairs. In 1869 Simrall again urged Mississippians to support congressional policies in the South, and when the Republicans came to power in 1870 Governor Alcorn appointed him to the state supreme court. In 1873, in one of the most celebrated Mississippi court decisions of the Reconstruction era, Simrall wrote the majority opinion sustaining the advanced and controversial civil rights bill enacted by the Republicans. Interestingly, it was not until after Reconstruction and his retirement from the bench that he became a Republican partisan. Simrall's long public career ended in 1890 when he served as the only regular Republican in the constitutional convention that disfranchised Mississippi blacks.

Whig editors were very much in evidence in the Democratic convention. The most prominent of these was George W. Harper of the *Hinds County Gazette*, who had no rival as a persistent Whig and opponent of radicalism from 1844 when he came to the state and established his newspaper until his retirement in 1884.

18. Governor Humphreys, a Whig, did not attend the convention because he feared that General Gillem might remove him from office for participating in antireconstruction politics. Nevertheless, he was very much available for consultation with the delegates, and his private secretary represented him in the convention as a delegate.

Present also were Whig journalists not known for their opposition to extremism. The fiery trio of McCardle, A. J. Frantz, and "Prince Edward" Yerger sought to put the convention on record as excluding Negroes from participation in the revived Democratic party.[19] But though the convention opposed black suffrage, the majority of the delegates rejected as inexpedient the extremists' proposal for the drawing of the color line, since in certain key counties conservatives hoped to persuade Negroes to vote with them in the election on the constitution.

The February convention, presided over by Union Whig John T. Lamkin, quickly perfected the state Democratic organization, chose delegates to the national convention, and drew up a declaration of principles for the party. An equal number of Whigs and Democrats were selected as delegates to the national convention and as members of the state executive committee; an effort was even made to divide committee assignments in the convention between the two old parties. Walker Brooke, one of the most influential Whigs in the river counties, chaired the important committee on resolutions. This committee brought in a report, which was adopted, calling on whites to organize thoroughly in their communities and use all "constitutional and peaceful means" to defeat the constitution that was being framed by the "unprincipled enemies of liberty."[20] The delegates proclaimed that the contest transcended the borders of Mississippi and even the South, since "the defeat of Radicalism in the approaching political struggle constitutes the only hope which the American people can reasonably cherish for the restoration of Constitutional Liberty, to ourselves and the coming generations of our posterity." It was the moral duty of all Americans, of both political parties, to unite their energies for the purpose of defeating "that odious and dangerous faction," the Radical party, which represented only a minority of the

19. Vicksburg *Times*, February 22, 1868. Two postwar northern settlers participated in the convention—Charles H. Townsend, who had been a delegate to the constitutional convention, and R. B. Avery, an adventurer who would later abandon the conservatives for the Republican party and become a confidant of Ames. Appearing also at the convention was the brazen R. C. Merryman, the Union League organizer in Lauderdale County and a native of Virginia who had achieved temporary sainthood in the eyes of Mississippi Bourbons by being expelled from the Black and Tan Convention.

20. Minutes of the state Democratic convention proceedings may be found in the Jackson *Clarion*, February 21, 1868, and the Vicksburg *Times*, February 22, 1868.

people. The purpose of the congressional Radicals was clear, the convention's statement of principles declared; it was "to give the balance of political power to the ignorant negroes of the South, [in order] to secure their own political ascendancy, not only over these States, but in the government of the United States, regardless of the true interests of the two races, and the prosperity and happiness of the American people." If successful, the Radical party would "inevitably ruin and degrade the republic" and would most likely culminate in the establishment of "a huge military despotism in the land." The Democratic delegates blamed Radical policies for the postwar economic recession and the attendant unemployment of large numbers of whites in the West and the Northeast. In essence, then, the convention adopted the Barksdale approach of placing the Mississippi reconstruction struggle in a national context and appealing to "fair-minded Northerners," believing that people of this persuasion now constituted a majority in the North and would aid the South's white leadership in overthrowing "the yoke of negro government."

The Democratic platform conceded little to the requirements of Congress that blacks be given the ballot and extended fundamental civil rights. Nevertheless, it avoided the more blatant expressions of racism advocated by Bourbons in the convention, perhaps a significant achievement in view of the emotionalism existing in the white community as the constitutional convention undertook its work. The delegates resolved:

> We will, in good faith and willingly, aid in securing to the colored race, security of person and property, and full guarantees against oppression or injustice as freedmen; cherishing against them no feeling of hostility, and desiring that they may elevate themselves in the scale of humanity by mental culture to any extent which they are capable; but their ignorance and incapacity to exercise the privilege of suffrage, and to discharge the responsibilities of making laws and holding office, forbid that we consent to invest them with these privileges, or to consent to any legislation designed to establish the political or social equality of the white and black races—much less the subordination of the former to the latter, as advocated by the Radical party.

The Democratic convention postponed a decision on the question of running candidates for the offices of the government that would be selected in the ratification election, deferring the matter to the state executive committee. They also gave the committee the responsibility for coordinating the activities of the county associations and scheduling speakers for a thorough canvass of the state prior to the election.

The Democratic meeting had hardly adjourned when it became apparent that thousands of Mississippi whites, regardless of their former political affiliations and despite their abhorrence of the work of the constitutional convention, were not convinced that the 1867 strategy of "masterly inactivity" should be abandoned. Demoralized by the preponderance of the Negro vote in Mississippi and believing that the high-riding Radicals in Washington and Jackson would impose their settlement on the state anyway, many whites preferred to ignore the political tempest swirling around them. As they perceived events, the only hope for deliverance from Radical domination rested with the success of the national Democratic party, and while awaiting redemption they rejected any action by local conservatives—specifically participation in the ratification election—that would tend to give legitimacy to congressional reconstruction. Since national political developments held the key to redemption, the impeachment proceedings in Congress, where their defender, President Johnson, faced removal at the hands of determined Radicals, received the close attention of conservatives in the spring of 1868. A verdict in favor of Johnson, they believed, would surely foretell the defeat of the Republican party in the national elections of the fall, and the bitter cup of military reconstruction would quickly pass from them.[21]

The problems associated with making a living during the hard times of early 1868 created an additional barrier to the Democratic effort to arouse white voters to political action. Most white Mississippians focused their attention in 1868 and for much of the Reconstruction era on pressing private matters, generally avoiding political affairs. However intense these citizens' opposition to black rights and Republican rule might be, their diaries and correspon-

---

21. Entries for February 17, 24, 1868, in Agnew Diary; Jackson *Clarion*, March 9, 28, 1868; Oscar J. E. Stuart to his niece, February 14, 1868, and Stuart to Anna G. Sessions, February 17, 1868, both in Dimitry Papers; Natchez *Weekly Democrat*, March 23, 1868; *House Miscellaneous Documents*, 40th Cong., 3rd Sess., No. 53, pp. 44–45.

dence indicate an overwhelming concern with private matters—family affairs, crops, gardens, sickness, death, religion, and the numerous mundane things in life.[22] People of all classes found a greater source of strength in the family circle than in the politics of Reconstruction, an activity that offered them little practical relief.

On the other hand the spectre of Radical domination and black equality motivated some whites to go beyond the normal bounds of political dissent and give birth in the state to the terroristic Ku Klux Klan. Although organized in neighboring Tennessee in 1866, there is no evidence that the Klan appeared in Mississippi before the meeting of the Black and Tan Convention. Reputedly, General Nathan Bedford Forrest introduced the organization into the state when he was supervising the construction of the Selma, Marion, and Memphis Railroad. Evidently he formed dens in Monroe County,[23] one of the few predominantly black counties where the Klan thrived during Reconstruction; however, this activity appears to have been the extent of Forrest's contribution to the organization of the order in Mississippi. Generally, societies of this secret order arose spontaneously, only rarely forming through any centralized effort of a group of shadowy organizers. And in fact, the Ku Klux Klan had only a fitful beginning in 1868 and was not at all the terror to Republicans during the ratification campaign that it later became.

The most fertile areas for Klan activity in the state, and the scene of most of the armed clashes between terrorists and Republicans until the revolutionary events of 1875 engulfed all of Mississippi, were counties where the proportion of blacks to whites was about equal. Early in 1868 the Ku Klux Klan and its somewhat milder associate in intimidation, the Knights of the Black Cross, sprang up in Kemper, Chickasaw, Clarke, Lauderdale, Franklin, and Pike counties, all with a fairly balanced black-white ratio in the population.[24] Elsewhere these societies of the night found little encour-

22. See, for example, the entries and items for early 1868 in the Agnew and Darden diaries; the Pinson Family Papers; and the Alexander B. Swanson and Mrs. Obedience Yates Family Papers, Mississippi Department of Archives and History.

23. Ernest F. Puckett, "Reconstruction in Monroe County," *Publications of the Mississippi Historical Society*, XI (1910), 128.

24. Meridian *Chronicle*, March 17, 27, May 20, October 22, 1868; *House Reports*, 42nd Cong., 2nd Sess., No. 22, Part II, Vol. I, 215–16.

agement from whites for a terror campaign against the Radicals.[25] Editor Garnet Andrews, who in 1875 would be one of the masterminds behind the celebrated Mississippi plan to rid the state of Republican control, expressed in 1868 the sobering view of many black-belt conservatives toward Klan activities when he wrote that white terrorists were more dangerous enemies to the South than all of the carpetbaggers and scalawags put together. "The Ku Klux Klan, if there be such an order," Andrews declared, has given "our enemies an opportunity to misrepresent us—to say nothing of the proneness of such organizations to breed strife and bloodshed. . . . Let us strike at the root of the evil and call the offenders to account."[26] In overwhelmingly black Hinds County, Barksdale condemned the activities of these clandestine associations as detrimental to the success of the Democrats in the forthcoming election on the constitution.[27]

Reasons other than the immediate political one caused whites in black districts to condemn the Ku Klux Klan. They believed that in a local confrontation between the races, which would probably result from Klan appearances in their midst, outnumbered whites would experience the swift, violent wrath of aroused blacks before order could be restored. The cause of civilization, as the conservatives put it, could not stand a racial war. Long tortured by the fear of slave revolts, these conservatives during the hard winter of 1867–1868 were reminded anew of the difficulties of maintaining racial order in the black counties. They viewed with grave apprehension any attempt to organize inflammatory white supremacist societies in their communities, a development that most assuredly would upset the delicate social balance.[28] Furthermore, black-belt planters realized that the employment of Klan tactics of coercion and terror would further disrupt the plantation labor system, the

25. For example, in northeast Mississippi where blacks were no threat to white supremacy the knowledgeable minister-teacher Samuel A. Agnew commented in his diary that a Klan unit had appeared near Corinth, but the organization was so obscure in the area that he had no idea what its purposes were. Entry for March 24, 1868, in Agnew Diary.

26. Yazoo City *Mississippi Democrat*, October 22, 1868.

27. Jackson *Clarion*, April 28, 1868.

28. Beulah (Miss.) *Bolivar Times*, August 27, 1870; Natchez *Weekly Democrat*, October 25, 1871, quoting the Carrollton *Conservative*; excerpts from conservative newspapers in the Jackson *Pilot*, April 18, June 6, 1871; Greenville (Miss.) *Weekly Times*, September 12, 26, 1874.

stability of which was crucially important for economic recovery. Betty Beaumont, a woman merchant in one of these counties who kept a journal of local affairs during Reconstruction, observed that the mere rumor of the organization of a secret white order in Wilkinson County was enough to cause alarm among thoughtful whites and to unsettle black tenants. Reports of the appearance of the Klan, Mrs. Beaumont wrote, were "driving our best labor from our midst, both black and white, which will eventually impoverish the country, as labor is its wealth. The colored element are aware of that fact. They know that the white man can make nothing if they leave the plantations, although there are many hard-working farmers; but their numbers cannot fill the places of thousands of negroes who are employed on all the plantations in Wilkinson County —one of the largest cotton-growing counties in the State."[29]

Throughout the state the presence of the military and the remnants of the Freedmen's Bureau caused unreconstructed whites to pause before joining terroristic societies for the purpose of overawing the new political element. The thoroughness with which General Ord had suppressed armed bands of men in 1867 was still fresh in the minds of Mississippians; and even though this resolute general had been replaced in command, most malignantly inclined whites in 1868 saw the wisdom of staying out of clandestine associations. The political campaign of that year was by no means free from violence and intimidation; however, organized acts of violence against the supporters of the constitution were rare. The secret societies that existed usually expressed their racial and political hostilities by preparing and sending relatively safe and pompous pronouncements to Republican leaders, indicating that the presence of these Radicals in Mississippi could no longer be justified and that in the name of humanity (their own) they should leave the state before bloodshed occurred. Although not oblivious to the interests of "humanity," the recipients of these tidings did not appear to be overly impressed by the attention given to their welfare by the Klan. The carpetbag editor of the Vicksburg *Republican* even suggested that such communications were mainly the work of "rattle-brained youngsters" and not the ghostly Ku Klux

29. Betty Beaumont, *A Business Woman's Journal: A Sequel to "Twelve Years of My Life"* (Philadelphia, 1888), 301–302.

Klan.[30] Nevertheless, when the campaign became heated and the stakes in the election assumed sacred dimension for many whites, individual acts of intimidation, economic coercion, and violence against Republicans occurred with unsettling frequency, despite the presence of the army.

The Democratic leadership viewed with alarm the reports of intimidation that came to its attention, believing that coercive tactics would backfire and result in a bloc Negro vote for the constitution. Furthermore, stories of Klan outrages, which the national Radical press would eagerly exploit, could easily erode sympathy in the North for the conservative cause and defeat the Democrats in the fall election.

At first the Democratic strategy was simply one of mobilizing whites into a solid phalanx of voters that would march to the polls and vote against the constitution and its hangers-on. Somewhat belatedly, and only after reports were received that a relatively large number of blacks in Arkansas had supported their former masters in that state's ratification contest, conservatives realized that some Negro votes were necessary for their success in the election. In an amazing bit of campaign effrontery, Democrats appealed for black support without first dropping the racist harangues on the depravity, irrationality, and inferiority of Negroes. When the campaign reached its climax in late May and early June, however, conservatives moderated their language and began carefully to cultivate the black vote. Planters, especially, were advised by the Democratic hierarchy to cease threatening to dismiss Republican laborers and to appeal instead to their reason.[31] Reminiscent of the unfruitful white courtship of the freedmen in 1867, conservatives invited blacks to free barbecues, where political food for thought was dispensed in a more lavish fashion than pork. The new Democrats, however, were determined to avoid the mistakes of 1867 and to overcome black suspicion of the conservative leadership. Such fire-eaters of late memory as Brown, Wiley P. Harris, and Barksdale, who had been conspicuous in the cooperationist rallies of the past summer, were persuaded to forego these gatherings lest blacks be-

30. Vicksburg *Weekly Republican*, May 5, 1868; Warren, *Reminiscences of a Carpet-bagger*, 37–38.
31. Jackson *Clarion*, March 28, April 4, 7, 16, May 12, 28, 1868; Forest *Register*, April 1, 1868; *Hinds County Gazette*, June 5, 1868.

come disturbed by their presence. Appearing in their places were
such stalwart Union Whigs as Brooke, Johnston, Shelton, and even
Potter, who had suppressed his resentment of the name "Demo-
crat" and joined the new white coalition in the fight against the
Radicals.[32] In 1867 these men, as pillars of the Constitutional
Union party, would have nothing to do with Negro voters.

The results of the conservative courtship were the same as in
1867; almost without exception blacks rejected Democratic overtures. At one rally near Vicksburg, for example, a large body of
blacks, estimated in the thousands, attended a Democratic barbecue and rally during the day, but when night descended they "proceeded at once to the [Union] League rooms, where the Democracy they had imbibed during the day was pretty thoroughly 'cussed'
out of them."[33]

In some areas—usually outside the plantation districts—local
Democrats sought to put the economic screws to Negroes who
refused to cooperate. Lists of blacks who supported the Republican
ticket at the polls were to be compiled, with the not-so-subtle
threat that these laborers would be discharged from employment
after the election. When it became clear that the vast majority of
blacks intended to vote Republican regardless, conservatives
changed their tactics and began recording the names of those
freedmen who sided with them, a much more manageable task because of the paucity of black Democrats. Those Negroes voting
Democratic would receive "whatever favors it may be in the power
of our citizens to bestow," influential conservatives promised.[34] Although the Democratic policy of economic coercion influenced
some blacks to avoid Republican politics as the campaign came to
an end, this instrument of political control failed to achieve appreciable results because labor was at a premium in postwar Mississippi, and few planters could be found who would issue threats
that might boomerang and result in the loss of valuable workers. In
fact, many planters were surprisingly tolerant of the political activ-

32. Natchez *Weekly Democrat*, June 8, 1868; Vicksburg *Weekly Republican*, June 9,
1868; *Hinds County Gazette*, June 5, 1868; Jackson *Clarion*, May 28, 1868; *House Miscellaneous Documents*, 40th Cong., 3rd Sess., No. 53, pp. 238–39.
33. Vicksburg *Weekly Republican*, June 9, 1868.
34. Jackson *Clarion*, March 30, 1868; Natchez *Weekly Democrat*, July 6, 1868; Meridian
Chronicle, July 10, 1868.

ities of their tenants, hoping thereby to avoid further discontent on their plantations.[35]

Although they failed to sway Negro voters, conservative leaders made rapid progress in arousing whites to political action after the constitutional convention adopted the proscriptive clauses in April. Whites throughout the state, now finally convinced that the first line of defense against the forces of radicalism must be formed at home, responded with enthusiasm to the Democratic call for a thorough organization of county associations of the party. State Democratic chairman John D. Freeman urged the county units to appoint committees in each precinct which, among other things, would have the responsibility of conferring with each white voter in their district on the importance of his vote. In case of plantation disorders Freeman directed the precinct committees to become the local instrument for "the preservation of order and domestic tranquility and . . . the suppression of all secret political associations designed to sever the interests of the planter and the laborer." Freeman therefore conceived of these committees as functioning in a far broader context than the political exigencies demanded for conservatives. "The people will not fail to perceive," he announced, that the precinct committee structure "may be useful alike for political, agricultural and social purposes."[36] Except in isolated cases, neither the Democratic committeemen nor the county associations ever performed the regulatory tasks that Freeman outlined; the presence of the military, the strength of the Republican party in the plantation counties, and planter concern for labor stability combined to prevent the implementation of this design.

As the campaign progressed, a debate raged among conservatives on the issue of running candidates for office in the election. At first, Democrats were reluctant to advance candidates for positions under the "Black and Tan" constitution lest this act give legit-

35. Report of Gillem for quarter ending September 30, 1868, in Freedmen's Bureau Records, Microcopy Roll 59; J. H. Chapman to S. C. Greene, July 1, 1868, in Freedmen's Bureau Records, Mississippi; *House Miscellaneous Documents*, 40th Cong., 3rd Sess., No. 53, pp. 270–71; entries for June 23, 25, 1868, in Darden Diary.

36. Freeman's instructions may be found in the Jackson *Clarion*, April 28, 1868. Conservative leaders called on every white man to campaign actively. As the Forest *Register*, April 1, 1868, expressed it, "let every household be a Democratic club and see that the members of each club vote. . . . By so doing your children will rise up and call you blessed."

imacy to the document and to Radical reconstruction. But the decision of Congress to have Alabama reconstructed under its new constitution with its victorious slate of Republican officials, despite the fact that a majority of the registered voters (as provided by the 1867 acts) had failed to go to the polls, convinced Democratic leaders in Mississippi that they should nominate candidates. It now appeared to them that in order to checkmate the Radical scheme they must defeat both the constitution and the Republican candidates.[37] There would also be a residual benefit in running candidates; the appearance of popular conservatives on the ticket would attract apathetic whites to the polls where they would vote not only for their heroes but also against the adoption of the constitution.

Democratic leaders met in Jackson on May 12 and 13 to nominate candidates for state office, though they hoped these candidates would not need to serve under the Republican instrument of government. Again, most of the prominent men of the old political parties were present, and on the first day a representative from each of the late antebellum factions in the state (secession Democrat, Douglas Democrat, and Union Whig) addressed the convention. The effort to balance these three elements continued as nominations were made, with Governor Humphreys, a Confederate hero of Union-Whig antecedents, selected by acclamation to head the ticket. In making these selections, the Democratic convention chose men who were not disqualified by the reconstruction laws or by the proposed Fourteenth Amendment—that is, those persons who before the war had not held office and then supported the rebellion. No effort was made to meet the stringent officeholding requirements of the new constitution, which disqualified everyone who gave voluntary aid to the Confederacy except private soldiers in the southern army or those individuals who had supported the work of the constitutional convention.[38]

Conservatives, however, adopted a different policy for the nomination of members of the legislature. The Democratic leadership urged local supporters to select men for this branch of the govern-

37. Natchez *Weekly Democrat*, March 23, 1868; Jackson *Clarion*, March 26, April 4, 7, 1868; Forest *Register*, March 25, 1868.
38. Jackson *Clarion*, May 12, 13, 19, 1868.

ment who were clearly eligible to serve under the proposed constitution in case it was adopted. As members of the legislature, these conservatives could serve as the last line of defense against the radicalization of the state.[39]

This policy resulted in the selection of many men who had never before supported the party. Several of the conservative candidates, such as Charles H. Townsend, were postwar settlers from the North whom one scalawag journal ruefully referred to as "worthless adventurers who feel no interest in the prosperity of the country and are destitute of honor."[40] Most of the Democratic nominees, however, were Union Whigs and life-long antagonists of the party of Jefferson Davis and Albert Gallatin Brown. The Democrats advanced for office very few private soldiers (who were exempt from the proscriptive clauses in the constitution). One interesting exception was "Private" John M. Allen of northeast Mississippi who cut his political teeth in 1868 when he ran for the legislature, thereby beginning a long and colorful public career that included several terms in Congress during the late nineteenth century.[41]

Even though dominant politicians of the past were missing from the Democratic ticket, they were by no means silent when the 1868 campaign reached its peak. Brown, Lamar, Hiram Cassedy, who was Brown's right-hand man during the secession storm before the war, and the Seal political clan of the Gulf Coast took to the stump with a new zest for life after several years of public disfavor. They found themselves sharing the platform with old adversaries like Watson, Brooke, and Sharkey, who had recently returned from Washington where he had been fighting Misssissippi's reconstruction battles before the Supreme Court. Speaking opportunities abounded for everyone; numerous mass meetings were held in every county and at times joint debates materialized between conservative and Republican campaigners. When the Democratic campaign crested in June, the white masses, now thorough-

39. *Ibid.*, May 6, 19, 26, 1868; Forest *Register*, March 25, 1868; New Orleans *Picayune*, June 5, 1868.
40. Meridian *Chronicle*, June 2, 6, 1868. This conclusion is also based upon the identification of a large number of the conservative candidates for state office, the legislature, and Congress. A few county associations, however, disregarded the advice of their state party leaders and selected candidates without regard to their qualification under the new constitution.
41. Entry for June 15, 1868, in Agnew Diary.

ly behind their leadership, were attending political rallies in larger numbers than at any time since 1860. The candidates for state office toured Mississippi, speaking in open fields before huge, enthusiastic audiences and denouncing the constitution as the crowning infamy of the Radical scheme to oppress the whites of the state.[42]

For their campaign efforts, Humphreys and Attorney General Charles E. Hooker on the eve of the election were forcibly removed from office by General Irvin McDowell, the new military commander in Mississippi, who charged them with obstructing the enforcement of the reconstruction acts. Convinced that McDowell's baseness could be traced to his embarrassment by Confederates at the first battle of Bull Run, conservatives characterized his actions now as politically designed to ensure a Radical victory at the polls and as "a gross, wicked, disgraceful, and indefensible exercise of arbitrary power by an audacious and unprincipled military tyrant."[43] Actually, McDowell had hesitated in making the removals; however, after reading the act of July 19, 1867, he decided that the issue "was not a mere question, on my part, of expediency or propriety, but simply one of obedience to law." To replace Humphreys, whose caretaker duties under military reconstruction had not been so strenuous as to prevent him from serving simultaneously as the state agent for the New York Life Insurance Company and president of the Planters' Insurance Company of Mississippi, McDowell appointed General Adelbert Ames.[44] A comic-opera affair ensued as young Ames maneuvered to take possession of the governor's office and the executive mansion without a show of bayonets. In the end, however, Humphreys forced Ames's hand, and the Confederate hero was unceremoniously evicted from both places by a squad of men in blue.[45] Thus Ames

42. Entry for June 2, 1868, *ibid.*; *House Miscellaneous Documents*, 40th Cong., 3rd Sess., No. 53, p. 289. James B. Murphy, *L. Q. C. Lamar: Pragmatic Patriot* (Baton Rouge, 1973), 94–95. For numerous announcements of Democratic rallies and speakers, see the issues of the Jackson *Clarion* for late May, 1868.

43. William H. McCardle to President Johnson, June 16, 1868, in Johnson Papers; *Hinds County Gazette*, July 10, 1868.

44. Irvin McDowell to Ulysses S. Grant, June 15, 1868, in Johnson Papers; James Hays to Benjamin G. Humphreys, April 26, 1868, in Governors' Correspondence, Vol. 69; *Hinds County Gazette*, January 3, 1868.

45. This comic opera affair may be followed in the correspondence between the two adversaries, reported in *Appleton's Annual Cyclopaedia*, 1868, pp. 514–15.

began his Mississippi career in controversy; in 1876 he would end it in the same manner.

Like the Democracy, the Republican party girded for political battle well in advance of the election on the constitution. But unlike the conservatives, Republicans experienced no rising crescendo of support as the campaign progressed. When the constitutional convention convened in January, 1868, the future appeared bright for the Republican party in the state, in spite of the white masses' implacable hostility to its organization and to the reconstruction program it represented. During the party's first few months of existence Republican organizers had demonstrated considerable vigor and resourcefulness in marshaling most black voters and a few hundred whites into a political machine that won a smashing victory in its maiden election in the state. With this success under their belts, elated Republicans had reason to believe that additional recruits could be added as the organization was perfected in the interior during the coming months. A Negro majority of almost twenty thousand registered voters also gave the Republican leadership cause for optimism. Of course, Republicans realized that this advantage could be lost at the polls by a conservative campaign of intimidation; however, they felt that despite their differences with General Gillem the presence of the military would blunt any general Democratic effort along this line. Once established in power under their own constitution, Republicans expected to be able to take care of themselves. Even the problem of overconfidence among some party leaders, and the intraparty divisions that usually resulted from such an attitude, held no terrors for them, since they believed that all differences among Republicans would vanish when they locked horns with "rebel" adversaries in the campaign. It was in such a spirit of confidence—and alienation from the white masses of Mississippi—that the majority of the Republican delegates in the constitutional convention had approached the task of drawing up an instrument of government for the state, and it was in this mood that these same men, along with fifty-eight nondelegates, organized themselves into a state Republican convention in order to prepare for the critical ratification contest.

The Republican convention met at the state capitol on February 5, 1868, and quickly drew up a platform, nominated candidates for state office, and selected a new state executive committee. Of the

130 delegates to the convention only 27 represented white counties, and the overwhelmingly black counties were especially favored.[46] This imbalance in representation reflected not only the
locus of Republican strength in Mississippi but also the difficulties
involved in organizing even a nucleus around which to build a local
party in the white counties. The resolutions adopted by the convention made no special appeal to whites, as moderates like Joseph
W. Field desired. Most of the delegates thought the anticipated
bloc voting of blacks would ensure the Republicans of continuous
victories at the polls. Preferring the ambiguity of the 1867 platform, especially on the crucial question of the proscription of Confederates, the convention simply affirmed its support of the Union,
equal rights for all, and Grant for president.[47] The majority also
ignored the claims made by white counties for places on the state
ticket; of the seven Republican nominations for state office, all
went to white delegates from black counties. The small minority of
Negro delegates remained fairly quiet during the proceedings, but
they were clearly disappointed that a member of their race did not
receive a place on the state ticket.[48]

For governor, the Republican convention chose carpetbagger
Beroth B. Eggleston, whose restraint and skill as president of the
constitutional convention had impressed both moderates and Radicals in the party.[49] The other nominations were divided equally
between carpetbaggers and scalawags, and although two of them,

46. The Jackson *Clarion*, February 6, 1868, provides a list of the delegates to the state
Republican convention.

47. *Appleton's Annual Cyclopaedia*, 1868, p. 511; New York *Tribune*, February 14,
1868.

48. New York *Times*, February 7, 1868. A correspondent to the New York *Tribune* (February 14, 1868) claimed that blacks at the convention did not seek a nomination to state
office for a member of their race. White delegates, according to this correspondent, had
no objection in principle to having a black man on the Republican ticket, but they professed
to know of no Negro who had the experience to qualify. Although many of the black
leaders who later played prominent roles in Mississippi politics had not arrived in the
state (*e.g.* Blanche K. Bruce and James J. Spelman) or had not reached political maturity
(*e.g.* John R. Lynch and James Hill), this reason appears dubious. James Lynch and Thomas
W. Stringer, both men of considerable intelligence and ability, were on the scene in
1868 and would have been excellent candidates. Lynch, especially, had impressive credentials for public office, including rapport with conservative whites such as Barksdale; but a
fear among some carpetbaggers that he would subvert their dominance of the Negro vote
and thus weaken the state Republican party temporarily blunted his rise to political prominence. Harris, "James Lynch," 52, 58.

49. New York *Tribune*, February 14, 1868.

Robert J. Alcorn and Andrew J. Jamison, had sometimes voted with moderate Republicans in the Black and Tan Convention, moderate leaders Field, Herbert, and Stovall were ignored in the selections. Only the choice of Eggleston for governor satisfied all elements of the party.

Even before the convention adjourned, conflict broke out among party leaders when Radicals objected to the selection of carpet-bagger Jonathan Tarbell as chairman of the state executive committee. Although now leaning toward radicalism, Tarbell, a former Federal brigadier, had been too willing in 1867 to temporize on the proscription issue to be acceptable to many Radicals.[50] Tarbell's executive committee, dominated by the safely Republican river counties, subsequently dragged its feet in preparing for the ratification campaign. One month before the election there was no party organization in some interior counties, and the state committee had done nothing, concerned Republicans charged, to remedy the situation. Specifically, these critics pointed out, the party hierarchy had failed to send prominent speakers into the interior to encourage the formation of local units and to convince blacks of the necessity for voting Republican in the election. The public criticism of the executive committee by leading Republican newspapers threatened a serious breach in the party on the eve of the election. "Members of that committee are huddled down in Vicksburg," carpetbagger Edward Stafford of the influential Jackson *Pilot* wrote, "and it is very questionable if they can be induced to do anything that does not begin and end with Warren county, and in the interests of a few managers of party machinery in that locality."[51] Even the Vicksburg *Republican* of Warren County found cause for alarm in the lack of vigor displayed by the party hierarchy. The carpetbag editor of this journal lamented:

> With an active, vigilant and unscrupulous enemy, marshaled by men of ability and experience, who are rapidly affecting a complete organization of their forces, we find ourselves upon the very eve of the battle, wholly unprepared for the struggle.
>
> At no time, and in no place, has a political party had so much to lose, as the Republican party of Mississippi has on the issue which is soon to

50. Jackson *Clarion*, February 9, 1868.
51. As reported in the Vicksburg *Weekly Republican*, June 9, 1868. See also the Meridian *Chronicle*, May 13, 1868.

be presented to the people. With a very large preponderance of the voting population of the State unmistakably favorable to our cause, to suffer defeat is a crime. To insure success we have but to organize, and [in] order to do this, we must have leaders—true, tried and determined.[52]

A more fundamental reason for the Republican division than the failure of the leadership to organize the campaign properly was the triumph of the Radical proscription policy in the constitutional convention. The adoption of the clauses in the constitution proscribing the political privileges of former Confederates came as a shock to moderate Republicans who had ardently desired and labored for a strong white party in the state. Republicans who were removed from the cockpit of political agitation in Jackson charged that the delegates in agreeing to the disabling clauses had overreacted to the attacks in the Democratic press. The convention, these Republicans declared, had grievously misread the true sentiments of the white people and thereby had seriously damaged the prospects for a strong and durable party in Mississippi. They claimed that thousands of whites were not nearly so hostile to the convention as the delegates had come to believe from reading such vituperative journals as McCardle's Vicksburg *Times*, Frantz's Brandon *Republican*, and even Barksdale's Jackson *Clarion*. In fact, they asserted, a large number of whites who could not forget the past excesses of the Democratic party and who, as young men in many cases, looked to the future would have voted for the constitution and affiliated with the Republican party had proscription failed in the convention. But alas it had not, and hopes for a strong biracial Republican party in the state had been dealt a severe blow, these disappointed moderates moaned.[53]

Confronted with the threat of social pressure from their conservative neighbors, many disillusioned moderate Republicans, especially of the scalawag class, during the height of the campaign curtailed their political activities and remained safely at home. A

52. Vicksburg *Weekly Republican*, March 17, 1868.
53. *Ibid.*, May 12, 1868; Meridian *Chronicle*, April 21, 28, 1868; clipping from the Kosciusko *Chronicle*, 1869, in Niles Scrapbook, Vol. XLI; Archie C. Fisk to William E. Chandler, July 4, 1868, in William E. Chandler Papers; George Stovall to William T. Townsend, July 19, 1868, in Fourteenth Amendment Relief Papers, Mississippi; Horatio N. Ballard to George S. Boutwell, February 13, 1869, in Papers on Conditions in Mississippi.

few, like Jason Niles, continued to stump for party candidates and for the ratification of the constitution "as a matter of policy," but in debate they were quick to indicate their opposition to the proscriptive features of that document.[54]

Some scalawags, however, refused to concede the white vote to the Democrats without a fight. In the forefront of this effort were James Lusk Alcorn and two young former Confederate officers, Jefferson L. Wofford, editor of the Corinth *News*, and John R. Smith, editor of the Meridian *Chronicle*, who tried to mollify whites on the proscription issue and direct their attention to the progressive features of the constitution, especially the provision for free schools. Alcorn, a Union Whig who briefly served the Confederate cause as a brigadier general of Mississippi troops, spoke in almost every county in the state, denouncing the past radicalism of the Democratic fire-eaters and stressing the basic conservatism of the proposed constitution.[55] Few politicians in Mississippi history have been as bold and vigorous on the stump as this proud and haughty planter-lawyer of the Delta. Threats and intimidation, especially when associated in his mind with his old political adversaries, seemed only to increase Alcorn's determination to express his convictions and to show his contempt for the Democracy. No other Republican in the state campaigned as much or as widely for the party during Reconstruction.

Excited by the canvass of 1868 and dismayed by evidence of the widespread intimidation of blacks during the election, Alcorn wrote Elihu B. Washburne, Grant's influential political mentor, giving reasons for his intrepidity, as well as that of his scalawag friends, in campaigning for the constitution and the new order in Mississippi. The recent gains by the northern Democrats, he said, had provided renewed hope for the disunionists, both North and South. Democratic leaders looked to the presidential election of 1868 for success, but if they failed, Alcorn predicted that they would inaugurate another civil war. "I am a Southerner; I love peace rather than war; I have hoped for honorable and favorable

54. Allen White to J. F. Farnsworth, February 9, 1869, and Stovall to Townsend, July 19, 1868, both in Fourteenth Amendment Relief Papers, Mississippi; clipping from the Kosciusko *Chronicle*, 1869, in Niles Scrapbook, Vol. XLI; Vicksburg *Weekly Republican*, June 30, 1868.
55. New York *Tribune*, June 22, 1868.

terms in the settlement of the question of restoration, but I had rather see the country charred by the flames of a ten years' war than see the Jeff Davis tyranny again revived in the land. The Republican party has every thing staked on the issue; they must play boldly or they are beaten."[56] Alcorn affirmed his friendship for "the poor, docile negro race," which would be oppressed if the Democracy triumphed in the struggle. "Can it be possible," he asked Washburne, "that the northern people have made the negro free, [but] to be returned, the slave of society, to bear in such slavery the vindictive resentments that the satraps of Davis maintain to day towards the people of the North? Better a thousand times for the negro that the government should return him to the custody of his original owner, where he would have a master to look after his well being, than that his neck should be placed under the heel of a society, vindictive towards him because he is free." It was this attitude that impelled Alcorn to affiliate with the Republican party and to stump the state in 1868, even though he was not a candidate for office. He converted few whites to the cause during the campaign, but he demonstrated to many that the Republican party of Mississippi had a vigorous champion "to the manor born."

Pointing out that Negro suffrage was an accomplished fact, Jefferson L. Wofford, who mixed his editorials in the Corinth *News* with campaign speeches, refuted the notion that the adoption of the constitution would result in "social equality" and racially mixed schools. Like most scalawags, he emphasized the positive in the Republican program. From the traditionally impoverished hills of northeast Mississippi, this young Republican editor especially appealed to the economic interests of the people and largely ignored the political mistakes of the past. Economic recovery would not occur, Wofford asserted, until the state was restored to the Union

56. James L. Alcorn to Elihu B. Washburne, June 29, 1868, in Washburne Papers. Alcorn was not the only Mississippian at this time to envision another civil war. The intensity of the political campaign in the state and the climactic struggle between President Johnson and Congress in the impeachment proceedings caused many excitable people to conclude that an armed conflict was virtually inevitable. Alcorn's own pessimistic view of the situation was based to a certain extent upon opinions expressed to him by "the ignorant classes." This view was also advanced by conservative editor George W. Harper, who declared that a war between the forces of the president and the Radicals was the only way "to arrest the march of the Destroyers." *Hinds County Gazette*, March 20, 1868. See also Yerger to President Johnson, March 25, 1868, in Johnson Papers, and the Natchez *Weekly Democrat*, August 3, 1868.

and a civil government that could advance the material interests of the people was formed.[57]

On the other hand, fellow scalawag John R. Smith of the Meridian *Chronicle* pitched his appeal to whites primarily on the Democratic party's tragic record and on the need for racial cooperation in Reconstruction affairs. Not only was the Democratic party the author of secession and ruin in Smith's view, but also the party in its hell-bent determination to advance the class interests of the "landed aristocracy" had suppressed the aspirations of laboring whites. He castigated the traditional leaders for their failure to provide a system of education for the state. The Democratic rulers "did not dare to educate" the masses because "they well knew that 'knowledge is power,' and that no educated people would have consented to occupy the station to which yeoman whites had been assigned."[58] In carrying his class analysis a step further, Smith claimed that by appealing to racial prejudices the landed aristocracy kept common whites docile supporters of the slave institution and black degradation. The fact that laboring whites had listened to such an appeal was absurd, he said. "A 'white man's party,' indeed! What cared these men for a man's color if he only worked? The real issue is not over a 'white-man's party,' but the *poor man's party*, and of equal rights to all. It is to secure the same rights before the law to the poorest as to the richest. This harms nobody. It is true Democracy. But only with the black man's help can the poor white man ever gain his just political influence in Mississippi." The Republican party was the poor man's party, Smith told his white readers, and it was pledged "to elevate labor, to educate the masses, and to enact laws as will secure you in the enjoyment of liberty and all your just and legal rights under the Government."[59]

Believing that he saw a weak link in the conservative coalition, Smith sought to arouse the traditional hostility of the Whigs to the Democratic party. He warned Whigs that although Democrats welcomed them to the party now, they would eventually be forced to take back seats while men like Davis and Brown again took control of the Democracy and the state. "Shall this hydra-

57. Corinth *Weekly News*, May 9, 1868.
58. Meridian *Chronicle*, May 12, 1868.
59. *Ibid.*, March 17, April 28, 1868.

headed monster rise up from the sea of blood and prevail upon the people of Mississippi to do him reverence again?" this intrepid scalawag editor asked. "Surely the people must be mad and recklessly insane if they bow the knee to this Molock again. The spirit of Calhoun and of Yancey still dwells in the bosom of those who worshipped at the shrine of these great conspirators."[60]

Despite the stalwart efforts of such scalawags as Alcorn, Wofford, and Smith to persuade whites to support the constitution and the Republican candidates in the election, the sinister image of the Radical party that was being constructed by Democratic spokesmen could not be overcome even by whites of good will toward the freedmen and the reconstruction acts. Before the adoption of the proscriptive clauses Republican strategists had hoped to obtain the votes of as many as ten thousand of the sixty-eight thousand whites who were registered.[61] But the fervor of conservative opposition to the constitution soon demonstrated to Republican leaders the futility of seeking white votes. Inevitably, then, the Republican campaign centered on the Negro vote.

In an attempt to marshal the complete black vote for the party, Eggleston and other Republican candidates for state office toured the state during the late spring. Often speaking from the same platform as the conservatives, these emissaries of the new order stressed the hypocrisy of the Democratic appeal to the Negro voter. The Democratic party, they reminded blacks, was the party of slavery, the Black Code, and the Ku Klux Klan; yet, with incredible gall, Democrats now sought black support against a constitution that would protect the rights of the race in Mississippi.[62] The real objective of the Republican campaigners, however, was not to convince blacks of the perfidy of the Democrats and the friendship of the party of emancipation; this was already an article of faith with them. Rather, these spokesmen sought to convince the black masses of the critical necessity for defying Democratic threats and marching as one to the polls on election day. The

60. *Ibid.*, January 22, March 13, 1868. A few weeks later Smith admitted failure in the Republicans' effort to alienate Whigs from their new Democratic allies; in fact, he sorrowfully reported, "we find many of that party to-day in the ranks of the rebel leaders." *Ibid.*, April 21, 1868.
61. Vicksburg *Weekly Republican*, April 7, 1868.
62. *Ibid.*, May 19, 26, June 9, 16, July 7, 1868.

use of prominent Republicans to bolster black courage proved effective in many white counties—a remarkable success in view of the inchoate state of Republican organizations there and the kind of discouragement that local Democrats provided for Negroes who planned to vote for the constitution. More might have been accomplished by this method of campaigning had the state party possessed a few thousand dollars for the purpose of sending financially embarrassed black leaders, like James Lynch, into the interior to embolden the freedmen on the eve of the election.[63]

In the predominantly black counties the Union League in the 1868 election attained its zenith of effectiveness as an instrument for uniting the new political element behind the Republican party.[64] But the league, whose clandestine and exclusive activities had already caused some leading Republicans to shun its councils, had to share the spotlight with the regular Republican associations. With little to fear from the local white minority in plantation communities, blacks in large numbers joined Republican clubs and sent representatives to county and district party meetings. Although white Republicans (mainly carpetbaggers) held the upper hand in these gatherings, black delegates from the beginning made their presence known, and increasingly during Reconstruction they came to exercise an influence on local party affairs and nominations that approximated the voting strength of their race in the area. Nevertheless, most black politicians during the first three years of the new order accepted without question the fundamental assumptions of the white Republican leadership regarding reconstruction and the political and legal dimensions of Negro rights.

Confident of success in the election, Republicans in the plantation counties often invited Democratic speakers to share the platform with them at local rallies. A typical Republican rally began with the formation of a black procession at the county courthouse. Usually involving several hundred persons, the massed group marched through the small downtown area to an open field outside of town, normally on the plantation of a sympathizer. A large

63. Fisk to William E. Chandler, July 4, 1868, in William E. Chandler Papers.

64. The Union League's effectiveness at this time is evidenced to a great extent by the intensity of conservative newspaper attacks on the organization. During other Reconstruction campaigns the league received no such special treatment. See especially the Jackson *Clarion* and the *Hinds County Gazette* issues of May, June, and July, 1868.

committee, formed several days in advance, prepared and dispensed food to the multitude, now grown to two or three thousand and including many whites. Despite the fervor of the oratory, harmony between the races almost always prevailed at these interracial gatherings in the black counties.[65]

The campaign came to a close in mid-June with apprehensive Republicans hoping that enough blacks in the white counties and in those where their majority was marginal (in addition to the safe bloc vote in the predominantly Negro counties) would brave conservative hostility and turn out to vote. Three weeks before the election the mood of the Republicans brightened when General Irvin McDowell, who had actually been appointed in January to replace General Ord but had been delayed in assuming command, arrived to take charge of the military district, supplanting the conservative Gillem. McDowell's removal of Governor Humphreys reinforced the Republican belief that in the time remaining the new commander would make a vigorous effort to ensure a free election.

Although Republicans would not admit it, Gillem had already made careful preparations for the election, which would be held under military supervision. On May 19 he had issued an election order outlining the precise procedure to be followed, and under this order balloting was to begin on June 22 and continue until registrars (who had earlier enrolled the voters) had had an opportunity to visit all of the precincts in their counties.[66] The election was consequently expected to take several days. Gillem provided detailed instructions to the registrars for opening and closing the polls, examining certificates of registration, securing the ballot boxes against fraud, counting the votes, and forwarding the returns to his headquarters. To further ensure a full and free expression of the will of the people, he ordered sheriffs to appoint a deputy

65. Vicksburg *Weekly Republican*, May 19, June 9, 16, 1868.
66. The counties were to be divided into three parts, with one registrar assuming responsibility for each area. Registrars were directed to appoint two assistants, who could qualify only if they were able to take the ironclad oath. Gillem's election order may be found in the *Journal of the Constitutional Convention of 1868*, pp. 749–53. For a detailed account of the military's preparation for this election, see Garner, *Reconstruction in Mississippi*, 205–208.

for each polling place who at the command of the registrar was to suppress any irregular conduct. A few days later the general selected ten army officers as election inspectors, directing them to spread out into the state, visit the precincts, and aid in any way to guarantee an untrammeled election.[67] Finally, Gillem ordered his unit commanders to place their troops on alert during the election and be prepared to move swiftly to any sites of trouble. Supplementing his force with five companies from Tennessee, Gillem divided the troops into detachments of from five to fifteen men to enhance their mobility and, he hoped, to provide an adequate distribution of soldiers throughout the state. Altogether Gillem had approximately 1,900 men, dispersed in sixty-three detachments.[68]

General McDowell soon disappointed Mississippi Republicans by approving his predecessor's arrangements for the election and by ignoring their plans for additional safeguards. As Republicans knew, Gillem's preparations did not cover the kinds of transgressions against the ballot that occurred before the voters entered the security of the polls, although Gillem later claimed that he had given his troops strict instructions "to allow no intimidation of any character whatever" in the contest. Even within the election machinery the military had devised there were weaknesses that permitted abuses of the right to vote. Many election officials, originally appointed by Gillem as registrars, were selected after their conservatism had been ascertained, and when the chips were down they permitted their conservative leanings to influence their official behavior. For example, although directed to prohibit the recording of names by observers at the polls, these officers looked the other way when Democratic poll watchers appeared with pencils in hand and started taking down the names of blacks who voted for the constitution. This practice, which Republicans claimed in-

67. Circular 5, May 29, 1868, in Records of the Fourth Military District. Gillem also took steps to ensure that agents of the Freedmen's Bureau and soldiers in his command would take no part in the debate on the constitution or the election. He directed that they "shall entirely abstain from public speaking, electioneering or endeavoring to influence voters; but this order is not to restrict [them] in their duty of instructing Freedmen as to their *rights* as electors." (The italics are Gillem's.) *Journal of the Constitutional Convention of 1868*, p. 753.

68. *House Miscellaneous Documents*, 40th Cong., 3rd Sess., No. 53, pp. 134–35; *Report of the Secretary of War, 1868*, p. 590.

timidated Negro voters, occurred at numerous precincts during the election.[69] Furthermore, county officials, who either had been appointed by the district commanders or had been elected by whites during presidential reconstruction, subtly assisted Democrats in keeping down the black vote. Some concealment of their anti-Republican activities was necessary to avoid removal from office for obstructing the reconstruction process. County officers of northern origins were especially effective in using their official positions to restrict Negro voting. Dr. Horatio N. Ballard, himself a native of the North and a member of the constitutional convention, explained to Massachusetts Congressman George S. Boutwell the effect such anti-Republican officials had on the election in heavily populated DeSoto County near Memphis:

> You can hardly conceive the number of ways by which at the time of registration and election these [northern] officers without open violation of orders are capable of immensely influencing the result. They are naturally looked to by the colored people for advice and direction. Just previous to our election the collection of the balance of the State, County and Convention taxes was pressed with tremendous vigor by the Sheriff, his deputies and the constables, at a time when there was the least money in the country—and the hardships occasioned thereby were systematically affirmed to the colored people as caused by their having voted for a convention—and to be relieved in [the] future they must vote down the Constitution. There was neither time nor opportunity to disabuse them of this error. This is but one of the many expedients resorted to.[70]

In addition, many troops openly sympathized with the conservatives, and on at least two occasions drunken soldiers broke discipline and attacked blacks who insisted on voting the Republican ticket. Usually, however, troops aided the Democratic cause by simply refusing to act on Republican complaints of intimidation and irregularities. Like the conservative election officials, sympa-

69. Report of Gillem for quarter ending June 30, 1868, in Freedmen's Bureau Records, Microcopy Roll 59; *House Miscellaneous Documents*, 40th Cong., 3rd Sess., No. 53, pp. 150–51, 193, 204; Vicksburg *Weekly Republican*, July 7, 1868; *Hinds County Gazette*, July 10, 1868.

70. Ballard to Boutwell, February 13, 1869, in Papers on Conditions in Mississippi. A constant theme of Republicans who complained about election irregularities was the pernicious influence of "disloyal" local officials. See, for example, letters in *House Miscellaneous Documents*, 40th Cong., 3rd Sess., No. 53, pp. 187, 256.

thetic men in blue preferred to look the other way when incidents occurred at the polls, as long as outright violence did not result.[71] Officers tended to take their duties more seriously than enlisted men; but when companies were divided and dispersed into remote areas of the state the detachments came under the command of racially prejudiced and easily flattered noncommissioned officers who made little effort to protect Republicans in their right to vote. It was in these backwater regions that intolerance of opinion was most oppressive and the greatest need existed for the scrupulous military enforcement of the reconstruction laws.[72]

The main aggressors against the free ballot during the election of 1868 were inflamed conservatives who were, according to one scalawag, "the idle, loafing, drunken portion of the [Democratic] voters." Although violence was rare because of the fear of military arrest and trial, rebellious whites devised a variety of ingenious tactics to carry the election for the Democratic party. In numerous cases, blacks en route to the polls were met by whites who reminded them that they would lose their jobs if they voted Republican; some were threatened with violence if they insisted on voting for the constitution.[73] William H. Gibbs, who became a sort of generalissimo of the Republican forces during and after the election, claimed that in some districts Democrats prevented the distribution of his party's tickets. Evidence to prove this charge is lacking, but a well-documented practice was the distribution to unsuspecting blacks of Democratic tickets that were similar to the gaudy, red, white, and blue ballots of the Republican party. In some cases, Democratic poll watchers challenged the registration cer-

71. Vicksburg *Weekly Republican*, June 30, 1868; *House Miscellaneous Documents*, 40th Cong., 3rd Sess., No. 53, pp. 25, 166, 255, 268–69. C. F. Johnson to Washburne, July 2, 1868, in Washburne Papers. The constitutional convention's Committee of Five, which investigated election irregularities, charged that many soldiers actually distributed Democratic tickets and advised blacks to support the conservatives. William H. Gibbs to Washburne, June 30, 1868, in Washburne Papers.

72. *House Executive Documents*, 40th Cong., 3rd Sess., No. 1, pp. 666–67. Even if the Federal forces had vigorously followed their instructions, they could not have prevented all acts of intimidation, since troop strength in the state was insufficient to protect every community from this kind of activity.

73. *House Miscellaneous Documents*, 40th Cong., 3rd Sess., No. 53, pp. 147, 259–60; Vicksburg *Weekly Republican*, June 30, 1868; Fisk to William E. Chandler, July 4, 1868, in William E. Chandler Papers; C. F. Johnson to Washburne, July 2, 1868, and Alcorn to Washburne, June 29, 1868, both in Washburne Papers.

tificates of blacks, and when their full (or proper) name was not recorded on the form conservative election officials barred them from the ballot box. Rumors of Ku Klux Klan activity were carefully repeated at the proper places, whether or not this secret society even existed in the area. The mere presence of a boisterous crowd of Democrats at the polls in communities where blacks did not have security in numbers served to discourage many from casting Republican ballots.[74]

These unscrupulous methods for reducing the black vote did not owe their existence to any systematic plan of subversion emanating from the state Democratic hierarchy, nor were they practiced in every county. But in those areas where intimidation was pervasive, many blacks and some whites who had planned to vote Republican were sufficiently cowed to stay away from the polls or to cast Democratic ballots. For whites who leaned toward the party of the new order, the threat of social ostracism (which was not always explicit) was sufficient reason for them to go fishing on election day. The absence of a resolute white Republican nucleus in those counties where blacks were in a distinct minority also caused many demoralized and frightened Negro voters to shun the polls or vote with their Democratic neighbors.[75]

The results of Democratic tactics were soon clear. From a possible Republican majority of approximately 17,000 (based on black registration alone, as revised immediately before the election), the constitution and the Republican candidates went down to defeat by a margin of 7,000 votes. Democrats won a comfortable majority in both houses of the legislature, a victory that became superfluous with the rejection of the constitution, provided Congress did not

74. Gibbs to Washburne, June 30, July 11, 1868, in Washburne Papers; entry for June 22, 1868, in Agnew Diary; Vicksburg *Weekly Republican*, June 23, 30, 1868; *House Executive Documents*, 40th Cong., 3rd Sess., No. 1, pp. 666–67; *House Miscellaneous Documents*, 40th Cong., 3rd Sess., No. 53, pp. 149–51. The harassment and intimidation of voters was not completely a one-sided affair. Democrats charged the Union League with such tactics, and this claim was sustained by the testimony of one Republican candidate for the legislature. Natchez *Weekly Democrat*, July 20, 1868; Jackson *Clarion*, April 1, 1869; *House Miscellaneous Documents*, 40th Cong., 3rd Sess., No. 53, pp. 292–93, 298. Nonetheless, Union League tactics of this kind paled in significance when compared to those employed by the Democrats during the campaign.

75. Meridian *Chronicle*, June 26, 1868; *House Miscellaneous Documents*, 40th Cong., 3rd Sess., No. 53, pp. 46, 257.

overturn the results.[76] As expected, the overwhelmingly black counties, with two exceptions, stood solidly behind the Republican candidates and the constitution, whereas the reverse was true for those counties where whites constituted a large majority. In densely black Warren County, for example, out of a total of 6,167 votes, Republicans received 4,851 of them. The Republican vote corresponded closely to the Negro registration of 4,794, before 1,026 voters of both races were added to the rolls on the eve of the election; reportedly only 140 blacks cast Democratic ballots in Warren, most of these being draymen, porters, barbers, and artisans in Vicksburg who depended upon white patronage for a living.[77] Twelve black counties went Democratic, though only two of these could be classified as overwhelmingly Negro; Republicans later presented strong evidence that black voters were systematically intimidated in six of these twelve counties.

White counties, on the contrary, voted solidly Democratic, except for Attala County where the mild-mannered and prestigious scalawag Jason Niles influenced opinion in favor of the constitution. In all but one white county, however, some blacks and a handful of white Republicans braved local opinion and voted Republican.[78] The extent of Republican participation in these counties varied with the precinct; for example, in Tishomingo County an impressive Republican vote was recorded (considering that the county was overwhelmingly white), but almost all of the ballots were cast at one precinct, Corinth, where military protection was available and where a white Republican leadership existed.[79]

Although many blacks were persuaded or forced to support the Democratic ticket in white or marginally Negro counties, few

76. Election returns may be found in *House Executive Documents*, 40th Cong., 3rd Sess., No. 1, pp. 590–602. The revised registration figures, unlike those of 1867, are not given by race; however, a correspondent to the Cincinnati *Commercial* who visited the district commander's headquarters after the books were closed reported that 86,000 blacks had registered and 69,000 whites. New York *Times*, July 7, 1868. Gillem later reported a total increase of 15,000 voters since the registration of 1867. *Report of the Secretary of War, 1868*, p. 591.

77. Vicksburg *Weekly Republican*, June 30, 1868; New York *Times*, July 7, 1868.

78. This county was traditionally turbulent Smith County in the piney woods; only two Republican votes were recorded there in 1868.

79. *House Miscellaneous Documents*, 40th Cong., 3rd Sess., No. 53, pp. 45–46. See also the entry for June 24, 1868, in Agnew Diary.

white Mississippians, whether in white or black districts, voted
Republican in the 1868 election. A comparison of the county election returns, which were not given by race, with the registration
figures, given by race in 1867, clearly demonstrates this point.
In only three counties, including Attala which went Republican,
is there evidence of a relatively large white vote for the constitution. With some allowance for black registrants who might not have
gone to the polls, even in these counties only two or three hundred
whites could have possibly voted "the mongrel ticket." In Copiah
County, where more than fourteen hundred whites were registered, only eight defied conservative opinion and cast Republican
ballots. At Okolona, of more than one thousand votes polled, only
one white man reportedly voted for the constitution.[80]

When reports of election irregularities began to pour into the
chamber of the Committee of Five at the state capitol, Gibbs and
his Republican associates descended upon Vicksburg to demand
that the district commander act on the complaints. First they approached McDowell, but he refused to intervene, pleading that
because he had just been removed from command by President
Johnson, he would leave the matter to his successor. His successor was none other than General Gillem who, with the platitudes
of conservatives ringing in his ears as he resumed control, rejected
the request of the Radical committee. A few days later Gillem
announced that although fraud and intimidation had been charged
by both sides, he felt sure the election had been reasonably free
and the constitution had failed to be ratified, the only one in the
southern states under congressional reconstruction to be defeated
at the polls. Mississippi therefore would remain under military
rule until Congress could provide further instructions.[81]

Thus ended the hard fought and bitter political contest of 1868,
which in the final analysis was decided by the suppression of Republican votes. Yet it is clear that had the constitution been stripped
of its proscriptive and partisan features the outcome would have
been different. White unity behind a militant campaign to carry
the election could not have been achieved if the constitution had

80. *House Miscellaneous Documents*, 40th Cong., 3rd Sess., No. 53, pp. 169, 257.
81. *Ibid.*, 6, 254; *Hinds County Gazette*, July 10, 1868; *Report of the Secretary of
War, 1868*, p. 603.

not included these inflammatory clauses.[82] By itself the extension of the ballot to blacks was not sufficient to arouse the white masses from their political lethargy to defeat the constitution. Despite their opposition to it, perceptive whites viewed Negro enfranchisement as a fait accompli, made so by Congress as a condition for the restoration of the state to the Union and perhaps irreversible with the emergence in the 1868 election of the popular Grant as the Republican standard-bearer.[83] Many white Mississippians could live with black suffrage, provided it was not used for radical purposes to reorder the society of the state. But the proposed constitution of 1868 had threatened to do just that. By proscribing the political rights of thousands of former Confederates, thereby reducing the conservative influence in the state, the constitution made likely the ascendancy of the most radical faction in the reconstructed government. Already the spectre of confiscatory taxes and the "social equality" of the races had been raised in white minds through Radical Republican pronouncements in and outside of the constitutional convention. The prospect that such Radical adventurers as Castello, Parsons, and the Negro Combash would control the new government filled Mississippi whites with the gravest concern and, at the risk of military intervention, incited them to conduct a campaign of intimidation in order to defeat the constitution.

In any analysis of the possible range of white political behavior

82. This was also the conclusion of Frederic Speed, the carpetbag editor of the Vicksburg *Weekly Republican*. Soon after the election he wrote: "Our misfortunes, as I conceive them, have come through our own violation of a sound principle. We asked for the great mass of our members a right which we sought to deny to a large number of those who previously exercised it. The result is before us. Let us in the future profit by the experience of the past. Let moderation in all things govern us, so that when next we are called upon to face the enemy, we may go into the struggle 'with a conscience void of offence.' " Vicksburg *Weekly Republican*, July 14, 1868. For a similar Republican view of the reasons for the party's defeat in the election, see A. H. Arthur to Joseph Holt, April 12, 1869, in Holt Papers. These two Republicans did not dismiss the significance of intimidation as a reason for their party's failure in the contest, but rather they insisted that campaign and election irregularities could have been avoided by the framing of a liberal constitution.

83. In a private letter to Joseph S. Fowler of Tennessee, Gillem expressed his strong opinion that Negro suffrage had not been an issue in the election, the foremost desire of the white people being a "settled government" under the terms outlined by Congress. But the clauses in the constitution "prescribing the qualifications of voters & office holders arrayed ninety nine out of one hundred white men against it." Gillem to Joseph S. Fowler, July 27, 1868, in Joseph S. Fowler Papers, Southern Historical Collection, University of North Carolina Library, Chapel Hill.

in 1868, the general condition of society at the time must be considered. The hard times of early 1868 served as a poignant reminder to many old citizens that economic recovery would not take place until the political tempest over reconstruction had subsided and Mississippi was restored to the Union. Under these dire circumstances, whites were not prepared to offer an effective opposition to a moderate Republican constitution that went no further than the congressional requirement regarding black political and civil rights and that promised an early end to the strife over reconstruction. Even the article in the constitution establishing schools for both races was viewed by many whites not as a radical imposition on the old citizens but as a means to achieve the immediate goals of economic and social rehabilitation. Despite the early fear that dominant Republicans would impose racial integration in the classrooms, planters in particular believed that labor stability might be advanced by the establishment of schools for the children of their Negro tenants. In addition, many whites who had long suffered from a lack of fundamental educational opportunities stood to benefit from the proposed system of schools, a fact that significantly reduced opposition to the constitution on racial grounds.

The convention's failure to write a document free of proscriptive features not only caused the defeat of the constitution but also greatly diminished Republican chances for a strong biracial party in the state. With a black majority of almost twenty thousand at the polls and at least five thousand whites prepared to support the party, the Republican future had been promising. Indeed, the prospect of the party's long-term success on a liberal platform would have recommended it to many whites who at first were not inclined to support the new order. But the adoption of the proscriptive clauses and the bitter ratification campaign that followed undercut the early Republican advantage and created an uncertain future for the party in Mississippi.

6

A Reconstruction
Stalemate

With the defeat of the constitution at the polls, Mississippi's reconstruction fate passed back into the hands of Congress. Republicans in the state realized that their task now was to persuade Congress either to reverse the official election returns or place "loyal men" in office preparatory to another vote on the constitution. Dominant Republicans in Washington obviously sympathized with their Mississippi brethren, but 1868 was a national election year, and faced with a revived Democracy in the North many Republican congressmen had no desire to remind northern voters of the continuing interference of Congress in southern affairs. Furthermore, congressional intervention prior to the election could be construed by voters as an attempt to restore Mississippi to the Union in time for the state to give its electoral votes to Grant.

Republicans in Mississippi, fearing that delay would be fatal to their cause, felt no election-year hesitation in insisting that Congress act soon on their case. Since the election on the constitution their position in the state had declined dramatically as thousands of blacks threatened to defect to the Democratic party. In some areas, including such important black counties as Adams and Hinds, Negroes were flocking to triumphant Democratic rallies where they were feted and flattered in appreciation of their supposed support for the conservatives in the election.[1] A history of the conservative courtship of the black voter should have suggested to worried Republicans that the affair would be broken off before the marriage was consummated. But the flirtation of the summer of 1868 was a more serious one than those of 1867 and the spring of 1868. What bothered Republicans now was the support local Negro leaders were giving the Democrats and the general uneasiness among rank-and-file blacks with carpetbagger management. At

1. Entries for July 7, 11, 1868, in Darden Diary; *Hinds County Gazette*, July 10, 17, 1868; Natchez *Weekly Democrat*, September 14, 1868; Address of the Mississippi Delegation in Washington to Republican Congressmen, clipping from the Vicksburg *Weekly Republican*, December 30, 1868, in Papers on Conditions in Mississippi.

least for populous Hinds County there was little exaggeration in
the jubilant George W. Harper's report that "the sensible negroes
everywhere are beginning to manifest the greatest disgust for the
carpet-baggists and scallawags, and are running into the Democratic lines with as much zeal as they went into the dens of the 'Loyal
League' twelve months ago."[2]

White Republicans realized that to check the defection of blacks
and regain the political initiative in the state they must first provide security for their followers. The election had demonstrated
that the political rights of Republicans could not be protected from
Democratic intimidation by the Gillem regime, with its retinue of
conservative officials. As Republicans saw it, the first step in rejuvenating the party and reconstructing Mississippi on a "loyal"
basis was to have Congress replace all officers in the state with men
recommended by the state Republican hierarchy.[3] This was not a
new idea; the constitutional convention had earlier and unsuccessfully petitioned Congress to give it the authority to remove all
"rebel" officials, most of whom had been elected under Johnson's
plan of reconstruction, and to replace them with "men of known
loyalty."[4] The insistence by Mississippi Republicans upon securing
the offices for friends of reconstruction seemed on the surface to
substantiate the recurrent conservative charge that the main interest of the Radicals was to obtain the loaves and fishes of public
office. Some Republicans may have had less than altruistic reasons
for seeking a clean sweep of the offices in the state. But the support for such an action was so pervasive in the party, coming from
moderates and Radicals, scalawags and carpetbaggers, and men
who evidently had little ambition to serve in office, it seems probable that most Republicans genuinely considered the success of the
congressional program of reconstruction dependent upon the state
and the ballot boxes being in the hands of friends. William H.
Gibbs, chairman of the Committee of Five, declared that Con-

2. *Hinds County Gazette*, August 14, 1868 (quote);. Natchez *Weekly Democrat*, September 14, 1868; Vicksburg *Herald*, August 29, 1868; *House Miscellaneous Documents*, 40th
Cong., 3rd Sess., No. 53, p. 277; clipping from the Vicksburg *Weekly Republican*, December 30, 1868, in Papers on Conditions in Mississippi.
    3. Archie C. Fisk to William E. Chandler, July 24, 1868, in William E. Chandler Papers;
William H. Gibbs to Elihu B. Washburne, July 11, 1868, in Washburne Papers.
    4. *Journal of the Constitutional Convention of 1868*, pp. 14–15.

gress must quickly give the Republicans "some show in the control of affairs in the State," or all would be lost. "If we are left in our present condition, there is but little hope for our party in the future."[5]

Even if Congress met the demand of Mississippi Republicans for the removal of all unfaithful officials, there would still be an important fly in the ointment. This obstruction was Gillem, who served by the grace of President Johnson and would probably appoint conservatives to positions vacated by Congress, even though the ironclad oath might be required of the new officers. Gillem was a protégé of Johnson, and although he was careful to avoid comment on the national struggle over reconstruction policy, he privately exulted when the Senate failed to remove Johnson from office. Gillem indicated his support for the reconstruction laws and black suffrage but at the same time cringed at the assaults of congressional Radicals on the Constitution, which, he said, "strike at the foundation of liberty and the existence of civilized society."[6]

Local Republicans had long realized that the ultimate source of their frustration with the military's management of affairs was Johnson, who despite Congress' ability to override his vetoes could still appoint and dismiss officers at will and influence their conduct. Not only did Republicans complain of their exclusion from state and local office by the Johnson-supported Gillem regime, but they also grumbled that their misfortunes were increased when the president awarded the federal patronage in the state to rebels.[7] Consequently, these Republicans persistently urged their friends in Congress to press forward in their impeachment effort against Johnson.[8]

The Senate's failure to remove Johnson from office, coming just before the defeat of the state constitution at the polls, dealt a serious blow to the hopes of Mississippi Republicans and caused them to despair for the future. Not willing, however, to abandon the

5. Gibbs to Washburne, July 11, 1868, in Washburne Papers.

6. Alvan C. Gillem to Joseph S. Fowler, May 30, July 27, 1868, in Fowler Papers.

7. Fisk to William E. Chandler, July 24, 1868, in William E. Chandler Papers.

8. *Journal of the Constitutional Convention of 1868*, p. 254; Charles W. Clarke to John Covode, August 31, 1867, in Covode Papers; Gibbs to Washburne, September 30, 1867, April 11, 1868, and James Lusk Alcorn to Washburne, June 29, 1868, both in Washburne Papers; Jackson *Clarion*, March 31, 1868.

field to the Democrats without a fight, they leveled their guns on Gillem, hoping that by picturing him as the abettor of rebels, Congress would be sufficiently aroused to enact some measure that would reduce the general's power and permit Republicans of the state to exercise a dominant influence in civil affairs. In a lengthy and bitter indictment of the election conducted under military supervision, Jonathan Tarbell, chairman of the state Republican executive committee, insisted that Congress take action against Gillem, whom he described as "a dangerous and fatal enemy" to the new order in Mississippi. In a later similar demand, Tarbell described the general as "a more artful, insidious, prejudicial and fatal enemy than Johnson himself."[9] Carpetbagger Ridgley C. Powers charged that Gillem had tolerated a "reign of terror" during the campaign and election, and a Gulf Coast Republican asserted that the general had not paid the slightest attention to Unionist complaints of mistreatment.[10] Concerned about their chances in the fall national elections, Republicans in Congress ignored the appeals for special legislation to bypass General Gillem in the management of affairs in Mississippi.

The difficulties of obtaining an early congressional decision were aggravated by the inability of state Republicans to agree on what course of action Congress should take. Although local Republicans were virtually unanimous in their belief that Gillem's influence and his "disloyal" officials must be eliminated, they could not agree on a plan for superseding or modifying military authority in the state. Nor could they agree on what should be done about the defeated constitution. Some Radicals wanted to have the document declared ratified and Republican candidates certified as the victors in the contests for office in the new government, but other party leaders feared this would be too high-handed a way to give birth to Republican rule. Moreover, there was no assurance that Republicans could control the new legislature, which the Democrats could claim to have won legitimately. Many Republicans preferred a provisional government, headed by one of their own who would be appointed governor by Congress and would serve until the state

9. *House Miscellaneous Documents*, 40th Cong., 3rd Sess., No. 53, pp. 274–87; Jonathan Tarbell to H. E. Paine, February 16, 1869, in Papers on Conditions in Mississippi.

10. Vicksburg *Weekly Republican*, December 6, 1868; C. F. Johnson to Washburne, July 2, 1868, in Washburne Papers.

was ready to vote again on the constitution. Supported by federal troops, the governor under this plan would have complete authority, and in advance of the election he would be expected to use his patronage power to give Republicans absolute control of the state. As a result, advocates of this proposal argued, Republicans would have no difficulty in carrying the state for the constitution by a margin of at least 20,000 votes. Even such moderate Republicans as Joseph W. Field, Jefferson L. Wofford, and James L. Herbert, who still had hopes for the development of a white-based party in Mississippi, urged Congress to approve the scheme, predicting that it would find acceptance among reasonable whites.[11]

As the issue became drawn out, a number of prominent Republicans, mainly of the moderate faction, began to doubt the wisdom of having another vote on the constitution with the proscriptive features included. A strong movement developed in the party to have Congress rule that the proscriptive clauses should be expunged before the constitution's resubmission to the voters.[12] Radical Republicans, on the other hand, would have no part of a scheme to repudiate any part of the document. Several of them denounced the proposal for a Republican provisional government, arguing that because of its impermanence such a government would be weak and therefore could be manipulated by the conservatives. They also insisted that a delay in acting on the constitution would give Democrats time to map a successful new election strategy. Condemning all notions of compromise, northerner Henry R. Pease declared: "We must have a loyal government by the loyal people and for the loyal people of Mississippi, or all is lost. Should Congress adopt a temporizing policy in our case and give us a quasi-loyal government, we have the alternative of packing our carpetbags and emigrating, or being delivered over to the tender mercies of the Ku-Klux democracy."[13] Furthermore, as Radical Charles W. Clarke pointed out, until the state was restored to the Union and civil government reestablished nothing could be done to im-

11. *Address to the Reconstruction Committee in Relation to Mississippi* (N.p., 1869); *House Miscellaneous Documents*, 40th Cong., 3rd Sess., No. 53, pp. 48–49, 167–68, 264; Fisk to William E. Chandler, July 24, 1868, in William E. Chandler Papers; *Hinds County Gazette*, December 30, 1868, March 24, 1869.

12. *Address to the Reconstruction Committee: Appleton's Annual Cyclopaedia*, 1869, p. 454; Meridian *Chronicle*, November 14, December 5, 1868.

13. *House Miscellaneous Documents*, 40th Cong., 3rd Sess., No. 53, pp. 258–59.

plement the education article in the constitution, "without which all permanent reconstruction must be a failure."[14]

Meanwhile, the Radical-dominated Committee of Five had gone to work on the task delegated to it by the constitutional convention. Empowered by that body either to proclaim officially the results of the election if the constitution were ratified or if it failed to reconvene the convention, the committee immediately after the election sought to reassemble the convention. General Gillem, as expected, refused to recognize the committee's authority, whereupon it dispatched a delegation to Washington to persuade Congress to pass a measure reconvening the convention.[15] Although the House of Representatives approved such a bill, the Senate squashed it.

Chaired by Gibbs, the Committee of Five next launched an investigation of the election with the obvious intent of buttressing Republican claims of widespread intimidation and fraud. The committee requested and received stacks of affidavits from Republicans of both races in all parts of the state attesting to the spirit of intolerance and violence that had characterized the campaign and election in their communities. Meeting behind closed doors in the capitol, committee members listened to the testimony of numerous Republicans but in a display of partisan rancor rejected out of hand conservative demands for a hearing. Angered by this refusal, Sharkey, Potter, and a few associates marched on the capitol, demanding entrance to the committee room. A clash was inevitable; fortunately, however, when violence broke out it was limited to a scuffle over a pistol that a Republican hanger-on drew on the conservative interlopers.[16] The elderly brigade of Union Whigs retreated, grumbling that their Union had been turned on its head by the Radical-instigated events of Reconstruction. Surely, the normally mild-mannered Sharkey, who as president of the

14. Clarke to James A. Garfield, January 29, 1869, in James A. Garfield Papers, Manuscript Division, Library of Congress. See also clipping from the Vicksburg *Weekly Republican*, December 30, 1868, and Gibbs to John A. Bingham, February 4, 1869, both in Papers on Conditions in Mississippi.

15. *House Miscellaneous Documents*, 40th Cong., 3rd Sess., No. 53, p. 6; Gibbs to Washburne, July 11, 1868, in Washburne Papers.

16. The written testimony appears in *House Miscellaneous Documents*, 40th Cong., 3rd Sess., No. 53, pp. 3, 33–34, 147–257.

Nashville Convention had handled the southern fire-eaters of 1850 with aplomb, found himself confounded by a different, more impatient breed of radicals in 1868.

After four months of work the Committee of Five startled Mississippians with a sweeping proclamation reversing the results of the late election and announcing that the constitution should go into effect immediately, with its retinue of Republican officers. Claiming that its investigation uncovered extensive fraud and intimidation in seven counties, the committee threw out the returns from these counties and proclaimed that the friends of the constitution had won the election by a majority of 3,380 votes.[17]

The committee's proclamation, which had no immediate effect because of Gillem's disapproval, was timed to coincide with the fall election and the anticipated national Republican victory. Gibbs and associates believed that after the election Republican congressional leaders, basking in their party's triumph and secure politically, would be receptive to the committee's solution to the Mississippi impasse.[18]

In a move to improve its prospects for congressional support, the Committee of Five obtained a call for a state Republican convention to meet in late November for the specific purpose of endorsing the proclamation. But it was obvious from the intraparty debate preceding the convention that no consensus could be achieved in favor of the proclamation, and the tactics of the Gibbs group revived the issue between Radicals and moderates over the necessity for substantial white support. Defeated earlier in their efforts to attract whites to the party, concerned moderate Republicans now received unexpected help from a group of northerners who had settled in overwhelmingly black counties. Several of these men were Gillem appointees, and a handful of the others had been associated with the Radical wing of the party. But, without

17. The proclamation, written by Gibbs, may be found in *ibid.*, 18–19, and for the majority of votes for the constitution as figured by the Committee of Five, see p. 5.

18. According to carpetbagger Lester Williams, who had canvassed for the constitution during the spring, the Committee of Five would not have issued its audacious proclamation had the Republicans failed in the fall election; as it were, Gibbs and his associates waited until two days after the election, then predated their proclamation to prevent suspicion. Williams divulged this information to Radical Congressman George S. Boutwell in a confidential letter which was subsequently published in several newspapers and in *House Miscellaneous Documents*, 40th Cong., 3rd Sess., No. 53, pp. 263–64.

rejecting the doctrine of equal political rights for blacks, most of them had become skeptical of achieving any permanent Republican success without making allowances for white opinion and attracting to the party the more independent-minded people of the state.[19] As aspiring planters and merchants, these newcomers perhaps also sought to check the triumph of a radical party that, they believed, threatened the agricultural recovery of the plantation districts.

Ironically, it was Grant's victory at the polls that persuaded these northerners to seek a reconstruction settlement that would be accepted by many of the old citizens and would be likely to bring political peace to the state. They declared that the general's triumph had put to rest the notion among whites that the reconstruction policy of Congress would not be sustained by the northern people; indeed, in a printed address to the congressional Committee on Reconstruction, they claimed that "a very large number of thinking white men of the State most heartily rejoice at the election of General Grant, believing that any other result might have put in jeopardy once more the pacific and final adjustment of our present troubles." Appealing to Congress to recognize this new development in Mississippi, leaders of the movement denied having a roseate view of affairs in the state, but added, "we do say that we confidently hope to derive material assistance and active support from a large number of the original Union men—[although] some may remain inactive and others go with the opposition. By this means we will divide the white vote, without which our party can never sustain itself. By dividing our adversaries we will conquer."[20]

Considerable evidence existed in late 1868 and early 1869 to support the moderate Republican belief that Grant's election had undermined formidable opposition to reconstruction and had persuaded many whites to seek an accommodation with the party of the new order. Grant's campaign slogan of "Let us have peace" appealed to numerous whites who were weary of postwar strife and

19. Meridian *Chronicle*, November 14, 1868; Vicksburg *Times*, December 11, 1868; *Address to the Reconstruction Committee*, 2–3.. These converts to the cause of reconstruction moderation claimed that they had earlier worked for the ratification of the constitution.
20. *Address to the Reconstruction Committee*, 4.

uncertainty and concerned about the stultifying effect that reconstruction politics were having on their attempt to recover from the staggering economic consequences of the war. On the eve of the election an east Mississippi Republican had reported the new political development in the state and predicted that "if General Grant is elected, white Republicans in Mississippi will be as thick as leaves in Val Ambrosa, and they will not be 'carpetbaggers' either, but gentlemen 'to the manor born.'"[21] A Republican correspondent to the Cincinnati *Commercial* observed at this time that a substantial minority of Mississippi whites favored the candidacy of the Hero of Appomattox, since only he could bring a restoration of peace and prosperity. Furthermore, this writer claimed, many of the old citizens who publicly went along with the popular preference for Democratic candidate Horatio Seymour had privately expressed the desire for a Grant victory. Even Jonathan Tarbell, a highly partisan Republican and chairman of the party's state executive committee, admitted after the election that thousands of whites were now on the political fence, waiting to see which way to jump.[22]

After the election influential Mississippi conservatives advised whites to cooperate with the new administration. Believing that Grant's election meant the triumph of moderate republicanism not only over the Democracy but over radicalism as well, prominent old citizens like Albert Gallatin Brown, Giles Hillyer, John W. C. Watson, and Horatio F. Simrall, most of whom had been reconstructionists in 1867, stepped forward to mold public opinion in support of equal political rights for blacks, political tolerance, and sectional reconciliation. Even Barksdale had kind words for Grant and those persons who had crossed the Rubicon to become Republicans after the election.[23] Summing up the pro-Grant feeling in the

21. Meridian *Chronicle*, October 17, 1868.
22. As reported in the Vicksburg *Herald*, September 17, 1868. See also the Hazlehurst *Copiahan*, March 13, 1869; the Vicksburg *Times*, February 23, 1869; the *Hinds County Gazette*, March 3, 1869; A. D. Jones to Benjamin F. Butler, April 13, 1869, and Tarbell to George S. Boutwell, January 14, 1869, both in Papers on Conditions in Mississippi. Although Mississippi, as an unreconstructed state, could not participate in the presidential election, rallies to support favorite candidates were held by both parties in the larger towns.
23. Vicksburg *Herald*, November 19, 21, 1868; *Hinds County Gazette*, January 6, 1869; Vicksburg *Times*, February 23, March 20, 1869; New York *Times*, January 12, 1869; *House Miscellaneous Documents*, 40th Cong., 3rd Sess., No. 53, p. 299; Jackson *Weekly Clarion*, March 18, May 6, 1869.

state, the editor of the Grenada *Sentinel* wrote that Negro suffrage was accepted as a fixed fact, and Mississippi whites could support a moderate party on this basis, provided that it rejected the political proscription of former Confederates. "We want the conservative masses of Mississippi, no matter to what political affiliations they formerly belonged, to come boldly up to the rescue and form a new party, whose power shall sweep the radicals of both extremes from the political arena," this editor declared. "We are tired of old issues, superanuated [*sic*] political hacks—men who carry the love of country in their pockets and whose patriotism never rises beyond an official position. . . . Let us shake off this lethargy which has nearly ruined us and move in a path that will lead us to the energy and spirit of the times."[24]

As representatives of the new political tendency, Brown, Simrall, and Watson went to Washington to inform the Republican Congress of the emergence of a genuinely cooperative spirit among a large number of whites in the state. Their specific purpose was to induce Congress to reject the efforts of Mississippi Radicals to have the constitution, with the proscriptive clauses, declared in force. Simrall told the Committee on Reconstruction that the results of the November election had ended the debate in his state on the congressional reconstruction settlement. The only issue remaining was the proscriptive clauses in the constitution. "The majority of our people," this Union Whig averred, "are ready to adopt the same constitution, if shorn by Congress of all unjust and irritating discriminations, especially its disabilities as contained in the franchise article." Insofar as political attitudes were concerned, "a large portion of the whites, it may be a majority, look with confidence and hope to the incoming administration," Simrall claimed. "By a liberal, confiding, and magnanimous policy towards them, the President-elect will find that they will give his administration a generous support."[25]

Brown, the old war horse of secession Democracy, insisted before the Committee on Reconstruction that party lines in Mississippi had been obliterated by the calamities that had occurred and people were now willing to affiliate with the party that would

24. As reported in the *Hinds County Gazette*, January 6, 1869.
25. Horatio F. Simrall, *Statement Made Before the Reconstruction Committee on the State of Affairs in Mississippi, February 6, 1869* (N.p., 1869), 1–2, 5–6.

give them peace and an opportunity to rebuild their society and economy.[26] Watson did not go as far as Simrall or Brown in promising white affiliation with the Republican party if it eliminated the proscriptive features of the constitution. The main thrust of his argument was that the document as a whole "was conceived and framed in the interest of a very small minority of the white population, and seemingly in direct antagonism to the property and personal rights of the bona fide citizens and property holders of the State."[27] Despite his reluctance to be associated with republicanism, this former Confederate senator conferred with Grant on three occasions, before and after his inaugural, regarding reconstruction and the constitution of 1868. In these discussions Watson evidently gave the president some assurance that important white support for the new administration would be forthcoming if it shunned the advances of the Radical Eggleston-Gibbs party and adopted a liberal and conciliatory policy toward Mississippi and the South.[28]

Thus with apparent support for Grant and for moderate republicanism mounting in Mississippi, many local Republicans saw an opportunity to realize their cherished hopes for a white power base for their party. They preferred, however, to work toward this goal through the regular Republican organization, avoiding the tainted association of the Brown-Watson "rebels." With a shaky hand, moderate Republicans carried their plan for a liberal reconstruction policy to the floor of the state party convention that met in Jackson in late November, 1868, to decide whether or not to endorse the proclamation of the Radical Gibbs committee.

Their hopes for success, however, were soon dashed. Heavily weighted in favor of the black counties, the convention shouted down moderate speakers Jefferson L. Wofford, a scalawag, and George F. Brown and Nelson Gill, carpetbaggers, when they spoke against the Committee of Five's action in proclaiming the ratification of the constitution and the election of the Republican candidates for office. By a vote of 79 to 25, the convention adopted a resolution calling on Congress to implement the proclamation,

26. Albert Gallatin Brown, *Statement on Mississippi Affairs, Filed by Permission with the Reconstruction Committee* (Washington, D.C., 1869).
27. John W. C. Watson, "Let Us Have Peace," in Papers on Conditions in Mississippi.
28. Jackson *Weekly Clarion*, May 27, 1869.

and it immediately dispatched a delegation of sixteen Radical Republicans to Washington to lobby for the cause.[29]

The Radical victory in the convention triggered a rupture in the party, with several alienated moderates declaring their intention to send their own delegation to Washington and present their case to Congress and President-elect Grant. Led by Wofford and Elza Jeffords, a Delta carpetbagger and Gillem appointee to the state supreme court, the bolters affirmed their devotion to Republican principles and insisted that they represented the true sentiments of the party. They reiterated the objections of moderates to the proscription policy and called for like-minded Republicans to rally behind them.[30] However, no ground swell of support developed. Although several prominent Republicans were dissatisfied with the action of the November convention, most of them like the powerful black orator James Lynch, remained loyal to the regular party.[31] Lynch's refusal to join the bolters frustrated their plans to sway large numbers of Negroes. Without a substantial following in the black community, dissident Republicans could not gain the support of local party functionaries who, if they expected to have a political future, could not defy the opinion of their Negro constituents. Several prominent white Republicans with moderate leanings, although admitting privately that the action of the November convention was rash and did not find favor with many party functionaries in the state, likewise rejected cooperation with the bolters.[32] Included in this group were the influential James Lusk Alcorn and the articulate Horatio N. Ballard. But even though they were unable to attract many prominent Republicans to their camp, once the die had been cast bolting moderate (or, as often referred to, conservative) Republicans felt compelled to pursue their risky

29. Meridian *Chronicle*, December 5, 1868; Vicksburg *Weekly Republican*, December 6, 1868; Vicksburg *Herald*, November 27, December 1, 1868. At least one delegation, the Rankin County one, headed by local black leader Cyrus Myers, was denied membership in the convention because it had already gone on record as opposing the Committee of Five's proclamation. Vicksburg *Times*, December 11, 1868.

30. *Address to the Reconstruction Committee*, 1, 4, 7.

31. Thomas W. Stringer to Boutwell, January 27, 1869, in Papers on Conditions in Mississippi; Harris, "James Lynch," 47–48.

32. Horatio N. Ballard to Bingham, January 7, 1869, in Papers on Conditions in Mississippi.

enterprise. Their chance for success rested with the national party leaders, especially with Grant.

By January, 1869, two Republican delegations from Mississippi had converged on Washington to exert pressure on Congress and President-elect Grant. When the Simrall group of conservatives arrived in February, the dissident Republican delegation joined them in an intense effort to win Grant's support, correctly believing that his influence would not be ignored by dominant Republicans in Congress. The Radical deputation placed their fate in the hands of Congress. The powerful Committee on Reconstruction in the House of Representatives indicated its sympathy for the Radical position but stopped short of recommending that the rejected constitution be declared in force. Instead, under the leadership of George S. Boutwell the committee proposed that the constitutional convention be reconvened with the authority to appoint a provisional governor and draw up a new constitution to be submitted to the people. The governor selected by the convention would obviously be in sympathy with the men of the new order, and preparatory to another ratification contest he would no doubt reorganize the election machinery to ensure an untrammeled ballot for the Republican majority.[33]

Mississippi Radicals, however, refused to support the Boutwell settlement, arguing that the delay that would inevitably occur if the plan were adopted would be fatal to the Republican cause in the state. Insisting that Republican victories in the fall had muted conservative opposition in Mississippi, Radicals declared that now was the time for Congress to put a loyal government in office under the constitution of 1868. They claimed that if placed in power the Republican party would quickly be able to consolidate its position and meet any future crisis that might occur.[34] Some Radicals promised that once in control of the state government they would soothe troubled white feelings regarding the new order and soon "win

33. *Congressional Globe*, 40th Cong., 3rd Sess., 1143.
34. Clarke to Garfield, February 12, 1869, in Papers on Conditions in Mississippi; J. R. Smith to Gibbs, February 27, 1869, in Fourteenth Amendment Relief Papers, Mississippi; Friar's Point *Weekly Delta*, March 10, 1869; U. Ozanne to Butler, March 24, 1869, in Butler Papers.

over to [our] way of thinking the entire conservative portion of the
well disposed citizens."[35]

Impressed by these arguments, but also wary of the political
repercussions that might occur in the North if they simply imposed the proscriptive constitution upon the people of the state,
dominant Republicans in Congress again postponed consideration
of the Mississippi question. This time they awaited the inauguration of Grant, who by virtue of his election to the presidency
had become the recognized leader of the Republican party and
whose support was now necessary for the continuation of congressional reconstruction in the South. Radical Republicans were well
aware that the general had been keeping close company with conservative delegations from Mississippi and Virginia, and they knew
that on one occasion he had expressed a strong opposition to the
proscriptive features of the proposed constitutions of these two
states. Nevertheless, Radicals hoped to secure Grant's cooperation, believing that as a political novice he would be amenable to
suggestions from congressional party leaders.[36]

When the new Congress met in March, 1869, soon after Grant's
inauguration, the reconstruction committee of the House of Representatives, now headed by Benjamin F. Butler, moved toward
meeting the new president's reservations regarding proscription
but without repudiating the position of the Mississippi Radicals.
On March 19 Butler introduced a bill in the House similar to the
Boutwell proposal in its stipulation that the constitutional convention would be reconvened and would select a provisional governor
to administer the affairs of the state until civil authority was restored.[37] More comprehensive than the Boutwell proposal, however, the Butler plan would placate Mississippi Republicans by
making it the responsibility of the federal government, and specifically the federal courts, to protect local political rights even after
civil government was reestablished in the state. A forerunner of
the Enforcement Acts of 1870–1871, the proposed bill imposed

35. N. A. M. Dudley to Legrand W. Perce, December 14, 1868, in Papers on Conditions in Mississippi.
36. New York *Tribune*, February 16, 1869; Jackson *Weekly Clarion*, April 1, 29, May 27,
1869.
37. The Butler bill may be found in the *Congressional Globe*, 41st Cong., 1st Sess.,
253–54.

a stiff penalty on any person found guilty of obstructing free speech, political activity, or the election process. Another innovative clause, probably designed to aid blacks in acquiring a freehold, required that all lands in the state that were sold for nonpayment of taxes "shall be disposed of only by sale in separate subdivisions not exceeding forty acres each." Butler's proposal, if enacted, would place Mississippi in the hands of the Republican party, with the federal judiciary as guarantors of the new regime's safety.

Many Mississippi Radicals, however, were still dissatisfied: the political proscription of former Confederates was not assured by the Butler plan. They believed, probably correctly, that the re-convened constitutional convention, although the same one that had framed the disabling clauses during a time of high emotions in 1868, would choose to avoid the issue now, especially since President Grant, moderate Republicans in Congress, and influential Republican journals like the New York *Tribune* had indicated their opposition to proscription. These Radicals had staked their dominance of the party and the state upon the principle of proscription, and the failure of their program would immediately lessen their influence. Only the imposition of the original constitution with its proscriptive features could save the day for the Radicals.[38]

Nevertheless, support in Congress for the Butler bill declined appreciably when the news leaked out of the White House that the taciturn Grant opposed it. In the debate on the floor of the House of Representatives, moderate Republicans, realizing that the course of events was now running in their favor, denounced the Butler plan as conceding too much to the Mississippi Radicals. For the moderates, John F. Farnsworth of Illinois introduced a substitute that would provide for the resubmission of the consti-tution to the voters, allowing them, however, to vote separately on the proscriptive clauses. Meanwhile the state would remain under military jurisdiction but with a new commander, appointed by President Grant.[39]

With Republicans divided there was little chance that Congress

38. Clarke to Garfield, January 29, 1869, in Garfield Papers; Jackson *Weekly Clarion*, April 29, 1869, quoting both Hiram T. Fisher, chairman of the state Republican executive committee, and the Meridian *Chronicle*.

39. *Congressional Globe*, 41st Cong., 1st Sess., 255–60, 345.

would pass either the Butler bill or the Farnsworth substitute during the spring session. Only the intervention of the president
could produce a decision on the Mississippi issue before Congress
adjourned. When debate ended on April 1 without a positive move
by Grant, the House of Representatives by an overwhelming majority voted to postpone consideration of the Mississippi question
until December when a new session would convene.[40] At first
Grant was content to go along with the congressional decision.
However, the dissident or moderate Republican delegation from
Mississippi, now reinforced in their lobbying activities by such
persuasive northern settlers as Alexander Warner and Archie C.
Fisk and by Grant's brother-in-law, Louis Dent, who owned a
plantation in the Delta but was living in Washington at the time,
descended upon the White House to encourage the president to
intervene and obtain a congressional decision on the question before adjournment.[41] Aware that Grant privately opposed the radical Butler bill, these Republicans argued that Mississippi's quick
readmission to the Union was essential to the restoration of the
state's social fabric, now threatened by widespread lawlessness,
demoralization, and economic rot. They urged the president to
take the initiative in securing congressional approval of the
Farnsworth substitute, though they avoided mentioning that with
the political momentum in Congress temporarily in their favor the
moderates wanted to strike before the Butler Radicals regained
the initiative and secured the president's support for a reconstruction settlement that would place the Gibbs-Eggleston faction in
power.

Faced with a similar political situation in Virginia, where conservatives already had begun to doubt Grant's early professions
of support,[42] the president agreed to intervene. On April 7 he sent
a brief message to Congress calling for swift congressional approval
of the separate-vote procedure for Virginia and Mississippi. Grant
did not specify what clauses in the two constitutions should be
voted on separately, but it was clear to his adherents in Congress

40. *Ibid.*, 437.
41. *Hinds County Gazette*, April 7, 1869; Jackson *Weekly Clarion*, April 1, 8, 29, May
6, 27, 1869.
42. Jack P. Maddex, Jr., *The Virginia Conservatives, 1867–1879* (Chapel Hill, 1970), 76.

that he wanted the proscriptive sections set aside. Declaring that the purpose of his party's reconstruction policy should always be "the absolute protection of all its citizens in the full enjoyment of the freedom and security which is the object of a republican government," the president assured his friends that the people of Virginia and Mississippi had met this requirement and Congress should thus aid them in eliminating "all causes of irritation [i.e., political proscription] as promptly as possible" to facilitate the completion of reconstruction.[43]

The next day Grant summoned Ben Butler to the White House to give his reasons for intervention on the side of the moderates and to prod Butler, as chairman of the Committee on Reconstruction in the House of Representatives, to support the administration's position. Rather than risk a break with Grant, with whom he had recently become reconciled after a long and bitter feud, the politically astute Butler not only acquiesced but agreed to influence the House to approve the plan. Disclaiming the need to explain his sudden shift of position to his startled colleagues, Butler on the same day that he visited the president reported out of the reconstruction committee a bill incorporating the recommendations contained in Grant's message of April 7. After a brief debate the new Butler bill, which was strikingly similar to the earlier Farnsworth measure, easily passed the House with no Republicans voting against it.[44] When the bill went to the Senate, Republicans saw an opportunity to advance the proposed Fifteenth Amendment a few steps closer to ratification. After the Senate had approved the Butler bill by a comfortable margin, Senator Oliver P. Morton offered an additional section requiring that the three unreconstructed states (Texas had been included in the provisions of the House bill) ratify the Negro suffrage amendment to the national Constitution before they could be restored to full fellowship in the Union.[45] This new requirement was not viewed as a significant departure from Grant's moderate proposal for these states, since by this time moderates, both northern and southern, had come to

43. James D. Richardson (comp.), A Compilation of the Papers of the Presidents (11 vols.; New York, 1896–1908), VII, 11–12.

44. New York Tribune, April 9, 1869; Congressional Globe, 41st Cong., 1st Sess., 633.

45. Congressional Globe, 41st Cong., 1st Sess., 653. In justifying his amendment, Morton said that his purpose was to speed up Negro suffrage in the North. Ibid., 654–55.

accept black suffrage as a fact, and also the president had given it his stamp of approval.[46] Even Mississippi conservatives eschewed criticism of the Morton amendment, believing that it placed no new substantive demand upon the unreconstructed states. In fact, Ethelbert Barksdale pointed out that the main purpose of the Fifteenth Amendment was to make Negro suffrage national, an action that was long overdue, rather than merely reinforcing its existence in three southern states.[47] The House immediately concurred in the Morton amendment, and it passed both houses by a strict party vote, with only three Republicans voting against it. The final measure actually permitted the president to determine the provisions to be voted on separately and also the dates for holding the elections in the three states.[48]

President Grant's vigorous intervention on the side of the moderates had indeed made a difference and suggested that the cause of moderate republicanism in the South might be the wave of the future. The president certainly had the support of his party in 1869, and if congressional cooperation in the early days of the new administration was a good index, party leaders in Congress would not insist on their hard-won prerogatives—won in their struggle with President Johnson—as long as Grant provided decisive and able leadership in protecting the bare bones of the reconstruction laws of 1867. A great deal depended upon the administration's implementation of what had emerged as a new (albeit ambiguous) Republican policy toward the South, specifically toward Mississippi, Virginia, and Texas. But also crucial to the success of the Grant policy of moderation was its reception by southern whites. Moderate Republicans in Mississippi who had bolted the regular party and well-meaning conservatives like Albert Gallatin Brown

46. For a contrary view, see Hans L. Trefousse, *The Radical Republicans: Lincoln's Vanguard for Racial Justice* (New York, 1969), 427–28.

47. William Gillette, *The Right to Vote: Politics and the Passage of the Fifteenth Amendment* (Baltimore, 1965), 93; Jackson *Weekly Clarion*, April 22, May 27, June 24, 1869; Vicksburg *Times*, May 5, 7, 1869. Several Republican senators, who favored the Fifteenth Amendment in principle, nonetheless believed that the Morton amendment was unwise in that it appeared to impose a new condition upon these states and violated congressional promises that this would not be done. *Congressional Globe*, 41st Cong., 1st Sess., 653; Edward McPherson, *The Political History of the United States [1865–70]* (New York, 1969), 410.

48. McPherson, *Political History*, 408–409.

and Horatio F. Simrall had promised the development of a strong Grant party among whites if the new administration abandoned proscription and the Radical faction in the region. Grant and his party in Congress had taken an important step in this direction. The success of the Republican new departure now largely depended upon the ability of friendly conservative leaders in Mississippi, Virginia, and Texas, in cooperation with moderate (and conservative) Republicans, to make real a Grant party in their states—and, not incidentally, to demonstrate that southern whites were indeed committed to the generally accepted results of the Civil War, that is, equal rights, justice, political tolerance, and an end to southern sectionalism. Political developments in Mississippi during the long campaign preceding the new election on the 1868 constitution would go far toward determining the fate of the Grant policy of conciliation.

7

Republicanism at the Crossroads

After four years of reconstruction frustration, uncertainty, and strife, many Mississippi conservatives hailed the action of the Republican president and Congress as a godsend and a national vindication of their struggle to defeat the forces of radicalism in the state. To the conservative leadership, the end of sectional recrimination and the dawn of national reconciliation appeared imminent. Effusive in their praise for Grant's intervention on their side, conservative accommodationists also passed out accolades to the dissident Republican delegation that had persuaded the president to take a hand in the matter.[1] For the first time since the rise of the party of the new order in the state, conservatives admitted that some distinctions should be made among individual Republicans regarding the purity of their motives and their integrity. The Yazoo City *Mississippi Democrat* expressed this view when it declared: "In Mississippi we have a class of Republicans whom we can no longer doubt to be true friends to the interest of the state." Such Republicans as native-born Joseph W. Field and Jefferson L. Wofford and northern newcomers Elza Jeffords, Archie C. Fisk, and Alexander Warner, by their successful efforts to rid the state of the proscriptive constitution and prevent a Radical ascendancy had placed the people "under obligations of gratitude that can never be forgotten."[2]

In handing out this measure of praise, conservative leaders had a more important purpose in mind than a mere expression of appreciation for the noble deeds of the insurgent Republicans. Their main objective was to obtain moderate Republican support for still another anti-Radical party in the state. The conservative effort to form such a coalition, which would be based on support for the president and his southern policy, began soon after Congress ap-

1. Jackson *Weekly Clarion*, April 22, May 13, 27, 1869; *Hinds County Gazette*, May 12, 26, 1869; Columbus *Southern Sentinel*, May 11, 1869.
2. As reported in the Jackson *Weekly Clarion*, April 15, 1869. See also *ibid.*, May 13, 27, 1869, and the Forest *Register*, August 18, 1869.

proved Grant's proposal for a new election. Although the traditional leaders like Brown and Barksdale planned to control the new party, they needed the cooperation of the dissident Republican faction to give their organization legitimacy in the eyes of national authorities, especially President Grant. Furthermore, there was the matter of the Negro vote. Mississippi's large black electorate, although demoralized by the course of events since the defeat of the constitution in 1868, remained suspicious of any effort by the old leaders to regain power. Protected by the military, blacks could be expected in the next election to provide the margin of victory for the regular Republicans if the old citizens were too noticeable in the anti-Radical party. To win at the polls conservatives needed some black votes, which, they believed, could be obtained if northerners like Jeffords, Fisk, and Warner, whose backgrounds as liberators and Republicans gave them standing in the black community as well as in Washington, were placed in conspicuous positions in the movement.

The promoters of a new conservative party were confident that they could form an anti-Radical coalition without calling themselves Republicans. Unlike in 1868 when whites achieved unity under the Democratic banner, in 1869 conservative spokesmen for the new departure could not expect to secure overwhelming white support for a policy of cooperation with a national Republican administration that favored Negro rights. Nevertheless, they expected to sway enough white votes so that, when joined by a substantial black following, they could be successful in future Reconstruction elections. In 1868 the participation of Union-Whig leaders in the campaign had been decisive in rallying the white masses to the Democratic banner and defeating the Radicals. Many Whigs, though not the die-hard, anti-Republican type, were only too willing in 1869 to abandon the Democratic party, especially the national organization, and form a conservative party that would be free of the Democracy's tainting influence. The events of April and the apparent commitment of the Grant administration to a liberal policy for the South provided these Whigs (and others who had never been Whigs but now preferred the leadership of this group to any other) with an opportunity to organize the kind of conservative, anti-Radical, nationally supported Union party that they desired.[3] They did not object to former secession Democrats affiliating with the new party, but they fully expected them to serve in the ranks and remain inconspicuous in party councils.

Some old-line Whigs were quick to applaud the cooperation of regenerated Democrats like Brown and Barksdale, who in the spring of 1869 played leading roles in persuading their adherents to accept the new conservative party's Union-Whig leadership. Barksdale, clearly having no intention of continuing in an inferior role after the party had gained power, urged Mississippians to sever all ties with the national Democratic party in order to demonstrate their good faith to finicky Whigs as well as to moderate Republicans.[4]

By early June, most of the newspapers had published their versions of a sound Union-Whig ticket for the forthcoming election. Intrastate regionalism and the post-1860 politics of the prospective Whig candidates were important considerations in these endorsements. In the river counties and in the southern part of the state, Union Whigs Charles C. Shackleford, Potter, and Simrall received strong support to head the conservative ticket. Those favoring a rock-ribbed Unionist who as governor would not be too enthusiastic for Negro rights advanced Shackleford, a planter-lawyer and former president of the Mississippi Central Railroad. Potter's record in defense of southern rights since 1865 made him the logical candidate for many conservatives, but it also made him unacceptable to influential moderates who feared the disapproval of the Grant administration and Congress if such a consistent foe of Republican reconstruction were nominated.[5]

The Union Whig who stood the best chance of attracting both black and white voters in the populous river counties was Simrall. With an impressive background as a professor of law, a member of the legislature of two states, and a participant in the Confederate "council" of Kentucky, Simrall came gradually to support recon-

3. Statements of Brown and Simrall, respectively, in the Jackson *Weekly Clarion*, April 29, May 27, 1869; *Hinds County Gazette*, May 5, 12, 1869; Vicksburg *Times*, June 30, 1869; Hernando *Weekly Press*, May 20, 1869.

4. Jackson *Weekly Clarion*, April 22, May 20, June 24, 1869; *Hinds County Gazette*, May 12, 26, 1869.

5. Vicksburg *Times*, April 23, 1869; *Hinds County Gazette*, May 5, 1869; Friar's Point *Weekly Delta*, May 5, 1869; Jackson *Weekly Clarion*, May 20, 1869.

struction on the terms laid down by Congress. His advocacy included, as he said, "the incorporation of the African race into the body politic" and an end to all forms of political intolerance in Mississippi. Simrall, who subsequently affiliated with the Republican party and served on the state supreme court, did not rest his case as a candidate on human rights alone, although these were fundamental to his vision of the future. In a publicized speech in Vicksburg soon after President Grant's intervention in the Mississippi question, this learned planter-lawyer outlined a program of material progress under national auspices that would have warmed the heart of Henry Clay. His speech also reflected the kind of expansive thinking that impelled a number of postwar moderates to cast their lots with the young and vibrant Republican party. Simrall declared on this occasion:[6]

> For myself, I am disposed to take my State from her isolation, and hitch her on to the car of progress, [placing] her in such condition that the rich streams that flow out from the national treasury may not float past her. . . . I want to open wide the door that people from the North, the East, and the West; from Europe, and if you please from Asia, may come in and dwell amongst us, and feel at home. I want no more strife, or contention, than such as legitimately belong to the field, the shop, the mart, and the profession. . . . Let there be absolute freedom of opinion of the tongue and pen, obedience to and enforcement of the laws, and soon, very soon, our State will arise refreshed like a strong man from his sleep.
>
> Now that China is open to American commerce, Mississippi can become the focus for the trade of the Orient with the Eastern U.S. and Europe. Then the center of the world's trade and power will be transferred to the United States, just as the Oriental trade had earlier made the Portuguese, the Dutch, and the British great.

The power of the federal government to make vast internal improvements was strengthened by the results of the war, Simrall contended. The time would come, he confidently predicted, when the railroads and the commerce of the nation "will radiate out from the center to the circumference of the Republic, like the spokes of the wheel." Strategically located in the great valley, Mississippi was destined to become a leading commercial state. But despite

6. Friar's Point *Weekly Delta*, May 5, 1869. Simrall's address may be found in the Jackson *Weekly Clarion*, May 27, 1869.

the popularity of Simrall's economic vision in financially starved Mississippi, his advanced position on human rights and national power, and, ironically, his ineligibility for office at the time due to Fourteenth Amendment disabilities, rendered him unacceptable as a candidate on a conservative ticket.

John W. C. Watson of Holly Springs was far more congenial to the conservative temper of whites. In fact, conservatives of north Mississippi were virtually unanimous in singing his praises and demanding that he be the proposed party's choice for governor.[7] Watson seemed the ideal candidate to meet the peculiar political needs of whites in 1869. He was the most prominent Union Whig in an area of the state containing a large class of yeoman whites, and he had served in the Confederate senate, which gave him some claim to the support of former southern nationalists who feared for the worst at the hands of an unsympathetic Union-Whig governor like Shackleford. In addition, he was not excluded from office by the provisions of the Fourteenth Amendment and had consulted with President Grant on reconstruction matters. Watson's early opposition to black suffrage would hardly recommend his candidacy to the Negro community, but the fact that he had long been sympathetic to black aspirations for education and his willingness by 1869 to extend to them the fundamental rights of citizenship might persuade some to vote for him. Unfortunately for the conservative cause, Watson became sick and left the state for treatment during the spring, leaving the old citizens in a quandary regarding a standardbearer who could meet the approval of all factions and perhaps the national administration as well.

In their efforts to organize an anti-Radical coalition, conservative leaders found, as before, that white opposition to Negro rights was the greatest barrier. Perceptive conservatives realized that unless they could convince the white masses to accept the principles of black suffrage and civil equality their movement would not be sustained by the Grant administration nor would they be able to attract black voters.[8] Despite a degree of recognition by whites that

7. Friar's Point *Weekly Delta*, June 2, 1869; Hernando *Weekly Press*, May 20, 27, June 10, 1869.

8. For an apparently candid statement by an anti-Radical spokesman suggesting the difficulties of the conservative support for Grant and Negro rights, see Albert Gallatin

political equality for blacks, at least in form, was inevitable, most could not imagine supporting a party that actively advocated such a damnable principle. Nevertheless, the apparent triumph of moderate republicanism nationally and Grant's willingness to abandon the southern proscriptionists had caused antipathetic whites to temper considerably their hostility toward Negro rights. Because of the delicacy of white racial attitudes and the need to avoid being labeled a Negro party, conservative leaders—many of whom had already demonstrated that they could be quite flexible when their racial preconceptions conflicted with political expediency—tied support for black equality with the less controversial themes of universal amnesty for Confederates, sectional and racial reconciliation, economic development, and the suppression of crime. Biracial "peace" meetings were held throughout the state with conservative speakers proclaiming the gospel of racial cooperation, equal justice for all, and support for the president.[9]

The resolution issued by conservatives in Choctaw County was typical of those adopted in the meetings. "It is with us now, as last year," the Choctaw resolution declared, "not so much shall the black man be enfranchised, as it is, shall the white man be disfranchised; and we are grateful to the black man for his magnanimity in conceding that we were as much entitled to this privilege as he, while subjected to the influence of the Radicals. . . . [As a result] we hail with grateful hearts the dawn of the doctrine of universal suffrage and universal amnesty as ominous of a better day ahead."[10] It soon became clear, especially to conservatives in the predominantly black counties, that few Negroes would be swayed by such appeals coming from men who as late as 1868 had denounced black aspirations for equal political rights. Moreover, their plan to obtain the support of dissident carpetbaggers in order to influence blacks to vote the conservative ticket failed to materialize because these northerners were unwilling to cut their ties with the Republican party. By the summer of 1869 conservative leaders had come to realize, in most cases reluctantly, that their

---

Brown's letter to several prominent old citizens of Jackson, published in the Vicksburg *Times*, April 29, 1869, and in other conservative newspapers.

9. New York *Times*, May 23, 1869; Jackson *Weekly Clarion*, April 22, 29, May 13, 1869.

10. Reported in the Jackson *Weekly Clarion*, August 5, 1869.

only hope of defeating the Radicals at the polls was to abandon their effort to form a homegrown party and give their support to the National Union Republican party.[11]

The National Union Republican party of Mississippi grew out of the schism in the regular state Republican party over proscription and the subsequent success of the insurgents in gaining President Grant's approval of their moderate plan for a new election on the constitution. After the president's action, other Republicans bolted the regular party. The time now appeared ripe for the organization of a liberal Republican party that would be free of the stigma of radicalism and proscription and would appeal to a substantial number of whites in the state.[12] Although they expected to attract whites to the party, the insurgents insisted that the new organization retain in undiluted form a Republican character and principles; conservatives who joined were expected to subscribe without reservations to a "true Republican" platform. Like the leaders of the aborted conservative movement, the organizers of the new Republican party recognized the need for attracting a sizable portion of the Negro electorate to their ranks. Since many of them were natives of the North and former Union officers and since Grant had apparently given his blessings to the movement, the party's founding fathers, operating out of Jackson and Vicksburg, believed they stood an excellent chance of winning the allegiance of blacks from the "political Philistines" of the Radical wing.[13]

While the iron was hot, fifteen moderate or insurgent Republicans met in Jackson in early June and issued a circular to the press, calling for a convention of all sympathizers to meet at the capitol on the twenty-third of the month to form the National Union Republican party of Mississippi. At least nine of the fifteen signers were former Union officers who had settled in the state and would play

11. *Ibid.*, June 10, 17, 1869; Forest *Register*, June 16, 1869.
12. George Moorman to William T. Sherman, June 12, 1869, in William T. Sherman Papers; Vicksburg *Times and Republican*, August 24, 1869, July 29, 1870; *Hinds County Gazette*, May 12, 1869; letter from Joseph W. Field to the Jackson *Weekly Clarion*, May 20, 1869.
13. Vicksburg *Times*, August 25, 26, September 12, 1869; Vicksburg *Times and Republican*, July 29, 1870; Forest *Register*, June 16, 1869, December 10, 1870.

leading roles in the party during its brief history.[14] Appealing to members of both races to join them and denouncing the Radicals for their proscriptive policies, the insurgents announced that they fully represented the Republican principles of equal rights, toleration, liberality, and forbearance. They claimed the support of President Grant and Congress and declared that the ultimate objective of their movement was to restore sectional and racial harmony in the state. "We do not understand that it is the mission of the Republican party to stir up strife; but, on the contrary, when truly interpreted, its highest aim . . . is to allay dissension, disarm prejudice, and restore law and order, by discouraging every useless and wanton attempt to array one class of citizens against the other." In their call for support the National Union Republicans assured Mississippians that they fervently desired "to see such a condition of affairs as will best enhance and promote the material interest and prosperity of our commonwealth."[15]

On June 23 delegates from fewer than one half of the counties assembled in the senate chamber of the capitol to give birth to the National Union Republican party. Dominated by men who could be classified as carpetbaggers, although a sympathetic conservative press preferred to describe them as "refined gentlemen" of northern origins, the convention nonetheless selected scalawag Wofford, a former major in the service of the Gray, as its president. Of the approximately seventy delegates in the convention only a handful were Negroes, and they had no influence in the proceedings. In the opening speech carpetbagger Frederic Speed of Vicksburg reaffirmed that the new organization would not deviate from the straight and narrow path of "true Republicanism." Disclaiming "the fatal heresy of proscription," Speed reminded the delegates that "we have come together as Republicans upon a truly Republican platform [one] recognizing the civil and political equality of all men."[16] The delegates then approved a platform which corre-

14. Field and Wofford were the only scalawags who have been identified among the signers of this call; Amos Draine of Madison County evidently was the only Negro in the group.

15. *Appleton's Annual Cyclopaedia,* 1869, pp. 456–57; Forest *Register,* June 16, 1869; *Hinds County Gazette,* June 16, 1869.

16. Jackson *Weekly Clarion,* July 1, 1869; Vicksburg *Times and Republican,* July 29, 1870.

sponded to the principles and purpose expressed in the early June circular. Although they had informally settled upon Louis Dent, the president's brother-in-law, as their nominee for governor, the delegates chose to postpone the selection of candidates for office until the election date had been set and the course of the campaign had become clearer. A gnawing feeling existed in the minds of these insurgent Republicans that Grant might not endorse their movement. They wanted to wait and make sure of both Dent's and the president's commitment to the cause before nominating a slate of candidates.

The election in Virginia in early July, 1869, would go far toward determining the policy of the Grant administration toward the new Republican party in Mississippi. In the Old Dominion carpetbagger Gilbert C. Walker, who insisted on being called a "liberal Republican," headed a conservative coalition that endorsed President Grant's reconstruction policy and indicated its support for the rights of blacks, universal male suffrage, and political amnesty for former Confederates. Radical Republicans, in a state where black voters did not constitute a majority of the electorate, sought desperately to convince the national administration that they were the "true Republicans" of Virginia and that Walker was only a stalking horse for a Democratic restoration.[17] Grant, however, remained neutral during the brief campaign. When the Walker ticket swept to victory on July 6, conservative observers from both North and South attributed it not only to the president's policy of permitting a separate vote on the proscriptive clauses in the Virginia constitution but also to his fundamental hostility to the party's Radical wing, inspiring him to give direct encouragement to the Walker movement. Much to their grief, conservatives would later discover that they had misjudged the meaning of the Virginia election.

Meanwhile, National Union Republicans in Mississippi hailed the triumph of the Walker party as a resounding affirmation of their course in forming a white-based Grant party in the state. Impressed by the success of the Walker strategy, a number of the traditional leaders who had shunned involvement in the organization of the party in June announced their support of the northern-led movement. One hundred and forty prominent old citizens is-

17. Maddex, *Virginia Conservatives*, 79–83.

sued an address to the people citing the "marvelous victory" of the conservative coalition in the "mother of States" and calling upon Mississippians to provide active and zealous support to the National Union Republican party. "We feel assured," the conservative address declared, that the ticket selected by the new party "will be composed of gentlemen actuated by conservative and patriotic principles and possessed of intelligence and capacity for office."[18] In the wake of the Virginia election, even conservatives who had never expressed kind words for any Republican faction or for the principle of black political equality contained in the congressional plan of reconstruction announced their endorsement of the National Union Republicans and advised their friends against entering a third-party ticket in the campaign.[19] Formerly a die-hard opponent of reconstruction, Arthur J. Frantz of the Brandon *Republican* confidently predicted that Louis Dent, who was now expected to be the new party's candidate for governor, "will get the support of all papers in the State except the organ of the proscriptionists [the Jackson *Pilot*] and a few of the ultra Democratic journals."[20] In the exhilaration of the moment, Barksdale declared that in view of the growing strength of the National Union Republicans he would not be surprised "to find that the Eggleston gang of Radicals entirely abandon the canvass long before the day of the election." Some conservatives frankly admitted that in joining the insurgents they only intended to espouse Republican principles until "nitroglycerin Radicalism" had been destroyed in the state; once redemption had been achieved they proposed to raise the Democratic standard again.[21]

The outpouring of white conservative support for the National Union Republican party almost immediately changed the complexion of the party, especially in the organization of its local units. Originally intended as a party of moderate or liberal Republicans, the handful of men committed to the perpetuation of Republican principles on the local level were swamped by the old citizens,

18. The conservative address may be found in the Forest *Register*, August 18, 1869, and the Jackson *Weekly Clarion*, August 12, 1869.
19. Forest *Register*, July 21, 28, 1869; Jackson *Weekly Clarion*, July 15, 22, 29, 1869; Vicksburg *Times*, July 25, 1869.
20. As reported in the Forest *Register*, July 28, 1869.
21. Jackson *Weekly Clarion*, July 29, 1869; Forest *Register*, August 25, 1869.

and even many supporters of the movement soon joined regular Republicans in labeling it a conservative party. Knowing the "rebel" stigma both northern and southern Republicans attached to the word "conservative," the carpetbag leaders of the state organization never ceased protesting the use of the label to describe their party.[22] But the damage had been done, and the image of the party as one controlled by former Confederates and Democrats was soon fixed in the minds of Republicans, including President Grant.

The liberalization and rejuvenation of the regular wing of the party in Mississippi paved the way for the Grant administration's repudiation of the insurgent Republicans. Although retaining the allegiance of the overwhelming majority of Republicans in the state, the regular faction could not receive the blessings of Grant and his cabinet unless it abandoned its proscription policy and adopted a more conciliatory posture in state politics. Soon after Grant's intervention in the Mississippi controversy in April, a group of moderate regulars and formerly unobtrusive Radicals quietly began the task of unseating the party leadership of stalwart Radicals or "bitter-enders" like Eggleston, Gibbs, Castello, Mygatt and Flournoy and moving the party toward a moderate platform. Many Republicans had long considered the devil-may-care proscription policy of the Eggleston-Gibbs faction to be unwise, but earlier they had neither the desire (or foolhardiness) to leave the party nor the leadership to lock horns with the aggressive stalwarts. But the reconstruction developments of April convinced them that they must take action if the party was to be saved. In addition, several of these skeptical Republicans, like Alcorn, were relatively late converts to the party and had had few opportunities to assert themselves in the state organization. Defying the bitter-end leadership, a group of reform Republicans met in Jackson in early May, indicated their acceptance of Grant's policy regarding the constitution, and urged the state party to go on record against the proscription clauses.[23]

The leadership in the movement to convert the Republican party into a positive instrument of "liberal" reform came from all three

22. Vicksburg *Times*, August 25, September 12, 1869; Vicksburg *Times and Republican*, July 29, 1870.

23. Jackson *Weekly Clarion*, May 6, 13, 20, 1869; *Speech of Hon. Geo. J. Mortimer at the Great Mass Meeting of the Republicans at Crystal Springs* (N.p., 1869), 7–8.

elements in the party—carpetbaggers, scalawags, and blacks. By far the most prominent of the new leaders was Alcorn, who since affiliating with the party in early 1868 had been waiting in the wings for an opportunity to demonstrate his political talents. This Delta planter, a sometimes supporter of the Confederate cause who had been selected to the United States Senate under the abortive presidential plan of reconstruction, feared the restoration to power of "the miserable Jacobins of secession" quite as much as did the Radicals, but he realized that a policy of political proscription was an unsound beginning for the development of his cherished Whig-Republican party in the state. Like other moderate Republicans, Alcorn also was disturbed by the implications of radicalism—mixed schools, so-called "social equality" for blacks, heavy taxes, political demagoguery, and the confiscation of land. He wanted to arrest these tendencies in the party before they had gained the upper hand.[24]

Joining the able Alcorn in the moderate effort to seize control of the party was carpetbagger Edward Stafford, the roly-poly editor of the influential Jackson *Pilot*. A native of upstate New York and a newspaperman in Missouri prior to moving to Mississippi after the war, Stafford's ability as an editor was unsurpassed among his Republican colleagues. In addition, few editors of Republican journals were as successful as Stafford in walking the thin line between radicalism and moderate republicanism; much of his broad influence in the party was due to his ambiguous and conciliatory position on controversial Republican issues. Although he had served on the Radical committee that attempted to persuade Congress to impose the defeated constitution upon the people of Mississippi, he remained in the background during the struggle and thereby avoided the stigma of proscription.[25]

The support of James Lynch was as important to the success of

24. James Lusk Alcorn to Elihu Washburne, December 5, 1868, in Washburne Papers. The interpretation of Alcorn as a moderate was not shared, at least publicly, by conservatives. During this early period of congressional reconstruction conservatives viewed Alcorn as a consistent Radical, only one level above the bitter-enders of the Eggleston-Gibbs persuasion. Friar's Point *Weekly Delta*, April 14, 1869; Jackson *Clarion*, July 11, 1867; Jackson *Weekly Clarion*, July 15, 1869.

25. Jackson *Weekly Pilot*, August 12, 27, October 22, December 3, 1870; Forest *Register*, July 16, 1870; Jackson *Weekly Clarion*, August 12, 19, 1869.

the moderate faction as that of Alcorn and Stafford. Always a moderate, Lynch's influence in the party had been in partial eclipse since the ascendancy of the proscriptionists in 1868, but with the surge of moderate sentiment after President Grant's intervention, this eloquent young black minister-politician regained his role as the leading representative of his race in the state. To promote the cause of moderate republicanism and black unity, Lynch entered the newspaper business as publisher and editor of the Jackson *Colored Citizen*. Although there are no extant issues of this short-lived newspaper, Lynch's approach and views during this crucial period of Mississippi Reconstruction may be found in the contemporary press. In an interview with a correspondent of the Cincinnati *Commercial*, the black leader declared that, though he appreciated the efforts of Mississippi Radicals on behalf of Negro rights, their policy of proscription had worked against the party's best interests, since whites had been alienated by it. At least the tacit support of a fairly large part of the white community was necessary for the success of Republican reconstruction. Without this support, he said, racial peace and economic security for Negroes could not be maintained, except by a standing army.[26] In a letter to a Maryland friend Lynch reiterated the hope that a substantial number of whites would eventually join the Republican movement. He wrote: "I have an earnest desire to see an element of the hitherto governing class incorporated into the Republican Party of Mississippi, to secure for it that confidence and sympathy which will prolong [its] existence and reconcile to each other both races. . . . I favor a policy that will make it the interest of the Southern people to ally themselves with the Republican Party, and secure to the colored citizens, despite prejudice against color, all of the benefits which should flow from their enfranchisement."[27]

With the national leadership leaning toward a balanced biracial

26. As reported in the Jackson *Weekly Clarion*, August 26, 1869. In an obvious reference to Radical carpetbaggers and his black rival Thomas W. Stringer, Lynch complained that "Designing politicians as unscrupulous as Satan, are preying like wolves upon the Freedmen, and they should be unmasked when they imperil their interests." Lynch proposed to use the *Colored Citizen* to unmask these demagogues and to promote black political, economic, and religious interests in the state. James Lynch to Matthew Simpson, December 3, 1868, in Matthew Simpson Papers, Manuscript Division, Library of Congress.

27. As reported in the New York *Times*, August 2, 1869.

party in Mississippi, Lynch, Alcorn, and associates believed that the time was ripe for the accession of a large number of old-line Whigs to the Republican party. Consequently, Republican orators and editors, including some chastened Radicals like Henry R. Pease, almost overnight launched a campaign to bring Whigs into the party. The initial reaction of the intended recipients of Republican beneficence was one of amazement and contempt. Commenting on the almost daily appeals to Whigs appearing in Stafford's Jackson *Pilot*, Dr. J. S. Davis, a prominent Union-Whig from northeast Mississippi, declared: "We are a little too smart to be honey-fuggled by the radical press."[28] Another Union Whig, claiming to represent the sentiment of all but one or two Whigs in his county, responded in a similar fashion and with some degree of misunderstanding concerning the forces in the Republican party behind the recruiting campaign.

> [We] have lately seen with unutterable scorn the attempts which are being made in this state to make Radicalism respectable by cloaking its naked villainy beneath the garb of old Line Whiggery. . . . Can any old Whig think without indignation of Henry Clay's name being associated with the dirty horde of foreign adventurers and home-made renegades who constitute the Radical party of Mississippi—the Egglestons, Barrys, Gibbses, Flournoys, and Jamisons, one half of whom have already been indicted for Penitentiary offenses and the other half of whom ought long since to have been hung? . . . Thank God the attempt to blend Whiggery and Radicalism is as contemptible in its failure as it is in its spirit. It is confined to one or two men who never had soul enough to appreciate the noble old party, or whose ambition would make them sell their Saviour for office. The great mass of the Old Whig party as well as its chosen leaders, indignantly spurn the unholy alliance.[29]

Most stalwart Radicals, demoralized by the swift course of events against their leadership, accepted with resignation the decline of their influence and the moderate strategy to develop a strong white element in the Republican party to complement the black majority. Believing that their eclipse would only be temporary and hoping

28. See especially the Jackson *Weekly Clarion*, issues of May, 1869; Davis' comment appears in the May 6 issue. See also the Friar's Point *Weekly Delta*, April 28, 1869, and the *Hinds County Gazette*, May 26, 1869.
29. Hernando *Weekly Press*, May 27, 1869.

that the party in the meantime would not be unduly compromised or contaminated by reactionary doctrines, some Radicals even breathed a sigh of relief to be rid of the albatross of proscription, although they had insisted earlier that the repudiation of this policy would lead to the state party's disintegration and the restoration of rebels to power. The vigorous and solid leadership provided by the Alcorn-Stafford-Lynch moderates after Grant's repudiation of proscription suggested to the stalwarts that republicanism could yet emerge virtually unblemished from the crisis. Furthermore, these Radicals reasoned, the party by suppressing its radical tendencies for a time and adopting a moderate posture could be restored to the good graces of the national leadership, without which there was little hope for the future of the new order in the state.

Only a few "bitter-enders" challenged the rise of the moderates and the need for a new departure by the party. Speaking for these ultras, the intrepid Flournoy, whose epithet "Old Osawatomie" suggested a strong resemblance to an earlier and more celebrated Radical, John Brown, never tired during the next two years of denouncing the party's surrender to expediency and moderation in the crisis of 1869. The danger to the party, he insisted, did not lie with Grant's southern policy or with the handful of bolters who had formed the sham National Union Republican party. The real danger lay elsewhere and was twofold. "First, we who are Radicals," Flournoy said, "see an evident disposition on the part of men who have never been fully identified with the principles of the party— eleventh hour men—to cast us out, to make scape-goats of us, and . . . brand us with infamy for having faithfully attempted to do the bidding of the party." Second, the white strategy of the new leadership would inevitably dilute the great Republican principle of equal rights for blacks, since the men who were being appealed to were lukewarm, if not hostile, to Negro rights. In effect, Flournoy complained, the emerging Alcorn faction in its mad haste to make Republicans out of sullen Whigs was diverting the true idealistic purposes of the party.[30]

When the state Republican convention met at Jackson on July 1,

30. Jackson *Weekly Clarion*, August 19, 1869; Jackson *Weekly Pilot*, February 12, August 12, 1870.

it was clear that the moderates had succeeded in persuading party functionaries to abandon the Radicals. For president of the body, the delegates ignored the claims of the bitter-enders and selected Armistead Burwell, a staunch wartime Unionist but a moderate on reconstruction issues. A revamping of the state executive committee followed, with moderates receiving four of the five positions. One of the new members of the Republican hierarchy was James Lynch, the first Negro to serve on this powerful committee. But it was the platform approved by the convention that best demonstrated the triumph of the moderates in the party. Declaring that "the enlightened spirit of the age" demanded that "the fossil remains of proscription must be numbered with the things of the past," the platform called for "universal amnesty and universal suffrage."[31] This included a recommendation that Congress remove all disabilities imposed by the Fourteenth Amendment on former Confederates, once the state had been restored to the Union. The platform also endorsed such well-known Republican principles as free schools for every child, the "full and unrestricted right of speech to all men . . . with the most complete and unrestrained freedom of the ballot," and the political and legal equality of all citizens. Still reflecting sound moderate republicanism, the convention called for the "reformation of the iniquitous and unequal taxation and assessments which, discriminating against labor and laborers, have borne so unjustly and unequally upon the people." In a special appeal for immigrants to bolster the economy, the delegates announced that, unlike the policy of the conservatives who sought only like-minded settlers to fill the labor void created by the results of the war, they wanted people of all races, nationalities, politics, and religious beliefs.

Finally, the July convention commended General Ames, who had replaced Gillem in March, for his directives reducing the state poll tax from two dollars to one, prohibiting local governments from levying an additional capitation tax, and opening the jury box to blacks. Probably a more important reason for this commendation was the young general's dramatic appearance before the conven-

31. *Hinds County Gazette*, July 7, 1869; Jackson *Weekly Clarion*, July 8, 1869. The Republican platform may be found in McPherson, *Political History*, 480–81.

tion and his declaration to the delegates that "you have my sympathies, and shall have my support" in the forthcoming campaign.[32]
This announcement gave the cause of the regular Republicans an
enormous boost and ensured the faithful that while Ames was in
command they would have the active assistance of the military.

The entrance of Ames into the cauldron of Reconstruction politics was unexpected. Except for his jury and poll-tax directives he
had done little to suggest that he might abandon his predecessors'
policy of political neutrality and cast his lot with the regular Republicans. Until July his appointments to fill the many vacancies created by the March, 1869, act of Congress requiring that all officeholders must take the ironclad oath were nonpartisan and elicited
the approval of the conservatives.[33] Radical Republicans disapproved of Ames at first, and even after he announced his support
for the party they viewed him for a time as an especial friend of
the now dominant moderate faction.

But once his cloak of neutrality had been discarded, Ames labored zealously for the regular Republican cause in the election.
He removed from office leaders of the National Union Republican
movement, including several carpetbaggers whom he had appointed earlier and also Wofford, one of the party's most prominent
organizers but a leading bolter in 1869. In fact, Ames almost over-
played his hand in his effort to fill offices with sympathizers of the
regular party. National Union Republicans, some having friends in
high places, bombarded Washington with requests for Ames's removal from command—an action that under the circumstances
would have been a major setback for the regular Republicans. Both
Secretary of War John A. Rawlins and General-in-Chief Sherman
favored the conservative, or "liberal" Republicans, but they refrained from public utterances of support because of the delicate
political nature of the Mississippi controversy. The kind of blatant
partisanship that Ames was practicing in Mississippi, however,
aroused the ire of the professionally minded Sherman, and for a
time during the summer the young general's removal appeared

32. New York *Times*, July 12, 1869; Jackson *Weekly Clarion*, July 8, 1869.
33. Vicksburg *Times*, May 5, 12, 1869; *Hinds County Gazette*, May 19, 26, 1869; Hernando *Weekly Press*, July 8, 1869.

imminent.[34] When Sherman called upon Ames to explain his departure from the accepted code of conduct for officers in the United States Army, the New Englander replied by claiming that it was absolutely necessary for him to enter the political arena on the Republican side in order to prevent the "rebels" from regaining power. The National Union Republican party, Ames informed his superior, was merely the stalking horse for the rebel Democracy; "they are the tools by which the democracy propose to deceive the world. They are important only so far as they aid in that scheme. . . . They actually have no power in the state—it is with those who use them."[35]

Although General Sherman failed to be impressed by Ames's defense, politically-minded members of the national administration, including President Grant, were in the process of reevaluating their southern policy and were beginning to view affairs in Mississippi and in other former Confederate states in much the same light as that of the young district commander. From Mississippi, Texas, and Tennessee, where a gubernatorial election was scheduled for August, representatives of both the conservative and regular Republican parties descended upon Washington soon after the Virginia election in July to obtain support for their factions. In conferences with President Grant and members of Congress the regular Republicans painted a bleak picture of how affairs in their states would develop if the administration continued to tilt toward conservative Republicans in the South as it had done in Virginia. At a hurriedly called cabinet meeting on July 13, Secretary of Treasury George S. Boutwell, the leading Radical Republican in the administration, denounced the conservative victory in Virginia and declared that the nation had grievously misinterpreted the government's policy of neutrality in that election; even men in high government and party positions had come to believe that Grant's southern policy called for the election of the Walker faction over the regular Republicans. They were mistaken, Boutwell said. But

34. New York *Tribune*, August 11, 1869; Jackson *Weekly Clarion*, August 5, 19, 1869; *Hinds County Gazette*, July 7, 1869; Adelbert Ames to John Eaton, September 13, 1869, in Eaton Papers; Vicksburg *Times*, October 28, 1869; Abel Alderson to Joseph Holt, July 18, 1869, in Holt Papers.

35. Ames to Sherman, August 17, 1869, in William T. Sherman Papers.

the damage to reconstruction had been done, and the only way now to check the disintegration of true republicanism in these states was for the administration to come out unequivocally in support of the regular party there.[36]

The president, with the approval of a majority of the cabinet, temporarily postponed a decision on the issue until southern political developments became clearer. Nevertheless, he was moved by Boutwell's arguments and indicated an increasing skepticism regarding the good faith and the political viability of "liberal Republicans" in Mississippi and elsewhere. In the July 13 meeting Grant did agree to Boutwell's recommendation that the Mississippi and Texas elections take place after the off year fall contests in the North but before Congress reassembled in December.[37] If the reconstruction elections were held at that time, the returns, which Boutwell and his Radical associates feared might go against them, would be too late to affect the contests in the North. When the Republican Congress met immediately after the northern elections it would be in a position to take swift action if the results had proved disastrous to the regular factions in Mississippi and Texas. As Boutwell reasoned, the fact that a concerned Congress would soon be scrutinizing the election returns should have a salutary effect on the outcome of the contests in these two states, perhaps providing the regulars with the boost necessary to win. Grant scheduled the elections for November 30, with the stipulation, as he had earlier recommended and Congress had authorized, that the proscriptive clauses be voted on separately.

A delegation of Mississippi National Union Republicans who arrived in Washington a few days after the July 13 Cabinet meeting immediately perceived that administration sentiment was running against them. Instead of asking for direct presidential support for their faction—an endorsement that now seemed farfetched—they pleaded with Grant to reaffirm his policy of neutrality in the southern contests. The president, according to the National Union Republicans' account of their meeting with him, agreed that such a policy was wise, but his continued support of it depended upon the

36. New York *Tribune*, July 13, 14, 15, 1869; Charles W. Ramsdell, *Reconstruction in Texas* (Gloucester, Mass., 1964), 275–76.
37. New York *Tribune*, July 15, 1869.

course of events in Virginia, where the newly elected conservatives had taken office, and also on the character of the ticket that the National Republicans nominated in Mississippi. These Republicans, in any case, would have to demonstrate their willingness to ratify and uphold the Fifteenth Amendment and also their ability to protect the life and property of all classes in the state.[38] The fact that the president was then staying at the Washington residence of Louis Dent, his brother-in-law, whose candidacy for governor on the National Union Republican ticket Grant had privately encouraged a few days earlier, probably influenced him to give the conservative delegation a far more sympathetic statement of the administration's position than actually existed at the time.

President Grant did not await developments in Virginia and Mississippi before abandoning his posture of neutrality and entering the southern struggle on the side of the regular Republicans. Two days after his conference with the National Union Republican delegation he informed Dent of his decision to support the opposition. "I am so thoroughly satisfied," Grant wrote, "that the success of the so-called Conservative Republican party in Mississippi would result in the defeat of what I believe to be the best interest of the State and country, that I have determined . . . [to] throw the weight of my influence in favor of the party opposed to you." In a closing comment, laden with irony in view of Grant's subsequent disposition to permit relatives to live at public expense, he declared: "Personally, I wish you well, and would do all in my power proper to be done to secure your success, but in public matters personal feelings will not influence me."[39]

Grant, however, had no desire to embarrass his brother-in-law with a public repudiation of the National Union Republican party; consequently the president's decision to aid the Alcorn-Ames party remained generally unknown, even by leading Republicans in the capital. But events in the South were inexorably moving the president to a public announcement of his new policy. Elections in Tennessee in early August produced an overwhelming victory for a coalition of conservatives and the end of legitimate Republican

38. Vicksburg *Times*, August 13, 1869; *Hinds County Gazette*, August 4, 1869; Jackson *Weekly Clarion*, August 5, 1869.
39. *Appleton's Annual Cyclopaedia*, 1869, p. 457.

rule in the state. As in Virginia, the coalition elected a "liberal" (conservative) Republican as governor but selected a legislature that flaunted its conservatism. There was even talk that the arch-enemy of Republican reconstruction (and of Grant as well), Andrew Johnson, would be sent to the United States Senate by the new legislature. True Republicans, whatever their differences, were appalled at the course of events. Insisting that the twin disasters in Virginia and Tennessee could have been avoided if the president had thrown his support to the regular Republicans, party leaders pleaded with Grant to state his position publicly and use his influence to defeat the schemes of the rebel-inspired conservatives in Texas and Mississippi before it was too late to save the party in the South.[40]

Soon after this appeal was made a meeting with Jonathan Tarbell, a persuasive carpetbagger of the regular faction in Mississippi, gave the president an opportunity to announce his new policy. Tarbell made notes during the conference, and he later asked Grant if his report of the meeting could be published. The president, after reading the report, agreed. Not only did Grant in his interview with Tarbell come out solidly for the regular Republicans in Mississippi but he also expressed support for General Ames and the campaign to remove "disloyal" officials from office. True Republicans in the conservative movement, the president remarked, were too few to have much influence; therefore he could only conclude that they were being used by the opponents of Republican reconstruction. Once in power the traditional leaders would quickly renounce the National Union Republicans and the principles expressed in their June platform. Developments in Virginia and Tennessee, Grant said, had proved that the real purpose behind the conservative Republican movement in the South was to circumvent all that had been accomplished by the congressional plan of reconstruction. This the administration would not tolerate.[41]

40. Thomas B. Alexander, *Political Reconstruction in Tennessee* (Nashville, 1950), 218–19; New York *Tribune*, August 6, 7, 10, 1869. In addition to the brutal murder of Major Joseph G. Crane by Edward M. Yerger, an election-associated riot in Mobile, in which a Democratic mob routed an excited gathering of blacks, contributed to the despair felt by many Republicans at this time because of the national administration's hands-off policy in the South. The Crane murder and the Mobile riot probably influenced Grant to abandon his early strategy and strike at the conservatives before it was too late.

41. New York *Tribune*, August 11, 1869; New York *Times*, August 12, 1869.

The fate of the National Union Republican party in Mississippi was sealed. Nevertheless, its supporters refused to admit defeat—at least publicly—and they predicted that Grant would yet see the wisdom of supporting the party. Ethelbert Barksdale even insisted that the president in publicly disowning Louis Dent and the conservative Republicans was only yielding momentarily to the pressure of Radicals like Boutwell. The ascendancy of the Radicals in the administration would be short-lived, he said, and the mild-mannered Grant would repudiate his endorsement of the Alcorn-Ames party and redeem the earlier promises he had made to his brother-in-law. Although under no such illusion regarding the president's decision, carpetbag editor Frederic Speed of the Vicksburg *Times*, the leading organ of the National Union Republicans, tried to cheer his disconsolate associates with the thought that by thoroughly organizing the party locally they could win the election without the administration's support. If this organizational feat were accomplished, defeat could only occur as a result of "the exercise of unjust and dishonest measures on the part of the Military Commander, such as we know Grant will not permit—whether he be for, or against us." [42]

Soft-pedaling their early promise that the party would be developed strictly along Republican lines, Speed and his northern friends now called for white support "to stay oppression and outrage." [43] These northerners, now reduced in number by defections to the regular party, still sought a large Negro vote and expected to secure it through the influence of cooperative local blacks who would be displayed at the state convention as prominent representatives of the black community in the National Union Republican party. They hoped that the increasingly conservative character of the party would not become common knowledge among the black masses until after the election.

On September 8 National Union Republicans met at Jackson to nominate their state ticket and to make final preparations for the fall campaign. Representing forty counties, the delegates had been selected by local meetings which in most cases were biracial. A few conventions in the plantation counties dispatched as many blacks as whites. Most of the local organizations, however, rejected racial

42. Jackson *Weekly Clarion*, August 19, 1869; Vicksburg *Times*, August 13, 25, 1869.
43. Vicksburg *Times*, August 13, 25, 26, 1869.

parity, though in most cases they included at least one or two Negroes in their delegations. Of the more than two hundred delegates, forty were black, representing thirty counties in the state.[44] Nevertheless, blacks exercised very little influence in the convention; they simply provided the biracial facade that the party's carpetbag leaders desired.

The white composition of the aberrant Republican convention was remarkable for its diversity and its mixed objectives. A handful of transplanted northerners, still insisting that they were Republicans despite their willingness to compromise the principles of the party of Lincoln and Sumner, dominated the convention proceedings.[45] At the same time the old leadership class was ably represented by Amos R. Johnston, C. P. Neilsen, and C. M. Vaiden, men who had consistently opposed congressional reconstruction but were now consorting with carpetbaggers and even accepting direction from these infamous adventurers in order to snare black votes and perhaps the support of the Grant administration as well. These whites, nonetheless, insisted on being called "conservative" rather than National Union Republican. As was true of previous efforts to organize an anti-Radical coalition in the state, Whigs were conspicuous in the convention, with Johnston serving as their leader.

Also present were a number of aspiring young bloods who had faithfully served the Confederate cause and after four years of waiting were impatient for political opportunity. William H. Hardy, Pat Henry, Joel P. Walker, Robert Lowry, and John M. Stone were young former Confederate officers who believed that the political future of the state rested with a conservative party that accepted the results of the war but stopped short of Radical, or even moderate Republican ideology. All of them cut their political teeth in the National Union Republican movement and then went on to greater heights as Conservative Democrats, with Stone and Lowry monopolizing the office of governor during the age of the Redeemers. On the other hand, a few of this class of ambitious

---

44. Jackson *Weekly Clarion*, August 5, 19, 26, September 2, 9, 1869; *Hinds County Gazette*, September 8, 1869.

45. The proceedings of the National Union Republican convention, including a list of the delegates, are in the Jackson *Weekly Clarion*, September 16, 1869.

young men in the convention, after some soul-searching, eventually cast their lots with the regular party. Among these were William
F. Fitzgerald, Reuben W. Millsaps, Harris Barksdale, and Fleet T.
Cooper. Except for Joseph W. Field, who died soon after the meeting, there were no scalawags of prominence in the convention,
strongly suggesting that despite the rhetoric of its founders the
new party was not viewed as respectable by true Republicans.

Still hoping to secure President Grant's endorsement—and the
key to the offices that went with it—the carpetbag-controlled convention chose Louis Dent to head the ticket. Several Whig delegates privately indicated their displeasure with the nomination,
pointing out that Grant had already repudiated his brother-in-
law's candidacy and that, furthermore, as a life-long Democrat who
had lived in California on the eve of the war, Dent would have
little appeal at the polls. Although he could be dubbed a carpetbagger, in fact he did not even have a residence in the state in 1869.
Dent's ties to Mississippi went back to the antebellum period, and
during the war he had extended charity to Confederates held in
military confinement. In 1865 he had leased a plantation in the
Delta, but had abandoned it in 1867 for the more congenial Washington setting. Dent's past was too unsound for any of the elements
in the National Union Republican party to view his candidacy with
enthusiasm. The old citizens in the movement preferred Simrall or
Watson as the nominee for governor; the small Union element
favored Lewis C. Nowell, a merchant of Pass Christian who had
friends in Washington and who had actively sought the nomination;
and several northerners in the party wanted to nominate Elza
Jeffords or Alexander Warner, both former Union officers with Republican credentials. But only Dent could marshal some support
among all three elements, mainly because each knew that if they
abandoned him all hopes that the president might change his mind
would be dashed.[46]

Dent headed a ticket composed of men with better than average
ability, but, with the exception of Jeffords, the candidate for lieu-

46. Lewis C. Nowell to John F. H. Claiborne, August 5, 1869, in John F. H. Claiborne
Papers, Manuscript Division, Library of Congress; C. B. New to Holt, June 21, 1869, in
Holt Papers; Hernando *Weekly Press*, June 24, 1869; New York *Tribune*, August 10, 1869;
Forest *Register*, September 1, 1869; Vicksburg *Times*, August 25, 1869.

tenant governor, they had little influence among the constituencies that they were supposed to represent. For the seven state offices, the National Union Republicans selected four northerners, three of whom, including Jeffords, had served as Union officers during the war, two antebellum residents and non-Republicans, Robert Lowry and Thomas S. Gathright, and one Negro, Thomas Sinclair, who was nominated for secretary of state. Supposedly all of these men would be acceptable to Congress—if the ticket won. Meeting after the state body had adjourned, district conventions selected all northerners except one as candidates for Congress. With these nominations the supply of northerners in the National Union Republican party appeared exhausted, and county conventions, like those held earlier in Virginia and Tennessee, dropped the Republican facade and nominated "Conservative" candidates for the legislature. Seemingly dominated by the same Whigs who had been conspicuous in anti-Republican parties since 1867, these local meetings nominated for office old citizens who were not disabled by the Fourteenth Amendment and also, in many cases, pliant and nondescript blacks.[47]

As sullen Whigs had predicted, the white masses showed little enthusiasm for the northern-dominated ticket of the National Union Republican party. Many conservatives resented Dent's nomination because of his relationship to President Grant. The whole scheme was a farce, many believed. Edward C. Walthall expressed the feeling of those whites when he wrote his friend L. Q. C. Lamar that the Dent movement was enough to disgust any man, "and it all comes of the ambition and folly of the would-be leaders who secretly rejoice that the old ones are embassed [sic] & are willing to send the country to the Devil in order to take their bows."[48] Others were disgusted not so much with the leadership or the platform of the National Union Republican party, which accepted Negro suffrage, but with the "spectacle of the educated and refined white people of the State fawning about a lot of ignorant Negroes

47. Vicksburg *Times*, October 28, November 12, 1869; Jackson *Weekly Clarion*, October 14, 18, 28, November 4, 1869.

48. Edward C. Walthall to L. Q. C. Lamar, October 14, 1869, in Lamar-Mayes Papers. The "new leaders" whom Walthall referred to were evidently the former Whigs in the hierarchy of both parties in the campaign—Alcorn, William H. Vasser, and Joshua S. Morris of the regular Republicans, and Johnston, Robert Lowry, and Harvey Walter of the National Union Republican party.

trying to persuade them to vote the Dent ticket." Equally disconcerting to most whites was the conservative policy of selecting a large number of blacks, many of whom were politically incompetent if not illiterate, as delegates to the state convention and as candidates for office.[49] Nevertheless, many whites, now sobered by the uncertain and unpromising course of reconstruction, did not reject out-of-hand the notion of black officeholding. But for it to be acceptable the number of Negroes chosen would have to be few and would have to include men of some ability, like James Lynch who, however, had declined a proffered nomination as lieutenant governor on the maverick Republican ticket.[50] This cautious policy was not followed by the conservatives, and even if it had been few competent blacks would have been willing to cooperate with "the bogus Dent party." The ruse involved in the National Union Republican movement was too obvious to attract local Negro leaders. For more than two years these blacks had been involved in a desperate struggle for equal rights under the congressional plan of reconstruction, and they had witnessed other attempts of conservatives to beguile them into abandoning the only party that stood for their interests. The new conservative snare offered no temptation to them.

In a quiet state of expectancy after receiving the president's nod of approval, regular Republicans met at Jackson in late September to nominate a state ticket and to perfect their plans for the November election. Committed by the July meeting to a liberal, nonproscriptive platform and still somewhat wary that political events of the summer in Virginia and Tennessee might be repeated in Mississippi, delegates to the convention were especially careful to avoid any appearance (at least in Washington) that the party had succumbed again to the dangerous fever of radicalism. Earlier, carpetbagger Edward Stafford had traveled up and down the trunk lines of the state seeking Republican support for moderate delegates.[51]

Stafford did his work well, although in the convention the mod

49. Forest *Register*, December 10, 1870, quoting the Vicksburg *Herald*; entry for November 29, 1869, in Agnew Diary.

50. For example, see conservative George W. Harper's description in the *Hinds County Gazette*, September 22, 1869, of the qualifications expected of a Negro candidate.

51. Jackson *Weekly Clarion*, August 12, 19, September 23, 1869.

erate leadership was forced to accept one Radical, Henry R. Pease, as the nominee for superintendent of education. Moderate Republicans were well represented in the nominations of Alcorn for governor, carpetbagger Ridgley C. Powers, lieutenant governor; scalawag William H. Vasser, state treasurer; Lynch, secretary of state; carpetbagger Henry Musgrove, state auditor; and scalawag Joshua Morris, attorney general.[52] Of these only Vasser's selection came as a surprise. A relatively obscure Union Whig and Roman Catholic of Monroe County who had donned the gray during the war, Vasser gave provincial northeast Mississippi a place on the ticket, and this fact, along with his known conservatism, was expected to swing numerous whites of the area to the support of the Republican party.[53]

The selection by acclamation of Alcorn for governor solidly affirmed the moderate ascendancy in the state Republican party. Although opponents of the new order insisted that this affluent and imperious Delta planter was "the very concentration of partizan malignity" and extremism,[54] he represented the element in the party that had long sought a racial balance in its membership without abandoning its progressive position on Negro rights and postwar reforms. Alcorn had spared no words in denouncing secessionists as a class. But to him they had never represented a majority of the whites of the state, and his plans, unlike those of the Radicals, did not include the political proscription of this class of citizens. To him, public opprobrium toward the secessionists should be limited to the main leaders of the movement, specifically the Brown-Barksdale faction which he scornfully referred to as the "Jackson clique."[55] Although some Whigs may have supported the Confed-

---

52. Conservative spokesmen during the campaign would not admit that this ticket was moderate. In commenting on Lynch's candidacy, Barksdale, in the Jackson *Weekly Clarion*, November 11, 1869, declared that if the black leader "is elected Secretary of State the office will be a manufactory for all the diabolic machinery which may be deemed necessary to perpetuate the reign of Blood, Terror, and Plunder, which the Jacobin schemers are striving with hellish intent, to inaugurate."

53. Entry for October 15, 1869, in Agnew Diary; application of William H. Vasser, March 17, 1869, in Fourteenth Amendment Relief Papers, Mississippi; Jackson *Pilot*, March 30, 1871.

54. Jackson *Weekly Clarion*, October 7, 1869; Vicksburg *Times*, October 28, November 12, 1869; Forest *Register*, November 3, 1869; Hernando *Weekly Press*, June 16, 1869.

55. Alcorn, *Views on the Political Situation*, 5; Alcorn to Washburne, December 5, 1868, in Washburne Papers; Alcorn, *Address*, 1869, pp. 2–3.

eracy, they were now the natural leaders of Mississippi whites, Alcorn insisted, and they could best seve the state by joining the Republican party. Only the Republicans, by virtue of congressional reconstruction, had the power to smash the diabolical political schemes of the Jackson clique and to lead the people out of the wilderness of despair that secession and war had created. Alcorn's analysis was flawed by the fact that some of the leading lights in the postwar "Jackson clique" were Union Whigs such as Potter and Johnston, and not Democrats, although Brown and Barksdale remained active in state politics.

In his acceptance address, which, in order to be precisely understood, he read to the hushed delegates in the Republican convention, Alcorn outlined a program of economic development for Mississippi that, he promised, would follow his party's victory at the polls and the restoration of the state to the Union. "Under the policy of internal improvements by the general government," Alcorn declared, Mississippi as a Republican state would "hold moral claims for large subsidies from the treasury of the United States." Included in the federal largesse for the state would be subsidies for railroads, funds for the construction of a harbor on the Gulf Coast, and money to restore the levees protecting the Delta.[56] However much historians have emphasized the peculiarly Whiggish roots of his appeal,[57] the fact remains that this part of Alcorn's program reflected little more than the common vision of the state's future that many conservatives and Republicans, even of the Radical persuasion, held during the postwar years.[58] Actually, continuing economic distress had unified the people on the need for boldness in the material development of the state and in the belief that federal money must and should be extended to assist in the work. This was a major reason why conservatives, for example, were anxious to complete the political process required by Congress. Although, unlike Alcorn, they were skeptical of receiving aid from a Republican Congress immediately, the conservative leadership continually

56. This address may be found in the Jackson *Weekly Clarion*, October 7, 1869.
57. Lillian A. Pereyra in her biography of Alcorn (*James Lusk Alcorn: Persistent Whig* [Baton Rouge, 1966]) goes further than most historians in attributing Alcorn's policies to his Whiggish economic concepts; in fact, she views him as a product of Hamiltonian ideology living in the age of Lincoln.
58. See Chaps. 14 and 15 herein.

expressed the belief that once the state was restored to the Union private northern capital would flow into Mississippi, and with this base for economic development the federal government could be persuaded to assist in the work of material progress.[59] An economic process of this kind could especially be applied to the Delta where northerners with a stake in the production and marketing of cotton were already petitioning Congress to finance the rebuilding of the levees and the drainage of the bottomlands.

The economic program that Alcorn projected in his acceptance speech only partly expressed his Republican creed. An advocate of Negro suffrage since 1865 (although admittedly for reasons of expediency then), this former slaveholder had consistently supported the Republican doctrines of equal political rights for blacks, the restoration of law and order, political tolerance, and free schools for both races. In 1867 he laid down a policy on the political rights of blacks which he did not abandon during Reconstruction. He declared that "the colored man comes, as well as the white man, within the scope" of his political thinking. "I propose to vote with him, to discuss political affairs with him, to sit if need be in political counsel with him, and from a platform acceptable alike to him, to me, and [to all citizens] to pluck our common liberty and our common prosperity out of the jaws of inevitable ruin."[60] Like many other Republicans from both North and South, Alcorn moved slowly toward voicing in public an acceptance of advanced rights for blacks; he remained, however, a steadfast opponent of racial integration in the public schools. In 1874 he supported Senator Sumner's civil rights bill guaranteeing equal rights for Negroes in public places and on public conveyances.[61] After receiving the praise

59. An excellent statement of this reasoning was expressed by conservative leader Amos R. Johnston in a speech delivered during the 1869 campaign. *Speech of Hon. Amos R. Johnston at Sardis, Mississippi, on the 13th Day of October, A.D. 1869* (N.p., 1869).

60. Alcorn to his wife Amelia, August 26, 1865, in James Lusk Alcorn Papers, Southern Historical Collection, University of North Carolina Library, Chapel Hill; Washington *New National Era*, June 4, 1874; *Harper's Weekly*, XIV (January 1, 1870), 2; Alcorn, *Views on the Political Situation*, 4.

61. *Speech of Hon. James L. Alcorn of Mississippi, in the United States Senate, May 22, 1874* (Washington, D.C., 1874). Alcorn's opposition to racial mixing in the public schools was perhaps more a matter of expediency, *i.e.*, the belief that the school system would die in its infancy if this issue were forced, than any deep-seated aversion to the principle of integration. See his letter of May 15, 1870, to the Washington *New Era*, quoted in the New York *Times*, May 23, 1870. In the same year Alcorn sought kind treatment at West Point for

of Frederick Douglass for a speech in the Senate favoring the Sumner bill, Alcorn wrote the distinguished black leader that he supported it partly because he now believed that the postwar amendments "had levelled the distinctions of race heretofore existing in the nation," and "Congress must proceed with strict reference to the text of the Constitution" as amended.[62]

Unlike Radicals such as Flournoy, Gibbs, and Albert T. Morgan, Alcorn seemed genuinely concerned with the aspirations of the white yeomanry, which since the war and the end of the slave labor system had become a vital element in the state's development. During the campaign of 1869 he proclaimed his broad purpose in leading the new order in Mississippi:

> The reconstruction to which I go forward is a reconstruction which will make rich and poor equal in fact before the law. I move on with it, guiding a harnessed revolution over the ruins of an oligarchy, to the erection of a government by the people and for the people. I go forward, fellow-citizens, to build up in accordance with the spirit of the age, in accordance with the will of the nation, a party new to the history of Mississippi—a party determined, while raising the State from her prostrate position under the foot of power, to erect it, not upon its point, but upon its base—the masses of the citizens.

Admitting that during the antebellum era he had been of the wealthy class, though never privy to its aristocratic designs, Alcorn declared that under Republican leadership "the 50,000 poor voters who have been dominated in the past by a wealthy class" will now have a chance "to strike for their independence. The small farmer who had been dragooned formerly by an insolent oligarchy will refuse to vote any more in the interests of the few." Alcorn proposed a coalition of yeoman whites, small merchants, and blacks who would follow him in "the erection of a government based on education, prompt payment [of public debts], equality before the

---

a black student from his state who had recently been admitted to the military academy (Jackson *Weekly Pilot*, June 11, 1870). He also had few qualms about blacks holding important state offices. As governor-elect, Alcorn supported Hiram R. Revels for the United States Senate and selected a Negro for a high position in the skeletal state militia. Later, while in the United States Senate, he journeyed from Washington to Jackson for the specific purpose of securing the selection of John R. Lynch as speaker of the Mississippi House of Representatives. John Roy Lynch, *Reminiscences of an Active Life: The Autobiography of John Roy Lynch* (Chicago, 1970), 80, 92.

62. Washington *New National Era*, June 4, 1874.

law, and a general system of legislation, having its foundation in strict justice to the rich and to the poor."[63]

The campaign of 1869 intensified in early October when Dent, after some hesitation, accepted Alcorn's challenge to a series of joint debates. A small, cigar-smoking man in his mid-forties, Dent surprised many with his vigor on the stump and his ability to show up his opponent's past record, but he was no match for the Delta planter whose stocky, impressive figure, booming voice, and campaign experience gave him an obvious advantage.[64] Soon the burden of the National Union Republican canvass passed from Dent and his northern associates to Amos R. Johnston, Robert Lowry, and other old citizens. Because of Alcorn's overshadowing presence in the campaign, conservative speakers directed most of their fire toward discrediting him in the eyes of the voters of both races.

The most telling effort of the conservative campaign was a speech by Johnston at Sardis on October 13. After exaggerating Alcorn's background as "a furious secessionist," this Jackson Whig arraigned the Republican candidate for his sellout to the extremists in his party "whose only purpose is to plunder the people of both races and enrich themselves by rapine, embezzlement and knavery." Johnston declared that "the mill-boy of the slashes," as conservative antagonists derisively labeled Alcorn, had no claim to the support of Mississippi whites, since "he has forsaken his poor downtrodden friends and countrymen in the hour of need." Ambition had ruined him. "Aspiring to Senatorial honors," Johnston asserted, Alcorn "wishes to use the Gubernatorial chair as a mere help to the Senate, and then we would have one R. C. Powers as Governor, who is one of the Northern Goths and Vandals, who came here to ravage the plains of our lovely people." The Republican promise to support universal political amnesty for former Confederates "was made with a mental reservation never to redeem it." Alcorn was a party to this effort to deceive the people, and he endorsed "the terrible oppressions" of General Ames, which were

63. As reported in *Harper's Weekly*, XIV (January 1, 1870), 2. See also the Jackson *Weekly Clarion*, December 2, 1869.

64. Jackson *Weekly Clarion*, October 14, 1869; *Nation*, IX (October 14, 1869), 305; *Hinds County Gazette*, December 8, 1869.

designed to carry the election at all cost for his Radical friends, Johnston informed his audience. The only way to avoid the despotism of the Alcorn-Ames "bitter-enders" and rebuild the waste places was for the state to be reconstructed under the auspices of the National Union Republicans.[65]

Turning to the blacks in his Sardis audience, Johnston assured them that the Dent party accepted in good faith their right to vote and would speedily ratify the Fifteenth Amendment if placed in control of the legislature. The conservative party would uphold its pledge that "you shall be the equal before the law with the white race, [with] the right to vote, serve on juries, give evidence in court, sue for and get all property rights, be as safe in your cabins as the rich white man is in his great house, and hold any office you may be elected to." Finally, Johnston told his black listeners, "my party is for common schools here and all over the state, not only for our children but for yours; and we want to be taxed to put those schools everywhere, with a fair division of the money between the races. We think it best that the schools should not be mixed, that the white and black children should be taught separately."

But despite the efforts of prestigious Mississippians like Johnston, the apathy of the white masses toward the Dent movement increased as the November election approached. Indeed, many conservatives, though remaining hostile to the regular Republican ticket, began to believe Alcorn's charge that the National Union Republican party was the brainchild of the "Jackson clique," which always seemed willing to betray the best interests of the people of the state.[66]

The action of a group of defiant Democrats who met at Canton on October 20 contributed to white disinterest and confusion. This meeting of "impracticables," as Barksdale called them, resolved that as the only true leaders of the Democracy in the state they would advise party faithfuls not to participate in the election. "Remaining firm in [the Democratic] devotion to the great doctrines of State rights," they announced their determination to retain a

65. *Speech of Johnston*, 3, 4, 6, 8.
66. Jackson *Weekly Pilot*, December 25, 1869, January 8, 1870; Hernando *Weekly Press*, January 6, 1870.

skeleton Democratic organization in the state and play "possum politics" white awaiting the call of the people.[67] The wait would be long; not until 1875 did the Democratic party regain its position as a viable political party in Mississippi.

Their campaign faltering around them, some spokesmen for the National Union Republican party adopted an anti-Negro appeal in order to rally white support for the Dent ticket. Choosing to forget their summer promises of a biracial party in the state, these conservatives easily fell back on a campaign technique that was more congenial to their tastes than the tactic of advocating fair play for blacks. The editor of the Forest *Register* exhorted his white readers to go to the polls and vote for the Dent ticket if they valued the superiority of their Anglo-Saxon blood and the greatness of their past civilization. Even Barksdale entered a wedge of racism into an otherwise racially mild series of campaign commentaries in the Jackson *Clarion* when he charged on November 11 that the school system authorized by the constitution would be mixed if the regular Republicans won the election. Turning from their denunciation of Alcorn, conservatives also tried to convince yeoman whites and "self-respecting" Negroes that if the Radical ticket were elected the carpetbag candidate for lieutenant governor, Ridgley C. Powers, "a monster in human form" according to George W. Harper, would become governor, since "the Mogul of the Radicals" (Alcorn) planned to secure an early election to the Senate. To have an adventurer of Powers' ilk in the governor's mansion would be far worse than having "the Eminent Man" there. On the eve of the election, the conservatives found one last straw in the wind—an old bogy in many an emotion-packed campaign in the past. They asserted that if the Radicals won the election, Alcorn and his carpetbag-Negro cronies in the legislature would fasten upon Mississippians the payment of the twenty million dollar debt from the repudiated Planters' and Union Bank bonds.[68] Then, in a final plea for support at the polls, Harper cried out, "People of Mississippi! Arouse yourself to action." A National

67. *Appleton's Annual Cyclopaedia*, 1869, p. 459; Jackson *Weekly Clarion*, October 28, 1869.

68. Forest *Register*, November 27, 1869; Jackson *Weekly Clarion*, November 11, 18, 1869; Vicksburg *Times*, November 12, 26, 1869; *Hinds County Gazette*, November 17, 1869.

Union Republican victory was "the only safety of the State from the preying of a fresh herd of carpet-bag and scallawag locusts" that would plunge their tentacles "deeper and deeper into the wealth of the State, to suck in and absorb it only for their own fattening."[69]

Tasting victory two months before the election, Republican campaigners ignored the charges against their party and its candidates and pushed home the argument that the National Union Republican movement had been born and nurtured by the "Jackson clique, the boastful hierarchy of the institution of slavery" whose ascendancy in the past had ruined Mississippi. Morris, Vasser, James Lynch, and Pease, along with Alcorn, crisscrossed the state, speaking at numerous rallies and assuring the people that their party no longer represented the proscriptionists and was the only true Republican organization in Mississippi.[70] Despite considerable white apathy toward the campaign, the old citizens, with a tradition of seeking entertainment at political rallies without making any particular commitment to party or candidates, turned out in large numbers to hear debates between representatives of the two sides. Tension mounted when certain "lying jail-birds and thieves of the carpetbag stripe" appeared at rallies to denounce the conservatives as rebels and to exhort the freedmen to vote against their old masters. Lynch reported to a friend in Washington: "Our canvass is a bitter one, nothing like it in the history of American politics."[71]

Violence occurred on several occasions during the campaign. At a rally in Durant carpetbagger William S. Barry, the Republican candidate for Congress in the district, was shot and wounded by a white assailant. After a similar incident in Sunflower County, racial war threatened to engulf several rural communities in this area of the Delta. Led by William T. Combash, a disreputable black who had served in the constitutional convention as a Republican but subsequently announced his support for the Democrats, a band of Negroes rose in virtual rebellion in Sunflower and adja-

69. *Hinds County Gazette*, November 17, 1869.
70. Alcorn, *Address*, 1869, p. 3; Alcorn to his wife Amelia, October 16, 1869, in James Lusk Alcorn Papers, Mississippi Department of Archives and History, Jackson.
71. Lynch to Simpson, October 6, 1869, in Simpson Papers.

cent Carroll County during late 1869.[72] Combash allegedly declared that his purpose was "to redeem his people from thralldom." The insurrection reached its height on November 17 when Combash at the head of an armed company of fifteen to twenty blacks marched into Greenwood, a village on the edge of the Delta in Carroll County, on the pretext of apprehending and punishing a conservative Negro who had been involved in a fight with one of the Combash group. When the marchers were repulsed by whites, Combash announced that he would return with five hundred men and sack the town. Quickly organizing whites in the area, the carpetbag sheriff pursued the insurgents and caught up with them several miles from Greenwood where they were entrenched along the Tallahatchie River. In the ensuing skirmish two of Combash's band were killed and the remainder fled. Soon after the battle, a squad of bluecoats sent by Ames arrived in Greenwood to restore order and security. The soldiers and a deputy sheriff tracked down Combash in early 1870, and, rather than face the imprecise justice of "Judge Lynch," he died in a fusillade of bullets.[73]

Less serious racial outbreaks occurred at Dry Grove in Hinds County and at West Point in the black prairie country. Five Negroes and three whites were wounded at Dry Grove in two skirmishes precipitated by a flare-up of tensions at a conservative rally. With excitement high at West Point as the fall election approached, the "accidental" wounding of a Negro by a white man over a private quarrel triggered a brief clash between armed bands of the two races. In both incidents the swift intervention of federal troops, on orders from General Ames, prevented a major racial confrontation.[74]

Although black-white tension was just below the surface throughout the campaign of 1869, as it had been in 1867 and 1868, this was accepted as a fact of life by most campaigners of both political

72. Vicksburg *Times*, November 26, 1869. A deserter from the army during the war, Combash was under indictment in 1869 for pilfering the property of his black roommate at Jackson while the constitutional convention was in session. Vicksburg *Weekly Republican*, June 28, 1868.

73. Vicksburg *Times*, October 15, 1869; Jackson *Weekly Clarion*, October 14, December 2, 1869, January 29, 1870; Friar's Point *Weekly Delta*, December 8, 1869; Rainwater (ed.), "Autobiography of Humphreys," 253.

74. *Hinds County Gazette*, November 3, 10, 1869; entries for November 11, 16, 1869, in Agnew Diary.

parties, and except for newcomers it apparently held few terrors. Political contests, especially in the South, were to some extent occasions for participants to prove their manhood, and many campaigners found exhilaration and challenge in the combativeness and excitement generated by these affairs. Alcorn, for example, despite his frequent denunciation of Klan-type violence, seemed to relish an encounter on the stump, as long as it did not become unmanageable. He described to his wife one such confrontation in north Mississippi during the 1869 campaign. "My canvass here has been reasonably pleasant; occasionally I have [had] a bout with blackguards. At Ripley I had an angry altercation with Bill Stricklin. I think he came out second best. I called him a liar, the crowd went out at the doors and windows of the church. I called to them not to leave, saying that Stricklin was a drunken cowardly vagabond." No one cared to refute the charge, and Alcorn, by his account, left town with the respect of the white yeomanry.[75]

The vigor with which General Ames acted against disturbers of the peace, despite the fact that his force in the state numbered fewer than eight hundred men, checkmated the activities of the Ku Klux Klan and other terror societies during the campaign. Only in northeast Mississippi, a predominantly white area, did Klan attacks as such occur during the fall of 1869. And even there the quick military apprehension of several Klansmen in Bladwyn, an action which, one observer caustically remarked, threatened to depopulate the town, suppressed this form of organized intimidation and violence in the area.[76]

Although Ames's vigorous efforts to maintain the social equilibrium in the state and prevent attacks on Republicans were commendable, he also played the role of military despot to ensure the success of his party in the election. The failure of the Republicans in the election of 1868 was indelibly impressed upon the young district commander's mind. This defeat had occurred, he

75. Alcorn to his wife Amelia, October 16, 1869, in Alcorn Papers, Mississippi Archives.
76. Entries for September 1, 2, 23, 1869, in Agnew Diary. A northern citizen from the turbulent town of Grenada was murdered in August by masked men. This seems to have been the only other incidence of Klan activity during the latter part of 1869. Petition of citizens of Grenada to General Ames, August 27, 1869, in Governors' Correspondence, Vol. 69. The petitioners, including, as they claimed, "the most prominent citizens" of the town, asked Ames to offer a reward for the speedy apprehension of the murderers.

believed, because local officials, including the election supervisors, were unsympathetic northerners or "rebels." Consequently, as the election approached Ames intensified his campaign, begun in July, to purge from office National Union Republicans and conservatives. After consultation with Ames, the state Republican executive committee in September issued a secret circular to local party organizers directing them to inform the committee of any officials in their counties who were not actively supporting the cause. The directive implied that those officers who did not meet this test would be summarily removed by Ames.[77] A few days later another circular from the state party headquarters—this one addressed to sheriffs—informed county officials that they had been assessed a certain amount of money "to pay the expenses of the canvass." Ames would dismiss any officer refusing to pay his pro rata share and would appoint a loyal Republican replacement. The amount of the levy varied with the county and was not excessive (for example, public officials in Hinds County were assessed a total of $250).[78] Although such political practices were not uncommon in nineteenth-century America, Ames's involvement while serving as district military commander tarnishes the image of idealistic crusader for freedom and tolerance that he sought to cultivate with Republicans in Washington and later with historians.[79]

The high-handed methods of Ames and the Republican hierarchy had the desired effect. Not only did it secure a free ballot for Republicans in the election—the ostensible purpose behind the policy—it also created a solid phalanx of industrious party workers whose jobs depended upon their diligence in organizing black voters and who could expect rewards from victorious party leaders. When news of Ames's test for officeholding was received in Memphis, St. Louis, and New Orleans, a migration of transients and adventurers descended on the border counties, all professing a

77. Ames to General Sherman, August 17, 1869, in William T. Sherman Papers; Jackson *Weekly Clarion*, August 19, 1869; Vicksburg *Times*, August 14, October 28, 1869; Forest *Register*, September 29, 1869.

78. *Hinds County Gazette*, September 15, 1869; Jackson *Weekly Clarion*, September 9, October 14, 1869.

79. Ames to Eaton, September 13, 1869, in Eaton Papers; Ames to General Sherman, August 17, 1869, in William T. Sherman Papers; Ames to E. Benjamin Andrews, February 29, 1896, in Adelbert Ames Papers, Mississippi Department of Archives and History; Ames to James W. Garner, January 17, 1900, in Garner Papers.

solemn dedication to Republican principles. After the fall election most of these newcomers found no future in the state Republican party; however, a few, not all of whom came solely for the perquisites of office, stayed on and played an important role in Mississippi politics in the 1870s. New arrivals during the campaign included such future black leaders and Republican stalwarts as Hannibal (Ham) Carter and Samuel J. Ireland.[80]

Conservative spokesmen wasted no time in working themselves into a frenzy over the activities of "the military tyrant" who "had prostituted the power delegated to him" for partisan and selfish purposes. To them, Ames's motive was simple: he expected to be elevated to the United States Senate by a grateful Radical legislature when it met. Ambition, the northern editor of the Vicksburg *Times* declared, "has taken hold of him." Ames "has been acting the part of a mean, low, abject tool in the hands of a few dozen scheming politicians, who as a reward for his subserviency, have promised to make him a Senator of the United States." He had, this conservative Republican editor asserted, disgraced the uniform of the army and made the political contest of 1869 a travesty upon republican institutions.[81]

Although they had failed earlier to persuade Grant to remove Ames, National Union Republicans saw the general's latest transgressions as offering a glimmer of hope that they might change the president's mind before the election. In late October, Archie C. Fisk, the carpetbag chairman of the conservative Republican executive committee, dispatched affidavits to Washington attesting to Ames's "tyranny" in packing local offices with political sympathizers in his resolve to carry the election for the Radicals. Then, in early November, Dent abandoned his debates with Alcorn and hurried to Washington for a final effort to persuade his brother-in-law to intervene on the side of his faction. Throughout the month

80. Vicksburg *Times*, November 7, 1869; *Hinds County Gazette*, November 24, 1869; Jackson *Weekly Clarion*, November 18, 1869; Jackson *Weekly Pilot*, December 4, 1869. Although directed by General-in-Chief Sherman to appoint conservatives to at least one of the three positions on the county boards of registrars to supervise the election, Ames refused to do so, and when the polls opened on November 30 there were few boards in the state that were not top-heavy with regular Republicans. Vicksburg *Times*, August 26, October 28, 1869; Jackson *Weekly Clarion*, November 25, December 2, 1869.

81. Vicksburg *Times*, August 14, September 26, October 28, 1869; *Speech of Johnston*, 1–2; *Hinds County Gazette*, November 3, 1869.

reports from the capital indicated that the circumspect president
had been impressed by the arguments of the National Union Republicans. When Dent dined with Grant on Thanksgiving Day,
conservative hopes soared. But the meeting produced only an
apology from the president for his opposition to Dent's candidacy
and his comment that if the election were not so near he would
remove Ames.[82] His resolution gone, Dent returned to Mississippi
to await the election returns.

With Ames officials in charge of the voting machinery and supported by an increased military presence in the state, the election passed quietly. Since the general permitted the presence of
conservative observers at the polling places, fraud on the part of
overzealous Republican election supervisors did not occur.[83] Few
elections in Mississippi between the Civil War and the reforms
of the twentieth century were as unfettered and as honest as this
one, despite conservative charges that the district commander was
determined to carry the contest for the Republicans by unscrupulous methods. Even more thorough than Ord in 1867 and Gillem in
1868, Ames gave careful instructions to election and law enforcement officials to ensure that no intimidation, no matter how innocuous or from what source, occurred at or near the polls. The
general's announcement that persons arrested for intimidating voters or for disturbing the peace would be tried by military commission contributed substantially to the good order that prevailed.
Under the circumstances, few antagonistic whites were willing to
intimidate Republicans and thereby risk an unpleasant exile to Dry
Tortugas to advance the cause of the weak Dent ticket.[84]

Blacks, untrammeled in their exercise of the ballot and carefully instructed by diligent Republican organizers of both races,

82. Vicksburg *Times*, October 28, November 6, 1869; Jackson *Weekly Clarion*, November 4, 11, 25, 1869; Forest *Register*, December 4, 1869. Even if Grant had agreed to intervene against Ames, it was too late for any presidential action to affect the outcome of the
election.

83. *Hinds County Gazette*, November 24, 1869; Jackson *Weekly Pilot*, December 4,
1869; General Order 55, October 14, 1869, in Records of the Fourth Military District.
Hoping to increase the voter turnout, Ames decreed that the election should be extended to
two days—November 30, as Grant had provided, and December 1.

84. General Order 55, October 14, 1869, in Records of the Fourth Military District.

flocked to the polls in 1869 in larger numbers than at any time during the Reconstruction era, with the possible exception of the local elections of 1871. Thousands of white voters, however, remained at home. Especially apathetic were whites in the northern counties, where suspicion of a "Jackson clique" and its role in the Dent movement loomed large in the minds of many. Reportedly, thirteen hundred of the twenty-six hundred eligible white voters in DeSoto County did not participate in the election; the number was higher in populous Tishomingo County where fifteen hundred chose to remain at home on election day. Even in the heart of Brown-Barksdale country whites showed little enthusiasm for voting, with hundreds refusing to go to the polls in Hinds County.[85] The extent of conservative inaction, however, was not nearly as great as in 1867 when perhaps no more than twelve thousand whites voted.

The massive black outpouring and white indifference gave the regular Republican party a staggering victory. Alcorn and his ticket captured 76,000 votes to 38,000 for the Dent party; regular Republicans won all five seats in the national House of Representatives, and they secured an overwhelming majority in both chambers of the state legislature. Since both parties endorsed the constitution, minus the proscriptive clauses which went down to an easy defeat in a separate vote, the document was ratified with fewer than 1,000 ballots cast against it.[86]

Although it could well have been a beginning, the election of 1869 did not produce the balanced biracial party that Alcorn and his moderate Republican associates had envisaged. Unfortunately for purposes of precise analysis, the election returns were not recorded by race, but a study of the county results correlated with the registration figures for 1869, which are available by race and

85. Hernando *Weekly Press*, December 16, 1869; *Hinds County Gazette*, December 8, 15, 1869; Jackson *Weekly Clarion*, December 16, 1869.

86. Complete election returns, by county, including the votes on the constitution and also on its separate clauses, may be found in General Orders, 1869, Records of the Fourth Military District, and in the Jackson *Weekly Pilot*, January 8, 1870. Some variance occurred in the ballots cast for state candidates. James Lynch, for example, in his race for secretary of state ran slightly behind Alcorn and others on the Republican ticket. The black leader secured 75,401 votes to 76,186 for the party's standard-bearer. County and local officers, except for members of the legislature, were not chosen in this election.

county, provides a reasonably clear indication of how the old citizens voted in the contest.[87] Alcorn carried forty-one counties, only fourteen of which possessed a majority of white voters. Of these fourteen counties, nine had black minorities of more than 40 percent of the registered vote. Given the pattern of white nonparticipation that existed in many counties and the large black turnout, Alcorn could have won with a solid Negro vote in all but Choctaw, a county with a turbulent (and Democratic) past, highlighted by the rise of a militant loyal league near the end of the war. This does not mean that "the Mogul of the Radicals" received only a scattering of white votes but rather that the number of the old citizens voting for him was not large. It is doubtful, then, that he attracted many Whigs to the Republican ticket. Most of them evidently felt that he was a renegade to the cause of conservatism and an instrument of Radical designs in the state.

The crucial fact in Alcorn's overwhelming victory was the support given him by the new electorate and, conversely, the almost complete failure of the conservatives to wrest black voters from the regular party. The Dent party, having transplanted northerners on the ticket, had hoped to win a substantial vote in the plantation counties where Negro registration was high, but the election returns indicate that the party was almost completely shut out in these counties. In percentage, the lowest counties for Dent had the highest Negro populations. At the extreme was Issaquena County in the Delta, which gave Dent only 32 votes out of a total registration of 1,843 (92 percent Negro), all of which probably came from the 112 registered whites. But even in a county such as Hinds, where the black registration was not as overwhelming (69 percent), the National Union Republican vote was embarrassing, especially since conservative spokesmen in the county had been very active in their efforts to win the Negro vote. Of a total registration of 6,945, Dent received only 1,415 votes. Even granted white apathy, the conservative party in Hinds secured almost all of its support from the 2,181 eligible whites. Virtually the same story was repeated in Warren, Holmes, and other plantation coun-

87. Official registration figures, as revised by Ames in November, 1869, are found in General Orders, 1869, Records of the Fourth Military District.

ties. Dent won only three black counties, all of which had a large white registration. In these counties the white voting population, despite considerable indifference, could have carried the day for Dent with little black support. Regular Republicans perhaps had not organized blacks as well in these three counties as in others where Negro voters constituted a majority and where they cast Alcorn ballots.

Although admitting that some whites were "attracted by the garish flame that Alcorn had lighted," conservatives in the aftermath of the election did not miss the point that blacks, not old Whigs, had produced the votes for the huge Republican victory. The majority of whites, shaken old citizens now argued, had refused to participate because their self-styled leaders had abandoned conservative, white supremacist principles, embraced carpetbaggers running for office on a Republican ticket, and accepted blacks into political fellowship. "Contaminated with negro suffrage," the conservative policy of conciliation had gained nothing but a "terrible humiliation" for the state, these whites declared.[88] "We are convinced," the editor of the Vicksburg *Herald* observed, "that with all this promising, drumming, and persuasion not one thousand negroes in the State were induced to vote the Dent ticket."[89] The lesson to whites was clear, the Forest *Register* exclaimed.

> We must look to [the] interests of our own race. The issues will henceforth be mainly based upon color, as the black men have seen fit to take the initiatory step of alienation in arraying themselves against the white man. Survey the field the best you can and you can but discern the antagonism, slowly, but surely, developing itself through the teachings of radicalism, suddenly assuming definite outline, fixed, tangible, and threatening. To meet this, it is our duty, paramount to all other considerations, to prepare for it as become men who aim to protect themselves and their property from the merciless blade of the semi-barbarian and the grasp of the agrarian.[90]

88. Vicksburg *Times*, December 10, 1869; Jackson *Weekly Clarion*, December 4, 1869, quoting the Meridian *Mercury*; *Hinds County Gazette*, December 15, 1869, quoting the Columbus *Index*; Oscar J. E. Stuart to Robert B. Mayes, December 3, 1869, in Stuart Papers.
89. As reported in the Forest *Register*, December 10, 1870.
90. *Ibid.*, December 4, 1869.

The Meridian *Mercury*, one of the few conservative newspapers that had not become "contaminated with negro suffrage" during the campaign, declared that in courting the favor of "slaves and menials" white people had "dragged the dignity of their Caucasian nature in the dirt." Now, "having been met with sneers of derision," whites were "stirred in the depths of their resentment with an antagonism they have vainly sought to repress. Henceforth the lines will be drawn sharply between the races in this State. The white men are not likely again to offer to fraternize with the negro, but accept sternly the issue of the 'irrepressible conflict' of [the] races."[91]

But this kind of blatant racism in defeat did not characterize the expressions of most conservative spokesmen or their political posture toward blacks during the early 1870s. Although quick to express their disappointment with the Negro's behavior in the election, most conservative leaders preferred to ignore the racial implications for the future of Mississippi politics. Some disappointed old citizens simply directed their criticism at those persons who had refused to vote, claiming that an active participation by whites could have carried the election for the conservatives despite Ames's high-handed methods and the solidarity of the Negro vote on the side of the Republicans. "The people have no one to blame but themselves for the result," the Meridian *Gazette* concluded. But many conservatives held the "Jackson clique" responsible for their terrible humiliation. The main object of the Dent movement, the Columbus *Democrat* asserted, had been to restore the Brown-Barksdale ring to power after years of political oblivion. The Port Gibson *Standard* labeled the whole business of 1869 "an ingeniously stupid Jackson scheme" which had no basis in popular support.[92]

One good thing, for sure, had come out of the election, anti-Jackson journals claimed. The influence of the clique had been broken and never again would the white people of the state turn to these "absolute despots" whose policies had resulted in social, political, and economic chaos. With a sigh of relief, the Grenada

91. As reported in the Jackson *Weekly Pilot*, December 18, 1869.
92. Jackson *Weekly Pilot*, December 25, 1869, January 8, 1870; Vicksburg *Herald*, January 19, 1870.

Sentinel published an obituary for the Jackson cabal and proclaimed the end of an era of rule by oligarchs.[93]

Barksdale weakly countered these assaults by blaming Ames and the Grant administration for the election disaster. The despotic activities of Ames, which were endorsed by Grant, had predetermined the results, and the campaign strategy of the conservatives had had no influence whatsoever on the outcome of the contest, Barksdale argued. There was, however, one consolation in the conservative defeat: the people would no longer be subjected "to the iniquities of the Ames administration," since his regime would be replaced by a civil administration under Alcorn. In fact, Barksdale now discovered that Alcorn, Lynch, and their Republican associates "may be more liberal than anticipated," and their control of the state would be a welcome relief from autocratic military rule.[94] George W. Harper, another "wire-puller" in the Dent movement, also suddenly realized that the triumph of Alcorn republicanism was not an unmitigated disaster. If the Republican leaders carried out in good faith their campaign pronouncements, this Whig editor said, there would be "no just ground for material opposition to them on the part of the white people of the State, although the white vote, in almost a solid body, was thrown against them in the election." Harper, who only three weeks earlier had charged Alcorn with leading "a fresh herd of carpet-bag and scallawag locusts" into the state, seven days after the election averred that if, as governor, Alcorn honored his campaign pledges, "we do not see why he may not be the most popular Governor Mississippi has ever had, and at the same time the most valuable one to the common interests of our people." But as a sine qua non for white support, Harper wrote, Alcorn would have to hold out to them "the olive branch instead of the negro." Down in Natchez, in an area of traditional white moderation in political matters, the people reportedly were reconciled to Alcorn's triumph, and they now looked to the new Republican administration to tackle some of the problems that had been left unsolved since the war.[95] As a whole,

93. Hernando *Weekly Press*, January 6, 1870; Friar's Point *Weekly Delta*, January 12, 1870.

94. Jackson *Weekly Clarion*, December 9, 1869.

95. *Hinds County Gazette*, December 8, 1869, February 26, 1870; Hernando *Weekly Press*, December 16, 1869; Natchez *Weekly Democrat*, December 16, 1869.

the old citizens of the state faced the future after the election of 1869 with far less gloom and foreboding than the rhetoric of the conservative canvass had suggested would be the case in the wake of defeat and certainly with less shock and demoralization than they had felt after the 1867 contest.

Republicans, from Alcorn down to the party organizer and voter on the plantation, made no attempt to conceal their elation over the party triumph. Nevertheless, surprised by the magnitude of their victory and exhausted by the long and arduous struggle for power, most of them preferred not to gloat over the political misfortunes of the conservatives. Even those Radicals of the old Eggleston-Gibbs faction who had been pushed aside during the campaign displayed a spirit of magnanimity toward their fallen foes, and some indicated that they now saw the folly of their earlier efforts to impose the proscriptive constitution upon the people.[96] Speaking for the moderates of the party, James Lynch, the first black man to win a state office in Mississippi, insisted that the triumphant Republicans should immediately honor their commitment to racial and political conciliation and thus lay the foundation for "a peaceful and prosperous commonwealth." Carpetbagger Hiram T. Fisher, an influential Republican editor who had vacillated between radicalism and moderation during the crisis over the constitution, assured the people that "the pledges made by our party will be faithfully redeemed; the personal animosities and disagreements engendered in the past will be overlooked and forgotten; and the demands of justice, patriotism and honor will be so met as to secure Mississippi a reign of uninterrupted prosperity."[97]

A policy of conciliation and liberalism toward former Confederates and toward opponents of congressional reconstruction, ascendant moderates declared in the afterglow of their greatest success, need not conflict with a strict observance of Republican principles by the new regime. Education for the masses, support for the removal of the Fourteenth Amendment disabilities imposed on Confederates, and integrity in government, Lynch asserted, were

96. A. W. Clapp to James A. Garfield, December 8, 1869, and Charles W. Clarke to Garfield, December 26, 1869, both in Garfield Papers; Jackson *Weekly Pilot*, December 4, 1869.

97. Jackson *Weekly Pilot*, December 4, 11, 1869.

the cardinal principles of republicanism (he did not include black rights on this occasion), and these tenets must be rigorously adhered to by the new administration if the party expected to succeed in the state.[98] After almost three years of often bitter struggle Lynch and his fellow Republicans were poised in early 1870 to assume control of the government and put into effect their promises of a new order for Mississippi.

98. *Ibid.*, December 11, 1869.

8

Restoration

The restoration of civil government under Republican control had to await the ratification of the Fourteenth and Fifteenth amendments and the approval of Congress for Mississippi's readmission to the Union. After the election of 1869 these actions were little more than formalities. On January 11, 1870, the new legislature, at the call of General Ames, met at the capitol for the specific purpose of ratifying the national amendments and selecting United States senators.[1] The legislature that would have the responsibility for constructing the new order begun by the constitutional convention of 1868 represented in a fairly balanced fashion all of the elements of the dominant Republican party. In the senate, where there were twenty-six Republicans and seven conservatives, scalawags numbered twelve, carpetbaggers nine, and blacks five. Of the eighty-three Republicans in the house of representatives (to only twenty-four conservatives) thirty-one were blacks and twenty each were carpetbaggers and scalawags; twelve Republicans have not been identified as to race and origins.[2]

In an atmosphere free of the conservative abuse and the internal tension that had characterized the constitutional convention of 1868, the legislature immediately went to work to meet the restoration requirements of Congress. The only difficulty was that of heating the dilapidated legislative chambers, through which the cold winter air blew almost unimpeded. Frantic efforts were made to repair the capitol, but these were not completed until the regular legislative session in March.[3]

1. Ames offered Alcorn the position of provisional governor until such time as Congress approved the restoration of civil government and the elevation of the victorious Republicans to power. Alcorn refused the tender, since it came from the military and would be subject, however briefly, to its authority. He preferred to await the complete restoration of civil government before assuming office. Jackson *Weekly Pilot*, January 29, 1870; *Appleton's Annual Cyclopaedia*, 1869, p. 462.

2. This information was compiled from data in the Jackson *Weekly Clarion*, December 9, 23, 1869, and the Jackson *Weekly Pilot*, January 1, 1870.

3. Jackson *Weekly Pilot*, January 8, 22, March 12, 1870.

The house of representatives quickly selected Franklin E. Freeman, a moderate carpetbagger of "comprehensive and expansive views," as its speaker, and simultaneous with the senate, where Lieutenant Governor Powers presided, it ratified both the Fourteenth and Fifteenth amendments. As they had promised in the campaign, conservatives in the legislature offered no real opposition to the amendments; only six representatives and two senators voted against the Fourteenth Amendment, whereas the Fifteenth passed the senate by a unanimous vote and received the approval of all but one representative.[4]

Next, the legislature turned to the more difficult business of selecting three United States senators, two for unexpired terms and the other for a full term beginning in 1871. It was no secret that Alcorn, once the Republican government had been established, wanted to serve in the Senate, where he could work for federal aid to restore the levees and where he could compete with the ablest politicians in the nation. As a result, before the campaign of 1869 had ended he promised his carpetbag associates that when the legislature met he would seek election to the Senate term beginning in 1871, leaving one of their own, Powers, in the governor's mansion. All factions in the party accepted this arrangement, including Alcorn scalawags, since Powers, although a northerner, was a political moderate. In the legislature the vote for Alcorn was almost unanimous, with only a handful of conservatives resisting the inevitable.[5]

A brief flurry of excitement occurred when candidates were nominated for the unexpired terms. Ames, whose assistance to the party during the election had been substantial, appeared hat in hand (some said sword in hand) to claim the senatorship as a reward for his service. Although grateful to Ames for his contributions to the party's success, many Republicans objected to his candidacy while he was still the military commander of the state; then, too, blacks preferred either James Lynch or scalawag Robert W. Flournoy for the long unexpired term. Resentful of Lynch's powerful influence with his race and suspicious of Flournoy's loyalty to the party because of his erratic behavior in the past, dominant

4. *Ibid.*, January 22, 1870; *Appleton's Annual Cyclopaedia*, 1869, p. 462.
5. Jackson *Weekly Pilot*, January 22, 1870; *Senate Journal [1870]*, p. 26.

carpetbaggers in the legislature opposed the selection of either of them for the unexpired Senate terms. Rather than risk a schism in the party at its very moment of triumph both Lynch, who had been elected secretary of state, and Flournoy withdrew as candidates before nominations were made.[6] This paved the way for General Ames's selection to the Senate, but it complicated the task of choosing a suitable person for the short term.

Since whites had received the long terms, blacks as a matter of principle expected to have one of their own tapped for the remaining seat. But white opposition was strong. When black legislators insisted on sending a member of their race to the Senate, white Republicans, unwilling to risk political oblivion by directly opposing their Negro colleagues, sought by subterfuge to defeat the move. They advanced as candidates several white Republicans who had influence among blacks and who might be acceptable to them. All fell short of the necessary majority, however, and finally, after a number of separate and joint ballots were taken, the name of Hiram Rhoades Revels, an obscure minister-missionary and state senator, was hoisted to the top. Only two additional ballots were necessary to make Revels the first Negro to serve in the United States Senate.[7]

Few men in public affairs have risen to the top as quickly as Hiram Revels. A free-born native of North Carolina and of mixed African-Indian descent, Revels after years of effective religious work among blacks in both the North and the South entered politics in Natchez in 1868 as a town alderman.[8] Virtually by accident, as a compromise candidate, he secured the local Republican nomination to the state senate in 1869, which was tantamount to election in the Natchez district. When the legislature assembled in January, Revels was invited to open the senate session with a prayer, and he gave a performance that, according to John R. Lynch, "made a deep and profound impression" upon his colleagues, in-

6. Vicksburg *Times and Republican*, March 29, 1870; Vicksburg *Herald*, January 14, 1870; Jackson *Weekly Pilot*, January 22, 29, February 12, 1870.

7. *Journal of the House of Representatives of the State of Mississippi for 1870* (Jackson, 1870), 30–31, 36, 38, 40, 42; *Senate Journal [1870]*, pp. 31–33.

8. Annie L. Pierson, biographical sketch of Hiram R. Revels, in Revels Subject File Collection; "Biographical Sketches of Mississippians: Hiram R. Revels" (MS in McCardle Papers).

fluencing many of them a few days later to support him for the United States Senate.[9]

The reaction to the election of a black man to the Senate was surprisingly mild. The Jackson *Clarion*, although carrying the racist blasts of out-of-state Democratic newspapers, soft-pedaled the dramatic event, indicating that it preferred Revels, "an honest negro," to a white Radical of the ilk of Ames for a Senate seat. The Vicksburg *Herald*, believing that conservative legislators in order to prevent the selection of a Radical had had a hand in the choice of Revels, informed its readers that the new black senator was "quite intelligent and liberal in his views" and, by implication, would do nothing to disgrace the Senate or the state.[10] After a few weeks of observing Revels' performance in Washington, Frederic Speed, the carpetbag editor of the Vicksburg *Times and Republican* whose support for the cause of Negro equality had never been very strong, announced that the senator "has had greatness thrust upon him, and no one can take umbrage at the manner in which he fills the duties imposed."[11]

Hiram T. Fisher of the Jackson *Pilot* led the Radical praise for the selection of Revels. Yet he found reason to point out to the disgruntled white Republicans that the new senator should not be considered "as a representative of the race of Ham, or of the true African-Ethiopian stock, rather than that of the Caucasian—for he is at least three-fourths of the latter race; and according to the opinion of many extreme, modern Ethnologists, has a sufficient predominance of the blood of the white race to give him not only intellectual but moral elements, which, if properly cultivated and cherished, may be raised to the highest point of human distinction."[12]

9. John R. Lynch, *The Facts of Reconstruction* (Indianapolis, 1970), 46–47; John Lynch, *Reminiscences of an Active Life*, 75–80.

10. Jackson *Weekly Clarion*, January 27, February 3, 1870; Vicksburg *Herald*, January 21, 1870. Reportedly, conservative legislators did some behind-the-scenes maneuvering to secure the election of Revels, rather than risk the triumph of an obnoxious Radical, like Beroth B. Eggleston, for the Senate position. A victory for Revels might also serve another purpose: the presence of a Negro in the United States Senate, some conservatives believed, would contribute to a reaction in the North against the Republicans.

11. Vicksburg *Times and Republican*, March 29, 1870.

12. Jackson *Weekly Pilot*, January 22, 1870. Fisher, nevertheless, reaffirmed his commitment to the elevation of the freedmen in society and indicated that blacks, even those without white blood in their veins, should be given office in keeping with their ability.

Refusing to be misled by any such racial syllogism, blacks in Mississippi rejoiced at the choice of one of their own for the Senate. Expressing the sentiment of his race, James Lynch hailed the development as an affirmation of Republican pledges of equal rights for the black race, and with his usual optimism exclaimed, "A glorious sunlight now shines upon the path of Mississippi that leads to a goal of prosperity of which her greatest patriots never dreamed."[13] A few weeks later, speaking at Baltimore on the eve of the ratification of the Fifteenth Amendment, Revels himself sounded a similar note of hope: "The seals of a new era are broken, and we stand to-night in the full radiancy of a period of time which has no counterpart in history."[14]

While blacks celebrated their success, Congress took up the question of restoring Mississippi to full fellowship in the Union under the constitution of 1868 with the newly elected officers. A brief effort by Benjamin F. Butler and a few of his Radical colleagues to restore the constitution's proscriptive features failed. However, with the lukewarm support of most moderate Republicans in Congress, Radicals managed to include in the readmission bill provisions requiring that the state never amend its constitution to deprive blacks of the ballot or their rights to hold office or share in the benefits of the school system outlined in the constitution. An additional clause reaffirmed Congress' determination to enforce the officeholding provision of the Fourteenth Amendment. This section, reflecting the Georgia imbroglio in which several conservatives were seated in the legislature without having their Fourteenth Amendment disabilities removed, required all legislators and officeholders to take an oath swearing that they either were eligible under the amendment or had secured the removal of their disabilities. On February 3, the restoration bill, somewhat modestly entitled "An Act to admit the State of Mississippi to Representation in the Congress of the United States," passed the House and two weeks later, after some debate, received the approval of the Senate. On February 23, President Grant signed the measure, thereby restoring Mississippi to full fellowship in the Union.[15]

13. *Ibid.*, January 29, 1870.
14. Washington *New Era*, March 10, 1870.
15. *Congressional Globe*, 41st Cong., 2nd Sess., 1013–14, 1356–66; McPherson, *Political History*, 576–77.

The question of seating Revels and Ames, however, still confronted the Senate. Although many Democrats in the North were terribly exercised over the elevation of a black man to the Senate, their representatives in Congress contented themselves mainly with the arguments that Revels had not been a citizen for the required nine years and that his certificate of election was not in order, since it had been signed by a military officer, Ames. After a brief debate on the issue, the Senate by an overwhelming majority voted to seat Revels. On February 25, in a dramatic moment before a packed and silent gallery, the first black to be selected to the United States Senate was escorted down the aisle of the chamber to take his seat—the seat that, some delighted in saying, Jefferson Davis had vacated in 1861.[16]

Far more open opposition developed over Ames's admission to this select circle. Fearing the political repercussions in the North that might follow the seating of Ames, who was in military command when chosen for the Senate, Republican members, even of the Radical persuasion, were sharply divided on the wisdom of accepting him into their fellowship. At first the Senate inclined toward rejecting Ames, especially after its judiciary committee recommended that he not be seated on the oblique ground that as a military officer on a duty assignment in Mississippi he could not hold state citizenship and therefore was not eligible to represent the people. Asked by the judiciary committee to explain his intentions in Mississippi, Ames botched his answer to such an extent that the Republican majority had no choice but to delay action on his case. Although he insisted to the committee that he was in the process of purchasing property in the state, he admitted, in all candor, that he probably would not have done so had the legislature rejected his candidacy for the Senate.[17] At the same time a handful of moderate Republicans in Mississippi beseeched the Senate to turn down Ames's appeal to be seated. In explanation, carpetbagger Frederic Speed of the Vicksburg *Times and Republican*, an aberrant Republican in 1869 who had returned to the party after the fall election, argued that not only was the manner in

16. *Congressional Globe*, 41st Cong., 2nd Sess., 1542–43; New York *Times*, February 26, 1870.
17. *Congressional Globe*, 41st Cong., 2nd Sess., 2125–26, 2130, 2334–38; *Nation*, X (January 27, 1870), 50.

which Ames had been selected for the Senate highly irregular, but the Radical general's elevation to the august body would defeat the efforts of Alcorn and his moderate associates to attract a substantial number of whites to the party. Conservative whites and many Republicans, Speed asserted, were thoroughly convinced that Ames had been "almost perfectly unprincipled in his administration of military power. The only principle he evinced was devotion to Ames and to ultra radicalism. He is not and never was, and never means to be identified with Mississippi. . . . He cares naught for its future prosperity, or the development of its resources. He hates the people."[18]

A majority in the Mississippi legislature did not agree with Speed. On March 24 the reconvened assembly passed a resolution imploring Congress to approve Ames's credentials. Bolstered by this reaffirmation of local Republican support for him, the Senate after a perfunctory debate agreed to seat Ames.[19]

The first signs of spring were beginning to appear in Jackson on March 10, 1870, when James Lusk Alcorn, attended by the eminent of his party in the state and joined by General James Longstreet, who had come up from New Orleans to witness the auspicious occasion, took the oath of office as governor of Mississippi.[20] Immediately preceding the administration of the oath this imposing scalawag delivered a stirring inaugural address to a sympathetic audience at the capitol. The moment was one of "special solemnity," and, Alcorn told his listeners, the feelings of triumph and pride usually characteristic of inaugural ceremonies had no place on the occasion of an old era ending and a new one beginning. "The Muse of History closes today a chapter of passion, bloodshed and social revolution and proceeds to write down" for Mississippi a new chapter whose theme will be peace and hope.[21]

As a result of the war the pernicious southern oligarchy had been overthrown by the emerging democracy of the North, Alcorn pointed out, and it was the responsibility of his administration to

18. Vicksburg *Times and Republican*, March 29, 1870; Blanche Ames Ames, *Adelbert Ames, 1835–1933: General, Senator, Governor* (New York, 1964), 298.
19. *Congressional Globe*, 41st Cong., 2nd Sess., 2314, 2349.
20. New York *Times*, March 11, 1870; Jackson *Weekly Pilot*, March 12, 1870.
21. Alcorn's inaugural address may be found in the *Senate Journal [1870]*, pp. 48–57.

make the democratic victory "a practical reality by ensuring all the blessings of a free government for the masses of the people." Alcorn reaffirmed his commitment to free schools for blacks and to the protection of Negro rights to hold property, vote, serve on juries, be secure from the lawless, and fill public office. Reflecting his recurrent vision of biracial cooperation in the reconstruction and development of the state, he promised that whites also would receive their full share of the benefits of the Republican order. He singled out for special attention "the poor white children of the State, who were permitted in the past to grow up like wild flowers, without training; the administration which we are about to inaugurate to-day is determined to extend a large proportion of its energies in educating" them.[22]

The extension of public benefits also required that the functions and powers of government be expanded, Alcorn declared. During the antebellum period the landed oligarchy had ruled only in the interest of twenty-five thousand slaveholding families, and its administration of affairs was inefficient and at times corrupt. Under the new order, this Delta scalawag claimed, five times that many families would need to be brought under the umbrella of government beneficence, and at the same time the functions of government would have to be expanded in order to meet the peculiar postwar needs of Mississippi society. Along with the creation of a system of public education, Alcorn indicated that action should be taken immediately to reorganize and enlarge the judicial system and form a militia to suppress the lawless. He also recommended the establishment of a department of public works to plan, promote, and give assistance to internal improvements in the state. This department's usefulness would not be immediate, however, since "so great are the demands upon the people for other services of the State that the present condition of [finance] is not opportune for any considerable expenditure from the public treasury on internal improvements."[23]

To the new governor, the crucial factor in achieving justice for the masses was the character of the men appointed to the courts. Accepting the principle that wealth, intelligence, and social posi-

22. *Ibid.*, 49–50, 53.
23. *Ibid.*, 50–51, 52.

tion should normally have a hand in public affairs—especially in the courts—Alcorn nonetheless declared in his inaugural address that these elements of leadership in the state were presently arrayed "against the spirit of our forthcoming laws." He therefore promised to exercise extreme caution in selecting men of the upper class for judicial positions, since "the laws for the protection of the rights and priviledges [*sic*] of the poorer class of our population must not be left subject to the interpretation of an opposition bar whose eminent ability does not scorn to enforce its subtle logic by bold brow-beating and arrogant exclusiveness." His appointees to the bench, he pledged, would be "in hearty accord with the mission of the men charged with the consolidation in the State of the work of reconstruction." He insisted, however, that the new judges should be lawyers of standing, whom "society cannot presume to ignore."[24]

Despite the new governor's expressed order of priorities that placed education and the protection of rights ahead of material development, he was far from being lukewarm regarding the need for public activity in the rehabilitation of the economic life of the state. An important result of the war, he declared, was the triumph in the nation of the northern spirit of material realism over the deleterious southern practice of political theorizing in the fashion of John C. Calhoun.[25] He indicated, as he had during the campaign of 1869, that the development of internal improvements, the restoration of the levees (which Alcorn believed was a federal responsibility), the establishment of public schools, and the suppression of the lawless were essential before Mississippi could be placed on the high road of economic well-being.[26]

Alcorn warned, however, against hastily committing the state to programs for economic development. The government would not have the financial means in the near future to undertake ambitious

24. *Ibid.*, 54.

25. *Ibid.*, 56–57. Alcorn's interpretation of the growing dichotomy between North and South during the antebellum period is not too much different from that of some latter-day historians. The obsession of the prewar South with "political theorizing," in Alcorn's language, becomes a southern exercise in "sublimated abstractions" in the lexicon of Arthur C. Cole and others. James G. Randall and David Donald, *The Civil War and Reconstruction* (Boston, 1969), 168.

26. *Senate Journal [1870]*, pp. 56–57.

schemes to assist material development. Not until public finances had reached a point where the state and local governments "can meet their ordinary expenses, not at a discount of twenty or thirty per cent on their paper, but at the par amount in money," should the new regime extend aid to various worthwhile enterprises.[27]

Another reason for caution in assisting economic development, the new governor announced, was the speculative impulse abroad in the land, which the state administration through its economic and financial policies should do nothing to encourage. The meagre capital in the state, whether private or public, should not be absorbed in the risky schemes being proposed in the name of material progress and gain. If the "mania of speculation" were not treated with firmness and foresight, he warned, it will, "as it has done elsewhere, not only plunge us into financial disaster, but may result in such bitter disappointments to individuals of enterprise as to leave behind it, for many years, a heavy discouragement upon measures of even healthy progress."[28]

In closing, Alcorn, a Whig partisan in many a political contest, could not resist the temptation, despite "the propriety of the occasion," to wish the Democratic party Godspeed on its road to dissolution. "The existence of that party as it now languishes out of life is a fact tied up in dazzling abstractions which the war has declared to be utterly impotent." All former Whigs, who had long possessed a sense of reality in matters of public policy, and also men of independent minds, who for various reasons had mistakenly followed the Democratic banner in the past, were morally bound to support the new order in the state insofar as it recognized the results of the war and confronted realistically the issues created by southern defeat. "On the very threshold of violence and revolution" as the new regime was being inaugurated, Mississippi had a right, the new governor declared, to expect all who in the past had stood for the Union, the Constitution, and the enforcement of the laws to stand once again against the headstrong spirit of irrationality and rebellion.[29]

27. *Ibid.*, 56.
28. *Ibid.*, 55.
29. *Ibid.*, 57–58.

As the Republicans began consolidating the work of reconstruction, Mississippi society after five years of freedom from the tramping of destructive armies and the roar of cannons still suffered from the ill effects of the war. Nevertheless, social and economic conditions had improved considerably since the bleak winter of 1867–1868, when political uncertainty and material deterioration had conspired to create an alarming social situation throughout the state.

The fundamental reason for this improvement lay with the agricultural economy's revival, which began with the harvesting of the 1868 cotton and grain crops and obtained full bloom during the next season. As might be expected, the rejuvenating key was a rise in the price of cotton, from fifteen cents per pound on the New Orleans market in December, 1867, to twenty-five cents in October, 1868.[30] But more was involved than an increase in the price of cotton. Paradoxically, the sociopolitical crisis of 1867–1868, climaxed by the bitter struggle over the work of the Black and Tan Convention, prepared the way for the economic upswing and for a significant easing of social tension and conflict between the races. White planters, sobered by the political turbulence of the spring and convinced that radicalism had been crushed with the defeat of the proscriptive constitution, went the extra mile in 1868 to cultivate the good will of their black laborers. For their part, Negroes, hoping to avoid during the coming winter the kind of crisis they had just survived and now realizing that politics offered no cure for their economic woes, returned to the fields and labored diligently for the success of the 1868 crop.[31] The cotton harvest thus proved bountiful and profitable for both planter and laborer.

Immediately, planters and their spokesmen began to praise blacks for their contribution to the cause of economic recovery and their willingness to shun Republican rallies in order to advance

30. A monthly tabulation of the price of cotton on the New Orleans market during the Reconstruction period may be found in James E. Boyle, *Cotton and the New Orleans Cotton Exchange: A Century of Commercial Evolution* (Garden City, 1934), 180–81.

31. Report of P. P. Bergevim for June, 1868, in Freedmen's Bureau Records, Mississippi; *Hinds County Gazette*, January 6, 27, 1869; testimony of John W. C. Watson in *House Miscellaneous Documents*, 40th Cong., 3rd Sess., No. 53, p. 298; Albert Gallatin Brown to Adelbert Ames, August 3, 1868, and Thomas J. Wharton to Ames, August 21, 1868, in Governors' Correspondence, Vol. 69; A. E. Netherton to Oscar J. E. Stuart, September 3, 1868, in Stuart Papers.

the state's material interests as well as their own. The Vicksburg *Herald*, an erstwhile critic of blacks for mixing farming with politics, expressed the new exuberant spirit of many planters when it declared:

> It is with no small degree of pleasure that we record the fact that from all parts of our State the negroes are represented as constantly improving in the art of self-government and are fast learning such ideas of economy as will ultimately result in demonstrating the fact that they are not incapable of becoming self-sustaining in the freedom they reaped as their part of the harvest of the late revolution. We are not disposed to oppress or oppose the black man in his honest effort at an honest living. This year's agricultural experiment has been fruitful of good results among the majority of those who, tired of waiting for the mule and homestead promised them by the Radical office seekers, went to work determined to win the promised prize in the only manner which it was possible for them to do so—by the sweat of their brows.
>
> Mississippi to-day exhibits a better prospect in all the financial departments than any of the States which have gone through the grades of a perfect reconstruction, and to no cause is the fact more clearly attributable than the defeat of Radicalism established in the last election.[32]

When all of the 1868 cotton crop had been marketed, it was clear that the agricultural interest of the state had received an encouraging boost toward recovery and perhaps financial independence. Mississippi farmers and planters had produced and sold 411,000 bales of cotton, receiving almost forty million dollars in return. These receipts exceeded by eleven million dollars the gross income from the poor 1867 crop.[33] The farmers' large grain yields rounded out the agricultural success of 1868. Normally, planters and farmers devoted almost all of their cultivated land to cotton, which had a cash value and was demanded by merchants in payment for provisions that had been advanced during the year. But the near starvation of many during the winter of 1867–1868 had shocked Mississippians into producing more foodstuffs, especially

32. Vicksburg *Herald*, November 25, 1868.
33. James L. Watkins, *King Cotton: A Historical and Statistical Review, 1790 to 1908* (New York, 1908), 174, 176; *Hinds County Gazette*, January 27, 1869; Vicksburg *Times*, February 23, 1869; Ross H. Moore, "Social and Economic Conditions in Mississippi During Reconstruction" (Ph.D. dissertation, Duke University, 1938), 71. The 411,000 bales that Mississippi produced in 1869 led the nation; Georgia was a distant second with 290,000.

corn. The 1868 corn yield was an impressive 35,519,000 bushels as compared to 19,657,000 in 1867.[34]

Nowhere in 1868 was agricultural change and success more evident than in the broad farm belt of central Mississippi, extending from Jackson to the Tennessee border. In this region, where the races mingled in about equal numbers, many whites who in the past had demonstrated a lack of enthusiasm for hard, sustained work under the hot sun took to the fields in impressive numbers and alongside black laborers produced large yields of both cotton and grain. By practicing economy, farmers of central Mississippi, as elsewhere, had relatively small provisions debts to meet at the end of the year, and they were therefore able to keep at home most of the proceeds from their staple crop. As preparations were made for a new growing season the Water Valley *Central Star* enthusiastically declared: "Central Mississippi is to-day in a flourishing condition, and with another abundant crop of cereals, will be the most inviting portion of the South to immigrants and capitalists."[35]

Not only in the farm country above Jackson but throughout the state the 1868 success gave debt-ridden Mississippians an opportunity to pay off their obligations, or at least a large portion of them. Furthermore, for the first time since before the war many men of the soil were able to make needed farm improvements, including the replacement of worn-out and outdated implements with innovative farm equipment from border and midwestern cities. The more optimistic observers predicted that if the newfound prosperity could be sustained for a year or two sufficient capital would accumulate to enable Mississippi to develop the kind of diversified economy that had been preached with fervor since 1865.[36]

The lessons learned from the 1867–1868 experience, however, were only partly retained. Encouraged by the remunerative cotton price and the cheerfulness with which black tenants stepped forward to make labor agreements for the new year, planters as well

34. *Merchant's Magazine and Commercial Review*, LX (February, 1869), 140; *Report of the Commissioner of Agriculture for the Year 1867* (Washington, D.C., 1868), 83; *Report of the Commissioner of Agriculture for the Year 1868* (Washington, D.C., 1869), 27.

35. As reported in the Jackson *Weekly Clarion*, March 11, 1869.

36. *Ibid.*, May 6, 27, 1869; Vicksburg *Herald*, November 24, 1868; Beaumont, *A Business Woman's Journal*, 346–47.

as yeoman farmers increased their cultivated acreage in 1869. Succumbing to the same boom psychology that had swept the cotton kingdom in the past, these farmers neglected the production of grain and other foodstuffs in order to expand the cultivation of the cash crop. Furthermore, growers of all classes failed to exercise the kind of financial prudence they had been forced to practice in 1868 when their credit "limit" was low.[37] The price of cotton, nevertheless, remained steady and lucrative, at no time during the picking season falling below twenty-two cents per pound. Although they had expected greater profits, farmers made money again in 1869. But, since they had purchased heavily during the year and had neglected to produce adequate foodstuffs, they were forced to turn over most of their proceeds to the local merchant or to commission houses in nearby commercial centers like Vicksburg and Memphis. Since the ultimate source of most of these provisions was the Midwest, a familiar cry was revived in Mississippi: "To make the State again prosperous the agricultural community must have their cribs and smokehouses upon their farms, and not in the great cities of the West."[38]

Blacks especially made progress in 1868–1869 on what appeared to be the road to self-sufficiency. Restored to the good graces of anxious planters after the successful crop of 1868, blacks found their labor at a premium in 1869. Not only were they able to command relatively lucrative labor contracts, at the rate of about twenty-five dollars per month where the wage system was employed, but many persuaded planters to rent farmland to them at a specific rate, payable when the crop was marketed. With more money available to pay wages and with black workers insisting on money payments for their labor, the sharecrop system, which had been introduced into the state on a large scale in 1867, declined in importance in 1869.[39]

37. Jackson *Weekly Clarion*, September 23, October 7, 1869; Forest *Register*, June 30, 1869; Vicksburg *Times*, September 12, 1869; *Report of the Commissioner of Agriculture for the Year 1869* (Washington, D.C., 1870), 22–23.

38. Boyle, *Cotton and the New Orleans Cotton Exchange*, 181; Jackson *Weekly Clarion*, February 3, 1870 (quote).

39. Vicksburg *Times*, September 12, 1869; Francis W. Loring and C. F. Atkinson (eds.), *Cotton Culture and the South, Considered with Reference to Emigration* (Boston, 1869), 114; Jackson *Weekly Clarion*, October 7, 1869. The decline in the sharecrop system was only temporary and was dependent on the status of the cotton market.

Working under terms which they perceived as advantageous, blacks gave close attention to the cultivation of their cotton plants during the spring and summer of 1869, and when the fleecy bolls opened in the fall they worked hard to pick them before the inclement weather of November and December set in. Their sweat and diligence in the field paid off. By the end of the year the plantation counties of west and north central Mississippi were full of reports of the good fortune of energetic black growers. Although probably none exceeded the two thousand bales of cotton that Isaiah Montgomery produced on the old plantation of his former master, Jefferson Davis, many blacks in 1869 realized enough money after paying expenses to put away some of it for the day when they would be able to purchase their own land.[40] In Carroll County, before the end of the picking season a large number of Negroes reportedly had liquidated their debts, and with the assistance of whites some of them were purchasing land. A Yazoo County planter wrote that freedmen on his plantation made more than three hundred dollars each after paying rent and "settling" for advances on the year's provisions. In Hinds County the Jackson *Weekly Pilot* boasted that numerous black families near Jackson had "cleared five hundred to twenty-five hundred dollars during the past year, and they are as happy and contented as people can be in their condition in life." The Republican journal continued, "Throughout the State this rate of remuneration, in proportion to the labor expended, has crowned the work of the colored people. In many instances they have purchased homes with their surplus means, and are laying the foundation of ease and wealth, while others have invested their money in plantation stock, supplies, &c., and have rented land to cultivate [during] the present year."[41]

Even in the white counties a few enterprising blacks overcame the racial barriers to agricultural success in 1869. One of them, Green Russell, a freedman of Leake County who had been educated in a northern mission school after the war, not only raised and

40. Jackson *Weekly Pilot*, January 15, November 12, 1870; Vicksburg *Times*, September 12, 1869; Jackson *Weekly Clarion*, December 30, 1869; Catherine Anderson McWillie to James McWillie, October 25, 1869, in William McWillie Family Papers, Mississippi Department of Archives and History.

41. Jackson *Weekly Clarion*, October 7, 1869; Richard Stephens to Joseph Holt, January 17, 1870, in Holt Papers; Jackson *Weekly Pilot*, January 15, 1870.

harvested seventy acres of cotton and corn but also taught a class of black children during the summer.[42]

An indicator of black economic progress in 1868–1870 was the remarkable growth of the Vicksburg branch of the National Freedmen's Savings and Trust Bank. Founded in late 1865 by northerners seeking to encourage the virtues of frugality and saving among former slaves, the Vicksburg office barely survived during its first two years of existence. Then, during 1868 freedman deposits in the bank spurted from $66,679 at the beginning of the year to $748,444 at the end, and in 1869 business with the Vicksburg branch rose to a high of $1,536,715 with 1,304 blacks depositing funds.[43] Most of the bank's customers were black residents of the Vicksburg area, and in 1870 more than one hundred of them purchased farms near the town.[44]

Buoyed by the material progress of their wards and unimpressed by rumblings of Bourbon white opposition to black ownership of property, Republican leaders, simultaneous with the inauguration of their rule in the state, predicted that Mississippi was on the verge of achieving their postwar ideal of a harmonious and prosperous biracial commonwealth. The key to this success had always been the elevation of the former slaves (though not necessarily to "social equality"), they said, and if the political and material advances of 1869 could be sustained the future was bright for blacks in the state. "The progress of the colored population in the acquirement of property has no parallel in the history of the country," the carpetbag editor of the Jackson *Pilot* claimed during the heady days of 1870, "and they have advanced equally in the attainment of practical education." Five years from now, he confidently predicted, "they will occupy ground in many instances far in advance of our white population and be comparatively independent

42. Forest *Register*, August 25, 1869.

43. For a report on the operations of the Vicksburg branch of the Freedmen's Savings Bank see the Washington *New Era*, March 24, 1870. The bank's mismanagement and a return of hard times on the land combined to cause the failure of the Freedmen's Savings Bank in 1874. Walter L. Fleming, *The Freedmen's Savings Bank: A Chapter in the Economic History of the Negro Race* (Chapel Hill, 1927), 51.

44. Washington *New National Era*, September 22, 1870. This modest trend toward black ownership of land did not begin until 1869–70. As a result of the crop success of 1868, approximately five hundred Negro families had homesteaded in Rankin County, according to the county sheriff. Jackson *Weekly Clarion*, August 5, 1869.

in earthly possessions."[45] In an even more sanguine mood, the northern-managed Vicksburg *Times and Republican* averred that the rapid fading away of prejudice against blacks "is apparent to every observant mind." An improved state of racial feeling was developing, and it "will gradually extend itself until there shall be nothing but the kindliest relations existing" between blacks and whites in Mississippi.[46]

Governor Alcorn affirmed this roseate view of black progress. Upon the completion of an intensive study of economic and social conditions in thirteen selected counties, including those in both plantation and nonplantation districts, he concluded that the increase of black property holding "is undoubted proof that the industry and thrift of the negro is developing with extraordinary rapidity the production of a mass of property-owners who constitute an unimpeachable guarantee that reconstruction goes forward to the consolidation of a society in which the reward of labor goes hand in hand with the safety of property."[47] As will be seen, this outpouring of hope soon lost its force and became a mere trickle of expectation for the future of racial equality and harmony in the state.

After years of seeing their communities languish and decay, town fathers and businessmen acted quickly in 1869–1870 to take advantage of the improved economic situation in the state. Merchants in railroad towns and in the river towns of Vicksburg and Natchez sprang to life and dispatched buyers to New York, St. Louis, and other northern and border centers to secure goods for the anticipated revival of trade in clothes, shoes, luxuries, farm equipment, and other manufactured products. George C. Kress of Vicksburg returned from New York with a large stock of "fashionable goods" that included hats for men, trunks, umbrellas, and walking canes. Another merchant, Meyer Bodenheim, filled a new, four-story building in Vicksburg with dry-goods articles from the North. But his competitor, Louis Hoffman, was assured of a larger trade with thirsty and convivial river planters after he installed a saloon on the

45. Jackson *Weekly Pilot*, January 15, 1870. See also the issues of April 2, 9, 1870.
46. Vicksburg *Times and Republican*, August 4, 1870.
47. *Annual Message of Governor Alcorn, 1871*, pp. 29–30.

first floor of his store.[48] In Natchez, where a fire had raked the downtown section in early 1868, commercial houses rose phoenix-like from the ashes when the farm economy improved during the following months. Throughout the state, merchants feverishly prepared their stores for the anticipated increase in business.[49]

The commercial revival of 1869–1870 also brought with it a frantic competition among towns for the proceeds from the successful cotton crops. As the economic situation on the land brightened, merchants scurried into the countryside to make business contacts before competitors from neighboring towns and wholesale drummers from distant places like St. Louis and New Orleans could preempt the trade. When threatened with a loss of their trade territory, merchants, assisted by town fathers and concerned citizens, urgently sought means to preserve their fresh prosperity and with it their hopes for the future. To retain control of the local trade, they turned, almost without exception, to the railroads—specifically projects for the extension of the railways into the interior. But the campaign to build these avenues of commerce, usually out of all proportion to their future value, stimulated an even more intense competition among commercial centers and led inevitably to financial disaster when the flush of prosperity faded.

Nevertheless, in the beginning businessmen and promoters in every important commercial center in the state expressed confidence in the ability of their own community to win out in the competition for trade supremacy in the area. The classic example of misplaced faith in its future greatness was Vicksburg. Recovering quickly after the war, this river port, near the mouth of the Yazoo where it flowed into the Mississippi, had moved during the immediate postwar years to root out the New Orleans factors and jobbers who had long controlled the provisions and cotton business of the southern Delta region and of the adjacent nonalluvial counties. By 1868 local merchants appeared to have succeeded in this objective, and their future seemed bright.[50]

48. Vicksburg *Herald*, September 29, 30, October 10, November 4, 24, 27, 1868; Jackson *Weekly Clarion*, April 1, May 20, 1869.

49. Jackson *Clarion*, April 3, 4, 15, 1868, August 19, 1869; Natchez *Weekly Democrat*, October 12, 1870; Beaumont, *A Business Woman's Journal*, 348; Jackson *Weekly Pilot*, December 17, 1870.

50. Harris, *Presidential Reconstruction in Mississippi*, 220–22; Vicksburg *Herald*, November 28, 1868.

During the early Reconstruction period both local promoters and visitors to Vicksburg busied themselves singing the praises of the town. Arthur J. Frantz of Brandon, after a visit in late 1868, predicted that because of its strategic location in the center of the cotton country and its easy access to water and railway transportation Vicksburg would grow rapidly and eventually become the largest city on the Mississippi River south of St. Louis. A lower branch of the transcontinental railroad, then being planned, was bound to cross the Mississippi at Vicksburg, thus making the new city the southern entrepôt for the long anticipated East-West line, Frantz indicated. Not only cotton but other southern products, such as lumber, tar, fruit, and cottonseed oil, would pass over this line and up and down the sinuous Mississippi. Already enterprising northerners were settling in Vicksburg, he said, and capital from the eastern money marts would soon follow.[51] After a brief visit a northern newspaperman foresaw a similar future for Vicksburg, emphasizing that its people seemed alive to the town's future importance and the requirements for commercial greatness. The Chicago *Times* echoed this sentiment, specifically claiming that "with the railway facilities that Vicksburg seems naturally designed to possess, no point on the lower Mississippi is a place of so great future promise."[52]

In Vicksburg, the leading evangelist of the new material gospel was editor William R. Spears of the *Herald*. Undeterred by the fact that Reconstruction politics were still unsettled and a military officer ruled (although benevolently) as mayor of Vicksburg, Spears in 1868 and 1869 constantly proclaimed the virtues of the town and envisaged the day in the not-so-distant future when the commerce between New York and the West coast would be funneled through Vicksburg. When the Southern Pacific Railroad was completed to Vicksburg, an event Spears and most of his associates believed inevitable, the city would become "the terminus between the Mississippi River and the Pacific Ocean on a line of railway which by its connections will shorten the distance between New York and the Pacific Ocean, and any other [eastern] point by at least two hundred miles." Furthermore, the lower Mississippi

51. As reported in the Vicksburg *Herald*, December 5, 1868.
52. As reported in the Vicksburg *Times*, August 13 (quote), December 4, 19, 1869.

Valley, which Vicksburg served, was "the great Eldorado of agricultural enterprise and the seat for the development of every enterprise in which profit and money are to be found."[53] The establishment in 1868 of through connections with New York via Norfolk or Charleston and then by water to Manhattan had provided an additional boost to the promotional spirit of the town, and, according to its leaders, ensured the decline of New Orleans as a competitor in the trade with eastern and British marts.[54] At this time Vicksburg promoters chose to ignore the threat of other railroad connections between the Mississippi Valley and the East Coast—connections that placed the town in a poor competitive position in its efforts to gain a large share of the East-West trade.

Even as this speculative spirit reached a fever pitch, developments were underway that would shatter Vicksburg's dreams of commercial greatness. Despite a long struggle, which extended into the late 1870s, the town never became the river terminus of the Southern Pacific route. But a more immediate interference with these grandiose plans came from the onslaught of drummers from Memphis, St. Louis, New Orleans, and even New York as business houses from these centers, in view of the sharp improvement in the cotton market in 1868–1869, sought to secure the region's lucrative trade.[55]

Business interests in Vicksburg reacted vigorously to the threat by pressing for the construction of a railroad connecting the town with the fertile Delta. In an effort to become the terminal of a Delta road, Vicksburgers demonstrated a willingness to follow almost any scheme that was proposed to build it. One highly dubious enterprise that attracted the support of some local people was the scheme mentioned previously in which a group of speculators proposed to construct an elevated railroad along the Mississippi from Memphis to Vicksburg. Predicated upon a federal donation of twenty thousand acres of land for each mile of the route, the

53. Vicksburg *Herald*, August 20, 1868. See also issues of August 21, September 19, November 6, 17, December 23, 1868, and the Vicksburg *Times*, March 12, September 24, 1869.

54. Vicksburg *Herald*, August 21, 28, December 23, 1868. Within fifty years, Spears confidently predicted, Vicksburg would be "second to no city in the Union in commercial importance." *Ibid.*, August 20, 1868.

55. *Ibid.*, December 5, 1868; Vicksburg *Times*, September 12, 1869; Vicksburg *Times and Republican*, February 15, 1873.

combined levee-railroad project was actually a gigantic land-grab scheme. Its instigators, most of whom lived outside of the state, had no intention of building the embankment, much less the railroad. Some anxious Vicksburg merchants nevertheless succumbed to the promoters' glib talk and pressed for congressional approval of the enterprise, as well as local encouragement of it. More perceptive townsmen saw that the elevated railroad, even if miraculously completed, would bring very little business to Vicksburg, since it did not penetrate the Delta but only followed the winding course of the river, where steamboats from St. Louis and New Orleans monopolized the trade.[56] Fortunately, Congress rejected the request of these land-grabbers. When the Republicans came to power in 1870, eager Vicksburg promoters had a number of more practical railroad schemes for the legislature's approval and material support.

The revival of the agricultural economy in 1868–1869 provided citizens of Jackson and Natchez with none of the Vicksburgers' immodest illusions of grandeur. Their confidence shaken by the vicissitudes of agricultural recovery after the war and by the surge of competition in their trade territory, merchants of these two towns sought simply to hold their own in the struggle for commercial survival. Even so, success for this course, they believed, depended upon penetrating the hinterland with iron rails. The piney woods and the rolling flatlands of "the Mighty East" had once been the special preserve of Jackson. But with the rise after 1860 of towns like Newton, Forest, and Meridian on the Vicksburg and Meridian Railroad and the funneling along the New Orleans line of an increasing volume of local trade to the Crescent City, Jackson, a town of only 4,234 people in 1870, found its business during this period circumscribed virtually to the area of its corporate limits. For a time Jackson merchants and town fathers had hopes of securing a privileged juncture with the ubiquitous Ship Island railway. They also maneuvered for a rail connection with the Yazoo Valley, which, they hoped, would undercut Vicksburg in the struggle to control the trade of the lower Delta. After the failure of their initial efforts along these lines, the Jackson leadership in 1869 dis-

56. Jackson *Clarion*, March 9, 1868; Vicksburg *Herald*, November 26, December 2, 1868; Jackson *Weekly Pilot*, June 11, 1870.

missed the railroad schemes as being beyond the financial means of the town.[57] Complaining about the lack of civic spirit in Jackson, carpetbag editor Hiram T. Fisher provided a somber description of conditions in the depressed state capital at a time when most communities were experiencing a degree of economic prosperity. "We never have seen our municipal affairs in a worse condition," lamented Fisher. "The sidewalks everywhere need repairs; there is no gas, and no prospect of there ever being any to light the streets. City warrants are almost worthless, and everything seems to be neglected."[58]

Barksdale, Fisher's most vigorous political adversary, expressed a similar concern for the fate of Jackson and, as a panacea for its difficulties, advanced a plan for the rapid development of industry. Aware that indigenous capital did not exist to attract important industrial enterprises to the town, Barksdale encouraged the townspeople to make an effort to accumulate a modest amount of money for industrial development.

> We can . . . [then] rely upon our own improved resources and the incoming of Northern labor and capital to develop the measures. There is no place in the State where an enterprising Northern company of capitalists could realize higher profits by manufacturing than in Jackson. Northern capital is superabundant. It is seeking profitable investment. Let us take some steps to *prove* to our Northern friends that they can find a highly lucrative investment for their money here, in the city of Jackson. Let us encourage them to come, and when they come, let us welcome them socially, and make their Southern home agreeable and pleasant; and let us take an interest in their business and aid them in their progress. . . . Without such steps, Jackson is doomed as a business place.[59]

A town of 9,057 people in 1870 (3,728 whites and 5,329 blacks), Natchez, overlooking the Mississippi, placed most of its hope for commercial success in the competitive postwar world on one railroad—the proposed Natchez and Jackson railway. Soon after the war leading citizens of Natchez, realizing that time was running out for river towns like theirs which possessed no railroad connec-

57. Jackson *Weekly Clarion*, April 1, 15, August 5, 1869; Jackson *Weekly Pilot*, December 25, 1869, January 8, 1870; Forest *Register*, March 19, 1870.

58. Jackson *Weekly Pilot*, December 18, 1869.

59. Jackson *Weekly Clarion*, August 5, 1869.

tion with the interior, had begun the promotion of a line to the
state capital. The road would run diagonally through a hinterland
that had traditionally been served by Natchez merchants. Unable
to obtain a charter before the state fell under military rule, promoters of the Natchez and Jackson Railroad had to await the restoration of civil control and the authorization of the new legislature
before resuming their efforts to secure the construction of this important line.[60]

Frustrated townsmen, more so than rural inhabitants, longed for
an end to the uncertainties of military reconstruction and the restoration of a civil government that would provide political stability,
restore business confidence, and assist with vital internal improvements. The fact that the new government would be Republican
might cause town dwellers regret, but after years of adversity the
stakes of economic recovery (as well as the new promises of commercial expansion) were too high for townsmen to quibble over the
postwar political settlement, provided that it was not very radical.
With Alcorn, a son of the Mississippi soil, at the helm practical-
minded men in the towns realized that, at least for a time, they
had little reason to fear Republican rule. Recurrent charges that
the new political element, constituting a majority in the state,
would transgress on property rights and stymie economic development were dismissed by town promoters as improbable. The moderate editor of the Natchez *Democrat* reminded its readers that
"Negroes are rapidly becoming tax payers, and as they must feel
the burden of taxation with us, it cannot be but they shall soon
be found nearly as anxious as the whites to correct the abuses that
make those burdens heavy." Besides, town dwellers were well
aware that Republican representatives in the new legislature,
whether white or black, were as much in favor of economic growth
and the construction of railroads as were the conservatives. In
Vicksburg and Natchez, Republicans and conservatives, blacks and
whites, northerners and natives, demonstrated an especially cooperative spirit in promoting the favorite railroad schemes of their
towns.[61] Throughout the state by early 1870 townsmen appeared

60. *Hinds County Gazette*, October 25, 1867; Natchez *Weekly Democrat*, December 16,
1869, December 14, 1870.
61. Natchez *Weekly Democrat*, March 10 (quote), October 12, 1870; William N. Whitehurst to W. B. Norman, March 26, 1870, in Whitehurst Papers; *Hinds County Gazette*,

to be sitting around waiting for the legislature to meet and legitimize, if not give aid to, their ambitious projects for material development.

An air of expectancy also pervaded the countryside with the improvement of economic prospects in 1869–1870. To be sure, a handful of editors, such as Alexander G. Horn of the Meridian *Mercury*, John A. Glanville of the Forest *Register*, and Arthur J. Frantz of the Brandon *Republican*, all former Whigs who now ironically were the spokesmen for the traditionally Democratic east, continued to fuel the fires of Reconstruction conflict. But a remarkable peace had set in on the political front after the state's readmission to the Union in 1870 and after Alcorn in his inaugural address assured the people that he would rule with moderation and in the interest of all classes. Except for "a few dyspeptic Democratic sheets [who] are doing their usual amount of croaking," the Republican newspaper organ in Jackson reported, the conservative press had applauded the governor's message and had indicated a readiness to extend a helping hand to the new administration. Even John D. Freeman, chairman of the state Democratic party in the campaign of 1868, announced his support of the new government, though without affiliating with the Republican party.[62] The editor of the Natchez *Democrat*, describing himself as an optimist, declared that "judging from the character of our Governor and Legislature we do not fear the occurrence in Mississippi of the villainy that has transpired in Louisiana. We stand then in anxious expectancy, not unmingled with hope, ready to praise where praise is due and to condemn where condemnation is deserved."[63]

John F. H. Claiborne, a former Democratic congressman, historian, and discreet Unionist during the war greatly influenced

October 5, 1870; Vicksburg *Times and Republican*, October 18, 1871; Jackson *Weekly Pilot*, March 26, 1870.

62. W. B. Tabor to Henry W. Barry, June 16, 1870, in Fourteenth Amendment Relief Papers, Mississippi; Jackson *Weekly Pilot*, February 26, March 26, 1870; *Hinds County Gazette*, March 16, May 11, 1870. On the defensive as a result of conservative denunciation of his role in the disastrous Dent movement, Barksdale was in no mood to view with hope the future under Republican rule. Nonetheless, he admitted that the Alcorn administration would be an improvement over the interregnum that had existed since the end of the war. Then, too, he found some comfort in Alcorn's inaugural address. Jackson *Weekly Clarion*, March 10, 17, 1870.

63. Natchez *Weekly Democrat*, March 3, 1870.

white Mississippians, particularly those along the Gulf Coast, to lay aside their intolerance of Republicans and accept the new regime. "We must cease the whip-poor-will cry of 'carpetbagger,' and give our support to the best men, no matter where they come from or to what party they belong," counseled Claiborne, who wrote under a poorly disguised pseudonym. "Men and parties are very much alike. They are neither angels nor devils; [they are] prone to run into excesses and become corrupt, but prefer to be honest and to do good, if properly encouraged. We must not assume that our opponents are all corrupt. This at once bars the door to conciliation and compromise, and the effect is most injurious to the public interests. Let us give praise and support where they are due, without caring what party elected the officer, or by what name he is known."[64] Expressing his faith in the future of the state under Republican rule, Claiborne pointed out that Governor Alcorn was "a man of great ability, of enlarged views, and with strong local attachments and great material interests in the State." The historian also announced his unqualified confidence in the new legislature. "The members are mostly young men, striving for distinction and position," Claiborne said.

> Many of them have invested all their capital here, their hopes, expectations and talents, and are, substantially, as much identified with us as the natives of the soil. The passions and the prejudices, natural incidents of civil war, have subsided upon a closer acquaintance with us, and they value the good will and favorable opinion of what was formerly considered "the rebel element" quite as much as any other men in the community. Many of them are men of education and talent; let us meet them in the proper spirit, and my word for it there is nothing to fear, but everything to expect from the majority in both branches of the Legislature. . . . Let us [teach] them to be moderate and liberal, and not trouble ourselves about parties and political scarecrows. I apprehend no proscriptive legislation. I expect wise and liberal measures; no confiscation in the shape of oppressive taxation, and no gambling away the credit and resources of the State.[65]

Conservative expressions of support for the new order, however qualified, were based on broad, practical considerations. The state's economic advancement depended upon an end to political

64. Vicksburg *Times and Republican*, April 10, 1870.
65. *Ibid.*

and social turbulence; furthermore, instead of courting the intervention of a hostile Congress in the political affairs of Mississippi, material progress could be enhanced considerably by a successful wooing of the national leadership. Sympathetic Republican authorities in Washington, many practical-minded conservatives believed, would extend aid for internal improvements, including the restoration of the levees, refund the more than eight million dollars paid by Mississippians to meet the cotton tax of 1865–1868, and contribute to the restoration of northern business confidence in the social stability of the state. To conservatives of this thinking the new Republican regime in Mississippi could advance the material interests of the state in the national capital. With military rule terminated and civil authority of the type approved by northerners restored, capital, "which had so long been timid by reason of the political uncertainty, will soon become bold and seek investment in enterprises of all kinds that promise profitable returns," the Natchez *Democrat* declared on the eve of Alcorn's inauguration. It continued:

> In the same degree that political agitation shall subside, labor will become more settled and reliable—the tide of immigration will begin to pour in, and the idle capital of the North will seek investment among us. Commercial confidence will be in some measure restored. Better feeling will prevail, and our people will settle down into a sense of security, thence to start again with redoubled energy upon the high road of progress, to a degree of prosperity heretofore unrealized. Radical misrule, if it shall prevail [which this editor doubted], may retard the realization of this prospect, but it cannot prevent it. Mississippi has a bright destiny before it.[66]

In a well-publicized letter to the new governor, which shocked die-hard opponents of republicanism, Freeman, "whilom Grand Duke of the Democracy," declared that since "it is now the acknowledged mission and duty of the Republican party to provide an economic system for the support, education and elevation of [blacks]," he would extend his influence in support of the administration. To emphasize his stand lest there be doubters, Freeman declared that he would "give the National and State administra-

---

66. Natchez *Weekly Democrat*, March 10, 1870. See also the *Hinds County Gazette*, February 23, March 16, 1870.

tion a hearty and zealous support in all measures calculated to develope to the utmost extent our material resources, and especially those that will have a tendency to develope the highest grade of civilization and physical comfort among our 'American citizens of African descent.' I am no friend to their continued debasement or expulsion from the State."[67] The Holly Springs *Star*, as well as other conservative newspapers, endorsed Freeman's remarks, claiming that "one by one the thinking men of the State are yielding to the inexorable logic of events, and are accepting the 'situation' which . . . by a wise and prudent course on the part of the Legislature in framing our laws, will secure to all our people, white and colored, the happiest combination of conditions and circumstances for the enjoyment of the most perfect peace and prosperity."[68]

The expression of such sentiments persuaded Alcorn and his moderate Republican colleagues that a large body of whites, mainly former Whigs but also Democrats, would stifle their prejudices, throw political caution to the wind, and affiliate with the party of progress and equal rights. In seeking the support of whites the new administration faced the dangerous prospect of alienating the element that had brought it to power and whose interest it had promised to advance when in office. The difficulties of bringing blacks and whites under a common Republican umbrella would tax the political dexterity and caution of an Abraham Lincoln. The first few months of the Republican ascendancy in large measure would determine whether or not Governor Alcorn and his associates could meet the high standards of leadership required to make real the vision of a biracial and progressive democracy for Mississippi.

67. *Hinds County Gazette*, May 11, 1870.
68. As reported in *ibid*. See also the issue of April 20, 1870.

9

The Emergence of the
New Order

The restored civil government of Mississippi, consisting at first of only seven elected executive officers and the legislature, had the formidable task of setting in motion the whole apparatus of the Republican order. A judiciary had to be created and men appointed to it; local offices had to be filled, although appointees of the military commander could be retained until after the local elections scheduled for the fall of 1871; state institutions, from the penitentiary to the university at Oxford, needed rehabilitation; and the reforms authorized by the new constitution had to be implemented. In addition, the question of public assistance to develop the economic resources of the state faced the Republicans when they assumed power in March, 1870. Finally, the security of the new regime and its supporters depended on the ability of Republican authorities to stem the tide of lawlessness that had plagued Mississippi since the early 1860s. These responsibilities of government required large outlays of money. Consequently, one of the first—and most formidable—tasks of the new Republican administration was to develop a financial system that could support the expanded activities of the state government.

The first step in creating a sound financial system was to restore the credit standing of the state government. With this in mind State Auditor Henry Musgrove, a carpetbagger, on taking office prepared an elaborate report on Mississippi's postwar financial problems and informed Governor Alcorn and the legislature that "our State at this time presents the anomalous condition of having no public debt, and yet her warrants are at a heavy discount, there being no funds in the Treasury to pay them." The amount of outstanding warrants (or state IOUs), which were selling at a 35 to 40 percent discount on the streets, he placed at $187,993.[1] These obligations, Musgrove said, had to be met before the Republicans

1. *Senate Journal* [1870], Appendix, 109; *Annual Message of Governor Alcorn, 1871*, p. 45.

launched into their program of reform. If money was not provided to redeem the warrants, the credit standing of the state, which had long suffered from the stain of repudiation, would continue to decline, making it virtually impossible for the government to borrow money to support its expanded functions. The difficulties of the situation were increased by the fact that revenues from taxes levied in 1870 could not be collected until the end of the year, which meant that money had to be borrowed in some form to provide for the immediate operating expenses of the new government. As in other matters, Alcorn took the initiative and secured the legislature's approval of an ambitious scheme to fund the warrants and to raise money for the immediate needs of the state.

Modeled after an arrangement employed by the postwar conservative regime in Alabama, the Alcorn plan called for the issuance of $500,000 in "certificates of indebtedness." These certificates, or "Alcorn money" as they were soon called, were to be issued in denominations not larger than five dollars or smaller than one.[2] Acceptable in payment for most state taxes, the certificates were circulated in small denominations for the expressed purpose of giving the common people an opportunity to use these notes in meeting their tax obligations. In the past state notes had only been issued in large denominations, and since tax collectors could not "make change" when tendered warrants in payment of taxes—a policy that was necessary to prevent rampant speculation—the poor had been virtually excluded from the privilege. On the other hand the large taxpayers had taken advantage of the system to avoid paying the face value of their tax obligations.[3] To cover the full amount of the certificates the legislature issued bonds which would bear interest at 8 percent annually and be redeemable, in series, during a four-year period ending on January 1, 1876.

At the same time, in order to improve the standing of the regular warrants, upon Alcorn's recommendation the legislature passed an act requiring out-of-state insurance companies doing business in Mississippi to deposit with the state treasurer an amount in warrants that would cover the almost one million dollars in premiums taken from the state by these firms. Expressing the hostility felt

2. *Laws of the State of Mississippi, 1870* (Jackson, 1870), 19–24.
3. *Annual Message of Governor Alcorn, 1871*, p. 45.

toward northeastern insurance companies because of their summary cancellation of Mississippi policies during the war, the act was also designed to protect future state policy holders from defaulting companies. This act caused the insurance companies to purchase and deposit in the state treasury $200,000 in outstanding warrants in 1870; the amount increased to $557,736 in 1871. The value of these notes, as well as that of other warrants, immediately appreciated. In this way, state warrants for a time were brought virtually to par value with greenbacks.[4]

The "Alcorn money," however, had to struggle to achieve respectability. Since additional taxes would be required to redeem the bonds the notes were based on, conservatives from the beginning tried to discredit the certificates of indebtedness, claiming that their issuance violated the clause in the United States Constitution prohibiting states from emitting bills of credit.[5] Nevertheless, it soon appeared to many, including conservative George W. Harper, that "those who cry most vehemently against the 'certificates,' and assert in the strongest terms their worthlessness, are either in the pay of, or partners in some of the many 'rings' in the State now engaged in deprecating said notes, [so] that those who may happen to hold them will be anxious to sell at very low figures."[6] Alcorn discovered by the fall of 1870 that "money brokers" were "employing all the appliances in their power to depress the current value of this issue in order to maintain the unfortunate depreciation of the State credit by which they grow rich at the expense of the tax-payer."[7]

Aroused to action, the scalawag governor called on the railroad companies in the state to receive the certificates of indebtedness

4. Jackson *Weekly Pilot*, April 30, 1870; *Senate Journal* [1870], 466; *Annual Report of the Auditor of Public Accounts to the Legislature of Mississippi for the Year 1872* (Jackson, 1873), 16; Vicksburg *Times*, August 10, 1871. Not all of the old citizens appreciated the action of the Republican administration in bringing the insurance companies to bay. Both the Natchez *Weekly Democrat*, January 31, 1872, and the Forest *Register*, April 9, 1870, complained that the state's policy would drive out many companies and cause those that remained to increase their premiums. An act of 1871 modified the arrangement and allowed the companies to collect 6 percent annual interest on the deposited money. *Laws of Mississippi, 1871*, pp. 105–10.

5. *Annual Message of Governor Alcorn, 1871*, p. 47; Jackson *Weekly Pilot*, December 3, 1870; Jackson *Weekly Clarion*, December 1, 1870.

6. *Hinds County Gazette*, November 23, 1870.

7. Jackson *Weekly Pilot*, October 22, 1870.

at par value, which would immediately appreciate their worth and ruin the "money brokers." When Henry S. McComb of the New Orleans, Jackson, and Great Northern road hesitated in acting on Alcorn's request, the governor, backed by the state's Republican journals, threatened to take action against the large companies for their failure to honor their debts to the Chickasaw School Fund. After this threat, McComb was more amenable to the governor's request, and at a hurriedly called meeting at Jackson Alcorn secured the railroad executives' promise to accept the certificates at face value.[8]

Alcorn was less successful, however, when he tried to persuade county officers to accept the certificates of indebtedness at par in payment for local taxes. Although some counties responded positively to his appeal "to rescue the tax-payers from a discount that adds to the burden of taxation as much as thirty per cent," others refused to do so for various reasons, not the least of which was the influence of powerful men who were involved in note speculation.[9]

After these modest successes in putting the state credit on a sound footing, the continuation of financial stability depended on a healthy flow of revenue into the treasury and the judicious use of these funds. Because of the poor condition of the state's postwar economy, although it had experienced some improvement in 1869–1870, appropriations for public programs and institutions would necessarily have to be in line with expected revenues. Additional money could still be borrowed by public authorities, but if the state was to avoid a rapid descent toward insolvency fiscal restraint would have to be exercised, at least until tax revenues increased.

The main source of revenue for the expanded governmental functions was necessarily the income from state taxes. In this regard, wise policy dictated that some consideration be given to the ominous fact that the value of agricultural lands, which under the Republican philosophy would carry the main burden of taxation, was only about one third that of 1860. In addition, when the Re-

8. *Ibid.*, October 22, November 12, 26, 1870; *Annual Message of Governor Alcorn, 1871*, p. 47.

9. Jackson *Weekly Pilot*, December 17, 1870; William Noonan to James Lusk Alcorn, March 26, 1871, in Governors' Correspondence, Vol. 73; Natchez *Weekly Democrat*, April 12, 1871.

publicans assumed power more than two million acres were held by public authorities for delinquent taxes. The new regime needed to make an early arrangement by which these lands could either be redeemed by their owners or sold, since, from the standpoint of government finance, they produced no tax revenues while in the hands of the state; in fact, the administration alone of the state-held lands cost the government thirty thousand dollars annually.[10] Under the best of circumstances criticism of Republican taxation and expenditures would develop, but in 1870 there was good reason to believe that by wise financial management, as well as an assist from the gods of agricultural economics, opposition could be kept within reasonable bounds and not be permitted to jeopardize the success of the new order.

The Revenue Act of 1870 became the basic tax law of the Republican era.[11] Based on the principle that property should pay its share of the expense of government, the act provided for the collection of a state tax of .5 percent on the assessed value of all real and personal property. This rate was .4 percent higher than the rate under the old regime, but the procedure for ascertaining the value of property was radically different. During the antebellum period the real estate owner determined the evaluation of his property for tax purposes, whereas under the new law the county assessor, who in 1870 was a Republican appointee, established the value. Nonetheless, the radical departure from past tax and assessment policies began and ended with this provision. Taxes on privileges, which ranged from ten dollars for lawyers and doctors to a thousand dollars for express and telegraph companies, followed policies laid down by the conservative government during presidential reconstruction.[12] Although there was some variation in specific levies, privilege taxes of the old and new regimes were similar in most cases: for example, the early Reconstruction tax of

10. *Annual Message of Governor Alcorn, 1871*, p. 44; R. A. Davis to G. W. Davis, March 13, 1870, in R. A. Davis Papers, Mississippi Department of Archives and History; *Senate Journal [1870]*, Appendix, 108.
11. *Laws of Mississippi, 1870*, pp. 24–38.
12. Governmental revenue provisions during presidential reconstruction may be found in *Laws of the State of Mississippi, 1865* (Jackson, 1865), 186–89, and *Appleton's Annual Cyclopaedia*, 1866, p. 520.

fifty dollars on all kinds of merchants was included in the Revenue Act of 1870.[13] Moreover, the new law retained the old system's poll-tax feature, increasing it from one dollar to two dollars. A supplementary act continued the tax on cotton, but lowered it from one dollar to fifty cents per bale. This continuation of the poll and cotton taxes threatened the Republican doctrine that the laboring man should be virtually free from taxation, since both levies would bear heavily upon this class. In fact, Radical Republicans in the legislature fought hard against the cotton tax, though they offered no opposition to the poll tax, which at that time was used strictly for revenue purposes and not as a requirement for voting.[14] In view of the uncertain results of taxing property, Republicans had accepted the practical necessity for imposing general taxes that could provide a dependable source of revenue.

The expenses of the new government, however, soon outran tax revenues, which did not enter the state treasury in any appreciable amount until 1871. Alcorn's certificates of indebtedness were also quickly absorbed by the needs of the administration. The expenses of maintaining the state government soared from $1,034,460 in 1870 to $1,729,046 in 1871, the largest amount spent in any year during Reconstruction. Tax receipts, however, totaled only $1,128,432 during the two-year period.[15] A small amount ($53,251) of state disbursements went to the new public school system, and $150,000 was distributed to the Chickasaw School Fund. Expenditures for state institutions and buildings, including the insane asylum, the penitentiary, the state hospital at Natchez, and repairs on the capitol and the governor's mansion, took some of the 1870–1871 appropriations. But the main outlays by the new regime followed traditional lines, being primarily used to meet judicial and legislative costs. Judicial and legislative expenses constituted 19 and 16 percent, respectively, of the total state budget for the two-year peri-

13. In a few cases the earlier tax on privileges was more than the 1870 one. The annual tax on express companies, for example, was one hundred dollars larger than that imposed by the Republican regime. *Laws of the State of Mississippi, 1866–1867* (Jackson, 1866–67), 412–14.

14. Jackson *Weekly Pilot*, May 28, June 18, August 20, 1870; Vicksburg *Times and Republican*, September 19, 1871. These taxes, except for the poll tax, did not include the school tax, which was to be levied by the county boards of supervisors.

15. These reports are found in *Senate Journal, 1871*, Appendix (for 1870); *House Journal, 1872*, Appendix (for 1871); and *Annual Report of the State Auditor, 1872*.

od. Furthermore, public printing contracts, a traditional expense, created problems for those who sought to practice economy. The cost of state printing increased from $52,876 in 1870 to $95,861 in 1871, although Alcorn made a strong effort to hold down these expenses. The cost of new property assessments also drew upon the administration's precious financial resources. During Alcorn's two-year tenure as governor the state spent $118,158 to have this work done.

In essence, the heavy expenditures of the Republican government of 1870–1871 went largely for restoring and improving governmental functions that had existed under the old regime but had fallen into severe neglect during the war and the early Reconstruction period. Very little was spent on new state programs or on the creation of new institutions to serve the public. Even so, tax revenues failed to meet the needs of the state government. By the end of 1871 tax receipts lagged $359,264 behind treasury disbursements. Then, in 1872 alone the deficit increased by $487,986. To meet state bills the old warrant system was continued under the Republicans, adding to the actual amount that the government and taxpayers had to pay for services and increasing the appetite for profit among speculators and cooperating officials who took advantage of the fluctuating value of the notes. Governor Ridgley C. Powers, in renewing the attempt at financial reform, correctly observed in his first message to the legislature, in 1872, that the warrant system "is an absurd attempt to conduct the finances of the State in utter disregard of commercial usage or justice, and will lead, if persisted in, to ultimate bankruptcy."[16]

The main abuse of good financial management, however, occurred at the local level. Overzealous and sometimes vindictive Republican assessors in a number of counties placed a value on real estate that was unrealistically high in relation to its actual earning capacity. This affected the amount of both state and local taxes that were due, raising the levies on this form of property far above what Republican policy makers in Jackson anticipated. In Carroll County general assessments were made covering all lands reportedly without regard to the value of individual properties. Assessors received

16. *Annual Message of Governor R. C. Powers to the Legislature of Mississippi, Session of 1872* (Jackson, 1872), 5.

a commission of 7 percent for their work, which in the relatively wealthy river counties brought some energetic officers compensations as high as $8,000 during the brief assessment period. In some counties the boards of supervisors, which had the authority to adjust assessments, reduced evaluations for state purposes in order, as Governor Alcorn complained, "to leave all the large margin for the taxes to be made payable for local expenditures."[17]

Moreover, boards of supervisors frequently abused their authority to appropriate money and to levy taxes for local purposes. Alcorn in a special message to the legislature on these abuses revealed that "contracts for court-houses, bridges, roads, are being let out in all parts of the State to an extent that threatens the people with grievous burdens." In Issaquena County, he reported, taxes had been imposed to the amount of 900 percent of the state levy in order to finance extravagant contracts for public works. Numerous counties overextended themselves early during the Republican era to finance railroad construction (see Chapter 16 for a discussion of local aid to the railroads). The fact that the tax collector, who was also the sheriff, received 5 percent of the amount collected increased this official's determination to do a thorough job.

On the surface and by late twentieth-century standards, the tax rates were not exorbitant in most counties. The levy of the reporting counties in 1872 ranged from $43.50 on the assessed $1,000 in Adams County to $12 in Grenada County; most of the counties reported amounts of about $25 on the $1,000. Some of the counties, however, where abuses had been most evident to Alcorn and others (for example, Issaquena and Warren) did not report their tax rates. And in counties with high levies the taxes quickly became oppressive. Almost uniformly operating on credit and profiting little from the crops of the early 1870s, landowners frequently found it impossible to pay taxes based on the overvalued assessments on their property. The inevitable result was that thousands of acres fell to the sheriff's hammer. This in turn removed land from the tax rolls, thereby compounding the difficulties of financing state and local

17. Message of Governor Alcorn to the legislature, February 8, 1871, in *Senate Journal, 1871*, pp. 419–20; Natchez *Weekly Democrat*, November 30, 1870; *Appleton's Annual Cyclopaedia*, 1871, p. 524; Jackson *Weekly Clarion*, February 24, 1871.

governments.[18] By 1874 approximately six million acres, or one fifth of the land area of Mississippi, were held by state and levee authorities for delinquent taxes.[19]

To cover expenses as tax revenues declined, county boards of supervisors and town officials turned for relief to the warrant device. The effect was intoxicating. The amount of warrants issued by local authorities is unknown; in fact, these officials did not always keep a close account of the amount they distributed. The white counties, which were controlled by Alcorn appointees until late 1871 when conservatives won the local offices, generally maintained some restraint in the issuance of warrants. On the other hand, the black counties, which in almost all cases remained under Republican control until 1876, suffered greatly from a flood of depreciated warrants. By 1872, Lowndes County had accumulated a debt of $191,000, much of which was in the form of outstanding warrants that had little chance for redemption. A local Republican editor found it impossible to ascertain the total amount of warrants issued by Warren County officials but discovered that during a two-week period in 1872 more than $15,000 had been printed and distributed. This carpetbag editor saw a conspiracy in such financial mismanagement. "There is a class of leeches in this county," he reported, "who buy and speculate in warrants, who desire to keep them as low as possible." In collusion with the board of supervisors, "a few vampires are growing rich from the misfortunes of our people. If ever there was a patient oppressed people, it is the tax-payers of Warren county."[20]

In 1872 Governor Powers recommended that the state government impose restrictions on the legislative powers of county offi-

18. *Senate Journal, 1871*, p. 422. *Journal of the Senate of the State of Mississippi, 1872* (Jackson, 1872), Appendix, 1445–46; Natchez *Weekly Democrat*, May 24, 1871; *Hinds County Gazette*, September 11, 1872. In addition to state and county taxes, town residents were required to pay a municipal levy. The total tax for Natchez citizens in 1872, for example, was $59.10 on every $1,000 of the assessed value of real estate and $69.10 on personal property. Natchez *Weekly Democrat*, August 21, 1872.

19. Testimony of State Auditor William H. Gibbs in hearing on "Vicksburg Troubles," *House Report*, 43rd Cong., 2nd Sess., No. 265, p. 530. This information is also contained in Gibbs's official report for 1874 in *Journal of the House of Representatives of the State of Mississippi, 1875* (Jackson, 1875), Appendix, 40.

20. *Senate Journal, 1872*, Appendix, 1442; Vicksburg *Times and Republican*, April 12, 1872; *Hinds County Gazette*, September 28, 1870, July 24, 1872.

cials to issue notes. He affirmed what critics were saying about the local warrant system and declared that these abuses in many instances amounted "to absolute oppression" and had created a class of "heartless speculators" who had accumulated "princely fortunes." Some warrants were selling as low as twenty-five cents on the dollar, but if they were redeemed, this carpetbag governor pointed out, taxes would have to be raised to pay their face value.[21] The legislature of 1872 acted to improve the standing of state notes by issuing bonds to retire them, but it refused to impose specific restraints on the more disturbing local issuance of warrants. Nonetheless, the legislature tempered the bent toward inflation by prohibiting county supervisors from levying taxes of more than $25 on the $1,000 of assessed valuation.[22] Despite the partial success of these efforts at reform, the damage had already been done to the monetary structure of the new order and to the hopes for Republican success in the state.

But when the Republicans came to power in 1870 they saw no cause to be alarmed by the financial prospects of the state. At the time the economy appeared to be on the road to a recovery which would provide an adequate tax base for the needs of the new government. With the state administration in good hands they envisaged a speedy restoration of public credit and the establishment of a sound monetary system. Reports that Reconstruction governments in other states were already experiencing financial difficulties were dismissed by Mississippi Republicans as either conservative propaganda or the product of the baleful Democratic legacy that southern Republicans had not had a chance to correct. With quiet confidence that the problems of finance would be solved, the new rulers in 1870 tackled the tasks of revitalizing and reforming the traditional functions of the state government and creating a public school system that would serve the children of both races.

Governor Alcorn and the legislature gave special attention to the early creation of the judiciary system authorized by the new constitution. The legislature's division of the state into circuit and

21. *Annual Message of Governor Powers, 1872,* p. 6.
22. Even so, exceptions were made to permit local governments to finance schools and to purchase railroad bonds. Natchez *Weekly Democrat,* April 24, 1872.

chancery districts posed few difficulties, but the stipulation that the courts should meet in each county three or four times a year raised the fear among many, including several Republican legislators, that despite the increase of judicial business the system would be entirely too expensive.[23]

Criticism of the judicial organization virtually ceased, however, after Alcorn announced his appointees to the courts. In the only important action of his administration that received the approbation of all political elements in the state, Alcorn appointed judges who possessed influence in their districts and also impressive legal credentials.[24]

Conservatives were especially relieved that the governor had rejected the claims of blacks for places on the bench. Alcorn's failure to tap a black man for the courts did not necessarily mean that he opposed Negro officeholding; he had earlier indicated his intention to give them a share in state patronage, and he had also supported Revels for the Senate. Later, as if to demonstrate his belief that competent blacks should be advanced to important positions, Alcorn worked successfully for the selection of John R. Lynch as speaker of the state house of representatives.[25] In 1870, however, when he had the responsibility for choosing a new judiciary for Mississippi, he was unable to find even one black lawyer whom he could support for the bench.

The Republican governor's selections for the three-man state supreme court were particularly prudent, although he simply retained two military-appointed justices, scalawag Ephraim G. Peyton and carpetbagger Jonathan Tarbell. The new member of the court, Horatio F. Simrall, was preeminently qualified, and his selection was not only designed to bring marked legal ability to the court but also was a part of Alcorn's political strategy to attract the Union-Whig element to his party. Peyton, a loyalist during the war and a faithful Republican in politics, was a jurist of average competence; at the first meeting of the high court he was named chief justice by his colleagues. Carpetbaggers hailed the gover-

23. *Laws of Mississippi, 1870*, pp. 40–46, 50–59; Jackson *Weekly Pilot*, April 16, 1870.

24. *Hinds County Gazette*, May 11, 1870; Jackson *Weekly Pilot*, May 15, 21, August 12, 1870; Forest *Register*, May 14, July 24, 1870.

25. Jackson *Weekly Pilot*, January 29, 1870; John Lynch, *The Facts of Reconstruction*, xx–xxii, 62; John Lynch, *Reminiscences of an Active Life*, 80.

nor's choice of Tarbell as evidence, despite discomforting signs in other patronage decisions, that Alcorn planned to deal justly with them in his appointments to office.[26] Actually, the governor preferred scalawag Jason Niles for the position, but he bowed to political wisdom and chose Tarbell instead.

In his appointment of judges to the circuit and chancery courts, Alcorn evinced no such respect for carpetbag wishes. To the fifteen prestigious circuit judgeships he selected thirteen prewar citizens of the state. The remaining two positions went to carpetbaggers, both of whom had considerable ability and influence with members of their class. Of the twenty chancellors chosen by him only two have been identified as northerners. Since local elections were not to be held until 1871 to choose district attorneys, Alcorn also possessed the authority to appoint these officials. Again, he turned to old citizens for his appointments, though in most cases they were acknowledged Republicans. He filled only two of these positions with carpetbaggers.

During the exuberant days of early 1870 most carpetbaggers, rather than create an early division in the party, swallowed their disappointment at being ignored by Alcorn.[27] After all, there were other emoluments outside of the governor's control that were theirs virtually for the asking—as congressmen in black districts, as federal appointees of President Grant, and as state legislators. Only when the powerful governor's mistakes multiplied did many of these newcomers, led by Senator Ames, abandon political caution and strike out at "Emperor Jeems." Nevertheless, some northerners, like moderates Stafford, Musgrove, and Powers, remained friendly with Alcorn and refused to carp when he slighted carpetbaggers in his appointments to office. (Actually, Stafford, Musgrove, and Powers had no personal reason for complaint: they all held offices in Alcorn's administration.)

Although slighting northern claims to judicial positions, Alcorn attempted to honor an earlier promise to consider enlightened, former Democrats for places on the bench to balance his known preference for Whigs. Prominent among the Democrats-turned-

26. Jackson *Weekly Pilot*, May 21, 1870; Oscar J. E. Stuart to Absalom M. West, August, 1874, in Stuart Papers.

27. See, for example, Charles W. Clarke's letter to James A. Garfield, May 8, 1870, in Garfield Papers.

Republican whom Alcorn appointed to the courts were William M. Hancock, a battling little judge from the piney woods whose possession of a derringer when on the bench had a salutary effect upon courtroom decorum, Green C. Chandler, a former Confederate colonel and a Gulf Coast Republican who after his appointment continued to play an influential role in the politics of the state, and Jehu A. Orr, a former United States and Confederate congressman who had supported Breckinridge for president in 1860. Although professing a strong interest in bringing old Whigs into the Republican party, Alcorn actually did little in a tangible way to attract Whig patriarchs. Except for Simrall, C. C. Shackleford, Jason Niles, and Arthur E. Reynolds, a former Confederate brigadier, Alcorn either ignored or refused to appoint prominent men of this political class. Sharkey, Yerger, Watson, Potter, John Watts, and Amos R. Johnston, all premier Whig lawyers, were passed over by the governor.[28] Their stout association with the conservative movement of 1869 made them undesirable candidates for places on a Republican court. At the same time some Whigs of lesser stature rejected Alcorn's advances because, as one of them crudely put it later, he feared "mixing with the shabby crowd of ignorant, disreputable asses who never stood upon my social plane in their lives."[29]

In addition to the judiciary, Governor Alcorn had the power in 1870 to appoint more than one thousand local officers, whose tenure would continue until after the fall election of 1871. Officials subject to appointment included sheriffs, county treasurers, assessors, county supervisors, mayors, town councilmen, and a host of minor officials. Alcorn could simply recommission incumbents from the military era, but he knew that if he expected to secure the support of whites of good will he must remove most of these men. In almost all cases the holdovers had been appointed by General Ames during the frantic political campaign of 1869, and their incompetence and partisanship had outraged not only the conservative masses but also many Republicans. Despite their undesirability, the new governor recognized that he must exercise extreme

28. Johnston, along with a former secessionist and a carpetbagger, did serve on an Alcorn-appointed commission to codify the laws of the state.
29. Stuart to Albert Gallatin Brown, November 4, 1875, in Stuart Papers.

caution in removing these men because many professed staunch Republican principles and were loyal to Ames. Alcorn also realized that if he appointed too many conservatives with the hope that they would become Republicans he would risk alienating many stalwart Republicans, even those who were not friendly to Ames. Therefore the governor avoided as much as possible the selection of men who had earlier opposed congressional reconstruction or had voted for Dent in 1869.[30]

During the first months of his administration Alcorn deferred to the wishes of Republican legislators on matters of local patronage. Soon, however, he soured on some of their suggestions and increasingly sought the advice of local Republicans and nonaligned moderates. Individuals of the latter class, whom Alcorn believed would inevitably join the party but in many cases never did, often worked in collusion with their moderate Republican neighbors to ensure that Ames's obnoxious appointees were rooted out. This situation developed especially in white counties where moderate Republicans were anxious to present a good front to fellow whites in order to attract them to the party.[31] Conversely, Republicans who had been appointed by Ames placed little confidence in the support of the old citizens and sought to extend their political lives through officeholding.

The patronage issue precipitated a bitter conflict within the party even before the new order had been solidly established. Although the governor's appointments were approved by the state senate, usually without debate or Republican opposition, the full odium of the patronage dispute fell on Alcorn's shoulders. Some disappointed Republicans, throwing political discretion to the winds, minced no words in attacking the governor for his perfidy. One letter to the Vicksburg *Times and Republican*, signed "Many Radical Republicans," expressed this faction's indignation at Alcorn's patronage policies and also illustrated their distorted interpretation of his actions. "His mask is thrown aside," they exclaimed, "and lo! he stands revealed, an old line Whig, racy of the

30. Forest *Register*, April 2, 1870; Hernando *Weekly Press*, June 9, 1870; Jackson *Pilot*, August 31, 1871.

31. Washington *New National Era*, September 14, 1871; Vicksburg *Times and Republican*, September 1, 5, 1871; J. J. Bradford to Alcorn, June 3, 1871, in Governors' Correspondence, Vol. 74.

soil of the South. In proof of which, look at the many honest and consistent Republicans [who] have been removed from office, to make place for wolves in sheep's clothing, whose Republicanism is racy of the soil itself." This class of pseudo-Republicans who once held positions of influence, these Radicals averred, "seem disposed to ignore 'carpetbaggers' unless it is directly to their interest to play lick-spittle" with them.[32]

All elements in the Republican party soon found fault with Alcorn's patronage policies. Southern Unionists of the Radical persuasion (especially in their hostility to former rebels) felt slighted by the governor quite as much as did northern Radicals. Along with a number of carpetbaggers and black leaders, scalawags who had long fought the good fight against the forces of the old order resented Alcorn's courtship of coy and reluctant Whigs and particularly his efforts to win their hand through patronage. Reflecting this sentiment, carpetbag editor Stafford of the Jackson *Pilot*, despite his close association with the governor, ridiculed the notion that a large number of Whigs could be drawn into the Republican party. Whigs as a rule, wrote Stafford, were too self-righteous and aloof from the realities of the postwar world to join in the work of establishing a new order in Mississippi; in fact, "the Whig party [had] died of too much respectability and not enough people." In their approach to Reconstruction politics, Stafford sarcastically remarked, Whigs "wind up with that delightfully self-soothing prayer so common in their ritual—'O, God, we thank Thee that we are not as other men are, even as these Republicans and Democrats.'" Most Whigs were regular Bourbons—forgetting nothing but not learning anything from their experience—and the Republican party would be rent with factionalism if the attempt to entice these men into the party continued.[33] An old Whig himself and a moderate Republican, the refined Jason Niles vented his disappointment with the governor on this score when he confided to his diary: "Alcorn is a demagogue; many of his superiors in honor are in the Penitentiary, and many of his superiors in morals and piety are in Hell." The fact that Niles was tendered an appointment to the circuit bench rather than to the state supreme court, which

32. Vicksburg *Times and Republican*, July 19, 1870.
33. Jackson *Weekly Pilot*, July 30, 1870.

he had high hopes of attaining, perhaps prompted this condemnation of Alcorn, which he wrote two days after receiving the news that he had been passed over for the high court.[34]

Alcorn also felt the wrath of a group of unabashed political opportunists of uncertain origins, as well as uncertain loyalty to the party, when he removed them from office. From Marion County, one such individual informed Alcorn that in replacing him and his associates with members of a competing faction the governor had destroyed the local Republican party. Who was to blame for this situation? he rhetorically inquired of Alcorn. "Why sir, no one but yourself," he shot back. "Now Genl, the people supported you at the last election in this County. We believed you to be the man in the proper place, but Sir we have been deceived by you."[35]

The sheer numbers involved and the incessant clamor for positions made inevitable the selection of men who were easy targets for criticism. (Alcorn later complained that for every office to be filled there were twenty applicants.)[36] On one occasion he chose a man for county treasurer whom the carpetbagger sheriff reported had come to the area "three years ago as the owner and keeper of a retail whiskey shop of the most humble grade, and has been in daily association . . . and affiliation with the old and invincible Ring of rule or ruin outlaws that have infested this community since the war." A more common problem for the governor was the question of which faction to support in counties where Republicans were divided. Contending factions almost invariably represented their opponents as rebels or corrupt adventurers. Which group should he believe? Frequently, in making a choice he was damned if he did, and damned if he did not.[37]

34. Entries for May 4, 6, 1870, in Niles Diary. For a more reasoned explanation of scalawag discontent with Alcorn's catering to unimpressed Whigs, see the letter from "Republican," himself a former Whig, in the Jackson *Pilot*, August 8, 1871. This early scalawag, who declared that he had no ax to grind on the patronage issue, warned the governor against office hunters "who under the good they have done as Old Whigs would ride into office to defeat the Republican party, for you can rest assured that of such is not the kingdom of heaven."

35. W. H. B. Lane to Alcorn, August 10, 1871; Bentonville Taylor to Alcorn, September 28, 1871, both in Governors' Correspondence, Vol. 74.

36. Vicksburg *Times and Republican*, September 1, 1871.

37. D. S. Salter to Alcorn, April 10, 1871 (quote), and Bradford to Alcorn, June 3, 1871, both in Governors' Correspondence, Vol. 74; Vicksburg *Times and Republican*, September 5, 1871; Jackson *Pilot*, August 31, 1871.

Discontented Republicans increasingly appealed to Senator Ames in Washington for support against the high-riding governor. Not fully understanding the situation in Mississippi, Ames hesitated in crossing swords with Alcorn lest he and his friends suffer defeat in a premature challenge to the powerful governor's authority in the party. Furthermore, during the first year of the Alcorn administration, it was not altogether clear, even to insiders, that the governor intended to exclude carpetbaggers per se from the perquisites of power.[38] In the river counties where northerners dominated the local Republican organizations, the scalawag chief executive had retained most of Ames's carpetbag appointees, and in a number of cases in which removals were made he had filled the positions with northerners, though not of the Radical wing. In addition, Alcorn's patronage policies did not appear to discriminate unduly against blacks, and except for a few Negro leaders most of them found little cause to criticize his actions publicly. Even after Ames kicked in the traces and went at Alcorn with a vengeance, powerful black politicians like James Lynch, Samuel J. Ireland, and Thomas W. Cardozo defended the governor's policies, and others like John R. Lynch remained silent.[39] Their support for Alcorn was all the more remarkable in view of the accelerating campaign of Ames and his Radical allies to make the black community their special preserve in the struggle for party supremacy.

Although other issues, such as the matter of suppressing the Ku Klux Klan, contributed to the estrangement between Ames and Alcorn, the patronage conflict seems to have been the catalyst that precipitated the break between these two powerful Republicans. Open warfare finally erupted during the summer of 1871 when Alcorn, abandoning his caution regarding local politics in the river counties, interfered in Warren County affairs and removed from office the carpetbag mayor of Vicksburg, J. C. Webber, along with several of his associates. Despite the strong protests of the influential Union League of Vicksburg, Alcorn persisted in his course

38. Jackson *Weekly Pilot*, June 11, 1870; Forest *Register*, April 2, 1870; Hernando *Weekly Press*, June 9, 1870.

39. Letter to the editor from "Civis" (Thomas W. Cardozo), September 14, 1871, and a letter to the editor from Samuel J. Ireland, June 6, 1872, both in Washington *New National Era*; Jackson *Pilot*, July 21, 1871.

of discharging undesirable county officials.[40] When Webber and his friends, including copublisher John B. Raymond of the Jackson *Pilot*, who had lost his contract for state printing because of Alcorn, appealed to Ames for support, the senator responded.

Actually, the political situation in Vicksburg was incredibly complex. Factionalism among the faithful was rife, and even observers who sought the truth about the affairs of the town and county could not tell the good guys from the bad. Ironically, carpetbagger Raymond, who became an influential confidant of Ames, had earlier been Alcorn's choice for county sheriff, but the senate failed to confirm his appointment. Alcorn could nevertheless claim several carpetbaggers as allies in the struggle with Ames, though not all of them were men of moderation or probity. Heading the list of Alcorn men in Warren County, until the governor dismissed him from office in the fall of 1871, was none other than the amiable and scampish erstwhile sheriff, Charles E. Furlong. Furlong's efforts to extend his control over all the Union Leagues in the county, including the one that Webber led in Vicksburg, probably had a great deal to do with the latter's removal as mayor.[41]

Once Ames had challenged the governor he took an immediate dislike to those Republicans, especially of northern vintage, who failed to join him in the fight. Convinced now that Alcorn was intent upon driving carpetbaggers from the state, Ames expressed the view that it was the height of either folly, dishonesty, or cowardice for northerners to refuse to take sides against "the Eminent Man." Even Supreme Court Justice Tarbell fell under the censure of the senator after he wrote that he would remain neutral in the power struggle. Ames dismissed Tarbell's action with the succinct comment, "Alas! How weak we poor humans are."[42] Soon he was admitting to his wife, the daughter of the volatile Benjamin F. Butler, that he was becoming obsessed with his abhorrence of Al-

40. Jackson *Pilot*, June 26, 1871; Adelbert Ames to his wife Blanche, June 20, 22, 1871, in Blanche Butler Ames (comp.), *Chronicles*, I, 289–90, 291; resolutions of Vicksburg Union League of America meeting, June 21, 1871, in Governors' Correspondence, Vol. 74; Vicksburg *Times and Republican*, September 23, 1871.

41. Jackson *Weekly Pilot*, June 11, 1870; Vicksburg *Times and Republican*, September 2, 12, 29, October 3, 6, 1871.

42. Ames to his wife Blanche, June 22, September 23, October 24, 1871, in Blanche Butler Ames (comp.), *Chronicles*, I, 291, 315, 342.

corn. He justified his opposition on the ground that "the Andrew Johnson policy of our governor" in preferring "democratic Ku Klux office holders" to carpetbaggers had encouraged the rebel element to reassert itself in the state. Unless Alcorn was repudiated, Democrats would be restored to power in the forthcoming local elections, Ames predicted. By the fall of 1871, as Alcorn prepared to resign the governorship and take his seat in the Senate, the young carpetbag politician could write that the warfare his rival had instigated against northerners "is raging more fiercely today than ever, and now comes the question, shall he whip me or I him in Washington?"[43]

Ames had clearly misjudged Alcorn's purpose in the imbroglio. When Alcorn used the word "carpetbagger," he meant a political adventurer in the state, whatever his origins, whose sole purpose was office and plunder. Consequently, his well-publicized "war on carpetbaggers" was designed to rid the state of this class of politician and was not a campaign to eliminate northerners per se from influence in the Republican party.[44] Those transplanted northerners who seemed committed to a broadly based party and who shunned the exclusiveness of the Ames fellowship found Alcorn friendly. Northerners who supported Alcorn or remained neutral in the power struggle—men like Tarbell, Furlong, Stafford, Congressman George C. McKee, Archie C. Fisk, Frederic Speed, and Lieutenant Governor Powers—generally had deeper roots in Mississippi than the Ames carpetbaggers. Insofar as their stand on vital issues was concerned, members of the Ames coterie tended to be more radical than Alcorn adherents, but this difference was not always clear, particularly after two or three years of the Republican ascendancy when the early idealism—albeit mixed with political opportunism and bitterness toward "rebels"—began to give way to cynicism and a concern for power and office alone.

The struggle between the Ames and Alcorn factions to dominate the party and in turn the state inevitably undermined the ability of Republicans to carry out their program of reform and sustain their

---

43. Ames to his wife, October 14, 26, 1871, *ibid.*, I, 332–33, 344–45.
44. For Alcorn's definition of a carpetbagger see the Vicksburg *Times and Republican*, November 2, 1873.

control. But these consequences of the virulent factionalism that soon pervaded the party were not so clear in the beginning when the new rulers, usually cooperating with each other although disagreeing on particulars, feverishly acted to implement the progressive features of the constitution of 1868.

10

Public Education: The Cornerstone of Mississippi Republicanism

The creation of a comprehensive system of public education for Mississippians of both races headed the Republican list of reforms for the state. Expressing the belief that education was "the energizing agent of modern civilization" and the corrective for the myopic sectionalism and moral degeneracy that they found in Mississippi society, education leaders in the new state government (principally carpetbaggers) burned the midnight oil in early 1870 to develop a detailed plan that would provide for the early opening of the schools.[1] On March 26, 1870, Superintendent of Education Henry R. Pease presented their proposal to the legislature for its approval. Sponsored on the floor of the house of representatives by carpetbagger Charles W. Clarke, who had written the draft of the education article in the constitution, the Pease plan became the basis for the assembly's debate on the organic law for the public school system.[2]

A few days after the plan had been introduced, Governor Alcorn sent the legislature a special message on education which on two significant points varied from the superintendent's proposal. First, in contrast to Pease's recommendation for the creation of a comprehensive system almost overnight, the governor proposed a policy of gradualism. Presenting statistics on the cost of public schools in other states, which had been compiled by the National Bureau of Education, and providing his own estimate of the expense involved in beginning a school system, Alcorn argued that if the state followed Pease's recommendation, it would be inviting financial disaster and the stillbirth of public education in Mississippi. The implementation of this ambitious plan, Alcorn declared, would cost the state approximately four million dollars during the first year and four hundred thousand dollars annually thereafter. Ac-

1. Harris, "Creed of the Carpetbaggers," 209–10.
2. *House Journal, 1870*, p. 139; Jackson *Weekly Pilot*, May 7, 1870; Vicksburg *Times and Republican*, April 15. 1870.

cording to the governor, the state did not have at the time the financial means to provide for a full-blown system of schools, and unless a policy of economy and caution was instituted in the beginning, the Republican party would abysmally fail to make good its pledge of a permanent and effective program of free education for the masses. In order to avoid the financial pitfalls, Alcorn recommended that the lawmakers "set the system going first in the cities, the towns, [and] the most populous districts"; then they should await the results of the work "before pressing it into those parts of the State which are thinly settled and so poor in resources as to condemn the system . . . to failure."[3]

The governor then called on the legislature to write into the organic law a provision requiring the separation of the races in the schools.[4] On this point the Pease plan was silent, since the state superintendent, backed by powerful carpetbag friends of education in the legislature, preferred to postpone debate on the inflammatory issue of mixed schools until the system had been firmly established and was receiving the support of whites. Several of these northerners, including Lieutenant Governor Powers, Clarke, and Albert T. Morgan, who would soon marry a mulatto schoolmistress, optimistically believed that the time would come in the not-too-distant future when the subject of racially integrated classrooms could be discussed dispassionately and without risking the destruction of the public school system. Meanwhile, they wanted no prohibition against school integration written into the law. On the other hand, Alcorn, along with many white Republicans of both northern and southern origins, foresaw trouble for the infant school system if the issue remained an open question; he insisted that crucial conservative support would be withheld if local school boards had the option of mixing white and black children in the classrooms. When criticized by the black editor of the Washington *New Era* for his opposition to the voices of integration in Mississippi, the governor reacted sharply in a letter to the newspaper. "I feel it my duty to go outside the proprieties of my office," he wrote, "to protest against those views as [being] a deadly injury to the cause of education at the South." The education of the people of

3. *Senate Journal* [1870], pp. 15–16.
4. *Ibid.*, 17.

both races, Alcorn announced, "is the measure of reconstruction nearest my heart," and he declared that he would not be deterred by extremists of either side from the achievement of this noble goal. Negro leaders in Mississippi, he claimed, also opposed the introduction of the destructive race issue into the school debate, since raising it could only revive the racial passions of the past. The political equality of blacks had been established through a vigorous effort on the part of Republicans; indeed, the governor claimed, considerable improvement in white attitudes toward the new order in the state and toward blacks had recently occurred.[5] Because of these encouraging developments, Alcorn entered a strong protest against any movement—and specifically the one designed to integrate the schools—that would impair the progress that had been made and damage Republican hopes for the future.

The debate on the school bill in the legislature raged intermittently into the summer. Without singling out the governor for criticism, carpetbag leaders in the assembly decried those who feared the costs of the comprehensive system outlined in the Pease plan and who confused the issue and disturbed blacks by insisting on a legal prohibition against racially mixed schools. Reminding the house of representatives that the laws of nature were not a matter for legislation, carpetbagger Charles A. Foster declared that the fears that racial integration would occur if the schools were organized under the Pease proposal were unfounded. Foster chided Republicans in the house for permitting the debate on mixed schools to snarl their efforts to provide a complete system of free schools for the state.[6]

Lieutenant Governor Powers, in what was hailed as the best speech delivered before the legislature on the education bill, asserted that the demise of racial prejudice itself, including the issue of mixed schools, depended upon the organization of the school system proposed by Superintendent Pease. Powers, reflecting the optimism of many carpetbaggers at this stage of the Republican experiment, declared that the implementation of the Pease plan, whether the schools were racially integrated or not in the begin-

5. As reported in the New York *Times*, May 23, 1870.
6. Jackson *Weekly Pilot*, June 18, 1870. See also the speech of Charles W. Clarke, as reported in *ibid.*, July 16, 1870.

ning (which should depend on local desires), would hasten the end of racial antipathy in Mississippi. Powers claimed that this would occur because schools by their nature open "the way whereby the truths of science and religion can gain access to the understanding of the people, and thereby raise them superior to their passions and prejudices, into the purer atmosphere of Reason and Truth."[7] Countering Alcorn's argument that the expense of the proposed system would exceed the ability of the people to pay, Powers claimed that a thoroughgoing program of education would actually be a measure of economy for the state. Education, he explained, would purify the morals of the people, both black and white, and crime and violence would thus be considerably reduced, obviating the need for an expensive judiciary and for extensive law enforcement agencies. Therefore, a comprehensive system of public schools, despite heavy initial costs, would in the long run contribute to the financial stability of the state.[8]

The forcible arguments of the lieutenant governor quieted Republican criticism of the education bill. Even Alcorn, who was beginning to see Powers as an influential carpetbag ally in his struggle with Ames, acquiesced in the proposal for the rapid expansion of the new school system. His only attempt to influence action on the education bill as the debate came to an end was to insist that county superintendents and district school boards be selected by the local people and not by the state board of education as provided in the Pease plan.[9] The leadership in the legislature disagreed, fearing that if these choices remained with the people the purposes of educational reform would be easily subverted in conservative dominated counties. A compromise of sorts was arranged, and in the final bill the power to appoint county superintendents was given to the state board of education, consisting of the state

7. Powers' address may be found in the *Mississippi Educational Journal*, I (February, 1871), 13–19, and in the *Senate Journal* [1870], pp. 436–40.

8. Charles W. Clarke's rationale for a comprehensive program of public schools was similar to that of Powers. "The opponents of this system of education say our State is poor and cannot afford the expense. I tell you, my friends, this system will make her rich," this young carpetbagger and sponsor of the Pease plan told the legislature. "With ignorance there can be no wealth—with education no poverty." Education also would produce virtue among the people, he said, and "as virtue increases, all the expenses occasioned by crime diminish," Jackson *Weekly Pilot*, July 16, 1870.

9. Jackson *Pilot*, June 11, 1870; *Annual Message of Governor Alcorn, 1871*, p. 18.

superintendent, the secretary of state, and the attorney general, whereas the elected county supervisors were authorized to select the local school boards.

The bill "to regulate the support, organization, and maintenance of a uniform system of public education for the state" passed the legislature by a strict party vote in early July and received the approval of Governor Alcorn on the Fourth.[10] Despite the power of the state board of education to appoint county superintendents and to oversee the law's implementation, the Mississippi public school system was far from being the centralized institution of control that historians have assumed these Reconstruction innovations to be. In fact, under the law of 1870 the burden of managing the school program was left to the counties, with the regular public officials, the school boards, and the county superintendents sharing in the responsibility.[11] An energetic and politically powerful state superintendent of education, with the support of the state board, might very well influence district school policies—which Pease did. But local school boards, consisting of six men appointed by county supervisors, had the tasks of selecting teachers, setting their salaries, providing facilities and textbooks, and establishing standards and rules for the schools. Upon the application of the school board for money, the county supervisors in the district (each county constituted a school district, and towns of five thousand or more people could form a separate unit) were required to levy a tax to support the system. The act, however, provided that this tax could not exceed ten mills on the dollar to support the construction of school facilities and the procurement of supplies, and it could not exceed five mills for teachers' salaries. On the other hand, the school tax could be quite small, depending on local desires.

To supplement county revenues for the schools, the law of 1870 provided for a state common school fund to be administered by the board of education at the capital. Consisting of a variety of revenue sources, including money derived from the sale of delinquent tax lands, fines collected from violators of penal laws, and fees received from liquor licenses—but not including revenues from ordi-

10. *Senate Journal* [1870], p. 445; *House Journal*, 1870, pp. 503–504.
11. The complete act may be found in *Laws of Mississippi*, 1870, pp. 1–18.

nary taxes except for the two-dollar poll tax—the state educational fund was to be distributed annually in proportion to the school population of the districts.

Although his authority over local school officials was limited, Superintendent Pease proved an able architect of the free school edifice in Mississippi. A native of New England, this short, unpretentious carpetbagger had had extensive experience in organizing southern schools before his election as state superintendent. As an officer in General Nathaniel P. Banks's army in Louisiana, he had assisted in creating behind the Union lines a system of education for blacks that served as a prototype for the school systems sponsored by the Freedmen's Bureau throughout the Mississippi Valley. In 1867 Pease took charge of the Mississippi bureau's educational program, which was entering a difficult stage of development after some initial success in 1865–1866.[12]

Faced with declining black enthusiasm for schools and decreasing northern financial support, Pease labored diligently for more than two years to revive the fortunes of the missionary schools in the state. In this he was partially successful. By July, 1868, enrollment in these schools had reached a high of 13,721 black students. A gradual decline then set in as the missionary associations reduced their commitments in the South until by 1870, on the eve of the creation of the state school system, only 3,475 pupils attended the bureau-assisted schools.[13]

The northern-sponsored schools fell far short of accommodating the approximately 150,000 blacks of school age in Mississippi. But the bureau-missionary program did bequeath to the public school system of the 1870s an example of Negro education which demonstrated to many skeptics that a little learning for former slaves was not a dangerous thing. In fact, some planters realized that schools for the children of tenants and field hands might in time contribute to labor and social stability, which to them was more important than giving vent to their racial prejudices.[14] Furthermore, the edu-

12. Jackson *Weekly Pilot*, May 7, 1870.

13. John W. Alvord, *Semi-Annual Report on Schools for Freedmen* (Washington, D.C., 1868), 35; Stuart G. Noble, *Forty Years of the Public Schools in Mississippi, with Special Reference to the Negro* (New York, 1918), 24.

14. Forest *Register*, February 26, 1870; Natchez *Weekly Democrat*, February 22, 1871; Jackson *Pilot*, March 31, 1871.

cational program of the Freedmen's Bureau gave a nucleus of black parents and teachers some experience with the workings of elementary schools, and this proved beneficial when the law of 1870 called for the rapid organization of common schools in the state. Although the instruction in bureau classrooms was quite rudimentary, some of the more apt pupils became teachers in the new system, and several former students in these schools rose to prominence in public affairs—John R. Lynch and James Hill, for example. The public system also inherited the modest buildings and equipment of the bureau-missionary schools.[15]

With only one clerk to assist in the administrative detail of the state office, Superintendent Pease went to work after the passage of the July law to put flesh on the bones of the ambitious public school system. First he visited several northern states, seeking practical information on the operation of common schools in the advanced systems there. But the real locus of authority in most school matters rested with the county superintendents rather than with the state leadership. Pease realized this, and in conjunction with his associates on the state board of education—Secretary of State James Lynch and Attorney General Joshua S. Morris—he sought to select county superintendents who were energetic and who, not incidentally, would follow his recommendations. Despite some criticism that strangers were appointed to these positions, the men selected as superintendents in most cases had been local residents for at least a few years, even though several were natives of the North.[16] As their accomplishments would soon indicate, most of them were men of considerable dedication to the cause of public education and of above average ability as administrators. After a testing period, they generally secured the good will of both races in their districts. Only a handful of blacks served as county superintendents, all in black districts. One of them, Blanche K. Bruce of Bolivar County, later served in the United States Senate.

The new superintendents, displaying a dedication of purpose and reasonableness of approach rare for a body of public officials engaged in creating an institution of the magnitude of the Recon-

15. Moore, "Social and Economic Conditions in Mississippi During Reconstruction," 212.
16. Vicksburg *Times and Republican*, July 28, 1871.

struction school system, traversed their districts in late 1870 performing a multitude of tasks preliminary to the opening of schools. Pease, in a series of circulars based on his experience with bureau schools and the information he had gathered in the North, provided the superintendents with some guidance, but only in matters of standards for teachers could he command their compliance. Nevertheless, local school officials usually cooperated with him, and his insistence on detailed annual reports from them promoted a degree of uniformity in the administration of the schools. As urged by Pease, the superintendents took the initiative in the appointment of district school boards, although the July law provided for their selection by the political boards of supervisors in the counties. The superintendents discovered, however, that the school board arrangement for launching and overseeing the school apparatus was little more than "a dead weight"—and an expensive one at that. Bypassing these officers on most matters, superintendents went directly to the boards of supervisors, which set local tax and revenue policies and appropriated most of the money for the schools. The superintendents also appealed to the people whose support was essential to the success of the free school experiment.[17]

Local superintendents soon realized that the serious shortage of competent teachers was a major obstacle to the infant school system's success. Black schools especially found it difficult to find qualified instructors, since few native whites, fearing social ostracism or worse, applied in the beginning to teach in these schools, despite the relatively high salary scale which ranged from $50 to $150 per month. In the black counties northern schoolmistresses, most of whom had entered Mississippi as teachers in the missionary schools, served with a handful of their former students as a nucleus for the development of Negro education under the new system. But their numbers were too few to staff even a majority of the black classrooms in 1871, and in deference to the sensitivities of the white masses, whose aversion to Yankee school "marms" approached the irrational, county superintendents usually made no effort to obtain qualified teachers from outside the state. Writing in the *Mississippi Educational Journal* in late 1871, Superintendent

17. *Mississippi Educational Journal*, I (February, 1871), 37; *Senate Journal, 1871*, pp. 1256, 1263, 1256.

Pease assured conservatives that the classrooms, as well as the school administrations, were overwhelmingly in the hands of the old residents, black and white. He declared that he did not know of a dozen northern school teachers who had come to the state since the enactment of the 1870 law.[18]

Conservative opposition to local whites teaching in these schools subsided in 1871, partly out of fear that northern teachers, with their advanced doctrine of the social equality of the races, would yet be hired to fill positions in the black schools. As a result many whites, both women and men, including some former Confederate soldiers who were now impecunious, sought and secured teaching positions in Negro schools. Nevertheless, in most counties the need for competent teachers in black schools continued to be great, and in order to staff the classrooms local school officials were forced to abandon Pease's relatively high standards of certification and employ unqualified instructors. In 1872 the usually optimistic Pease dolefully admitted that the majority of the teachers in the public schools "are most lamentably deficient in professional training and skill, and I regret to say that in some instances teachers have been employed who were disqualified on account of immorality."[19]

Pease early sought means for improving the quality of instruction in the schools. He encouraged county superintendents to organize district institutes to instruct teachers in the latest pedagogical techniques, and the first of these meetings, extending for three days, was held in March, 1871, at Lexington, in Holmes County, the vanguard of educational advance in Reconstruction Mississippi.[20] At the same time Pease and his associates went before the legislature and lobbied for the creation of a system of public normal schools for the training of teachers. But only two small training institutions were established during Reconstruction, since many Republicans, including Governor Alcorn, preferred to

18. *Mississippi Educational Journal*, I (February, 1871), 31, (March, 1871), 91, (November, 1871), 268; Jackson *Pilot*, April 29, May 11, June 20, 1871.

19. Vicksburg *Times and Republican*, September 8, 1871; *Mississippi Educational Journal*, I (February, 1871), 31–32, 43, (April, 1871), 135; Moore, "Social and Economic Conditions in Mississippi During Reconstruction," 177 (quote).

20. *Mississippi Educational Journal*, I (March, 1871), 90. The school law of 1870, which Pease drafted, required that a teachers' institute be held annually in each congressional district; Pease, however, found it impossible to enforce this requirement.

train teachers in the state colleges rather than in normal schools that would be relatively expensive to begin.

Education officials experienced more success in their efforts to obtain physical facilities for the school system than in their attempts to provide it with competent teachers. Whites, especially in the black and racially balanced counties, responded in a positive and often impressive fashion to the appeals of county superintendents for the donation of school sites, buildings, and materials to construct classrooms. With no funds appropriated for educational purposes even by early 1871, the material assistance of property-holding whites was essential to inaugurate the educational experiment on a reasonably sound footing. Biracial cooperation also contributed, for in many places where schoolhouses did not exist whites provided the materials and blacks the labor in raising the buildings. This example of the races working together pleasantly surprised Pease and his associates in educational reform.[21]

By May, 1871, Pease could report that land for more than five hundred schools had been donated by individuals. On these sites, and on others that had been purchased or leased by school authorities, several hundred log schoolhouses had been raised. In addition, numerous churches opened their doors on week days to the onrush of eager schoolchildren. As a result of this enthusiastic response, Pease estimated that public funds had been required to construct fewer than one hundred of the more than three thousand schools in operation in early 1871. In a heady moment, Pease confidently assured the people of Mississippi that when the vast educational program had matured it would cost annually no more than four and one-half mills on the dollar of their taxable property. At this time many were prepared to believe him.[22]

The large number of old citizens who were willing to cooperate in the free school experiment was not surprising in view of earlier, though abortive, efforts to provide some form of public education for the white masses. Once the issue of mixed schools had been laid to rest, as it apparently had been by the school law of 1870,

21. *Senate Journal, 1871*, pp. 1252, 1256, 1262, 1284; William H. Lynch to James Lusk Alcorn, 1871, in Governors' Correspondence, Vol. 73.

22. Along with those of the county superintendents, Pease's report and analysis for the first few months of the operation of the school system may be found in *Senate Journal, 1871*, pp. 1233–89.

whites could reflect more dispassionately upon the benefits of public education and recall that some of the state's most revered leaders had in the past worked to establish a free school system for Mississippi.[23] And their efforts had produced some results. As early as 1846, the legislature, at the urging of the popular and progressive Governor Albert Gallatin Brown, enacted a measure designed to secure for every white child "the advantages of a liberal education." But the responsibility for creating, financing, and managing the system had been left to the counties and larger towns. Lacking central direction and uniformity, the common school program had fallen short of the goals of Brown and its early promoters.[24] Furthermore, the developing, semifrontier character of the state had placed a higher premium upon brawn power than upon the cultivation of minds, and many whites, both of the planter and yeoman class, preferred to use their surplus money to speculate in land and slaves rather than provide tax revenues for public education. Most antebellum Mississippians believed that the responsibility for the education of the young should be left to individuals and not public authorities; the state should only become involved when necessary to provide the rudiments of learning for the more ambitious of the dispossessed whites.

Despite the state's failure to create a viable public school system during the 1840s and 1850s, friends of free education had made considerable progress in this direction when the drums of war interrupted their efforts. In 1860 education reformers could point with a measure of pride to the 1,116 free schools which had enrolled 30,970 students, or approximately one fifth of the white children in the state.[25] After the war the Whig-dominated government during presidential reconstruction moved toward reviving the com-

23. In their efforts to stimulate interest in the new school system, carpetbag promoters reminded the old citizens that precedents for public education were deeply rooted in Mississippi history. See especially the *Mississippi Educational Journal*, I (March, 1871), 57–62. This journal, established by carpetbaggers Hiram T. Fisher and Pease in early 1871 to promote the cause of free schools in the state, appeared particularly sensitive to white opinion during its brief existence of less than two years.

24. Humphrey, "Public Education for Whites in Mississippi," 26; *Mississippi Educational Journal*, I (March, 1871), 56–57.

25. Humphrey, "Public Education for Whites in Mississippi," 26–27; Elsie Timberlake, "Did the Reconstruction Regime Give Mississippi Her Public Schools?" *Publications of the Mississippi Historical Society*, XII (1912), 76.

mon school system. At the same time school promoters, in greater numbers than before, proclaimed the gospel of public education, claiming that a uniform and efficient program of free schools was more than ever a necessity for the state. B. F. Larrabbee, a long-time advocate of common schools, warned whites that despite the hard times of the postwar period "public education is a vital interest that cannot safely be deferred. . . . The value of every man's property is at stake, and, more important still, the security of our domestic, religious and social welfare is involved."[26] A state teacher's convention, meeting in Jackson in January, 1867, at the same time that the legislature was considering an ambitious plan to revive public education, lobbied for the measure and came out squarely in support of schools for blacks as well as whites. A number of the traditional leaders of the state seemed impressed by Larrabbee's arguments and the proposal of the teachers' convention. Although normally shying away from the issue of black schools, several prominent conservatives strongly endorsed efforts to provide education for the masses, without mention of race. Even Barksdale, whose view of the role of government was usually negative, from the columns of the Jackson *Clarion* proclaimed the virtues of public education and promised the people: "establish a system of common schools on a permanent basis in Mississippi, and you have laid the foundation of her future greatness and prosperity."[27] With military reconstruction imminent, the legislature of early 1867 refused to establish the proposed system of schools.

A number of conservative leaders continued to promote the doctrine of free education, and a few, like former Governor Brown, expressed the belief that with Republican reconstruction the education of blacks was essential. These conservatives argued that blacks, now that they had acquired political rights, if left mired in ignorance would be an easy prey for outside political adventurers. An educated black electorate would shun the fellowship of demagogues and vote with their old masters. Moreover, conservative support of public schools for Negroes, seemingly their most cher-

26. Jackson *Clarion*, February 2, 1867. See also *ibid.*, September 27, 28, 1866, January 30, 1867, and the Meridian *Semi-Weekly Gazette*, April 24, 1867.

27. Jackson *Clarion*, January 30, April 24, 1867; Meridian *Semi-Weekly Gazette*, April 20, 1867.

ished goal in freedom, would go a long way toward restoring labor stability in the state. A program of schools for black children, they said, would improve the work morale of black parents. Some conservatives even believed that education would make the black man a more skilled and efficient farm laborer.[28] Certainly, they asserted, a black's respect for the law would increase in proportion to his educational experience. In the conservative rationale for a biracial system of common schools (which after the passage of the reconstruction laws could hardly be avoided), there was no thought that the Negro was capable of attaining the same high degree of learning as whites. He was expected merely to achieve a level of enlightenment commensurate with "the full extent of his capacity."[29]

Most whites at this time, however, held antagonistic attitudes toward Negro education. They viewed with alarm the use of precious revenues to support an experiment they believed would not appreciably improve the habits of the former slaves. School funds in the hands of Radicals, they presumed, would be squandered not only in a quixotic effort to provide blacks with a modicum of learning but also to indoctrinate them to hate their former masters and support the Republican party in future political contests. They had reacted defiantly to the work of the Black and Tan Convention of 1868, believing that the education article in the new constitution was a diabolical plot to mongrelize the races. Even after passions had subsided after the triumph of moderate Republicans in the 1869 election, an undercurrent of opposition to public education—especially schools for Negroes—continued in Mississippi.

Just before the public schools were organized under the law of 1870, Thomas S. Gathright, headmaster of a prestigious academy near Macon who in 1876 would become the first conservative state superintendent of education, denounced the new system as "an unmitigated outrage upon the rights and liberties of the white people of the State." The purpose of the school law, he argued, was "to demoralize our people and to proselyte our children in the interest of a political party hostile to the dignity, interests and sen-

28. Jackson *Clarion*, May 9, June 11, August 29, 1867; Meridian *Semi-Weekly Gazette*, August 29, 1867; Natchez *Weekly Democrat*, February 22, 1871; Liberty (Miss.) *Advocate*, December 22, 1866.
29. Forest *Register*, February 26, 1870.

sibilities of the white people of Mississippi. . . . It is the most flagrant enactment known to me in the history of legislation." Nevertheless, Gathright denied that he opposed the principle of public
schools; what he sought was a reform in the law guaranteeing
whites a share of the school fund in proportion to the taxes they
paid.[30]

Taking his cue from Gathright, Harper, the dean of Mississippi
editors, asserted that the main object of the carpetbag-conceived
scheme of public education "was to punish, in every possible way,
the white people, and especially the property-holders of the State."
He pushed further to claim that carpetbaggers also had designed
the school bill in order "to feed a flock of hungry managers at the
expense of the very money which is required to furnish the women
and children of the State with bread and meat."[31]

Such hyperbole had its effect on white attitudes, but with the
actual organization of schools in 1871 the posture of defiance was
soon spent as the people began to get a closer look at the workings
of the Republican program of education. At first they felt a sense
of relief that the system was no Radical vehicle for the inculcation
of a partisan spirit among blacks or for the naked oppression of
white taxpayers. As the program further unfolded, many conservatives expressed approval of what they saw and offered a helping
hand in the development of the schools, despite the fact that the
1870 law was not changed to protect white property owners against
extravagant tax levies by Republican officials.

In 1871 from throughout the state, with the exception of the
sparsely settled piney woods of southeast Mississippi, school officials and local Republican leaders flooded Superintendent Pease's
office and also the state newspapers with encouraging reports of
an improving spirit among whites toward the schools. Radical Republican Robert W. Flournoy, who toured northeast Mississippi
promoting the cause and seeking fair treatment for the area's black
minority in the organization of the schools, wrote as early as February, 1871, that he detected a friendly sentiment for public educa-

30. Widely published in the state, Gathright's diatribe may be found in the *Hinds County Gazette*, October 12, 1870.
31. *Ibid.*, December 28, 1870.

tion. He was sure, at any rate, that the old citizens "are disposed to give it a fair trial."[32] Reporting the establishment of sixty-six schools in the bipartite Delta tableland county of Yazoo, Radical Albert T. Morgan's territory, a Republican wrote during the late summer that "the best feeling prevails" toward the school program. "The citizens of the county without reference to politics, have manfully supported the free school system. White men, natives of the county, as well as colored men, teach in colored schools, and all these are alike protected by public sentiment."[33]

The conservative Yazoo City *Banner* echoed this feeling, and with a measure of pride observed that "we, indeed, have good schools, and we are glad to know it." Where formerly "strangers" had run the few schools in Yazoo, under the law of 1870 local people were engaged in the work of organizing schools for all the children of the county. "We hope soon to see a perfect educational system established here," the editor wrote. And down in Adams County (Natchez), William H. Lynch, brother of John R. Lynch, happily informed Governor Alcorn that "the feeling here among all classes towards the Public Schools is all that could be desired."[34]

Many conservative spokesmen who only a few months before had denounced the law of 1870 as "an outrage upon the white people" were now caught up in the exhilaration of creating from scratch a system of schools in their districts. Most of the whites who still opposed remained silent as the sentiment of their neighbors swung decidedly in favor of the reform. E. G. Wall, a one-armed Confederate veteran who had recently founded *Southern Field and Factory*, a monthly devoted to the state's economic development, urged white farmers to abandon their apathy and opposition to the school law and take immediate advantage of its benefits.[35] The editor of the Canton *Citizen* was even stronger in his expression of support. He declared: "The cause of education should be in the

32. *Senate Journal, 1871*, p. 1275; *Mississippi Educational Journal*, I (February, 1871), 42; entries for February 22, 23, 1871, in Agnew Diary.

33. Vicksburg *Times and Republican*, September 8, 1871.

34. As reported in the Jackson *Pilot*, December 14, 1871; William Lynch to Alcorn, 1871, in Governors' Correspondence, Vol. 73.

35. *Mississippi Educational Journal*, I (February, 1871), 53; *Southern Field and Factory*, 1 (February, 1871), 85.

future the paramount interest of the people of Mississippi. She is now far behind most of her sister States in the diffusion of education among her people. The work has been nobly started, and unless obstructed by adverse legislation, we shall, in five years, be far ahead of most of the Southern States in the advantages afforded for free school education."[36]

Most county superintendents warmly confirmed reports of increasing popular support for schools. Carpetbagger Liberty C. Abbott, superintendent in Marshall County (Holly Springs), informed Pease in early 1871 that "the free school system is working admirably" and he anticipated no problems in sustaining biracial support for it.[37] In overwhelmingly white Calhoun County, the superintendent wrote that far from violence erupting in his district when black schools were organized, as had reportedly occurred in a neighboring county, calm prevailed; in fact, "the mass of the citizens from all portions of the county have given the school officers their hearty co-operation." Charles A. Benjamin reported that school officials in Panola, a county in north Mississippi characterized by both plantations and small farms and where five Ku Klux Klan dens reputedly had existed two years before, "have yet to experience the first sign of *opposition* to the system, either overt or concealed, much less any outrages upon persons or buildings." On the contrary, he said, whites as well as blacks had cooperated in a significant way in the formation of schools. Benjamin did report "a little indifference regarding the establishment of colored schools, but no opposition; while in many cases the white people have interested themselves strongly for them, and aided us, and them in locating their schools."

Similar reports emanated from the overwhelmingly black river counties. Superintendent W. V. Onslow of Bolivar County informed Pease that in his section of the Delta both planters and black laborers were assisting in the work of establishing schools. Pease was told that in Tunica County teachers "can pursue their avocations in colored schools without fear of violence, molestation or insult." Even in the piney woods, where indifference and suspi-

36. As reported in the *Mississippi Educational Journal*, 1 (February, 1871), 53.
37. These reports are found in *ibid.*, (April, 1871), 133–37.

cion rather than hostility generally characterized the attitude of whites toward the school experiment, a ray of hope could be found in 1871. Superintendent D. H. Thompson wrote that the people of Smith County favored popular education, "provided the taxes don't press too heavy at first." As elsewhere, Thompson indicated that teachers and school officials were treated with respect, and certainly, he reported, the school buildings had not experienced any depredations at the hands of the county's few reactionaries.

Many whites, however, retained their early hostility toward the Republican system of education, even though their numbers dwindled in 1871. Opponents of the system generally remained inactive, biding their time until opposition to the schools became popular again. A handful of Bourbon newspapers manifested no such reluctance to attack the school program, although they usually took pains to assure their readers that they were not enemies of public schools per se. In 1871 the Columbus *Democrat* assumed the leadership of the disheartened opponents. "We favor public schools," the editor of this journal gratuitously remarked, but they must be "organized by tax-payers for the benefit of white children. We would leave the negroes to take care of themselves, convinced that if they possess the motive power, which has elevated the white race from ignorance to intelligence and civilization, they will develop [schools] in due time." As matters stood, he was "an uncompromising enemy of that system of public schools devised by the Black Republican Party of Mississippi."[38] Harper of the *Hinds County Gazette* expressed alarm that the school system was operated by "northern scoundrels and ruffians" who at home were "inmates of jails, and pest and bawdy-houses." Consequently, "this school business is an oppression and an infamy—a disgrace to the age—a machine for plunder and robbery," Harper wailed. "Our people are powerless—they are in the hands of the Phislestines [sic]."[39]

Such tirades, the exception rather than the rule, did not lead to any pattern of intimidation or violence to break up the schools, even in turbulent east Mississippi, an area pictured by historians

38. As reported in the Jackson *Pilot*, March 22, April 12, September 23, 1871.
39. *Hinds County Gazette*, April 5, 26, 1871.

as teeming with Klansmen bent upon the destruction of the Republican school program.[40] To be sure, the Klan and other terroristic societies were quite active in early 1871 in the easternmost tier of counties (bordering on equally disorderly counties in Alabama), but except for their operations in two of these counties little evidence exists of a pattern of attacks against the infant school system there. The isolated attacks on the school system and its personnel were part of the emotional fallout from the broader Klan objectives in the region, and even in the two afflicted counties, Winston and Monroe, these assaults were secondary to the Klan's main political and social purposes. Furthermore, the campaign of violence and burnings proved short-lived. Inspired to a great extent by federal arrests under the new Enforcement Acts, as well as by a rising aversion to reports of depredations on the schools, public opinion quickly swung against the terror movement.

When the Klan fever was at its height, the schools in Monroe and Winston suffered severely. In Monroe, a plantation, small-farm county where blacks nonetheless held a comfortable majority at the polls, Superintendent Allen P. Huggins, an active Republican, was severely whipped and twenty-six of his schools reportedly were closed by the Klan. Characterized by a former Confederate

40. Based mainly on scattered and suggestive testimony in the congressional *Ku Klux Klan Report, Mississippi*, historians have inaccurately left the impression that opposition to the public school system, or rather to the abuses of it by the Republicans, as James W. Garner preferred, was the fundamental cause of Klan terror in the eastern counties. Garner, *Reconstruction in Mississippi*, 359–63; Noble, *Forty Years of the Public Schools in Mississippi*, 36–37; Allen W. Trelease, *White Terror: The Ku Klux Klan Conspiracy and Southern Reconstruction* (New York, 1971), Chap. XVIII. Trelease devotes very little attention to reported outrages upon the school system in the state, although he entitles his chapter "Mississippi: The Campaign Against Schools." Wharton grossly exaggerates the opposition to the schools when he writes: "In the hill counties of the eastern and northern portions of the state, small farmers, aggrieved by poor crops and rising taxes, rode out at night to destroy the educational system so strongly denounced by their leaders. During the fall and winter of 1870 and the spring of 1871, the counties of Winston, Monroe, Choctaw, Lowndes, Pontotoc, Lee, Noxubee, and Chickasaw experienced a reign of terror. Teachers were tortured and murdered, or, at best, ordered to leave the county. No free school was safe from attack, but the violence centered on the schools of the Negroes." Wharton, *The Negro in Mississippi*, 245. A Study of the reports of school officials and the newspapers, especially the Republican Jackson *Pilot* and the Vicksburg *Times and Republican*, has led me to the opposite conclusion. This is not to suggest that there were no threats or attacks on obnoxious teachers in eastern counties, but these were isolated and were motivated more by the Klan's detestation of the teachers' direct political and social activities than by their work in establishing free schools.

officer as "mossbacks, deserters and bushwhackers" during the war, Klansmen in Winston in March, 1871, burned all of the county's schoolhouses and churches where blacks were taught. These attacks, however, only temporarily snarled the work of school organization in the two counties.

At the end of 1871 Pease and his associates took justifiable pride in the progress that had been made in creating a public school system in Mississippi. Hailing the work as "truly marvelous," Pease reported that 2,601 schools (1,739 white and 862 black), employing 2,655 teachers and instructing 111,686 pupils (66,257 whites and 45,429 blacks), had been established during the year.[41] The efforts of 1871 fell far short of reaching all of the 304,762 children of school age (five to twenty-one years of age) in the state, but a large proportion of youngsters under fifteen, particularly of the white race, were receiving the benefits of the new system.[42]

The next year was even better, for although by northern standards many of these schools were primitive and small (one-room buildings in most cases), an estimated 4,650 schools existed by the end of 1872 with 148,780 students enrolled. Pease again reported that steady progress was being made in white attitudes toward the schools. "Irrational prejudices and passions are gradually giving way to reason and an enlightened conservatism," he announced. Pease associated this development with a broader change occurring in the state. "The masses of the people, including a large proportion of the wealthy and intelligent classes, are beginning to demand a conformation to the great fundamental changes in our state and nation, particularly with reference to popular education."[43]

Reports in 1872 that the Ku Klux Klan had been crushed in the eastern counties and attacks against schools in the area had ceased provided additional reason for optimism. In Monroe Coun-

41. Pease's report for 1871 may be found in the *Senate Journal, 1872*, Appendix, 134–92. His statistical summary is on page 398 of the appendix. These figures were based on reports from fifty-two of the sixty-nine counties, most of the delinquent ones being small districts.

42. Compiled by the county superintendents, statistics on the number of children of school age in the state may be found in the *Mississippi Educational Journal*, I (November, 1871), 265.

43. *Journal of the Senate of the State of Mississippi, 1873* (2 vols.; Jackson, 1873), I, 709–10.

ty, the new superintendent (Huggins had resigned to go to the legislature) wrote that opposition to public education had died out and "the people were clamoring for their schools."[44] In neighboring Lowndes County, where the Columbus *Democrat* had earlier urged whites to resist paying taxes to support the Republican program and where several teachers reportedly had been threatened by the Klan, J. N. Bishop, the young carpetbag superintendent, indicated in 1873 that during the past two years "there has been no act of violence or marked demonstration on the part of any person showing hostility to the public schools or teachers. There are those who are not in sympathy with our school system, but prudence or past teachings have convinced them of the fact that open violence is not the way to win. In all my official visits in the county, I have been treated, without exception, kindly and with all the hospitality I could desire."[45] And in Chickasaw, another formerly turbulent county, the scalawag superintendent reported that "lawlessness seems to have yielded to a moral sentiment [and] the advocates of the free school system are so far in the ascendancy as to place its future beyond doubt."[46]

From Lauderdale County (Meridian), where a bloody race riot had occurred in March, 1871, the superintendent informed Pease that during 1872 "there has been every indication that the bitter prejudices against the colored schools have been allayed and are fast disappearing." Those black schools that were burned during the racial disturbance had been rebuilt, and other schools had been opened. "Some who were [the system's] most violent enemies are now its warmest supporters." Members of the old establishment in the county, who were formerly wealthy but reduced in circumstances by the war, "felt that the small school tax required to establish and sustain the Public Schools, if not saved to them in the diminished tuition fees for the education of their own children, is returned to them a hundred fold in the enterprise it will quicken, in the increased value of their property, and the general prosperity engendered by the dissemination of knowledge."[47]

44. *Ibid.*, 877.
45. *Journal of the House of Representatives of the State of Mississippi, 1874* (Jackson, 1874), Appendix, 844.
46. *Senate Journal, 1873,* I, 822.
47. *Ibid.*, 860.

Educational advance continued into 1873, and the benign attitude of most whites toward the system was generally sustained.
The conversion of private schools into public institutions, a process
that had begun slowly with the establishment of the first common
schools in 1870, increased in tempo in 1873. In early 1870, before
the implementation of the public school law, there were 41,965
students enrolled in 1,542 private schools of varying quality.[48] Although state tuition was extended to students in these schools
under the law of 1870, which in effect was a public subsidy to
private education, most of the schools operated on a financial shoestring and soon found it desirable to merge with the expanding
public system. By the end of 1873 only 500 private schools with
an estimated enrollment of 12,000 students existed in the state.
Disbandment was so rapid during this year that several local school
officials announced the demise of the private system in their counties.[49] Students from the defunct private institutions increased the
enrollments in the public schools during the last three years of
the Republican era. By 1875 attendance in the public schools had
risen to 168,217 (78,404 white children and 89,813 black).[50]

Despite these rosy developments in public education, by 1874
the school system was in trouble—a condition that, not incidentally, corresponded with the increasing political difficulties experienced by the Republican party in the state. In terms of enrollment
the system had not achieved the results that its Republican founders had envisaged necessary to attain a society of learning and virtue in Mississippi. Never more than 52 percent of the school-age
population attended the public schools during the Republican
period. Indifference and neglect toward schools rather than opposition characterized the viewpoint of thousands of the poor of
both races as they labored to grub out an existence on the land
during the lean years following the war. Poor parents, needing the
assistance of their children to make ends meet, frequently ignored

48. *Report of the Commissioner of Education for the Year 1870* (Washington, D. C.,
1870), 201; *House Journal, 1874*, Appendix, 847–48, 857, 921. The statistics for students
in private schools included the more than three thousand blacks receiving instruction in
bureau-sponsored classrooms.
49. *House Journal, 1874*, Appendix, 718, 847–48.
50. *Report of the Commissioner of Education for the Year 1875* (Washington, D. C.,
1875), 232.

the long-range benefits of the public schools for the more immediate, practical consideration of working the land. Even during the
winter months there was always work to be done, and for many
dirt farmers school attendance only interfered with the traditional
system of family labor on the farm.

On the other hand there were many common people who saw in
education the main hope of the future for their children. Many
of them, like their indifferent neighbors, were impecunious and
generally landless, made so, temporarily as they believed, by the
war and the economic and social instability that followed it. But
their ambitions and willingness to strive for financial independence
and standing in their communities had not been diminished by
their present difficulties. More perspicacious than their demoralized neighbors who viewed their straitened circumstance in the
traditional, rigid pattern of the poor, these people observed that
they were no worse off than many who had held upper-class rank
during happier days. They thoughtfully concluded that under postwar conditions of virtual economic equality their chances for success were as good as anyone's. Unable to send their children to the
few private schools still in existence, yet long exposed to arguments in favor of education, white men of this thinking (the counterpart of the more prosperous middle-class American of the twentieth century) naturally turned to the public schools to educate
their sons and daughters.

A large number of blacks, inspired by freedom and the Republican rhetoric of equality, opportunity, and racial progress, viewed
the benefits of public schooling in a similar light. They too believed that the road to success and moral rectitude lay largely
through education. Neither race seemed to have had an advantage
over the other in school registration, although school statistics indicate that in the beginning whites took greater pains to enroll
their children than did blacks. By 1875 black school registration
had passed white enrollments, with attendance in the public schools
closely corresponding to the state's racial composition. Even the
number of teachers in the schools reflected generally the black-
white ratio in the population, although the difficulties of finding
qualified black teachers posed a special problem for county superintendents. On the matter of compensation, Negro instructors ex-

perienced little discrimination: in 1875 the difference between white and black salaries on the average was only five dollars, and this apparent inequity in favor of whites could be explained by the lower qualifications among black teachers.[51]

Nevertheless, after the halcyon days of 1871–1873, most blacks and whites responded to the public schools with indifference rather than support. Already, Superintendent Pease and his associates had turned to the principle of compulsory education as the solution to the problem of lagging enrollments. Professing a debt to European models of public education, Pease in his annual report of 1872 entered a strong plea for a state law requiring the school attendance of all children between the ages of eight and fourteen. He argued that public sentiment was ripe for a compulsory law, and he even claimed that the upper class strongly favored such a measure. When the legislature of 1873 rejected a bill incorporating his recommendation, Pease intensified his campaign for compulsory education, and he was joined by a chorus of support from local school officials.[52] In 1874 Thomas W. Cardozo, Pease's black successor as superintendent, and Governor Ames, realizing that the Republican educational structure in Mississippi was now on shaky grounds, took up the cause of universal education. But even in the Republican camp the political winds had shifted away from reform, and despite the importunities of Cardozo and Ames, party leaders in the legislature refused to press the issue. As the Republican order crumbled, in a final and futile gesture in early 1876, Governor Ames called for a law compelling school attendance.[53]

Perhaps more than any other reason, including the endemic race issue and the emotionalism generated by Reconstruction politics, the problem of finance proved the undoing of the Republican dream of creating an effective system of education in Mississippi. Some of the money difficulties experienced by education officials stemmed from the excessive demands that the new system,

51. *Ibid.*
52. *Senate Journal, 1873,* I, 741–46; *Report of the Commissioner of Education for the Year 1873* (Washington, D. C., 1875), 213; *House Journal, 1874,* Appendix, 722, 889, 911, 916.
53. *Annual Report of the State Superintendent of Public Education to the Legislature of Mississippi, for the Scholastic Year 1874* (Jackson, 1875); *Annual Message of Governor Adelbert Ames to the Legislature of Mississippi, Session of 1876* (Jackson, 1876), 17.

along with other governmental activities, placed upon the tax resources of the state. These requirements, coming before Mississippi had fully recovered from the Civil War, proved too great a
financial burden to sustain a first-rate program of schools or to retain the confidence of the white people in a Republican-adminis-
tered system of public education.

In the beginning Republicans placed their hopes for the financial
success of the school system on a healthy restoration of the state's
agricultural economy. The economic revival of 1869–1870, in full
swing when the Republicans came to power and launched their
education enterprise, convinced these optimistic reformers that
the political triumph of the new order had ushered in a period
of prosperity, and they expected adequate school revenues to be
available on a long-term basis. The recovery, however, soon collapsed, and property values, which had never come close to regaining their prewar levels, continued their downward path. In
1870 the assessed value of both real and personal property in the
state was a modest $177,278,000 (it was $509,472,902 in 1860); by
1875 it had plunged to $116,518,000—and much of this value, at
least in farm lands, was based on the hope that a degree of agricultural prosperity would soon return and income would increase.[54]
Since the Republican founders of the education system placed the
main burden for its support on property taxes, the fortunes of the
public schools declined in proportion to the fall in property values.
Unable to pay the taxes levied against their property, many planters and farmers saw their land fall to the sheriff's hammer. Once
these properties had been seized by public authorities—although
indulgent sheriffs, both Republican and conservative, frequently
permitted former owners and tenants to continue working the land
—they were no longer subject to taxation. By 1875 at least one
fifth of the land area of Mississippi was held in this fashion and
therefore out of the reach of the tax collector.[55]

The burdens of financing the school system, as well as the benefits from it, were unevenly distributed. Although state officials uni-

54. *A Compendium of the Ninth Census (June 1, 1870) Compiled Pursuant to a Concurrent Resolution of Congress and Under the Direction of the Secretary of the Interior*
(Washington, 1872), 638; *Annual Report of the Auditor of Public Accounts to the Legislature of Mississippi, for the Year 1875* (Jackson, 1876), Doc. Q.
55. State auditor's report for 1874, in *House Journal, 1875*, Appendix, 40.

formly disbursed the Common School Fund, which was largely a supplementary source of money for the schools, county boards of supervisors determined the local tax rate for educational purposes. In some districts, mainly those in the Republican-dominated river counties where the enthusiasm for black education exceeded the financial realities of the time, supervisors imposed heavy taxes upon the land, only to see large tracts of it transferred to the custody of the sheriff when owners could not pay their taxes. On the contrary, in some counties—the majority of which, according to Pease, had the greatest need for education—supervisors by 1873 were resisting the idea of levying school taxes because, they said, deteriorating economic conditions would not permit it.[56] With facilities of the crudest sort and teachers of marginal literacy, schools in these and many other counties were forced for lack of money to close their doors after the completion of the minimum four-month session required by the law of 1870. Needing at least $1,500,000 to sustain a reasonably effective program of education in Mississippi, school officials were rarely able to raise $1 million for school purposes in any year during the Republican era.

Inefficiences and outright peculation in the collection and reporting of miscellaneous state taxes designated for the Common School Fund contributed to the dearth of money. Special Commissioner F. A. Clover, a carpetbagger appointed by Governor Ridgley C. Powers to investigate government affairs, revealed in 1873 that at least two thirds of the justices of the peace and chancery clerks since the passage of the school law had failed to report or forward to state officials those fines they had collected that were legally earmarked for the Common School Fund. He indicated that "in many instances these fines are embezzled, amounting in the aggregate, to a large sum of money." The legislature, however, ignored Clover's recommendation that it pass legislation to end this corrupt practice and ensure that all fines find their way into the school fund.[57]

56. Jackson *Pilot*, February 1, March 17, 1871; *Senate Journal, 1871*, p. 422; Greenville *Weekly Times*, November 7, 1874, March 27, 1875; report of Pease for 1872 in *Senate Journal, 1873*, Appendix, 721.

57. Report of Special Commissioner to Examine Administration of State Departments, January 21, 1873, in *Senate Journal, 1873*, p. 1100. The Vicksburg *Times and Republican*, May 24, 1875, estimated that $100,000 had been lost by the mismanagement of school revenues.

In addition, many tax officials displayed a remarkable indifference toward collecting the required license fees from dramshop
proprietors and liquor dealers. In an embarrassing number of cases
their lack of zeal was obviously the result of some monetary consideration on the side. Some collectors also winked in approval
when impecunious citizens balked at paying the two-dollar poll tax
that was set aside for the school fund. According to state Auditor
William H. Gibbs, by 1876 the public school system of the state
was losing annually between $75,000 and $90,000 in revenues because of poll-tax evasions alone.[58]

At the same time the Republican-dominated legislature showed
little disposition to aid the schools by tapping some traditionally
privileged sources of tax revenue. Except for landed and personal
property, Republicans, like their conservative predecessors in
power, found it desirable to exempt from taxation altogether or
impose only trifling levies on commercial and industrial properties.
The railroads, by far the largest industrial enterprise in the state,
avoided taxation until 1875 when a duty of seventy-five dollars per
mile of track was imposed on them; even then some powerful companies ignored the levy.[59] Manufacturing companies almost completely escaped taxation during the Republican era. After 1872 textile and woolen enterprises were exempt from taxation, and the
numerous sawmills that emerged in south Mississippi during Reconstruction generally avoided the small state levy placed on all
businesses.[60] Commercial establishments, especially those with
fairly extensive assets, also had no reason to complain of Republican tax policies. The Revenue Act of 1870, the basic tax law of the
Republican period, assessed merchants a sum of fifty dollars each
regardless of the size of their business and required banks and
insurance companies, of which there were few in the state, to pay
a tax of one hundred dollars.[61] School finances might have been
improved had all economic interests in the state been required to
carry a fair share of the tax burden.

58. State auditor's report for 1874, in *House Journal, 1875*, Appendix, 39; *Annual Report
of the Auditor of Public Accounts to the Legislature of Mississippi, for the Year 1876*
(Jackson, 1877), 9.
  59. *Annual Report of the Auditor, 1875*, p. ix; *House Journal, 1874*, p. 17.
  60. *Laws of the State of Mississippi, 1872* (Jackson, 1872), 65–67.
  61. *Laws of Mississippi, 1870*, pp. 27–29.

These shortcomings by no means complete the story of the Republicans' failure to provide a solid financial foundation for their educational system. But in one area—the administration of the federal lands granted to the state during the antebellum period for educational purposes—Republicans in clear conscience could concede the greater share of mismanagement and negligence to the old regime. The federal endowment consisted of two grants: Sixteenth Section lands, totalling 661,001 acres, which were donated to the state when it entered the Union, and, in lieu of Sixteenth Section lands, 147,550 acres in the area ceded to the United States by the Chickasaw Indians during the 1830s. Both of these trusts suffered grievously at the hands of antebellum officials. As occurred in other states, Sixteenth Section lands were turned over to local officials who proceeded to lease them to private companies and individuals. Imperfectly accounted for from the beginning, leased lands produced little revenue for prewar common schools in Mississippi, and the disruptive events of the Civil War virtually completed their alienation from the public domain. Nonetheless, the titles to the land, however obscured by the loss of records and the pyramid of leases, still resided with the state. But neither the conservatives of the Johnson era nor the Republicans of the 1870s adopted a uniform policy to regain these lands for the school fund. Beset by other problems, the state board of education waited until 1874 to try to untangle the jumbled status of the Sixteenth Section lands; however, in their report to the legislature the members of the board admitted that the task of making the property available for educational purposes was a hopeless one.[62] As with properties held by the state for nonpayment of taxes, most of the Sixteenth Section lands, although regularly farmed or exploited for their timber, yielded no tax revenue.

No antebellum problem inherited by the Republicans proved more vexatious or more subject to manipulative pressures than that of the Chickasaw endowment. The origins of the imbroglio went back to 1848 when the Mississippi legislature sold most of these

---

62. *House Journal, 1874*, Appendix, 872–74, 892; W. W. Wade to Alcorn, January 31, 1871, in Governors' Correspondence, Vol. 73; *Report of the State Superintendent of Education, 1874*, pp. 93–94; *Annual Report of the State Superintendent of Public Education, to the Legislature of Mississippi, for the Year 1877* (Jackson, 1877), 15–16.

lands for approximately $800,000, which became a trust fund for future common schools in the twenty-two counties of the old Chickasaw cession. In 1856 all of this fund was loaned at 8 percent interest to four railroad companies that were in the process of constructing trunk lines in the states. Completed by the time of the Civil War, all of these railroads except the New Orleans, Jackson, and Great Northern, which was cut by the early Federal occupation of the Crescent City, took advantage of the state's need for money during the war to pay off the loan in grossly inflated state and Confederate treasury notes. After the war the conservative administration of 1865–1867 declared the whole proceeding invalid and announced its determination to force the railroad companies to honor their original debt to the Chickasaw Fund.[63] But military reconstruction intervened, and despite the efforts of General Ames to secure the compliance of the railroads (see Chapter 2), the settlement of the matter was delayed until civil government was restored.

When Alcorn became governor in 1870, he instituted judicial proceedings against the railroads to recover the money. The Mississippi supreme court ruled in favor of the state, but the 1872 legislature followed the decision with an act permitting the railroads to discharge their obligations with depreciated state warrants. The act also allowed a third party to assume responsibility for the Chickasaw loan in exchange for the first mortgage bonds of the roads, which the state held and had guarded jealously in case the railroads repudiated their obligations.[64]

In pursuance of this act, a group of Columbus bankers, headed by Abram Murdock and backed by a New York financial house, contracted with Governor Powers to pay in warrants the amount due from the New Orleans, Jackson, and Great Northern Railroad.

63. *Biennial Report of the State Superintendent of Public Education to the Legislature of Mississippi, for the Years 1880–81* (Jackson, 1882), 9; *Journal of the Senate of the State of Mississippi, October, November, and December Session of 1865* (Jackson, 1866), 139–40; New Orleans *Picayune*, October 18, 1866.

64. *Hinds County Gazette*, May 25, 1870; Jackson *Weekly Clarion*, April 14, 1870; *Mississippi Central Railroad* v. *State of Mississippi*, 46 Miss. 157–222 (1871); *Laws of Mississippi, 1872*, pp. 391–92. Meanwhile, out of regular tax revenues the state was distributing to the Chickasaw counties a sum of money ($64,000) that almost equaled the amount due them from the interest on the loan. Most of these counties, however, misapplied the money, using it to assist in the construction of local railroads. The legislature of 1873 ordered a halt to this practice. Vicksburg *Times and Republican*, March 16, 1873; *Laws of the State of Mississippi, 1873* (Jackson, 1873), 17–18.

But before the full amount was paid (a sum of $370,000, including interest), Powers injudiciously transferred to the Columbus speculators the railroads' first mortgage bonds—the only collateral the state possessed for the Chickasaw loan. At first the New Orleans railroad refused to make an arrangement with the Murdock group to liquidate the debt, but Powers, finally recognizing the danger to the state's interest in the matter, threatened to obtain the revocation of the company's charter if it did not honor its commitment. The managers of the railroad needed no further reminder of their responsibility to the Chickasaw Fund, and they resumed payments on the loan.[65]

The other railroad debtors to the Chickasaw Fund, having failed to make a settlement under the 1872 law, bombarded the legislature with demands that they be given relief from their obligations. The legislature responded with an act affirming the companies' right to pay off their debts in state warrants and permitting them to make their payments in five installments. The accumulated interest on the loans was cancelled, but the provision in the earlier law allowing an outside party to assume the debt was not renewed.[66]

The settlement was not final. Lawyers for the railroads found reasons to take the state to court on the matter and thus delay payment. The litigation had scarcely begun when the legislature transferred (with conditions attached) the state's interest in the Chickasaw Fund first to the aspiring Vicksburg, Pensacola, and Ship Island company, which made use of $110,000 of it before failing, and then to the equally aspiring Greenville, Columbus and Birmingham Railroad. The next year, however, the so-called Redeemers recaptured the fund.[67] Then, in 1878, in order to secure legislative approval of a plan to merge the New Orleans road with the

65. Message of Governor Powers to the legislature, in *Senate Journal, 1873*, I, 13–14; Vicksburg *Times and Republican*, February 15, August 8, 1873; Annual Message of Powers, January 20, 1874, in *House Journal, 1874*, p. 20; *Journal of the House of Representatives of the State of Mississippi, 1876* (Jackson, 1876), 632–35.

66. Vicksburg *Times and Republican*, February 15, March 16, 1873; *Journal of the House of Representatives of the State of Mississippi, 1873* (Jackson, 1873), 1905; *Laws of Mississippi, 1873*, pp. 119–20.

67. *Laws of Mississippi, 1873*, pp. 562–63; *Annual Message of Governor Ames, 1876*, p. 16; *Laws of the State of Mississippi, 1875* (Jackson, 1875), 81–83. Fortunately for the interest of the school fund, managers of the Greenville enterprise were unable to construct the minimum five miles of track before the Redeemers revoked the grant. *Laws of the State of Mississippi, 1876* (Jackson, 1876), 275–76.

Mississippi Central, the managers of the consolidated company agreed to assume the Chickasaw debt of the latter railroad. But the amount of the settlement was considerably less than the original loan and accumulated interest.[68] In the end, the state had only $162,839 to show the Chickasaw counties for their once magnificent $800,000 school endowment not including the subsequent interest on it that had been lost.[69]

When sufficient revenues, from whatever source, did not materialize, harassed local officials adopted the pernicious warrant system to finance the schools. Since the worth of the warrants was always based on anticipated tax revenues, which rarely matched the amount of notes issued in any one year, they seldom attained par value with greenbacks and specie. Only United States currency, supplemented in some counties by Alcorn's certificates of indebtedness, was accepted in payment of taxes, whereas depreciated warrants were paid out for services and salaries.

This method of financing school obligations was especially hard on teachers, who were forced to hawk their salaries on the streets for as little as forty and fifty cents on the dollar, depending on the locality. Only speculators, who could afford to wait until currency was paid into the treasury, profited from the warrant system of finance. Although carpetbag Governors Powers and Ames made a special effort to convert state finances to a strictly cash basis, when the Redeemers came to power in 1876 warrants were still very much in evidence and public school finance was in disarray.[70] In addition to undermining the effectiveness of the Republican experiment in public education, the failure of its founders to develop a solid financial structure for the system so stigmatized the concept of educational reform and progress in Mississippi that it was decades before the people were willing to make the sacrifices necessary to implement the Reconstructionists' grand design.

68. *Laws of the State of Mississippi, 1878* (Jackson, 1878), 223; *Biennial Message of Governor J. M. Stone to the Legislature of Mississippi, Session of 1880* (Jackson, 1880), 21.

69. *Biennial Report of the State Superintendent of Public Education to the Legislature of Mississippi, for the Scholastic Years 1889–90 and 1890–91* (Jackson, 1892), 16–17.

70. J. W. Armstrong to Alcorn, July 1, 1871, in Governors' Correspondence, Vol. 74; Jackson *Pilot*, July 20, 1871; *Senate Journal, 1873*, pp. 828, 876; *Annual Message of Governor Ames, 1876*, p. 10.

Higher education in Mississippi did not receive the same enthusiastic attention from the Republicans as did the public schools. Republicans conceived of public, elementary education as the broad cornerstone for the kind of society that they wanted to see in the state—a society free of the blighting influences and practices of the slavery-secessionist past. The elevation of the freedmen to their full potential, the end of the rampant lawlessness that plagued the state, the development of political tolerance, and the material rehabilitation of the state, Republicans believed, all depended upon an educated citizenry.[71] To achieve these objectives education must be made available to the masses of both races. In a speech before the legislature in 1870, Powers expressed the expectations of most Republicans regarding public education. He declared that a system of schools was "a reform vast in its objects—because it is based upon the broadest principle of benevolence and charity, and is intended to reach all classes of our people; a reform salutary in its influences—because its effect will be to remove the clouds of ignorance and prejudice that envelope society and obstruct all genuine advancement and prosperity; a reform that will be lasting—because it is directed toward the rising generation, and is intended to enlighten and develop the youth of the country."[72]

On the other hand many Republicans were lukewarm toward higher education, believing that it offered few benefits for the masses and would contribute little to the reconstruction objectives of the new order. The University of Mississippi, as most Republicans probably thought, had in the past served only the wealthy planter, and because of insufficient funds if for no other reason, there was little likelihood during Reconstruction that the advantages of a college education could be extended to all classes. Furthermore, the presence on the faculty of L. Q. C. Lamar, one of the leading fire-eaters of 1860–1861 and a die-hard opponent of

71. Extant issues of the ephemeral *Mississippi Educational Journal*, founded in February, 1871, are rich in articles and editorials illustrating Republican, and especially carpetbagger, faith in the regenerative and ameliorative power of public education. For other extensive expressions of the broad virtues of a common school system, see editorials in the Jackson *Pilot*, October 8, 1870, March 31, April 9, 1871.

72. Powers' speech, made when he was lieutenant governor, may be found in the *Mississippi Educational Journal*, I (February, 1871), 13–19, and in the *Senate Journal* [*1870*], 436–40.

congressional reconstruction, was enough to cause some otherwise friendly Republicans to hesitate in their support of the university. The more radical black leaders in the state, realizing that the university even under Republican management would continue to admit only white students, opposed the restoration of the institution as a center of privilege in Mississippi.[73]

Finally, the need to train teachers immediately for the public schools weakened Republican support for the university. A number of influential Republicans, mainly of the carpetbag class and including Pease and Powers, were convinced that only a system of inexpensive, conveniently located normal schools could quickly supply the large need for properly prepared elementary school teachers. These men, reflecting the mania for normal schools that was then sweeping the North, rejected the notion that the state university might be expanded to train students in pedagogical skills. Despite their efforts, only two state normal schools were established, and both of these grew out of missionary colleges that had been created for blacks after the war.[74]

The virtual collapse of private college education in the state as a result of the war and the financial depression that followed placed a premium upon the restoration and expansion of the University of Mississippi. When the Republicans came to power in 1870, only two private colleges remained.[75] Mississippi College, the Baptist institution at Clinton, had closed its doors during the war and though burdened with a heavy debt had reopened in 1867 with a president, one instructor, and a handful of students. The college, serving Arkansas and Louisiana Baptists as well as those of Mississippi, languished for the remainder of the Reconstruction period, although the student enrollment increased to 126 in 1873.[76] Along the coast, Pass Christian College, founded by the order of Christian Brothers in 1866, survived into the 1870s due mainly to the "liberal aid" of New Orleans patrons. Its high-water mark was

73. Jackson *Weekly Pilot*, April 23, August 27, 1870; *Senate Journal, 1872*, pp. 541–42.

74. Report of Pease for 1872 in *Senate Journal, 1873*, pp. 734–35; *House Journal, 1874*, pp. 425–26, Appendix, 721, 827–28; Jackson *Weekly Pilot*, April 23, 1870.

75. A few private colleges like Oakland College near Rodney survived the war only to fall victim to the financial crisis of the postwar period. Jackson *Clarion*, October 8, 1867.

76. *House Journal, 1874*, Appendix, 1014. Baptists in Louisiana and Arkansas also contributed a modest sum of money toward sustaining the institution. *Report of the Commissioner of Education for the Year 1874* (Washington, D.C., 1875), 232.

reached in 1873 when eighty students were enrolled, most of them following a commercial curriculum. During the early 1870s protestant denominations established six small institutions "for the superior instruction of young ladies"; all six were authorized by the legislature to confer college degrees.[77]

Products of the northern missionary impulse that accompanied the freeing of slaves, two private colleges for blacks arose after the war to provide Mississippi freedmen with some opportunity for advanced training. Shaw University at Holly Springs, established in 1866 by the Northern Methodist Episcopal Church, struggled to survive, though it provided little more than elementary instruction, until the state assumed control in 1870 and with mixed results converted it into an all-black normal school.[78] Tougaloo University, a few miles north of Jackson, had a much more promising beginning. Endowed with a grant of land, including several small buildings, this institution opened in 1869 as a result of the combined efforts of the American Missionary Association and the Freedmen's Bureau. From the beginning the quality of its instruction, mainly in the hands of young ladies who were graduates of "the best training schools in the North and West," was superior to that given blacks at Shaw University and later at Alcorn University. At the invitation of the missionary society, the state in 1872 established a normal-school department at Tougaloo, which ensured the institution's financial success. Student enrollment there continued to increase during the Republican era, reaching a high of 287 in 1874.[79]

Despite some Republicans' indifference to the problems of higher education, authorities in Jackson did not permit the state university to languish, as occurred in several southern states during Reconstruction. The vigorous support of Governor Alcorn in 1870–1871 proved the salvation of the struggling school at Oxford. Alcorn

77. *Report of the Commissioner of Education for the Year 1871* (Washington, D.C., 1872), 257; *Report of Education Commissioner, 1873*, p. 217, and *1875*, p. 237. As with other institutions in the state, these female schools were incorporated and boards of trustees formed that included both Republicans and conservatives. See *Laws of Mississippi, 1873*, pp. 429–34, 442, 445.

78. When the state assumed control in 1870, "university" classes were being taught in a local Methodist church. Jackson *Weekly Pilot*, March 5, 1870; *Laws of Mississippi, 1870*, p. 161.

79. *Report of the State Superintendent of Education, 1874*, pp. 14–15; *Laws of Mississippi, 1872*, pp. 55–56; Wharton, *The Negro in Mississippi*, 254–55.

was convinced that the university could be transformed into an institution that would provide not only the enlightened leadership of the future for the state but also qualified teachers for the emerging public schools, and he early secured the legislature's approval of a university reorganization act. The scalawag governor followed up this action with a plea that the legislature "fill out the opportunity presented in the University by bringing its advantages within the reach of the poor." He specifically proposed, and the lawmakers approved, two types of grants for students—a tuition-free scholarship for the poor and a complete, expense-paid grant for the student in each county who scored the highest grade on a special examination. The legislature, however, appropriated less than one half of the $100,000 that Alcorn requested for the general support of the university.[80]

Under the reorganization act, the governor received the authority to appoint a new board of trustees, with himself as chairman. Instead of selecting a partisan board of Republicans, which would have alienated the white community from the university, Alcorn chose the directors from prominent and moderate men of both parties who were in sympathy with higher education in the state. The board, which served for most of the Republican era, consisted of eight Republicans (including three carpetbaggers) and five conservatives. Carpetbaggers Alexander Warner and Jonathan Tarbell worked well on the board with such prominent men of the past as Civil War Governor Charles Clark and Absalom M. West, a Confederate general and the state's most influential railroad man.[81]

One of the first acts of the new board of trustees was to approve a sweeping reform of the curriculum, making the institution a university (although of modest size) in reality as well as in name. Modeled after an innovative curriculum at the University of Michigan and recommended by Chancellor John N. Waddel after his extensive visit to northern universities, the new program of studies at Oxford was divided into three divisions—college preparatory education, arts and sciences, and professional education. A student

80. Jackson *Weekly Pilot*, April 23, 1870; *Annual Message of Governor Alcorn, 1871*, p. 23.

81. John N. Waddel, *Memorials of Academic Life: Being an Historical Sketch of the Waddel Family* (Richmond, 1891), 470, 472; Jackson *Weekly Pilot*, August 12, 20, 27, September 3, 1870; Vicksburg *Times and Republican*, October 3, 1873.

under the new curriculum could select a course of study in his field without having to take all of the courses in that division.[82] Postgraduate courses leading to the master of arts and doctor of philosophy degrees were also instituted, but none was conferred during the Republican era. Under the new organization, the university grew at a moderate rate. Enrollments increased from 120 students in the fall of 1870 to 360 in 1871 and 302 in 1872.[83]

These achievements, however, failed to quiet conservative criticism that Alcorn and his Republican cohorts had politicized the University of Mississippi. Even after Alcorn admonished the university to "purge its halls of the old vice that has haunted them so long—political faction," the Jackson *Clarion* ironically claimed that the institution "had been ruthlessly seized by the spoilsmen who have determined to Radicalize it." Only in a limited sense, however, was the university politicized by the Republicans. Chancellor Waddel's fear that the institution might be ruined if it did not respect the political sensibilities of dominant Republicans caused him to instruct his faculty not to offend the board of trustees or the legislature by teaching the doctrine of states' rights or by venerating the Lost Cause. In fact, Waddel imposed a rigid censorship on political discussions and activities on the campus, although the board of trustees suggested no such policy. Only on two occasions was this prohibition violated, both times by students who made "indiscreet speeches" of an anti-Republican character at commencement ceremonies.[84] Although obviously affronted, Republican trustees scrupulously avoided using the board's authority to punish the students or the university for the incidents. After three years of service on the board, Tarbell, one of the more politically sensitive trustees, could say with little exaggeration: "No political question or consideration has ever intruded itself into the deliberations of the trustees. Even the political bias of individual trustees has never been indicated by, nor could it be learned from any word or act on the Board. The ambition of all has been to place the institution on a basis which no State administration would

82. Jackson *Weekly Pilot*, December 24, 1870.

83. Cabaniss, *History of the University of Mississippi*, 84–85; Waddel, *Memorials of Academic Life*, 470.

84. Jackson *Weekly Clarion*, October 27, 29, 1870, July 24, 1873; Waddel, *Memorials of Academic Life*, 472; Cabaniss, *History of the University of Mississippi*, 82.

see reason to change. If ever a great enterprise was undertaken in a spirit of impartiality, sincerity and disinterestedness, with a purpose to be governed by conscience, judgement and duty, the trustees of the State University have labored in that spirit."[85]

The board of trustees demonstrated a remarkable degree of restraint in its relations with the old faculty of the university. Despite demands from the Republican press that the faculty be "reconstructed," the trustees refused to replace conservative members with men who, as the Jackson *Pilot* described them, were "profoundly alive to the fact that they are living in the latter half of the 19th century, when the world is a blaze in the spirit of industry, enterprize and freedom." The board even refused to remove the obstreperous Lamar from the faculty, thus frustrating his efforts to become a martyr at the hands of the Republicans. With some bitterness at the failure of the trustees to cooperate in his scheme, Lamar ultimately resigned his position as professor of law.[86] He was replaced by Thomas W. Walton, a former Confederate whose advocacy of central power as opposed to states' rights exceeded even the advanced views held by many Radical Republicans on the issue.[87]

Professor Walton's political pronouncements and the Republican trustees' expressions of disapproval at the student speaker's anti-Union remarks during the 1873 commencement inspired Mississippi Bourbons to unleash a late Reconstruction barrage of criticism at the university. This time Bourbon newspapers called on parents to withdraw their sons from the institution and send them to out-of-state colleges. If their children remained at the university, one editor warned, parents would have to submit "to the humiliating spectacle of having them trained up under the supervision of public thieves and robbers, and their minds imbued with the worst principles of scallawag [*sic*] and carpet-bag politics."[88]

85. Vicksburg *Times and Republican*, October 3, 1873. See also clipping from the Kosciusko *Chronicle*, n.d., in Niles Scrapbook, and the Jackson *Weekly Pilot*, September 3, 24, 1870.

86. Jackson *Weekly Pilot*, April 9, 1870. Lamar's hopes for political martyrdom in this affair are suggested, but not explicitly stated, by Murphy, *L. Q. C. Lamar*, 98.

87. Thomas W. Walton to Ridgley C. Powers, February 24, 1872, in Governors' Correspondence, Vol. 72; Jackson *Weekly Clarion*, January 30, 1873.

88. Jackson *Weekly Clarion*, July 24, 1873, quoting the Crystal Springs *Monitor*.

Despite the Bourbon campaign to discredit the university, conservative support of the institution wavered only slightly. The great issue that could have alienated whites, the bugbear of racial integration, had been scotched by the Republican board in 1870 when Flournoy, the "John Brown of Mississippi Radicals," had unsuccessfully attempted to secure the admission of black students to the university.[89] The 1871 establishment of Alcorn University for blacks satisfied whites that their university at Oxford would not be "mongrelized" under the Republican regime. Furthermore, the creation in 1872 of a department of agriculture in the university under the terms of the federal land grant act of 1866 and the vigorous, but unsuccessful, effort of the Republican board of trustees to save the $320,000 in the endowment from the depredations of the railroads kept most public-spirited whites from joining the Bourbons in their attacks.[90] Nevertheless, legislative appropriations, which never exceeded $50,000 in any year, fell far short of the needs of the university, and when Governor Alcorn's system of student scholarships, instituted in 1871, was swept aside during the last year of Republican rule, enrollments in the university declined to 131 students, 46 of whom matriculated in the preparatory division.[91]

Alcorn University arose out of the need of white Republicans, principally Governor Alcorn and his moderate associates at the capital, to relieve black pressure for the racial integration of the University of Mississippi. Only a few black leaders—and these mostly in the legislature—during the first year of Republican control demanded the admission of blacks to the institution. But when scalawag Flournoy launched his integration crusade in late 1870 other blacks manifested restlessness on the subject. After Flournoy threatened to test the issue before the federal courts on the ground that Negro exclusion from the university violated the Fourteenth Amendment, carpetbaggers in power bestirred themselves and threw their support behind the governor's plan, originally ad-

89. *Ibid.*, December 1, 1870; Jackson *Weekly Pilot*, October 8, 15, 1870.

90. Vicksburg *Times and Republican*, October 3, 1873; Waddel, *Memorials of Academic Life*, 466–67; *Senate Journal, 1873*, I, 19; Columbus *Press*, July 12, 1873.

91. *Annual Message of Governor Alcorn, 1871*, p. 23; *Laws of Mississippi, 1875*, p. 168; *Journal of the Senate of the State of Mississippi, 1880* (Jackson, 1880), 259.

vanced in 1870, for an all-black college.[92] White Republicans, while professing their own color blindness, nonetheless argued that the forced admission of black students into the university would destroy higher education in the state and would retard the development of the emerging public school system. In supporting dual colleges for the races, carpetbagger Edward Stafford, editor of the Jackson *Pilot*, rationalized that on the matter of race "we have to take mankind as we find it; and what we would like to have, and what we can obtain, may be two [different] things, owing entirely to circumstances beyond our control. . . . Wisdom's dictation is, that we do the best we can for the moral, material and educational advantage of all, and we will have discharged a solemn obligation we owe to the youth of the State."[93]

The bill creating Revels University (later changed to Alcorn University) passed the legislature in 1871 by an overwhelming vote.[94] Even several black legislators who had earlier opposed the plan for fear an all-Negro university would establish "a precedent which we were working hard to break down—that of separate institutions for the races," grudgingly gave their support to the bill.[95] Black opponents were mollified when the governor selected an all-Negro board of trustees for the college and appointed former United States Senator Hiram R. Revels as its first president. At Governor Alcorn's insistence, the legislature awarded the new institution three fifths of the proceeds from the college land grant fund (an endowment that amounted to $192,000 by 1873), leaving only two fifths for the agriculture department at the white university. The legislature also appropriated $50,000 from state revenues for the support of Alcorn University.[96] The largesse of the governor and

92. Jackson *Weekly Clarion*, December 1, 1870; Jackson *Weekly Pilot*, May 17, 1871; *Special Message of Gov. James L. Alcorn, on the Subject of the Establishment of a University for the Colored People, Etc.* (Jackson, 1871).

93. Jackson *Weekly Pilot*, October 8, 1870.

94. In the senate only three votes were cast against the bill; one black senator and two conservatives opposed it. *Senate Journal, 1871*, pp. 589–90; *Journal of the House of Representatives of the State of Mississippi, 1871* (Jackson, 1871), 932.

95. Washington *New National Era*, April 4, May 2, 1872.

96. Confirmation of officers for Alcorn University, May 13, 1871, in Governors' Correspondence, Vol. 74; *Laws of Mississippi, 1871*, pp. 716–21; Natchez *Weekly Democrat*, May 24, 1871; *Report of Education Commissioner, 1874*, p. 232.

the white-dominated legislature persuaded many skeptical black leaders, like young John R. Lynch, already an influential member of the state house of representatives, and Thomas W. Stringer, the only Negro senator to vote against the bill creating the institution, that Alcorn University would receive its fair share of financial support from the state. Consequently, for some blacks the impulse to obtain equality of treatment in the state's public institutions gave way in the founding of Alcorn University to a feeling of pride in the college; a few even went so far as to boast that it would develop into a leading center of learning in the Mississippi Valley.[97]

Black opposition to the institution, however, soon resurfaced. Local elections in the fall of 1871 had spawned a sense of militancy and independence among blacks that had not existed before. Negro members of the new legislature arrived in Jackson determined to make their majority at the polls felt and to effectuate a real equality of treatment. One of their first targets was Alcorn University, which opened its doors to students in February, 1872. Now convinced that white Republican motives for founding the school had been less than pure and reinforced in their position by Senator Ames's opposition to the college, black legislators introduced a bill to abolish the institution. With the support of a number of white Republicans, who in most cases feared the political consequences of opposing their black colleagues on the issue, the bill passed the house of representatives where 41 of the 107 members, including Speaker John Lynch, were Negroes, but failed in the senate where blacks held only 5 of the 37 seats.[98]

Established on this shaky foundation, Alcorn University, located near Rodney, had a fitful existence for several years. Although 117 students were enrolled by the end of the first year—none of whom was prepared for advanced academic work—the institution suffered from neglect at the hands of its Republican patrons. Both white and black Republicans, some still hoping to integrate the white university, soon regarded Alcorn University as strictly an

97. Washington *New National Era*, May 2, 1872, March 20, 1873; Natchez *Weekly Democrat*, May 24, July 19, 1871.

98. Natchez *Weekly Democrat*, March 27, 1872; Washington *New National Era*, April 4, 25, 1872; *Congressional Globe*, 42nd Cong., 2nd Sess., Appendix, 395; *House Journal*, 1872, pp. 541–42.

agricultural and mechanical training school.[99] Even with this limited purpose the administration of the college proved unequal to the task of developing a first-rate institution. President Revels, an amiable, scholarly man of reasonable competence, was out of his element in the maelstrom that existed at the new college. Not only was Revels forced to contend with inadequate facilities and an apathetic state administration, but he also encountered bitter internal strife among faculty, students, and the superintendent.

When Ames became governor in 1874, he removed Revels from office quite as much because of his political support of Senator Alcorn as for his inability to manage the college.[100] But the removal of Revels, who was popular with the students, triggered a protest on campus and caused the students to either leave school or boycott classes. Labeled a "rebellion," not only by conservatives who delighted at any chance to belittle blacks, but also by black and white Republicans at the capital, the incident was free of violence and the destruction of property except that one overzealous student "clipped the tail" of a trustee's horse. The legislature reacted by ordering the dismissal of Dr. John M. Thompson, Revels' incompetent successor as president, and the replacement of the board of trustees, the faculty, and "all other officials connected with the University."[101] Ames, however, retained Thompson, although the new board, consisting of both white and black Republicans, characterized him as "a man capable of becoming the facile tool of any man or set of men, good or bad, or of any political party for any purpose." When the Redeemers came to power in early 1876 and restored Revels to the presidency, only fifty students were enrolled at Alcorn University, and the all-black college languished in "a miserable, deplorable, disgraceful condition."[102]

99. *Senate Journal, 1873*, I, 19–20; Washington *New National Era*, May 16, 1872; *Report of Education Commissioner, 1873*, p. 217.

100. *House Journal, 1875*, pp. 437–39; Adelbert Ames to Frank C. Harris, August 4, 1874, in Letterbook of Governor Adelbert Ames, D, Mississippi Department of Archives and History.

101. Ames to John M. Thompson, November 3, 1874, in Governor Ames Letterbook, B; *House Journal, 1875*, p. 438; W. H. Furniss to Ames, January 27, 1875, in Governors' Correspondence, Vol. 96; *Laws of Mississippi, 1875*, p. 127.

102. Report of Jonathan Tarbell to Governor Ames on conditions at Alcorn University, December 25, 1875, in Governors' Correspondence, Vol. 96; Hiram R. Revels to John M. Stone, December 11, 1876, in Governors' Correspondence, Vol. 110.

In essence, then, Republican efforts to achieve a society of virtue and enlightenment through public education—especially elementary education—failed. Nevertheless, a beginning was made in mass public schooling and the state university, however deficient in the appurtenances usually associated with institutions of higher education, remained open. The establishment of Alcorn University, the white ploy to defuse the Radical demand for the racial integration of the University of Mississippi, quickly relegated black higher education to an inferior status. But, as moderate Republicans argued, the admission of blacks to the state university, no matter how desirable in principle, would have destroyed white support for the institution and raised the bugbear of integration in the public schools. Of the higher institutions of learning in the South during Reconstruction, only the University of South Carolina opened its doors to black students. The results of this experiment in biracial education were mixed, and the university virtually folded for lack of white patronage. By the same token the integration of the New Orleans public schools, the only school system to be racially mixed during the period, undermined the efforts of Louisiana Republicans to gain white support for public education in the state. Unlike Mississippi, where as many as 78,404 whites were enrolled in the dual system of schools in 1875, interior whites in Louisiana during Reconstruction boycotted the public schools because they feared the classrooms would be integrated.[103] Until progress had been made in changing fundamental racial attitudes, the imposition of racially mixed schools in Mississippi would have been premature and destructive not only of the modest gains made in public education for both races but also of Republican control in the state.

The structure of the free school system staggered into the twentieth century when with a burst of activity during the 1950s and 1960s it achieved the comprehensiveness (and perhaps the quality) that its founders, the much-maligned carpetbaggers, scalawags, and black Republicans, had long ago envisaged. It might not be

---

103. Information on the integration of the University of South Carolina and the desegregation issue in Louisiana is taken from William P. Vaughn, *Schools for All: The Blacks & Public Education in the South, 1865–1877* (Lexington, 1974), 89–91, 101, 111–14. Although based on the data that Vaughn presents, my conclusions regarding the effects of these experiments in mixed schools are different from his.

claiming too much to say that their failures, due primarily to their overzealousness and their grave misunderstanding of the financial prospects of postwar Mississippi, contributed ultimately though inadvertently to the twentieth-century success of their educational dream. When Mississippians finally committed themselves whole-heartedly to the cause of public education, they took a lesson from the Reconstruction past, which had been ingrained in the minds of each succeeding generation, and planted their system on solid financial ground, designed to get the most out of their still meager tax resources.

11

The Reconstruction of Public
Institutions and Services

The new order's attempts to provide a progressive foundation for the rehabilitation and development of the regular public institutions also fell short of early Republican promises. When the Republicans assumed power in 1870, the state penitentiary, the insane asylum at Jackson, the state hospitals at Natchez and Vicksburg, and the deaf and blind institution were struggling to survive after years of largely unavoidable neglect. Furthermore, the care of the poor, traditionally a county responsibility, had almost completely collapsed in the wake of the war, although the Freedmen's Bureau had briefly offered some assistance to indigents. A major effort was needed merely to resuscitate the institutions that served the public. But the prospect of restoring them in a way that would immediately meet expanded postwar needs was farfetched because of the straitened financial conditions existing during the 1870s. Nevertheless, a wise management of available resources and a genuine dedication to humanitarian reform by the state's new rulers could go far toward creating a solid base for the future development of these institutions and the effective expansion of their services.

In the work of rehabilitating the institutions, the vexatious problems of the state penitentiary provided the Republican regime in Jackson with its most difficult challenge. When the Republicans came to power, responsibility for the prison was in the hands of merchant-planter Edmund Richardson, who had secured a three-year lease to the institution in 1868. Most of the 194 convicts under Richardson's control were laboring on his plantations in the Delta; the others were employed in the penitentiary itself, producing goods in competition with Jackson artisans. Not only did Richardson receive free labor under the lease, he also received an annual appropriation of $18,000 for the maintenance of the penitentiary facilities.[1] As on other matters during the feverish early days of

1. Report of committee to investigate conditions in penitentiary, June 23, 1870, in Governors' Correspondence, Vol. 72, hereinafter cited as penitentiary conditions report, 1870; Jackson *Weekly Pilot*, May 15, 1870; Vicksburg *Times and Republican*, May 12, 1872.

Republican rule, Governor Alcorn sent a message to the legislature regarding the convict lease system; in it he called for the immediate end of the arrangement, despite the expense to the state that would be incurred in returning the prisoners to public control. "The utilitarian view of the question," the governor told the legislature, "should be made subordinate to the moral considerations entering into the reformation of criminals and the punishment of crime." Alcorn also expressed his outrage at the inhumane treatment of prisoners under the lease system. "The shocking spectacle of a group of men followed by keepers with loaded rifles, ready to shoot them as though they were dogs, lowers that sentiment of well ordered society which surrounds human life with sanctity."[2]

The "utilitarian view" of convict leasing, however, prevailed in the legislature, and even Alcorn soon lost his zeal for changing the system. Faced with heavy, immediate expenses for other public services, to be financed from a virtually empty treasury, Republican lawmakers permitted Richardson to retain control of the convicts until his lease expired in late 1871. For the state to resume the responsibility for the prisoners without gravely overcrowding the penitentiary would have required the expensive construction of new buildings—a burden the Republican regime was not prepared to undertake at the time.[3] When some legislators grumbled about Richardson's ties to the old regime, carpetbag editor Edward Stafford of the Jackson *Pilot* reminded his Republican associates that the financial stakes in the matter were too important to quibble about the contractor's politics. "We don't care a rye straw who are the lessees of the Penitentiary," Stafford callously declared, as long as they "relieve the State of the burdens of forty or fifty thousand dollars a year, and take control of the institution, make the necessary improvements, put in machinery, and manage the labor so that it shall not come in contact with honest labor outside."[4]

The decision to continue the lease with Richardson, despite his political conservatism, hinged on the report of a biracial committee Alcorn had appointed to investigate conditions among the convicts. This report, the result of an apparently thorough study, awarded

2. *Senate Journal* [1870], Appendix, 58.
3. *House Journal*, 1872, p. 112; penitentiary conditions report, 1870.
4. Jackson *Weekly Pilot*, July 9, 1870.

high marks to Richardson for his humane treatment of the prisoners, both on his plantations and in the penitentiary at Jackson. Only six convicts had died during the preceding year, which to the committee was a remarkably low figure in view of the wretched condition of most of the convicts before Richardson received them. Confidential interviews with each prisoner on Richardson's Delta plantations convinced the committee that the convicts strongly preferred labor in the cotton fields to incarceration in the cramped quarters of the state penitentiary. They concluded that the interest of the state and the prisoners would be better served by continuing Richardson's lease.[5]

Then, in 1871 the impending expiration of the Richardson lease produced a flurry of activity at the capital. Representatives of interested groups and individuals buttonholed legislators in an attempt to secure the lucrative prison concession. Other lobbyists, acting for town artisans and mechanics' associations, insisted that the legislature develop a convict work system that would avoid competition with "manufacturers." Still others, thinking of the vast internal improvements planned for the state, argued that the prisoners should be employed, under state supervision, on "public works." A few urged that the inmates be kept in the penitentiary and taught a trade that would be useful to them after their release.[6]

The confusion gave the incumbent Richardson the advantage over his rivals. He reportedly ensured the success of his lobbying campaign with an outlay of some $20,000 to buy the support of key legislators. The result was a "monstrous" bill, "an immense fraud," as a Republican editor labeled it, which, if approved by the governor, would provide Richardson with a concession of major proportions. The old contract paled in contrast to the new bill which gave Richardson a fifteen-year lease on the penitentiary and its inmates, who now numbered 240 and were increasing as the effectiveness of law enforcement improved and as more crimes were classified as felonies. Far from paying the state for the convicts' labor, Richardson would immediately receive $120,000 from the government to construct new prison walls and facilities and

5. Penitentiary conditions report, 1870.
6. Jackson *Pilot*, April 2, 4, 12, 20, 23, 28, May 6, June 2, 1871; Jackson *Weekly Clarion*, April 13, 1871.

purchase machinery to produce goods, and he would be granted $18,000 annually to feed and clothe the prisoners. One critic calculated that "if properly handled" Richardson could realize an annual profit of $67,500 from the lease.[7]

Since the bill passed at the end of the legislative session, Governor Alcorn conveniently permitted it to lapse without his signature.[8] Powers was in the governor's chair when the Richardson bill was revived during the next session of the legislature, and he immediately calmed the fears of those who believed that the combination of a carpetbag governor and a Republican legislature would bring ruin to the state. On the grounds that the measure illegally absolved the state of its responsibility for the administration of justice and made "extravagant demands upon the public treasury," Powers vetoed the Richardson bill. In his veto message, he also denounced the whole principle of convict leasing as "wanting in humanity" and declared that he would develop a plan to return the prisoners to the penitentiary.[9]

Meanwhile, as arranged by Alcorn during the closing days of his administration, the prisoners continued under the control of lessees. Powers permitted Richardson to retain temporary use of the inmates and the industrial equipment in the prison itself, but he terminated the merchant-planter's lease on the convicts outside of the penitentiary walls. The governor leased these convicts to Confederate hero and former Ku Klux Klan leader Nathan Bedford Forrest for work on the construction of his Selma, Marion, and Memphis Railroad. Despite the questionable character of this arrangement in view of Forrest's background, which also included the occupation of slave trader, Powers actually believed he was acting in the best interest of both the prisoners and the state. Since the 1870 penitentiary report, conditions among the plantation convicts had deteriorated sharply, and Powers in awarding these men to Forrest was convinced that their removal from the disease-in-

7. Natchez *Weekly Democrat*, May 24, 1871; Memphis *Avalanche*, May 4, 1871; Vicksburg *Times and Republican*, May 12, 1872; Jackson *Pilot*, April 23, 1871; *Senate Journal, 1872*, p. 24.

8. Natchez *Weekly Democrat*, January 31, 1872. Conservatives and a handful of Republicans in the legislature voted against the Richardson bill. Jackson *Weekly Clarion*, May 18, 1871.

9. *Senate Journal, 1872*, p. 24.

fested Delta to the more salubrious uplands to aid in railroad construction would be an act of humanity. Furthermore, Powers, an advocate of railroad development as an important key to northern-style material progress, reasoned that using convict labor would hasten the completion of the important Forrest road and thereby contribute substantially to the economic revival of the depressed northern part of the state. As a temporary expedient the contract with Forrest worked well for the prisoners, resulting in better treatment for them and a marked improvement in their health under the benevolent care of a railroad physician.[10]

Powers' permanent plan for the penitentiary, introduced early in the legislative session of 1872, called for the construction of a new prison to accommodate all of the state inmates. Powers complained that the grounds of the old penitentiary, which were wedged into the town of Jackson, were entirely too small for the necessary expansion, and he asked the legislature to authorize the purchase of five hundred acres of land north of the capital as a site for the new penitentiary. In order to save the taxpayers' money, the governor proposed that convicts be put to work on the buildings of the new prison. Those convicts who were not needed for this purpose could be "hired out for short periods, by the board of control, to labor on other public works, or elsewhere, until such time as they can be given employment within the Penitentiary walls."[11] The burden of supporting these convicts would fall on the contractor; in fact, the governor hoped that the leases would supplement prison construction funds.

The ultimate purpose of Powers' plan, as he told the legislature, was to end the baleful policy of leasing the penitentiary and its inhabitants to private contractors—a practice that worked "to corrupt public morals, degrade industry, pervert justice, and thwart the true objects of punishment." The construction of a new, enlarged prison under state control would obviate the need for this system, Powers said.

The carpetbag governor also proposed a set of "full and explicit

---

10. *House Journal, 1872*, p. 112; Nathan B. Forrest to Ridgley C. Powers, April 2, 1872, in Governors' Correspondence, Vol. 79; report of superintendent of the state penitentiary for 1872, in *Senate Journal, 1873*, Appendix, 562.

11. *Annual Message of Governor Powers, 1872*, pp. 9–11.

provisions" for the management of the penitentiary. In addition to the appointment of a superintendent for the institution, he recommended the creation of a board of three inspectors, one from each section of the state, to maintain a close supervision over penitentiary affairs. Since the vast majority of inmates were black, he asked that provision be made to employ members of the race as prison guards. Powers also called on the legislature to write into the penal law explicit prohibitions against "the cropping of the hair of female convicts" and using corporal punishment on inmates of either sex (although stocks might still be employed in extreme cases). Finally, reflecting his often-expressed belief that the main purpose of imprisonment was to reform the malefactor, he recommended that a special effort be made to teach inmates a skill and to give them moral training.[12]

After a delay instigated by the vigorous opposition of Richardson and his allies in the legislature, the 1872 assembly enacted Powers' plan for the penitentiary.[13] The governor immediately selected the three-member board of inspectors, choosing a carpetbagger, a Negro, and a scalawag, to represent the three elements in the Republican party. Pending the construction of the new prison, the board, with the governor's approval, leased for three years those convicts who were not working on the penitentiary plus the old facility's machinery to a company headed by W. P. Dunnavant and William M. Forrest, son of the Confederate hero. Instead of the state compensating the lessees, as it had Richardson, under the terms of the new lease the contractors agreed not only to bear the expense of the prison but also to pay the state $8,000 annually for the inmates' labor and $666 monthly for the use of the penitentiary machinery. Unlike the usual leasing arrangement, the state retained sole responsibility for guarding and disciplining the convicts.[14]

The governor's clever plan for ending the convict leasing system

12. *Ibid.*; Vicksburg *Times and Republican*, May 12, 1872, April 22, 1873; *Senate Journal, 1872*, p. 24; *Appleton's Annual Cyclopaedia*, 1872, p. 545; report of superintendent of the state penitentiary for 1872, in *Senate Journal, 1873*, Appendix, 561, 563–64.

13. Vicksburg *Times and Republican*, May 12, 1872; *Laws of Mississippi, 1872*, pp. 67–82.

14. Contract between board of inspectors of the state penitentiary and W. P. Dunnavant and Company, May 6, 1872, in *Senate Journal, 1873*, Appendix, 604–606.

soon went astray. Although the state almost immediately realized a small profit from the Dunnavant contract, the arrangement did not prove remunerative for the lessees, who worked the convicts both within the prison walls and on Forrest's railroad in north Mississippi. Consequently, in January, 1873, Dunnavant and Forrest surrendered their lease, leaving Powers and his board of inspectors with the immediate task of finding some means for supporting the convicts who could not be accommodated in the congested and ramshackle prison.[15] To make matters worse, the construction of the new prison became snarled—and was ultimately abandoned by Republican authorities—when Henry Musgrove, the fastidious state auditor, arbitrarily refused to issue the warrants for the purchase of the new site, claiming that some community in the state would be delighted to donate a tract of land for the penitentiary. Despite Powers' efforts, the legislature, which from the beginning had been sharply divided on the governor's prison program, endorsed Musgrove's action.[16] As a result, with room for only one half of the convicts in the old prison and without an additional appropriation from the legislature, the Powers administration was forced to continue the lease system, this time using several lessees, including the irrepressible Edmund Richardson who employed prisoners in railroad and levee construction.[17] Dismayed by the failure of the legislature to support his program for penal reform, Governor Powers, in his last message on the subject, admitted that under the circumstances the use of convicts on such "public works" as the railroads and levees was preferable to their incarceration in the crowded prison. Furthermore, he rationalized, the system of leasing the prisoners to private contractors would provide some relief for hard-pressed taxpayers.[18]

The system of convict leasing now settled into the harsh and

15. *Appleton's Annual Cyclopaedia*, 1872, p. 548; report of board of inspectors of the state penitentiary for 1873, in *House Journal, 1874*, Appendix, 84.

16. Vicksburg *Times and Republican*, January 24, February 2, 1873; Jackson *Weekly Clarion*, February 6, 1873.

17. Vicksburg *Times and Republican*, May 24, June 4, 1873; Jackson *Weekly Clarion*, May 1, 1873; report of board of inspectors of the state penitentiary for 1873, in *House Journal, 1874*, Appendix, 84–85. Contracting for one hundred of the prisoners was Henry S. McComb of the New Orleans railroad who put his convicts to work constructing the extension of his road from Durant to Kosciusko.

18. Vicksburg *Times and Republican*, April 22, 1873.

degrading pattern usually associated with this late nineteenth-century phenomenon in the South. A legislative committee in 1874 reported an increasing number of incidents involving abuses committed against convicts by agents of the lessees.[19] The Ames administration, the last Republican one, did little to prevent this mistreatment of convicts by their keepers. The proportion of the penitentiary population under lease to private individuals during the last year of Republican rule increased after the legislature of 1875 authorized the use of convict labor on plantations as well as on public works. With a few exceptions, white Republicans and conservatives voted for this act, which in effect gave the system of convict leasing an entrenched status in the state. Black legislators, who formed a plurality in the house of representatives but not in the senate, opposed it, since almost all of the prisoners leased out to private contractors were Negroes.[20] By the end of the year, 373 of the 513 prison inmates were in the hands of lessees and completely removed from the jurisdiction of the state. The number would continue to increase under the Redeemers.[21] In addition, upon Governor Ames's recommendation the legislature authorized local boards of supervisors to employ county prisoners (*i.e.* those awaiting trial or serving short terms) on county roads and public works.[22]

The penitentiary law of 1875 also initiated the practice of subleasing prisoners. When Ames became governor in 1874, he removed Powers' board of prison inspectors and replaced them with members of his own faction. Simultaneous with the passage of the 1875 law, the Ames board, with the governor's approval, awarded the convicts to O. C. French and Charles S. Jobes. Granted without any other bids being entertained, the lease specifically gave French and Jobes the privilege of subletting the prisoners, which they immediately did at a profit to themselves. Predictably, Rich-

19. *Senate Journal, 1874*, pp. 203–205.

20. *House Journal, 1875*, pp. 304–305; *Journal of the Senate of the State of Mississippi, 1875* (Jackson, 1875), 253. Conservatives in plantation districts opposed the act of 1875 because it brought the lessees, whose labor costs were cheap, into direct competition with planters who had to meet the demands of free labor. Greenville *Weekly Times*, September 11, 1875.

21. *Annual Message of Governor Ames, 1876*, p. 17.

22. *Annual Message of Governor Adelbert Ames to the Legislature of Mississippi, Session of 1875* (Jackson, 1875), 4–5.

ardson, whose appetite for prison labor could hardly be satisfied, received the lion's share of the convicts under this arrangement. Even more revealing is the fact that carpetbagger French, a Republican floor leader in the legislature and a close associate of Ames, later admitted that he had influenced the legislature to pass the liberal penitentiary law in order to bring this scheme to fruition. Once established, the practice of subleasing took firm root in Mississippi, further removing the prisoners from the relatively benign control of state authorities.[23]

By the end of his term as governor, Ames, the epitome of the Radical Republican in the state, had succumbed to the expedient arguments of those who supported the convict lease system. Ames explained that although it had been forced on the state by the inadequacies of penitentiary facilities, the system nonetheless had relieved the public of a large expense. And the convict actually stood to gain under the lease arrangement, the governor claimed, since in working outside the penitentiary walls, he "received a much less severe punishment than the law intended he should receive when it consigned him to the narrow limits of the prison."[24]

Ames, however, did make a gesture toward returning the prisoners to the penitentiary when he attempted to establish a state-controlled cotton factory for their employment. A building was constructed for the purpose, but funds ran out before the machinery could be purchased.[25]

Republicans approached the management of the state insane asylum far more sympathetically than that of the penitentiary. Concern for the plight of the mentally sick and defective was strong not only among men of the new order but also among the old citizens. Inspired by Dorothea Dix and led by Albert Gallatin Brown, Mississippians during the late antebellum period had thrown off many of their antiquated notions regarding the care of the insane and had built an impressive asylum at Jackson. The war and the dis-

23. William Noonan, superintendent of the state penitentiary, to Travis Rhodes, August 10, 1875, in Governors' Correspondence, Vol. 98; *The Testimony in the Impeachment of Adelbert Ames, as Governor of Mississippi* (Jackson, 1877), 126–28, 155.

24. *Annual Message of Governor Ames, 1876*, p. 18.

25. *Journal of the Senate of the State of Mississippi, 1874* (Jackson, 1874), 203–205, 362; *Annual Message of Governor Ames, 1875*, pp. 4–5.

ruption that followed ended this progress for a time, although the asylum, in disrepair and crowded with patients, had remained open during this period. Nevertheless, during the institution's most difficult period, 1868–1869, only the extension of aid by the military rulers saved it from dissolution. When civil government was restored in 1870, the responsibility for the reconstruction of the insane asylum passed to Governor Alcorn and the Republican legislature.[26]

Alcorn took a keen interest in the asylum—and within ninety days of his inauguration he had assembled and sent to the legislature two reports that included recommendations for the institution's rehabilitation. In his first report he called for an emergency appropriation of $5,000 to meet the immediate needs of the asylum—a request the legislature quickly approved. Then, with the endorsement of the lawmakers, he reorganized the administration of the asylum, placing it under his general supervision.[27] Alcorn selected the able William M. Compton, a physician and erstwhile Republican editor from Holly Springs, as superintendent and charged him with the actual work of reconstruction. Although Compton continued to dabble in politics, he gained the confidence of all elements in Mississippi, and by the end of his eight-year tenure as superintendent he had become a recognized mental health leader in the South.[28]

Alcorn's second message to the legislature, based upon a hurried survey by Dr. Compton of conditions in the asylum, contained an elaborate recommendation for the institution's restoration and development. The main requirement, the governor said, was for an extensive expansion of facilities, including the construction of two new wings. As matters stood, 150 patients were crowded into accommodations that had an optimum capacity of 110. In addition, Alcorn estimated that more than 400 Mississippians needed care though they could not be admitted to the asylum because of a lack

26. An excellent account of the antebellum movement to improve care of the insane and the early history of the asylum was written by William M. Compton, the Republican superintendent of the institution. This report is found in *Senate Journal, 1871,* Appendix, 64–104.

27. Jackson *Weekly Pilot,* April 2, 1870; *Laws of Mississippi, 1870,* pp. 153–55.

28. Yazoo City *Herald,* May 12, 1876; Greenwood (Miss.) *Yazoo Valley Flag,* February 1, 1878.

of space. The trauma of war had increased the number of mentally sick people in the state, the governor reported, and because of the impoverishment of their families these individuals could no longer be cared for privately. Humanity dictated that the state quickly assume responsibility for them.[29]

Alcorn also pointed out to the legislature that blacks in freedom could be expected to augment the insane asylum's population. Believing, as did other southerners, that blacks in slavery had been virtually free of mental disorders, the governor predicted that the freedmen's "anxieties and strivings of the brain" would increase the number of insane among Negroes to a rate more nearly that of whites. To Alcorn this meant that asylum facilities should be more than doubled, to take care of anticipated needs as well as to alleviate immediate overcrowding. "The dictates of humanity and law," this scalawag governor declared, called for the state to provide the black insane with "housing and treatment in all respects equal to those provided for whites," regardless of cost.

Although the constitution of 1868 required that public funds be withheld from any institution except schools that made any distinction among the citizens, Alcorn emphatically recommended that the racial segregation of the asylum begun during military reconstruction should be continued. He explained that, "while anxious" to give "the colored people, not only their rights of the present, but whatever is possible of requital for the past, I am not the less solicitous to maintain in an operative form all the benefits of those charities to the afflicted among the whites. If a mixture of races be made a condition of participation of our public charities, no matter how you may regard the wisdom of the objection, that condition will act among the whites, to a great extent, as a virtual exclusion. We must deal with this fact as we find it." Although he was not willing to recognize the principle of segregation for the other state "charities," he asked the legislature to give the superintendent of the insane asylum "ample authority in law" to keep the races separate in that institution.

29. Alcorn's message is contained in the report of Compton for 1870, *Senate Journal, 1871*, Appendix, 100–103. A recent and enlightened act of the legislature that committed the criminally insane to the insane asylum rather than incarcerating them in the penitentiary, Alcorn indicated, would also add to the demands placed on the institution.

The legislature of 1870 again acted with alacrity to approve the governor's proposal for the asylum, except that it avoided the sensitive race issue he had raised. Manifesting a bipartisan spirit of liberality toward the mental hospital, the assembly appropriated $150,000 for extensive repairs and for two additional wings. The new facilities were designed to double the asylum's capacity, as Alcorn had recommended, and to make possible the removal of black patients from an old bowling alley on the grounds to a modern wing of the hospital. Issued in depreciated state warrants, the money appropriated by the legislature, however, proved insufficient to complete the improvements. Not until 1872, and after supplementary funds had been made available, were the new wings of the asylum finished. The hospital was then able to accommodate three hundred patients, which for a time met the admission demands placed upon it.[30]

The benevolence of the legislature, the active interest of Governors Alcorn and Powers, and Superintendent Compton's wise management of available resources allowed the mental hospital to enjoy a degree of success unknown to the other public institutions of the state during the Republican era.[31] Even the Redeemers, when they came to power in 1876, praised the asylum's Republican administration and the enlightened treatment of the patients by Dr. Compton and his staff. Redeemer Governor John M. Stone, who had been the lone conservative on the asylum's board of trustees during the early Republican period and therefore had a firsthand knowledge of the doctor's unique qualifications, retained Compton as superintendent. In 1878, however, the state senate refused to confirm his reappointment, ending the Republican party's control of the one public institution in Mississippi it had managed to hold onto.[32] Compton's dismissal was purely political, as State

30. *Ibid.*, 63; *House Journal, 1872*, Appendix, 566–67; *Senate Journal, 1873*, pp. 22, 616. The policy of issuing warrants to meet the expenses of the insane asylum, as well as those of other state functions, continued to work against improving the institution to a standard that Compton and his staff sought. However, by reducing some services, postponing the payment of salaries, and ignoring repairs, the administration managed to weather the difficulties created by the fluctuation of warrants. *House Journal, 1874*, Appendix, 22.

31. *House Journal, 1872*, Appendix, 591; *Senate Journal, 1873*, p. 22; *Annual Message of Governor Ames, 1876*, p. 19.

32. *Journal of the Senate of the State of Mississippi, 1876* (Jackson, 1876), 576–77; Yazoo City *Herald*, May 12, 1876; William McWillie to John M. Stone, January 31, 1878, in Governors' Correspondence, Vol. 115.

Senator William D. Peery, a conservative floor leader, admitted. "Dr. Compton has an almost national reputation as an able physician, and has made an efficient Superintendent," Peery explained, "but the objection to him is that he has furnished a large part of the brains and vindictive hate that has fed the Radical party since 1869, and the Senators feel that to [retain] him in a place of honor, and profit, and trust would be to warm up the old snake to bite us again in future elections."[33]

During Reconstruction the state also operated small general hospitals in Natchez and Vicksburg for the care of indigents. The hospital in Natchez, a three-story brick building with a capacity of about one hundred patients, was donated to the state by its private directors in 1858 with the unusual but promising stipulation that the facility be supported mainly by a local tax on liquor. This fulsome financial arrangement did not continue after the war, and, lacking adequate support from state or public authorities, the hospital barely survived during the first five years of Reconstruction.[34]

The Vicksburg hospital was approximately the same size as the one in Natchez and had originated as a joint state-city enterprise during the late antebellum period. Also supported by a local liquor tax, which continued to be indifferently collected after the war, the institution was managed by city authorities with rare interference from the state. The legislature, however, required that it be open to all citizens of the state. Like the Natchez hospital, the one in Vicksburg suffered from postwar neglect. The establishment of indigent hospitals by the Freedmen's Bureau in both towns temporarily provided some relief for these impoverished institutions, and in 1869 District Commander Ames extended state funds to the Vicksburg facility but not to the one in Natchez.[35]

When the Republicans assumed control the state hospitals were

33. Greenwood *Yazoo Valley Flag*, February 1, 1878. Dr. Compton died a hero's death, attending to the needs of victims of the yellow fever epidemic that devastated his hometown, Holly Springs, in October, 1878. At its next meeting the Mississippi State Medical Association, which he had helped found, adopted a tribute to Compton which praised him as one of "the very first psychologists of his day and generation" and a superintendent of a mental institution whose record "has been but rarely equaled, and never excelled." Printed tribute to Compton in Elizabeth Craig Papers, Mississippi Department of Archives and History.

34. George S. C. Hussey to James Lusk Alcorn, March 14, 1870, in Governors' Correspondence, Vol. 72.

35. E. Swift to Alcorn, March 30, 1870, *ibid.*; Jackson *Pilot*, January 26, 1871; Vicksburg *Times and Republican*, February 21, 1873.

crowded with patients, many of them old, infirm, mentally disturbed, and blind, and most of them black indigents. Officials of both hospitals reported to the new administration in Jackson that they would soon be forced to close their doors and discharge the helpless patients unless some provision for their care was made immediately. In keeping with their early concern for the unfortunates in Mississippi society, Governor Alcorn and his Republican associates in the legislature acted in 1870 to save the hospital by appropriating about ten thousand dollars for each institution and reorganizing both to ensure direct state supervision.[36] Infused with new life, the hospitals appeared on the verge of fulfilling, at least in a modest way, their purpose of administering to the medical needs of the poor in the area.

The Republican regime, however, soon hedged on its commitment and finally abandoned the charity hospitals to their fate. The lawmakers' indifference to these institutions, coupled with a dispute between the senate and the house regarding the amount to be allotted for their support, resulted in their receiving no appropriation in 1872. Governor Powers, though opposed in principle to state involvement in what he considered to be relief to the poor (traditionally a local matter), hurried to Natchez and Vicksburg to make the necessary financial arrangements to keep the hospitals open. Acting without any real authority, the carpetbag governor arranged sufficient credit to meet the patients' needs, and with an assist from the trustees, who even used personal collateral to obtain supplies for the hospitals, Powers averted a disaster. Rather than risk a future crisis of this kind, which could bring the sudden ousting of many forlorn patients, the governor in 1873 recommended to the legislature that the state sever its relations with the hospitals. He would make adequate provisions, however, for each hospital's current needs and provide funds through 1875 to phase out the state's obligation.[37] When the Redeemers came to power in 1876, a movement was launched to revive the Natchez hospital but for reasons

36. Vicksburg *Times and Republican*, February 21, 1873; *Senate Journal, 1871*, Appendix, 444.

37. E. J. Castello to Powers, April 6, 1872, in Governors' Correspondence, Vol. 79; Natchez *Weekly Democrat*, May 29, 1872; *Senate Journal, 1873*, Appendix, 683–84; *Laws of Mississippi, 1873*, pp. 127–28; *Annual Report of the State Treasurer for the Year 1875* (Jackson, 1876), 7, Statement A.

of economy the legislature refused to take a hand at this time; however, in 1884 both hospitals were reestablished as state institutions with a small amount of financial support from the legislature.[38] In essence, then, after a sputtering attempt to sustain the modest antebellum beginnings made in providing free medical treatment for the poor, the new order in Mississippi, with other priorities to fulfill and with limited means, chose to abandon the two charity hospitals at Vicksburg and Natchez.

The care and training of the blind and deaf received the careful attention of the Republicans of the 1870s. The Institution for the Blind had been established in Jackson in 1848 as a result of the impulse toward reform inspired partly by Governor Brown. When the Republicans took charge of the school in 1870 only twenty-one students were enrolled, representing perhaps one fifth of the state's blind population. The new regime made two significant operational changes but did little to improve the institution's deteriorating physical plant. First, a school in simple handicrafts was created within the institution, requiring only a small outlay of state money. Second, upon the recommendation of Governor Alcorn and in accordance with the constitution's nondiscriminatory clause, the legislature directed that the blind in the black community be admitted to the school. Nevertheless, by 1876 only five of the thirty-five students were black, and no provision had been made to accommodate Negro females. The failure of public authorities to provide funds for the transportation of blind youths to the institution prevented its full use by the poor of the state.[39]

Like the blind school, the Institution for the Deaf and Dumb had been established during the prewar period but its facilities had been destroyed by General Sherman's forces during the war. Instead of appropriating a fairly large amount of money to construct a new school, the hard-pressed conservative regime during presidential reconstruction made arrangements with the Louisiana in-

38. *Senate Journal, 1876*, p. 95. During the 1873–74 interim period both hospitals managed to survive as local public facilities, but with considerably reduced capacity. Richard A. McLemore (ed.), *A History of Mississippi* (2 vols.; Hattiesburg, 1973), II, 521, 523.

39. *Appleton's Annual Cyclopaedia*, 1870, p. 514; *Senate Journal, 1873*, p. 22; *Annual Message of Governor J. M. Stone to the Legislature of Mississippi, Session of 1877* (Jackson, 1877), 13–14.

stitution in Baton Rouge for the care and instruction of the state's deaf-mutes. In 1871 through the efforts of the Alcorn administration, a new school for the deaf was constructed in Jackson, and the students who had been sent to Louisiana were returned. Racially integrated from the beginning and endowed with training facilities, this institution reached the height of its Reconstruction development in 1872 with forty-four students in attendance. Republicans kept a close rein on the budgets of the deaf and blind schools, normally appropriating a modest sum of between ten thousand and fifteen thousand dollars annually for each one.[40] Even Mississippi conservatives had praise for the efficient and economical administration of these two institutions under Republican control.[41]

The traditional responsibility for poor relief rested with the county and town governments rather than with the state. Although the Freedmen's Bureau, which is frequently but inaccurately associated with the Republican order, provided some direct aid to the indigent, Republicans of the Reconstruction era made no change in the local system of care for paupers. The searing effects of the war, throwing large numbers of citizens upon the public for charity, seemed to require a more centralized and efficient system of relief than had existed under the old regime. But the poor laws enacted by the men of the new order were lifted almost verbatim from the code of 1857.[42]

Even so, two systems of pauper relief had emerged in Mississippi by the 1870s. Some counties and towns provided a poorhouse which normally accommodated between twenty-five and seventy-five people, including blacks in Republican counties. In other counties public authorities contracted with private citizens for pauper support.[43] The definition of the word "poor" varied with the

40. Jackson *Pilot*, June 2, 1871; *Appleton's Annual Cyclopaedia*, 1870, pp. 514–15, and 1871, p. 523; *Senate Journal, 1873*, p. 23.

41. Vicksburg *Times*, April 27, 1874; *Senate Journal, 1876*, pp. 109–110. More than in the case of the insane asylum, the Republican governors of the 1870s attempted to keep the deaf and blind institutions free of politics. Governor Alcorn even went so far as to appoint George L. Potter, a Bourbon on Reconstruction issues, to the board of trustees of the blind school.

42. *The Revised Code of the Statute Laws of the State of Mississippi* [1857] (Jackson, 1857), 210–15; *The Revised Code of the Statute Laws of the State of Mississippi, As Adopted at January Session, A. D. 1871, and Published by Authority of the Legislature* (Jackson, 1871), 427–32.

43. Jackson *Pilot*, March 31, 1871; *Hinds County Gazette*, December 18, 1872; *Senate Journal, 1872*, p. 156. Although incorporated towns were authorized to operate poor

locality, but usually only the most wretched were eligible for relief.

The practice of awarding private contracts, begun during the 1860s by the conservatives, grew into the main means of support for the forlorn poor during the Republican period. Abuses quickly developed. In some counties the sole object of private contractors, Republicans admitted, "was to make a speculation"; consequently, "the pauper list [was] constantly liable to be enlarged by those contractors who reap the benefit."[44] Governor Powers in 1872 called for an end of the contract system and the establishment in every county of a public farm for paupers, which would include an "infirmary," since most of the poor who became wards of the public were enfeebled and in need of medical attention. Those who were healthy, the governor declared, could be put to work on the poor farm or on local public works, constructing and repairing bridges. But the tightening ring of financial distress in the counties provided an excuse for indifferent legislators, whose main interests by 1872 lay with railroad matters, printing "jobs," and other perquisites of power, to reject Powers' proposal for reforming the system of care for the poor.[45]

Actually, few Mississippi Republicans wanted the state to impose standards for the care of the aged and infirm or to create programs to alleviate the plight of the poor, although the majority in the constitutional convention of 1868 had attempted to provide emergency relief for the sufferers of the winter economic crisis. Except for the care of the insane, the blind, and the deaf, which all could agree should be administered by the state, Republicans, as well as the old citizens, viewed the responsibility for social welfare as a local matter. Even if handled by county and town authorities, programs to assist the unfortunates in society were to be kept at a minimum (*i.e.* at prewar levels) and were to be purely humani-

---

· houses, few did, and the responsibility for the care of paupers thus fell almost entirely on the county boards of supervisors.

44. *Senate Journal, 1872*, pp. 156–57. Reform Republicans also complained of the "loose, reckless and extravagant manner" in which some pauper houses were managed in counties that had rejected the contract arrangement as a substitute for the traditional method of poor relief. Specifically, they claimed that purchases for the poor houses were frequently approved by the county boards of supervisors without proper justification or accountability for the transactions. Vicksburg *Times and Republican*, February 21, 1873.

45. *Senate Journal, 1872*, pp. 156–57.

tarian in form.[46] Government intervention, Republicans assumed, would neither attack the source of poverty nor correct the problems experienced by the downtrodden. The only cure for "social depravity," they insisted, was the development of "universal education in morals and mind," which would be considerably advanced by the establishment of public schools and the continued supremacy of the party of equal rights and political tolerance.[47] In 1870–1871 the hegemony of that party appeared in jeopardy as a result of rampant lawlessness in the state, highlighted by a terrorist campaign of intimidation and violence against Republicans in several counties.

46. This interpretation conflicts with that of some revisionist Reconstruction historians regarding Republican achievements in the area of social welfare and services. See, for example, Wharton, *The Negro in Mississippi*, 175; Kenneth M. Stampp, *The Era of Reconstruction, 1865–1877* (New York, 1965), 183–84; Allen W. Trelease, *Reconstruction: The Great Experiment* (New York, 1972), 137–39.

47. For this emphasis on moral training as a corrective for the ills of society, see the *Mississippi Educational Journal*, I (March, 1871), 84; I (December, 1871), 297 (quote); I (January, 1872), 353–60; I (February, 1872), 382–90.

12

The Security of the
New Order

Governor Alcorn and his Republican associates had hardly settled
into office when they were confronted with a surge of lawlessness,
cresting in 1871 with a wave of Ku Klux Klan terror in the easternmost counties. The prevalence of night-riding terrorists, the most
ominous aspect of the deterioration of law and order in Mississippi,
cannot be fully understood unless viewed in the context of the
general lawlessness that prevailed and the reasons for its existence.

Although military reconstruction had restrained crime and violence, a resurgence occurred during the last months of army control. After civil government was restored in 1870 the drift toward
lawlessness in some areas of the state became epidemic.[1] Governmental authority was especially weak in marginally Republican
counties and in communities that were overwhelmingly white and
anti-Republican but were saddled with a slate of obnoxious appointed officials. Under these conditions, in which the officers of
the law were held in disrepute (though this attitude was not universal in the white counties), the local governments were strained
and incapable of suppressing the unruly. And these were the areas
where crime and violence became rampant in 1870–1871. This
condition ultimately affected other parts of the state and prepared
the ground for the flare-up of Ku Klux Klan activity in the more
lawless counties.[2]

The weakness of local governments was not the only reason for
the sharp increase in crime in Mississippi at this time. The harsh
resumption of the economic depression in late 1870 also contributed to social unrest. As the fall cotton crop moved to the market
the price began to drop, and in December, when most of the cotton was ginned and sold, the price plummeted to fourteen cents
per pound on the New Orleans market. This was a decline of ten

1. See especially the Vicksburg *Herald*, August 29, October 1, December 9, 1868; Jackson *Weekly Clarion*, April 29, 1869; Jackson *Weekly Pilot*, April 2, 1870.
2. Vicksburg *Times*, March 22, 1870; *Senate Journal, 1871*, pp. 1214–15; Jackson *Weekly
Clarion*, April 13, 1871.

cents since 1869 and equaled the lowest price for cotton since the war. Because cotton occupied such a predominant position in the state's economy, almost all elements of society—businessmen, professionals, farmers, planters, artisans, laborers, and railroad men—suffered when the market collapsed and the agricultural depression resumed its destructive course.[3]

Furthermore, the new economic crisis struck precisely at the time when the first payment of taxes under the expanded Republican order fell due. Unable to meet the taxes, thousands of farmers and planters lost property to the sheriff's hammer. By mid-1871, 666 printed pages were required to list all of the forfeited lands held for sale by the state. Instead of the economic revival that Republicans had promised once civil government was restored under their auspices, Mississippians had again been frustrated in their efforts to recover from the postwar depression. Indeed, as many conservatives had feared from the beginning, the taxes to support the new government seemed so heavy as to preclude all hope for economic rehabilitation as long as the Republicans held power.[4]

Economic conditions continued to deteriorate in 1871, despite a slight rise in the price of cotton during the latter part of the year, and again deprivation stared Mississippians in the face. Reports of economic stagnation and social stress emanated from all areas of the state. Traveling by train through north central Mississippi, one observer was pained to see large and fertile tracts of land covered with grass.[5] A northern traveler had a similar tale of woe concerning conditions along the route of the Mississippi Central Railroad. "It was a sad sight," he reported, "to pass plantation after plantation, some of them with almost palatial residences, all of them surrounded with several out-buildings, large and small, and see the air of desolation that hung over everything. The most desirable fields upon which the human eye ever rested, whose fertility is inexhaustible, lying idle and deserted, the wild grasses taking the place of rich crops of former days, the houses tenantless, or if

---

3. Boyle, *Cotton and the New Orleans Cotton Exchange*, 181; C. Byrd to Oscar J. E. Stuart, January 22, 1871, in Dimitry Papers; *Hinds County Gazette*, October 12, 1870; Vicksburg *Times and Republican*, January 31, 1871.

4. Byrd to Stuart, January 22, 1871, in Dimitry Papers; Vicksburg *Times and Republican*, August 15, 1871.

5. Jackson *Pilot*, January 28, 1871.

occupied, by some colored family, living in a room or two, and all seemingly going rapidly into decay." He estimated, perhaps with some exaggeration, that not more than one tenth of the land was in cultivation.[6]

In the fertile Mississippi Valley, a Republican editor reported that "fences are torn down and going to decay, weeds and briars are growing up, where all those products that give life and permanence to a country should be found in abundance. Commerce and manufactories are steadily decreasing . . . and very many are reduced to absolute want."[7]

From south Mississippi, Hiram Cassedy, an influential secessionist in the crisis of 1860–1861 who would later affiliate with the Republican party, wrote in 1871: "This country is in a woeful decline in all the pursuits and means of life. Beyond doubt it is in a worse condition to day by 50 per cent than it was on the day of the surrender." The human effects of this situation were staggering, Cassedy said. Hopes had been shattered again, producing a kind of endemic demoralization that caused people to be callous of the rights of others. "It is now a mere struggle for animal existence without even the perception that in such a condition it is better not to be than to be."[8]

As the economic recession deepened, denunciation of Republican tax policies became wider and more intense. Even Governor Alcorn admitted that grass-roots complaints against inequitable assessments and burdensome taxes were a legitimate criticism of the Republican regime. Alcorn especially pointed the condemning finger at county boards of supervisors for imposing "extravagant schemes" upon the people, and he asked the legislature to put a halter on the property assessment and taxing authority of these officials.[9] "Driven by the force of surrounding circumstances," the

6. W. K. Verbeke to the editor of the Harrisburg (Pa.) *Patriot*, December 24, 1872, in M. B. Hillyard (comp.), *Letters Descriptive of the Climate, Soil and Resources of Central Mississippi and of the Country Adjacent to the New Orleans, St. Louis & Chicago Railroad* (McComb City, Miss., 1876), 11–12.

7. Vicksburg *Times and Republican*, January 18, 1872.

8. Hiram Cassedy to Stuart, August 23, 1871, in Stuart Papers. For other descriptions of the deplorable state of affairs at this time, see *Southern Field and Factory: A Monthly Magazine Devoted to Agriculture, Horticulture, Manufactures, and Mechanic Arts*, I (March, 1871), 115–16; II (March, 1872), 95, hereinafter cited as *Southern Field and Factory*; and the Vicksburg *Times and Republican*, January 11, April 25, 1872.

9. Jackson *Weekly Clarion*, January 19, 26, 1871; *Senate Journal, 1871*, pp. 419–22.

legislature of 1871 passed an act designed to correct errors in the assessment and valuation of property. But it declined to reform the tax law of 1870 or check the abuses of local "Shylocks who are employing themselves in the art of converting the sweat and blood of the toiling masses into greenbacks and 'Certificates of Indebtedness' for their own enrichment," as the Jackson *Clarion* described these officials. George W. Harper compared the tax measures of the Republicans and their indifference toward reform "at a time of the most wide-spread impoverishment" ever known in the state with the British Parliament's arbitrary taxation of Americans before the Revolution. Based on reports of casual comments by Hinds County carpetbaggers, Harper claimed that the real purpose of the Republican tax program was to bring property "to the Sheriff's block" in order to punish political opponents.[10]

Barksdale of the *Clarion* echoed this sentiment, declaring that the confiscatory taxation policies of the carpetbaggers gratified their twin passions for political gain and vengeance against former rebels. He warned the "spoliators" that all classes, including black tenants, would suffer as a result of their narrow and vindictive legislation, since agriculture was the sole basis for the general welfare of the state.[11]

When the legislature of 1871 failed to respond to pleas for tax relief, a group of "tax-payers" petitioned the state supreme court for an injunction against the collection of "illegal taxes" by local officials. Claiming that the "intrinsically wicked features" of the 1870 law had been perverted by local officers "into a worse engine of fraud and tyranny than was designed by its authors," these petitioners argued that the courts had traditionally intervened to protect citizens from the abuses and corruption of tax collectors. The Alcorn-appointed court refused to act, however, though Justice Horatio F. Simrall issued a dissenting opinion chastising the two-member majority for ignoring the courts' historical responsibility in such matters.[12]

Conservative charges against tax extortions by the Republican "ring of plunderers" continued throughout Reconstruction, the in-

10. Jackson *Weekly Clarion*, January 26, 1871; *Hinds County Gazette*, May 17, November 29, 1871.
11. Jackson *Weekly Clarion*, February 24, 1871.
12. *Ibid.*, May 25, 1871.

tensity varying in proportion to the degree of economic distress on the land. In 1871, and again in 1874–1875, when agricultural conditions were particularly severe, the volume of denunciation in the press and on the platform became overwhelming. Under these circumstances, even some Republicans joined in the criticism of the tax system and called for rigorous reforms, only to retreat when conditions improved and when their conservative associates in tax reform appeared more interested in making political capital than in tackling the intricacies of public finance. Most conservative opposition to Republican tax policies remained political, and only a few spokesmen—and these of the Bourbon or extreme conservative persuasion—called for the nonpayment of "illegal taxes" or a more radical form of resistance. Nevertheless, the venom that characterized the denunciation of the "carpetbag malignants" and their tax program assumed a threatening meaning in the minds of dispossessed whites, and combined with the latent racial prejudices of the white masses, it triggered a violent response—or, at least an acceptance of the legitimacy of violence—among many yeomen against local Republicans and their black "minions." The barrage of extreme anti-Radical propaganda, which was only partly believed by the conservative leadership, convinced many whites of the actual existence of an evil conspiracy to plunder the land, rob them of their fundamental rights, and defile the purity of the white race. They believed that with the instrument of government in the hands of Radical adventurers their only recourse was through violence and intimidation.

The force of this provocative influence, however, was weak in the predominantly black and planting districts, the traditional center of power in Mississippi. In these areas dominant conservatives had compelling economic reasons for shunning extreme political tactics and for keeping the lid tight on local racial prejudices. Here, the difficulty of securing and maintaining black labor stability clearly overrode any inclination the whites in these districts felt to overthrow Republican rule and reduce Negroes to political impotency through violence and intimidation.

As before, whites in the plantation counties found the main source of their economic troubles in the failure of the new labor system. But in 1870–1872 the criticism had a different ring. Instead of attacking the Negro's presumed tendencies toward idleness or even his participation in politics, which was now viewed as a fact of life and which, many believed, could be considered separately from purely economic matters, planters directed their criticism at the stultifying sharecrop arrangement for working the land. C. M. Vaiden, a prominent planter, agricultural reformer, and erstwhile conservative politician of Carroll County, in calling for an end to the sharecrop system and a return to the practice of paying wages to laborers, absolved blacks of the blame for bringing on the current economic crisis and instead pointed a condemning finger at the planter class. Lacking confidence in the future after the war, planters, he said, had adopted the sharecrop system as an expedient, never realizing that it would assume a degree of permanence, with disastrous results. To Vaiden, it was clear that despite the money pinch the wage system would work for those planters who operated efficiently, as the experience with wage labor had proven even during the poor crop year of 1870.[13]

Other farm leaders echoed these sentiments and some, in addition, sharply criticized local merchants for their insistence on cotton—and more cotton—to satisfy debts under the crop lien arrangement. Appeals for the reform of the agricultural system that had developed since the war were heard everywhere. *Southern Field and Factory*, a monthly of the New South genre that began publication in Jackson in January, 1871, filled its columns with admonitions for planters and farmers to return to the wage system, seek repeal of the crop lien law protecting merchants, diversify their crops, practice economical and scientific farming methods, and, where black labor was unavailable, send overseas for immigrants. Some farm spokesmen even suggested that large estates should be divided, voluntarily of course, and sold cheaply to immigrants and blacks.[14] A group of prominent businessmen, planters, and politicians of both parties who had earlier organized as the Planters, Manufacturers, and Merchants' Association, met in December, 1870, and affirmed these principles, including a resolution "that inasmuch as there are many persons in our State who from

13. *Southern Field and Factory*, I (April, 1871), 36.
14. *Ibid.*, I (January, 1871), 2, 76; I (March, 1871), 97–98, 115; I (April, 1871), 187, 193; I (May, 1871), 236–37; Jackson *Weekly Clarion*, January 26, 1871.

.their former condition of servitude are without lands, that we recommend the division of large tracts of land into small tracts of forty or eighty acres, and the sale of the same upon the most favorable terms to the colored people that they may soon become better citizens, and have more interest in the welfare of the State." They also called on planters to adopt "a higher standard of integrity and good faith" in future labor contracts with blacks.[15]

Although many planters ignored the appeals for agricultural change and a more equitable opportunity for blacks in the economic life of the state, a general policy seems to have prevailed in the plantation counties to conciliate Negroes in order to achieve maximum labor stability. The demand for labor in this area was now too great for planters to be narrowly guided by the prejudices and practices of the past in their relations with blacks.[16]

Whites in the plantation counties were motivated to adopt this new policy by another and more ominous consideration as well. In counties with an overwhelming black population, whites had come to realize that a failure to satisfy black aspirations during a time of deprivation and rising lawlessness, combined with the unsettling presence of the Ku Klux Klan in the eastern counties and adjacent states, could quickly bring serious racial disorders. In any such confrontations, most whites expected to suffer a horrible fate at the hands of enraged blacks before military forces could be dispatched to restore order. In their view, all reasonable steps should be taken to minimize the threat of social chaos; certainly racial agitation should be discountenanced during times of stress, though blacks and whites might not always agree on what constituted agitation. Racial turmoil had been a major concern of conservatives during the political crisis of 1868. Then, in late 1869 the William T. Combash "insurrection" in Sunflower County, followed by reports of Negro flare-ups in other black counties, brought home to whites in the plantation districts the fearful consequences of social unrest and heightened their interest in racial conciliation. The assumption of political power by local Republicans also motivated planters in

15. The minutes and resolutions of this convention may be found in the Jackson *Pilot*, January 26, 27, 1871.
16. *Southern Field and Factory*, II (March, 1872), 95, 97–98; Greenwood (Miss.) *Times*, July 5, 1873.

these counties to seek a modus vivendi with blacks as a possible means of avoiding the excesses of Radical rule. At any rate, whites in the plantation counties realized that they could ill afford to alienate the black majority or their leaders. As a result concessions were made to Negro laborers that, despite the vicissitudes of the agricultural economy, contributed to a reduction in racial tension in most of the predominantly black counties.[17]

Nevertheless, the black counties did not entirely escape the general lawlessness that pervaded the state in 1870–1871. Faced with a struggle to make ends meet, a disquieting number of Mississippians of both races and in all sections of the state turned to theft to satisfy their needs or desires. Never completely checked by military reconstruction, a wave of horse stealing, cattle rustling, moonlight butchering of hogs, cotton pilfering, and petty thievery of all kinds swept the state. A rash of incendiary attacks accompanied this descent into lawlessness; in one such attack, unrelated to politics, Governor Alcorn himself lost property amounting to more than seventy thousand dollars.[18] But the most glaring form of lawlessness was the deadly violence, both political and nonpolitical, that flared in 1870–1871 and shook the Republican order to its roots.

Since antebellum days Mississippians had been uncommonly violence prone. The irritations and frustrations of postwar life, which were probably more directly related to the everyday difficulties of eking out a living than to political setbacks, accentuated this propensity. The quick resort to the pistol or the bowie knife was curbed somewhat by the military rulers, but with the restoration of civil government and the strains placed on individual behavior by

17. Beulah *Bolivar Times*, August 27, 1870; Greenville *Weekly Times*, September 12, 26, 1874; Vicksburg *Vicksburger*, August 7, 1874, quoting the Port Gibson *Standard*; Jackson *Weekly Pilot*, January 29, February 12, 1870; entry for November 11, 1869, in Agnew Diary. William H. Lynch, a Natchez black leader, wrote Alcorn in 1871: "Never do I remember a time when a better feeling existed than now exists among all classes in my county." William Lynch to James Lusk Alcorn, 1871, in Governors' Correspondence, Vol. 73.

18. Evidence of the increase in all kinds of criminal activity is extensive. See the following: Vicksburg *Times*, March 22, 1870; *Senate Journal, 1871*, p. 1213; *Hinds County Gazette*, November 9, 16, 1870; Jackson *Weekly Pilot*, October 8, November 12, 1870; Jackson *Pilot*, March 19, April 8, 1871; E. G. Robinson to Stuart, October 2, 1870, in Dimitry Papers; Robert Somers, *The Southern States Since the War 1870–71* (1871; Tuscaloosa, 1965), 249; Thomas B. Carroll, *Historical Sketches of Oktibbeha County (Mississippi)* (Gulfport, 1931), 140–41.

the hard times, a full revival of the baleful practice occurred. The old habit of carrying concealed weapons became fashionable again. Governor Alcorn claimed at the apogee of Klan activity in the eastern counties that this deadly custom was a greater source of violence than the white terror societies. "The suppression of the pistol and knife," he told the legislature, "will do as much in Mississippi as the suppression of the sword did in England, for asserting the sanctity of human life." Contributing also to the increase in violent crimes was the proliferation of dramshops, "those nurseries of crime," as Alcorn called them, which served a strong, on-tap brew to those who sought a seemingly easy way to forget their postwar troubles.[19]

Whatever the stimulus to violence, quarrels between neighbors over matters that would appear insignificant to a later generation often erupted into bloodbaths that were not always satisfied by a single confrontation. Few condoned such violence, but many accepted it as an unpleasant fact of life, and some, forgetting its prewar origins, claimed that the state would continue to be plagued by such fury as long as it suffered from Radical rule.[20]

Others knew better, and Republicans, especially transplanted northerners, were shocked. "The heart is sickened and pained with the frequency of life taken suddenly and by violence," carpetbagger Jonathan Tarbell lamented. "Two neighbors, life-long friends, perhaps members of the same church, have a slight difference; high words pass; instead of giving reason sway, or referring the subject to the courts, or to friends, one rushes for his pistol or shot gun with which he violates one of the most direct and peremptory commandments, 'thou shalt not kill.' . . . It is unchristian, barbarous and a stain upon society."[21] Writing soon after he became governor, northern war hero Powers was appalled by the sight of numerous "belted knights of spurious courage who are daily seen in public places, ready on slight provocations, under the inspiration of evil spirits, to display implements of war."[22]

The most brutal episode of nonracial violence during this time

19. *Senate Journal, 1871*, pp. 1213–14. See also *Annual Message of Governor Powers, 1872*, p. 3, and *Senate Journal, 1873*, I, 10.
20. See, for example, the Jackson *Weekly Pilot*, April 2, 1870, and the *Hinds County Gazette*, May 17, 1871.
21. As reported in the *Hinds County Gazette*, June 16, 1869.
22. *Annual Message of Governor Powers, 1872*, p. 3.

occurred at Winona in late 1870. At a ladies' concert A. J. Brantley, the unpopular conservative mayor of the town, was assassinated by William and Henry Ringer and this was quickly followed by the fatal shooting of a Brantley relative in the streets of Winona. When Sheriff Moses H. Tuttle, a former colonel in the Union army, refused to pursue the murderers because of the townspeople's sympathy for the Ringers, William F. Brantley, a former Confederate brigadier general, came from Choctaw County to avenge the deaths of his kinsmen. He never made it to Winona; on the outskirts of the town the Ringers ambushed him. Still another Brantley relative, state legislator Thomas P. Conner, ventured to Winona to settle accounts with the Ringers, but he too met a violent death, which was followed by the burning of the town block where the Brantley family lived. Pro-Brantley bands from Choctaw County now threatened to march on the town, but warfare was averted when Governor Alcorn dispatched agents of his newly formed Secret Service to reestablish order. Although there was not much chance for convictions, the Secret Service secured the indictment of the Ringers for the death of Mayor Brantley. A degree of peace and legitimate authority was restored, and the town settled into the normal pattern of crime and violence that prevailed in many areas of the state.[23]

A few miles north of Winona, in Panola County, a spate of murders, violent assaults, and armed robberies occurred in 1871, culminating in a shoot-out between Sheriff Urbain Ozanne's forces and brigands under the leadership of John Murdock. Associating his lawless activities with the Ku Klux Klan's political purpose of ridding the county of Radicals, Murdock, who had had a longer experience as an outlaw than as a defender of white supremacy, gained the support of many old citizens who saw him as their champion against the "Tennessee carpetbagger" Ozanne, one of the most hated Republicans in the state. But with the support of Circuit Judge Ephraim S. Fisher, an influential member of the antebellum supreme court, Ozanne chased Murdock and his cutthroats out of the county in 1871.[24]

23. Jackson *Weekly Pilot*, October 8, November 12, 1870; *Hinds County Gazette*, November 9, 16, 1870; William A. Morest to L. M. Hall, August 27, 1870, and Hall to Alcorn, November 5, 1870, both in Governors' Correspondence, Vol. 72.

24. Jackson *Pilot*, February 15, March 19, April 14, 1871; W. C. McGowan to Adelbert Ames, September 3, 1869; and C. Rodney Taylor to O. H. Crandall, September 17, 1869,

No political motives were attached at this time to the murders of the mayor of Brookhaven, Sheriff Ansel H. Prewett of Pike County, and Republican State Senator-elect William S. Gambrell of Noxubee County.[25] Governor Alcorn reported that seventy-four state indictments for murder alone were returned in 1870, a number that did not include many unapprehended offenders. According to Alcorn's figures, whites accounted for forty-one of these homicides, blacks for thirty-three.[26]

Many Mississippi Republicans closely associated general violence in the state with the depredations of the Ku Klux Klan, and thus conservative newspapers during the height of the lawlessness chose to ignore or minimize the incidents. Conservatives reasoned that too much publicity for these violent acts would play into the hands of Republicans who sought federal intervention to sustain their political power in the South. But despite this conservative news blackout, by 1871 Republican congressmen and President Grant had enough "outrage" evidence of a political and racial character to justify launching a federal campaign against the perpetrators of terror and violence throughout the South.

The Ku Klux Klan and other secret white societies emerged from this environment of violence, disrespect for the law, material deprivation, and demoralization that accompanied the confusion of authority in the state. Few phenomena in American history have been as enshrouded in myth as the Ku Klux Klan. For decades after its fiery appearance on the southern scene, the Klan was extolled as the defender of white nobility and rights against rapacious Radical adventurers, backed by Negro votes and federal bayonets. Only since the 1930s have historians taken a more realistic view of the organization's terroristic activities. The debunking of the old myth has received the most impressive treatment in the work of Allen W. Trelease, whose specialized volume, *White Terror: The Ku Klux Klan Conspiracy and Southern Reconstruction*, appeared in 1971.

Despite many admirable qualities, however, Trelease's account

both in Governors' Correspondence, Vol. 69; Kyle, "Reconstruction in Panola County," 79–81.

25. Jackson *Pilot*, December 11, 18, 1871; John D. Moore to Alcorn, January 23, 1871, in Governors' Correspondence, Vol. 73; H. Murray Quin to William N. Whitehurst, January 10, February 5, 1871, in Whitehurst Papers. Gambrell was killed by a Negro laborer.

26. *Senate Journal, 1871*, p. 1215.

of the Ku Klux Klan in Mississippi fails to place the phenomenon in its full historical context. Based primarily on the partisan and in some cases defective testimony before the congressional investigation committee of 1871, the book, as it relates to Mississippi, mainly chronicles violent incidents perpetrated by the Klan in the eastern counties. Trelease's story is largely two dimensional, with white conservatives, whether Klansmen or not, lumped together as villains and intrepid Republicans as the heroes.[27] Furthermore, Trelease was misled (as other writers have been) by some of the testimony in the Ku Klux investigation. He erroneously concludes from the Mississippi testimony that the Republican school system, specifically Negro education, was the main target of the terror societies in the state. As explained in Chapter 10, herein, this was not the case. To be sure, racial hostility and political alienation provided the raison d'etre for the white terror movement, but its presence in Mississippi was more complex and more limited in relation to the general lawlessness in the state than Trelease has judged.

Even though the Klan saw the light of day in Mississippi during the exciting political contest of 1868, it was not very significant until the restoration of civil government in 1870. At first it affected almost exclusively a tier of counties on the Alabama border, from Lauderdale (Meridian) to Tishomingo (Corinth); at its zenith in 1871 the Ku Klux reached into north central Mississippi. Although Nathan Bedford Forrest organized dens in 1868 along the route of his proposed railroad in north Mississippi, the Klan was largely dormant in the area until the convulsion of 1871. Further west and south, the resistance of both planters and local Republican officials prevented the penetration of the secret order into the fertile and overwhelmingly black counties. Ku Klux operations in Panola and Attala counties proved to be the closest that the conspiracy came to the Republican strongholds in the west. In the south, the Klan threatened the right flank of the plantation counties with the establishment of dens in Amite County.[28]

27. See especially Chap. XVIII in Trelease's *White Terror*.
28. *Ku Klux Klan Report, Mississippi*, I, 73, 583, 586; Jackson *Pilot*, September 2, December 4, 26, 1871; McGowan to Ames, September 3, 1869, in Governors' Correspondence, Vol. 69; anonymous agent to Hall, July 30, 1870, in Governors' Correspondence, Vol. 72.

Piney woods whites of southern Mississippi—along a belt of sparsely populated wilderness extending from the Gulf Coast to as far as one hundred miles into the interior—were never really affected by the terror movement. Removed from the mainstream of Mississippi and southern developments, the folk of the pine barrens seemed reasonably well satisfied with their homegrown and appointed corps of Republican officials, who served until after the local elections of late 1871. One of these officers, Circuit Judge William M. Hancock, who for a time was chairman of the state Republican executive committee, became a legend in the southeastern counties for his intrepid activities against wrongdoers and his even-handed administration of justice. To ensure respect for Republican authority, Hancock frequently presided over his court with a derringer in his pocket and dared the obstreperous to defy him. Nevertheless, except for Republicans like Hancock, the support for black rights in the overwhelmingly white counties of the south was no greater than in those areas seething with Klan activities. But, since there was obviously no threat of black domination and outside Republican interference was minimal, conservatives of the piney woods had no compelling need to employ terror tactics against blacks and their white allies.[29]

From beginning to end, the center of Ku Klux operations in the state was in the east. Bordering on Alabama, except for turbulent Winston County, the Klan-infested area was the scene of a plethora of Klan depredations which included threats, whippings, murders, and the destruction of property, directed mainly against black Republicans. Local Klansmen were frequently aided and abetted by border ruffians from Alabama who had become masters in fear tactics at the expense of blacks in their own communities. Although the overriding purposes of the Klan in east Mississippi, as well as in other parts of the South, were political and racial, the terror

29. Jackson *Weekly Pilot*, June 11, 1870; Legrand W. Perce to Benjamin F. Butler, December 23, 1869, in Fourteenth Amendment Relief Papers, Mississippi; William H. Hardy, "Recollections of Reconstruction in East and Southeast Mississippi," *Publications of the Mississippi Historical Society*, IV (1901), 122–23. The moderating influence of the historian John F. H. Claiborne, who lived at Bay St. Louis and filled the columns of seacoast newspapers with admonitions for people to accept the new order of things, also contributed to the region's opposition to the Klan. Ames to "Mr. Casey," July 19, 1873, in Claiborne Papers, University of North Carolina Library.

phenomenon also had an economic dimension. The hard times of late 1870 and 1871 contributed by exacerbating racial hostility among the deprived white yeomen of the area. According to the reliable Lieutenant Governor Powers, who owned several plantations in the east, and other observers, in addition to their political objective white terrorists sought to restrict the labor competition of local blacks.[30] A fertile strip of plantation lands, worked primarily by blacks, existed adjacent to predominantly yeoman white communities in all of the eastern counties. The planters' efforts to secure more black tenants for the labor-starved plantations worked at cross purposes to hard-pressed yeoman attempts to hold down competition and regain their livelihood. However, deprived whites of the border country did not blame the planters for their troubles; instead, they directed their wrath at blacks who were being courted for their labor and who were receiving the lion's share of available wages. The crisis of terror, not only in the east but in the other regions of the state where the Klan rode, occurred precisely at the time when economic distress was again prevalent in Mississippi.

Most eastern yeomen never joined the Klan; however, many of them gave either open encouragement or watched in silent approval when masked men forayed into their communities. Whatever their opinion of Ku Klux tactics, they refused to cooperate with local Republican officials in their efforts to suppress the terrorists.

On the other hand eastern planters, as those in the west, tried generally and with varying degrees of enthusiasm and success to check the onslaught of terror lest their labor system suffer. But unlike their western counterparts, they were not always able to restrain the violent forces around them, and when the Klan moved into their communities they were forced to wait out the storm.

In two Klan counties, Winston and Lauderdale, where the planter class was insignificant and Republican control was most precarious, yeoman passions went virtually unrestrained. These also were counties where the economic motive most clearly merged with the political one to inspire Klan violence. Here Ku Kluxers kept both

30. Testimony of Powers, *Ku Klux Klan Report, Mississippi*, I, 590; Jackson *Weekly Pilot*, November 19, 1870; Jackson *Pilot*, September 2, 1871.

black and white Republicans in a constant state of fear in 1870 and 1871, whereas their activities in the other eastern counties, though a cause of great concern, were sporadic, clandestine, and fraught with some peril for the terrorists. There is evidence to suggest that some of the counties receiving Ku Klux visits did not develop their own Klansmen but depended for their terror on forays from dens in Winston County or across the Alabama line.[31] Ku Klux societies arose in an irregular fashion with very little supervision from above, although dens frequently cooperated with each other.

Many of the Klansmen were so wretched that even such Republican stalwarts in east Mississippi as Sheriff William W. Chisolm of Kemper County confused them with the common criminals who had long plagued the border country.[32] Probably a majority of the guerrillas were young men, a significant number of whom had not served in the army during the war, either because of youth or for personal reasons. Now, under the cover of darkness and secret oaths, they sought to prove their manhood. A Republican editor bore witness to the lowly and disreputable character of the night riders when he described a group of Winston County Klansmen who appeared before the federal court at Oxford. "All who saw them," he wrote, "agreed that there never appeared, in a courthouse or elsewhere, a harder looking set of crabs than those men from Winston County. 'Cut-throat' spoke out from the faces of two-thirds of them, and one gentleman, a former Confederate officer, remarked when they came in, that he knew most of them, and that during the war he had chased them, and arrested some of them as 'mossbacks,' deserters and bushwhackers."[33] A Republican of Union County reported that the Klansmen in his area were deserters who had returned after the war and were now marauding under the popular shield of antiradicalism. From Tishomingo County scalawag J. M. Patrick, who had been threatened with violence by the Ku Klux Klan, said that the Klansmen in his county numbered

31. Testimony of Powers, *Ku Klux Klan Report, Mississippi,* I, 583–90; Jackson *Pilot,* September 2, 1871; A. J. McHenry to Alcorn, January 5, 1871, Henry B. Whitfield to Alcorn, April 6, 1871, W. W. Chisolm to Alcorn, October 4, 1871, all in Governors' Correspondence, Vol. 74.

32. Chisolm to Alcorn, October 4, 1871, in Governors' Correspondence, Vol. 74.

33. Jackson *Pilot,* August 1, 1871. "Moss-backs" were southerners who went into hiding during the war to avoid conscription into the Confederate army.

only about sixteen or eighteen men and did not have "one respectable gentleman among them."[34] Even the night riders who came looking for "Old Osawatomie" Flournoy in 1871 were reportedly outlaws who had been stealing and marauding in the county since the end of the war.[35]

Nevertheless, the dregs of Mississippi society had no monopoly on Klan membership. The sons of respected citizens affiliated with the society, and some former Confederate officers joined and led Ku Klux units on their forays. Prominent Mississippians, however, seem to have shunned membership in the terror organizations. In addition to Forrest, whose work as an organizer of dens in northern Mississippi was significant, there is evidence that only one other prominent individual of the old order belonged to the Klan. This was Samuel J. Gholson, a former United States congressman, Confederate brigadier general, and speaker of the state house of representatives, who reputedly served as chief of the Monroe County Klan in 1870–1871. More significant than the number of respectable men who rode with the terrorists was the encouragement and rationalization frequently given to Klan activities by conservative newspapers and influential community leaders. When the Meridian *Gazette* and the *Mercury*, in the hotbed of Ku Klux violence, were not pronouncing Klan threats a hoax, they were justifying the need for some such extralegal association to protect the rights of the people against Republican misrule. At the height of the terror, and soon after the bloody Meridian riot of 1871, these newspapers were crying for a revival of "the spirit of '76" to withstand Radical assaults on the liberties of whites and, by implication, they were encouraging young men to rally to the ghostly order's standard.[36] "All our troubles," declared the *Gazette*, "are attributable to the revengeful and reckless adventurers sent here by the [Republican] party to persecute the white people and inflame the negroes to malicious and incendiary deeds. There is no disposition to maintain any murderous organization; we have nothing of the kind in the State."[37] The Columbus *Index*, viewed as an extreme journal

34. W. S. Cannen to Alcorn, April 27, 1871, and J. M. Patrick to Alcorn, April 5, 1871, both in Governors' Correspondence, Vol. 74.

35. Jackson *Pilot*, May 20, 1871.

36. *Ibid.*, April 6, 19, June 9, 1871.

37. As reported in the *Hinds County Gazette*, April 5, 1871.

even by many Bourbons, openly expressed the need for the violent chastisement and even lynching of some of the more obnoxious Radicals in the state. After an unsuccessful Klan attempt to put an end to Flournoy's activities in Pontotoc County, the *Index* sanctimoniously declared: "We are opposed to lawlessness, but we could have heard of the hanging of this ungodly wretch with a very great degree of fortitude, consoling ourselves with the conviction that 'his loss was Mississippi's gain.'"[38] Z. P. Landrum carried the *Index*'s message to the floor of the Mississippi house of representatives, although he refused to recognize the existence of the Ku Klux Klan. Pointing out his support for the Union in 1860–1861, Landrum told the state representatives that the Radicals' tyrannical reconstruction policies, especially the laws of 1870–1871 to suppress the rights of the southern people, were too much for him to bear. "Let a flag now be raised against the Government by anybody in behalf of the oppressed South and in vindication of their rights, and I will be the first to rally under that flag," he excitedly promised. But then he backed off from his bravado by meekly predicting that the people would soon be relieved of their yoke without a resort to arms.[39]

In Scott County, an area with close ties to the eastern part of the state, John A. Glanville temporarily discontinued the publication of the Forest *Register* in order to issue *The Ku Klux*, a weekly ostensibly designed to keep the people abreast of the Klan trials then being held in the federal courts. Glanville's declaration that his journal "looks to the interests of the masses of the nation on the broadest and most catholic basis" masked his determination to keep the spirit of the organization alive during this difficult period.[40] Close to the scene of Klan activity, the Aberdeen *Examiner* blamed the Radical Republicans for the outburst of terror and warned them of greater violence unless they abandoned their "reckless course" in governing the state. "For many months," the *Examiner* charged the Republicans, "you have devoted your satanic energies to the spoilation of an already impoverished people.

38. As reported in the Jackson *Pilot*, May 22, 1871.
39. *Hinds County Gazette*, April 19, 1871; Blanche Butler Ames (comp.), *Chronicles*, I, 251.
40. Forest (Miss.) *Ku Klux*, November 14, 1871.

The men who pay the taxes have petitioned you time and again for relief, and you sneeringly ignore their prayers. Is it your purpose to force the people into open rebellion? If not give to the press and our peacefully disposed people—a vast majority—the moral support that can alone be derived from generous, respectable legislation."[41]

The Jackson *Clarion*, a more moderate newspaper with a larger circulation than the extremist journals, simply ignored the presence of the Klan until the spring of 1871 when evidence of its operations in east Mississippi became overwhelming. Then, though calling for a halt to its violence, Barksdale justified the Klan's existence on the grounds that it had formed to protect whites from "Loyal League conspiracies" and the tyranny of corrupt Radical officials. If the legislature of 1870 had passed a law permitting the people to elect their local officials immediately instead of waiting until the fall of 1871, there would have been no Ku Klux outrages "committed upon our borders," Barksdale averred.[42] Nearby, Harper filled the columns of the *Hinds County Gazette* with railroad matters during the period of greatest Klan activity in the state. He hardly mentioned the night riders or the violence in the east except to attack Senator Ames and his Republican allies for raising the issue in Congress.[43]

A handful of conservative journals and leaders, however, chose not to ignore the presence of the Klan and the serious implications of its activities; indeed, a few meetings were held denouncing racial and political violence.[44] Some of the traditional leaders, at the height of the violence but without mentioning the Klan, were calling on whites to accept the tenets of the emerging conservative "New Departure," which recognized the Fourteenth and Fifteenth amendments as "accomplished facts" and accepted the doctrine of equal rights for all.

Most of the Ku Klux Klan's outspoken opponents were in the

41. As reported in the Jackson *Weekly Clarion*, April 6, 1871.
42. Trelease, *White Terror*, 297; Jackson *Weekly Clarion*, April 13, 1871.
43. *Hinds County Gazette*, issues of March-July, 1871. When impelled to mention the disorder in the east, Harper blamed "bad public officers" and gangs of "base and infamous negroes who have been used by very corrupt men for the worst of purposes." *Ibid.*, March 15, 1871.
44. Entry for July 21, 1870, in Agnew Diary; Jackson *Weekly Pilot*, December 3, 1870; report of a meeting in Marshall County, in Jackson *Pilot*, April 4, 1871.

western and non-Klan counties, since the conservative editors or leaders of east Mississippi rarely possessed the wisdom or the temerity to denounce the organization's depredations. William Ward of the Macon *Beacon*, however, was a notable exception. Surrounded by a sea of blacks in Noxubee County, Ward, an erstwhile poet, declared of the Klansmen:

> These midnight banditti are doing more to thwart the peace and prosperity of our country than a wise legislation of years can counteract. Our people should personally endeavor to remove these foul ulcers that now and then break out where bad blood exists, and apply remedies that will finally restore these diseased parts to healthy action. It can be done calmly and soothingly, but it must be done firmly. It should be made disreputable to aid or countenance such outrages, and the very perpetrators will then pause and look back with horror on the deeds of darkness which they have blindly committed.[45]

Although the conservatives' New Departure strategem, introduced both nationally and locally in 1871, was designed primarily to capture black and moderate votes for the Democratic party, its object also was to calm rising racial tensions and stifle Klan activities. Located almost exclusively in non-Klan districts, editors and spokesmen of the New Departure stressed that the continued abuse of blacks was politically shortsighted in a state where black voters predominated. Furthermore, they predicted, the toleration of anti-Negro activity would prolong the economic recovery of the state and lead to further social dislocation. Shunning comment on the Klan terror that was then sweeping the east lest they feed material to the "outrage mills" of the North, the New Departurists had no qualms about attacking anti-black extremists, whom they labeled "Bourbons." Inspired by the reasoned arguments of Brown and Claiborne, the leading apostles of the New Departure, the editor of the Carrollton *Conservative* captured the spirit of the movement when he wrote:

> Extremism, either way, is what the people are beginning to be most heartily tired of. We have to adapt ourselves to the altered surroundings of a new era. . . . Ideals and prejudices that found birth and were

45. As quoted in Garner, *Reconstruction in Mississippi*, 345n. For denunciations of the Klan by non-Republican, western Mississippi newspapers, see excerpts in the Jackson *Pilot*, April 18, June 6, 1871.

cherished in another day, under other circumstances, should be discarded and not permitted to stand in our way. . . . It is equally true that it is unwise to trust our affairs to the counsel and management of the impracticables, who are utterly unable to realize the requirements of the new situation.

Whether considered in the abstract, the 14th and 15th amendments are constitutional; they are in operation and practically recognized as the law of the land. It is a waste of time therefore and a catching at shadows to discuss them at all. . . . What may be obtained in the discussion of the 14th and 15th amendments and in disputing their validity now, we fail to see, unless it be to insure a more extended lease of power to corruption and wrong.

The opprobrious terms that it is the custom of some of our contemporaries to use in referring to the large class of our population who are now equally citizens with the white people, we shall eschew. We believe it right to be the friends of these people for the sake of the peace and welfare of both ourselves and them. And the disposition to be friends with them shall not end in mere words."[46]

As did other advocates of the New Departure, this editor referred to the extreme Democrats as Bourbons who "would hold out against destiny itself."

Although the New Departure movement did not persuade Klansmen to cease their depredations, it served to still white passions in areas untouched by Ku Klux bravado. But something more than weak admonitions or resolutions from west Mississippi conservatives was needed to halt the onslaught of the terror societies. Republicans realized this fact quite clearly. They understood that only force would stay the Klan's power and restore order and security in the affected communities. Republican leaders, however, could not agree on the means to be used in suppressing the lawlessness. Most moderate Republicans, including Governor Alcorn, believed that the state's law enforcement resources should be fully utilized before asking for federal intervention against the guerrillas, as demanded by Radicals like Ames.[47] Still hoping to entice a

46. As reported in the Natchez *Weekly Democrat*, October 25, 1871. For the New Departure views of Brown and Claiborne, see the Jackson *Weekly Clarion*, December 1, 1870 (Brown), and the Natchez *Weekly Democrat*, October 26, 1870 (Claiborne). See also the Natchez *Weekly Democrat*, June 7, 14, July 5, 1871, and the Vicksburg *Times and Republican*, July 14, August 20, 1871.

47. Somers, *Southern States Since the War*, 249; Jackson *Weekly Pilot*, December 3, 1870.

large number of whites into their party, Alcorn and his associates felt that a quick and timorous call for federal troops would not only alienate whites from the regime but would also be an admission of Republican weakness and inability to rule. Such an admission, which moderate Republicans refused to make in 1870–1871, would undercut the new order in the state before it had a chance to prove itself.

With moderates firmly in control of the Republican party in 1870—and before the full force of Klan attacks had occurred— most Radical Republicans went along with Alcorn's strategy. As approved by the legislature, the governor's plan provided for the outlawing of masks and disguises in public, the creation of a state investigative agency known as the Secret Service, and the organization of the militia, units of which were to be outfitted and called into service at the governor's discretion. Furthermore, a law was passed classifying as a felony the surreptitious entry of any house. At the same time the governor received the power to offer rewards not to exceed five thousand dollars for information leading to the arrest of Klansmen.[48] Although many conservatives opposed these measures, especially the creation of the Secret Service which Barksdale claimed would be used against the political opponents of the Republicans, a number of moderates grudgingly approved the acts, since they wanted lawlessness suppressed without the odious resort to federal intervention.[49]

Alcorn's hurriedly organized Secret Service consisted of Chief L. M. Hall and six agents, hardly a force to threaten the liberties of the people. This small crew infiltrated selected dens of the Klan, secured membership lists, and identified the perpetrators of a number of the unsolved violent crimes in the state. Nevertheless, few indictments resulted, since witnesses out of fear or sympathy refused to testify, and in some cases jealous local officials, piqued by the presence of Alcorn "spies," declined to cooperate in apprehending the lawbreakers. Hall and his agents therefore produced meager results. Even Republicans soon soured on the Secret Service, preferring to believe, along with conservatives, that the fifty

48. Jackson *Weekly Pilot*, March 26, August 20, 1870; *Ku Klux Klan Report, Mississippi*, II, 864–65; *Laws of Mississippi, 1870*, pp. 89–92.
49. Jackson *Weekly Clarion*, April 7, 1870; *Hinds County Gazette*, April 27, 1870.

thousand dollars appropriated for the agency had been squandered. Consequently, the legislature of 1871 permitted this modest state investigating agency to die a silent death, precisely at the time when it was most needed to aid in combating the rampaging Klan in the eastern counties.[50]

The wise use of the militia offered the best hope for suppressing the Klan and other lawless elements by internal means and without federal intervention. In fact, during the summer and fall of 1870 the Alcorn administration appeared alive to the importance of organizing the militia into an effective force for fighting the Klan, as Governor Powell Clayton had done in Arkansas. Alcorn placed Edward Stafford, who had helped organize Union forces in St. Louis in 1861, in charge of enrolling the militia. In selecting brigadier generals to command the districts, the governor divided the positions equally between carpetbaggers and scalawags. No blacks received appointments to the high command, although Alcorn appointed at least three blacks to command militia forces in plantation counties and several were granted commissions to form local units. Racial separateness was normally maintained within the units; however, there were a few racially mixed militia companies.[51] Stalwart Republicans recoiled in dismay not so much at Alcorn's failure to select blacks for the militia hierarchy but because he had excluded Radicals from it. Moreover, Stafford's enrollment (but not activation) of a large number of former Confederate soldiers, constituting one fourth of the state's militia force, appalled Radical Republicans. In some Klan-infested counties the mere selection of former rebel officers to command paper militia units was viewed by Radicals as a complete surrender by the state administration to the forces of terror.[52]

Enthusiasm for raising militia units was strongest among the blacks of the plantation counties, where a military force was least

50. Anonymous agent to Hall, July 30, 1870, Hall to Alcorn, November 5, 1870, and payroll of Secret Service, August 27, 1870, all in Governors' Correspondence, Vol. 72; Hall to Alcorn, April 7, 1871, *ibid.*, Vol. 74; Vicksburg *Times and Republican*, March 3, 1872.

51. *Laws of Mississippi, 1870*, pp. 132–43; Jackson *Weekly Pilot*, August 20, September 3, 17, 24 October 1, 1870; Natchez *Weekly Democrat*, October 12, 1870; Jackson *Pilot*, November 27, 30, 1871; *Senate Journal, 1871*, Appendix, 426.

52. Natchez *Weekly Democrat*, March 29, 1871; Jackson *Weekly Pilot*, December 24, 1870.

needed to combat Ku Klux terrorism. Although they had no weapons or compensation, since the legislature had failed to provide money for such purposes, blacks turned out several times a month to drill and receive instruction not only in martial techniques but in political affairs as well. At this time racial tensions do not appear to have been exacerbated by black martial display, since no effort was made to conceal these activities or threaten local whites. To ensure against trouble, some conservatives in the predominantly black counties appeared at the militia rallies and joined in the work of instruction. Near Natchez William T. Martin, a former Confederate major general and president of the aspiring Natchez and Jackson Railroad—which was to be financed by local railroad bond elections that needed black votes to carry—participated with black leader John R. Lynch and his Republican allies in forming the first Negro militia company in the county.[53]

Complaints soon reached Jackson, however, that the militia festivities were interfering on a large scale with the harvesting of the 1870 crop. Major General Stafford reacted vigorously to this threat to the planting interest of the state. Endorsed by Alcorn and several carpetbaggers who had extensive agricultural holdings in the plantation counties, Stafford through the columns of the Jackson *Pilot* admonished blacks to abandon the drill field for the cotton field. Harvesting the cotton crop, he told black laborers, was a "more pressing and necessary duty to yourselves and the State" than "making a little military display."[54] Stafford's admonitions, Radical Republicans' lukewarm acceptance of Alcorn's militia policy, and the legislature's refusal to appropriate money for the purchase of arms and accoutrements for military units brought the early death of the black militia movement in the western counties.

In the eastern counties where a show of force was most needed, Alcorn's militia plans never got off the ground. The main reason for this failure was neither Republican timidity nor the governor's inability to find whites who could be depended on to counter the Klan and protect blacks in their rights, though many Republicans doubted that an effective militia could be raised in the east. Alcorn

53. Natchez *Weekly Democrat*, October 5, 12, 1870.

54. Jackson *Weekly Pilot*, October 29, 1870. See also the issue for November 12, 1870, and the Natchez *Weekly Democrat*, February 1, 1871.

failed mainly because he waited until the Ku Klux had established a strong position in the area before acting. When he finally attempted to organize an eastern force, the legislature refused the necessary funds to equip and activate it.[55]

Frustrated in his efforts to combat the terror, Governor Alcorn in late 1870 announced his determination to take drastic measures against the Klan. "I will, if sustained by the Legislature," he declared, "sink the State in financial ruin" rather than see it "dragged under the heels of a terrorism which obtains a surrender of the first condition of Liberty—Law and Order."[56] When the legislature met in early 1871, Alcorn backed up his words by asking for the authority and money to raise and sustain indefinitely an elite, swift-striking cavalry regiment that would be able to meet Klan challenges wherever they might occur. The governor also requested the authority to change the venue, or place of trial, of individuals accused of felonies in cases where justice could not be obtained because of local prejudices. Such an arrangement would transfer accused Klansmen from the fear-infested east to solid Republican counties where the guilty more likely would be convicted. Alcorn would also have the affected counties pay the state rewards for information leading to the apprehension of Klansmen. In the wake of the Meridian riot in March, Alcorn even bent, though by no means all the way, to Radical demands for federal intervention and had two detachments of troops sent to east Mississippi.[57]

A strange combination of bedfellows in the legislature, however, defeated the governor's cavalry proposal. With reports of the "outrages" committed by a similar military organization in North Carolina (the militia under Colonel George W. Kirk) ringing in their

55. In late 1870 Alcorn sent Stafford into the eastern counties to organize white units and Samuel J. Ireland, a black colonel, to form Negro companies. Despite some initial success in recruiting militiamen, the units were never operational because of a lack of money. *Senate Journal, 1871*, Appendix, 424, 425; message of Governor Alcorn to the legislature, April 1, 1871, as reported in the Jackson *Weekly Clarion*, April 6, 1871. Even at the height of Klan terror, some eastern Republicans still believed that an effective militia could be raised to put down the Ku Klux Klan, and they preferred this method of restoring order to the uncertainties of federal military intervention. See Henry B. Whitfield to Alcorn, April 6, 1871, in Governors' Correspondence, Vol. 74.

56. Jackson *Weekly Pilot*, December 3, 1870.

57. Jackson *Pilot*, March 18, 1871; Jackson *Weekly Clarion*, March 23, April 6, 1871; Charles Jordan to Alcorn, March 8, 1871; and B. F. Moore to Alcorn, March 11, 1871, both in Governors' Correspondence, Vol. 73.

ears, several moderate Republican members expressed fears that such a force would be used to oppress the innocent and joined with conservative legislators in opposing the cavalry bill. But the decisive element in the defeat was the lack of support from influential Radical Republicans.[58] By this time Radicals were committed to a policy of seeking federal intervention for the suppression of the Klan, since they preferred to believe that this method offered an easy and uncomplicated, if not the only, means for restoring order and security. Radical legislators were encouraged in their opposition to Alcorn's efforts by Ames who in early 1871 used the forum of the United States Senate to attack the governor for his failure to protect Republicans in the state.[59] After this speech few Ames partisans in the legislature were willing to support any anti-Klan proposal originating with the governor, although the cavalry bill, if properly implemented, offered some hope for success against the terrorists.[60] Almost the same combination of conservatives, moderate Republicans, and Ames Radicals defeated the governor's change of venue bill, making it virtually impossible for the state courts to secure the indictment, much less the conviction, of Klansmen.[61]

Simultaneous with Alcorn's belated effort to suppress the Klan, Congress was debating a bill that would authorize extensive federal intervention to put down white night riders in the South. Mississippi's failure to curb Klan activities in the east contributed to the congressional decision to enact the measure on April 20, 1871. The two most notorious incidents of Klan outrage, which occurred near Aberdeen and at Meridian, received considerable attention in

58. Jackson *Weekly Clarion*, May 18, 1871; letter from Alcorn in the *Hinds County Gazette*, June 5, 1872; *Senate Journal, 1871*, p. 417.

59. *Congressional Globe*, 42nd Cong., 1st Sess., 194–98; and 42nd Cong., 2nd Sess., 569–71; letter from Alcorn to the New York *Tribune*, as reported in the Jackson *Weekly Clarion*, April 13, 1871; Jackson *Pilot*, April 6, 1871.

60. The example of the militia's suppression of the Arkansas Klan in 1868–69 demonstrated that southern military units, if in capable hands—which they probably would have been under Alcorn and Stafford in Mississippi—could overcome the societies of the night. For the success of the Arkansas militia, see Trelease, *White Terror*, 161–71.

61. *Hinds County Gazette*, June 5, 1872. Only in one circuit court, meeting at Corinth, were Klansmen "held to answer" by a state court for their depredations. The prosecution of six Klansmen in this court nonetheless failed to halt terrorist activities in Tishomingo County. H. Mask to Alcorn, April 19, 1871; and A. Worley Patterson to Alcorn, May 5, 1871, both in Governors' Correspondence, Vol. 74.

Congress during the debate on the so-called Ku Klux Klan bill. Near Aberdeen, Allen P. Huggins, the carpetbag chief of Monroe County, received a vicious whipping at the hands of the Klan. This act of violence provoked Benjamin F. Butler to brandish the victim's soiled shirt before a startled House of Representatives, thus instituting the popular Republican pastime of "waving the bloody shirt" and increasing congressional support for the Ku Klux Klan bill.[62]

A bloody racial riot at Meridian in March, 1871, was of much greater importance in provoking Congress to action against the Klan. The conflagration in this east Mississippi railroad center had its origins in the forays of Alabama Klansmen into Lauderdale County for the main purpose of apprehending alleged violators of labor contracts. Although most of the "respectable" whites of Meridian and the surrounding countryside viewed the Alabamians as desperadoes, nothing was done to aid local Republican officials in their efforts to check the terror. Even after the assassination of two black members of the county board of supervisors in late 1870, which was followed by reports of other attacks on blacks, prominent conservatives still refused to lift a finger to curb the border ruffians. Instead, they blamed the turbulence on the Republicans' failure to provide good government in the county.[63]

Republicans indeed had demonstrated a lack of capacity in managing county affairs and enforcing the law. The main Republican officials in Lauderdale County, Sheriff Robert J. Mosely, a timid and vacillating former Confederate officer, and Mayor William Sturges of Meridian, a carpetbagger who was referred to by his lawyer as a "man so utterly without principle, so vindictive and embittered that nothing good can come out of him," proved incapable of handling the crisis that engulfed the county in early 1871.[64]

Despite Sturges' shortcomings, blacks rallied to his support in

62. Trelease, *White Terror*, 290; Stanley F. Horn, *Invisible Empire: The Story of the Ku Klux Klan, 1866–1871* (Boston, 1939), 151.

63. John W. Fewell to Robert E. Leachman, February 27, 1871, in Governors' Correspondence, Vol. 73; Jackson *Weekly Pilot*, November 19, 1870; *Ku Klux Klan Report, Mississippi*, I, 6–7.

64. Fewell to Leachman, February 27, 1871, in Governors' Correspondence, Vol. 73. See also J. R. McLaurin to Alcorn, January 31, 1871, *ibid.*, and testimony of William C. Ford in *Ku Klux Klan Report, Mississippi*, I, 7.

a series of nightly meetings in late February and early March. Encouraged by the mayor, they paraded and shouted their defiance of the Klan in the streets of Meridian, punctuating the demonstrations with the firing of weapons. A confrontation of the races was virtually inevitable—and it soon occurred. On the night of March 4, soon after a black rally had been addressed by Negro leaders William Clopton [Dennis], J. Aaron Moore, a member of the legislature, and Warren Tyler, a fire broke out in the store of Theodore Sturges, the mayor's brother. The fire quickly consumed a city block and threatened the entire business district. The origin of the fire was unknown, but even level-headed whites suspected that it was the work of a black incendiary. An effort by the inebriated William Clopton to persuade blacks to quit the fire engines and permit the town to burn convinced the old citizens that the speeches of the black political leaders had inspired the work of arson.

The next day, Sunday, March 5, armed bands of both races began to appear in the streets. In order to satisfy whites, and thereby hoping to avert an invasion from the Alabama border, Sheriff Mosely arrested Clopton, Moore, and Tyler on vague charges of making incendiary speeches. In the case of Moore, however, white auditors were prepared to testify that he had constantly exhorted his followers to pursue a policy of harmony and peace with whites. On Monday the three black leaders were brought before William Bramlette, a justice of the peace, for arraignment.[65] With armed men very much in evidence, tension gripped the courtroom during the hearing. When Tyler objected to the testimony of James Brantley, a white man, the latter advanced on him with a walking stick. Tyler, who somehow had secured a pistol, fired at the charging Brantley. The shot missed the intended target but hit Judge

65. As was true of other racial disturbances in the state during Reconstruction, despite a fairly large body of testimony on the Meridian riot the incident's causes and many facts relating to it have been obscured by the racial passions and partisanship of the witnesses. The above account of the affray was pieced together from several sources, the most important being the reports in the Jackson *Pilot*, March 8, 1871, that were given by a "reliable" witness and by J. Aaron Moore soon after his arrival in Jackson. The testimony of William C. Ford, the prosecuting attorney in Meridian and a moderate Republican, was also of considerable use. Ford's testimony is in the *Ku Klux Klan Report, Mississippi*, I, 96–99. See also the *Senate Journal, 1871*, Appendix, 1128–81, for the testimony of witnesses before the committee of the state legislature investigating the riot. Much of the same testimony is found in the *Ku Klux Klan Report, Mississippi*, I, 6–205.

Bramlette in the head, killing him instantly. Whites quickly drew their pistols and commenced firing on the blacks. When the smoke of battle had cleared, in addition to Bramlette, two blacks lay dead and Clopton hobbled from the room with a leg wound. Other blacks, including Tyler and Moore, fled for their lives.

White vigilantes now seized control of Meridian and the surrounding countryside. Within five minutes after the courtroom melee armed whites discovered Tyler's hiding place and riddled him with bullets. Taken into protective custody by the sheriff, the wounded Clopton met his death at the hands of a lynching party during the night. Three other Negroes were also lynched before the night was out, though Moore managed to escape town and make his way through the woods to the safety of Jackson. Meanwhile, a "citizens' committee" escorted Mayor Sturges to the railroad station where he was put on a northbound train, never to be heard from again. By the time the white savagery had run its course a few days later—when federal troops arrived in Meridian at Governor Alcorn's request—perhaps as many as thirty blacks had been killed.[66] After passions had subsided, Circuit Court Clerk B. F. Moore, a Republican, attempted to place in perspective the events surrounding the violence. "The negroes have acted badly," he wrote Governor Alcorn. But far worse, "the whites have committed, & applauded outrages committed which History must hand down as only equalled by the most uncivilized of the Human Race."[67]

The Meridian riot shook the confidence of Mississippi Republicans in their ability to preserve the new order and protect the liberties of the blacks. It convinced most of them, including moderate Alcorn supporters though not the governor himself, that extensive federal intervention must soon come if the Klan contagion were to be contained and suppressed. A caucus of Republican legislators appealed over Alcorn's head for Congress to take "prompt and thorough measures to suppress outrage and violence in all parts of the State."[68] Answering this and similar pleas from other southern states, Congress in April passed and President

66. B. F. Moore to Alcorn, March 11, 1871, in Governors' Correspondence, Vol. 73.
67. *Congressional Globe*, 42nd Cong., 1st Sess., 196; Jackson *Pilot*, March 10, 1871.
68. *U.S. Statutes at Large*, XVII, 13–15.

Grant signed the Ku Klux Klan bill. This measure at last provided Mississippi Republicans with the instrument of federal authority necessary to end the terror in the eastern counties and provide security for their regime.

The Ku Klux Klan law of 1871 extended federal jurisdiction to incidents of Klan violence and intimidation. Briefly, the act empowered the president to use troops to assist the federal courts in bringing Klansmen to justice. The president was also empowered to suspend the writ of habeas corpus if necessary to destroy the Klan. (President Grant did not use this authority in Mississippi.) Significantly, in view of the reluctance of state juries to indict or convict Klansmen, the law gave United States district attorneys the authority to purge federal juries of Klan sympathizers when hearing or trying cases under the act.[69]

Mississippi conservatives were surprisingly quiet upon the passage of the Klan bill, perhaps because they knew that earlier laws to enforce the Fourteenth Amendment had not resulted in serious federal intervention in local affairs. In the hands of the federal judiciary in the state, the act of 1871 might also prove to be a nullity, since the main responsibility for its enforcement would be up to District Judge Robert A. Hill, a longtime resident of Mississippi. But when Hill and United States District Attorney G. Wiley Wells, a Holly Springs carpetbagger, announced their determination to apply the full force of the law against offenders, conservatives, both moderate and Bourbon, unleashed a barrage of invective against the "kidnap law," claiming that it was conceived by southern carpetbaggers out of "the lust of power and plunder." Specifically, they averred, the Ku Klux Klan law was designed to retain adventurers in power "by bayonet interference in disregard of the right of the people to select representatives of their own choice." Fortunately, according to the conservative version, the Radicals "in their cowardly and vindictive persecution of Southern whites under pretence of punishing Ku Kluxism" had overshot their mark. A reaction against these excesses would inevitably occur in the North and would hasten the overthrow of the Radicals in Wash-

69. Jackson *Pilot*, June 21, 1871; Jackson *Weekly Clarion*, July 13, November 2, 1871; Vicksburg *Times and Republican*, February 23, 1872.

ington along with "the carpet-bag plunderers and their aiders and abbetors to the manor born" in the South.[70]

Undaunted by such attacks, District Attorney Wells, whose jurisdiction was northern Mississippi, with the vigorous assistance of United States Marshal James H. Pierce launched a roundup of white terrorists that attracted national attention and became the model for the swift arrest and prosecution of Klansmen in other southern districts. Since the April, 1871, law could not be applied retroactively, Wells issued warrants against violators of the Enforcement Act of 1870. The Ku Klux Klan Act, however, provided the means for bringing these violators to justice. Under this act, United States troops were made available to aid in apprehending suspects, a task which had proved impossible for the handful of federal marshals and deputies in southern states under the previous laws. Unlike the procedure in South Carolina, troops in Mississippi did not actually make arrests, but went along with federal marshals and their deputies to provide support and later guarded Klansmen who awaited trial. Occasionally they were dispatched, at the request of civil officers, to trouble spots to restore confidence in the government and serve as a warning against further violence.[71]

Troop strength in Mississippi was never large during the period of enforcement. The force consisted mainly of infantry companies which lacked the swiftness and effectiveness of cavalry units in operations against terrorists. When the Ku Klux Klan law was en-

---

70. Trelease, *White Terror*, 399; Everette Swinney, "Suppressing the Ku Klux Klan: The Enforcement of the Reconstruction Amendments, 1870–1874" (Ph.D. dissertation, University of Texas, Austin, 1966), 253, 259; J. H. Pierce to Amos T. Akerman, August 21, October 12, 1871; and G. Wiley Wells to Benjamin H. Bristow, October 16, 1871, both in Source-Chronological File, Northern Mississippi, January, 1871–December, 1875, General Records of the Department of Justice, Record Group 60, National Archives, Microcopy Roll 1.

71. Swinney, "Suppressing the Klan," 258–59; Sefton, *United States Army and Reconstruction*, 262; John S. McNeily, "The Enforcement Act of 1871 and the Ku Klux Klan in Mississippi," *Publications of the Mississippi Historical Society*, IX (1906), 165. After the initial arrests of the spring and summer of 1871, a show of military strength was not usually necessary to obtain the apprehension of Klansmen. However, local federal officials insisted that the presence of troops in nearby garrisons was essential to the permanent suppression of the Klan. Pierce to Akerman, October 12, 1871; Wells to George H. Williams, July 8, 1872, in Source-Chronological File, Northern Mississippi, RG 60, NA, Microcopy Roll 1.

acted, the federal contingent in the state consisted of approximately 200 men, all of whom were infantrymen stationed at Jackson. The number was increased to 262 after the law passed and to 328 in 1872, including two units of cavalry; in addition, posts were established at Meridian, Oxford, Aberdeen, and Holly Springs. In 1873, after the terror had subsided, the War Department reduced troop strength in the state to 144, and the next year it dropped to only 45. As during military reconstruction, the old citizenry found little fault with the troops themselves, who were as unobtrusive as possible. Except when under the direction of federal marshals and their deputies, almost all of whom were carpetbaggers and the real villains in the conservative scenario, troops remained close to camp and refrained from any act that could be classified as military intervention in civil affairs.[72]

Confronted by troops, Klansmen who did not flee the state meekly surrendered to federal arresting officers and in the northern district were taken to Oxford to await arraignment before Judge Hill. The hearings, the first in the South after the passage of the Ku Klux Klan law, opened in June before a tense and crowded courtroom. In seeking indictments District Attorney Wells was ably assisted by Harvey W. Walter, a prominent conservative lawyer of north Mississippi and the Whig candidate for governor in 1859, whose services for the government were obtained through the friendly intervention of Governor Alcorn. Heading the defense for the first group of suspected terrorists were L. Q. C. Lamar, at the time a law professor in the university, and Samuel J. Gholson, a reputed Klansman.

Courtroom violence was not long in occurring. In the course of the hearing, the hot-blooded Lamar contemptuously referred to Deputy Marshal C. H. Wissler, a man with a jaded past, as an "assassin" who was unfit to be in the courtroom. The offended officer immediately threw his hand behind him, which was the customary challenge for a shoot-out. Without asking for an explanation Lamar charged Wissler with a chair, but the blow intended for the deputy struck United States Marshal Pierce on the head when he stepped between Lamar and Wissler. For a moment, some of the

72. Vicksburg *Times and Republican*, July 1, 1871; New York *Times*, September 9, 1871.

Klansmen in the room rallied to Lamar's side, but other defense attorneys quickly restrained them. Soldiers now poured into the courtroom and with the click of their guns, in preparation for an order to fire, restored peace. Lamar immediately apologized to the court for his part in the fracas, and as a result he received only a brief suspension as an attorney for the arrested Klansmen.[73] Ironically, Pierce, a native of Kentucky and a vigorous foe of the Klan, supported Lamar in his race for Congress in 1872 and opposed Republican exploitation of the Oxford incident.

Violence and disruption in the federal courtroom during the Klan trials began and ended with the Lamar-instigated disturbance. The early indictment of twenty-eight Klansmen for the murder of a local black leader had a sobering effect upon suspected terrorists and their sympathizers, although the accused men in this case, released on bond, were welcomed home to Aberdeen as returning heroes. While the iron was hot, District Attorney Wells during the summer of 1871 hurriedly hauled arrested night riders before federal grand juries in Judge Hill's court, and by September he had secured 175 indictments under the Enforcement acts. The work continued into the fall and the first half of 1872. When he ceased his anti-Klan campaign during the summer of 1872, Wells reported that he had obtained a total of 678 indictments, of which 262 had resulted in convictions. Left unsaid in his report was the fact that almost all of the convictions involved compromises out of court in which the defendants agreed to make open confessions in court or to plead nolo contendere in exchange for suspended sentences or minor fines. Only one Ku Klux Klan case in Mississippi went before a trial jury, and this resulted in a conviction.[74]

The government's policy of negotiating with indicted night riders came about because of the uncertainty of achieving a trial con-

73. The main sources of information for the courtroom incident are eye-witness accounts in the Republican Jackson *Pilot*, June 27, 29, 30, 1871, which appeared immediately after the event. See also McNeily, "The Enforcement Act," 142–43, and Murphy, *L. Q. C. Lamar*, 100–101.

74. Jackson *Pilot*, July 15, 1871; New York *Times*, September 9, 1871; Allen P. Huggins to Akerman, June 14, 28, 1871, in Source-Chronological File, Northern Mississippi, RG 60, NA, Microcopy Roll 1; *Senate Executive Documents*, 42nd Cong., 3rd Sess., No. 32, p. 11.

viction of Klansmen. Evidence in Klan cases was largely circumstantial, and alibis were easy to obtain. Juries also were unreliable, as Judge Hill observed, although the federal prosecutors had authority to fill the jury box only with individuals who favored the Ku Klux Klan legislation—a policy they followed in securing indictments but evidently hesitated to use in obtaining convictions.[75] Furthermore, the abuse that the conservative press was sure to hurl at trial proceedings discouraged federal officials from seeking the full application of the law against Klansmen. The publicity that would inevitably accompany a courtroom trial, they believed, might undermine the good effect that the arrests and indictments appeared to be having in the community. As early as July, 1871, a Republican official in the hotbed of Klan activity in the east wrote that after the Oxford hearings the terrorist movement in his county had ended. "Everything is quiet here," he wrote to Governor Alcorn. "The parties charged in the McLachlin case [a pending Klan case] are . . . absolutely crushed by the prosecution at Oxford."[76] A report in the New York *Times* in September claimed that the indictment proceedings had broken "the bar of prejudice and sympathy" that the "better classes" of the state had had with the Klansmen, and "a sentiment against the outrages is being built up among the people." At the same time a report came out of northeast Mississippi that even District Attorney Wells was treated with considerable respect when he appeared in Corinth to attend a Klan hearing.[77] Under the circumstances, Judge Hill, who more than Wells favored the lenient policy of disposing of Klan indictments, believed that an effort should be made, despite the risks involved, to cultivate "the moral influence of the right thinking men of the State," without which the enforcement program would ultimately fail. In this policy he had the support of most moderate

75. Swinney, "Suppressing the Klan," 266. In addition, lengthy trials by jury were expensive, which was an important consideration for federal officials in the state who were chronically in need of more funds to continue the work of obtaining arrests and indictments against suspected terrorists. Wells to Attorney General Williams, April 2, 1872, in Source-Chronological File, Northern Mississippi, RG 60, NA, Microcopy Roll 1.

76. C. A. Sullivan to Alcorn, June [July] 12, 1871, in Governors' Correspondence, Vol. 74.

77. New York *Times*, September 9, 1871; Corinth *News*, as reported in the Vicksburg *Times and Republican*, August 1, 1871.

Republicans, but Radicals, including Senator Ames and several federal officers in the state, complained privately of his mildness in dealing with the terrorists.[78]

Nevertheless, when Judge Hill convened the court for the southern district of Mississippi at Jackson he pressed the grand jury to investigate thoroughly all cases of violations under the Enforcement laws.[79] Already District Attorney Eugene P. Jacobson, seeking to emulate the successful example of his colleague in north Mississippi, had sent marshals and deputies, accompanied by troops, into Lauderdale and neighboring counties scouring for Klansmen. Partisanship, or more accurately, vindictiveness against the Bourbons or "rebels" of the area, partly inspired carpetbagger Jacobson in his search for violators of the Klan act. Except for Lauderdale County, terrorist activity had been light in the southern district. Still, Jacobson saw fit to send expeditions into neighboring Newton County where no Klan activity had been reported. He also ordered the arrests of the Bourbon editors of the Meridian *Mercury* and the *Gazette* in Lauderdale County. Many of those taken into custody in Lauderdale were suspected of participating in the Meridian riot of March, 1871, but the arrest of editor Alexander G. Horn of the *Mercury* followed a series of blistering editorials in which he castigated the "Reign of Terror" that Jacobson had instituted with the dispatch of his "agents of villainy" into the area. When their cases appeared before Judge Hill, both Horn and the editor of the *Gazette* were released.[80] In all, Jacobson, a congressional medal of honor recipient for heroism at Chancellorsville, secured 165 indictments, as well as the only trial conviction that occurred in the state.[81] Most of the indictments evidently ended in "confessions" before Hill and suspended sentences.

The vigorous federal campaign against Klansmen had the de-

78. Swinney, "Suppressing the Klan," 267; Wells to Attorney General Williams, April 2, 1872, in Source-Chronological File, Northern Mississippi, RG 60, NA, Microcopy Roll 1; Garner, *Reconstruction in Mississippi*, 290.

79. Jackson *Weekly Clarion*, July 20, 1871.

80. Jackson *Pilot*, July 11, 21, November 23, 1871; W. Burwell to Ridgley C. Powers, December 8, 1871, and E. D. Beattie to Powers, December 8, 1871, both in Governors' Correspondence, Vol. 79. Excerpts from the editorials of the Meridian *Mercury* may be found in the Jackson *Weekly Clarion*, July-August, 1871.

81. *Senate Executive Documents*, 42nd Cong., 3rd Sess., No. 32, pp. 34–35.

sired effect. By early 1872 a black writer from DeKalb informed the editor of the Washington *New National Era* of the terror organization's virtual demise in once turbulent east Mississippi. "It is impossible," he wrote, "to describe the feeling of consternation and alarm that the action of the court has produced among those hell-deserving wretches and their friends. They see the hand-writing on the wall, and like Belshazzar they tremble and fear."[82] Although Klan activity had ceased, this writer, like other blacks in the east, feared a revival of the terror if federal jurisdiction in such matters was weakened. At the same time District Attorney Wells was reporting to his superiors in Washington that the enforcement program in his district, which included most of the Klan country in the east, had completely routed the terrorists. "At the present time, there is hardly a person of respectability or standing in the district who will attempt to excuse this class of offenders, and matters are in a quiet and peaceable condition," Wells indicated.[83] On the other hand, Jacobson, convinced that the conservative press would continue to keep the spirit of intolerance and violence alive in the state, would admit to no such happy state of affairs in his district.[84] However, the indictments that he procured in 1871 and early 1872 ended political violence in south Mississippi until the summer of 1874 when white leagues arose in Vicksburg to challenge Republican authority. An excellent indicator of Republican success in subduing the Klan and achieving a large measure of security for the new order was the revival of "politics as usual" in 1871, which culminated in the generally free fall election and another Republican victory at the polls.

82. Washington *New National Era*, March 14, 1872.

83. *Senate Executive Documents*, 42nd Cong., 3rd Sess., No. 32, pp. 11–12. See also the Vicksburg *Times and Republican*, June 1, 1873, and Wells to Attorney General Williams, July 8, 1872, in Source-Chronological File, Northern Mississippi, RG 60, NA, Microcopy Roll 1.

84. Eugene P. Jacobson to John F. H. Claiborne, November 8, 1872, in Claiborne Papers, University of North Carolina Library.

13

New Directions in the Politics of Reconstruction

The defeat of the Dent party in 1869 temporarily shattered organized opposition to the Republican party in the state. Controlling the state and local governments (Governor Alcorn had retained or appointed all local officials), Republicans with a majority of 30,000 at the polls maintained the upper hand in Mississippi politics in 1870–1871, despite the threat posed by the Klan in some districts. Conservatives, demoralized by the success of the Republican juggernaut and without a statewide political organization to challenge the new order, struck out in a number of directions in an effort to develop a party that would be strong enough eventually to overcome the Republican advantage. The conservative fragmentation became so great that for a time it appeared that every county was determined to consider only its own situation in relation to Republican strength and organize a party that would be successful locally. The outpouring of white animosities toward blacks and the ready resort to terrorism in some communities occurred partly because no strong statewide organization existed to moderate local political behavior. The suppression of the Klan by federal authorities, however, for a time discredited violence and intimidation as a political tactic and reinforced the moderate emphasis on regular political means to overcome Republican control. Actually, very few conservative leaders had ever advocated violence or intimidation as methods for resisting Republican rule. As federal authorities penetrated the interior to apprehend Klansmen during the summer of 1871, the ranks of those who had condoned or explained away Klan attacks become noticeably thin. By the fall political campaign conservative rhetoric, though still fierce, no longer inspired whites to violence against the Republicans or blacks.

Despite the recognition by most whites that the defeat of the Republicans would have to come through the normal political process, the quest for conservative unity proved an elusive one. Conservatives had united in 1868 under the Democratic banner in the struggle to head off the political proscription of former Confederates and prevent the "mongrelization" of Mississippi. But the situation had changed since then. The new government had not produced the orgy of radicalism that whites had expected from the Republicans. Although weakening by 1870, the stigma of secession and ruin still marked the Democratic party in the minds of many Mississippians, including not a few who had voted the Democratic ticket before the war but were now hostile to it. Furthermore, too many conservatives, especially in the white counties of north Mississippi, still associated Democratic leadership with the discredited "Jackson clique."[1]

Then, of course, there were the old-line Whigs who, despite their support of the Democratic revival in 1868, found it very difficult to join their old rivals in a permanent political organization that would probably be controlled by Democrats and would be affiliated with the national Democratic party. In 1870 they rejected the efforts of Democrats to bring them into a new anti-Radical coalition.[2] Most conservative leaders realized that without the support of such influential Whigs as Benjamin G. Humphreys, George W. Harper, Robert Lowry, and George L. Potter, a resuscitated Democratic party would fail, shattering the prospects for the organization of a viable conservative coalition in the state. The outlook for a Democratic revival appeared so bleak in 1870 that carpetbagger Stafford announced the party's demise, proclaiming that it was "deader than Lazarus . . . and a greater miracle than that which raised [him] would be required to resurrect it."[3] Many conservatives, including Brown, the old war-horse of the party who during the postwar era consistently advised against resurrecting the Democracy, agreed that rigor mortis had set in and Mississippi whites should seek another organization to lead it out of the wilderness of radicalism.[4]

1. Vicksburg *Herald*, January 19, 1870.

2. Vicksburg *Times and Republican*, August 9, 1870; *Hinds County Gazette*, August 17, October 5, 1870; Natchez *Weekly Democrat*, October 12, 1870.

3. Jackson *Weekly Pilot*, August 12, 1870.

4. *Hinds County Gazette*, October 6, November 30, 1870; Natchez *Weekly Democrat*, October 26, 1870.

At the same time the majority of old Whigs rejected Governor Alcorn's invitations to join the Republican party, claiming that his party was as radical as the party of secession and ruin.[5] After a few months of observing the performance of Alcorn, some Whigs, according to one of them, could commend the governor for his efforts "to save us from extreme and ruinous legislation," but they could not approve "the extreme radical legislation of the Republican party in Mississippi" nor could they "affiliate with and endorse many of the men from abroad who hold present power in that party."[6] To a majority of Whigs the most appalling radical aspect of the Republican party was its commitment to Negro political rights, especially since they believed that these rights could be manipulated by carpetbag adventurers to the detriment of good government and in violation of the United States Constitution. Horn of the Meridian *Mercury* summed up the historical position of Whiggery toward radicalism when he wrote:

> The old Whig party, in the days of its greatness and purity, was the natural foe of Radicalism in all its forms. It fought the Democracy because its tendency was, to push republicanism—not using the term in a party sense—into radical or ultraism. We grant that the Whig party favored a strong government, but it wanted a decent one. It was for rule of the intelligent, and the most abhorrent idea of all to it was, the putting of public affairs in the keeping of the ignorant groundlings of society. So far was it from enfranchising the inferior races that it could hardly tolerate "universal suffrage" as applicable to whites only. Its tendency was to check and to hedge in the profane rabble, and not to turn it loose, in the spirit of a wild fanatical howling of democracy, to trample intelligence and decency and honesty in public affairs out of sight—as has been done by the Radical party of this day.[7]

What Whigs like Horn really desired was not the revival of their old party, which they realized would be impractical, but the organization of an anti-Radical party that would be called "Conservative" and would bear the imprint of Whiggery. Although they could not all agree on what principles of antebellum Whiggery might apply

5. Forest *Register*, October 15, 1870; Jackson *Weekly Clarion*, March 3, 1870, quoting the Iuka *Gazette* and the Meridian *Mercury*; *Hinds County Gazette*, August 10, September 21, November 30, 1870; Harris, "A Reconstruction of the Mississippi Scalawag," 26.

6. *Hinds County Gazette*, August 10, 1870.

7. As reported in the Jackson *Weekly Clarion*, March 3, 1870.

to the peculiar setting of Mississippi politics in the 1870s, most Whigs professed a strong attachment to the idea that the Constitution should be restored to its "primitive vigor" and politics should be cleansed of extremism and corrupting influences. The concept of union was particularly appealing to them, but they denigrated the idea of a consolidated government, considered by many Republicans to be a result of the war. Although still attractive to some, the old party's support for internal improvements, a protective tariff, and a central banking system had lost its meaning for most Mississippi Whigs in the cauldron of Reconstruction politics. Only old-line Whigs, they believed, could provide the leadership that would avoid the pitfalls of Democratic extremism and demagoguery and unify conservatives into a party that would sweep the Republicans from power. As C. B. New, a Gulf Coast Whig put it, "if we are ever to arrest the progress of Radicalism, good and honest men of all parties should unite upon a Whig basis, and organize a great Conservative or People's party."[8]

With this purpose in mind, Whig editors Harper of the *Hinds County Gazette* and Robert M. Brown of the Grenada *Mississippi Central* issued a call for a "Whig Consultation Convention" to meet in Canton in November, 1870. The meeting was not to be a full-blown conservative gathering but was designed to prepare a set of principles, which would be Whiggish in tone, for the subsequent organization of an anti-Radical party. Opposition to the consultation meeting immediately developed, and the ridicule from both Republicans and Bourbons that greeted the call went far toward discrediting the convention before it ever met. "Just think," Republican Stafford declared, "a meeting of Whigs, eighteen years after the party was defeated, dead and buried"; evidently Brown and Harper were "getting a few fossils together."[9] The Bourbon press, including a few editors who had once been Whig stalwarts, charged that the real objective of the consultation movement was the formation of a third political party in the state, which inevitably would further weaken the anti-Republican forces.[10]

8. *Hinds County Gazette*, July 13, August 10, 17, September 21, 28, October 26 (quote), 1870; Jackson *Weekly Pilot*, June 11, 1870.
9. *Hinds County Gazette*, July 13, October 12, 1870; Jackson *Weekly Pilot*, November 26, 1870.
10. *Hinds County Gazette*, October 5, 1870.

The real blow to the hopes of "the fossils" came when Whig party patriarch William L. Sharkey announced in a public letter, published in many conservative newspapers, that he could not support the Canton convention. Only the state Democratic party, though currently moribund but with a parent national organization ready to assist in its revival, could rescue Mississippi from Radical usurpation and misgovernment, he declared. The Harper-Brown movement would only make more difficult the work of reorganizing the Democratic party and defeating the Radicals. "The party questions on which the Whigs and Democrats formerly divided are utterly obliterated," Sharkey told former Whigs. "The party now known as the Democratic party is an opposition party, a new party of Whigs and Democrats united for the purpose of restoring the Constitution to its primitive vigor by utterly abrogating every innovation that has been made upon it." [11]

Because of general conservative opposition, the Canton convention was a bitter disappointment for its promoters. Fewer than twenty Whigs attended, the most prominent of whom was John W. C. Watson, the leading Whig of north Mississippi. [12] After the "old line Whig fizzle" at Canton, this group never again attempted to organize a conservative coalition in Mississippi that would be free of the tainting influence of the Democratic party. Even so, old party antagonisms continued to work against a political union of whites.

By the summer of 1871—a few weeks before the crucial local elections—the debate over the New Departure strategy had emerged as the main cause of contention among conservatives. The New Departure doctrine, which recognized the postwar amendments and black political equality as "accomplished facts," developed mainly out of the need of conservatives in overwhelmingly black areas of the South to find some formula for capturing a sufficient number of Negro votes to overthrow the "corrupt adventurers" who dominated the local governments. Although national Democrats gave the movement respectability and encouragement in 1871, the roots of the New Departure were southern. In Mississippi these roots actually went back to the grudging sup-

---

11. Forest *Register*, October 15, 1870; Natchez *Weekly Democrat*, October 19, 1870.
12. *Hinds County Gazette*, November 30, 1870.

port such prominent Democrats as Barksdale and Brown had given the reconstruction acts in 1867. After the cooperationist failure, the policy of accommodation was revived in the Dent movement, only to be discredited for a time by the crushing defeat of the National Union Republicans in the election of 1869. By 1871, however, the conservative need for a scheme to win black votes seemed greater than before in view of perceived Republican excesses and the approach of the first local elections since the imposition of Negro suffrage. A resort to violence and intimidation, as practiced in the white counties, was politically counterproductive for conservatives in predominantly black counties and, it appeared, would inevitably lead to "a war of races" and economic chaos.[13]

Old fire-eater Brown and Paul A. Botto of the Natchez *Democrat* in 1871 constantly beat the drums for the New Departure. An accommodationist platform, Botto insisted, was "the only perfectly feasible plan for overthrowing the Radical party and restoring that proper respect for constitutional restrictions, without which our government will inevitably go to ruin." The postwar amendments, which New Departurists accepted in good faith, did not really alter, as Bourbon critics claimed, "the original theory and character of the Federal government as designed and taught by its founders." Still, Botto found cause to warn conservatives who supported this policy against deceiving blacks on the matter, believing that such a course had defeated earlier efforts to win black support for the conservative party. He wrote:

> If we wish to induce colored men to co-operate with us in an effort to overthrow the party in power, or to cooperate with us in anything connected with politics, we must honestly assure and convince them that we fully recognize the political rights which have been conferred upon them, and are perfectly willing in all good faith, and without reservation, mental or otherwise, to guarantee to them, so far as we can, the continued enjoyment of these rights, to the extent that we shall not favor or countenance any movement to make discrimination in the matters of political rights on account of race, color or previous condition of servitude.[14]

13. For examples of the conservative belief in the destructiveness of white extremism in black districts, see an excerpt from the Vicksburg *Evening News*, as reported in the Jackson *Pilot*, June 2, 1871, the Natchez *Democrat*, October 25, 1871, and the Jackson *Weekly Clarion*, August 14, 21, 1873.

14. Natchez *Weekly Democrat*, September 20, 1871.

New Departure advocates generally ignored the question of black political capacity and, for that matter, the burning issue of "social equality" which Bourbons were constantly throwing in their faces. Rather, they stressed the corrupt and disastrous consequences of the oppressive taxes imposed on the citizens by Radical demagogues. In their appeal to blacks, accommodationists especially argued that because of the heavy tax burden Negro laborers had little hope of becoming independent farmers. Botto pointed out that blacks who bought land after the fairly prosperous year of 1869 had lost their farms to the sheriff's hammer in 1871, and the economic status of Negroes would not improve until they threw off the yoke of local carpetbaggers and the demagogues of their own race.[15]

Bourbons reacted quickly to this campaign. Charging that New Departure advocates had sold out to the Radicals, Bourbons urged Mississippi whites to repudiate the accommodationist heresy and to organize the Democratic party on the uncompromising principle of white supremacy. When the controversy became intense during the summer of 1871, a number of prominent conservatives did not know which way to turn. Generally decisions were made on the basis of the size of the local black electorate and the prospects for the success of a local "reform" ticket if an appeal were made to the Negro voter. The influential Harper was a conservative who found himself in a quandary over the New Departure; he finally supported the movement because it appeared "universal" and expedient as a tactic for overcoming the Republican majority in his county.[16]

Former political alignments made little difference in the division on the New Departure issue. Prominent fire-eating Democrats of the past like Brown, Hiram R. Cassedy, and Jacob Thompson, who had served in Buchanan's cabinet, could be found vigorously advocating the acceptance of the new political doctrine, whereas old-

15. See especially *ibid.*, issues of August-October, 1871; see also a "Mississippian," writing in the Jackson *Weekly Clarion*, June 29, 1871, for an excellent statement of the appeal of the New Departure for some conservatives.

16. Natchez *Weekly Democrat*, July 5, 1871; Hiram R. Cassedy to Oscar J. E. Stuart, August 23, 1871, in Stuart Papers; Jackson *Pilot*, April 18, July 8, 1871. For Harper's decision to support the New Departure, see Thomas B. Alexander, "Persistent Whiggery in Mississippi: The Hinds County Gazette," *Journal of Mississippi History*, XXIII (April, 1961), 84–85.

line Whigs of the stature of Sharkey, McCardle, and Humphreys maintained a die-hard opposition to the postwar amendments. Whatever their political backgrounds, many of the conservatives who accepted the New Departure approach only grudgingly did so, admitting their distaste for the whole business and suggesting that their support for black political equality would extend no further than the overthrow of local Republican authority.

When the revived Democratic state executive committee met in July, it was seriously split between the friends and foes of the New Departure. Because of the divisiveness of the issues, as well as the lingering conflict between ultra Whigs and Democrats, the committee decided not to call a state convention to prepare for the election.[17] The county organizations that emerged to direct the campaign reflected the political fragmentation of Mississippi conservatives on Reconstruction issues. In Marshall County the anti-Republican party took the name "Conservative"; in Tishomingo, "Democratic-Conservative"; in Choctaw, the "White Man's Party"; in Adams, the "Citizens' Reform Ticket"; and in Warren, where conservatives fused with moderate Republicans, the "Reform Party."[18] Local splits still occurred; and were especially severe in the handful of white counties where conventions had adopted the New Departure platform. Even though the conservative leadership manifested a united front by the time of the election, the early divisions reduced the anti-Republican strength at the polls.

The Republicans also entered the political contest of 1871 with serious intraparty divisions, though of a different kind than those of the conservatives. The focus of Republican factionalism was Governor Alcorn, whose patronage policies and attempts to develop a white-based party had antagonized many Radical Republicans —and some who were not Radicals. Led by Senator Ames and Flournoy, Republican opponents of Alcorn feared that his policies would produce a "hybrid" party which would sell out to the Democrats at the first crisis, as had occurred in Virginia and Tennessee.

17. Vicksburg *Times and Republican*, July 14, 1871.
18. Jackson *Pilot*, September 25, November 1, 1871; Vicksburg *Times and Republican*, November 1, 1871.

Furthermore, several Republican leaders in the legislature had been alienated by the scalawag governor's free use of the veto power to block favorite party measures. His 1870 veto of a district printing bill, which would award all public printing to "loyal" newspapers, brought down the wrath of Republican editors, both Radical and moderate, on Alcorn's head. Claiming that the Republican press could not survive without "public patronage" and believing that the governor had earlier committed himself to assisting these newspapers, Frederic Speed of the powerful Vicksburg *Times and Republican* denounced "the treacherous Alcorn" for his veto and called on the legislature to override it.[19] This veto also raised the ire of state Senator Charles Caldwell, one of the most influential blacks in the legislature. In voting to overrule the governor's action, Caldwell declared, "I do not propose to assist in any manner in giving support to the Democratic journals of the country, which, even now, are counseling the shooting down of negroes who happen to hold offices and who are honestly endeavoring to discharge their duties. These papers have already done enough mischief, by encouraging lawlessness; and I cannot give my consent to strengthen[ing] them, by giving them public patronage."[20] Outraged legislators, however, failed to override the public printing bill veto. Despite prophesies of doom, the Republican press survived and most of the editors, at least publicly, made their peace with Alcorn.

Black leaders found racial reasons to complain of Alcorn's policies. In 1870 the governor stymied the efforts of state Senators William H. Gray and Robert Gleed to pass a strong civil rights bill that would prohibit racial discrimination on public transportation, though in this case he was careful not to attack the principle of integration. Indeed, he ultimately signed a weak provision guaranteeing black rights on public transportation.[21] His stand against racial mixing in the public schools was stronger, but except for Senator Gray black leaders refrained from criticizing the governor on the issue, since they were well aware that even white Radicals shied away from any such concession to "social equality." Alcorn's

19. Forest *Register*, July 23, 1870; Vicksburg *Times and Republican*, July 17, 24, 1870.
20. *Senate Journal, 1870*, p. 504.
21. *Ibid.*, 3; Jackson *Weekly Pilot*, May 28, June 25, 1870.

determination to bring prominent whites into the party, a development that would probably inhibit the emerging black leadership
in the state, caused some Negroes to pause in their support of the
governor. .Then, at the time of the Meridian riot when he mini-
mized the significance of Klan terror in the state, they joined with
white Radicals to appeal over the governor's head for federal intervention. Black disillusionment with Alcorn was reinforced by his
conflict with Flournoy, who, before Ames emerged as champion
of the blacks, was viewed as the special friend of Negro rights.[22]

The Alcorn-Flournoy vendetta contributed greatly to an early
revival of the struggle between moderates and Radicals for supremacy in the party. Soon after Alcorn had led the party to victory
in 1869 Flournoy launched a series of attacks on him and other
moderate Republicans, charging them with the abandonment of
black rights and loyal men in the state. The attacks on Alcorn,
mainly from the columns of Flournoy's Pontotoc *Equal Rights*, became especially severe and personal after the governor offered,
then withdrew, an appointment to Flournoy as a brigadier general
in the militia. By 1871 this north Mississippi Radical was referring
to Alcorn as the "arch deceiver" and a "ravenous office hunter"
who should be repudiated by all true Republicans.[23]

Encouraged by the efforts of the intrepid Flournoy, other Radicals on the eve of the 1871 campaign hoisted the red flag of radicalism. The influential Jackson *Pilot*, again under Radical control,
announced its intention to crusade for the adoption by the party
of the advanced principles of republicanism. It proclaimed:

> Republicanism is, from its very nature Radical. Without being deep-
> ly planted in the minds and hearts of the people—and that is the true
> interpretation of Radicalism as connected with Republicanism—it
> would never have accomplished anything. Had the fathers of the anti-
> slavery movement been mere make-believe lovers of freedom, mere
> half-way friends of the colored race, the freedman would at this mo-
> ment be just where he was twenty-five years ago. Indeed, even in
> religion, there must be Radicalism or there is no progress, no conver-
> sions of sinning souls. Anything that is right, if advocated at all, must,

22. Jackson *Pilot*, August 21, 1871.

23. *Ibid.*, January 26, July 31, 1871; newspaper clipping, 1870, in Niles Scrapbook;
Jackson *Weekly Pilot*, February 12, August 12, 1870; Jackson *Weekly Clarion*, January
12, 1871; *Hinds County Gazette*, October 12, 1870.

in the nature of things, be radically advocated to have the proper effect.

Out upon the very term, Conservatism! And conservative Republicanism be hanged! The very word, meaning a tendency to preserve; opposition to change; is diametrically contrary to the spirit of the age; contrary to progress; fossilizing in its tendency; going backward, crablike, at a time when the hearts of men—even of politicians—cry out, "Excelsior!" "Forward! March!"[24]

From Washington, Senator Ames informed local Radicals that he supported their attempts to unseat the moderates and particularly Alcorn. Not until the fall, however, did he return to the state to seek the leadership of the Radical movement. Mississippi Radicals, no matter how much they proclaimed the need for a revival of radicalism, were not united on a specific platform as they had been in 1868. They seemed more anxious to show their contempt for Alcorn than to formulate a set of principles for the party's guidance. Except for Flournoy, who announced his support of mixed schools, white Radicals, mainly of carpetbag vintage, shunned a commitment to advanced rights for blacks, although many of them accepted the principle of equal treatment on public transportation and in such public places as theaters.[25] They also expressed a greater concern than moderates for the security of Negroes and for their right to participate in public affairs. The issue of political proscription, a major tenet of this faction in 1868, was dead, but Radicals in 1871 found reasons to be alarmed at the moderate program to bring former rebels into the Republican party. These issues, however, were frequently obscured, perhaps by design, in the intensifying struggle between the Radicals and the Alcorn faction.

The reaction of Alcorn to the Radical challenge was predictable. After striking at Flournoy, he turned the power of his office on John B. Raymond and A. N. Kimball, the proprietors of the Jackson *Pilot*. On the pretext that public printing had been awarded illegally to the *Pilot* in 1870, the governor removed Kimball and Raymond as the state printers at a time when the legislature was not in session. Then, acting on his authority to

24. Jackson *Pilot*, June 13, 1871.
25. *Ibid.*, September 25, 1871; Adelbert Ames to his wife, September 23, 1871, in Blanche Butler Ames (comp.), *Chronicles*, I, 315; Harris, "Creed of the Carpetbaggers," 214–15.

appoint a new printer in the absence of legislative action, he gave
the patronage to his cousin Robert J. Alcorn and carpetbagger
Hiram T. Fisher. They immediately established the Jackson
Leader and appointed Dr. William M. Compton, the superintendent of the insane asylum, as editor. Shocked by the swift course
of events, the *Pilot* proprietors nonetheless refused to admit
defeat. They secured a temporary order from the courts restraining
Alcorn and Fisher from exercising the printing concession, only to
lose when the case was adjudicated by the state supreme court.[26]
While awaiting the court's decision, they instigated misconduct
charges against Compton, accusing him of having "improper
relationships" with female patients of the insane asylum. Much to
the embarrassment of the *Pilot* managers, both the board of
directors of the asylum, headed by Governor Alcorn, and the
grand jury of Hinds County exonerated Compton of any guilt. The
Pilot men, however, would have the last laugh, though not until
the imperious Alcorn had given up the office of governor to take
his seat in the Senate. When the legislature met in 1872, it
returned the state printing to Kimball and Raymond—an action
that reputedly had Democratic support.[27]

When the Republican state convention convened in late August,
1871, to prepare for the fall election, the state printing issue
threatened to disrupt the party. A few days before the convention
met Alcorn stunned a Republican audience at Vicksburg with a
bitter tirade against his enemies in the party, and he even singled
out for abuse State Auditor Henry Musgrove, a moderate who had
supported him in the past. The Jackson *Leader* followed the
governor's harangue with a series of editorials insisting that the
convention endorse his administration of the state, a proposal that
the Vicksburg *Times and Republican* denounced as being "dangerous, wicked and disorganizing in its tendencies and purposes."[28]

The expected struggle in the convention, however, did not
occur. Anti-Alcorn delegates realized that the "Disorganizer-in-

26. Vicksburg *Times and Republican*, July 8, 14, 30, 1871; Jackson *Pilot*, July 12, 20,
September 26, 1871.

27. Vicksburg *Times and Republican*, August 5, 1871; *Hinds County Gazette*, February
21, 1872.

28. Vicksburg *Times and Republican*, August 9, 30, 31, 1871; Jackson *Pilot*, August 22,
29, 31, 1871.

chief" would soon be vacating the governor's office to take his seat in the Senate, and in the interest of party harmony for the fall election many of this faction resisted the impulse to nail Alcorn to the wall for his war on party faithfuls. Moreover, moderate strength was still strong in the Republican party and especially in the powerful state executive committee chaired by Lieutenant Governor Powers, an Alcorn ally. In fact, moderate delegates secured the convention's approval of a resolution endorsing Alcorn's leadership, despite the rearguard efforts of a handful of determined Radicals to prevent it. A few days later a "Colored Men's Convention," consisting of black political leaders in the state, adopted a resolution introduced by John R. Lynch that commended the Alcorn administration. His vanity reinforced by these resolutions, the governor nonetheless was not content to let well enough alone. In a major address to the Republican convention soon after the delegates had endorsed his administration, he launched another assault on his critics in the party and followed it up by removing a number of them from office.[29]

Although Alcorn's attacks on fellow Republicans included scalawags as well as carpetbaggers, the impression prevailed that he was determined to rid the party of northerners, however much they had contributed to the success of the new order. Even some moderate scalawags deprecated his "war on the carpetbaggers," realizing that his policy held ominous implications for the future of the balanced party they desired. Partly because of the governor's impulsiveness, many moderates and friendly black leaders ultimately aligned with the Ames faction. Ames did not fail to see the opportunity presented by the emerging Republican dissatisfaction with the "Eminent Man" during the fall campaign. While he canvassed for the Republican ticket in the black counties—his first experience on the stump—Senator Ames was building support for himself among disaffected Alcorn men and other Republicans. The decisions of Henry R. Pease and State Senator Alexander Warner, influential carpetbaggers who were former opponents of Ames, to join their political fortunes with him went far toward making the young New Englander the rising star in the Mississippi Republican

29. Washington *New National Era*, September 14, 1871; Jackson *Pilot*, August 9, 31, October 2, 1871; Vicksburg *Times and Republican*, September 1, 7, 1871.

firmament. Ames's marriage in 1870 to the daughter of the powerful Benjamin F. Butler, now a confidant of President Grant, gave an additional boost to his campaign to win party control. Furthermore, his vigorous support of the Ku Klux Klan Act endeared him to the black masses, who feared for their liberties if the violence contagion spread.[30] Everywhere that he campaigned in the plantation counties, Ames received an enthusiastic reception from blacks. He reported to his wife one such rally in Vicksburg: "The applause at times was long and continuous. At the close of my speech they gave me three cheers, three cheers for your Father, and adopted resolutions approving my course in urging the passage of the Ku Klux bill."[31]

Dismayed by the course of events, moderate Republicans, who viewed the rise of the radical Ames with great misgivings, lashed out at Alcorn for his failures. Jefferson Wofford, a former Confederate officer and the leading Republican in the hill country of northeast Mississippi, declared that despite the probable success of the party in the fall election, Alcorn in abusing the carpetbaggers, "the positive element of the Republican party in this State," had opened a division that would be difficult to close.[32] Nevertheless, Wofford and other moderates still hoped that once the election was over and Alcorn had left the state the new governor, Powers, might reverse the trend toward radicalism and retain control for moderate republicanism.

In the counties other issues arose in 1870–1871 to divide Republicans and threaten their political dominance. Although the factionalism generated at the state level obviously affected local intraparty relationships and weakened the forces of harmony, grass-roots divisions had an origin and existence peculiarly their own. The most striking cause of local Republican divisions was what in the late twentieth century would be called "black power," which developed out of the desire of blacks to control local offices in proportion to their strength at the polls.[33] This movement was a phenomenon of the predominantly black counties, where Negroes

30. Ames to his wife, October 24, 26, 1871, in Blanche Butler Ames (comp.), *Chronicles,* I, 342–43, 344–45.
31. Ames to his wife, October 17, *ibid.,* I, 334–35.
32. As reported in the Jackson *Pilot,* October 2, 1871.
33. Washington *New National Era,* October 26, 1871.

could afford the luxury of challenging their white leaders without risking Republican defeat at the polls. Rarely, however, did black power advocates achieve complete success. Usually a handful of white Republicans, mainly carpetbaggers, realized before it was too late the folly of opposing black aspirations for local influence and position; as a result they made their peace with the movement and thereby retained their offices. Those whites who lost out in the struggle with black Republicans frequently bolted the party and either joined short-lived, independent Republican factions or affiliated with local "reform" parties organized by New Departure conservatives. In some plantation counties, such as Madison and Claiborne, the white leadership was too entrenched and aspiring Negro leaders too divided and unskilled for the black movement to succeed within the Republican party. Consequently, in those counties some blacks bolted the local organization and immediately became the recipients of conservative goodwill and the focus of New Departure schemes for a fusion ticket. When locally prominent Negro politicians remained in the regular party, the bolters found themselves isolated from their black constituency and they were politically destroyed.[34]

The greatest measure of success for black assertiveness occurred in Adams County. With blacks comprising 81 percent of the registered voters and with several able leaders of the race available, including State Senator J. M. P. Williams and John R. Lynch, this county was ideal for a black attempt at political control.

The struggle for dominance in Adams County began in December, 1870, when Williams announced to a meeting of his followers in Natchez that "the time had come for blacks to rely upon themselves more and upon their hitherto white leaders less."[35] The white leadership, headed by carpetbaggers Edward J. Castello, the "wheel-horse" of the Radical faction in the constitutional convention of 1868, and Congressman Legrand W. Perce, foolishly rejected any compromise on the policy of white control of the party. By August it was clear that the Williams faction had overcome the fears of Negro precinct leaders that they would be left high and dry

34. Cassedy to Stuart, August 23, 1871, in Stuart Papers; Vicksburg *Times and Republican*, October 6, 8, 11, 19, November 7, 26, 1871; Jackson *Pilot*, September 18, November 2, 4, 1871; Jackson *Weekly Clarion*, October 12, 1871.
35. Natchez *Weekly Democrat*, December 7, 1870.

politically if a black revolt failed. Confident now of support at the grass roots, Williams and his associates laid their plans to raise the black standard at the county convention. Seeing the handwriting on the wall, Castello abandoned his Radical posture and sought the support of Governor Alcorn (which, unfortunately for the white Republicans, came at the time when the governor's political fortunes were ebbing). The Castello ploy did not work. The county convention, consisting of twenty-six blacks and three whites, selected Lynch as chairman of the executive committee and nominated an almost completely black slate of candidates for local office and for seats in the legislature. Only carpetbagger O. C. French, who had cooperated with the black movement, survived the purge of the Adams County leadership.

In Natchez itself, where the black advantage at the polls was not very great, a handful of white Republicans managed to retain some influence in the party as well as their places on the town board of aldermen. Nevertheless, blacks controlled the board and the office of mayor until late 1872.[36] Eventually factionalism developed in the black power structure, making possible the triumph in the city of a coalition of disgruntled Republicans of both races and New Departure conservatives. But in the county, blacks retained control even after the redemption of the state from Republican rule.[37] In view of white fears it is interesting that black political dominance in Adams County and Natchez did not contribute to racial strife or black arrogance toward whites. The success of the New Departure in winning the support of conservative landowners and businessmen—although unsuccessful at the polls—made possible a relaxed racial climate in the county and a considerable degree of biracial cooperation in public affairs, such as railroad development.

36. *Ibid.*, April 3, August 9, October 11, 1871. Writing years later, John R. Lynch attempted to minimize the black effort to dominate the local Republican party. In his writings, completed during the age of segregation, Lynch was anxious to demonstrate to a critical public that Negroes had not sought to dominate the southern governments during Reconstruction and, indeed, had acted as if the color of their skins, or the way white Republicans viewed them, made no difference. John R. Lynch, *Some Historical Errors of James Ford Rhodes* (Boston, 1922), vii; John R. Lynch, *The Facts of Reconstruction* (Indianapolis, 1970), Chap. III; John Lynch, *Reminiscences of an Active Life*, Chap. XIII.

37. Although Lynch emerged as the most significant black politician in Adams County, he did not possess complete power over the local party. The leadership of the organization was collective, with as many as six blacks, including Lynch, in control. Natchez *Democrat*, August 29, 1874.

Adams became the elusive model for other experiments in local black dominance.[38]

Nowhere was the incipient black power movement more subject to misdirection and abuse than in Warren County. Similar to Adams County in racial composition, Warren by 1871 had produced no Negro leaders of outstanding ability. Factionalism had been rife in the local party since the beginning of Reconstruction, and carpetbag adventurer Furlong made the most of the situation to advance his ambitions in the county. He took the position of sheriff for himself and selected a group of black subalterns for the other offices in the county and town governments.[39] These men were not as well educated or as able as Furlong—and no more honest. Even Thomas W. Cardozo, a recent black arrival who would soon rise to a position of leadership in the Vicksburg "Ring," admitted that the organization had put Negroes in office who were "totally unfit" for public service. By 1872 the corrupt Furlong organization had milked Warren County of thousands of dollars. When white Republicans sought a voice in party matters, they became targets of abuse for Furlong's minions who used color-line politics to maintain the ascendancy of the machine in Warren. Although Alcorn in 1871 removed him as sheriff in an attempt to break his hold on Vicksburg politics, Furlong won election to the position a few weeks later. The carpetbag editor of the Vicksburg *Times and Republican* lamented that the majority of the county's voters were the "abject slaves of Charles E. Furlong." Demoralized by their lack of influence in public affairs, almost all of the white Republicans in Vicksburg, which included a fairly large community of northern businessmen, virtually ceased to attend party meetings. In 1871 some assisted in the founding of the "Reform Party" and in 1873 became leaders in the first taxpayers' league in the state.[40] Unlike the situation in Adams County, many Warren County conservatives rejected conciliation on a New Departure

38. Jackson *Times*, June 2, 25, August 7, 1875; Natchez *Democrat*, September 17, October 22, 1875.

39. Vicksburg *Times and Republican*, September 14, October 3, 6, 1871; Jackson *Pilot*, September 18, 1871.

40. Washington *New National Era*, December 21, 1871; Vicksburg *Times and Republican*, September 16, October 8, 15, November 26, 1871, April 13, 1872; Jackson *Pilot*, November 1, 1871.

platform, and, inspired by the vitriolic McCardle of the Vicksburg *Herald*, agitated for the adoption of a color-line policy that would match the black one. When racial tensions became intense, insurgent blacks, principally Cardozo, I. D. Shadd, Ham Carter, and Peter Crosby, deposed Furlong and established complete black control of the Ring, employing virtually the same tactics that the discredited carpetbagger had used, although control of the organization was now more diffuse and unstable. Nevertheless, at least two of the new leaders—Shadd, a newcomer to Mississippi who became speaker of the state house of representatives, and Carter—were men of apparent integrity and political ability.[41]

The Ring's hold on Vicksburg ended in 1872 when Governor Powers appointed carpetbagger Benjamin A. Lee as mayor. Lee, the cashier of the Freedmen's Bank in Vicksburg and a man of considerable prestige among the town's northern residents, produced a few significant reforms but failed to create a balanced Republican coalition that could successfully challenge the Ring for control of Warren County.[42] These conditions made Vicksburg a tinderbox of racial and political conflict that would ultimately explode in 1874.

When the chips were down in the fall of 1871, intraparty strife, whether the result of Alcorn's policies, the black power movement, or personal rivalries, gave way to the need for Republican unity at the polls to meet the conservative challenge. Protected by the federal Enforcement acts, thousands of Republicans shouted and paraded for the success of the party in the local elections and for control of the new legislature. Leaders of the party, representing all factions, canvassed the state for the cause. Ignoring the river counties, where Republican success was assured regardless of what

41. Vicksburg *Times and Republican*, May 7, 1872, February 23, 1873; Vicksburg *Vicksburger*, March 11, August 8, 1874; Jackson *Times*, July 17, 1875; Washington *New National Era*, December 21, 1871. Although black leaders in Warren County could act in unison against Furlong and other whites who threatened their position, rivalries among them existed from the beginning. For example, Cardozo and Carter early became bitter enemies in the struggle for influence in the black community. Vicksburg *Times and Republican*, January 13, 1872, August 14, 1873.

42. Vicksburg *Times and Republican*, January 19, March 12, 13, 14, May 23, 1872. The opportunity to appoint Lee as mayor occurred when the Ring-controlled mayor died in office.

faction won (and probably also not wanting to get involved in the intraparty struggles raging there), James Lynch, perhaps the best orator in the state, campaigned for party candidates in the largely white interior of Mississippi. In debates with conservative speakers he appeared before large white as well as black audiences. At Holly Springs he spoke to hundreds of white men who attended a Republican rally. Conservative Harvey W. Walter, Whig candidate for governor in 1859, followed Lynch into the piney woods to give him competition on the stump, but after an embarrassing effort he excused himself from further debate for "business reasons."[43] Alcorn, in a series of four joint debates with Robert Lowry, the leading conservative campaigner, brought his immense talents on the stump to the aid of Republican candidates. Then, at Oxford the popular Lamar came out of political retirement to meet him in debate. The conservatives claimed that Lamar got the best of the governor, but this seems unlikely in view of Alcorn's skill on the platform and his commanding presence before a crowd. Powers, Pease, and Congressman George E. Harris, a scalawag, also campaigned extensively for Republican candidates. The conservatives, on the other hand, had to be content with a largely local effort, with the notable exception of Lowry's wide-ranging canvass.[44]

Republican orators hammered on the achievements of the new order, especially emphasizing that the party had secured for blacks the rights guaranteed by the Fourteenth and Fifteenth amendments. They also attempted to demonstrate that, despite repetitious conservative charges, Republicans had wisely managed state finances and were the harbingers of future economic prosperity. Some still engaged in the old polemics regarding disunion and slavery, but much less often than before. A number of Republican campaigners appealed to "poor whites" to throw off the yoke of "the old haughty slaveocracy" and aid the Republican party in constructing a society that would reduce ignorance and poverty.[45]

Conservative speakers sounded the usual charges against the Republicans—corruption, alien and demagogic control of the state,

43. Jackson *Pilot*, September 19, October 11, 12, 23, 1871.
44. Pereyra, *James Lusk Alcorn*, 143; Jackson *Weekly Clarion*, October 5, 1871; Jackson *Pilot*, October 19, 1871; Vicksburg *Times and Republican*, November 7, 1871.
45. Jackson *Pilot*, August 1, 24, September 6, October 24, 1871; Vicksburg *Times and Republican*, September 22, 1871.

heavy taxes, financial mismanagement, the suppression of political opponents by the Ku Klux Klan Act, and radicalism in general. An appeal to white racial passions was rarely heard from the stump, mainly because conservatives were seeking black votes, even in areas that had not adopted the New Departure platform, and Negroes frequently attended the rallies, especially when Republicans occupied the same platform.[46]

Neither side possessed a campaign treasury, and speakers who visited other communities had to pay their own transportation expenses and impose upon the hospitality of their political friends for free lodging and meals. As was customary in nineteenth-century America, the political parties depended largely upon local enthusiasm and initiative to promote the campaign and the candidates. The more elaborate rallies were characterized by the presence of colorful floats and eye-catching signs during the day and transparencies at night, accompanied by the booming of a cannon. As the cannon fire announced the beginning of the rally, hundreds of country people of both races flocked to town to attend the festivities, which, in addition to its political appeal, constituted a major source of diversion for them.

Black participation in these rallies was at its height in the 1871 campaign. Secret Union League meetings had been virtually abandoned as an instrument of Republican control, and Mississippi blacks, in the most relaxed campaign during Reconstruction, turned out in droves to attend political marathons. An observer reported one such rally in Yazoo City, which occurred three months before the election. He wrote: "Before midday the city was a perfect jam—men, women and children, horses, wagons, and all sorts of vehicles so wonderfully commingled as to constitute a picture seldom seen—while the roads for miles in the country continued to be lined with other thousands on their way to the grove two miles distant from the city, where a stand had been erected to accommodate the speakers, invited guests and the brass band." The overwhelmingly black crowd was addressed by carpetbagger Albert T. Morgan, the Republican leader in Yazoo, Negro politician-minister Thomas W. Stringer of Vicksburg, and three local

46. For campaign developments see the October and early November, 1871, issues of the Jackson *Weekly Clarion* and the Jackson *Pilot*.

black leaders. After spending most of the afternoon listening to speeches, this correspondent noted, "the whole company gave themselves up to refreshing the inner man. Every family was provided with a basket of provisions, to which ample justice was done. Then came the march to the town, and at six o'clock, while passing through the principal business streets, a halt was ordered in front of General [William R.] Miles' law office, from the balcony of which the General discoursed for a while on the duties and responsibilities of the newly enfranchised, ending in an appeal to them to vote [for a bond subscription to] the Mobile and Northwestern Railroad."[47] Another speech was made on the same topic, and at eight o'clock, while the cannon boomed from the outskirts of Yazoo City, the crowd filtered home. "No disturbance of any note occurred to mar the proceedings of the day," this Republican writer proudly noted in concluding his account.

Election day, November 7, passed off quietly, except in Vicksburg where a McCardle-Furlong confrontation at the polls almost precipitated a racial fracas.[48] In an election that was remarkably free of intimidation and fraud, both Republicans and conservatives turned out in larger numbers than in the crucial 1869 election. The Republicans marshaled 83,588 votes, the largest vote for the party during the Reconstruction era. With a total of 61,307 the conservatives came within two thousand ballots of 1868, when, in addition to the outpouring of white voters, intimidation and economic coercion had won some black votes for the Democratic party.[49]

Since no state offices were to be filled by the election, the aggregate vote had little significance for Mississippians. Their interest was focused on the county races where local officers and members of the new legislature were selected. The returns indicated that the Republicans again had won a comfortable majority in the legislature, although not as large as in 1869. On the other hand they lost thirty-eight of the sixty-nine counties to the conservative co-

47. "Fidus" to editor of the Jackson *Pilot*, August 4, 1871. William R. Miles was a New Departure conservative and the leading railroad promoter in Yazoo County.

48. Vicksburg *Times and Republican*, November 8, 9, 1871; Washington *New National Era*, November 23, 1871.

49. Election Returns, 1871–1900, Records of the Secretary of State of Mississippi, File F, Mississippi Department of Archives and History. The state totals, which are not given in these records, were compiled from the county returns for local offices and the legislature.

alition.[50] As before, the strength of the parties followed racial lines: Republicans won only three white counties, whereas the conservatives captured one black county. From these returns it is clear that the conservatives' New Departure policy influenced few blacks to vote the anti-Republican ticket. In fact, in several counties where the black registration was overwhelming, conservatives offered only token opposition to Republican candidates.[51] In the white counties, the struggle to "redeem" the local governments from the Republicans brought a temporary end to yeoman apathy and an outpouring of white voters.

The election returns of 1871 also demonstrated that the incipient Negro movement designed to win a greater share, or even absolute control, of local offices had been remarkably successful. In the black river district, Negroes swept the contests for membership on the powerful county boards of supervisors as well as the minor local offices. At least five blacks, perhaps as many as eight, won election to the important position of sheriff; one of them was Blanche K. Bruce, who used the office as a stepping-stone to the United States Senate. Blacks were not very successful in winning control of towns in the Negro counties, mainly because of the relatively large white population there. They won the office of mayor in Natchez and gained a majority of one on the board of aldermen; the other aldermen were carpetbaggers with close ties to the business community. In Vicksburg, the largest town in the state, blacks secured a majority on the board of aldermen, but they supported carpetbaggers for the offices of mayor and city marshal and scalawags for city judge and town assessor.[52] Jackson, a white town surrounded by a sea of blacks, went Republican in 1871 but avoided Negro control.[53] Small black-belt towns like Woodville, Fayette, Port Gibson, Greenville, Yazoo City, and Raymond seem to have elected biracial administrations, consisting of white merchants of both parties and blacks who, however, were not very influential in

50. Jackson *Semi-Weekly Pilot*, November 16, 1871; Jackson *Weekly Clarion*, November 23, 1871.

51. Election Returns, 1871–1900.

52. Natchez *Weekly Democrat*, November 22, December 6, 1871; Washington *New National Era*, December 21, 1871; Vicksburg *Times and Republican*, December 8, 1871; *Hinds County Gazette*, December 27, 1871.

53. Wharton, *The Negro in Mississippi*, 167.

local politics. The real power in local affairs during Reconstruction lay with the county governments, and except for the position of sheriff, blacks controlled most of these offices in the Negro counties after the election of 1871.

The legislative contests also produced gains for blacks. Although they only increased their number from 6 to 7 in the senate, where half of the seats were subject to election and where influential carpetbaggers held sway, blacks secured 42 of the 64 seats captured by the Republicans in the house of representatives. The selection of John R. Lynch as speaker of the house reflected the rising influence of blacks in this body and the reality that Negro members, if they asserted themselves, could clearly control the Republican caucus. At the same time conservatives increased their strength in the lower house, winning 45 of the 109 seats in that body.[54]

The election of 1871 demonstrated that the white Republican leadership could ill afford to ignore black demands for influence and position, especially in the counties where black voters were in an overwhelming majority. Furthermore, the state leadership now had to contend with the fact that thirty-nine counties had been "redeemed" by the conservatives, a success that would inspire a greater effort by anti-Republicans to overcome Republican rule in the state.

Nonetheless, some Republicans viewed the campaign and the election returns with hope for the future of the new order. The opposition of many whites to the resuscitation of the Democratic party in the state, a development that moderate Republicans were anxious to report and perhaps exaggerate, combined with the solid Republican victory in the contests for seats in the legislature, caused these Republicans to conclude that their party had weathered the early opposition to its existence and was now established on a firm foundation. The editor of the Jackson *State Leader*, the Alcorn organ, expressed the belief that "time and the experience of personal association" had eroded "the old prejudices and asperities" which had endangered the state in the beginning of congressional reconstruction. "Democrats have found that the Republican party is not a party of 'corrupt adventurers and ignorant negroes.'

54. All but two members of the newly elected legislature have been identified as to party, race, and origins.

. . . And, on the other hand, Republicans are pleased to know that all the Democrats and Conservatives are not intolerant bigots. . . . As far as we may be permitted to judge from the outgoings of politicians, there is [sic] no substantial principles dividing the two parties in the State now. . . . We may take it, then, that the principles of Republicanism have been accepted in this State by all the people." This editor insisted that it mattered little that some of the candidates in expressing New Departure principles concealed their thoughts "in a mental reservation," since people who supported the ticket took them at their word and agreed to their progressive doctrine.[55] From Vicksburg, the moderate *Times and Republican* declared: "The Republican party is in power for at least two years to come, and it was never anything like so powerful as it is now." If Republicans ruled well during this period, especially managing with "the strictest economy and retrenchment in every way," the party's lease on power would be long and the people would never again be exposed to "the curse of democratic rule."[56] As time would prove, these Republicans were overly sanguine in their interpretations of the party's 1871 election success and in their belief that politics had settled into a normal pattern.

55. Jackson *State Leader*, January 4, 1872. See also the Jackson *Pilot*, December 21, 1871.

56. Vicksburg *Times and Republican*, February 3, 1872.

14

A Reconstruction Peace:
The Powers Years

Carpetbagger Ridgley Ceylon Powers replaced Alcorn as governor of Mississippi on November 30, 1871. The new governor inherited the difficult tasks of reconciling the divergent elements in his party, consolidating the new order in the state, and assuring conservatives that the Republican party was not hostile to the interests and rights of the white masses or the material well-being of the state. More so than such carpetbag governors as Robert K. Scott of South Carolina, Gilbert C. Walker of Virginia, and Henry Clay Warmoth of Louisiana, Powers brought to the governor's chair a rich educational background and several years of political experience in his adopted state.[1] Furthermore, unlike his carpetbag successor as governor, Adelbert Ames, his interest and commitment to the state seemed strong, and many years later, as an old man living in retirement in California, he recalled with misty affection his life and career in Mississippi.[2] As lieutenant governor he had demonstrated his desire to make republicanism as palatable as possible to the old citizens, even at the risk of alienating some Radical friends in the party. Powers' reputation for conciliation and his mild demeanor made him a sound choice to follow the imperious Alcorn in office.

Born in a log cabin in Ohio, Powers attended the local common schools and the Western Reserve Seminary where he finished high in his class.[3] He taught school for several years during the 1850s in

1. The career of Powers in postwar Mississippi politics has been virtually ignored by historians of Reconstruction. Richard N. Current in his seminal essay, "Carpetbaggers Reconsidered," published in *A Festschrift for Frederick B. Artz* (Durham, 1964), 139–57, does not include Powers in his list of the nine carpetbag governors in the South during Reconstruction. Regarding Powers' role as governor, James W. Garner only comments, "Few of the 'carpet baggers' won the respect and confidence of the native whites to such an extent as did Governor R. C. Powers." *Reconstruction in Mississippi*, 281. Wharton, *The Negro in Mississippi*, makes passing references to Powers.

2. Ridgley C. Powers, "Biographical Memoranda in Reference to Ridgley Ceylon Powers" (August 21, 1907, in Ridgley C. Powers Folder, Subject File Collection, Mississippi Department of Archives and History).

3. Biographical information on Powers has been pieced together from the following sources: *Hinds County Gazette*, October 22, 1870; Vicksburg *Times and Republican*, Janu-

Lincoln's home county in Illinois, where in 1858 he cast his first Republican ballot. Powers left the teaching profession in 1859 to enter the University of Michigan. As editor of the student newspaper, he led a movement to bar secret societies from the campus, a success that resulted in his dismissal from school. The future carpetbagger then entered Union College at Schenectady, New York, and received a degree in 1862. At the commencement ceremony he was awarded a gold medal for having written and delivered the best oration in his class.

After graduation Powers enlisted in an Ohio regiment in the Army of the Cumberland and rapidly rose to the rank of lieutenant colonel. He participated in thirteen major battles and numerous skirmishes, winning high military honors in the battles of Franklin and Nashville. Powers came to Mississippi soon after the war and purchased a two-thousand-acre plantation in the rich eastern prairie country. He shunned politics at first, but with the promulgation of the "Black and Tan" Constitution in 1868 he got into the thick of the fight for its ratification. His yeoman work for the cause resulted in his selection as chairman of the state Republican executive committee and his nomination in 1869 for lieutenant governor.

As the state's first lieutenant governor, he presided over the senate "with an impartial rectitude that commanded the admiration of his political friends for his ability and the esteem of his political opponents for his fairness," according to a scalawag associate.[4] While serving as acting governor for the absent Alcorn, Powers vetoed a Delta development scheme that would have defrauded Mississippi of thousands of acres of fertile lands. From the beginning of his political career this midwestern carpetbagger was a persistent advocate of a comprehensive system of public education in the state; in the debate in the legislature on the 1870 bill to establish public schools he made the most important speech in its support.

The tone of his administration as governor was set in his first message to the new legislature that convened in January, 1872. Announcing that Ku Klux terrorists had been suppressed in the

ary 25, 1872; Jackson *Pilot*, October 11, 1871; Powers, "Biographical Memoranda of Powers"; William M. Compton, "Ridgley C. Powers, Governor of Mississippi" (MS written *ca*. 1872, in Garner Papers).

4. Compton, "Ridgley C. Powers," 10.

eastern counties and political violence was no longer a threat to the security of the new order, Powers told the lawmakers that "the people are now free to devote their entire attention and energies to bettering their material condition." The state administration, he said, could contribute significantly to this new direction by a wise policy of retrenchment and reform in government. Specifically, taxes should be reduced. "Taxation, which is always more or less distasteful when it is made unreasonable or unjust," Powers informed the legislature, "renders a government burdensome and kindles among the people a restless spirit of insubordination which is liable to provoke serious consequences. Public confidence becomes weak, enterprise dies out, and business stagnates. It is your duty to lighten as far [as] possible this burden by making only such demands upon the pockets of the people as are absolutely necessary to promote the general welfare." A halt must be made, the governor said, to the state's steadily increasing indebtedness and the rampant issuance of warrants by all units of government in Mississippi.[5]

Powers devoted much of the message to public education and specifically to the need for reform in the financial administration of the school system. "The present condition of the country demands that all the moneys available for school purposes shall be applied as far as possible to the employment of teachers, and opening schools," Powers maintained. "Costly school houses, elegantly furnished and supplied with libraries and apparatus, may be the out-growth of the system in future years, but they cannot be thought of now, while the great body of the children of the State are entirely without school advantages." True to the republican spirit that motivated many members of his party during the 1860s, Powers declared that "it is better that *all* should have the opportunity of acquiring the rudiments of an English education in log school-houses, than that the entire fund should be exhausted in procuring elegant accommodations for the few."

The carpetbag governor called for no reduction in support for the benevolent institutions of the state. He asked the legislature, however, to apply a sharp pruning knife to its own expenses, the second largest item of expense in the state budget. He especially

5. *Annual Message of Governor Powers, 1872*, pp. 1, 3–4.

pointed out that the cause of economy in administering state affairs would be well served "by a short and active session" of the legislature. He also recommended that the legislature drastically reduce public printing, a favorite issue with critics of Republican rule, and adopt a general incorporation bill that would greatly decrease the demand for private or special legislation. Finally, he urged the enactment of a measure that would require all contracts for state work or services to go to "the responsible bidder" and not to loyal party men.[6]

Preferring to believe that the age of political and racial intolerance was coming to an end, Governor Powers ignored the question of civil rights for blacks on public transportation and in public places. This issue would soon be felt in the legislature as a result of the black power movement's success in the fall, 1871, election and the strenuous efforts of Charles Sumner to secure a national civil rights law. The governor's only concession at this time to the Radical contention that a great deal still needed to be done to protect the new order was to recommend that the legislature pass a stringent law against carrying concealed weapons, which, he said, as practiced in Mississippi was "a standing menace against the laws of the country."[7]

Although Radicals received Powers' message with some puzzlement, conservatives and moderate Republicans expressed pleasure that the address had stressed the harmony of material progress and reform rather than the specter of "social equality." Some moderate Republicans predicted that Powers would succeed where Alcorn had failed as governor. A conservative writer declared that the people of the state should now be "thankful that chance, or something worse, put Alcorn where he is and saved us from the further infliction of his verbose, egotistical and hard-to-be parsed messages, and his vindictiveness against his own people who have not all yet learned to praise and admire [him]." If Powers' actions approximated his rhetoric, Mississippi would be in good hands for the next three years, conservatives concluded.[8]

6. *Ibid.*, 6–9, 14–15.

7. *Ibid.*, 3.

8. Vicksburg *Times and Republican*, January 17, 19, 1872; Natchez *Weekly Democrat*, January 14, 1872 (quote); Jackson *State Leader*, January 13, 1872; Compton, "Ridgley C. Powers," 10.

It was soon clear, however, that the new governor was not the master of his own house, and specifically of the Republican-dominated legislature. In the beginning Powers had little trouble securing the passage of a bill funding outstanding state warrants; however, the tax measure required to retire these notes more than doubled the rate of general state taxes, from four dollars per thousand of assessed value to eight and one-half dollars. Powers and State Auditor Musgrove believed that the retirement of the depreciated warrants and the return to a cash basis for meeting expenses would substantially reduce the cost of operating the government. These two officials predicted that through this and other proposed economy measures state expenses could be cut by one fourth "without doing violence to any of her interests."[9]

Powers, "a quiet, unassuming man," could not, however, muster enough strength in the legislature to secure the passage of his other reform proposals. Bills to reduce salaries and fees for public offices, shorten judicial sessions, tighten the expensive voter registration procedure, hold sheriffs to a strict accountability for enforcing the revenue law and forwarding tax receipts, and lower the rates for public printing were introduced only to be brushed aside for "private bills" and other matters. A prod by Powers midway through the session failed to nudge the legislature in the direction of reform.[10] Legislative leadership, especially in the lower house, was diffuse and virtually nonexistent. Twenty-five-year-old John R. Lynch proved an able speaker of the house, but a tangled skein of divisions and animosities among Republicans in this body made almost impossible the passage of a systematic program of retrenchment and reform. Lobbyists for the officials who would be affected by the economy measures took advantage of the leadership vacuum and successfully flooded the legislature with arguments against the bills they wanted defeated. Even judges and district attorneys journeyed to the capital to lobby against the salary and fees bill. Absenteeism also plagued the work of the legislature, prolonging the 1872 session by forty days at an expense of $56,000,

9. Natchez *Weekly Democrat*, March 27, April 24, 1872; Vicksburg *Times and Republican*, March 2, 1872; *Annual Report of the Auditor, 1872*, p. 9.

10. Entry for October 15, 1872, in Agnew Diary; Vicksburg *Times and Republican*, March 8, 1872; *Senate Journal, 1872*, pp. 65–66; *House Journal, 1872*, pp. 289–91.

according to a Republican critic.[11] Except to admonish the legislature to take action, Powers made little effort to coax individual Republicans to support his proposals. Furthermore, like the lobbyists whom he deplored, the governor diverted the legislature's attention from reform with recommendations for internal improvements, mainly aid for railroad construction (see Chapter 16 herein), which found a more friendly reception in the assembly than proposals for economy in government.

On the eve of adjournment the legislature frantically passed three "reform" bills. Powers vetoed one of the bills, permitted the second, a revised fees and salaries bill, to lay over until the next session, and signed the third. The evidence is strong that the legislature deliberately designed all three measures to be faulty in order to ensure their veto, which in addition to defeating the cause of genuine reform would also place the odium of its failure upon Governor Powers. The bill the governor signed drastically reduced the rate to be paid to public printers, to such a low level that the printing could not be done at a profit for the contractors. In approving the bill Powers turned the tables on Radicals A. N. Kimball and John B. Raymond, again the state printers, who had intrigued to prevent a reduction in the rates.[12]

When the 1873 session of the legislature convened Powers renewed his plea for retrenchment and reform. He admitted that the efforts under the funding act of 1872 designed to bring state warrants to par and retire them had not worked: "As a consequence, State and county credit is at the mercy of speculators, and paper which should represent par value, is frequently sold from forty to sixty cents on the dollar." He now found a simple remedy for this dilemma. "Prohibit, by rigid enactment," he told the legislature, "the drawing of warrants upon any fund in excess of estimated collections, and place Boards of Supervisors under bonds corre-

11. Jackson *Weekly Clarion*, January 16, 1873; Vicksburg *Times and Republican*, February 4, March 15, 1872.

12. Vicksburg *Times and Republican*, April 9, 10, 18, 1872, October 17, 1873; Natchez *Weekly Democrat*, April 17, 1872; Thomas H. Woods to Ridgley C. Powers, December 28, 1872, in Governors' Correspondence, Vol. 80. Powers subsequently vetoed the fees and salaries bill because, as he pointed out, it increased the compensation for local officers, including sheriffs, who were already overpaid, and reduced the salaries of judges and chancellors, who were underpaid with depreciated state warrants. Vicksburg *Times and Republican*, January 25, 1873.

sponding in amount to the importance of their transactions." Powers reiterated his view that the state and local governments should be operated entirely on a currency basis. "Warrants have no standard value, and the shrewd and the crafty profit by their fluctuations at the expense of the poor and the ignorant, and to the detriment of public credit."[13]

Also in the name of economy, Powers called on the legislature to initiate constitutional amendments that would provide for biennial legislative sessions and for the scheduling of local elections to coincide with the national contests. At the same time he recommended that further restraints be placed on the taxing and spending power of local governments.[14]

As in 1872, the legislature brushed aside the governor's reform program. The assembly agreed to restrict appropriations to anticipated tax revenues for the year; otherwise it rejected outright Powers' recommendations. Nevertheless, the legislature without the support of the governor passed two significant retrenchment bills designed to demonstrate their goodwill on the burning issue of economy in government. The first measure proposed to reduce by almost one half the number of circuit judges and chancellors in the state. Powers immediately vetoed the bill, declaring, "The theory on which it is based makes the judicial department subservient to the Legislature. If the Legislature . . . has the power to remove one Judge and destroy his district, it may in succession remove all the Judges and gerrymander judicial districts to suit the caprice of dominant factions." The legislature was not impressed with his argument against the bill; it quickly overrode the veto.[15]

The second retrenchment measure passed by the assembly was a revised fee and salary bill. As before, the legislature waited until the last day of the session to approve the bill, then deliberately filled it "full of clerical and other errors," as a Republican revealed, in order to ensure a gubernatorial veto.[16] Powers did not disappoint the legislature. He vetoed the bill and, as expected, brought down on his head the criticism of the conservative press.[17]

13. *Senate Journal, 1873*, I, 12.
14. *Ibid.*, I, 25–26.
15. *Ibid.*, I, 1145–46; *Laws of Mississippi, 1873*, pp. 19–26.
16. Vicksburg *Times and Republican*, October 17, 1873.
17. Jackson *Weekly Clarion*, May 1, 1873.

An even greater source of conflict between the governor and the legislature was Powers' attempt to check the proliferation of local legislation that if enacted would have increased the authority of county and town officials at the expense of the state government. Powers made frequent use of the veto power to block this type of legislation; in one day alone he vetoed five local bills. "Passing laws for counties as though they were independent governments is an abuse of legislative functions, and the tendency of all such pernicious enactments is to unsettle governments and produce confusion and discord," he lectured the legislature. His standing with powerful legislators of his party was not enhanced when he labeled one such bill as "ridiculous, absurd, and impracticable."[18] Although commendable in the name of good government and administrative uniformity, Powers' policies severely damaged his bid for the leadership of the Republican party in Mississippi which, he hoped, would be confirmed by his nomination as the party's candidate for governor in 1873. His policies also damaged the efforts of Republican moderates to retain control of the party and the state in the face of a surging Radical challenge.

On two matters, however, the governor and a majority in the legislature could agree. These were civil rights and internal improvements. It was during the Powers era that blacks made their strongest bid for equality of treatment in public places and on public transportation, and, perhaps surprising in view of his heavy emphasis on political harmony and material progress, Governor Powers gave measured support to the cause.

The question of advanced civil rights for blacks had arisen as early as the constitutional convention of 1868 when Negro delegates unsuccessfully sought a section in the state bill of rights that would provide equality of treatment for their race in public accommodations. The attempt was not a very strong one, since blacks held relatively few seats in the convention and at the time were more concerned with winning political and basic legal rights than in pressing for "social equality." But the first Republican legislature had scarcely convened when blacks, whose representation had

18. *House Journal, I, 1873*, pp. 1928–30; Vicksburg *Times and Republican*, April 26, 1873; *Senate Journal, 1873*, pp. 1582–83 (quote).

grown since the 1868 convention, announced their purpose to effectuate the equality promises contained in the congressional reconstruction program, as they interpreted it. On March 16, 1870, Senator William H. Gray, a young minister-politician of Washington County in the Delta, introduced a bill to prohibit racial discrimination on public transportation and in public places. The fat was in the fire, and a serious division between white and black Republicans in the legislature immediately threatened. Even the Radical Albert T. Morgan cringed when the bill was introduced. Rising from his seat, Morgan reminded the senate that such impositions had been disastrous to republicanism in Louisiana, and Gray's bill, if it received support, would cause trouble in Mississippi.[19] Gray, however, persisted in his course and issued a strong plea for the bill's passage. In defense of the bill, the black senator focused on the mistreatment that Negroes received when traveling on railroads. "This bill asks for nothing but what is just and right," he told the lawmakers. "It does not demand social equality; I don't want social equality. . . . But I don't believe after having paid a first-class fare that it is right that my wife should be thrust into a car filthy with tobacco juice and almost suffocating from its tobacco smoke, and where she is subject to the annoyance of the vulgar and obscene conversations of a set of rowdies." In closing, he warned white members of the legislature that if they voted down the bill, "You will be digging your own political graves, whether you be Republicans or Democrats."[20]

Submitted to the senate judiciary committee, the Gray bill emerged shorn of the provision that would protect the rights of blacks in public establishments. The measure, which made it a misdemeanor for any official of a public transportation facility to discriminate against passengers on account of race, fairly easily passed the senate with no white Republicans voting against it. The amended bill purported to give substance to the clause in the constitution guaranteeing "the right of all citizens to travel upon public conveyances" without infringement. This half loaf, which avoided

19. *Senate Journal* [1870], 84; Jackson *Weekly Pilot*, March 19, 1870.
20. Jackson *Weekly Pilot*, March 19, 1870. Gray later moderated his tone toward white Republicans in a formal speech on the amended civil rights bill. He especially indicated his appreciation for the dedication of Republicans, both white and black, to the cause of political rights for blacks, and he insisted that his race would forever be loyal to the party.

the inflammatory issue of mixing the races in public places, appeared to white Republicans to be the easiest way of dealing with Gray's measure without alienating their black associates and thereby destroying their influence in the black community.[21]

But victory was not to be that easy for the white Republicans. In the house of representatives, where Negroes were the most numerous element in the party caucus (although not a majority in the house), blacks secured the passage of an amendment to the bill that closely followed the original Gray measure. Then, when the bill became bogged down in conference committees, blacks in the house attached a nondiscrimination clause to a general railroad incorporation bill in an effort to obtain the support of powerful carpetbaggers like O. C. French who were keenly interested in railroad development and wanted this bill to pass. The maneuver worked. The approved railroad bill included the provision that would make it a penal offense, rather than a misdemeanor as stated in the original bill, for any person to violate black rights on a railroad chartered by the legislature.[22]

Not surprisingly, Governor Alcorn vetoed the railroad incorporation bill. Actually, Alcorn was not hostile to some form of protection for blacks when traveling by train. What he sought was a civil rights formula that both moderate blacks like James Lynch and most white Republicans could support. The poorly framed clause in the railroad measure, Alcorn declared in his veto message, was ambiguous and unenforceable, despite the strong medicine the bill prescribed for violators. At the same time Alcorn's newspaper organ promised blacks that the governor would support any bill the legislature passed that was just and capable of providing meaningful protection for their rights on public conveyances. The language in the veto message, however, suggests that Alcorn preferred a law guaranteeing separate first-class accommodations for Negroes on passenger trains and not the racial integration of the white cars.[23]

This veto sent French and other railroad supporters scurrying

---

21. *Senate Journal* [1870], 268.
22. *Ibid.*, 427, 472, 500, 544; Jackson *Weekly Pilot*, May 15, 21, 1870; Vicksburg *Times and Republican*, April 10, 1870; *House Journal, 1870*, pp. 344–45.
23. Jackson *Weekly Pilot*, May 28, June 25, 1870; *Senate Journal* [1870], 3.

back to the legislature to secure a speedy acceptance of Gray's civil rights measure, which is what militant black legislators had sought from the beginning. The bitter fight that ensued, however, obscured the issues involved in both bills. As a result friends of the railroad interest failed to obtain the necessary votes to override the governor's veto of their pet bill, and advocates of the comprehensive civil rights bill had to settle for a compromise measure that would protect black rights only on public transportation, a position that white Republicans had earlier been willing to concede.[24]

Signed by Alcorn, the act to prohibit racial discrimination on public carriers soon proved a broken reed for hopeful blacks. Although the language of the law was quite explicit, the burden of prosecution rested with the wronged individual and not with the state. Consequently, only those blacks, mainly of the leadership class, who insisted on their rights under the law were permitted first class accommodations. Such exercises in Negro assertiveness, however, were exceptional and fraught with difficulties and even dangers for the blacks who attempted to sit with whites. "If you watch some of our leading men . . . when they go into the cars," Thomas W. Cardozo complained to the readers of the Washington *New National Era*, "you will see that they invariably go into those provided for 'Jim Crow.' It makes me blush when I see it, especially when the laws of the State confirm their right to travel in any car they please." He added, "My skirts, however, are clear of this dereliction of duty, as I have on all occasions, when not smoking, taken seats in first-class cars, and I have never been interrupted."[25]

White violence against the attempted integration of passenger cars occurred only along the Mobile and Ohio Railroad in the Klan country of east Mississippi. At Columbus State Senator Robert Gleed was forced from a first-class compartment into "the car for niggers" by an armed white mob. This incident made clear to other blacks in the east the fate that awaited them if they insisted on riding in the "ladies' car" on the railroad.[26]

Except for the Mobile and Ohio, which could hardly afford to

24. *Laws of Mississippi, 1870*, pp. 104–105. Only eleven white Republicans, all in the lower house, voted against the civil rights bill in the legislature. *House Journal, 1870*, p. 558; *Senate Journal [1870]*, 268, 544.

25. Washington *New National Era*, January 18, April 4, 1872.

26. *Ibid.*, February 1, 1872; W. F. Simonton to Powers, June, 1872, Governors' Correspondence, Vol. 80.

defy the anti-Negro sentiment of its white customers in the east, railroad managers, fearing that the powerful black contingent in the Republican legislature would attack their privileges, trod softly on the matter of rights for Negroes aboard their cars. These companies added "equal" first-class cars for blacks in an attempt to lessen the pressure for integration and reduce the number who would insist on sitting with whites. Evidently most conductors, acting under careful instructions from their management, sought as unobtrusively as possible to accommodate the few blacks who asked for seats in the white cars. Negroes soon discovered, however, that they could not obtain redress in court when conductors refused to comply with the law or the rules of their companies. In 1871 a case brought by Ham Carter, an emerging black leader in the state, against the Mississippi Central Railroad for violating his rights under the 1870 act ended in failure and the virtual collapse of black efforts to ride in first-class compartments. The fact that Carter was forced to pay court costs provided additional discouragement for blacks in their efforts to secure justice on the railroads.[27]

The worst indignities experienced by blacks traveling in Mississippi occurred on the steamboats. Since the steamboats were owned by non-Mississippi companies and in most cases operated mainly on out-of-state waters, the companies did not feel the political need, as the railroad companies did, to comply with the civil rights act. Blacks who sought first-class rooms on steamboats were ushered to the Negro "bureau" or "Texas" compartments. On some boats these accommodations, according to the sensitive Cardozo, were little more than "stalls—called by the captains state-rooms for the colored" whereas on others "they are in the shape of shelves, with an old greasy straw-bed, all in one large apartment, without curtains or any other enclosure for ladies! And, as a general thing, our table is set in the kitchen or in the pantry, where our ears ring with the rattling sound of a hundred dishes in a tub of greasy water; and this is done, too, after charging us the same fare that first-class white passengers pay."[28]

27. Jackson *Weekly Pilot*, March 26, May 21, 1870; Vicksburg *Times and Republican*, April 28, 1872; Natchez *Weekly Democrat*, May 30, 1871.

28. Washington *New National Era*, January 18, November 22, 1872. See also the Natchez *Weekly Democrat*, May 17, 1871.

Negro gains in the local elections of 1871, accompanied by an increasing black awareness of the ineffectiveness of the 1870 law and the indignities of second-class treatment in public, produced a flurry of activity in the legislature of 1872 for a stronger and more comprehensive civil rights law.[29] Led by Gray in the senate and Carter in the house of representatives, Negro legislators advanced a bill designed to guarantee black rights on public conveyances and in public places. Except for the omission of equal rights in schools and churches, the measure followed the provisions of Charles Sumner's national civil rights bill, which at the time was being rejected by the Republican Congress because it was too radical. The penalty for violators contained in the Gray-Carter proposal, however, was more severe than in the Sumner bill. Hotel owners, railroad and steamboat officials, and, in fact, proprietors of almost any kind of public business who denied equal treatment to Negroes could be fined a maximum of one thousand dollars and imprisoned for three years.[30]

The black effort to achieve equal rights in public crested precisely at the time when Governor Powers embarked on his policy to seek a broad base of support for republicanism in the state, one that would emphasize political conciliation and economic progress. As on the issue of retrenchment in government, a clash between the carpetbag governor and blacks in the legislature over additional rights for the race appeared inevitable, since on the surface Negro demands conflicted with Powers' policy. The differences, at least those stated publicly, were more apparent than real. Despite his reputation as a moderate Republican, Powers had been sympathetic to black rights since his entrance into Mississippi politics. In 1870 he had expressed confidence that prejudice against blacks would eventually disappear. "I have no sympathy with the great outcry that is levelled against the rights of men solely on the ground of color," he declared at that time. He could see some reason for refusing to occupy the same railroad car or steamboat berth or sit in a meeting hall with drunkards, robbers, and repro-

29. A weak public accommodations bill was introduced in the legislature of 1871, but it failed to pass either house. Natchez *Weekly Democrat*, March 22, 1871; Jackson *Pilot*, March 2, 1871.

30. Natchez *Weekly Democrat*, March 27, 1872; Washington *New National Era*, April 4, 1872.

bates, "but to refuse to come into such proximity with men because they happened to bear a different complexion from my own, would be to acknowledge a mean prejudice, unworthy of an age of intelligence." The revolution that had elevated blacks "to the dignity of citizenship" would not cease, Powers predicted, "until their rights are recognized, and they have assumed their proper place in society."[31]

Powers saw nothing contradictory between his policy of political harmony and material development for the state and the principle of equal rights for blacks. One would not necessarily come at the expense of the other. In fact, the two might very well reinforce each other. He believed that political reconciliation and economic prosperity could only come after the rights of all Mississippians had been secured. "When all classes are placed upon an equal footing before the law, and in all respects equally protected in their rights, there [will] be no danger of a conflict, there [will] be no cause of any," he asserted.[32]

When he became governor, Powers was prepared to let "the revolution" take its course without pressing the issue of additional civil rights legislation. Although black rights in public had obviously not been achieved, he felt that considerable progress for the race had been made with the suppression of the Klan and the moderating of conservative attitudes toward the new order. If the question of Negro rights were revived, it might undercut the racial and political progress that had been made and divert attention from the more pressing issues of financial reform and economic development. Nevertheless, the black drive in the legislature for an advanced civil rights bill hit a responsive chord in Powers. Tying it with his program of retrenchment and reform, the governor announced to the legislature his support for "a liberal policy of legislation which shall secure all citizens in their equal and just rights, and provide for the rigorous and economical administration of the State Government. . . . The future prosperity of the State demands it at your hands."[33]

Despite Powers' qualified support for further legislation to pro-

---

31. *Senate Journal* [1870], 439–40.
32. Vicksburg *Times and Republican*, April 22, 1873, quoting Powers.
33. *House Journal*, 1872, p. 291.

tect black rights, he remained silent when the Gray-Carter civil rights bill was introduced. Even if the governor had actively supported the measure, the key to its success was the position of moderate Republicans in the legislature, especially in the senate where blacks and their Radical allies were relatively weak. Moderate Republicans throughout the state appealed to their associates in the assembly to stand firm against the Radical measure. The Vicksburg *Times and Republican* expressed the view that behind the bill were "a half dozen idiots of both races" who sought "a little ignoble and infamous capital by striving to enact that the two races, without the consent of either, shall be hurled into each other's faces in the cars, in the steamboats, in the places of amusement and in the hotels." Dominant Republicans in the legislature, this carpetbag editor wrote, should "recognize the fact that the pathway of the colored man through life shall not be higher and shall not be lower than the path of the white race, but that it shall be seperate [*sic*] and distinct, and yet be equal."[34] Such an open expression of Republican hostility to black aspirations was rare, but it followed an attempt by a young Negro politician to take a seat in the white section of a Vicksburg theater. Although denouncing the whites who "mob-like rushed to the assistance of the usher" during the confrontation, the editor felt compelled, perhaps by the polarization of racial attitudes around him, to resist publicly any measure that extended equal rights to blacks in public places.[35]

The Vicksburg incident also motivated black leaders in the legislature to be more militant in their demands for the passage of the Gray-Carter bill. As a result of black pressure the measure easily passed the house of representatives, where only five white Republicans risked their political fortunes to vote against it. In the senate, scalawag Joseph Bennett sought to secure the measure's defeat by introducing a bill to guarantee blacks "equal but separate accommodations" in public places. The maneuver failed, and the senate approved the Gray-Carter bill by a close vote with most of the moderate members conspicuously absent. With Powers prepared to sign it, "the social equality abomination," as conservatives la-

34. Vicksburg *Times and Republican*, March 30, 1872. See also W. C. Ford to Powers, March 23, 1872, in Governors' Correspondence, Vol. 79.
35. Vicksburg *Times and Republican*, March 3, 5, 1872.

beled the civil rights measure, appeared to be a reality. But a preposterous thing occurred: the bill was lost or stolen, depending on the view of the teller (but more likely the latter), before it arrived on the governor's desk.[36]

Chagrined by the mysterious disappearance of the civil rights bill, Gray and Carter, instead of reviving it as the session approached adjournment, attached the substance of the measure to a railroad bill that was conveniently under consideration by the legislature. The maneuver succeeded in the house of representatives but failed by a vote of 14 to 15 in the senate. Thwarted again, angry black legislators left Jackson vowing to renew the fight early in the next session.[37] Throughout the state their Negro constituents joined them in feeling betrayed over the incident. In Natchez aroused blacks exercised their local power to make amends for the loss of the bill. Here, the black-dominated board of aldermen passed an ordinance prohibiting the renting of the popular city-owned Institute Hall to any group that discriminated among its patrons on account of race. The conservative reaction to this imposition became so strong that Mayor Robert H. Wood, a black man who was anxious to maintain harmony in the town viewed by many Republicans as a showcase of biracial democracy in the Mississippi Valley, agreed to accept a separate seating arrangement for the races in the hall. Not all blacks, however, were satisfied with the compromise. At a time when the politics of the New Departure was at its zenith in Natchez, a local black made a pointed observation about the issue when he wrote: "It strikes my mind as very inconsistent on the part of the Democrats to ask the colored voters of Natchez to support them politically and in business, when they never have conceded to them any rights as citizens unless they were compelled by circumstances over which they have no control."[38] This sense of outrage contributed to the growth of black solidarity in the state and a determination to resist the emerging liberal Republican movement which proposed to compromise their rights (see pages 456–68 herein).

36. Jackson *Weekly Clarion*, March 14, April 11, 1872; Washington *New National Era*, April 4, 25, 1872.

37. Washington *New National Era*, April 25, 1872.

38. Natchez *Weekly Democrat*, April 17, 1872.

When the legislature met in January, 1873, blacks reintroduced the civil rights bill. This time the struggle would not be long, and nothing mysterious would happen to the bill before it became a law. By a vote of 61 to 41, with only three white Republicans opposing, the measure easily passed the house of representatives. The senate quickly agreed to the bill with all Republicans voting for it, even Joseph Bennett. On February 7 Governor Powers invited all the members of the legislature and many others to the mansion to witness the signing of the measure that Gray and his associates in the legislature had worked for since the beginning of Republican rule in Mississippi.[39] The governor hailed the event as "an advanced step in the enlightened tendency of the time." Mississippi, he said, "is entitled to the distinction of being the first State in the Union to guarantee, by statutory enactment, full civil as well as political rights to all her citizens, without distinction."[40] Even the Vicksburg *Times and Republican* found reason to applaud the enactment of the bill.

No doubt such an impressive degree of white Republican support for the civil rights measure reflected political considerations, since Republican politicians could not win election to office or maintain local influence in the party unless they were able to retain black support. Even in the white counties the strength of the party rested with its black constituency (probably no more than five thousand Mississippi whites ever supported the party). Although blacks in these areas tended to be more conservative and more willing to follow white leadership, by 1873 they were aware of the debate on the civil rights bill at the state capital, and they pressed for its enactment. Nevertheless, political considerations were not the only reasons for white Republican support of black rights in public places. Their close and congenial association with blacks over a period of time, their reaction to the conservatives' abuse of the Gray-Carter bill, and their obvious reflection on the not-so-radical implications of public rights for Negroes, particular-

39. Jackson *Weekly Clarion*, February 27, 1873; Washington *New National Era*, February 20, 1873. The civil rights act of 1873 was in the form of an amendment to sections 2731 and 2732 of the Revised Code of 1871. *Laws of Mississippi, 1873*, pp. 66–69.

40. Vicksburg *Times and Republican*, April 22, 1873, quoting an address by the governor to the legislature.

ly in view of the mild effect that the 1870 guarantees regarding public transportation had had, all worked to persuade white Republicans that the extention of additional rights would not be socially catastrophic. By 1873 even moderate Republicans were willing to concede the rights contained in the Gray-Carter bill, which, they believed, would probably result in selective integration at worst. Indeed, Alcorn would soon be speaking in the United States Senate in favor of Sumner's civil rights bill.[41]

Meanwhile, Radicals were shifting to a more extreme position on civil rights. A few weeks after the passage of the public accommodations measure Flournoy in a speech at the capitol called for the racial integration of the state's public schools, and black leaders joined in the demand.[42] When the Radicals gained control of the state Republican convention later in 1873, they resolved to recognize "no distinctions as now existing by law, in the rights of all children of the State to equal privileges, and access to all public schools, colleges or universities, and should any institutions of learning deny to any child, on account of race or color, its equal rights, we pledge ourselves to enforce said rights by appropriate legislation."[43] Victorious Radicals, however, made no significant effort to implement this platform when they came to power in 1874. Other matters, especially the pressing issues of retrenchment and tax reform, diverted their attention, and only a handful of black legislators reminded their white colleagues of the party's pledge to break down the hardening dual system of public schools. Stymied by his own wing of the party in his efforts to eradicate, at least legally, the last vestiges of racial discrimination in Mississippi, Gray led an attempt to integrate the white schools in his hometown of Greenville. Although there was no immediate cause to fear a violent reaction, since blacks were in an overwhelming majority in the county and in control of most of the offices, Gray, whose radicalism was frequently tempered by a concern for racial harmony,

41. See the Vicksburg *Times and Republican*, June 24, 1873, "Economist" to the editor, October 8, 1873; and *Speech of Alcorn in the Senate, 1874*.

42. Vigorously applauded by the blacks in attendance, the speech was referred to by the Jackson *Weekly Clarion*, March 20, 1873, as "the most Radical deliverance" since Reconstruction began. For the position of the black leadership on the issue, see the Washington *New National Era*, July 24, 1873.

43. Vicksburg *Times and Republican*, August 30, 1873.

abandoned the effort after a brief debate with school officials.[44]

But in 1873 blacks seemed satisfied with the passage of the civil rights bill, and they turned out in mass meetings to celebrate the event.[45] Their delight was really more cautious hope than jubilation, in view of the failure of the 1870 civil rights act to guarantee equal treatment for them on public transportation facilities. Even so, their hope was short-lived, but before it died the state supreme court had placed its stamp of approval on the new law.

In June, the court handed down a decision on the civil rights law which was the most sweeping judicial affirmation of black rights in Mississippi, and perhaps in the nation, during the Reconstruction era. The case originated when Ham Carter, co-author of the civil rights bill, was refused a seat in the white section of the Angelo Concert Hall in Jackson. Carter secured a warrant for the arrest of the doorkeeper, George Donnell, who had barred him from the white area. The intrepid legislator won his case before Chancellor E. W. Cabaniss, a scalawag, and Donnell, who was ordered jailed for violating the new law, appealed to the state supreme court for a writ of habeas corpus. William Yerger and William L. Nugent, two of the ablest lawyers in the state, represented Donnell before the high court; they argued that the 1873 act was unconstitutional on the grounds that it interfered with property rights. If forced to seat blacks in the white section, the defense insisted, the proprietor of the theater would lose business, which inevitably would result in the depreciation of his property.[46]

Attorney General Joshua S. Morris ably argued the case for the state and Carter. He deflected the issue from property rights to human rights. Not only was the civil rights act in accordance with the doctrine of "the equality of all men before God," Morris asserted, but it also conformed to the spirit of the Fourteenth Amendment which had raised a suppressed class "to a plane of absolute legal equality with the hitherto dominant caste." Blacks "have been invited, and have accepted the invitation, to enter the race of life as competitors with the white man for the goal of a higher and

44. Greenville *Weekly Times*, October 10, 1874.
45. Washington *New National Era*, May 22, 1873.
46. *George Donnell* v. *State of Mississippi*, 48 Miss. 661–82 (1873).

nobler civilization." Morris argued, "It is very plain, upon admitted facts, that the colored people will have to be admitted by law to, or excluded by law from, all places of public amusements." Since the Fourteenth Amendment explicitly prohibited state action discriminating against blacks, by implication the state had the responsibility for protecting their rights in public, which was the objective of the civil rights act of 1873. Furthermore, the scalawag attorney general argued, black political power in the state was on the rise, and unless whites extended rights to them now, blacks at some future time might gain power and withhold the same rights from their former oppressors. Morris believed that the law "seeks only to preserve the peace between two classes, who, whatever may be the real or supposed differences in social rank, are perfectly equal before the laws of God and man."[47]

The supreme court agreed with Morris and sustained the lower court decision againt Donnell. Justice Horatio F. Simrall, an old-line Whig who became a Republican after Governor Alcorn appointed him to the court, delivered the court's unanimous opinion. Simrall declared that the civil rights act was a logical result of black freedom and the ratification of the Fourteenth Amendment. He brushed aside the defense's contention that the act violated property rights under the Constitution, saying that common law precedents gave the legislature the right to regulate businesses which had "a *quasi* public relation to the communities," a category that included theaters. Finally, Simrall revealed that this kind of enactment came under the reserve power clause of the Constitution; therefore "the large subjects of the general welfare, safety, happiness and prosperity of the people of the state are committed to the legislature, to be advanced and promoted by legislation."[48] The civil rights act fell into this category.

Despite the court's decision, the civil rights act of 1873, like its predecessor of 1870, had virtually no effect on the treatment of blacks in public. Already the informal code of racial separation in public places and on public conveyances was becoming rigid. The new law would not disturb this trend.

47. *Ibid.*, 665–66, 668–69.
48. *Ibid.*, 673–82.

At the time the law was passed conservatives, though disturbed, expressed no real fear that it would be enforced. They seemed more alarmed that incidents of racial violence would occur when blacks tried to assert their rights under the law. Barksdale charged that "the worst feature of the measure" was "the attempt to compel association between the races in violation of natural laws, and in disregard of the peace and good order of society. While it will produce strife, it will not accomplish the object designed by its authors, who insist on legislating colored people into association unnatural with the whites."[49] The Natchez *Democrat* dismissed the act, predicting that the effect "will be only to involve a few lawsuits for damages, which will terminate . . . in the defeat of the party claiming pretended rights which no law can force people to accord to [blacks]. With this, and probably a few conflicts, the matter will end, and the law stand inoperative as a monument to the folly of those who enacted it." To demonstrate that he was not hostile to the legitimate rights of blacks, the New Departure editor of the *Democrat* declared that without intermingling the races, "every steamboat and railroad ought to be compelled by law to furnish to all decent and well-behaved colored people accommodations and fare equal in every respect to those furnished to white people paying the same rate of fare." He believed that "if this were done, we are satisfied that no colored man with common self-respect and a sense of decent propriety, would think of desiring to obtrude himself at a table, or in a car or cabin where he knew his presence was distasteful to those for whom that particular place was reserved."[50]

Proprietors of public establishments, however, could not take a chance on the *Democrat*'s prediction coming true. Threatened by the loss of their white patronage if even token integration occurred, hotel and restaurant owners and managers of public amusement places put signs on their doors announcing that they were no longer open for public business, but instead had converted their establishments to accommodations for selected guests. Only those persons who had received "invitations" would be served, and they

49. Jackson *Weekly Clarion*, February 6, 1873.
50. As reported in *ibid.*, February 20, 1873.

would be expected to make a contribution toward defraying the expenses of the services and accommodations. "All of the hotels are strictly private, the same little proscribed bureau has its place on the steamboats, and colored passengers wishing to purchase at the bar, or procure tickets must 'come around on the outside,' " a black from Hurricane wrote of this system one year after the passage of the civil rights bill.[51]

In addition to Ham Carter, a number of blacks in 1873 asserted their rights under the law. A black demonstration occurred at Vicksburg when a Negro was refused a ticket to a lecture in the public hall. Later in the year blacks "grossly intruded" upon whites "at a private performance" in the Vicksburg Opera House. Whites subsequently abandoned the hall to the blacks, and theatrical companies canceled their performances for the winter season because they feared, as a Bourbon editor explained, that "the disgraceful scene will be re-enacted to their detriment and financial injury."[52] In Hazlehurst, a minor disturbance occurred when a handful of Negroes, inspired by an "outsider" from Vicksburg, tried to rent a hotel room and eat in a local white restaurant. Although a warrant was issued for the arrest of the proprietor of the restaurant, the case evidently was dismissed on a technicality.[53] Normally blacks were turned away from white accommodations in the quiet way experienced by Congressman John R. Lynch when he took a seat at a white table in the dining room of the railroad station at Holly Springs. He was asked to leave, and he did so without protest and before white racial passions could be aroused.[54]

By the middle of 1874 the early apprehension of some conservatives that the civil rights act would be enforced had largely vanished. Proprietors of public establishments brought down their private club signs (perhaps because they feared losing their licenses at the hands of the Ames administration) and continued to serve their white patrons as if the law did not exist. Only rarely did a black man "create a scene" to secure his rights in public,

51. Washington *New National Era*, May 28, 1874.
52. *Ibid.*, May 22, 1873; Vicksburg *Vicksburger*, January 1, 1874.
53. Jackson *Weekly Clarion*, April 10, 1873. An attempt to integrate a Pascagoula bar was successful at this time. Vicksburg *Times and Republican*, April 22, 1873.
54. Wharton, *The Negro in Mississippi*, 231.

and except for a few instances on the railroads he was unsuccessful in his efforts.[55]

If Governor Powers expected to gain political advantage from his support of civil rights for blacks, he was soon disappointed. At the same time his plan to form a coalition of moderates based on political conciliation and economic progress went astray. As early as the campaign and election of 1872 it appeared that the Powers strategy might flounder on the shoals of Reconstruction and racial antagonisms, although there were clearly many prominent men of both parties who looked to the governor—more than to Senator Alcorn who was temporarily in political exile in Washington—to head off the rise to power of the Radical Ames.[56] Ironically, as time would prove, the national emergence of liberal or moderate republicanism in 1872 contributed significantly to the failure of the moderate cause in Mississippi.

Nevertheless, the election year began on a good note for the cause of political moderation in the state. The local elections of 1871 had demonstrated again the folly of conservative efforts to dislodge Republican control of the state government and the predominantly black counties. Among conservative leaders the elections had increased interest in the politics of the New Departure, which in essence was a policy of divide and conquer, even though several of its spokesmen were evidently sincere in their professed support for some black rights. But difficulties abounded for New Departure advocates. Governor Powers' policy of retrenchment and reform complicated their efforts to win a following among moderate Republicans, and at the same time the white masses showed little enthusiasm for an alliance with moderate carpetbaggers like Powers.

55. In a matter-of-fact fashion, scalawag Jason Niles reported in 1874 that William Gray had occupied a berth in a white sleeping car on a train in the state. Entry for November 10, 1874, in Niles Diary. See also the Pascagoula *Star*, October 3, 17, 1874, for other instances of racial mixing on the railroads. The decisions of the United States Supreme Court during the late Reconstruction period, of course, went far to vitiate federal enforcement of the guarantees in the Fourteenth Amendment and to discourage blacks in their efforts to obtain equality of treatment under the law. LaWanda Cox and John H. Cox (eds.), *Reconstruction, the Negro, and the New South* (New York, 1973), xx–xxi.

56. Absalom M. West to Powers, December 24, 1872, in Governors' Correspondence, Vol. 80; Vicksburg *Times and Republican*, January 25, 1872; Natchez *Weekly Democrat*, February 14, 1872.

The complications of working out a political coalition aside, the 1872 swing toward moderation among conservatives offered a glimmer of hope that the day of the Bourbon in Mississippi politics had passed. Nowhere was this more apparent than in the retirement early in the year of a number of Bourbon editors and the abandonment of the "billingsgate" style of journalism by most of those who remained. The Bourbon retreat appeared virtually complete in March when the proprietors of the Vicksburg *Herald* forced McCardle, the most popular of the extreme journalists, to resign as editor. In removing McCardle, the owners admitted that his intemperate editorials had lost their appeal to west Mississippi readers; consequently, merchants were turning elsewhere to advertise their wares and the *Herald* was losing money. By April only A. J. Frantz of the Brandon *Republican* continued to belch forth the fire and brimstone editorials associated with bourbonism in the state.[57]

Speeding the decline of bourbonism and the rise of the New Departure was the formation of the national Liberal Republican party. A movement by old Republicans to reform the national government and withhold federal support from the reputedly corrupt carpetbag regimes in the South, the Liberal Republican party offered cooperative conservatives in Mississippi the opportunity to take a major step toward redeeming the state from Republican rule. Accommodationists rejoiced when the Liberal Republican convention at Cincinnati adopted a platform of "universal suffrage and universal amnesty," since it fitted well with the state's New Departure doctrine. But their rejoicing turned to dismay when the telegraphic wires flashed the news that the old southern nemesis, Horace Greeley, had been selected as the party's candidate for president. Be that as it may, they had no alternative but to support Greeley against Grant's bid for reelection. In endorsing the Greeley candidacy, most conservative spokesmen pointed out that a Democratic ticket, if offered, could not succeed against the regular Republicans, and Greeley was the only hope Mississippi had to be rescued from "the most disgraceful government that ever

57. Natchez *Weekly Democrat*, March 20, April 10, 1872; Columbus *Index*, as reported in the *Hinds County Gazette*, February 12, 1872; Vicksburg *Times and Republican*, March 15, 24, April 9, 1872.

outraged any people." The Macon *Beacon* put the matter succinctly: "We certainly prefer Greeley or the devil to Grant, but we're not going into hysterics over it."[58]

Hamilton H. Chalmers, a leading advocate of the Greeley-conservative alliance, insisted that the purpose of the movement was not to take away the rights of blacks, as the Republicans, North and South, claimed. The conservative party in Mississippi, he declared, "is pledged in every conceivable way to a maintenance of the legal rights of the negro as now established by law" and the Fifteenth Amendment.

> If the Northern man who hesitates to trust us will not believe in our good faith he should be able to realize the fact that the ballot works its own protection, and that no political party ever existed which, as a matter of policy, could afford to wage war against a large, and in my State preponderating class of voters. Why, then, does the South support Mr. Greeley? I answer in a word, because he, of all men, seems to typify that sentiment of kind feeling and fraternity towards the South which appears at last to be making some headway in the northern heart, and because he, of all Republicans, first and most forcibly realized the fact that the South was being plundered and robbed by a set of men, who, to use his own language, were "desperate adventurers, destitute of education and character, who had crept down South in the rear of the Federal army for the purpose of plundering a people already impoverished."

Chalmers claimed that under Greeley "the whole power of the national government will not be brought to bear in the future as it has been in the past to support these men; but that we shall be at least permitted to fight out our political battles with them fairly at the polls without Federal interference either military or pecuniary."[59]

The Greeley pill was far more difficult for Mississippi conservatives to swallow than his apologists would admit in public. Thomas E. Tate, an old Unionist of Pike County and a Greeley supporter, doubted that any self-respecting Democrat would support the *Tribune* editor. Greeley's record as an abolitionist, his advocacy of radical reforms, and his support for a high protective tariff had made

58. Natchez *Weekly Democrat*, May 29, 1872. This issue carried a number of excerpts from editorials on the Greeley candidacy that appeared in various state newspapers.
59. *Ibid.*, September 11, 1872.

him an anathema to the Democrats in the past. Tate did not expect old Democrats to "drink so bitter a draft" as Horace Greeley. Lamar, who during this campaign came out of political retirement to begin his rise to a position of leadership in the conservative party, wrote to a northern friend that Greeley "has ever been the living embodiment and concentration of all that we of the South and of the Democracy are accustomed to regard as unsound and pestilent in politics." Greeley's biography, Lamar said, "should be entitled 'A History of the Aberrations of Human Reason, as Illustrated by the Life and Writings of an American Editor.'" Nevertheless, Lamar campaigned for the New York editor, since his candidacy offered the only hope for the overthrow of "a vile despotism" in the South.[60]

With the same lack of enthusiasm, a makeshift state convention of conservatives met at Jackson in late June to consider a course of action for the fall campaign. Only forty of the seventy-one counties sent delegates, which led critics to compare it with the Dent party that was "gotten up" by the Jackson clique in 1869. Thirty blacks, almost all of them politically inexperienced, were brought to the convention as showcase delegates to promote the cause of the New Departure in the Negro community. Old-line Whigs could not complain about being ignored by the delegates. As its chairman, the convention selected John W. C. Watson, the most prominent Whig of north Mississippi, and he in turn chose a state executive committee whose membership was balanced between the old parties. The convention also sent a delegation to the national Democratic convention at Baltimore that was almost equally divided between Democrats and Whigs. On the crucial issue of fusion with the Liberal Republicans, the convention endorsed Greeley and instructed the Baltimore delegation to oppose the selection of a Democratic candidate.[61]

A barrage of conservative criticism greeted the action of the state convention and a revival of the Bourbon spirit appeared in

60. T. E. Tate to William N. Whitehurst, May 15, 1872, in Whitehurst Papers; L. Q. C. Lamar to Charles Reemelin, July 15, 1872, in Edward Mayes, *Lucius Q. C. Lamar: His Life, Times, and Speeches, 1825–1893* (Nashville, 1896), 170; Murphy, *L. Q. C. Lamar*, 109. See also the Brandon (Miss.) *Republican*, May 30, 1872.

61. Columbus (Miss.) *Democrat*, July 6, 1872; Natchez *Weekly Democrat*, July 3, 10, September 11, 1872; New York *Times*, July 6, 1872.

the offing. "Horace Greeley is virtually the father of the Radical party," the editor of the Columbus *Democrat* exploded. How could the conservative convention endorse the candidacy of a man who had been a leading instigator of the troubles of the South? he asked. When a small group of second-line Republicans, most of whom had been inconspicuous in Mississippi politics since their advocacy of the ill-fated Dent movement, met and formed a state Liberal Republican party, the parallel with the 1869 fiasco became clear to Bourbon critics. The Greeley-New Departure coalition, a "Democrat" wrote, was also "like the Know-Nothing movement of former years, great in appearance but small in reality."[62]

Mississippi Republicans entered the political contest of 1872 with confidence that their ranks would hold firm against the seductions of the Greeley-conservative alliance. Their confidence in the black voters, as well as in many whites, was not misplaced.[63] United States District Attorney G. Wiley Wells expressed the feeling of many Republicans in the state when he wrote that if the conservatives won the presidential election in the fall "the situation would indeed be deplorable; no man with union proclivities could remain in the state, while the condition of the freedmen would be much worse than when in slavery." The national Liberal Republicans attempted to lure Alcorn into the party with a promise of a cabinet position if they won. He rejected their overtures but at the same time revealed to his wife: "I intend that Grant shall let me control affairs in Mississippi or I will make him feel my weight." Although the president did not permit him to "control affairs" in the state, the scalawag senator remained loyal during the campaign.[64] His cousin Robert J. Alcorn bolted the party and became chairman of the Liberal Republicans' state executive committee,

62. The Columbus *Democrat*, July 6, 1872, contains several excerpts from statements of conservatives denouncing the action of the state convention.
63. Alexander Warner to William E. Chandler, April 13, 1872; and O. C. French to Chandler, July 17, 1872, both in William E. Chandler Papers. Some moderate conservatives, disgusted by the Greeley movement, revealed to local Republicans that they were prepared to speak publicly for Grant if he would promise that his administration "for the next four years would be liberal & conciliatory" toward the South. A moderate Republican delegation was sent to Washington to secure such an assurance, but it failed. Jonathan Tarbell to Chandler, October 23, 1872, *ibid.*
64. G. Wiley Wells to George H. Williams, April 2, 1872, in Source-Chronological File, Northern Mississippi, RG 60, NA, Microcopy Roll 1; "Indian" (James Lusk Alcorn) to his wife Amelia, April 13, 1872, in James Lusk Alcorn Papers, Mississippi Department of Archives and History.

and one of the senator's sons also joined the movement. In addition to Robert Alcorn only three other prominent Mississippi Republicans, Jefferson L. Wofford, William M. Hancock, and Joseph Bennett, threw political caution to the wind and announced their support of Greeley. All four were impelled to bolt the regular party more by local Republican divisions than by any commitment to the Liberal Republican cause.[65]

In fact, the only threat to the regular Republicans in the election came from local party divisions, most of which had been present during the 1871 campaign. In addition to the presidency, congressional seats were to be filled. In all but one of the Republican district conventions to choose the party's nominees for Congress, disruptions threatened serious splits in the organization. Black disaffection erupted in three district meetings when Negro candidates failed to secure the nominations. In one of these conventions, at Vicksburg, fights broke out as the frustrated supporters of James Lynch, who obviously was the choice of the black masses in the district, sought to prevent the nomination of carpetbag incumbent George C. McKee. When McKee received the nomination (through bribery, Lynch supporters charged), Hancock, the bantam-rooster Radical of the "Mighty East," walked out of the convention and announced his support for Greeley. The demoralized Lynch went north to Indiana to canvass for Grant rather than remain in Mississippi during the campaign.[66]

In the fourth district convention, the success of John R. Lynch in deposing the carpetbag incumbent led to the walkout of many of the white delegates. Only the candidacy of Flournoy against Lamar in the northernmost congressional district received the approval of all elements in the local party. As in 1871, on election day the Republicans closed ranks and supported the party nominees, although in the disaffected districts Grant received a higher vote than the congressional candidates.[67]

Although the congressional campaigns exacerbated Republican

65. Natchez *Weekly Democrat*, July 3, 31, August 14, 1872. Surprisingly, all four were able to return to the good graces of the regular party after the election.

66. A. C. Fisk to William E. Chandler, August 13, 1872, and John B. Raymond to O. C. French, August 3, 1872, both in William E. Chandler Papers; Natchez *Weekly Democrat*, August 14, 1872; Columbus *Press*, July 12, 1872; Harris, "James Lynch," 58–59.

67. H. Murray Quin to Whitehurst, November 1, 1872, in Whitehurst Papers; Natchez *Weekly Democrat*, August 21, September 11, November 13, 1872.

factionalism, the contests proved a godsend to the faltering conservative cause. They advanced congressional candidates like Lamar in the north and Hiram Cassedy in the south, both old Democrats of New Departure sentiments who could rally whites to the polls on election day. Even though the conservative party leadership, in the face of Bourbon taunts, maintained an appearance of support for Greeley with torchlight parades and meetings in Natchez and other centers of the New Departure, the Liberal Republican's goose was cooked well before the election. Typical of the situation was Jefferson County, where a Republican reported to Governor Powers that President Grant "is constantly gaining ground while Greeley is losing. . . . You might find a needle in a haystack almost as soon as you could find a Greeley man in this county."[68]

Nonetheless, on election day a surprising number of Greeley needles were found in the Mississippi haystack. As expected, however, Grant easily carried the state (and the nation), but Greeley's 47,287 votes to Grant's 82,406 was larger than anticipated considering white apathy and hostility toward the New York editor. Of the seventy-one counties in the state, Greeley won twenty-seven, five of these being new counties carved out of larger white units.[69] The *Tribune* editor's respectable showing at the polls was due more to the attraction of the conservative congressional candidates than to any appeal Greeley might have had. Most conservatives who rode to town to vote for Lamar or Cassedy for Congress in most cases took the time to vote for Greeley as the lesser of evils in the presidential election. And even a few blacks, without threat of intimidation or violence, cast ballots for the man who had befriended their race long before U. S. Grant became a Republican.[70]

68. Abel Alderson to Powers, October 18, 1872, in Governors' Correspondence, Vol. 80. See also the Natchez *Weekly Democrat*, September 4, October 23, 1872.

69. The election returns for 1872 may be found in *Mississippi in 1875: Report of the Select Committee to Inquire into the Mississippi Election of 1875, with the Testimony and Documentary Evidence* (2 vols.; Washington, D.C., 1876), II, 137–45. This document is sometimes referred to as the Boutwell Report but will be cited hereinafter as *Mississippi in 1875*. For extensive reports of white apathy in the election, see the Hernando (Miss.) *Weekly Press and Times*, December 5, 1872, and the Natchez *Weekly Democrat*, November 20, 1872.

70. Perhaps even more than in the election of 1871, the state during the 1872 campaign was "perfectly peaceable," as Governor Powers reported. "There is no probability of any

The conservative strength in the 1872 election, however, declined by 14,000 votes from that of 1871, whereas the regular Republicans polled almost the same number of ballots as in the previous contest. Republicans in 1869 had won all of the congressional seats; in 1872 they lost one—to Lamar, who at the time of his election was still ineligible to hold office because of Fourteenth Amendment disabilities. Congress removed his disabilities soon after the election, an action that gave him the opportunity to appear on a national stage where he could promote the New Departure doctrine of sectional reconciliation and harmony.[71]

The Republican victory by an almost two to one margin, coming after the success of 1871, convinced many in the party that no compelling reason existed for them to follow a policy of conciliation and moderation toward conservatives in the state, as advocated by Powers and Alcorn.[72] The Republican ascendancy appeared safe behind a bloc of black voters and federal protection, which Grant's victory seemed to reinforce. Many Republicans who had earlier favored a policy of developing a racially balanced party now joined the Ames Radicals in rejecting any realistic effort to win the good will of the old citizens. To Ames and the growing Radical wing, the strategy to attract a large number of whites to the party had from the beginning been an illusion born of conservative intrigue and moderate Republican gullibility. The Liberal Republican-New Departure alliance represented still another attempt to exploit moderate Republican sentiment. Although the conservatives had failed in the election, Republicans in the future, stalwarts insisted, must not be misled by those who preached political conciliation, retrenchment and reform in government, and racial harmony. Such expressions, Radicals said, were only weapons to discredit Republican rule, divide Republican voters, and rally whites behind a campaign to restore the old rebels to power and circumvent the

---

disturbance during the coming election," he wrote the military commander of the Department of the Gulf on the eve of the voting. Powers to W. H. Emory, October 28, 1872, in Governors' Correspondence, Vol. 80.

71. Murphy, *L. Q. C. Lamar*, 109–10.

72. Evidence for the solidification of this attitude among Republicans can be found in the Vicksburg *Times and Republican*, August 21, 26, 1873, and the Jackson *Weekly Clarion*, December 5, 1872.

rights of blacks. By accepting the Powers-Alcorn strategy, Republicans would be playing into the hands of their enemies.

Since the suspicious loss of the civil rights bill in the spring of 1872, the black leadership had moved to a more militant position not only in their quest for bona fide racial equality but also in their demand for greater political influence in the state. The Powers-Alcorn strategy of moderation threatened to cut short this black drive toward political power. Although Governor Powers had signed the 1873 civil rights bill, blacks viewed with suspicion his consorting with men who had formulated the Black Code of 1865. Furthermore, his emphasis upon financial reform and material progress threatened to divert attention from the unfulfilled black demand for equality in public places and on public transportation. Despite the governor's good intentions blacks believed that conservatives would take advantage of him, to the detriment of the reconstruction settlement in the state. To many blacks, the impressive Republican victory of 1872 was an affirmation of their struggle for meaningful rights and for greater influence in the government.

The death of Secretary of State James Lynch soon after the election removed from the scene the only black moderate who might have been able to swing substantial Negro support to the Powers-Alcorn wing in a showdown with the Ames Radicals. Lynch's struggle to free blacks from carpetbag adventurers in the Jackson area was well known, and, despite a decline in his influence among local black leaders primarily because of his affinity for hard liquor, he still enjoyed the confidence of the masses of his race—a support surpassing that of any other black leader in Mississippi Reconstruction. Rather than press for public rights for blacks, during the last two years of his life Lynch turned his attention to criticizing the state's economic system, specifically the debilitating sharecrop and crop-lien arrangements. He seemed to view the economic quagmire that blacks found themselves in as a greater threat to their liberties than the emerging pattern of social segregation. Lynch believed that members of his race had a better chance of controlling their destinies through economic progress, which would include the purchase of land from willing planters, than through additional laws guaranteeing their rights in public.[73] After his death in December, 1872, the Powers-Alcorn faction advanced former Senator Hiram R. Revels as its spokesman in the black community. The mild-mannered Revels, however, had never enjoyed any real influence with the black masses, and his speaking tours for the moderate cause in 1872–1873 fell flat.[74] He also failed to win the support of local Negro leaders who now looked to such young blacks as John R. Lynch, Ham Carter, and William H. Gray for state leadership.

The erosion of Republican support for Governor Powers escalated in 1873, a year that would be climaxed by a bitter gubernatorial election. The carpetbag governor's increasing disposition to appoint conservatives to office and his hobnobbing with "railroad corruptionists" caused many Republicans to turn against him. The list of anti-Powers Republicans soon included the powerful editor of the moderate Vicksburg *Times and Republican*, though the opposition of this carpetbag journalist may very well have stemmed from the governor's failure to appoint him as superintendent of the state penitentiary, a position he had desired.[75] In April Powers concluded that his effort to win control of the party had faltered. His ambitions whetted by election year politics, he now made several rash moves that shattered his influence in the party. He weakened his support among moderates by approaching Ames with a plan to compromise their differences. Under the Powers plan, according to Ames, the governor would support the New England carpetbagger's return to the Senate if Ames would endorse his candidacy for governor. Although Powers claimed to control the party in a majority of the counties—a claim some independent observers confirmed—Ames believed that the offer of compromise was an artful move by a man whose political strength was waning.[76]

73. For a fuller treatment of Lynch's economic views as well as his political activities at this time, see Harris, "James Lynch," 55–59.

74. Adelbert Ames to his wife, October 3, 1872, in Blanche Butler Ames (comp.), *Chronicles*, I, 386–87.

75. John J. Smith to Powers, March 27, 1873, in Governors' Correspondence, Vol. 80; Jackson *Weekly Clarion*, June 26, 1873; Washington *New National Era*, August 21, 1873; Vicksburg *Times and Republican*, July 20, 27, August 7, 9, 1873.

76. Ames to his wife, April 14, 1873, in Blanche Butler Ames (comp.), *Chronicles*, I, 444–45; Jackson *Weekly Clarion*, May 15, 1873, citing the Memphis *Appeal*.

In May Powers announced his intention to implement the 1870 militia law by partially organizing the thirty thousand men who had been enrolled but never formed into units. A few days later he began to issue commissions for the creation of seventeen companies and five divisions in the state. He instructed Adjutant General William W. Dedrick, a carpetbagger, to make no distinction on account of race in the organization of the units. However, the units were not integrated, few blacks received commissions, and the brigadier positions that were authorized all went to whites.[77]

The governor's action in organizing the militia immediately aroused a storm of protest from his enemies in the Republican party and from some who had been careful in the past not to criticize his policies. Black leader Cardozo, who had earlier supported the Powers administration, expressed disbelief that the governor would take such a step after his repeated statements that peace and quiet prevailed in the state. Unlike the situation in Louisiana, there was no need to organize militia units in Mississippi, Cardozo declared, and the distribution of arms to whites who had worn the gray and blacks who had worn the blue would invite racial strife. Radicals Mygatt, Flournoy, and Ames echoed Cardozo's criticism of the governor's action, and even Senator Alcorn opposed his political ally's militia policy. "To arm a people who may be brought in collision by the merest accident," a Republican wrote, "is the height of folly." A few days after Powers issued his militia order, reports circulated that men of both races had formed companies and applied for state arms. They claimed that if they did not organize quickly, members of the other race and political party would gain the upper hand in the contest for local military dominance.[78]

Ames Republicans quickly seized upon the issue, claiming that since the militia was not needed in the state the governor's only purpose in organizing it was a political one. Cardozo charged that Powers' policy of granting militia commissions, instituted a few weeks before Republicans selected delegates to the state convention, was designed to win the support of key local Republicans for

77. *House Journal, 1874*, Appendix, 679–80, 682.
78. "Civis" (Cardozo) to the Washington *New National Era*, July 3, 1873; Vicksburg *Times and Republican*, June 10, 12 (quote), 17, July 6, 1873; Robert W. Flournoy to Powers, June 14, 1873, in Governors' Correspondence, Vol. 80.

his gubernatorial candidacy. Throughout the early summer the editor of the Vicksburg *Times and Republican*, who was no friend of the Radicals, filled the columns of his newspaper with attacks on the governor, insisting that ambition and power had motivated Powers in the affair. "Have We a Military Dictator?" this carpet-bag editor asked, and he then went on to explain why the answer should be yes.[79] Ames, who suspected the worst in Powers, expressed confidence that the governor's maneuver would not affect the outcome of the contest for the Republican nomination. "The Militia will do no harm to me, and I believe little good to the Gov. though its purpose was to do a world of good to him and accomplish my destruction," he indicated to his wife.[80]

Even though political considerations may have played a part in his militia decision, Governor Powers in organizing a limited number of units was actually carrying out a policy announced in his annual message to the legislature, delivered in January. At that time he called for a legislative appropriation to outfit "a small proportion of the militia," which might be needed to suppress a flare-up of violence, now that the federal forces in the state had been reduced to a few dozen troops. The continuation of racial and political violence in Louisiana evidently caused Powers to fear that such disturbances might spill over into Mississippi. The legislature refused to act on the governor's request, but in March Congress passed a law that provided money for the states to purchase arms and accoutrements for militia units. Mississippi's share of this appropriation was $31,114, which made possible the implementation of Powers' plans for an active militia even without legislative support.[81]

Although Ames was the chief beneficiary of Powers' political blunders, his nomination for governor by the Republican convention was far from certain when the campaign for delegates began in July. The carpetbag senator's standing among blacks had been high since his vigorous support of the Ku Klux Klan bill in 1871. But by 1873 "Old Osawatomie" Flournoy had emerged as a rival for the leadership of Mississippi blacks and the Radical wing of the party.

79. Washington *New National Era*, July 3, 1873; Vicksburg *Times and Republican*, June 8, 1873.
80. Ames to his wife, July 4, 1873, in Blanche Butler Ames (comp.), *Chronicles*, I, 473.
81. *Senate Journal, 1873*, I, 24, *House Journal, 1874*, Appendix, 679–80; Powers to Emory, October 28, 1872, in Governors' Correspondence, Vol. 80.

In May, after corresponding with several Negro politicians, Flournoy advanced a platform calling for the enforcement of full rights
for blacks, including the racial integration of the public schools and
colleges. He also called for a "sweeping reduction in taxes" at all
levels of government. Flournoy admitted that Republicans could
legitimately differ on the best means for accomplishing tax relief.
"But the question of mixed schools," he claimed, "is no longer an
open one, about which Republicans may differ."[82]

Soon after Flournoy's platform appeared in the press several
black leaders announced their support of him for governor. The
Pontotoc scalawag, these blacks declared, was the only prominent
white Republican in the state to advocate the full measure of rights
for their race under the postwar amendments and the Declaration
of Independence. A letter from a group of "colored citizens of
Mississippi," appearing in the Washington *New National Era* on
July 24, expressed concern over carpetbag adventurers' abuse of
the trust blacks had placed in them. Negro votes had put them in
office, these citizens pointed out, but much to their dismay, the
carpetbaggers had not "come up squarely to the organic law of the
land, giving us every right guaranteed by the national compact.
. . . We are afflicted by two evils—heavy taxes and a sort of hybrid
dual school system—that is, separate schools for the races. Both
are curses! the latter—the dual [system]—is transmitting to posterity the prejudices of to-day." Flournoy promised to correct both
evils. Using their increasing influence, blacks planned to demand
at the state convention that the party nominate Flournoy for governor, select members of their race for three of the other six state
positions to be filled in the election, and adopt a platform supporting the dismantling of the dual system of public schools.[83]

Their plans to put Flournoy in the governor's mansion soon collapsed. Black support for Flournoy had never been organized, and
although blacks were able to dominate the party organization in
several river counties it was a far more difficult task to wrest control of the state party and its patronage from white Republicans.

82. Columbus *Press*, July 12, 1873; Vicksburg *Times and Republican*, July 30, 1873;
Flournoy to the editors of the Jackson *Pilot*, May 27, 1873, as printed in the Jackson *Clarion*,
June 19, 1873.

83. Washington *New National Era*, July 24, 1873. See also the issues of July 10 and
August 21, 1873.

Both carpetbaggers and scalawags, with a few exceptions, easily found reasons to oppose Flournoy's candidacy. Powerful carpet-baggers, even of the Radical wing of the party, had never really trusted Flournoy because he had been a large slaveholder before the war and was still a wealthy landowner in Pontotoc County.[84] Coming from outside their group, Flournoy had long been a threat to the carpetbaggers' influence in the Negro community. Scalawags of the Alcorn-Powers wing—and not a few carpetbaggers—ab-horred his campaign for the racial integration of the public schools and the University of Mississippi; in addition, his caustic attacks on Alcorn and other moderates had caused many Republicans to doubt his capacity for executive leadership. Except for his own journal, the Pontotoc *Equal Rights*, no white Republican news-paper raised Flournoy's standard during the campaign. Indeed, the Jackson *Pilot*, the leading Radical newspaper in the state, turned its editorial guns on "Old Osawatomie" in an effort to discredit him among Republicans who would otherwise support Senator Ames.[85]

The vigorous effort of Ames's friends to win delegates to the county conventions, which in turn selected those to the state con-vention, was the decisive stroke in the campaign. Organized and determined, local Ames politicians toured their counties in what was known as "mule riding," since the main means of transporta-tion was by mule or horse, in an effort to obtain delegates to the county conventions. Even before the state convention assembled on August 27, it was clear that the mule-riding canvass for Ames had been extremely effective.[86] Nevertheless, the anti-Ames Re-publicans had one final card to play against the senator. On the eve of the convention they attempted to divide the black support

84. Tarbell in a lengthy letter to John C. Churchill (February 20, 1868, in Fourteenth Amendment Relief Papers, Mississippi) outlined the carpetbaggers' case against Flournoy. Actually, Flournoy had supported equal rights for blacks before Tarbell and many of his carpetbag associates had joined the effort to elevate the freedmen to first-class citizenship. As early as November, 1865, Flournoy had written to Thaddeus Stevens that he was "anxious to see the negro have all the rights of a citizen, and I wish to see him . . . protected in those rights" by federal authority. Flournoy to Stevens, November 20, 1865, in Thaddeus Stevens Papers, Manuscript Division, Library of Congress.

85. Jackson *Weekly Clarion*, June 19, 1873.

86. Ames to his wife, June 28, 1873, in Blanche Butler Ames (comp.), *Chronicles*, I, 468; Vicksburg *Times and Republican*, July 29, August 9, 1873.

for the New England carpetbagger by putting Blanche K. Bruce, the popular Negro sheriff of Bolivar County, at the head of the Republican ticket. When Bruce refused to cooperate, probably in part because he already had his eye on the United States Senate, the effort collapsed, and Ames easily defeated Powers for the gubernatorial nomination. (Flournoy had abandoned the contest.) Ames's main support came from the black areas where local carpetbaggers and black leaders could ignore with impunity the pleas of moderates for a ticket that would attract a significant white vote.[87]

The real contest in the Republican convention occurred over the nominations to the other state offices. Aspirants for these six offices were numerous and aggressive.[88] The strong demand of black delegates that three of the offices go to members of their race complicated the problem of selecting a ticket that would avoid serious disaffection in the party. White Republicans were willing to give blacks two places on the ticket, but not three. Trouble erupted when the ascendant Ames faction dismissed the claims of Carter, a leader in the fight for the civil rights bill, and selected Alexander K. Davis, a nondescript black of Noxubee County, for lieutenant governor. The nominations of blacks James Hill for secretary of state and Cardozo for superintendent of public education, which came after a vigorous fight, did not still black disappointment in the convention's slight of their first choice for lieutenant governor —the man who would become governor if Ames returned to the Senate in 1874, as many expected. On the other side of the hall, moderate disaffection boiled when the convention failed to renominate the able Henry Musgrove for state auditor.[89]

The conflict over the offices deflected interest in drafting the platform. As a result, with little debate, the convention adopted a radical civil rights plank, as mentioned earlier, committing the party to legislation that would end the dual system of education in the public schools and the university at Oxford.[90]

87. Ames to his wife, August 16, 1873, in Blanche Butler Ames (comp.), *Chronicles*, I, 524; Vicksburg *Times and Republican*, August 12, 28, 30, 1873.
88. "Civis" to the Washington *New National Era*, September 11, 1873; Ames to his wife, September 3, 1873, in Blanche Butler Ames (comp.), *Chronicles*, I, 547–48.
89. Washington *New National Era*, September 11, October 23, 1873; Jackson *Weekly Clarion*, September 4, 1873.
90. Vicksburg *Times and Republican*, August 30, 1873.

"Blind with rage" at the Radicals' success, as Ames reported, Senator Alcorn appeared before a large meeting of followers in Jackson on August 29 and announced that he would become a candidate for governor in order to save the Republican party and the state from the New England carpetbagger and his coterie of "corrupt adventurers." At the same time he called for a convention of reform Republicans, or opponents of Ames, to meet and to nominate a ticket for the fall election. Alcorn emphatically denied that he was bolting the party or leading his supporters into a fusion with the Democrats. "I am a Republican of the true faith," he declared. "I have not lost my faith. I have only turned on plunderers and thieves."[91]

To implement their plans, a group of Alcorn devotees—numbering no more than forty men—met in Jackson on September 18. Referring to their organization as the "Republican party of Mississippi," the "delegates" adopted a platform that endorsed the Grant administration, denounced the nominations of the Ames convention, called for retrenchment and reform in government, and announced that the party's "first and highest duty," if elected, would be "to give protection and security to the laboring classes, and equal rights to all the people, Northern and Southern, colored and white."[92] The Alcorn convention also declared that it "unalterably" opposed any payment on the repudiated Planters' and Union Bank bonds, a debt "contracted by locofoco Democracy, and by them repudiated." The postwar issue over these bonds had been rekindled and would climax during the 1873 campaign.

Alcorn Republicans in their platform and in the fall canvass especially leveled their guns on the white members of the Ames ticket, whose only aim, they said, was self-aggrandizement and public plunder. They characterized Ames as an "irresponsible non-resident" who had done nothing for the state during his tenure in the Senate. William H. Gibbs, the Radical candidate for state auditor, they charged, was a carpetbagger who was "notoriously debaunched," which Ames himself had once admitted, whereas scal-

91. As reported in the Jackson *Weekly Clarion*, September 4, 1873. Ames expressed pleasure that Alcorn had bolted the party, since "It is the easiest way for us to get rid of him. He will make a great noise, but it will be the last of him." Ames to his wife, September 12, 1873, in Blanche Butler Ames (comp.), *Chronicles*, I, 560.

92. The Alcorn platform may be found in the Vicksburg *Times and Republican*, September 21, 1873, and in *Appleton's Annual Cyclopaedia*, 1873, pp. 514–15.

awag George H. Holland, the nominee for state treasurer, was "wholly incompetent." Alcorn supporters also singled out for special treatment O. C. French, an Ames crony and power on the state Republican executive committee, whose shady dealings in the legislature had created concern among reform Republicans.[93] To avoid arousing Negro hostility to their movement, the bolters refrained from attacking the three blacks on the Ames ticket; two of these politicians, Davis and Cardozo, would later become the only high-level officials during Reconstruction to be indicted on charges of misconduct in office.

As expected, the Alcorn convention nominated their hero for governor and selected a ticket that contained four scalawags, one carpetbagger (Henry Musgrove), and two blacks (Thomas W. Stringer, a founder of the Republican party in the state, and J. D. Webster, a mediocre black leader from the Delta). Despite the solid Republican credentials of its candidates, the Alcorn party suffered greatly from the stigma attached to the Dent and Greeley bolters. Several prominent moderates in the old party, such as Governor Powers, though giving tacit approval to the new party refused to publicly endorse it.[94] At the same time President Grant, nudged by Benjamin F. Butler, quietly spread the word that he favored the Ames faction. Alcorn's support of a late 1872 Senate resolution to investigate corruption in the administration probably had as much to do with Grant's endorsement of the Radicals as did the influence of Butler on the side of his son-in-law Ames.[95] Nevertheless, more Republicans joined the Alcorn crusade than had supported the early aberrant movements. But this support was far short of the strength needed to win the election of 1873. Consequently, the Alcorn machinators, as the bolters of 1869 and 1872 had done, looked to Mississippi conservatives to provide the bulk of the votes they needed.

When the new party made its appeal to conservatives for support, Ames Republicans immediately labeled the Alcorn candidacy a Democratic affair, charging that the movement owed its incep-

---

93. Vicksburg *Times and Republican*, September 27, October 14, November 2, 1873.

94. Ames to his wife, September 15, 1873, in Blanche Butler Ames (comp.), *Chronicles*, I, 564.

95. Pereyra, *James Lusk Alcorn*, 162; *Hinds County Gazette*, January 3, 1872.

tion to intrigue between disappointed Republican claimants for office and Jackson-clique conservatives. They pointed to the disbandment of the Democratic-Conservative party, one day before the Alcorn convention met, as proof of a previous commitment by the Brown-Barksdale group to deliver white votes to Alcorn if he should raise the standard of revolt against the Radicals.[96] Actually, this interpretation of the events leading to the disbandment of the Democratic party and the alliance of a number of its leaders with the Alcorn faction was only partly correct.

Even before the conservatives abandoned their party organization in September, the Democratic-Conservative hybrid, weakly revived in 1872, seemed destined for extinction in Mississippi. The election of 1872 had demonstrated again the futility of a conservative coalition against the Republican party on a statewide basis. White apathy in the face of a well disciplined Republican majority of registered voters, which included eighty thousand blacks and an estimated five thousand whites, caused many conservative leaders to despair in their attempts to regain control of the state.[97] By 1873 Mississippi's redemption from Republican rule seemed remote.

As before, the conflict between New Departurists and Bourbons on the one hand and old Democrats and Whigs on the other added to the difficulties of keeping the Democratic-Conservative party alive. Both New Departurists and Bourbons threatened to vote with the Republicans in the election of 1873 if the other faction gained control of the party. Others announced their determination to be neutral. Still other conservatives proposed, regardless of what faction won out in the Democratic party, to support "a tolerable" Republican in hopes of averting the election of "an odious wretch like Ames." Such pronouncements exaggerated the intent of their authors, but at the same time they contributed significantly to the difficulties of organizing an anti-Radical coalition. "We have never known a time since the birth of Radicalism when there

96. Vicksburg *Times and Republican*, October 1, 1873.

97. Jackson *Weekly Clarion*, May 15, August 14, 1873; Natchez *Weekly Democrat*, October 23, 1872; Greenwood *Times*, August 16, 1873. Warren A. Ellem estimates scalawag strength at nine thousand voters, the bulk of whom, he claims, were located in the Delta counties. This estimate seems high, and I have found no evidence to support his view that the Delta, an area inhabited by relatively few whites, possessed a large scalawag concentration. Warren A. Ellem, "Who Were the Mississippi Scalawags?" *Journal of Southern History*, XXXVIII (May, 1972), 228, 240.

was so little organized opposition to it in Mississippi as there is to-day," the Holly Springs *Reporter* soberly declared in July, 1873.[98]

But New Departure conservatives found a ray of hope in the growing political sophistication of blacks. More than ever before, New Departurists seemed to believe that blacks in local politics were willing to throw off the yoke of the "carpetbag adventurers" and cooperate with moderates in a "reform" coalition. Negroes, these conservatives insisted, were beginning to realize that local corruption and mismanagement, as well as the heavy tax burden, worked against their material advancement; as a result they were beginning to see their political interests in the same light as did their white neighbors. Barksdale went so far in his espousal of the accommodationist doctrine to endorse the Louisiana Unification movement, although at the time he probably did not know that it called for conservative acquiescence in the principle of racially integrated schools. Some hopeful New Departurists even viewed the black power movement as an opportunity for a conservative-Negro fusion, since they believed that its main purpose was to overthrow carpetbag control, which in turn would make possible a black alignment with local reformers. The main stumbling block to biracial cooperation in a moderate coalition, New Departure advocates believed, was the continued existence of the Democratic organization, which blacks could never agree to support. To these conservatives, as well as to a number of Whigs like former Governor Humphreys who felt uncomfortable with the name Democratic and its past association, the Democratic party had to be dissolved before they could exploit the changing political attitudes of blacks.[99]

Hiram Cassedy, a power in the antebellum Democratic party and an influential postwar accommodationist, expressed clearly the New Departure position in 1873 in a public letter to the Jackson *Clarion*, written after a tour of the western counties. He was con-

98. Jackson *Weekly Clarion*, July 24, 1873, citing the Natchez *Democrat* and the Columbus *Index*; Greenwood *Times*, July 12, August 9, 1873; Vicksburg *Times and Republican*, May 4, 1873, quoting the Canton *Mail*.

99. Greenwood *Times*, August 16, 1873; Jackson *Weekly Clarion*, July 10, August 7, 1873; Vicksburg *Times and Republican*, August 28, 1873.

vinced that "organized state opposition to the Republican party" along present lines "is worse than fruitless."

> It is positively pernicious. Defeat is certain on that basis, and the result of repeated defeat is beginning already to tell on the spirits of men whose high-toned integrity was never doubted. The fact is that there is no *practical principle* on which sensible men can divide. Old issues have become extinct, and party names have lost their prestige. The Democratic name serves no other purpose now than to arouse fears, North and South, by which alone [Republicans] are enabled to keep up their organization. Here Democrat, with the colored people, is synonomous with slavery, and its attendant consequences. North it stands for the losses and calamities of the war, and arouses fears that by some unknown means the success of that party might disturb the results of the war as now settled.[100]

Although Alcorn had many enemies among the old citizens, his bolt from the Republican party gave a decisive boost to Democratic-Conservative sentiment favoring the party's disbandment, a move that would leave conservatives free to vote for the "Eminent Man." Led by delegates from the overwhelmingly white east, Bourbons in the state Democratic-Conservative convention that met in Meridian on September 17 nonetheless put up a vigorous fight to prevent the adoption of a resolution dissolving the party. Their efforts were in vain; by a vote of 100 to 45 the convention dismantled the Democratic organization and freed its members to vote for whomever they chose in the fall election.[101]

Alcorn and his aberrant band of Republicans expected to reap a rich harvest from the action of the Meridian convention. The Vicksburg *Times and Republican*, the leading Alcorn organ, could hardly believe the news. "We can scarcely realize that we have no organized opposition in our State to the Republican party," the carpetbag editor of this journal exulted. "Peace had come at last. . . . No more intolerance! No more persecution! . . . Now, there comes suddenly, the dawn of an era of mutual good feelings." It

100. Written on August 23, 1873, this letter appeared in the Jackson *Weekly Clarion*, September 4, 1873.

101. *Ibid.*, September 25, 1873; Henry, *Editors I Have Known*, 306; William H. Hardy and Toney A. Hardy, *No Compromise with Principle: Autobiography and Biography of William Harris Hardy* (New York, 1946), 120. A motion to endorse Alcorn's candidacy failed to pass. Clay Sharkey, "Essay number 48," in Sharkey Papers.

behooved Republicans, he said, "to meet the voluntary dissolution of the opposition, not with derision and suspicion, but with prompt, practical measures of reform in the State, county and municipal governments."[102]

Reform, then, became the catchword of Alcorn Republicans in their campaign to entice conservatives to support their ticket in the election. From the beginning, however, they fought a losing battle. Twenty-six of fifty-three conservative newspapers surveyed by a correspondent of the New York *Times* indicated their opposition to the work of the Meridian convention.[103] Led by McCardle, these journalists claimed that the conservatives should have entered a candidate of the stature of Humphreys, the hero of the Bourbons, and taken advantage of the Kilkenny fight in the Republican party. As Greeley had been in 1872, Alcorn was a bitter pill for most conservatives to swallow. Placing the candidate in the select company of Judas Iscariot and Benedict Arnold, a "Whig" writer proclaimed to the world, "There never has lived in the tide of time a public character more unprincipled and corrupt than J. L. Alcorn."[104]

Bourbon bitterness toward Alcorn was so great that Ames expected many of them to vote for him. When he campaigned along the railroad in east and north Mississippi, Ames marveled at the presence of large numbers of whites at the Republican rallies. In Tupelo he spoke, as he reported, "to the largest gathering ever seen in this usually lawless place, but they listened attentively for two hours and fifteen minutes. Although they are usually hostile to carpetbaggers, they seem to be planning to vote for me, if they vote at all, and not for Alcorn." At Ripley, Corinth, Holly Springs, and other towns in this predominantly white area, he spoke to racially mixed audiences and was "continually amazed at the effect" he was having on whites. The carpetbag candidate attributed his success to the fact that, in contrast to his opponent, he was honest and straightforward in his speeches.[105] No doubt observers, in-

102. Vicksburg *Times and Republican*, September 23, 1873.
103. New York *Times*, September 21, 1873.
104. Jackson *Pilot*, September 25, 1873; Crystal Springs (Miss.) *Monitor*, October 2, 1873; William H. Hardy, "Recollections of Reconstruction," 148; Washington *New National Era*, October 2, 1873 (quote).
105. Ames to his wife, September 18, 21, 30, October 2, 5, 1873, in Blanche Butler Ames (comp.), *Chronicles*, I, 571–72, 583, 587, 589–90.

cluding many of his own supporters, had underrated Ames's ability on the stump, and his appeal to whites during the campaign did not breathe the kind of defiance and disdain for the old citizens that his reputation among conservatives suggested. Actually, he appealed more to the audience's reason than did Alcorn, whose method was to lash out at his opponents in a free-wheeling manner that left no time to discuss such practical issues as retrenchment, aid for internal improvements, and governmental reform.[106]

As he had expected, in the river counties Ames found an enthusiastic reception for his campaign. At Mayersville in the Delta, he arrived in town on the same day that Alcorn was speaking. Ames attempted to arrange a joint debate, but Alcorn refused and held a meeting, supported by a brass band, at another place in town. According to Ames, although Alcorn's "band attracted at first, he had not been on the stand five minutes before all the colored people left him . . . and came to me, and Alcorn had to adjourn his meeting and come to where I was."[107] At another rally, Ames believed that every black in the county "had presented himself" and demonstrated support for his candidacy. "There were two four-horse carriages decorated with flags, and having my name in large letters pasted on every conspicuous place," he observed. "Even the rough, country wagons had on their sides my name— and the colored people had it tied or fastened on their hats—hundreds of them."[108]

Although blacks were solidly behind him, as he claimed, Ames misinterpreted the significance of the large number of whites who turned out to hear him speak. Their presence was due partly to a curiosity to see the "Great Mogul" of the Radicals, and his appeal to their good senses did not change their opposition to him. Furthermore, campaign oratory and display, of whatever party, was a traditional social outlet for many farmers who lived an isolated and uneventful existence. The excitement of the 1873 canvass brought many whites to the Republican rallies. But as the election results indicated, when compared with earlier Reconstruction returns not

106. For representative speeches made by Alcorn during the campaign, see the Vicksburg *Times and Republican*, October 14, November 2, 1873.

107. Ames to his wife, October 18, 1873, in Blanche Butler Ames (comp.), *Chronicles*, I, 603.

108. Ames to his wife, October 5, 1873, *ibid.*, I, 590.

many whites other than party faithfuls voted the Radical ticket in 1873.

A more intense struggle occurred over the election of members of the new legislature. In the election of 1871 conservatives had somewhat reduced the huge Republican majority in the legislature. In 1873 they expected Alcorn Republicans to cooperate with them in their effort to gain control of the assembly. But when conservatives failed to permit moderate Republicans on their local tickets, many nonaligned Republicans threw their support to Ames and the Radicals.[109] The every-man-for-himself campaign in the counties worked against both Alcorn's candidacy and the conservative campaign to win a majority of the seats in the legislature.

Despite the large rallies and the importance of the legislative contests, the campaign aroused little interest in old Reconstruction issues. The matter of black rights, including the advanced civil rights plank in the Ames platform, failed to create much debate. Not that whites had abandoned their racial prejudices, but rather all parties were now committed, at least in their public pronouncements, to a measure of equal rights for blacks; it thus behooved conservatives and Alcorn Republicans not to attack this part of the Radical program if they expected to win Negro votes. Only the Bourbons, who seemed to be faltering, stood to benefit from injecting the race issue into the campaign and arousing white racial passions. Furthermore, with the experience of the ineffective civil rights laws of 1870 and 1873 fresh in their minds, many whites realized that the Ames platform calling for racially mixed schools would never be implemented; therefore they saw no reason to agitate an issue that no longer threatened white supremacy.

Instead, conservatives joined Alcorn Republicans in hammering hard on the issues of corruption, heavy taxes, and extravagance in state administration. But a cynical public had been served these issues before, only to be disillusioned by defeat at the polls and the continuation, as the old citizens believed, of the same practices. The white masses also knew that only on the local level had friends of Ames held power; the state government generally had been in the hands of the Alcorn-Powers wing of the party. One issue that emerged during the campaign, however, was too ominous for many

109. T. E. Tate to Powers, November 8, 1873, in Governors' Correspondence, Vol. 81.

people to dismiss lightly. This was the question of the repudiated bonds of the Planters' and Union Banks.

A source of political contention since their repudiation during the antebellum period, these bonds when the Republicans came to power had a face value of more than thirty million dollars, including accumulated interest. Most of the bonds were held by British and northeastern speculators, who had purchased them for about six cents on the dollar. The success of their investment depended upon the recognition by state authorities of the validity of the bonds. Presuming that the Republican government of Mississippi was no more honest or perceptive than those in Louisiana and South Carolina, lobbyists for these speculators descended on the legislature in 1871. They pointed out to the lawmakers that until the stain of repudiation had been removed from the state's reputation investment capital would not flow into Mississippi nor would its bonds be marketable in eastern centers. Their plan called for the legislature to accept the legitimacy of the principal and impose a tax on property to pay the future interest and ultimately the principal of the debt. In case their arguments failed to persuade a majority of the legislature, the bond lobbyists were prepared "to make very favorable arrangements" with hesitating members.[110]

They soon discovered, however, that neither their arguments nor the extension of "very favorable arrangements" to cooperating legislators could achieve in 1871 the result they desired. This setback for the lobbyists owed a great deal to the influence in the legislature of the Radical Albert T. Morgan and Lieutenant Governor Powers. Revealing that speculators alone held these bonds, Powers in a speech before the senate announced that Mississippi was not "morally bound to satisfy the demands of a horde of speculators by bankrupting the State to pay a debt if not actually barred by the statute of limitations, at least repudiated by the highest power in the State—the people."[111]

The bond speculators, however, had planted a seed that would grow, and two influential Republican journals, the Natchez *New South* and the Jackson *Pilot*, with or without making "very favorable arrangements" announced—though in a somewhat guarded

110. Jackson *Pilot*, February 8, 1871; Vicksburg *Times and Republican*, September 12, 29, 1871; New York *Times*, April 5, 1871; Natchez *Weekly Democrat*, April 10, 1872.
111. As reported in the Jackson *Pilot*, February 8, 1871.

fashion in the case of the *Pilot*—their support for honoring the debt.[112] In early 1872 with the legislature again in session, the New York *Times*, in the heart of the eastern money marts, added its endorsement to the efforts of the bondholders. If Mississippi really wanted to throw off the unfortunate Democratic heritage of repudiation, restore public credit, and open the state to incoming capital, it should honor its obligation to these bonds. With an influential friend like the New York *Times* in their corner, the bond speculators renewed their pressure on the legislature. But the presence of Powers in the governor's office was a constant threat to their scheme; a two-thirds majority of the legislature would be required to overcome his opposition to any bill recognizing the debt. Despite their vigorous efforts, the plan failed even to win a simple majority of the legislature in both 1872 and 1873.[113]

During the political campaign of 1873 Alcorn Republicans and conservatives charged that if Ames were elected governor the bonds would be redeemed. Based on an innocuous inquiry that Butler, Ames's father-in-law, had made regarding the total Mississippi debt, the anti-Radical scenario cast the "corrupt" Butler in the role of the bondholders' agent, whose intent was to impose his evil influence upon Ames and secure the new state administration's approval of the speculators' redemption scheme. Actually, there is no evidence that the bondholders contacted Butler about such a scheme. When queried by Ames, Butler denied any connection with it; in fact, he insisted that he had never heard of the Planters' and Union bonds until the charge was made in the newspapers. At any rate, both parties in the 1873 election announced their determination to oppose all efforts of the bond speculators to secure payments on the repudiated debt. Then, in 1875, an amendment to the state constitution initiated by the last Republican legislature prohibited the state government from ever redeeming the bonds.[114]

112. *Ibid.*, September 8, December 26, 1871; Vicksburg *Times and Republican*, August 24, 1873.

113. New York *Times*, March 28, 1872; Natchez *Weekly Democrat*, April 10, 1872; Vicksburg *Times and Republican*, February 18, 20, 25, May 1, 1873.

114. Vicksburg *Times and Republican*, September 21, October 29, 1873; Jackson *Weekly Clarion*, September 4, 1873; Blanche Ames to Adelbert Ames, September 17, 1873, in Blanche Butler Ames (comp.), *Chronicles*, I, 567; *Journal of the Senate of the State of Mississippi, 1880* (Jackson, 1880), 465.

Nevertheless, the bondholders did not accept defeat, and sporadic efforts were made to secure payment until 1934, when the United States Supreme Court freed Mississippi of any obligation to pay the antebellum bonds.[115]

Frustrated in their campaign to head off the Ames juggernaut, anti-Radicals in the 1873 campaign took a page from Louisiana's shady Reconstruction history in an attempt to gain time for their cause. Governor Powers and Attorney General Joshua S. Morris, both being anti-Ames Republicans who nonetheless had refused to bolt the party with Alcorn, suddenly discovered in late September that the section of the 1871 law providing for an election in 1873 was unconstitutional. They claimed that the election should be held in the fall of 1874.[116]

In order to obtain the necessary legislation to validate the scheme, Powers called a special session of the legislature and asked it to postpone the election until 1874. Such an action, the governor claimed, would "save the State from imminent discord and disgrace, and consequent financial embarrassment, to say nothing of still graver consequences." One of the grave consequences he referred to was obviously the expected triumph of the Radical party if the election were held as scheduled. The Vicksburg *Times and Republican*, which supported Alcorn, was candid in explaining the purpose behind the postponement movement. "A large number of Republicans, those of heretofore unquestioned loyalty to the party" were supporting Powers' scheme "because they are totally disgusted with the Ames ticket . . . and while they lack the independence and moral courage to come boldly out and proclaim their opposition, they are quite willing, aye, anxious, that it should be slaughtered by a postponement of the election until 1874."[117]

When the legislature met in special session in late October to consider Powers' request, it was soon clear that the house of representatives favored postponing the election. But in the senate the

115. Reginald C. McGrane, *Foreign Bondholders and American State Debts* (New York, 1935), 221–22.

116. Ames to his wife, September 24, 1873, in Blanche Butler Ames (comp.), *Chronicles*, I, 577; Vicksburg *Times and Republican*, September 21, 24, 1873.

117. *Appleton's Annual Cyclopaedia*, 1873, p. 515; Vicksburg *Times and Republican*, September 30, 1873. See also J. J. Smith to Powers, October 5, 1873, in Governors' Correspondence, Vol. 81.

Ames Republicans held the upper hand by a slight majority. The anti-Ames forces, however, attempted two maneuvers that almost succeeded. Joseph Bennett, the moderate Republican presiding officer, announced that two Radical senators were ineligible to hold seats in the body, since they also held local public offices. The issue of their eligibility had not been raised during the regular session of the legislature; consequently, the clerk of the senate, an Ames man, ignored Bennett's opinion and with support from the floor continued to include the names of the two senators in the roll calls.[118]

A greater threat to the slim antipostponement majority in the senate occurred when the Powers forces "decoyed," as Ames described it, two Radical senators to New Orleans for a "spree," with the intention of keeping them there until the issue had been decided. Actually, both were willing accomplices, since by their absence they hoped to avoid taking a public stand on an issue that had divided the Republican party and would be dangerous to their political careers.[119] Not to be outdone, Ames men immediately went to New Orleans and persuaded the wayward senators to return. The trip to Jackson of one senator, Alston Mygatt, produced a flurry of activity by both parties in a final effort to obtain his vote. "A squad of men on both sides took the down train to meet him— our side to guard, theirs to capture," Ames reported to his wife. "Our side was successful—and at about half past three . . . he was brought to see me at his own request." Later, Mygatt "was safely ensconced in the middle of a bed between two of our friends." The next morning he was taken to the senate where he voted with the majority (including conservatives John M. Stone and Hiram Cassedy, Jr.) against the postponement of the election.[120] Five days later the Radical ticket swept to a solid victory at the polls—a victory that Ames claimed would have been greater if the postponement scheme had not caused many Republicans to stay at home, believing that the election was not being held.

118. Ames to his wife, October 25, 28, 29, 1873, in Blanche Butler Ames (comp.), *Chronicles*, I, 613, 617, 619.

119. Ames admitted that his friends used the same weapons—money and whiskey— to win the support of key senators. Ames to his wife, October 26, 1873, *ibid.*, I, 616.

120. Ames to his wife, October 30, 1873, *ibid.*, I, 621–22; Jackson *Weekly Clarion*, November 13, 1873.

Again in a contest that was generally free of intimidation, Ames captured 69,870 votes to 50,090 for Alcorn.[121] Ames won thirty-five of the seventy-two counties, though only seven of these were white counties, and all seven had a black registration of more than 40 percent. As in 1869 and 1872, white apathy was apparent in the election, but most who cast ballots for conservative candidates for local office and the legislature also voted for Alcorn.[122] The total vote in the gubernatorial contest was 24,000 fewer than in the election of 1871, when only local offices and seats in the legislature were at stake. Ames received 14,000 votes fewer than the aggregate for Republican candidates in 1871, which suggests that Alcorn, though failing to carry a black county, won many regular Republican votes, especially in white counties where moderate Republicans controlled the local party machinery.

The Republicans won the legislature again, capturing twenty-three seats in the senate to thirteen for the conservatives and winning seventy-six seats in the lower house to only forty for their opnents.[123] Party cohesiveness in the senate, however, was threatened by the presence of five anti-Radical Republicans, although only one, Furlong, had actually bolted the party to support Alcorn. The increase in the number of blacks in both houses of the legislature, especially in the house of representatives, was even more significant. These victories reflected the continued demand of blacks for office and influence in proportion to their voting strength and included nine seats in the senate (three more than in the senate of 1872–1873) and fifty-five in the house of representatives (an increase of thirteen seats). Although four votes short of a majority in the lower house, blacks could control party caucuses and therefore the legislative proceedings of the house. Even in the senate, where the able and experienced William H. Gray, Charles Caldwell, and Robert Gleed held forth, Negroes, if united, could

121. The state election returns may be found in *Mississippi in 1875*, Documentary Evidence, II, 144–45.
122. The results of many of the 1873 local contests are found in Election Returns, 1871–1900.
123. Most of the new legislators are identified as to race and party in the Jackson *Weekly Clarion*, November 20, 1873. The identification of the remaining members has been made from a miscellany of sources; in addition, the *Clarion's* list has been checked for accuracy against other sources.

be expected to exercise an important influence over legislation, particularly since white Republicans were divided.

Governor Powers still had one card to play in his effort to prevent the inauguration of the Radical Ames. He appealed to the state supreme court to invalidate the election and order a new one for the fall of 1874. With the matter before the Alcorn-appointed court, conservative hopes soared, despite warnings by Republicans and some conservatives that invalidating the election might result in disorders and federal intervention on the side of the Radicals, as had occurred in turbulent Louisiana.[124] Even many moderates, like the editor of the Natchez *Democrat*, in their apprehension for the future of the state under the opportunistic Ames and his faction, could see no harm in testing the issue before the court. "It would be the height of pusilanimity and cowardice to yield the field without a stubborn battle before the highest judicial tribunal in the State," the Aberdeen *Examiner*, a Bourbon sheet, declared.[125] On January 19, 1874, however, the field was yielded when the court ruled that the election was valid and the victors should take office immediately. Powers and his supporters accepted defeat with good grace, and on January 22 Adelbert Ames became governor of Mississippi.[126] After seven years of trying, radicalism—or what passed for radicalism in the Reconstruction South—had triumphed in the state. Its success would depend less on the idealism that still found expression among some Radicals than on the manner in which the new regime met the practical problems that continued to plague the state and on its ability to keep the conservative opposition defused. By 1874, with republicanism collapsing in other southern states, this was a tall, but not impossible, order for Ames and his Radical associates.

---

124. Vicksburg *Times and Republican*, November 19, 1873; Jackson *Pilot*, as reported in the Jackson *Weekly Clarion*, November 13, 1873.

125. As quoted in the Jackson *Weekly Clarion*, November 27, 1873. This issue of the *Clarion* contained several excerpts from conservative statements on the issue.

126. Pascagoula *Star*, January 25, 1874; Vicksburg *Times and Republican*, January 23, 24, 1874.

15

The Search for Agricultural Salvation

In addition to progress along the more visible political, racial, and educational lines, the permanence of the new order in Mississippi depended to a significant extent on the economic recovery of the state. Economic rehabilitation was essential not only to provide the financial base for the new regime's ambitious programs, but also to persuade Mississippians that Republican rule would restore the material well-being of the people, as a number of the new leaders had promised from the beginning. If postwar doldrums lingered, Republicans would become convenient scapegoats for whites who expected the worst from the new government. Any hope that Republicans might have of securing the confidence of the old citizens would be dashed by the continuation of the agrarian depression.

As a result Republican leaders like Alcorn and Powers, especially during the early 1870s, took an active interest in policies to revive the economy of the state. However, they soon found themselves hamstrung by a lack of money, the reluctance of the people, even within the Republican party, to commit the state government to a policy of economic intervention unless it would aid their own area, and the confusion of tongues in the legislature and among officials regarding what level of government should be involved and what policies should be adopted to advance the state's material interests. Furthermore, most of the problems associated with recovery and growth were beyond the capacity of the state government to remedy.

Governmental action could do little to change the main contours of the state's economic development. Mississippi entered the 1870s dependent upon cotton more than ever before, which made material progress difficult regardless of who controlled the government or what public economic policies were developed. Most of the material and financial problems could be traced to the people's overriding dependence on cotton. Even the labor problem, a matter of considerable concern to planters, was only an offshoot of the state's subservience to King Cotton.

This dependence on cotton, however, was not by design. The staple formed the basis for the credit system of the state, and without credit, as made increasingly available under the crop lien or cotton mortgage arrangement, provisions could not be secured to sustain the population during the year. Because of the continuing postwar depression, broken only by the relatively good yields of 1868 and 1869, money to diversify the economy and break the hold of King Cotton had not accumulated in Mississippi. Outside capitalists who extended credit to local merchants expected to be repaid in cotton, since, though chronically depressed, it always had a cash value in the international market. In turn, merchants demanded cotton from the growers in payment for the provisions that had been advanced during the year. The crop lien act of 1867, passed during the closing days of presidential reconstruction, protected merchants in their arrangements with the cultivators.

In addition to the financial reasons for growing cotton, Mississippians were skilled at producing the staple and, lacking other economic opportunities, preferred to continue what they knew best. Unfortunately for the agricultural interest of the state, the international demand for cotton, which set its price, declined during the 1870s, and the grower, whether planter or farmer, received less and less for his crop.

Despite constant admonitions from farm leaders and editors to reduce cotton production and plant more grains,[1] farmers were forced to increase their acreage in the fleecy staple in order to offset the drop in its value. After all, they still had to meet their expenses, which in most cases were fixed costs unaffected by the vicissitudes of the cotton market. Demoralized growers literally mined the land to grow cotton; they possessed neither the money nor the incentive to make improvements or to conserve the soil. Since land was cheap in relation to labor, the planter or farmer was more interested in how much cotton he produced per unit of labor than in his yield per acre.

In 1869, the last good crop year during Reconstruction, Mississippi growers produced 564,938 bales of cotton, which brought

1. See, for example, the Jackson *Clarion*, February 12, 1868, the Jackson *Weekly Clarion*, April 6, 1871, and *Southern Field and Factory*, I (January, 1871), 2; I (April, 1871), 149; I (October, 1871), 337–38; III (March, 1873), 98–101.

$65,167,227 on the market. In order to take advantage of what appeared to be an improving market for the staple, they planted 650,000 bales in 1870, only to see the price plummet and their receipts decline to $46,280,000. This condition continued, and in 1875, the last year of Republican control, a harvest of 670,000 bales brought only $38,560,500.[2] By this time growers saw very little of the cotton income, since it went to merchants to pay off debts for provisions under the crop lien system. Any leftover money was usually given to the tax collector for current taxes or to redeem tax-forfeited lands. Few were so free from encumbrances that they could legitimately abandon the land and seek new opportunities in Texas or elsewhere. Nevertheless, many demoralized farmers, especially yeoman whites, pulled up stakes during Reconstruction, frequently leaving the local merchant in the lurch for provisions that had been advanced. When they found conditions no better in Texas and other exotic western places, some farmers returned to Mississippi to renew their struggle to make ends meet on the credit terms that the merchant demanded.[3] By 1880 an estimated three fourths of the land in the river counties and one half in the upland counties were encumbered with liens held by merchants and others who had advanced supplies to hapless farmers. In all of the counties most of the provisions supplied under these liens were "imported" from either the Midwest, Tennessee, Kentucky, or southern ports like New Orleans.[4]

Blacks, of course, were at the bottom of the economic ladder and suffered worse than yeoman whites under the debilitating credit system. Yet the laws protecting merchant liens provided impecunious blacks their only opportunity of securing credit and supplies for the growing season. Despite increasing demands for the repeal of the crop lien law, which came more from whites than from

2. These figures have been taken from a table compiled from several sources by Ross H. Moore, in his "Social and Economic Conditions in Mississippi During Reconstruction," 71.

3. Entries for April 20, 1868, August 29, October 5, 27, 1869, in Agnew Diary; *Hinds County Gazette*, November 17, 1869; Brandon *Republican*, January 4, 1877.

4. Eugene W. Hilgard, *Report on Cotton Production in the United States* (Washington, D.C., 1884), Part I, 153, 155. An excellent account of the emergence of the postwar "furnishing merchant" may be found in Harold D. Woodman, *King Cotton and His Retainers: Financing and Marketing the Cotton Crop of the South, 1800–1925* (Lexington, 1968), Chap. XXIV.

blacks, the Republican administrations retained the state's legal support for the system. In 1874 a repeal bill actually passed the legislature, only to be vetoed by Governor Ames.[5] The Republicans' failure to repeal the measure led some Bourbon critics to charge (erroneously) that the crop lien law "has never benefitted any one except a few lazy and worthless negroes, for whose benefit it was passed by a Radical Legislature." Elaborating, one Bourbon critic declared that the law enabled the black laborer "to go to the merchant, give a lien upon his growing crop, get provisions for the year, and then loaf around until they were eaten up, swindle the merchant, and compel the good men of the country to pay the merchant big prices in order to make up his losses." He admitted, however, that shrewd and unscrupulous merchants had taken advantage of black farmers and had "gobbled up" numerous plantations in order to make money from supplying black tenants at exorbitant prices.[6]

On the other hand, Judge Ephraim S. Fisher, a scalawag, found that the merchant who took advantage of black laborers was frequently ruined also. "The merchant, selling on credit," Fisher observed, "always doubled his profits, and the ignorant class, thus making themselves the dupes of merchants, bought twice as much as they really required. The result now is that both are ruined. . . . Legislation, instead of discountenancing this state of things, has been used to build it up, by laws regulating supply liens on crops, abbreviated deeds of trust and mortgages."[7] Since only the merchant, who in turn operated on credit from commercial centers, was protected by the lien law, the system undermined the businesses of artisans, blacksmiths, and even professional men who had to extend credit to clients under extremely risky conditions. As a result the crop lien system imposed a serious handicap on the efforts of the people to regain economic self-sufficiency.[8]

5. *Southern Field and Factory,* I (April, 1871), 194; *Annual Message of Governor Alcorn,* 1871, p. 38; Armistead Burwell to James Lusk Alcorn, January 6, 1871, in Governors' Correspondence, Vol. 73; *Journal of the Senate of the State of Mississippi, at a Called Session Thereof, December 17, 1874* (Jackson, 1875), 20; *Hinds County Gazette,* December 7, 1870.

6. Brandon *Republican,* February 10, 1876.

7. Ephraim S. Fisher to Joseph Holt, February 10, 1874, in Holt Papers.

8. Yazoo City (Miss.) *Herald,* January 28, 1876; Brandon *Republican,* February 10, 1876.

For Mississippians the difficulties of overthrowing the tyranny of King Cotton and its credit system and establishing a solid economic foundation were compounded by the expansion of the sharecrop arrangement. Born of the postwar need for poor farmers to secure land to work and for impecunious planters to obtain laborers without having to pay scarce wages, the system soon became pervasive in the state.[9] Farm spokesmen continuously warned that share-cropping was "false in theory and ruinous in practice." A resolution adopted by the state Planters, Manufacturers, and Mechanics' Convention of 1870 declared that the system was "exhaustive of present values and inimical to the improvement and permanent prosperity of the farm, and must eventuate in the utter and hopeless ruin of the landed estates of the country."[10] In addition, C. M. Vaiden, the most influential farm spokesman in the state, insisted that the sharecrop system more than anything else had contributed to the demoralization of the black cultivator and the consequent labor instability in the plantation districts. "Let the planters persist in this folly," he said, "and in ten years their ruin will be the result." Vaiden and other agricultural spokesmen called for the restoration of the wage system of compensation.[11] Although a few planters managed to pay wages to their laborers (at a rate of between fifteen and twenty dollars per month during good years), the vast majority, mainly because of their own financial demoralization, were either unwilling or incapable of providing wage payments to black tenants.

This somber condition in agriculture was reflected in the continued depressed value of land. Reduced in worth by an average of 65 percent after the war, agricultural property during the 1870s remained generally at the 1865 price level, but at times of acute distress lands frequently sold for less. Lands valued at about ten dollars per acre in 1865 in the cotton belt of central Mississippi were priced from an average of eight dollars in Madison County to

---

9. An account of the origins of the sharecrop system is found in Harris, *Presidential Reconstruction in Mississippi*, 182–84. See also James L. Roark, *Masters Without Slaves: Southern Planters in the Civil War and Reconstruction* (New York, 1977), 142–43.

10. *Southern Field and Factory*, I (January, 1871), 15.

11. *Ibid.*, I (April, 1871), 149 (quote), 187, 193–94; Carrollton *Mississippi Conservative*, June 13, 1874.

twelve dollars in Holmes County in 1872.[12] Property in the Delta, however, appreciated at a moderate rate during Reconstruction, although in 1873 some rich bottom lands could be purchased for as little as five dollars an acre. Because of the complexities and uncertainties surrounding the titles to the land and the encumbrances on much of the property in Mississippi, there were few buyers for the thousands of acres available for sale as a result of tax forfeitures or mortgage foreclosures. By 1874 the state alone claimed one sixth of the total acreage of Mississippi, which did not include properties held by the levee boards in the Delta.[13]

Land devaluation and tax forfeiture were nowhere more apparent than in the Yazoo-Mississippi Delta—and here it was tied to the problem of constructing a durable levee. The situation in the alluvial district produced a maze of land and tax complications that severely retarded for two decades the agricultural development of the fertile region. Consisting of four million acres of the richest land in North America, the Delta had been on the verge of a massive agricultural expansion when the Civil War wiped out the makeshift levee that protected the lowlands from periodic floodings.[14] The war also wiped out the ability of antebellum levee authorities to pay off the debt of more than fifteen million dollars contracted in building the old embankments. The old-line Whig regime of 1865–1867 understood all too well the need to restore the credit standing of the two levee districts before major work could begin on a permanent system to control the waters of the Mississippi. The Liquidating Levee Board was thus created to settle prewar claims against the district boards.[15] Rather than solving the intricate problems facing these authorities and local landowners, the new board only complicated the situation, although the

12. *Report of the Commissioner of Agriculture, 1867* (Washington, 1868), 106; table of average price of lands for Mississippi counties in *Southern Field and Factory*, II (March, 1872), 141.

13. Vicksburg *Times and Republican*, April 29, 1873; J. A. Nash to William N. Whitehurst, April 27, 1873, in Whitehurst Papers; report of the state auditor for 1874, in *House Journal, 1875*, Appendix, 40.

14. When the antebellum period ended, only one tenth of the Delta was under cultivation; the remainder was either being held for speculation or was swampland mainly in the possession of the state.

15. Harris, *Presidential Reconstruction in Mississippi*, 189.

credit of the levee boards was strengthened by the effort to pay off the debt. The real difficulty was that planters, who held most of their property for speculation or future cultivation in case conditions improved, could not (or would not) pay the tax. Many claimed correctly that their lands had already been forfeited to the authorities for failure to pay either their state or levee taxes, and therefore they were not liable for the new levy. In Sunflower, the hardest hit county, more than nine tenths of the agricultural lands had fallen into the hands of the Liquidating Levee Board and were no longer subject to taxation.[16]

The state caretaker administrations during military reconstruction had done nothing to halt the drift toward economic confusion and stagnation in the Delta. When the Republicans came to power in 1870 the situation called for drastic action.[17] It was soon clear that the legislature and Governor Alcorn, who had supervised the construction of the antebellum levee and later had served as president of the Liquidating Levee Board, had little faith in the old system of reclamation. Alcorn believed that Mississippi, along with other states in the valley, should focus its attention on securing federal aid and supervision for the development of a unified system for controlling the waters of the Mississippi and draining Delta lands.[18] Alcorn quickly obtained the passage of a legislative memorial asking Congress to provide two million dollars and five million acres of land to help restore the levees. In a letter of transmittal, the governor placed the request for assistance on high national grounds. The war had dealt a blow to the supremacy of the United States in the international cotton trade, he declared, and a European combination, led by the Manchester Cotton Supply Association, was determined that "America must continue as but a tributary rather than as a master of the cotton market." The salvation of the nation's cotton trade, Alcorn asserted, depended on the agricultural development of the Mississippi Delta, where the rich soils, when protected from inundation, produced one bale of cot-

---

16. Robert L. Brandfon, *Cotton Kingdom of the New South: A History of the Yazoo Mississippi Delta from Reconstruction to the Twentieth Century* (Cambridge, Mass., 1967), 44; Wade, "Lands of the Liquidating Levee Board," 284.

17. See Chap. 2 herein.

18. Pereyra, *James Lusk Alcorn,* 77–78.

ton an acre in contrast to the one-third to one-half acre yields of the uplands.[19]

As it had done earlier, the Republican Congress rejected the Mississippi appeal for aid to restore the levees. When Alcorn later went to the Senate, the campaign for federal assistance intensified, and in 1875 he almost secured the approval of a $3,420,000 appropriation for levee construction.[20] The defeat of this bill, however, dashed the hopes of Mississippians for any federal aid for this purpose in the immediate future.

While attempting to persuade the federal government to undertake the responsibility for the reconstruction of the levees, Alcorn insisted that the Liquidating Levee Board should complete its work of restoring the credit of the levee districts before bonds were issued for the construction of new embankments. The legislature of 1870, on the other hand, attempted to raise to $200,000 the ceiling on the amount that the levee commissioners of the southern district could borrow; indeed, one half of this sum had already been borrowed without the authorization of the levee board. The legislature also proposed to continue the special tax on Delta lands and the one cent per pound levy on cotton that the conservative regime of 1867 had imposed for levee purposes.[21]

When Governor Alcorn vetoed the legislative program for the Delta,[22] many legislators sought to revive the scheme for the construction of an elevated railroad along the Mississippi. Proposed in 1868 by a group of "capitalists," the railway embankment would also serve as a levee to protect the bottomlands from the river's overflow. The underlying purpose of the scheme, as had already been demonstrated in Louisiana, was land speculation, not internal improvements. Nevertheless, a growing number of Republicans preferred to believe that with proper safeguards the adoption of the plan would relieve the state and the Delta of the vexatious problems associated with levee construction. Carpetbag editor

19. *Laws of Mississippi, 1870*, pp. 634–37; Alcorn to "Gentlemen," May 25, 1870, copy in Governors' Correspondence, Vol. 72.

20. Jackson *Weekly Clarion*, May 8, 1873, March 25, 1875.

21. Message of Alcorn to the house of representatives and the senate, June 8, 1870, in Governors' Correspondence, Vol. 72.

22. In his veto message Alcorn particularly denounced the levy on cotton as "a tax on labor, and as such violates . . . the best interests of the State and the people." *Ibid.*

Hiram T. Fisher used the columns of the Jackson *Pilot* in early 1870 to influence the legislature to approve the scheme. "Private enterprise," he told the lawmakers, "builds all the railroads and most of all the public works. That kind of organization can manage with more economy than States can. It can bring more energy and skill to bear upon the work, and experience shows that private enterprise alone is capable of making effectual a great work like the one under consideration."[23]

The proponents of the elevated railway scheme, however, did not reckon with the opposition of Governor Alcorn. He appeared before the legislative committee studying the proposal and persuaded its members that the enterprise was a fraudulent operation to divest both the federal and state governments of thousands of acres of land and of millions of dollars in the form of bond endorsements. As a result the committee killed the scheme for that session. Revived in 1871, it passed the house of representatives but was defeated in the senate, never again to be considered by the legislature.[24]

Meanwhile, the confused issue of tax titles to the forfeited lands in the Delta assumed paramount importance in the effort to expand the area for agricultural development. Three authorities—state, Liquidating Levee Board, and the levee district board—vied for control of these lands, which by 1874 amounted to more than one third of the property in the Delta. Between 1867 and 1872 the Liquidating Levee Board held the upper hand in this contest, mainly as a result of the influential Alcorn's support. Nevertheless, uncertainty regarding the titles persisted, and few purchasers could be found to take the property off the hands of the board. Consequently, the board was denied a source of revenue both from the sale of the property and from taxes on it, although planters continued to cultivate many of the lands. The chronic confusion over tax titles and the fact that at one time or another much of the area had been subject to forfeiture also depreciated the value of lands that were actually free of tax liens. Many hard-pressed landowners, who for several years had held property for speculation or future cultivation, wanted desperately to sell their unimproved

23. Jackson *Weekly Pilot*, April 9, May 7, 15 (quote), 21, 1870.
24. *Ibid.*, June 4, 11, 1870; Jackson *Pilot*, April 20, 21, 1871.

lands, but they could find few buyers who were willing to gamble on property that conveyed no clear title.[25]

When Alcorn resigned as governor in late 1871 to take his seat in the Senate, the tables were turned on the Liquidating Levee Board. Unable to obtain adequate tax support while Alcorn sat in the governor's chair, the district boards had borrowed heavily, even after the scalawag governor had killed the bill that would give them the authority to raise money in this fashion. The legislature of 1872–1873, with Governor Powers' approval, threw its support to the two district boards, agencies that had the responsibility for actually constructing and maintaining the levees. The new legislation, in effect, gave these boards priority to the tax lands and the power to tax and raise money for levee purposes. The state government's action threatened the investments of the Liquidating Levee Board bondholders, and with the encouragement of the board itself they instituted suits in both the state and federal courts to protect the value of their bonds. Their official claim was that the new legislation had deprived them of their property without due process of law.[26]

Until a definitive court decision was rendered in 1877, the tangled skein of affairs continued in the Delta and opened the door to widespread mismanagement and fraud by local officials. Alcorn in 1874 complained that the levee board for the northern district had issued one million dollars in bonds since 1871, but had little to show for it. Even the levee that had been completed, he revealed, "has been constructed in the most insufficient and unsatisfactory manner and at prices three or four times the value of the work." He asked for the opportunity to appear before the legislature for the purpose of exposing "a system of outrage and plunder in the levee Districts whereby the people of the whole State are now

25. Robert W. Harrison, *Levee Districts and Levee Building in Mississippi: A Study of State and Local Efforts to Control Mississippi River Floods* (Stoneville, Miss., 1951), 41–42; Wade, "Lands of the Liquidating Levee Board," 286–87, 296–97; petition of citizens of Bolivar, Washington, and Issaquena counties, December, 1870, in Governors' Correspondence, Vol. 73; *Report of the Levee Commissioner of the State of Mississippi, January, 1872* (Jackson, 1872), 6–7; *House Journal, 1875*, Appendix, 40.

26. Alcorn to A. K. Davis, December 17, 1874, in Governors' Correspondence, Vol. 96; Harrison, *Levee Districts*, 46–47.

being robbed of thousands of dollars annually."[27] The Ames-dominated legislature refused to grant Alcorn a hearing, but it did launch an investigation into the failure of the levee boards to account for their expenditures—an investigation that was aborted by the overthrow of the Republican regime in 1876.[28]

Meanwhile, carpetbagger Charles W. Clarke, commissioned by Governor Ames to investigate the collection of taxes in two Delta counties, reported another source of fraud in the levee districts. Because of the confusion over who was responsible for collecting public revenues on certain lands, some tax collectors, Clarke said, appropriated the taxes for their own use, then settled their accounts with the state auditor by simply claiming that the levee district or the Liquidating Levee Board had priority in the receipt of tax revenues from the lands. These officials were almost invariably Republican, black as well as white. But a number of planters were also involved in cheating against the public interest. Clarke revealed that some planters would redeem their lands from one set of officials, then keep the property off the tax rolls by claiming that another authority had tax titles to it—a contention that was not easily refuted in view of the confused pattern of land titles in the Delta.[29]

Facing impeachment at the time, Governor Ames was not able to act on Clarke's report. The new conservative regime, however, quickly imposed a solution. The legislature abolished the Liquidating Levee Board and placed the tax-forfeited lands in the hands of the state auditor. Little improvement in the situation occurred, however, except in the diminution of fraud; by 1878 the state held more than one half of the lands of the Delta.[30]

But already, an 1877 state supreme court decision had forced a settlement that went far toward clearing up the complications surrounding the tax titles. This decision, rendered in the case of *Gibbs* v. *Green*, invalidated the efforts of the state and the old levee dis-

27. Alcorn to A. K. Davis, December 17, 1874, in Governors' Correspondence, Vol. 96.

28. *Laws of Mississippi, 1875*, pp. 173–74.

29. Charles W. Clarke to Adelbert Ames, January 3, 1876, in Governors' Correspondence, Vol. 100.

30. *Laws of Mississippi, 1876*, pp. 166–73; Brandfon, *Cotton Kingdom*, 46.

tricts to repudiate or reduce the obligations (mainly bonds) of the Liquidating Levee Board, although it permitted the consolidation of all the tax-forfeited lands under the administration of the state auditor. The court also ruled that these lands were to be sold on easy terms to purchasers, with the proceeds going to retire the bonds at par value.[31] At one swoop the supreme court had restored the credit standing of the Delta, made mandatory the sale of state-held lands there, and given prospective purchasers confidence in the conveyance of titles to this property. Even though a durable levee was not completed during these years (seventy-eight miles of new embankment was built between 1865 and 1882, thirteen miles less than was abandoned),[32] the settlement of the land imbroglio made possible the large-scale agricultural development of the Mississippi Delta beginning in the 1880s. Unfortunately, this development—or more accurately, exploitation—was controlled by outside capitalists for their own aggrandizement, which prevented the state from realizing very much benefit from it.[33]

Although fighting a losing battle, farm spokesmen during Reconstruction never tired of calling for agricultural diversification and the adoption of scientific methods of cultivation as means to improve conditions on the land. Beginning publication at Jackson in early 1871, *Southern Field and Factory* filled its columns with exhortations for Mississippi farmers to plant crops other than cotton. The leading agricultural reformers in the state contributed numerous and lengthy articles to the crusade for diversification and farm improvements. The promotion of wheat and corn production, and even that of rice for the Delta, received a great deal of attention, but considerable space was also given in the journal to the economic benefits of producing fruits and vegetables for midwestern markets. In addition, a strong appeal was made for planters and farmers to breed stock and plant pasture grasses.[34] Agricultural

31. Brandfon, *Cotton Kingdom*, 48; *W. H. Gibbs, Auditor, et al.* v. *Joshua Green*, 54 Miss. 592–612 (1877).

32. In constructing these levees and maintaining the old ones, the levee boards spent $3,557,918. Harrison, *Levee Districts*, 53.

33. Brandfon, *Cotton Kingdom*, Chaps. III–V.

34. See especially *Southern Field and Factory*, I (January, 1871), 2, 3, 35, 76, 96; I (March, 1871), 97–98; I (October, 1871), 349; I (November 1871), 393.

diversification, C. M. Vaiden insisted, would cause money to accumulate in the state, which then could be used to develop industry, "not cotton fabrics only, but nearly every thing needed here."[35] Charles E. Hooker, a leading conservative politician as well as a farm leader, in a plea for agricultural change declared that the present system was exhausting the soil and impoverishing the people of the state in order "to pay tribute to the North, West and East, for that which we could better produce ourselves, and the whole country north of the Ohio river was studded with the monuments of *our* folly."[36]

The newspapers of the state, both conservative and Republican, also promoted the cause of diversification. In calling for the introduction of livestock breeding practices, the carpetbag editor of the Jackson *Pilot* labeled as absurd the policy of sending farm proceeds to the Midwest to purchase mules and horses and to pay for the products of packing houses. Mississippians could easily succeed in stock breeding, he predicted, if they would only abandon their all-consuming passion for cotton.[37]

As instruments for promoting innovation in farm practices, agricultural societies sprang up throughout the state during Reconstruction. In 1868 local farm associations appeared in several counties, and the following year county fairs were held under the auspices of these organizations.[38] In January, 1869, a group of farm leaders, planters, and businessmen, responding to a call by James M. Wesson, president of the only significant textile plant in the state, met in Jackson and formed the Mississippi Planters, Manufacturers, and Mechanics' Association. In keeping with its purpose to promote agricultural reform and economic diversification, the association immediately laid plans for a state fair to be held in the fall to propagate the gospel of change and to serve as a showcase for the products of a diversified economy. The state fair was an instant success, probably due more to its social and enter-

---

35. *Ibid.*, I (January, 1871), 4.
36. Jackson *Weekly Pilot*, October 29, 1870.
37. *Ibid.* See also *ibid.*, December 16, 1869, the Jackson *Pilot*, January 13, 1871, the Vicksburg *Times and Republican*, July 31, 1873, and the *Hinds County Gazette*, November 23, 1870.
38. Vicksburg *Herald*, November 26, 1868; Jackson *Weekly Clarion*, March 4, 1868.

tainment features than to its educational value.[39] Actually, the movement toward agricultural organization and the promotion of a diversified economy was not new, having emerged in a sporadic fashion during the antebellum period. Its development after the war, however, led to a more uniform and persistent attack on the evils of King Cotton and his retainers.

A political chill in 1870 threatened the gains that had been made by the reformers. The omission of Governor Alcorn from the list of speakers at the state fair caused Republicans to complain of the political bias of the state planters' association.[40] The issue soon lost its force when the society invited prominent Republicans like carpetbagger Alexander Warner and blacks Matthew T. Newsom and Robert Gleed, both Radicals, to participate in its next meeting. Soon the Republican press gave its support to the planters' association, and in 1871 the legislature gave the organization a charter, an annual appropriation of nine thousand dollars to help finance the state fair, and a permanent site on state property for the event.[41] As a result of this assistance the state fair, though it failed in its original purpose of moving Mississippi toward self-sufficiency, emerged during Reconstruction as an exciting social diversion for many people who lived a dull and drab existence. On one day in 1871 five thousand people attended the fair, which almost equaled the total attendance for the largest one held during the antebellum period. Subsequent fairs during the 1870s were even more popular. Even Governor Ames, who normally disliked mingling with former rebels, attended the one of 1874, where horses owned by his carpetbag associates swept the racing contests. The governor's day was ruined, however, when he was thrown into the presence of Jefferson Davis and was forced to shake hands with the nation's most infamous "traitor."[42]

Inspired by the efforts of Governor Powers on behalf of economic development, the legislature of 1872 directed that boards of supervisors collect and make available accurate monthly data on

39. Natchez *Weekly Democrat*, September 7, 1868; Jackson *Weekly Clarion*, June 10, November 25, 1869.

40. Jackson *Weekly Pilot*, November 5, 1870.

41. Jackson *Pilot*, January 26, 28, 1871; *Laws of Mississippi, 1871*, pp. 628–32.

42. Jackson *Semi-Weekly Pilot*, December 11, 1871; Jackson *Weekly Clarion*, December 5, 1872; Ames to his wife, October 29, 30, November 1, 1874, in Blanche Butler Ames (comp.), *Chronicles*, II, 46–48.

the crops in their counties. *Southern Field and Factory*, edited by E. G. Wall, a former major in the Confederate army, was given a contract to publish the information and was also encouraged in its work of propagating the gospel of agricultural reform. But a recommendation by Powers that the legislature provide for a state experimental farm failed to pass, despite the support of Wall and other farm leaders.[43] Republican legislatures enacted a few minor measures designed more to promote than to aid the cause of agriculture change. In one area of concern—relations between planters and laborers—the legislature refused to intervene.

Despite the efforts of the reformers, little progress was made during Reconstruction toward agricultural self-sufficiency. The production of most crops, including cotton, did not reach the yields of 1860. Corn production, for example, fell sharply from 29,057,682 bushels in 1860 to 15,637,316 in 1870, only to rise to 21,340,800 during the 1870s when the most intense effort was being made to get farmers and planters to increase their acreage in the crop. Little attention was paid to the reformers' plea for larger wheat yields; 587,925 bushels were produced in 1860, 274,479 in 1870, and only 218,890 in 1880. On the other hand, yields from oats, rice, and tobacco increased more than 100 percent above the 1860 levels, although these crops remained minor in comparison to cotton and corn. In addition, the production of wool went from 665,959 pounds in 1860 (288,285 in 1870) to 734,643 pounds in 1880.

At the same time the efforts of Mississippians to meet their own livestock needs met with failure. The value of livestock in 1880 was $24,285,717 as compared to $41,891,682 in 1860. Although the population of the state had increased by more than 340,000 (to 1,131,597) in the two decades since secession, the number of horses, hogs, and beef cattle remained below that of 1860. Only in the replacement of milk cows and mules did Mississippians during the 1870s recover from the war-inflicted depredations on livestock.[44]

43. *Laws of Mississippi, 1872*, pp. 63–64; *Southern Field and Factory*, II (March, 1872), 131.

44. Comparative crop statistics for 1860, 1870, and 1880 are found in *Compendium of the Tenth Census (June 1, 1880), Compiled Pursuant to an Act of Congress Approved August 7, 1882* (Washington, D.C., 1888), 662–63, 665–67, 669–71, 674–81.

The agricultural reformers of the early 1870s had also promoted the development of truck farming and fruit growing in the state. Although the statistics for these activities are incomplete, it is clear that the gains made held promise for significant agricultural diversification along these lines. A few farmers near the New Orleans, Jackson, and Great Northern Railroad began raising vegetables in 1870 and shipping them to urban markets in Louisville, St. Louis, and Chicago. This trade, however, developed slowly during the late nineteenth century.[45] A more important innovation was the development of peach farming along the same railroad. Inspired by the success of William Hester, an agricultural reformer and later a Grange leader who shipped peaches to the Midwest in 1869, farmers in the Terry-Crystal Springs area a few miles south of Jackson developed a thriving peach culture to supplement the local cotton economy. The height of peach production during Reconstruction was reached in 1873 when 40,000 boxes were sent to New Orleans and the Midwest where they sold for $32,000. Efforts to grow peaches along the railroad north of Jackson failed because of the vagaries of the climate, the mishandling of the peaches by careless railroad agents, and the pervasiveness of cotton cultivation in the area.[46]

Agricultural reformers also prepared the way for the rapid spread of the Patrons of Husbandry, or the Grange, in Mississippi. Entering the state in 1871, Grange chapters dotted the countryside by the end of 1872, and by 1875 the organization could claim a membership of thirty thousand whites dedicated to the amelioration of conditions among the agricultural masses.[47] Planters as well as farmers were encouraged to join the movement, and such early agricultural reformers as C. M. Vaiden, A. Q. Withers of Holly Springs, and William D. Gibbs of Yazoo County, all of the planter class, became Grange leaders. Following the example of their brethren in the Midwest, Mississippi Grangers devoted some at-

45. Jackson *Weekly Pilot*, May 15, 1870; Griggs (comp.), *Guide to Mississippi*, 8.

46. Jackson *Weekly Clarion*, December 16, 1869; Vicksburg *Times and Republican*, July 31, 1873; E. G. Wall (comp.), *The State of Mississippi: Resources, Condition, and Wants* (Jackson, 1879), 12, 166; *Southern Field and Factory*, I (November, 1871), 393.

47. *Southern Field and Factory*, I (August, 1871), 250–52, 290; III (March, 1873), 120–21; D. Sven Nordin, *Rich Harvest: A History of the Grange, 1867–1900* (Jackson, 1974), 29.

tention to attacks on the railroads and other economic interest groups, which they charged with suppressing the right of farmers to gain a just return for their labor. But mainly they confronted the specific ills that they perceived in Mississippi agriculture. Grange leaders unremittingly called for an end to the debilitating credit system, coupled with a demand for the repeal of the crop lien law of 1867 which, they claimed, worked for the benefit of merchants and to the detriment of farmers. To aid the farmers in freeing themselves from the credit system and from grasping merchants, a number of local Granges established cooperative stores where producers could sell their cotton and purchase supplies without paying the exactions of the middlemen. These mercantile endeavors, however, were frequently mismanaged, and others fell victim to the same problems that affected all economic enterprises in the state—mainly, a dearth of money and an inability to borrow at reasonable rates from outside capitalists.[48]

The Grange promoted the cause of crop diversification and independence from cotton quite as much as did the agricultural reformers. It also stressed the need for farmers to practice "the strictest economy until the farming interests are put on a cash basis."[49] The Grange, as was its policy in other states, attempted to relieve the dull monotony of farm life with inexpensive but frequent "social reunions" and meetings, in which women as well as men participated. This part of the Grange program received a more enthusiastic response from farmers than did its program for agricultural change. The admission of women to membership at first created some opposition to the order, but the vitality they brought to the movement soon dispelled this objection. Furthermore, as Grange editor E. G. Wall pointed out, there were thousands of widows of Confederate soldiers in the state who were independent farmers. "Would you deny them the privilege to meet with their brother farmers, to consult together for their

---

48. *Southern Field and Factory*, I (September, 1871), 328–29; James S. Ferguson, "The Granger Movement in Mississippi," (M.A. thesis, Louisiana State University, 1940), 88, 147–48; Pascagoula *Star*, November 21, 1874; Jackson *Weekly Clarion*, August 21, 1873; Vicksburg *Vicksburger*, March 12, 1874.

49. *Southern Field and Factory*, II (October, 1872), 459–60; III (October, 1873), 445.

mutual interest and protection?" Wall asked those who opposed the order on sexual grounds.[50]

Reflecting planter interest, the organization increasingly turned its attention to the labor problem. Grange leaders called for the end of the sharecrop-tenant system and the reinstitution of wage payments to plantation laborers. Mainly, however, they emphasized immigration as a solution to the labor problem. By 1874 the Grange seemed consumed with the desire for settlers, both from the North and from Europe, believing that white newcomers would provide the energy necessary to revitalize the farm economy. The state Grange convention of 1874 went so far as to send a carpetbagger to the Midwest to promote the agricultural resources and society of Mississippi and entice settlers to the state.[51]

Editors and spokesmen of both political parties and the early agricultural reformers joined in the mania for immigration that swept the state during Reconstruction. Although their purposes and emphases frequently differed, most promoters insisted that Mississippi's material recovery and future prosperity depended upon a large influx of settlers.

Planter spokesmen who were conservative in politics generally sought settlers to replace black workers and reinforce labor stability in the plantation districts. During the five years immediately after the war this purpose was obvious in the various schemes planters employed to induce immigrants to the state.[52] Immigration promoters denied, however, that their efforts were inimical to the interests of blacks; they insisted that by supplementing black labor with that of immigrants labor stability and efficiency would be restored and all classes would benefit. They desired to fill the "waste places" with cultivators, not to drive out Negro tenants whose employment would continue to be necessary in the labor-starved plantation areas. Although they rarely admitted it, black belt and river county planters also hoped to bring in a sufficient

50. *Ibid.*, II (October, 1872), 456.

51. Jackson *Weekly Clarion*, September 24, October 8, 1874; Pascagoula *Star*, March 13, 27, 1875.

52. William J. Sykes to the editor, *De Bow's Review: After the War Series*, IV (November, 1867), 420–21; Meridian *Semi-Weekly Gazette*, October 9, 1867; Jackson *Clarion*, February 10, 1867; Vicksburg *Times*, March 5, 1867.

number of white settlers to offset the local political advantage that blacks and their white Republican allies held.

A convention of old citizens who were interested in securing settlers met in Jackson in March, 1868. The timing of the meeting reflected not only planter dismay over the "Black and Tan" Convention then in session, but also economic fears that had been spawned by the hard times of the winter. Addressed by John Everett, a British immigration agent, the convention adopted a plan to organize "Freehold Land and Colonization" companies in interested counties. The scheme called for each company to purchase and sell or rent land to settlers whom Everett would send from Europe. All persons subscribing land would receive stock certificates in the company. Although a number of meetings were held in 1868–1869 to organize county land and immigration companies, the plan was too much of a will-o'-the-wisp to gain the cooperation of enough landowners for its success.[53] The only successful attempt during Reconstruction to secure immigrants directly from Europe resulted from the dispatch of an agent of the Mississippi Central Railroad to Sweden. He returned with "several hundred" immigrants who were settled as landowners or tenants along the road in north Mississippi.[54]

A more vigorous effort was made in 1869–1870 to secure settlers from the Midwest. Even political Bourbons joined in the chorus for northern settlers. The tide of immigration "will soon set towards this State," the Bourbon editor of the Forest *Register* announced. "Mississippi is the first State on the Continent in point of value of agricultural products to the number of her population. . . . The lands here are cheap, and we look for vast numbers of emigrants from the Eastern and Middle States in the next four years. Most of these will be industrious and thrifty men and women, and some of them will be men of capital. It depends entirely on the men who live in the several counties of the State where the vacant lands are for sale, whether any large portion of this number shall settle

53. Jackson *Clarion*, March 31, April 1, 7, May 2, 1868; Vicksburg *Times*, December 15, 1868.

54. Jackson *Weekly Clarion*, December 16, 1869, December 12, 1872.

amongst them."[55] Despite such platitudes promising land for settlers and encouragement to "men of capital," the main thrust of
the immigration societies was toward securing agricultural laborers
on a contract basis. The Chicago German Society, an agency founded to find employment and land for recently arrived Germans in
the Mississippi Valley, dispatched from three to four hundred
laborers to north Mississippi in 1869. Working either on shares or
for wages of about ten dollars a month, most of them, however,
"were obliged to leave after four or five months" because they were
"unable to stand the treatment, live on the food and work in the
same manner as the former slave."[56] Even the Young Men's Christian Association of Chicago organized and furnished transportation to Mississippi for footloose young Europeans. In addition,
individual planters, local societies, and Mississippi railroad companies dispatched agents to Chicago, Rockford, Racine, and other
midwestern towns to obtain agricultural laborers.

Ethelbert Barksdale toured the Midwest in early 1870, making
contacts with immigration agencies and sending back reports on
the desirability of contract labor. Nevertheless, he became increasingly sensitive to midwestern criticism that Mississippi planters were attempting to replace black slavery with white slavery.
Consequently, he ended his tour with an appeal for landowners
to divide their estates and sell to settlers on favorable terms.[57]
In cooperation with the Mobile and Ohio Railroad, which agreed
to transport immigrants at a rate of one cent per mile, a society
in Okolona reportedly placed two thousand midwestern laborers
and homesteaders in the community. More than the local immigration associations, railroad managers sought settlers who would
purchase land along their lines and increase the freight traffic.
However, instead of promoting diversification and the economic
self-sufficiency of the newcomers (as well as that of the old citizens
along their lines), the railroads encouraged the production of cot-

55. Forest *Register*, December 11, 1869. Northern politicians, or carpetbaggers, of
course, were not welcomed by these immigration promoters.

56. Jackson *Weekly Clarion*, December 16, 23, 1869, February 10, 1870; *Hinds County
Gazette*, December 29, 1869, February 23, May 11, 1870; Jackson *Weekly Pilot*, December
25, 1869, September 17, 1870.

57. Jackson *Weekly Clarion*, February 10, March 3, 1870.

ton, since its transportation to market in exchange for foodstuffs provided them with a reliable source of freight revenues.[58]

The flurry of immigration activity in 1869–1870 brought no significant results. Most of the laborers returned to the Midwest or went west to seek opportunities where economic and social conditions were better. A former Union soldier who was active in Mississippi immigration efforts during Reconstruction later revealed that the movement of 1869–1870 served more "as drains for an idle, vagabond class who were imposed on us by Labor agencies at so much per head than as a means of procuring the kind of accessions to our population which [were] so much needed."[59] Nevertheless, many of the immigrants were independent, upward-bound homesteaders who subsequently left Mississippi because of their dismay at the poverty, the lack of respect for the law, and the general political uncertainty and shrillness that prevailed.[60] No doubt many settlers in abandoning the state were partly motivated by a desire to escape social and economic competition with blacks, but this does not appear to have been their main motive in leaving. Like immigrants to other regions, they came to Mississippi seeking economic opportunity and a congenial social climate. When they did not find these, they sought the American dream elsewhere.

Simultaneous with the movement to attract white immigrants, an effort was made by planters and entrepreneurs in the Mississippi Valley to secure Chinese workers. A "Chinese Immigration Convention" met in Memphis in July, 1869, to map plans for tapping this source of cheap labor. Although Civil War Governor Isham Harris of Tennessee presided over the convention, it was mainly a Mississippi affair. The delegates formed an immigration company and made preparations to send an agent to San Francisco to contract for Chinese laborers. General Nathan Bedford Forrest, who attended the meeting, subscribed five thousand dollars to

58. *Ibid.*, October 14, 1869, February 10, 1870, April 13, 1871; *Hinds County Gazette*, February 23, 1870.

59. As reported in the Jackson *Weekly Clarion*, December 12, 1872.

60. See especially the remarks of General Lieb, an officer in a Chicago immigration agency, concerning the reasons for the newcomers' disillusionment with Mississippi and their decision to leave the state. Jackson *Weekly Pilot*, September 17, 1870. See also the Vicksburg *Times and Republican*, September 17, 1871.

the company and announced his desire to employ one thousand Chinese in the construction of his railroad in north Mississippi. Representing Yazoo Valley planters, former Confederate General William R. Miles hurried to San Francisco during the summer to secure favorable terms with immigration agencies before the expected demand raised the price of "coolie labor."[61] At the same time Stephen Duncan, the scion of "the greatest planter and slaveholder in the United States in the fifties," and other Adams County planters dispatched an agent to join Miles in the quest for Chinese immigrants.[62]

The enthusiasm for Chinese workers was short-lived. Although two or three hundred Chinese were brought to the plantation districts (only fifty-one remained in 1880), the promoters of the enterprise encountered problems that they had not anticipated.[63] The fees charged by the contracting agencies in San Francisco and the travel expenses across the continent for the immigrants proved excessive for Mississippi planters who were already heavily in debt. Even Forrest abandoned his plans to emulate the Central Pacific Railroad in its use of Chinese laborers. Furthermore, a number of Protestant ministers in the state and at least one Ku Klux Klan den raised their voices against the large-scale introduction of pagan Chinese who, they charged, would lower the moral standards of the people. The opponents of Chinese immigration brought in a northern minister to influence the Republican leadership against the movement. Speaking on the state capitol grounds and elsewhere, he denigrated the moral habits of the Chinese and charged that their introduction into the Mississippi Valley would be accompanied by a lively trade in opium and prostitution.[64]

Most Republicans needed no such moral suasion to place them solidly in opposition to Chinese immigration. A large Chinese pop-

61. Jackson *Weekly Clarion*, July 15, 22, 29, September 2, 1869.
62. McLemore (ed.), *History of Mississippi*, I, 343; *Hinds County Gazette*, August 4, September 1, 1869.
63. U.S. Bureau of the Census, *Tenth Census of the United States: 1880, Population* (Washington, D.C., 1883), p. 3.
64. Jackson *Weekly Clarion*, September 2, October 28, 1869, December 1, 1870; Jackson *Weekly Pilot*, January 22, 1870; synopses of the testimony of N. N. Adams, W. T. Harris, and Elijah Smith of Pontotoc County, before the United States District Court at Oxford, 1871, in Source-Chronological File, Northern Mississippi, RG 60, NA, Microcopy Roll 1.

ulation in the state would depreciate the value of Negro labor, since under contracts of eight to ten dollars a month they would be working for less compensation than blacks received. The effect would be either to drive Negroes out of the state or make them even more dependent on the planters for their livelihood. Demanding that Congress prohibit the system of labor contracts, the Republican editor of the Jackson *Pilot* argued that "the spirit of modern civilization is utterly opposed to Coolie traffic. Wherever it has been in existence, it is as pitiful as slavery itself."[65]

Yeoman whites also found the "Coolie traffic" to be inimical to their interests. A Hinds County "Plowman" claimed that "nine-tenths of the laboring white people of the South are against it" on the grounds that Chinese labor would compete with them for the little revenue that could be realized from the land. The Chinese, yeoman whites insisted, would benefit the large planters to the detriment of the poor, who constituted an overwhelming majority of the region's people.[66]

The 1869–1870 mania for immigrants also spawned a land-grabbing scheme in the Mississippi Valley that almost succeeded in defrauding the state of 200,000 acres of rich Delta lands. Formed in 1868, the Mississippi Valley Navigation Company, composed of outside speculators, proposed to put into service several safe, low-pressure steamboats and to provide free transportation for immigrants to the state in exchange for 200,000 acres of land at fifty cents an acre. Under the proposal the company would not pay for the land immediately, but would issue bonds to the state which would be liquidated when immigrants purchased the land from the company. In 1868 the company obtained the support of the Republican regime in Louisiana to a similar scheme, but it had to wait until Mississippi was restored to the Union in 1870 before pressing for the approval of the proposal there.[67]

A bill to effectuate this land-grab enterprise was introduced into

65. Jackson *Weekly Clarion*, August 5, 26, 1869; Jackson *Weekly Pilot*, April 9, June 18, 1870. Not all Republicans opposed Chinese immigration. Flournoy employed twenty-four Chinese laborers on his plantation in 1871. *Southern Field and Factory*, I (March, 1871), 106.

66. *Hinds County Gazette*, September 1, 1869. Many whites, of course, objected to the introduction of Chinese into the state because of the color of their skins.

67. Vicksburg *Herald*, August 8, 9, 1868; Jackson *Weekly Pilot*, June 4, 1870.

the legislature in 1870, and the powerful but evidently naïve editor of the Jackson *Pilot* announced his support of the measure, arguing that its implementation would be a boon to immigration. Not so convinced of its public benefits, carpetbagger Charles A. Foster, a Republican floor leader in the house of representatives, declared, "Whatever may be said of the low-pressure of the proposed boats, [the scheme] is certainly a very high-pressure upon the property and resources of the State." He wondered why the state could not sell these lands directly and cheaply to immigrants or to its landless poor.[68] Foster's opposition led to the bill's defeat in this session, but a vigorous effort by the company's lobbyists in 1871 secured its passage. Fortunately for the public interest, Lieutenant Governor Powers, acting for the absent Governor Alcorn, vetoed the measure. In registering his disapproval Powers correctly claimed that the whole business was an attempt to defraud the state of 200,000 acres of fertile land. When the veto was sustained, the navigation company abandoned its scheme. For his action in protecting the state's interest, the Natchez *Democrat* declared that Powers "entitled himself to the profound gratitude of all honest men."[69]

Republicans, though not all in agreement, differed from the conservatives in their immigration policies. They insisted that only settlers of skill and enterprise should be encouraged to come to the state. Complaining that the South was "over stocked with non-producers," the carpetbag editor of the party organ in Vicksburg, who was the most active Republican promoter of immigration in Mississippi, denounced the conservative movement to attract farm workers. He frequently called for a campaign to attract northern and European settlers who would quickly add wealth to their new communities and bring about a diversification of the economy of the state.[70]

Politics also entered into the promoter's view of the type of immigrant the state needed. Republicans charged, with some truth, that an important purpose behind planter efforts to secure

68. Jackson *Weekly Pilot*, July 16, 1870.
69. *Senate Journal, 1871*, pp. 496–97; Natchez *Weekly Democrat*, May 3, 1871.
70. Jackson *Weekly Pilot*, December 18, 1869, April 23, May 7, June 4, 1870; Loring and Atkinson (eds.), *Cotton Culture*, 89; Vicksburg *Times and Republican*, September 17, December 14, 23, 1871, April 18, 1872.

white farm laborers was the conservative need for reliable voters to counterbalance the large black registration in the plantation counties. These Republicans believed that the influx of a higher class of immigrants would redound to the benefit of their party, since, as men of intelligence, they would not be swayed by the Democrats' old fogy notions and would inevitably affiliate with the Republican party. Moderate carpetbaggers, in fact, looked to the infusion of northerners of this class to provide the party with the kind of racial balance they felt was essential to the preservation of its hegemony in the state. On the other hand, most Radical Republicans, assuming that they were secure behind their black ballots and fearing that a migration of whites into Mississippi would lessen their political advantage, remained aloof from the crusade to attract settlers.[71] Moreover, black leaders for economic reasons viewed the movement with considerable wariness, concluding that the introduction of white farm workers would depress the value of Negro labor, which despite the financial pinch was relatively high during Reconstruction.

Nevertheless, the Republican-framed constitution of 1868 had committed the party to the creation of the office of commissioner of immigration and agriculture. Gaining control of the state government at the peak of the conservative effort to secure white immigrants, Republicans at first refused to implement this constitutional provision, although Governor Alcorn recommended that it be done. Then, during the Powers years, partly as a result of the Republican shift away from political issues toward economic matters, the legislature established the immigration "bureau." At the same time the Republican majority, passing over a carpetbag associate of Powers, elected black legislator Richard Griggs as the first commissioner.[72] With the selection of Griggs, "an unlettered negro," according to the Jackson *Clarion*, any support that the conservatives might have given to the agency vanished. Far from being in a position to encourage immigration, Griggs's presence in the office would repel it, Barksdale charged. "The knowledge among Europeans that [this] important office had been confided

71. Jackson *Semi-Weekly Pilot*, November 23, 1871; Harris, "Creed of the Carpetbaggers," 219–20.
72. *Laws of Mississippi, 1873*, pp. 103–105; *House Journal, 1873*, pp. 1967–71.

The Day of the Carpetbagger

to one of his race and class as the representative of the intelligence and property of the State, would be sufficient to turn their minds away from all thought of emigrating to Mississippi."[73]

Although infrequently voiced, a real concern of conservatives and many moderate Republicans was that as commissioner Griggs would use the resources of the state government to promote black settlement and would ignore the overpowering need for white immigrants. Many river planters had no objection to an influx of contract black laborers from Alabama and Georgia as an emergency step toward solving their labor problem, but most whites, especially in the upland and piney woods districts, opposed the migration of Negroes to the state, for political, if for no other, reasons. An exodus of blacks into Mississippi, they reasoned, would only swell the Republican majority and make more difficult the redemption of the state from the rule of the adventurers and the ignorant.[74]

Sensitive to these criticisms, Griggs made a special attempt to keep the affairs of his office free of racial favoritism. His main problem was not conservative opposition; it was the inadequate financial support that his Republican colleagues in the legislature gave to the immigration program. Griggs had no money to establish contacts with immigration agencies, much less to send agents to Europe or to the North, and his clerical staff was restricted to five part-time clerks, three of whom were also members of the legislature. He was able, however, to secure reduced fares for prospective settlers from railroad companies that had not already adopted such a policy.[75] Then, in 1874, the legislature provided funds for the publication of a lengthy pamphlet promoting the resources of the state and describing state and federal lands that were available for purchase. In addition to this data, the pamphlet, entitled *Guide to Mississippi*, contained articles by prominent Republicans and the historian John F. H. Claiborne on various aspects of the life and economy of the state.

The act authorizing the publication of the promotional tract also

73. Jackson *Weekly Clarion*, April 24, 1873. See also the *Hinds County Gazette*, December 18, 1872, April 30, 1873.

74. See the comment of the Bourbon editor of the Forest *Register*, as reported in the Jackson *Weekly Pilot*, January 30, 1875, and also the Jackson *Weekly Clarion*, August 7, 1873.

75. *House Journal, 1874*, Appendix, 534; Griggs (comp.), *Guide to Mississippi*, 34.

created a liberal plan for the sale of state lands to settlers. The measure provided that the head of any family, including current citizens of Mississippi, who settled on state lands could be granted a maximum of 160 acres at five cents an acre. Payment for the property was not due until the end of the third year of residence, whereupon the homesteader would receive title to the land provided that his residence had been continuous and that he had cultivated the property. Since the state held more than 4,500,000 acres of delinquent tax lands, which were specifically included in the measure, in addition to unknown but substantial quantities of land obtained before the war from the federal government, the act of 1874 on the surface offered an excellent opportunity for the acquisition of land by thousands of the dispossessed citizens, as well as by immigrants.[76]

The program, however, faltered from the beginning. The state's title to the tax-held lands was not legally strong, and it could be wiped out entirely by an act of the legislature abating delinquent taxes. Already, in 1874, the clamor for abatement was heard as the economic decline continued, but the Republican legislature at first refused to act. In 1875 support for abatement reached into the Republican leadership, and with the approval of Governor Ames an act was passed providing for the restoration of those properties surrendered to the state before 1874.[77] Under these circumstances prospective homesteaders shunned the proffers of land on state-held tax properties. Even had there been no confusion regarding titles, many landless farmers, with continuing obligations to meet under the crop lien system, simply would not have been able to take advantage of the opportunity to settle on state lands, which in many cases were in inaccessible places and in poor soil districts. Furthermore, like the tax-held properties, titles to the older state lands were in disarray.[78] To make matters worse, except for funds to publish the *Guide to Mississippi*, Griggs and his associates did not have the means to publicize the availability of the cheap lands under the act of 1874. As a result the Republican

76. *Laws of the State of Mississippi, 1874* (Jackson, 1874), 62–65; *House Journal, 1875*, Appendix, 40; Jackson *Pilot*, January 20, 1871.
77. *Laws of Mississippi, 1875*, pp. 11–12.
78. *Ibid.*, 90–91; Jackson *Pilot*, January 20, 1871.

policy to provide homesteads for the landless of both races failed for some of the same reasons that beset the federal homestead program of 1866, which had also been designed for the poor of the South.[79]

White fears that with a black man as commissioner of immigration Negroes would flood into the state seemed to be confirmed by a large migration of Georgia and Alabama blacks to the river counties in 1873–1875. Actually, this exodus had developed quite apart from any policy or effort by Griggs, although Bourbons charged that the commissioner and his agents had inspired the movement. Deteriorating economic conditions in Georgia and Alabama caused mass restlessness among blacks there, and labor-starved planters of the river counties, taking advantage of the situation, dispatched agents to entice them to the bottomlands as tenants or contract workers. Griggs's responsibility for the migration was limited largely to answering queries of interested planters and representatives of blacks, as well as finding employment for Negroes who came to Jackson seeking assistance.[80]

In an unofficial capacity, local black leaders became involved in the exodus as agents of the planters. Sheriff Merriman Howard of Jefferson County made arrangements in Georgia for the shipment of blacks to fill the labor needs of planters in his county. William A. Pledger, a black politician and editor from Athens, was his contact in that state, and at least once Pledger came to Mississippi with a consignment of black workers. Henry P. Jacobs, a former state senator and a Natchez minister, went to Georgia seeking black immigrants and asked the editor of his hometown newspaper to publicize his availability as a labor agent for planters.[81] So many black ministers were involved in the enterprise,

79. For a general discussion of the application of the Homestead Act of 1866 in the South, see Paul W. Gates, "Federal Land Policy in the South, 1866–1888," *Journal of Southern History*, VI (August, 1940), 303–30. An account of its effects in Mississippi can be found in Harris, *Presidential Reconstruction in Mississippi*, 92–93.

80. Pascagoula *Star*, January 11, 18, 1874; Jackson *Weekly Clarion*, December 11, 1873; Jackson *Weekly Pilot*, January 16, 1875. Ames believed that blacks were fleeing to Mississippi in order to escape political oppression in Georgia, Alabama, and Tennessee. Ames to R. S. Fisher, January 15, 1876, in Combined Letterbook of Governors Adelbert Ames and John M. Stone, 1876, Mississippi Department of Archives and History.

81. William A. Pledger to Merriman Howard, January 3, 1876, in William A. Pledger Letterbook, John E. Bryant Papers, Duke University Library; Natchez *Democrat*, December 18, 1874, January 12, 1875.

reports circulated in the Alabama black belt that "some negro preachers are at the bottom of this wholesale exodus," and they pontificate "that it is the will of God that negroes should move to Mississippi." These ministers reportedly instilled in the minds of blacks the idea that successive crop failures were proof that God wanted them to leave Alabama and go to the Mississippi "Promised Land."[82]

The movement reached flood tide during the winter of 1873–1874. Observing that the migration resembled the movement of troops during wartime, a correspondent reported in early January that "ten thousand [blacks] have passed Meridian up to this time, and thousands are waiting for transportation."[83] During the winter the cars of the Vicksburg and Meridian Railroad were constantly filled with Negroes going to the plantations in the river counties. A fleet of covered wagons shuttled between Alabama and the Delta bringing laborers and their families, while other immigrants reached their destinations by foot. Although compensation for their labor was generally higher in the bottom country than in Alabama or Georgia, blacks found no promised land in Mississippi; only a few, however, returned to their old homes.[84]

The number of blacks migrating to Mississippi is impossible to determine, but a comparison of the census reports of 1870 and 1880, before and after the exodus, gives a clear indication of its significance. In the river counties (including all of the Delta), the black population leaped from 115,298 in 1870 to 187,812 in 1880.[85] The tier of plantation counties bordering on the river district and the black prairie belt of east Mississippi also experienced a large influx of Negroes during the decade. There, the black population of 174,375 in 1870 soared to 230,557 in 1880. This represented a gain of 127,686 in the black population of the plantation districts,

---

82. Pascagoula *Star*, January 18, 1874.

83. *Ibid.*, January 11, 1874.

84. Jackson *Weekly Clarion*, December 11, 23, 1873; Pledger to Merriman Howard, January 3, 1876, in Pledger Letterbook, Bryant Papers.

85. Historians have frequently discounted the reliability of the census of 1870 for the southern states, mainly because it was taken and compiled by Radical appointees who presumably were incompetent to perform such intricate tasks. Nevertheless, for Mississippi, a comparison of county statistics of the censuses before and after with the one of 1870 gives the clear impression that the Reconstruction count was no more defective than any other federal census.

and 62 percent of the increase for the whole state.[86] Since few blacks moved into these counties after the revolution of 1875—in fact, hundreds left the state to seek opportunities in Kansas and other places during the late 1870s—almost all of the increase occurred during the first half of the decade and mainly in 1873–1875.

Whites responded to the black immigration threat and the bankruptcy of the cotton economy with renewed efforts to entice white settlers to the state. This time they sought the assistance of moderate Republicans in an attempt to lure midwestern "men of industry and capital" to Mississippi. Unlike the movement of 1868–1870 which received its inspiration from the planters' need for labor, the immigration crusade of the late Reconstruction period gained its stimulus from a strange combination of interests. Almost simultaneously, agricultural reformers in the plantation districts, Grange leaders throughout the state, railroad managers, and town entrepreneurs became involved in a campaign to publicize the opportunities in Mississippi for northerners of energy and money. Appeals for farm laborers or mention of the virtues of cotton cultivation were almost totally ignored in these promotional efforts. Instead promoters stressed the opportunities for independent, diversified farmers and for small capitalists to invest in industry and commerce and exploit the forest resources of the vast piney woods. As an added inducement, they pointed out the advantages of the climate of the "Sunny South" over that of the "cold and cheerless" Midwest.[87]

Promoters of the new immigration made a special effort to convince midwesterners that regardless of their political affiliation they would be welcomed in the state and their political views respected. In response to a midwesterner's query at the height of the movement, editor Paul A. Botto wrote, with only a slight exaggeration from his Natchez perspective: "Every man's right of political opinion is as sacredly respected here as anywhere; that no man

86. The plantation counties represented only about one third of the state's land area. In addition to these counties, but not included in this analysis, were areas with a marginally Negro or predominantly white population that had some relatively large agricultural units worked by blacks.

87. Hillyard (comp.), *Letters Descriptive of Mississippi*, 65; Pascagoula *Star*, August 8, 1874, March 13, 27, 1875; *Hinds County Gazette*, September 16, 1874; Vicksburg *Times*, April 18, 1874.

is ever persecuted for his politics, and that every man who comes here to be of us and with us in the struggle to redeem our material prosperity, is welcomed with open arms, and enjoys as much of the confidence of the people as his good conduct entitles him to. Some of our best citizens are Republicans in politics, and very many of them are Northern men. And we all wish there were many more of this stamp."[88]

Not all proponents of the new immigration would admit that "some of our best citizens are Republicans," but all emphasized that the day of social ostracism and sectional recriminations was past in Mississippi. Lest there be doubters, the promoters compiled testimonials of northern visitors and residents as evidence of the state's changing social and political climate and rushed the statements northward to influence prospective settlers.[89] A midwestern sojournor in the state assured the readers of the Cincinnati *Commercial* in 1875 that former Confederate leaders "have accepted the decision of war as Americans—unification, emancipation and all. These men invite immigration. They need what the north have [sic] in abundance and to spare—people and implements for successful husbandry. There is a universal desire to see the country brought forward to its best condition, socially, politically, agriculturally, commercially—every way."[90]

These northerners also revealed the milk and honey opportunities of a land that needed only capital and enterprise to become like the Midwest. Alexander Clark, a northern visitor, wrote home in early 1875 that the area along the route of the north-south trunk line "offers rare inducement to industry and capital, and will, ere long, become equal in society and in every essential to good homes in the fairest sections of the East and West." The northern visitor and those of his kind living in the state found only one drawback. "The only disturbing element here is among ambitious politicians; and this is largely an imported element from the North, intent on speculation, office-getting, and a proscriptiveness which is as anti-

88. Natchez *Democrat*, March 13, 1875.
89. M. B. Hillyard, the Delaware-born secretary of the Mississippi Valley Company, an immigration and land corporation, has conveniently compiled and published these statements, most of which appeared in northern newspapers during the mid-1870s. *Letters Descriptive of Mississippi, passim.*
90. *Ibid.,* 94.

Republican as the caste of slavery times." A midwesterner wrote, "The great need is the establishment of mutual confidence between the races; and the great curse is the interference, for mere personal emolument, of foreign politicians, who seem to live and move only to accomplish mischief, at whatever cost to the manhood or the Americanism of the people." Another northerner believed that Mississippi "has had enough of carpetbaggers; let us now send her intelligent cultivators of the soil."[91]

Ironically, when the promoters of the new immigration dispatched an agent to the Midwest in their most ambitious effort to attract settlers, they chose a carpetbagger for the task. Their representative, moderate Republican Henry Musgrove, did not really fit the carpetbag stereotype and was only identified as one when he consorted with the Radicals in his party. In 1874, when "Modest Mus" was selected by the state Grange for the midwestern mission, he was on the black list of the Republican hierarchy in Jackson, since he had recently run for lieutenant governor on the aberrant Alcorn ticket. During the months since his retirement as state auditor, Musgrove had emerged as a leader in the Hinds County Grange and as a strong advocate of economic diversification and midwestern immigration.[92]

Musgrove's mission took him to several midwestern centers, and at Springfield he delivered a long New South style address in the Illinois state house. In this speech, Musgrove reminded his audience of the traditional ties between the upper and lower Mississippi Valley and asked midwesterners to once again turn their attention to economic cooperation with their southern brethren. His only reference to war issues was to point out that the reconstruction policy of Congress had succeeded in Mississippi. In case prospective immigrants found the civil rights act of 1873 a deterrent to settlement in the state, Musgrove indicated that blacks had not insisted on these guarantees, and as a result race relations were generally good.[93]

While in the Midwest, Musgrove arranged for newspapermen of the region to tour Mississippi by rail. The entourage arrived in

91. *Ibid.*, 48–49, 94–95, 104.
92. Jackson *Weekly Clarion*, September 24, 1874; Pascagoula *Star*, March 13, 27, 1875.
93. Vicksburg *Times*, January 25, 1875.

Jackson on March 19, 1875, and was given a royal welcome by prominent men of both political parties as well as by leading businessmen. At an impressive banquet held the night of their arrival and presided over by Ethelbert Barksdale, paeans were sung to the Union and to material development. Champagne corks popped as prominent conservatives mingled with their counterparts of the Republican party in a rare demonstration of social forbearance during the Reconstruction era. Governor Ames and the black leadership were conspicuously missing, however.[94] The blacks' absence from the feast reflected the triumph of the spirit of sectional reconciliation and material progress and the decline of the national commitment to black equality.

After visiting Jackson the excursionists went south on the New Orleans Railroad, into the piney woods. Their trip into the largely undeveloped pine barrens revealed the northerners' main economic interest in Mississippi. They looked for investment and speculative opportunities in the natural resources and transportation facilities of the state rather than involvement in the pursuit of the elusive Jeffersonian agrarian dream—a dream that had a better chance for fulfillment in the West or elsewhere.

The results of the late Reconstruction campaign to attract white immigrants, like those of the earlier movement, were meager. Whether from the North or Europe, men seeking new opportunities preferred the West or the bustling commercial centers of the North to what they perceived to be an impoverished, inhospitable, and politically turbulent South. Although there is little in the promoters' records to suggest it, many prospective immigrants were probably deterred from settling in the region by their animus toward blacks. George Torrey, who was sent to England by a local society to secure immigrants, reported "great prejudice among the laboring classes" against blacks, and this proved a sticky problem in attracting settlers. He added, however, that "in all cases after talking to them, I find that their prejudices are easily removed."[95] The foreign-born population in Mississippi actually declined during the decade, from 11,191 in 1870 to 9,209 in 1880. In spite of the vigorous efforts to attract midwesterners, the number of

94. Jackson *Weekly Clarion*, November 19, 1874; Jackson *Weekly Pilot*, March 27, 1875.
95. George Torrey to the Jackson *Weekly Clarion*, February 6, 1873.

natives of this region in Mississippi also declined, from 3,281 in 1870 to 3,125 in 1880. Even the traditional pattern of white immigration from the Carolinas, Georgia, and Alabama came to a virtual standstill during the 1870s; almost all of the 96,502 growth in the white population during this period was due to natural increase.[96] The increase of unskilled people of both races added to the difficulties of adequately sustaining the already overextended agricultural economy, and it further reduced the standard of living in Mississippi. The nature of the population and the commitment, however necessary, to a one-crop economy also served as a formidable barrier to the development of the state's nonagricultural potential.

96. U.S. Bureau of the Census, *Ninth Census of the United States: 1870, Population* (Washington, D.C., 1872), 328–39; U.S. Bureau of the Census, *Tenth Census of the United States: 1880, Population*, pp. 484–91. Missouri is included in the midwestern population statistics.

16

New Economic
Frontiers

Since the antebellum period, nonagricultural opportunities had appealed to the material instincts of Mississippi entrepreneurs, but the economic success of slavery and cotton had dampened organized enthusiasm for their exploitation. After the war indigenous capital was not available to develop the full economic potential of the state. The necessary capital to pursue new commercial opportunities, to create a first-rate transportation system (which had been started but not completed when the war intervened), to exploit the magnificent forest resources, and to develop a nascent industry had to come ultimately from the outside. This reality became clear early in the Reconstruction period, but difficulties abounded as first conservatives, then Republicans, led the public attempt to attract money to the state and develop new dimensions in the economy.[1]

The greatest hope for a new economic departure existed in the vast piney woods of south Mississippi. Comprising about one fourth of the state, this area was sparsely populated in 1870 and almost wholly undeveloped. Although during the nineteenth century it was referred to as a single region, the pine country actually consists of two geographic areas. One region, extending southward about twenty miles below an east-west line from Jackson to Meridian and to about fifteen miles from the Gulf Coast or Mississippi Sound, consists of rolling hills and streams, covered by long-slash pine. Approximately 10 percent of this area was cultivated during the late nineteenth century, and black labor competed with white in the struggle to succeed on the infertile lands. Along the coast is a second geographic division, generally similar to the pinewood interior, but the land here is flat, marshy, and almost completely unsuitable for agriculture. During the postwar period the inhabi-

1. For an account of the state's conservative attempts to find a new direction for the economy immediately after the war, see Harris, *Presidential Reconstruction in Mississippi*, Chaps. XI and XII.

tants of the seacoast were less isolated than the people of the interior and therefore less provincial in their views and attitudes. The pine-hill yeomen looked to the coast dwellers for guidance rather than to the state leadership in Jackson, whose chronic neglect of their interests was proverbial. The people along the coast still suffered from a lack of adequate communication and transportation with the outside world, although the completion of the coastal New Orleans and Mobile Railroad in 1870 had stirred their interest in internal improvements and whetted their appetite for the economic development of the area. Writing after the war, historian John F. H. Claiborne, the region's leading promoter, declared:

> THE GREAT WANT of this country is a railroad, with proper feeders, to lift this mighty forest, and bring it, as it were, to the lap of the ocean. For a hundred miles at a stretch, at any point of the compass, one may ride through these ancient woods and see them, as they have stood for ages, untouched by the hand of man. . . . Here we have a field for enterprise far more extensive [than in the northern woods]— virgin forest—a benign climate—a coast exempt from storms—capacious harbors with access to all the markets of the world. A railroad could develop these great resources, and build up an important commercial entrepot on our beautiful sea coast.[2]

Actually, the exploitation of the forests did not wait for the construction of Claiborne's much-delayed Ship Island Railroad into the interior. This development, mainly in the form of timbering, however, was restricted to the periphery of the piney woods where transportation was available. Following antebellum precedent, postwar lumbermen did not always feel the need to purchase or lease the land that they exploited, preferring instead to cut their timber at no cost to themselves from the area's sprawling federal domain. (The federal government owned 4,728,513 acres in Mississippi in 1870, most of which was in the piney woods.) Governor Alcorn brought this pernicious practice to the attention of federal authorities, but nothing was done to check the depredations on public lands until 1877, and then the government's efforts were only partly successful.[3]

2. *Report of the Mississippi Centennial Managers*, 28–29. See also Griggs (comp.), *Guide to Mississippi*, 11–12.

3. Nollie Hickman, *Mississippi Harvest: Lumbering in the Longleaf Pine Belt, 1840–1915* (Oxford, Miss., 1962), 70; Jackson *Pilot*, January 8, 1870; Griggs (comp.), *Guide to*

Immediately after the war sawmills sprang up along the New Orleans, Jackson, and Great Northern Railroad and along the Pearl River near where it empties into the Mississippi Sound. Most of these enterprises were small and primitive.[4] A much more promising development occurred along the Pascagoula River near the small community of that name. Here fifteen relatively large and modern sawmills were established by 1870; the number would increase to eighteen by 1875.[5] Although the credit and machinery came from northern sources, the Pascagoula mills were owned by local entrepreneurs, as were the small, "peckerwood" sawmills located elsewhere in the piney woods. Pascagoula lumberman Walter Denny, who had served in the state legislature during the war, reportedly accumulated more than $100,000 during Reconstruction from the products of his steam-driven mills at Pascagoula. Denny and other lumbermen in the area sent most of their lumber to New Orleans and to Texas ports, but cargoes were also shipped directly to New England, Latin America, and Europe. By 1874 more than three hundred vessels (reportedly three fourths of the shipping on the Mississippi Sound) were involved in carrying Pascagoula lumber to distant markets, and the port had become the second largest lumber port on the Gulf. The value of Pascagoula's trade was estimated at $1,000,000 annually.[6] In addition, three small shipyards emerged to take advantage of the proximity of naval stores and the demand for light-draft vessels. By 1874 three schooners had been constructed and outfitted in these yards, the first ocean-going vessels to be built at the site of what would become a busy twentieth-century shipyard.[7]

Nevertheless, a sandbar at the mouth of the river severely restricted the lumber trade at Pascagoula and threatened the town's emergence as a leading port on the Gulf. The Noyes channel, en-

---

Mississippi, 34; Pascagoula *Star*, November 30, December 7, 1877. The special government agent charged with stopping the depredations on federal property estimated in 1877 that since the war more than fifty million dollars in timber had been illegally cut and taken from public lands. Pascagoula *Star*, January 11, 1878.

4. Harris, *Presidential Reconstruction in Mississippi*, 226.

5. Jackson *Weekly Pilot*, February 19, 1870; *Senate Journal, 1873*, I, 17–18; Hickman, *Mississippi Harvest*, 48.

6. Pascagoula *Star*, January 4, February 7, June 6, 1874; *Senate Journal, 1873*, I, 17.

7. Pascagoula *Star*, March 6, 21, 1874.

gineered by private means during military reconstruction (see Chapter 2), had temporarily made possible the entrance of light-draft vessels, but the bulky and more profitable cargoes had to be transshipped to vessels lying in anchor about five miles out in the Mississippi Sound. The lumber trade was also hampered by the fact that there was no port of entry at Pascagoula, which meant that ships had to come there in ballast to pick up their lumber cargoes.[8]

When civil government was restored in 1870, local lumbermen and their allies launched a campaign to secure public assistance for harbor improvements and the establishment of a port of entry at Pascagoula. The first Republican legislature and Governor Alcorn, a Delta planter whose economic vision for Mississippi rarely extended as far south as the Gulf Coast, ignored the appeals for aid. Powers, Alcorn's successor, however, took an active interest not only in Pascagoula affairs but also in the development of the whole piney woods region. The impending exhaustion of the timberlands around the Great Lakes, this carpetbag governor told the legislature in 1873, placed Mississippi in an enviable position, since it possessed a large forest that was virtually untouched by lumbermen. The demand for building materials in the expanding cities of the Northeast had already turned the eyes of timber merchants southward, Powers revealed, and the state could contribute to their interest by making the internal improvements necessary for the convenient exploitation of the piney woods.[9] Already the governor had directed State Engineer Thomas S. Hardee to study and report to him on the harbor situation at Pascagoula. Hardee reported that an expenditure of $200,000 for harbor improvements there would "give Mississippi a permanent seaport and harbor far superior to that of Mobile." This sum, Hardee believed, could be obtained from the federal government if state authorities would demonstrate their interest in the project by appropriating $20,000 to $25,000 for the preliminary work. Once improvements had been made—and Pascagoula declared a port of entry—Mississippi would have a seaport that could serve as a terminal for the long-desired trans-piney woods railroad.[10]

8. *Ibid.*, January 4, February 28, 1874.
9. *Senate Journal, 1873,* I, 17.
10. Report of Thomas S. Hardee to Ridgley C. Powers, March 18, 1873, in Governors'

Governor Powers immediately acted to have the Hardee report implemented. He requested and received a legislative appropriation of $25,000, but on the condition that no more than $8,000 be spent annually on the improvements. Powers himself may have advised the legislature to attach this condition to the appropriation, since he possessed a fetish for the careful administration of state expenditures. The policy soon proved impractical. Issued in depreciated state warrants, the amount of money for each year was too little to launch the work.[11]

At Powers' suggestion the legislature of 1873 appealed to federal authorities in Washington to aid the Pascagoula project. As a result an officer of the United States Corps of Engineers was dispatched to the Gulf Coast to study the situation. His findings gave a ringing endorsement to the state's plans for the harbor, and he estimated that the necessary improvements could be made for as little as $42,000. In justification, the engineer pointed out that there were 1,300 miles of navigable waters that flowed into the Mississippi Sound at Pascagoula, most of which passed through rich timberlands.[12] But because of the past "political constitution of this region" and "the depressing circumstances attending the late war," the development of the area "has not been such as its favorable location and natural advantages would suggest." He found, however, that the Pascagoula area had lately become a beehive of activity, and lumbering "has now grown to grand proportions." The port, he wrote, "ships lumber to Europe, South America, and distant countries, besides supplying a large portion of that required for home consumption." The lumber trade also had brought other businesses in its train, "and with each succeeding year the prospects for the future of this country grow brighter and brighter." He concluded that the economic development of the Gulf Coast would be significantly advanced by federal aid for the improvement of the Pascagoula harbor.

Buoyed by the engineer's report as well as by the locally commissioned and equally optimistic report of General Braxton Bragg,

Correspondence, Vol. 80. This report may also be found in the Jackson *Weekly Clarion*, May 1, 1873.

11. *Laws of Mississippi, 1873*, pp. 129–30; E. F. Griffin to John M. Stone, June 16, 1876, in Governors' Correspondence, Vol. 108.

12. *Laws of Mississippi, 1873*, pp. 131–32; *Senate Journal, 1873*, I, 18; Pascagoula *Star*, February 28, 1874.

Pascagoula promoters in 1874 intensified their efforts to secure federal aid. Local editor Melancthon Smith, a Bourbon in politics, felt confident that Congress would now come to their assistance. "Mississippi has never received a dollar from the General Government in such aid, while millions have been expended upon other states, and we have no fears that this, our first application will be refused; on the contrary, we have assurances . . . that it will be granted." [13] The "assurances" came from George Hannah, a wealthy Michigan lumberman who had recently invested in a mill at Pascagoula and was lobbying intensely for federal aid for the project. Mississippi's delegation in Congress, dominated by Republicans, also entered the campaign to secure congressional approval. These efforts, however, came to naught. After years of lavish expenditures on western and northern developments, Congress was becoming wary of appropriating money for internal improvements. Furthermore, the Republican majority had no taste for extending aid to a section of the country, lately in rebellion, which might soon become Democratic again.

This congressional indifference, combined with the financial pinch created by the Panic of 1873, caused Pascagoula to languish during the mid-1870s. Their credit extended beyond repair, many lumbermen lost their sawmills to northern capitalists, who temporarily gave the trade new vigor. [14] In the end, however, the shipping disadvantages that had plagued the area during Reconstruction, along with the town's failure to secure a railroad into the interior to tap timber and agricultural areas not served by water, were too great to overcome. Although Pascagoula continued to develop at a moderate pace, it never became the emporium on the Gulf that its promoters had envisioned.

Other settlements along the Gulf Coast, principally Pass Christian, Biloxi, and Shieldsboro (Bay St. Louis), received a boon to their development from an unexpected source—the resort trade. Like Pascagoula, these communities had looked northward for rail-

13. Pascagoula *Star*, February 28, 1874. See also the issues of January 4 and February 1, 1874.
14. *Ibid.*, June 19, 1875. In 1875 Governor Ames attempted to revive state interest in the removal of the bar at the mouth of the Pascagoula River, but the legislature rejected his plea for an appropriation to aid the work. *Annual Message of Governor Ames, 1875*, pp. 8–9.

roads that would connect them with the interior. But they changed their focus soon after the 1870 completion of the New Orleans and Mobile Railroad, which brought with it a summer migration of citizens to the Gulf Coast "watering places." Although a small resort business had developed before the war, sustained by a few steamers plying the coast, the coming of the railroad transformed summer tourism into a thriving trade. Even the federal troops in turbulent New Orleans were sent to the Mississippi coast during Reconstruction to escape the heat and sickness of the city.[15]

Residents of formerly sleepy Gulf Coast villages now spent the winter months feverishly constructing hotels, boarding houses, and family cottages, securing provisions in New Orleans for the tourist season, and expanding shell roads along the coast. By 1875 only Pass Christian of the Gulf communities did not have a hotel; this town, with a resident population of about 1,500, could boast of numerous attractive cottages and boarding houses extending along a five-mile shell road. Shieldsboro (which changed its name to Bay St. Louis in 1875), had a population of almost 2,000 and claimed a "front street" of seven miles in length, dotted with resort facilities, including a hotel for blacks. Perhaps the most remarkable growth occurred in the historic village of Biloxi where the resident population mushroomed from 954 in 1870 to more than 1,500 in 1874. Six hotels and numerous boarding houses arose almost overnight to accommodate the 4,000 to 5,000 visitors who after the completion of the railroad came from Mobile and New Orleans.[16]

Along the coast regattas were held and boat trips to the offshore islands were arranged to entertain vacationers, but visitors mainly amused themselves in conversation, drinking, eating, and absorbing the sun and sea breeze. At times the resort facilities were strained to capacity; even the vacationing Senator Ames found himself placed in a room with four other men. The only threat to the new prosperity that coastal citizens saw was the effort by the antiliquor forces in the legislature to pass a strong temperance law.

15. Jackson *Pilot*, March 30, 1871; Jackson *Weekly Clarion*, January 16, 1873; Pascagoula *Star*, June 6, 1874, June 26, 1875; Adelbert Ames to his wife, August 15, 1873, in Blanche Butler Ames (comp.), *Chronicles*, I, 523–24.
16. Pascagoula *Star*, June 6, 1874, June 26, 1875.

Such a measure was enacted in 1874, but it proved a dead letter on the coast, since the law required local action to restrict or prohibit the sale of alcoholic beverages.[17] Few residents of the resort towns could be persuaded to support any such proposition.

In essence, the Reconstruction era witnessed the emergence of the resort industry along the Mississippi coast. Nevertheless, the trade was modest, and it would remain at Reconstruction levels until the twentieth century. One drawback to continued growth was the remoteness of the coast to the interior. To visit the Mississippi coast, interior residents were forced to travel a long route by train to Mobile or New Orleans, and then transfer to the New Orleans and Mobile Railroad to complete their trip. The impecunious condition of the people, and the fact that the summer months were the busiest time of the year for those involved in the agricultural economy, further restricted the number of interior residents who used the resort facilities. During Reconstruction and for many years after, most vacationers on the coast were residents of New Orleans and Mobile.[18]

A notable exception to this pattern was the migration of state carpetbaggers to the resort towns during the summer months. Generally having more money to spend than their neighbors, carpetbaggers came to the coast to escape temporarily the political turmoil that swirled around them and the hostile treatment some received from interior whites. Ames found so many northerners at Mississippi City in 1873 that he labeled it "a Northern watering place." At Shieldsboro, where he bought a house, Ames could not avoid crossing paths with his carpetbag foe, Governor Powers. Although perhaps with an exaggeration that reflected his own animus toward the interior, Ames in a letter to his wife explained the social attraction of the coast for carpetbaggers. "The people are mainly from the south of Europe and French [*sic*]," he wrote. "You hear a foreign language spoken most everywhere. It is very unlike Mississippi. Down here on the coast they do not seem to care or even know much of Mississippi or any other kind of politics. In this particular it is more pleasant than up country where

17. *Ibid.*, May 2, 1874; Jackson *Pilot*, July 30, 1875; Ames to his wife, August 11, 1873, in Blanche Butler Ames (comp.), *Chronicles*, I, 518.
18. Pascagoula *Star*, June 26, 1875; Jackson *Pilot*, July 30, 1875.

every Democrat looks upon you and treats you as an enemy."[19]
Not surprisingly, he found the coastal inhabitants "far superior
to the whiskey drinking, pistol carrying Anglo-Saxons" of the
interior.[20]

Despite the boost to the Gulf Coast economy that the resort trade
provided, the emergence of southern Mississippi still depended
upon the development of the vast piney woods interior. On its
western periphery the New Orleans, Jackson, and Great Northern
Railroad furnished the means and inspiration to exploit the forest
resources. Numerous "peckerwood," or small, sawmills arose along
the road immediately after the war, but their development was
limited by the logging distance from the railroad and a shortage of
capital. Then, during the 1870s northern lumbermen and speculators moved into the area and purchased the best timberlands for
fifty cents to five dollars per acre. Some lands were bought in anticipation of the construction of feeder lines into the interior. The
midwestern newspapermen who visited the piney woods on Henry
Musgrove's promotional tour in early 1875 were attracted by the
opportunities for the exploitation of the timberlands, and, although admitting that many of the best forest lands had been
claimed, they returned home to encourage a further northern infusion of money and enterprise into the area.[21]

As had been the custom, northern entrepreneurs did not always
restrict their cutting operations to lands they had purchased. Char-
acteristically, until federal agents interfered during the 1880s,
lumbermen sent loggers into the public domain or accepted timber
at their mills without inquiring about its origin. The federal Homestead Act of 1866 restricted the sale of public lands, but it served
only as a paper barrier to the exploitation of Mississippi timberlands. Then in 1876, a new law opening public lands to unrestricted private entry increased the interest in the piney woods and
substantially reduced the size of the public domain. The main
deterrent for rapacious timbermen was never federal land policy

19. Ames to his wife, August 12, 15, 16, 1873, in Blanche Butler Ames (comp.), *Chronicles*, I, 520, 524.
20. Ames to his wife, August 10, 1875, *ibid.*, II, 131.
21. Vicksburg *Times*, May 18, 1874; Jackson *Weekly Pilot*, March 27, 1875; Hillyard
(comp.), *Letters Descriptive of Mississippi*, 117–21, 145, 150.

(nor state policy, since Mississippi held some of the lands in the piney woods), but rather it was the difficulty of transporting the felled trees from the interior to the mills either on the rivers or on the New Orleans railroad.[22]

The most remarkable illustration of northern enterprise in the piney woods during the postwar period occurred at McComb City. Located on the New Orleans railroad in Pike County, fifteen miles from the Louisiana border, and begun in 1872, this Yankee city in the wilderness was designed by Colonel Henry S. McComb, the Delaware entrepreneur and president of the railroad, to be a model for subsequent settlements in the area. The town was carefully laid out on an elevated site, chosen by McComb to avoid the malarious conditions of the lowlands, and stringent building and behavior codes were imposed by officials of the colonel's Mississippi Valley Company. Regulations imposed by the company (the town was not incorporated until 1877) prohibited the sale or consumption of alcoholic beverages within two miles of the town and also required that all houses be two or more stories in height. A religious man, McComb brought in churches of several denominations as well as schools. He also moved the railroad's machine shops from New Orleans to his city in the wilderness. The town's raison d'etre, however, was to exploit the timber resources of the piney woods, developing not only sawmills but also manufacturing finished lumber products, such as furniture.[23]

The Mississippi Valley Company was able in the beginning to attract skilled workers and capital from the North, mainly due to the efforts of M. B. Hillyard, the indefatigable secretary of the company. As a result McComb City in the mid-1870s appeared destined for the greatness that its promoters envisaged. By 1874 it had a population of about one thousand, most of whom were from the North, with eighty-two two-story houses lining the main, and virtually the only street of the town. In addition, McComb City

22. Hickman, *Mississippi Harvest*, 70, 72, 79; Samuel G. Thigpen, *Pearl River: Highway to Glory Land* (Kingsport, Tenn., 1965), 90; Pascagoula *Star*, January 11, 1878.

23. Hillyard (comp.), *Letters Descriptive of Mississippi*, 33, 38, 95–96. In addition to McComb, the Mississippi Valley Company included such influential railroad men as Absalom M. West, the president of the Mississippi Central Railroad, a subsidiary of the McComb system, and Thomas A. Scott of the Pennsylvania Railroad, whose appetite for southern development could hardly be satisfied.

already claimed to have "the finest hotel in the state." Flanking the town were three modern sawmills and the large railroad engine shops. The Yankee flavor in the town did not seem to bother the old citizens of Pike County. Farmers who had managed to eke out a marginal existence in the largely wooded county rushed into town to obtain jobs. For a time the compensation was good; one white laborer reported that he received $2.50 a day in wages at one of the company's sawmills. Although they did not move to McComb City, two of the area's most prominent citizens, Hiram Cassedy and Brigadier General Evander McNair, C.S.A., actively promoted the enterprise.[24]

Nevertheless, the town's development soon slowed. The tight national money market that began to affect the Mississippi Valley Company in 1874, the poor economic conditions in the state, the inability of the company to establish a finished products industry in the town, and McComb's own financial difficulties conspired to prevent the realization of the dreams of its founders. In 1880 McComb City had a population of only 1,982, and it would continue into the twentieth century as a small town of little promise.[25]

The economic activity along the New Orleans railroad in south Mississippi was on the edge of the piney woods. The opening of the region to large-scale development and settlement depended, as Claiborne had insisted, on a system of railroads traversing the pine country. Historically—and it would not change during Reconstruction—the effort to construct these roads was inspired mainly by the desire of old and struggling commercial centers like Vicksburg and Jackson and aspiring ones like Meridian and Forest to secure a convenient outlet to the sea. The development of the piney woods along the route to the coast was only secondary to their schemes. Indeed, the local competition for a railroad connection with a Gulf port created a situation that made unlikely the early completion of a railway network for southern Mississippi.

Most of the plans for a railroad running from central Mississippi to the sea focused on the development of a terminal near Ship

24. *Ibid.*, 43–44, 95–96, 167, 169; Jackson *Weekly Clarion*, April 16, 1874; W. L. Robinson to Oscar J. E. Stuart, May 3, 1872, in Dimitry Papers.

25. U.S. Bureau of the Census, *Tenth Census of the United States: 1880, Population*, 236.

Island, a deep-water point. In a series of articles on the desirability of a port at this location, the Forest *Register* claimed that "the *God of nature* marked the spot as a suitable place, in every way, to build up one of the finest and largest commercial cities in the South." Belying its political bourbonism, this newspaper blamed the past generation's obsession with state and local rights for the failure to establish a seaport that would be a source of great wealth for the state. Again, in 1870, the *Register* declared: "Mississippi City [near Ship Island] must be baptized into the family of commercial marts. The State must stand godfather to her. The cotton regions of the North-centre, and the timber regions of the South-centre must have a direct outlet to the sea."[26]

In response to the growing demand for a seaport, a group of Gulf Coast entrepreneurs advanced a scheme to dredge a canal from Ship Island to the shore at Mississippi City, a distance of five miles, where dock facilities would be constructed. Calling themselves the Harrison Harbor Company, these businessmen appealed to the legislature of 1870 for a charter that would include a grant of land within a ten-mile radius of the port. The legislature refused to act at this time on the grounds that the work could not be completed without federal aid. When national assistance was not forthcoming (actually there seems to have been no significant attempt by Mississippi officials to secure federal aid for the project), a charter, under the terms requested, was granted to the Harrison Harbor Company in 1871.[27] Eight black opponents in the legislature issued a strong protest against the creation of a company that would "deprive the people of their natural right to the free use of the rivers, bays and harbors of the State. . . . The effect of placing this Act upon the statutes of the State will be the merciless oppression of the poor by soulless corporations."[28] Perhaps partly because of such fears, the state government, unlike several other southern state governments during Reconstruction when chartering internal improvement companies, did not endorse the company's bonds. The modest amount of land the com-

26. Forest *Register*, June 30, 1869, March 26, 1870. The writer of the articles, of course, expected Forest to secure a railroad connection with the new port.
27. Jackson *Weekly Pilot*, July 9, 1870; *Laws of Mississippi, 1871*, pp. 501–508.
28. Jackson *Pilot*, February 17, 1871.

pany received from the state soon proved an inadequate basis for
financing the construction of the Ship Island canal. Consequently,
the Harrison Harbor scheme never left the drawing boards. Because of the legislature's indulgence in this will-o'-the-wisp enterprise, the state lost valuable time in developing a seaport on the
Mississippi Sound.

The belief during the early 1870s that port facilities would soon
be available at Mississippi City stimulated considerable interest
in the construction of railroads leading to the harbor.[29] Interest
was heightened by the likelihood that Congress would revive its
1856 promise of a federal land grant of 652,800 acres upon the
completion of a road from central Mississippi to the Gulf. Carpetbag Congressman George C. McKee, whose district would be affected by the grant, in 1870 introduced a bill to obtain the land.
The measure, however, failed to pass, and the 1856 promise was
never honored, although the legislature during and after Reconstruction regularly applied for the grant.[30]

When the legislature met in 1870, the first since early 1867, promoters of various railroad schemes marched into the capitol demanding liberal charters and state aid for their enterprises. One
group of audacious promoters, styling themselves the Ship Island
Railroad and Navigation Company, asked for the privilege of building a road from Canton to Mississippi City with branches running
to all of the leading commercial centers in the state. To accomplish
their scheme, these developers called upon the legislature to grant
the proposed railroad all state lands within fifteen miles of its route.
The intent to defraud the state of its lands which in 1870 were
substantial, was obvious in a provision of the incorporation bill permitting the company's directors to dispose of the charter without
legislative approval, an action that would leave the state with no
legal recourse to preserve its interest. Reflecting the mood of the
legislature, which rejected the bill, the Jackson *Pilot* referred to
the scheme as "a monstrosity." The editor was not willing "to see
the State give away all her rights to a few incorporators, who claim
the privilege of putting their franchises up for sale to the highest

29. *Ibid.*, July 8, 1871; Forest *Register*, March 26, 1870.
30. Jackson *Weekly Pilot*, April 30, 1870; *Hinds County Gazette*, May 11, 1870; *Laws
of Mississippi, 1878*, pp. 251–56.

bidder, pocket proceeds and let the public interest take care of itself, and the road get built when it can."[31]

The lobbying activities of vested interests to win the railroad
prize were so intense—one overzealous promoter attempted unsuccessfully to bribe Governor Alcorn and members of the legislature—that State Senator John C. Shoup, a Pontotoc scalawag,
was impelled to offer a bill taking the project entirely out of private
hands. He proposed that the state, using convict labor, build the
Ship Island Railroad and then operate it as a source of revenue.
Although Shoup's proposal received some support from towns that
expected to benefit from it, the bill received little support in the
legislature. After considerable debate over the route of the road,
the legislature chartered the Ship Island, Mississippi City, and
Paducah Railroad Company and authorized it to construct the line
from the Gulf Coast to the Tennessee border in Tippah County.
The company, however, received no special privileges from the
state, in spite of the fact that its list of incorporators included white
politicians of both parties.[32] Without either federal or state aid the
construction program of the Ship Island Railroad floundered, and
in 1872 Colonel William C. Falkner, president of the Ripley Railroad, assumed control of the company, renamed the line the Ship
Island, Ripley, and Kentucky Railroad, and within a year completed the portion from Middleton, Tennessee, to Ripley, a distance
of twenty miles. At this point progress on the road came to a halt,
and although Falkner had developed a friendly association with
Governor Powers he failed to secure the state support necessary
to continue construction.[33] After Reconstruction the Redeemers
extended some aid to the road, but only sixty-two miles had been
constructed by 1889 when a northern firm assumed control of it
and subsequently completed the line.[34]

31. Jackson *Weekly Pilot*, April 2, 1870.

32. Forest *Register*, April 30, 1870; speech of Alcorn, reported in the Vicksburg *Times and Republican*, October 14, 1873; *Laws of Mississippi, 1870*, pp. 283–95.

33. McLemore (ed.), *History of Mississippi*, II, 308; William C. Falkner to Powers, March 20, 1872, in Governors' Correspondence, Vol. 72.

34. *Laws of Mississippi, 1878*, pp. 224–27; John H. Lang, *History of Harrison County* (Gulfport, 1936), 82. Colonel Falkner was the great-grandfather of the famed writer William Faulkner, who used his ancestor as the model for one of his most significant characters, John Sartoris. The colonel himself wrote a popular novel, *The White Rose of Memphis*, which was set on the Mississippi River.

Vicksburg also cast covetous eyes toward the harbor at Ship Island, and in 1871 it obtained a charter for the Vicksburg, Pensacola, and Ship Island Railroad. Wisely downplaying its railroad ambitions lest competing towns become alarmed, Vicksburg at first made no attempt to secure special privileges for the road or to compete with other companies for the limited state resources available for railroad construction. Vicksburg promoters insisted that their main purpose in the Ship Island enterprise was to break the commercial monopoly that New Orleans had upon their town and state. Actually, Vicksburg had developed a grand design to build a railroad empire in the Mississippi Valley with the town as a focal point. The plan included the development of the Gulf Coast line, the construction of a railroad into the Delta, and the completion of the East-West railroad to the Pacific with Vicksburg as its connecting point on the Mississippi.[35]

The efforts of Vicksburg promoters to win adequate local assistance for the Ship Island scheme soon faltered, and they appealed to the legislature for help. Here they had powerful friends. A bill was passed making available to the railroad at two cents per acre all tax-forfeited property within a ten-mile swath of land on both sides of the road. Under the terms of the act the burden of clearing the titles to the lands, a difficult task at best, rested with the company. To protect the state's interest, the act prohibited the railroad from obtaining any of the land until twenty-five miles of track had been laid.[36] This form of aid proved of no immediate benefit to the Vicksburg, Pensacola, and Ship Island Railroad. The company critically needed money (or convertible assets) with which to begin the construction of the road. In order to obtain such assistance, Vicksburg promoters again turned to the legislature. With the reluctant approval of Governor Powers, the legislature in 1873 made available to the railroad the state's interest in the Chickasaw School Fund (a potential sum of $800,000), installments of which were to be delivered to the company at the rate of $10,000 per mile of completed track. The railroad completed eleven miles

35. Vicksburg *Times and Republican*, July 21, 1871, January 16, 1872; *Laws of Mississippi, 1871*, pp. 237–52.
36. Vicksburg *Times and Republican*, June 23, 1872; Natchez *Weekly Democrat*, April 10, 1872; *Laws of Mississippi, 1872*, pp. 281–82.

of track and received $110,000 from the trust fund before violating its charter privileges, whereupon the watchful Ames administration ceased payments in accordance with the 1873 act.[37] Cut off from state support, construction on the Vicksburg, Pensacola, and Ship Island Railroad sputtered and finally came to a halt in 1874 with the completion of less than twenty miles of track. Although the state escaped serious loss in the enterprise, the city of Vicksburg found itself saddled with a bonded debt of $400,000 and no railroad to show for it.[38]

Other railroad schemes to cross the piney woods were no more successful than the Vicksburg-inspired road. One ambitious project, the Meridian, Red River, and Texas Railroad, was designed to run southwestwardly from Meridian through the heart of the piney woods to Riverside in Wilkinson County where it would cross the Mississippi en route to Texas. The railroad received a thirty-year exemption from state taxes and considerable encouragement from those who dreamed of a trans-Mississippi road that would link up with the projected Southern Pacific (or Texas-Pacific) Railroad. The promoters of the road included General James Longstreet, William H. Hardy, a rising railroad entrepreneur from Meridian, and scalawag William H. Noble who secured a $400,000 subscription to the railroad in Wilkinson County by virtue of his control of the black vote there. Nearby, Natchez, which had high hopes of becoming a river terminal for the Southern Pacific, lashed out at the proposed railroad as a logrolling scheme that would bankrupt the counties subscribing to it. Natchez also used its powerful influence in the Republican legislature to prevent the extension of state aid to the project. As a result the Meridian, Red River, and Texas Railroad came forth stillborn, with only Wilkinson County having subscribed to its bonds.[39]

Hardy and Longstreet also became involved in a plan to build a

37. *Laws of Mississippi, 1873*, pp. 562–63; *Annual Message of Governor Ames, 1876*, p. 16. For a discussion of the abuse of the Chickasaw School Fund by both Republican and conservative regimes, see Chap. 10 herein.

38. Moore, "Social and Economic Conditions in Mississippi During Reconstruction," 140–41.

39. *Laws of Mississippi, 1871*, pp. 119–29; Jackson *Pilot*, March 23, 28, July 20, 1871; Vicksburg *Times and Republican*, February 29, 1872; Natchez *Weekly Democrat*, May 17, July 19, 26, 1872.

railroad from New Orleans to Meridian, where it would connect with the troubled Alabama and Chattanooga line. Incorporated in Louisiana in 1868 as the New Orleans and Northeastern Railroad, the company received a Mississippi charter in 1871. When local aid to begin the work of construction was not forthcoming, scalawag Congressman John L. Morphis introduced a bill into Congress that would give the road the extensive federal lands along its proposed route. The bill, however, failed to pass. After Reconstruction Hardy revived the New Orleans and Northeastern project, and, aided by the Erlanger firm of Paris, construction on the road began in 1881 and was completed in 1884.[40] Of all the schemes initiated during Reconstruction to traverse the piney woods and exploit its lands, the New Orleans and Northeastern Railroad was the first to be completed—and this occurred almost a decade after the collapse of Republican rule in the state.

The intense desire of Mississippians to develop the piney woods and secure alternate routes to the Gulf provided the opportunity for one of the most daring schemes of the Reconstruction era. This was the Mobile and Northwestern Railroad, which in 1870 received its charter from the Mississippi legislature. As proposed, this road would cross the heart of the piney woods on a direct line from Mobile to some point on the Vicksburg and Meridian Railroad in central Mississippi.[41] It would also bisect the Delta, reaching the Mississippi River opposite Helena, Arkansas, where the line would connect with railroads leading to the grain-producing areas of the West.

The Mobile and Northwestern project developed out of the desire of Mobile promoters to divert the vast trade of the Mississippi Valley from New Orleans to their city. Despite its control of the Mobile and Ohio Railroad through eastern Mississippi and northward to Illinois, the port of Mobile had languished after the war as the trade of the area flowed to New Orleans, Savannah, and other coastal cities. The hope of Mobile merchants lay in tapping the rich agricultural lands of the lower Mississippi Valley and,

40. *Laws of Mississippi, 1871*, pp. 160–72; Natchez *Weekly Democrat*, February 28, 1872; William Hardy and Toney Hardy, *No Compromise with Principle*, 207–12.
41. *Laws of Mississippi, 1870*, pp. 255–56.

to a lesser extent, in opening the timberlands of southern Mississippi to exploitation.[42] The scheme's principal architect was Colonel William D'Alton Mann, the commander of the Seventh Michigan Cavalry Regiment during the war who had settled in Mobile in 1865. Bringing money with him to invest in the town's capital-starved economy, Mann quickly rose to a position of prominence as a merchant and as the new proprietor of the prestigious Mobile *Register*. Because of his political conservatism he gained the confidence of the old citizens, while as a former Union officer he was admitted to the fellowship of Republicans who controlled Reconstruction affairs. The bridge to both sides placed him in an excellent position not only to advance his personal fortunes but also to perfect his scheme for the Mobile and Northwestern Railroad.[43]

The success of Mann's enterprise depended on the cooperation and assistance of Mississippi, where almost all of the track would be laid. To secure a liberal charter and the state's largesse for the project, Mann rushed to Jackson in 1870, soon after the Republicans took office. Accompanying him was Republican Congressman Legrand W. Perce of Natchez, whose political association with Governor Alcorn and members of the legislature, Mann hoped, would sway the necessary support for the enterprise. Mann also took a plan for the annexation of the Mobile area to Mississippi, the prospects for which, he correctly believed, would whet Mississippians' appetite for the railroad. His lobbying campaign in this session of the legislature, however, was tempered by the failure of other schemes to divest the state of its wealth. At first the Mobile entrepreneur asked only that the railroad be granted a liberal charter, including a tax exemption for thirty years. He gave his word that the road would never again seek the financial aid of the state, since, he said, it could obtain adequate support from prominent New York capitalists and from the merchants of Mobile.[44] Accepting Mann's promise at face value and expressing the belief that the completed railroad would attract "vast sums of money in

42. *The Mobile and North-Western Railroad* (New York, 1871), 5–6; Jackson *Pilot*, April 18, 1871; Jackson *Weekly Clarion*, February 2, 1871.
43. For Mann's background see the Mobile *Register*, February 11, 1868, the Jackson *Pilot*, January 8, 1870, and his obituary in the New York *Times*, May 18, 1920.
44. Jackson *Weekly Pilot*, April 16, June 25, July 9, 16, 1870; *Hinds County Gazette*, May 11, 1870; Vicksburg *Times and Republican*, September 19, 1871.

mills and manufacturing" to the piney woods, Edward Stafford of the Jackson *Pilot* urged the legislature to approve the charter. With the support of the *Pilot* and Alcorn, whose son Milton was one of the incorporators, the chartering bill, including a modified tax exemption clause, was easily enacted. In the senate, only scalawag Alston Mygatt and blacks Charles Caldwell and Thomas W. Stringer saw that the chartering act was only the first step by Mann and Mobile interests in a raid on the assets of the state. "Mississippi has made three attempts to work her own ruin," Mygatt remarked. "The first was repudiation; the second adopting the ordinance of secession; the third, granting a charter to the Mobile and Northwestern railroad."[45]

As Mygatt and his associates predicted, when the legislature convened for its 1871 session, Mann returned to Jackson—this time with an open hand. Lacking state and local aid, the company did not have the money or credit to begin constructing the line. Mann first secured the passage of a resolution memorializing Congress to aid the railroad by granting alternate sections of public lands up to a distance of fifteen miles on each side of the proposed route. Congress, however, ignored the appeal. Meanwhile, Mann and his Mississippi allies had organized a series of rallies for the purpose of pressuring the legislature to extend state aid.[46] The campaign was highly successful. Supported vigorously by most of the members from the counties along the proposed route, the legislature granted the Mobile and Northwestern Railroad all of the state lands within twenty miles of the road on both sides, a total of 1,048,450 acres, including tax-forfeited lands. In the same act the legislature sold to the railroad at the nominal price of two cents an acre the state swamp or overflowed lands, which had been granted by Congress in 1850 to finance internal improvements. The size of this donation was an estimated 744,879 acres. Despite its generosity, the legislature did provide a safeguard for the state. The act required that at least forty miles of track be completed before the Mobile and Northwestern could receive title to

45. Jackson *Weekly Pilot*, July 16, 1870; *Senate Journal* [1870], 548; *House Journal*, 1870, p. 788; Vicksburg *Times and Republican*, March 2, 1873 (quote).

46. *Laws of Mississippi, 1871*, pp. 780–81; issues of the Jackson *Weekly Clarion* for February-April, 1871, and the Jackson *Pilot* for the same period.

the state lands, and eighty miles before it could obtain the swamp-lands.[47] Even so, twenty-five Republicans and one conservative in the house of representatives condemned the act as "a palpable violation" of the constitution of 1868, since it assigned to a corporation lands that had been reserved for the public schools. Furthermore, they charged that under this law millions of acres were "wantonly wrested from the State to enrich a corporation whose greatest aim is to gather up the wealth along its route and pour it into the lap of a foreign metropolis." The grant, these protesters claimed, was "one of the most gigantic and enormous subsidies ever made by any State to private corporation, and when we consider the extreme poverty of the State of Mississippi, and the fact its only resources are the few acres of land it possesses, by this bill reduced almost to nothing, we stand amazed at the action of members sworn to protect the interests of the people they represent."[48]

Not satisfied by this largesse, Mann, along with other railroad promoters, pressed for the passage of a bill that would provide an outright grant of money for railroad construction. Again, he was successful. Known as the Subsidy Law, this act appropriated four thousand dollars per mile to any railroad that constructed twenty-five miles or more of track. Companies that hoped to benefit from the subsidy, however, had to act quickly, since under the law's provisions the first twenty-five miles had to be completed by September 1, 1872, and the remainder by September, 1875.[49]

Unlike most railroad issues, the enactment of the Subsidy Law immediately raised a political storm. Barksdale, who had been inexplicably silent a few days earlier when the legislature donated state lands to the Mobile and Northwestern, denounced the act as an "enormous steal" concocted by the "lobby-vultures" that had been hanging around the capitol. He claimed that until its expiration in 1875 the measure could add as much as one million dollars a year to the already oppressive burden carried by the taxpayers of the state. Other conservatives joined Barksdale in labeling the

47. Jackson *Pilot*, April 18, 1871; *Laws of Mississippi, 1871*, pp. 221–22; *The Mobile and North-Western Railroad*, 8–9, 33, 35–36.

48. *House Journal, 1871*, pp. 893–95.

49. *Laws of Mississippi, 1871*, pp. 745–48. For Mann's role in the passage of the Subsidy Law, see the Jackson *Weekly Clarion*, June 19, 1873.

Subsidy Law another Radical scheme to plunder Mississippi and in calling for its repeal.[50]

Although the bill was indeed a Republican one—a carpetbag editor defended it as "the best measure that has passed any legislature since the war"[51]—many conservatives, especially those residing along proposed railroad routes, supported the law after its passage. From Aberdeen, a town at a strategic location on Forrest's Memphis to Selma railroad, a conservative editor entered a "solemn protest against the ill advised effort" of Barksdale and others "to make political capital against a measure that is to-day far more popular with the Democracy of the State than with the Radicals."[52] Conservatives of Natchez, stymied in their efforts to build the Natchez and Jackson Railroad, saluted the Republican authorship of the Subsidy Law and expressed the view that it was "one of the wisest measures of the session." They conceded, however, that the measure "opens wide a door to speculation and corruption, and may lead to lamentable results, so far as the credit of the State is concerned."[53] The conservative editor of the Fayette *Chronicle*, on the line of the proposed Natchez Railroad, was also willing to overlook the "jobbery" involved in the bill's passage. "We don't know what motive prompted the Legislature to pass this Act, nor do we care, so that the roads are built. The Legislature may have had in view the stealings they could make out of the scheme; but we can stand a pretty big 'steal' if we can get railroads in the State."[54] In Vicksburg the *Times and Republican* was so certain of the broad support for the law that it erroneously reported that only Bourbon Democrats opposed it.[55]

But despite this support, when the legislature met in January, 1872, a block of conservative members, backed by a handful of Republicans and Governor Powers, introduced a bill to repeal the Subsidy Law on the grounds that it violated the clause in the constitution of 1868 prohibiting state aid to private corporations.[56]

50. Jackson *Weekly Clarion*, May 18, June 22, 1871; *Appleton's Annual Cyclopaedia*, 1871, p. 524.

51. Vicksburg *Times and Republican*, March 2, 1872.

52. As reported in the Jackson *Pilot*, June 3, 1871.

53. Natchez *Weekly Democrat*, May 17, 1871, January 24, 1872.

54. As reported in the Jackson *Pilot*, June 3, 1871.

55. Vicksburg *Times and Republican*, March 2, 1872.

56. *Ibid.*, January 18, 1872; Jackson *Weekly Clarion*, February 8, 1872.

Mann, whose railroad stood to gain more than any other road under the provisions of the law ($2,480,000 if it could meet the 1875 deadline for construction) rushed to Jackson to renew his lobbying activities. He immediately went before the committee studying the repeal bill and persuaded it to refer the question of the law's constitutionality to State Attorney General Joshua S. Morris. Meanwhile, Mann hired Morris on a legal retainer for the railroad and on January 10 advanced him five hundred dollars. On either January 9 or 10 Morris rendered his official opinion. He declared that the subsidy act was constitutional and, furthermore, that under its provisions the companies had "acquired vested rights which the Legislature could not affect by its repeal." An investigating committee selected by the Republican legislature and chaired by Robert Lowry, a conservative and later a Redeemer governor, concluded that Mann in employing Morris and paying him five hundred dollars "expected and intended to influence and control the Attorney General in obtaining the opinion . . . and if the Attorney General was not influenced and controlled by the five hundred dollars, it was [a] remarkable coincidence."[57] Mann, however, was not prosecuted for bribery, and Morris was permitted to serve out his term in office without impeachment charges being brought against him. By the time that this wrong doing was revealed, the legislature, influenced by Morris' opinion, had reaffirmed its support of the railroad subsidy program.

The subsidy issue itself was soon an academic one. Except for the Ripley Railroad, none of the aspiring railroads in the state was able before the act expired to complete the twenty-five miles of track necessary to qualify for a grant. The Ripley Railroad received $81,968 in warrants under the Subsidy Law, only to discover that the scalawag state treasurer would not honor the notes. McComb of the New Orleans railroad, however, arranged for Governor Powers to accept the depreciated warrants in return for a reduction by that amount of the Chickasaw Fund debt that his road owed the state.[58] Efforts by Mann and others in 1873 to renew the

57. This account of the "Subsidy Scandal" is based on the report of the Lowry committee, which contained a majority of Republicans although chaired by a conservative. *House Journal, 1873*, pp. 1532–72. The quotes appear on page 1532.

58. *Annual Report of the Auditor, 1872*, p. 14; *Appleton's Annual Cyclopaedia*, 1872, p. 547.

subsidy program met with a quick rebuff by legislators of both parties and both races who were beginning to view the whole issue of railroad construction in a more critical light. Disclosures regarding Mann's shady activities, which a handful of conservatives like Harper and Republicans like Mygatt had pointed out when the Mobilian's influence was at its height, contributed by the late Reconstruction period to a growing public opposition to aid for railroad construction.[59]

In a desperate effort to retain state support for his scheme, Mann in 1873 revived the campaign for Mobile's annexation to Mississippi. His Mobile *Register* beat the drums for annexation, a tactic designed to convince Mississippians, especially the Republican administration, that Mobilians fervently desired to become a part of the Magnolia state. In an incredible bit of effrontery, Mann's *Register* complimented the people of Mississippi on the "wise provision" in the constitution of 1868 that had "saved the state from carpetbag plunder" and heavy debts and asked them to annex Mobile and thus rescue it from the misrule of Alabama Republicans. Governor Powers was receptive to the idea, although he had long since soured on Mann's railroad (in 1872 he had secured the suspension of a part of the 1871 act granting the company certain state lands along its route). Then, as authorized by the legislature the governor appointed a three-member commission, which included two prominent conservatives, to open negotiations with Alabama for the annexation of Mobile County. Unfortunately for the success of the scheme, the Alabama senate refused to enter negotiations with the commissioners and the annexation movement, as well as Mann's efforts to secure additional state aid for his railroad, collapsed.[60]

The woes of the Mobile and Northwestern Railroad were not all caused by the defeat of Mann's schemes to secure direct state assistance for its construction. In addition to state aid, the railroad needed considerable local support in the form of stock and bond subscriptions before it could get off the drawing boards. As required

59. Jackson *Weekly Clarion*, March 6, 13, 20, June 19, 1873; Vicksburg *Times and Republican*, March 2, 1873.

60. As reported in the Vicksburg *Times and Republican*, February 20, March 2, 1873; *Senate Journal, 1872*, pp. 509–10; Jackson *Weekly Clarion*, February 13, March 20, 1873.

by the constitution of 1868, this aid could only be secured by the approval of two thirds of the local electorate. With this in mind, Mann in 1871 opened his campaign to win county and town support at the polls for large bond issues to aid his road. The ambiguity of the charter regarding the railroad's route at first assisted this predatory promoter in his efforts to secure local support. He went from community to community promising each that it would be on the route, provided the county approved a large subscription to the railroad's bonds. This stimulated a far broader interest in the road than would otherwise have been the case. Promoters arose in almost every town, however small, that had a chance for the road. They expressed concern that the Mobile and Northwestern would leave their communities high and dry and make their rivals prosperous unless local voters acted quickly to provide the aid that Mann demanded. Barksdale, who was lukewarm to the project at first, became an ardent supporter in 1871 when he realized that the capital city might be bypassed unless Hinds County voters approved a forthcoming bond subscription to the railroad.[61]

Throughout 1871 and early 1872 a series of promotional rallies were held in prospective counties. Activity was especially intense in Rankin, Hinds, Madison, and Yazoo counties, where because of their relative wealth and the competitive impulse of merchants and leaders in the main towns (Brandon, Jackson, Canton, and Yazoo City) Mann expected to secure a large subscription to the railroad. In these rallies, which fell far short of generating the enthusiasm of a political meeting, local Republican and conservative leaders joined Mann on the platform and proclaimed the virtues of the road. Enthusiasm soared in late 1871 when Mann reported that he had signed a contract with a New York firm to begin the construction of the line, a report that failed to mention that the continuation of the work, after the initial surveying had been completed, would depend upon an immediate payment to meet construction expenses.[62]

61. Brandon *Republican*, May 30, 1872; Jackson *Weekly Clarion*, February 16, May 8, 1871; *Hinds County Gazette*, April 17, May 1, 1872.

62. Jackson *Pilot*, May 2, October 28, November 9, 1871; Jackson *Weekly Clarion*, June 8, July 13, August 17, October 26, 1871; Mobile *Register*, October 24, 1871.

After an early success in Yazoo County, where he secured voter approval of a $600,000 subscription, Mann soon discovered that competition for bond issues from other projected railroads threatened to undo his campaign. In Hinds and Yazoo counties, the Vicksburg, Yazoo City, and Grenada and the Yazoo City, Raymond, and Crystal Springs railroads also had agents canvassing for local subscriptions and using their influence "to flop Mann overboard and allow him the privilege of taking care of himself." After the Yazoo election Harper of the *Hinds County Gazette* and the carpetbag editor of the Vicksburg *Times and Republican* joined in a campaign to defame Mann "as a purchaser of corrupt Legislatures" and discredit the Mobile and Northwestern enterprise. Other editors awoke to the perfidy of the Mobilian, especially when they discovered that their towns were not on the proposed route of the railroad.[63]

This campaign and the revelations of Mann's role in the Subsidy Law scandal destroyed local confidence in the railroad before subscription voting occurred, except for the election in Yazoo County. In Holmes County, blacks defied their carpetbag leaders to vote with the conservatives against a proposed $300,000 bond issue for the Mobile and Northwestern. Even Yazoo County found cause to repudiate its commitment to the road. As a result Mann received nothing of the $5,500,000 that he expected to obtain from local sources.[64] With his railroad scheme coming apart at every turn and unable to secure financing in New York, Mann scurried to Europe in search of the necessary money. He failed in his mission, but ever the irrepressible entrepreneur, like Jim Fisk and other counterparts in the North, he secured a franchise to operate a set of boudoir cars between Paris and Vienna. By June, 1873, even Mobile promoters admitted that the Mobile and Northwestern was bankrupt and that the road would not be built. A disillusioned but wiser Barksdale concluded that Mann was "the prince of Humbugs" and "a corruptionist of the deepest dye"

63. *Hinds County Gazette*, April 17, 1872, and issues of May–July, 1872; Vicksburg *Times and Republican*, September 8, 1871, March 29, April 27, 1872; Jackson *Weekly Clarion*, February 15, 1872.

64. *Hinds County Gazette*, May 1, July 24, 1872; Jackson *Weekly Clarion*, February 15, 1872; *The Mobile and North-Western Railroad*, 9–10.

whose escapades could easily have brought Mississippi to ruin had he not overstepped himself.[65]

Railroad development in the state during Reconstruction was not limited to proposed roads designed to open the piney woods for development or to establish a direct route to port for interior communities. Even Mann's shenanigans, at least during the first two years, failed to dampen enthusiasm for the creation of a network of interior railroads to provide markets for agricultural production and to expand the economic opportunities of the state. In the end— and before the close of the Reconstruction period—the effort to extend the railroad system failed because of a lack of financial support, which reflected the impoverished condition of the people and the poor credit standing of the local and state governments. As in the case of the piney woods projects, money simply was not available to construct the roads. Even the established trunk lines fell victim to the money pinch.

At the beginning of the Republican era, enthusiasm was high for railroad development. Republicans and conservatives frequently vied with each other in their expressions of support for the construction of railroads. In addition to railroads being "the great civilizer of nations," the carpetbag editor of the Jackson *Pilot* declared that the expansion of lines in Mississippi would have a marvelous effect: lands would appreciate in value, economic activity would be stimulated, new enterprises would arise, tax revenues would increase, and a large number of immigrants would be attracted to the state. By encouraging economic diversifications, railroad proponents argued, the roads would aid in breaking the pernicious hold that King Cotton had upon the people. "The most striking and real want of Mississippi is railroads," the Vicksburg *Times and Republican* announced, and a program of internal improvements along this line "will certainly bring prosperity and population."[66] Railroad development should transcend the politics of Reconstruction, Botto of the Natchez *Democrat* told his read-

65. Jackson *Weekly Clarion*, June 19, 1873.
66. Jackson *Pilot*, March 28, June 22, September 5, 1871; Vicksburg *Times and Republican*, January 7, 1872; Natchez *Weekly Democrat*, December 14, 1870, September 13, 1871; Forest *Register*, April 30, 1870.

ers.[67] The editor of the Vicksburg *Times and Republican* agreed, saying, "We must, above all things, keep this matter out of politics. The two subjects have no necessary or legitimate connection. Railroad building is strictly a matter of business, affecting the interests of all alike, and here at least is one common ground upon which all can meet and be friends. If we attempt to make a political question of it, we shall very likely spoil everything."[68]

Most railroad promoters did not believe that the clause in the constitution of 1868 prohibiting the extension of the state's credit to assist private corporations would be a significant barrier to railroad development. The provision could be easily flanked by a state program of direct aid to the roads. Nevertheless, the Subsidy Law of 1871 and sporadic attempts to grant state lands to aspiring railroad companies produced more confusion and charges of logrolling than anything else. By 1872 it was clear that, despite the state's award of educational trust funds to two favored railroads, the main burden of meeting construction costs would fall on the shoulders of the local governments. Able railroad managers might be able to tap some outside money sources for the support of the roads, but this assistance would be severely limited, since capitalists viewed Mississippi enterprises and the likelihood of Mississippians meeting their financial obligations as extremely risky undertakings.[69] Furthermore, local commercial competition for roads compounded the difficulties of any company obtaining the meager public funds that were available for railroad construction.

The case of the Natchez, Jackson, and Columbus Railroad best illustrates the plight of one of these aspiring roads. Chartered in 1870, without state aid, to build a railroad from Natchez to Jackson and ultimately to Columbus, the company owed its inception to the desire of Natchez promoters to draw interior trade to their town. Natchez had earlier failed to secure a railroad connection with the interior, and after the war its citizens believed that their economic woes were due in large measure to this fact. The com-

67. Natchez *Weekly Democrat*, December 7, 1870.
68. As reported in *ibid*.
69. For an analysis of the dampering effect that the stain of repudiation had upon railroad enterprises in the state, see Mygatt's speech before the state senate, as reported in the Vicksburg *Times and Republican*, March 30, 1872.

pletion of the railroad, Botto informed fellow townsmen, was "the only way we can escape the dry rot which is impoverishing us all." Once this line was finished, Natchez had visions not only of becoming a river terminus for the Southern Pacific Railroad but also a link in a chain of roads extending into Mexico.[70]

From the beginning the promoters of the Natchez railroad steered carefully to avoid the pitfalls of Reconstruction politics. The incorporators and board of directors of the company included all political elements. William T. Martin, the most prominent conservative of Natchez and a former major general in the Confederate army, served as president of the road, and black leaders Hiram R. Revels, William H. Lynch, and Henry P. Jacobs of Adams County and Merriman Howard of Jefferson County were involved in its affairs, though usually in a tangential fashion. In addition, Samuel J. Ireland, the leading black politician of Claiborne County, was employed by the company to solicit private subscriptions to the road's stock. When the campaign to secure public support for county and town subscriptions to the railroad bonds began, black leaders and carpetbaggers spoke on behalf of the company from the same platform as Martin and his conservative associates.[71] The overwhelmingly black composition of the electorate in the counties along the route of the road dictated this biracial and nonpartisan method of canvassing for local subscriptions, since a two-thirds majority at the polls was required to approve bond issues. The commitment to New Departure politics in Adams and neighboring counties was partly motivated by the need for local Republican cooperation in the Natchez and Jackson Railroad scheme.

The bipartisan strategy for promoting the Natchez railroad succeeded in Adams County where $600,000 in bonds was approved and in Hinds County where $225,000 was subscribed. But in Jefferson County the railroad campaign suffered an important reversal, not for political reasons but because of the vigorous opposition of the Rodney community. Rodney, near the Mississippi River, had long served as the small commercial center for the interior

70. Natchez *Weekly Democrat*, December 14, 1870, August 7, 1872, March 6, 14 (quote), 1875.

71. *Ibid.*, October 12, 1870, July 12, November 15, 1871; *Laws of Mississippi, 1870*, pp. 221–22; *Hinds County Gazette*, October 5, 1870.

of the county, including Fayette, the county seat, which was on the route of the proposed Natchez railroad. Citizens of Rodney had no desire to pay taxes for the construction of a railroad that would build up Fayette and other communities. In the first election black politician James Cessor of Rodney rallied his followers against the $300,000 bond subscription, and it went down to defeat in the county, followed by rumblings of discontent against the road in nearby Claiborne County.[72]

Promoters of the Natchez railroad immediately launched an intensive campaign in Jefferson County to secure a reversal of the decision. Prominent Republicans of the area descended on Rodney and other recalcitrant communities in the county to elicit black voters' support. Outdoor meetings were held and barbecue was served in a liberal fashion to the assembled throng of blacks. These rallies usually culminated in a vigorous debate between spokesmen of the two sides. At all of the meetings Cessor made an appearance in an effort to counter the steamroller campaign of the railroad forces. When the antirailroad campaign faltered, Cessor introduced politics into the debate, claiming that the railroad project was a plot by Natchez conservatives to make themselves wealthy. He also reminded his audiences of General Martin's background as a slaveholder and a Confederate officer. Cessor's strategy had the desired effect; once again Jefferson County voters refused to approve the bond subscription.[73]

From this point, the fortunes of the Natchez and Jackson Railroad declined. Martin soon experienced problems in marketing the bonds issued by Adams and Hinds counties to support the construction of the road. Under the circumstances, Republican officials in Hinds found cause to delay the delivery of most of their bonds to Martin's office, and the few Adams County bonds the railroad sold brought only sixty-three to seventy cents on the dollar. With this money, supplemented by private subscriptions, the first spike was driven at Natchez in January, 1873. Construction,

72. Clay Sharkey, "Essay number 37," in Sharkey Papers; Jackson *Pilot*, March 25, 1871; Natchez *Weekly Democrat*, December 13, 1871.

73. Natchez *Weekly Democrat*, June 19, July 10, 26, 1872. Natchez retaliated against Rodney for this second defeat. Its merchants instituted a line of freight wagons between Fayette and their town, thereby drawing off trade from Rodney's main interior market. *Ibid.*, August 7, 1872.

however, proceeded at a snail's pace, as Martin scurried from town to town along the route futilely seeking money. By 1875 only nine miles of track had been laid, and $300,000 in Adams County bonds remained unsold. Disillusioned by the slow progress of the road and evidently fearful that Martin might dispose of the bonds at a ruinous discount (actually he had scrupulously protected the county's interest in the matter), the Republican board of supervisors ordered that the bonds be returned to the county and destroyed.[74]

As a result the Natchez railroad's collapse appeared imminent. Martin and his associates, however, made a desperate appeal to Natchez merchants to save the railroad by subscribing enough money to complete the portion to Fayette. "The question at present seems not to be how much would the railroad improve the value of property and increase our trade and facilities of intercourse," the board of directors told the merchants, "but whether without it our property will have any value or our diminished trade be left to us at all." President Martin elaborated: "Trade had steadily been diverted from us; the city of Natchez is full of vacant houses, going to decay. Every department of trade and industry languished; our population is decreasing; our young men and mechanics, the hope of the country, are seeking elsewhere a field of labor. Rents will scarcely pay taxes, repairs and insurance, and the delinquent tax list is swelling enormously year by year."[75] Only the completion of the railroad to Fayette could revive the town, Martin declared.

The appeal bore fruit. Martin raised $100,000, of which $42,000 was subscribed by the already overburdened directors of the railroad, and the road continued its crawl toward Fayette, reaching that small town in 1876. To negotiate this twenty-six miles of Mississippi countryside, the road had cost Adams County taxpayers a total of $450,000. At the same time no profits had been realized by the company, and Martin had yet to receive a penny in compensation for his labors. Nevertheless, with the completion of the line to Fayette the rate of construction increased, and by 1882 the railroad had reached Jackson.[76]

74. *Ibid.*, December 26, 1871, May 29, 1872, August 12, 1874, February 6, 1875.
75. *Ibid.*, February 6, 1875.
76. *Ibid.*, March 21, 1875, March 28, 1876; *Hinds County Gazette*, August 30, 1882; affidavit of William T. Martin, November 30, 1876, in Mississippi Railroad Papers.

Despite the heavy expense involved, an outside observer commented that the promoters of the Natchez road had approached the task of railroad building with a caution and saneness lacking in similar projects in the state. He wrote:

> Usually communities go mad on the subject of railroads, and in grasping at imaginary moonshine projects of stupendous magnitude, fail to secure the solid advantages that would result from enterprises of more moderate pretensions. They attempt to build at once long lines of railway, the utility of all parts of which depends on the completion of the whole. The counties along the whole line are called on to issue bonds, which are sold or hypothecated at a ruinous discount to *nonresident capitalists*—work is begun and then suspended, and the people along the line of the projected railway are burdened with a heavy annual tax and a frightful debt in the future without being able to reap any of the advantages which they expected would compensate them for their burden.

Natchez promoters had avoided these pitfalls by financing the road as it was constructed and restraining their ambitions for a railroad empire.[77] Their neighbors to the North, in Vicksburg, had exercised no such restraint in mapping their grandiose designs.

Immediately after the war Vicksburg experienced a surge of economic activity convincing its residents that the town would become a great commercial center. Although a thin layer of euphoria continued into the 1870s, a sobering mood had replaced the early optimism by 1870, as merchants from St. Louis, Memphis, New Orleans, and elsewhere began to compete for the lucrative trade of the region. One Vicksburger complained that even though the town, near the mouth of the Yazoo River, "should get the lion's share of the rich trade of the valleys of the Yazoo, Tallahatchie, Sunflower and Deer Creek [the Delta country], she only gets the scraps of the feast after the lions of New Orleans and St. Louis have satiated themselves." The crunch became so severe that by 1874 Vicksburg reportedly handled only one bale of cotton of every ten produced in the Delta, an area that had earlier been the city's special trade preserve.[78]

The steamboat, not the iron horse, provided the means by which outside interests siphoned off Vicksburg's Delta commerce. Pos-

---

77. As reported in the Natchez *Weekly Democrat*, April 8, 1875.
78. Vicksburg *Vicksburger*, September 1, 1874.

sessing superior financial resources, St. Louis and New Orleans merchants established regular and relatively cheap packet service on the Mississippi and its tributaries above Vicksburg. The intruders set freight rates that discriminated against Vicksburg merchants, and by 1871 they had developed a virtual monopoly of the river trade. By far the most significant of the steamboat cartels was the White Collar line, operated by a group of St. Louis merchants for the purpose of diverting the lower Mississippi Valley trade to their doors. These entrepreneurs also secured an agreement with the Vicksburg, Shreveport, and Texas Railroad by which they were able to supply communities along the route of the road with goods at a lower price than that charged by Vicksburg merchants. East of the river, New Orleans merchants employed the same combination of rail-steamboat rate discrimination to root Vicksburg out of its interior trade. Nevertheless, steamboats continued to dock at the Vicksburg wharf, and trade was active, though now it was controlled by outside interests, leaving the merchants of the Hill City to wither in the same doldrums that affected less promising interior towns.[79]

A slow agony gripped Vicksburg as its dreams of a commercial empire vanished. Some townsmen lashed out at the "Rip Van Winkle" attitude of the leading businessmen and their failure to contest their rivals' control of Delta commerce. Others, of both political parties, blamed the unstable political situation in the county and town for their economic troubles, although even the editor of the Bourbon *Vicksburger* admitted that this was not the main reason for the town's decline. Goaded by the local press, Vicksburg merchants, many of whom were transplanted northerners, took a financial risk in 1871 and dispatched a packet, the *Rubicon*, into the Delta to compete with the St. Louis and New Orleans controlled steamboats. This boat was successful, but it was no real challenge to the supremacy that outsiders were establishing in the Mississippi bottomlands.[80]

79. Vicksburg *Times and Republican*, October 27, November 9, 18, 1871, January 25, 1873.

80. *Ibid.*, November 18, 29, 1871, February 9, 21, 1873; Vicksburg *Vicksburger*, September 1, 1874. Once they had gained control of the trade, the interloping steamboat lines raised their fares, much to the dismay of planters at noncompetitive places in the Delta who had earlier turned their backs on Vicksburg merchants in order to do business with the outsiders. Vicksburg *Times and Republican*, February 11, 1873.

Vicksburg's lethargy in combating the steamboat monopoly could be traced mainly to its blind faith in the iron horse as the harbinger of future prosperity. The obsession of its townsmen with railroad development left little room for any other activity in the way of internal improvements for this river port. Unlike Natchez, which kept a keen eye on its river traffic (despite an unpropitious location) and restricted its railroad activity to the construction of one road at a time, Vicksburg neglected its river interests and struck out in all directions to build a railroad empire. The editor of the Vicksburg *Evening News* expressed the prevailing sentiment of the local citizenry when he declared: "Railroads are essential for the growth and prosperity of any town, and railroads Vicksburg must have if we would ever realize our greatness and importance as a people."[81] Another townsman boasted, "When the railroad system is perfected it will give a prominence to the city that can scarcely be anticipated by its most sanguine friends."[82]

The perfection of the railroad system included the construction of the Southern Pacific, or Texas-Pacific, Railroad with Vicksburg as its terminus on the Mississippi. Residents firmly believed that their town would become the great river port for this transcontinental railway. Their confidence was based not only on the Hill City's strategic location in the Mississippi Valley, but also on the completion of a portion of the line, the Vicksburg, Shreveport, and Texas Railroad (later the North Louisiana and Texas Railroad) as far as Monroe, Louisiana. When the Cincinnati commercial convention of 1870 announced its support for the Vicksburg position, the citizens of the town assumed that the terminus was theirs. The thought of the completion of the road filled their minds with dreams of commercial glory and town growth.[83]

During the 1870s both Republican and Democratic governments in Mississippi labored to secure federal aid for the construction of the transcontinental railroad. Jefferson Davis, a past leader in the southern effort to secure the road, spoke at the Memphis commercial convention of 1875 and urged the completion of the rail-

81. As quoted in the Jackson *Pilot*, June 30, 1871.

82. *Ibid.*, August 2, 1871.

83. Vicksburg *Herald*, September 18, November 28, 1868; Jackson *Weekly Pilot*, October 15, 1870; Vicksburg *Times and Republican*, March 30, 1872. Vicksburg contributed $57,000 to the completion of the Vicksburg, Shreveport, and Texas Railroad. Taylor, *Louisiana Reconstructed*, 340.

road with Vicksburg as its eastern terminus. During the same year
the Radical legislature and Governor Ames petitioned Congress to
endorse the bonds of the Texas-Pacific in order to advance construction work on the road. When Ames was overthrown, the Redeemers repeated the Republican plea for federal aid for the project, and, as C. Vann Woodward has ably told, the decision in the
disputed election of 1876 hinged to a great extent on the struggle
over the elusive southern railroad to the Pacific.[84]

Not only did Vicksburg seek to enlarge its commercial opportunities, it answered every threat to its traditional trade territory
with a plan for a railroad to thwart its competitors. For example,
though an excellent waterway connected the two towns, Vicksburg
embarked on a campaign to build a road to Yazoo City when it appeared that the Delta town would construct a railroad to a point
on the Mississippi Central line. The Hill City also reacted to the
Mobile and Northwestern threat to penetrate the Delta, as well as
to a scheme originating in the village of Raymond to lay a road
across Yazoo County. A Vicksburg company was quickly organized
to build a railroad through Yazoo County to Canton. When citizens
of the town hesitated in their support of the project, the Vicksburg
Times and Republican reminded them that "Vicksburg must guard,
with Argus vigilance, all her avenues of trade. The Raymond and
Yazoo and the Mobile and Northwestern roads will literally strip
this market of all the cotton produced in the sections through
which they traverse, unless we do something to counteract it."[85]
Even the Vicksburg, Pensacola, and Ship Island Railroad, designed
mainly to provide the town with a direct line to the Gulf Coast,
was partly conceived to check the intrusion into Vicksburg territory of the proposed Natchez and Jackson road. At the same time,
in an effort to improve its commercial advantage at the expense
of its rivals, Vicksburg became involved in the New Orleans, Baton
Rouge, and Vicksburg Railroad, the so-called "backbone line" that
had been conceived in Louisiana as an unabashed railroad jobbery
to swindle the state out of thousands of acres of public lands.

84. *Laws of Mississippi, 1875*, p. 212; *Laws of Mississippi, 1876*, pp. 94–95; C. Vann
Woodward, *Reunion and Reaction: The Compromise of 1877 and the End of Reconstruction* (Boston, 1951), Chaps. IV and V especially.
85. Vicksburg *Herald*, November 17, 18, 1868; Vicksburg *Times and Republican*, December 15, 1871, February 20, 1872 (quote); *Laws of Mississippi, 1870*, pp. 205–14.

When it became clear that if completed, the road would benefit New Orleans at the expense of Vicksburg, local promoters soured on the project.[86]

The most ambitious undertaking by Vicksburg to counter its rivals was the Memphis and Vicksburg Railroad. This road, to be built northward from Vicksburg through the heart of the Yazoo Valley, was designed to divert trade from Memphis in the upper Delta and St. Louis in the lower. Although ostensibly projected to terminate at Memphis, there was no assurance that this would be the case, since the management centered in Vicksburg would probably find cause to deny the Tennessee river port a rail connection with the Delta if and when construction on the road neared the town. Chartered in 1870, the Memphis and Vicksburg Railroad included among its incorporators many of the most influential political leaders of Vicksburg and the Delta. Heading the list of incorporators (and later serving on the railroad's first board of directors) were Governor Alcorn, scalawag A. S. Dowd, carpetbagger Charles W. Clarke, and black leader Thomas W. Stringer. Civil War Governor Charles Clark was the most prominent Delta conservative affiliated with the new company.[87]

Stringer was the only Negro associated with the Memphis and Vicksburg Railroad, and this tokenism was resented by river country blacks. Negro leaders in the Delta claimed that since their race held political power along the route of the projected road blacks should be adequately represented on the board of directors. The carpetbag editor of the Vicksburg *Times and Republican* viewed the situation in a different light. "We would remind our colored friends," he said, "that this is no political matter; it is simply a business transaction. Every man votes according to the amount of his capital invested. If they can and will subscribe stock enough, they can elect every member of the Board."[88] This response ignored the question of why white stockholders would vote only for whites as directors of the company—except for Stringer whose political fortunes were in decline. The Memphis and Vicksburg's

---

86. Jackson *Weekly Clarion*, April 15, 1869; Woodward, *Reunion and Reaction*, 88.

87. *Laws of Mississippi, 1870*, pp. 316–26; Vicksburg *Times and Republican*, December 15, 1871; Jackson *Weekly Pilot*, November 12, 1870.

88. Vicksburg *Times and Republican*, August 10, 1871.

policy of ignoring blacks in the management of the railroad, in contrast to the Natchez and Jackson company's approach, contributed to the road's failure to secure bond and stock subscriptions in several Delta counties.

Political divisions among the white directors of the Memphis and Vicksburg Railroad also retarded its development. Inspired by McCardle of the *Herald*, the conservative members of the board of directors so vigorously resisted the majority's appointment of Alcorn as company president that he not only refused to serve but also withdrew his support for the road. Gaining control of the board, conservative directors selected as president Wirt Adams, a Confederate hero and a Democrat—an action that severely damaged the railroad's campaign to win bond subscription elections in the Republican-dominated river counties. Even in Vicksburg, where enthusiasm for a Delta railway was highest, the new leadership of the company after the vote on the initial subscription of $100,000 had difficulty persuading the voters to approve additional bond issues.[89]

At the same time that they were opposing the grant of state lands to the Mobile and Northwestern Railroad, State Senator Mygatt of Warren County and other proponents of the Memphis and Vicksburg road were pressing the legislature for an extension of the railroad Subsidy Law. Snarled in their construction program by the lack of local support, the managers of the Memphis and Vicksburg had not been able to qualify during the required period for the $4,000 per mile subsidy under the original act. When the extension bill failed to pass, they had no choice but to wait out the remainder of the Republican era and hope that the next regime would be more friendly to their interests.[90] The Redeemers, however, delayed until 1881 their response to the company's pleas for aid and then granted the road more than 774,000 acres of tax-forfeited Delta lands. Nevertheless, the company was unable to capitalize on this bonanza, mainly because of conflicting titles to the properties. Collis P. Huntington, the great railroad entrepreneur, and New York financier Richard T. Wilson picked up the pieces of the Memphis and Vicksburg Railroad, merged it with the

89. *Ibid.*, November 15, 18, 1871, June 21, 1872.
90. *Ibid.*, January 7, March 30, 1872, February 11, 1873.

remnants of roads south of Vicksburg, and in 1884 completed the construction of the trunk line from Memphis to New Orleans.[91]

Their inability during Reconstruction to build a railroad northward through the heart of the Delta drew Vicksburg promoters into an alliance with a northeast Mississippi group to construct a line diagonally through the area. In 1872 the moribund company that had been chartered to build the road from Vicksburg to Yazoo City joined with the Grenada, Houston, and Eastern Railroad to form the Vicksburg and Nashville Railroad. The charter recognizing the merger exempted the company from taxation for a period of thirty years. The immediate ambition of the railroad's managers was to construct a line from Okalona to Grenada; however, bankrupt Vicksburg interests hoped that once this objective had been achieved the road would be completed to their town.[92] Like other railroads, this one had no chance for success unless it could secure extensive state aid, which depended on political influence at the state capital. Since the proposed road cut a swath across a large area of Mississippi, including several large Republican counties, the managers of the Vicksburg and Nashville, led by former Confederate brigadier and company president William F. Tucker, found themselves in a good position to secure state financial assistance. Furthermore, when they appeared at the capital in 1873 the fever for railroad development was at its height; no fewer than eleven railroads received charters during that legislative session, though all were short lines and none secured direct state aid.

The lobbying activities of the Vicksburg and Nashville promoters proved highly successful. Managed through the legislature by carpetbaggers F. M. Abbott and Finus N. Little, both representing affected counties, a bill was passed and signed by Governor Powers that loaned the college land-grant fund to the railroad. Amounting to about $320,000, the fund, which in 1871 had been given to the state by the federal government to support agricultural education, was extended to the railroad on the condition that five miles of track be completed before the company received the first payment of $40,000. The act, passed by a bipartisan vote, also

91. *Laws of the State of Mississippi, 1882* (Jackson, 1882), 838–49; Brandfon, *Cotton Kingdom*, 70–71.

92. *Laws of Mississippi, 1872*, p. 287; Vicksburg *Times and Republican*, February 24, 1872.

required that the loan, bearing 8 percent annual interest, be secured by the railroad's first mortgage bonds and that it be repaid within ten years. The governor was responsible for ensuring that these conditions had been met before the fund could be distributed. The legislature, and Powers at first, chose to ignore the fact that the Vicksburg and Nashville had no assets at the time and would probably have none until it was completed. In a separate act the lawmakers arranged to sell the Vicksburg and Nashville Railroad all of the tax-forfeited lands lying within ten miles of its route for two cents an acre.[93]

Opposition to the raid on the college land-grant fund immediately flared. The trustees of the University of Mississippi, several of whom were influential Republicans, announced their determination to resist through the state courts the alienation of the fund. Even in Vicksburg, the projected terminus of the railroad, the *Times and Republican* admitted that the donation of the education fund was not its idea of the proper method for aiding the road. Senator Alcorn rushed to Jackson to inform Powers of the risk involved in the transaction and persuaded him to withhold any distribution of the money to the railroad. Powers, who evidently had signed the bill in hopes of advancing his own political fortunes during the upcoming gubernatorial contest, saw the truth in Alcorn's argument. Despite Tucker's enraged objections, the governor announced that he would not permit a distribution of the fund until the company provided adequate security for the loan— an improbability in view of the unpromising condition of the road.[94]

In a move designed to increase the railroad's political clout, the directors of the Vicksburg and Nashville selected Republican State Senator Little to replace the conservative Tucker as president of the company.[95] This succeeded in keeping at bay the opponents of the road in the legislature. But when Ames became governor in 1874, he bombarded the legislature with requests for the repeal

93. *Senate Journal, 1873,* II, 1582, 1669, 1683–84; *Laws of Mississippi, 1873,* pp. 516–18, 558–61.

94. Vicksburg *Times and Republican,* July 15, August 3, 1873; William F. Tucker to Powers, July 26, 1873; statement of Alcorn [1873], in Governors' Correspondence, Vol. 81.

95. Vicksburg *Vicksburger,* August 5, 1874.

of the law granting the agricultural land-grant scrip to the railroad before it became eligible for the first installment.[96] "Let this law stand," he told the legislature, "and there will spring from it a corporation which, if ruled by the spirit of the legislation that gave it birth, will sooner or later blight, if not destroy, nearly every other interest in the State." Ames affirmed his support for internal improvements but insisted that such projects must stand the test of economic competition. "A commercial necessity must breathe life into all enterprises for pecuniary profits, and that road which depends solely on state and county subscriptions, and is undertaken with money borrowed thereon, enticing no other capital, must be of problematical success." The Vicksburg and Nashville Railroad was one such road. If completed, Ames pointed out, this railroad "would run through but one county untraversed by railroads, and would be but a feeder to two great railroads. . . . The history of railroads has taught that only through roads, which carry the products of a county to market, are successful, and especially is this the case in sparsely settled sections" like the one covered by the projected Vicksburg and Nashville Railroad. Despite Ames's strong political influence with the lawmakers, Little and the friends of the railroad held the upper hand in the legislature, and the distribution act was not repealed until 1876 when the Redeemers, at Ames's request, acted to save the fund.[97]

Meanwhile, Ames privately assured the opponents of the scheme that he would never approve a distribution of the agricultural scrip unless ordered to do so by the state supreme court. When he sought a judicial confirmation of his position, the Republican state supreme court, much to his surprise, sustained the right of the company to receive the money. Fortunately for the public interest, the railroad failed to lay the required five miles of track before the law was repealed. When the struggle for the control of the agricultural land-grant fund ended in 1876, not one cent of it had been transferred to the railroad. A few weeks after this de-

96. Message of Governor Ames on the Vicksburg and Nashville Railroad [March, 1874], in Blanche Butler Ames (comp.), *Chronicles*, I, 662–66; *Annual Message of Governor Ames, 1875*, pp. 6–7.

97. *Annual Message of Governor Ames, 1876*, pp. 11–16; *Laws of Mississippi, 1876*, pp. 64–65.

cisive defeat for the company, the Vicksburg and Nashville Railroad announced its failure.[98]

At the end of Reconstruction Vicksburg had little but a large debt to show for its ambitious efforts to lace the hinterland with railroads. Less than twenty miles of track had been laid, all on the Vicksburg, Pensacola, and Ship Island Railroad, and, as one Vicksburg spokesman admitted, "the whole material assets" of the companies chartered to build the railroads "would not pay one half the interest on the debt" accumulated in aiding the projects. Vicksburg and Warren County had issued almost one million dollars in bonds to aid these enterprises; fortunately, an undetermined amount of the securities were not sold and therefore were returned to local officials.[99] Those bonds that were marketed sold far below their face value, which inevitably increased the future burden on the local taxpayers who had to redeem the full amount. When payments could not be made, various refunding schemes were approved, further increasing the debt. The only alternative was the repudiation, in whole or part, of these obligations. This solution required the approval of the legislature, which during Reconstruction refused to give its approval mainly because of Mississippi's sad legacy of repudiation.

Although its debt was the largest in the state, Warren County was not alone in its accumulation of railroad obligations. In 1872 Hinds County voters subscribed $550,000 in bonds to three railroads, only one of which (the Natchez and Jackson Railroad) was ever completed. At the same time Madison County invested $250,000 in the ill-fated Vicksburg and Canton Railroad. One year later three Delta counties, despite already being encumbered with heavy levee debts, subscribed $650,000 to a projected feeder line from Greenville to Winona on the Mississippi Central Railroad. In the southwestern corner of the state Wilkinson County voted $400,000 to the Meridian, Red River, and Texas, a railroad that

98. George H. Holland to E. W. McClure, April 27, 1874, in Letterbook of the State Treasurer of Mississippi, April 2, 1874—December 16, 1874, Mississippi Department of Archives and History; *The State* v. *Vicksburg and Nashville Railroad Company*, 51 Miss. 361–75 (1875); Natchez *Democrat*, May 16, 1876.

99. Vicksburg *Vicksburger*, October 18, 1874; Wall (comp.), *Mississippi*, 146–47; Vicksburg *Times and Republican*, February 20, 1872. Even to the west, the Vicksburg, Shreveport, and Texas trunk line made little progress toward Texas. Not until 1884 did the tracks reach Shreveport. Taylor, *Louisiana Reconstructed*, 340.

never got off the drawing board.[100] Most of the counties and towns covered by General Forrest's Selma, Marion, and Memphis Railroad, running diagonally across north Mississippi, committed themselves to the bonds and stock of the company. During the early 1870s Forrest had labor crews busy grading the road, building bridges, and even laying crossties, but he did not have the means to secure the expensive rails needed for the line's early completion.[101]

Most local commitments were made in 1872–1873 when the fever for railroad construction was at its height. Railroad intrigue and violated promises by company officials were not conducive to continued public enthusiasm for the roads. But opposition mainly developed when it became clear that the construction of the railroads would cost far more than glib promoters had promised. The expense could be met neither by the communities along the route nor by the state. A number of counties and towns soon sought relief from their burdensome railroad debts, despite the serious implications of repudiation. As early as 1872 a few county boards of supervisors simply refused to levy a tax to meet the payments on the bonds issued by their counties. The legislature acted quickly to halt this practice, passing a bill the same year that required the state auditor of public accounts to impose the necessary tax when local authorities refused to act. A provision of the law, which also held the railroads accountable for good faith in meeting the terms of their agreements with local officials, gave the auditor some leeway in the matter, and carpetbag Auditor Henry Musgrove rejected the appeal of two railroads to intervene against delinquent local authorities.[102]

In 1874 the state supreme court, with old-line Whig Horatio F. Simrall delivering the opinion, provided the mechanism for additional relief from railroad burdens. It ruled that two thirds of the registered voters, rather than two thirds of those voting in the election, must have actually approved a local bond issue to

100. *Hinds County Gazette*, February 28, April 3, 10, 1872; Vicksburg *Times and Republican*, January 2, 1873.

101. Jackson *Weekly Pilot*, December 25, 1869; *Senate Journal, 1873*, I, 15; Wall (comp.), *Mississippi*, 147.

102. *Laws of Mississippi, 1872*, pp. 101, 105–106; Jackson *Weekly Clarion*, December 11, 1873; E. W. Smith to Henry Musgrove, June 27, 1873, in Mississippi Railroad Papers.

make it binding on the people.[103] Since the turnout at these elections was usually small and short of the necessary two thirds, most counties now had the legal means to repudiate their railroad obligations. It must be remembered also that in many cases before the railroad received the bonds a certain amount of track had to be laid. Few companies during Reconstruction were able to qualify for any assistance under this condition. In fact, only 120 miles of track were constructed during the 1865–1875 period, 37 of which were completed in 1873.[104]

The efforts of Governors Powers and Ames—though in a mild form in the case of Powers—to point out and prevent abuses of the public interest by the railroads contributed to the changing sentiment toward the roads. Their criticism of railroad schemes and the dangers of overcapitalization of local roads especially inspired opposition to the projects in the predominantly Negro counties where promoters sought to beguile blacks into voting large subscriptions for their lines. Although blacks were usually no more vulnerable than their white neighbors to the facile assurances of railroad backers, Mann, Martin, Little, and other railroad men had concentrated most of their efforts on convincing Negro voters of the desirability of bond subscriptions. Even Forrest, reputedly the first grand wizard of the Ku Klux Klan, had adjusted to Reconstruction political realities in order to obtain financial support for his road. In 1872 he publicly endorsed the New Departure movement signifying conservative acceptance of the postwar amendments to the Constitution.[105] The greater wealth, at least relatively, of the plantation counties, as well as the belief that Negroes could be easily persuaded to vote for bond issues that landowners would have to redeem in taxes, also caused railroad proponents to curry the favor of blacks. But by 1875 Republican disillusionment with railroad projects had dried up this source of bond subscriptions.

Finally, a rising crescendo of criticism against the established

103. *Frank Hawkins et al.* v. *Board of Supervisors of Carroll County*, 50 Miss. 735–66 (1874).

104. John F. Stover, *The Railroads of the South, 1865–1900* (Chapel Hill, 1955), 61; *Commercial and Financial Chronicle: Banker's Gazette, Commercial Times, Railway Monitor, and Insurance Journal*, XIX (January 3, 1874), 6.

105. *Hinds County Gazette*, February 14, 1872.

trunk lines contributed to an emerging new reality in matters of railroad development, affecting both Republicans and conservatives. Most of the controversy involving the old trunk lines focused on Henry S. McComb, the flamboyant and energetic Delaware capitalist who dreamed of creating a railroad empire in the Mississippi Valley. McComb, a round-faced former colonel in the Union army, began his rise to railroad prominence when in 1868 he formed the Southern Railroad Association and obtained a sixteen-year lease to the debt-ridden Mississippi Central Railroad.[106] He permitted Absalom M. West, for many years Mississippi's leading railroad entrepreneur, to continue as president of the road, a wise decision that defused local opposition to the imposition of eastern control. McComb's plans of empire extended far beyond the Mississippi Central Railroad, and he had no desire to arouse the enmity of Mississippians before he had consolidated his position in the area. Believing that McComb was the kind of northeastern capitalist who would advance railroad development in the region, the influential West sang his praises and defended him against critics. Indeed, West's support gave McComb more credibility as a railroad manager than he deserved based on his background, which included involvement in the Credit Mobilier scandal.[107]

McComb's early completion of the long-projected extension of the Mississippi Central from Jackson, Tennessee, to Milan in that state, where a connection with the Louisville and Nashville Railroad was made, seemed to confirm the belief that the coming of the Delaware entrepreneur was a harbinger of railroad progress. To cap this success, with the aid of the Illinois Central McComb now pushed the road farther northward, reaching Cairo, Illinois, in 1873.[108] The completion of the railroad gave the Mississippi heartland a trunk line to the Midwest. It also increased the value

106. *The Southern Railroad Association: Lease of the Mississippi Central Railroad; Agreement for Milan Extension; and Articles of Agreement Between the Trustees, June 25, 1868* (Wilmington, Del., 1868), 3–14.

107. Jackson *Weekly Pilot*, October 29, 1870; Jackson *Pilot*, April 13, 1871; Jackson *Weekly Clarion*, January 23, 1873. McComb also gained control of the Mississippi and Tennessee Railroad, which junctured at Grenada with the Mississippi Central, by the simple method of appointing its head, Samuel Tate, as president of the Southern Railroad Association (thus bringing Tate's road into his organization) and then, a few months later, replacing him in the office with his own man. Jackson *Weekly Pilot*, September 24, 1870.

108. Jackson *Weekly Clarion*, November 13, 1873.

of the southern portion of the line, the New Orleans, Jackson, and Great Northern Railroad, and provided merchants in the Crescent City with hope that their city would regain its commercial supremacy in the Mississippi Valley. McComb quite early had calculated the financial benefits that would accrue from the completion of the trunkline—and in 1870 he acted to gain control of the whole route.

The colonel's covetous designs on the New Orleans railroad immediately encountered the opposition of P. G. T. Beauregard, the distinguished president of the road, and the somewhat mild opposition of state officials in Jackson. The main stockholders in the company were the states of Mississippi and Louisiana and the city of New Orleans, with the latter two holding a majority of the shares. In 1870 when McComb made his move to obtain control of the railroad, Mississippi's investment in the company was valued at $448,735, or 13 percent of the total capitalization. The state's financial interest in the railroad dated back to 1841 when it had received a federal grant of 500,000 acres for the purpose of internal improvements. The antebellum state government, as explained earlier, also had loaned a part of the Chickasaw School Fund to the New Orleans railroad, and by 1870 the amount of this obligation exceeded $300,000. Mississippi authorities had long fought the efforts of New Orleans merchants to merge the Mississippi Central and the New Orleans, Jackson, and Great Northern into one company. Such a consolidation, they feared, would not only minimize the state's influence in the management of the railroad, but it would also permit the new directors to adopt discriminatory practices designed to benefit the port city at the expense of interior farmers and merchants. Many Mississippians felt that if McComb succeeded in his scheme to control the entire road, New Orleans would be the main beneficiary and their communities the losers. Nevertheless, the colonel's success in extending the Mississippi Central northward had gained some state support for him at a time when enthusiasm for railroad development was high. In addition, the fact that McComb was crossing swords with a rebel hero struck a sympathetic chord in the minds of many Republicans. At any rate, the Republican administration that came to power in 1870 was more interested in securing the construction of the long-promised extension of the New Orleans railroad to Aberdeen (from Canton) and also the repayment of the Chickasaw loan than in who controlled the road.[109]

McComb understood the divided mind of Mississippians regarding his consolidation activities and believed that the state would pose no serious threat. As a result, when he acted in the spring of 1870 to gain control of the New Orleans railroad, he completely ignored his few Mississippi critics and directed his efforts toward obtaining control of the Louisiana and New Orleans stock, which together represented a majority of the shares. On the pretext that the company's securities were virtually worthless, McComb, actively supported by Louisiana Governor Henry Clay Warmoth, secured the approval of the legislature and the city to purchase the stock at a price of four dollars per share, which was worth at least six dollars and probably more. The bill authorizing the sale of the Louisiana stock was reputedly eased through the legislature by bribes amounting to $80,000.[110]

The Confederate "Napoleon in Gray," however, was not prepared to surrender the railroad without a fight. When McComb and his men, including Peter Starke, a former brigadier in the Louisianan's command and a representative of the Mississippi stock, attempted to occupy the company's offices in New Orleans, Beauregard had them arrested as trespassers. His victory was short-lived. A few days later McComb returned with a court order from a local Republican judge directing Beauregard to turn over the management of the company. When Beauregard surrendered the building, McComb had achieved his goal of consolidating the trunk line running from New Orleans to Tennessee, a line that would soon be extended to the Ohio River.[111]

McComb's coup aroused more opposition in Mississippi than he had anticipated. Even Republicans who at first had applauded his victory over Beauregard soon had second thoughts and called for

109. Jackson *Weekly Pilot*, April 16, May 21, June 4, July 16, 1870; Harris, *Presidential Reconstruction in Mississippi*, 199–201; *Hinds County Gazette*, February 7, 1872, quoting the Vicksburg *Herald*.
110. Francis Wayne Binning, "Henry Clay Warmoth and Louisiana Reconstruction" (Ph.D. dissertation, University of North Carolina, Chapel Hill, 1969), 186–87; Jackson *Weekly Pilot*, April 16, 1870; Jackson *Weekly Clarion*, May 6, 1869.
111. Jackson *Weekly Pilot*, April 30, May 7, 1870; Jackson *Weekly Clarion*, May 5, 1870.

an investigation. The conservative Jackson *Clarion* denounced the coup as an "extraordinary and scandalous" proceeding and demanded that the Alcorn administration protect the state's interest in the matter. Reports reached McComb that some Mississippians were urging the legislature to revoke the road's charter and seize its equipment in the state.[112] Governor Alcorn's Whiggish predilections restrained him from recommending any such radical attack on property rights; however, he asked the legislature to give him authority to act through the courts to force the New Orleans railroad to return its part of the Chickasaw School Fund to the state. The scalawag governor also asked the legislature to order the company to begin immediately the construction of the Aberdeen extension. If the McComb directorate refused to honor the state's demand, Alcorn then was prepared to seek a revocation of the railroad's charter.[113]

Alarmed by the threats from Mississippi, McComb rushed to Jackson, bringing in his train the affable Governor Warmoth to aid in persuading state Republican leaders to go easy on the railroad. The Delaware adventurer assured Alcorn and legislative leaders that construction of the Aberdeen extension would begin soon and would be completed to Kosciusko within twelve months, provided the company received a moderate amount of state aid for the project. At the same time McComb refused to commit himself to the repayment of the Chickasaw loan. Although McComb's personal appearance in Jackson and his promise regarding the Aberdeen extension allayed some opposition, Alcorn warned him that his administration would not stand by and permit outside capitalists to dominate the state's transportation facilities.[114]

Sobered by this experience, McComb during the next year worked to improve his image in Mississippi. When Robert E. Lee died he draped the offices of the railroad in mourning—a demonstration of respect that even the Republican Alcorn approved. He also agreed to accept at face value the state's certificates of indebtedness, and he loaned $30,000 to Alcorn, which the governor insisted was purely a private matter and would not influence his

---

112. Jackson *Weekly Pilot*, April 16, 1870; Jackson *Weekly Clarion*, April 14, 28, 1870.
113. Alcorn's message on the subject is in the Jackson *Weekly Pilot*, May 21, 1870.
114. *Ibid.*, June 25, 1870.

public decisions regarding the railroad. Finally, McComb purchased new equipment for his railroad, improved the track, and increased the efficiency of its operations, causing the Jackson *Pilot* to conclude that the colonel was rapidly making it into "one of the finest railroads in the United States."[115]

McComb's campaign to cultivate goodwill in Mississippi had the desired effect by the time of the 1871 legislative session. Complaining that his organization did not have the financial resources to build the extension to Aberdeen, he proposed to the legislature that the state surrender its stock in the company as a means of assisting the work. The stock, which the colonel claimed was not worth very much, could be converted to funds for the construction of the extension. The legislature and Governor Alcorn accepted the proposition, but with one condition. Before Mississippi surrendered its stock, McComb would have to complete the extension as far as Kosciusko or, as an alternative, provide the state with $200,000 in company bonds.[116]

Even with this incentive, McComb hesitated. The required route from Canton to Kosciusko had few advantages for his company, since much of it ran parallel to the Mississippi Central Railroad, which he controlled. The cost of construction was too great and the potential return too little for the colonel to build the extension unless the state forced him to do so by threatening to revoke the charter. In spite of the reputation for opulence which he carefully cultivated, McComb was chronically short of cash, managing during most of the period to remain one step ahead of the sheriff's hammer.[117] Consequently, he reappeared before the legislature in 1873 seeking a new point of departure for the Kosciusko-Aberdeen branch as well as an extension of the time limit for completing the first part to Kosciusko. He secured both concessions, although Durant, the new place of departure, was only fifteen miles from Kosciusko. While he had the initiative, he asked the legislature to legitimize his railroad empire, and despite the threat of a veto by Governor Powers, which did not materialize, the trunk line from Cairo to New Orleans was chartered as the New Orleans,

115. *Hinds County Gazette*, October 26, 1870; Jackson *Pilot*, February 9, May 21, 1871.
116. *Laws of Mississippi, 1871*, pp. 178–80.
117. John F. Stover, "Colonel Henry S. McComb, Mississippi Railroad Adventurer," *Journal of Mississippi History*, XVII (July, 1955), 184, 186.

St. Louis, and Chicago Railroad.[118] With his position now legally secure, McComb dropped the pretext of southern management of the road; he obtained the election of a board of directors consisting largely of northerners, mainly from New York and Philadelphia.[119]

Since these latest McComb moves came at the time when the Grange movement was at its height in the state, a flood of criticism was unleashed on the Republican administration for permitting the Delaware adventurer to take such liberties with the state's interest. Most of the critics, however, failed to note that a bipartisan majority had approved most of the measures benefiting McComb. Barksdale, in recounting the sordid history of McComb's intrigues and the legislature's collusion in the schemes, compared these abuses to "the same dangerous and corrupt [railroad] influences that have aroused the people of the Western States to the highest pitch of indignation."[120]

The New Orleans, St. Louis, and Chicago Railroad, however, did not prosper. McComb's debts caught up with him, and in 1876 his entire railroad system passed into receivership. An investigation of the colonel's management disclosed that he had misapplied at least $600,000 of company funds, including $100,000 in cash receipts that he had purloined for personal use just before the railroad fell into receivership.[121] In 1877 the Illinois Central bought McComb's railroad at a foreclosure sale, but the official merger of the two roads did not occur until 1880. In the end, Mississippi had only fifteen miles of track (the Kosciusko extension was completed in 1874) to show for its lost stock in the New Orleans railroad and for its indulgence in the bold machinations of Henry S. McComb.[122]

The other trunk lines—the Mobile and Ohio, the New Orleans and Mobile, the Vicksburg and Meridian, and the Memphis and Charleston which ran for only thirty-five miles in the state—experienced no such manipulation at the hands of railroad adventurers.

118. Ames to his wife, April 11, 1873, in Blanche Butler Ames (comp.), *Chronicles,* I, 439; Jackson *Weekly Clarion,* June 12, 1873; *Laws of Mississippi, 1873,* pp. 567–72.

119. Stover, "Colonel Henry S. McComb," 186.

120. Jackson *Weekly Clarion,* June 12, 1873.

121. *Ibid.,* March 15, 1876; Stover, "Colonel Henry S. McComb," 188–89.

122. *Commercial and Financial Chronicle,* XX (August 1, 1874), 119; affidavit of James C. Clarke, December 22, 1877, in Mississippi Railroad Papers; *Laws of Mississippi, 1880,* pp. 268–69.

Nevertheless, these roads, especially the Mobile and Ohio, came under increasing attack for their violations of the public interest. Even before Mississippians lost faith in McComb, the people in the eastern part of the state were excoriating the Mobile and Ohio for its discriminatory freight rates and its subservience to Mobile's interests. The company adopted the long-short haul formula for fixing rates in order to eliminate competing forms of transportation and to protect Mobile businessmen against competing merchants along the railroad.[123] Critics also attacked the Mobile and Ohio for holding almost one million acres of land in east Mississippi and refusing to sell any of it. According to one critic, this railroad, in contrast to what it claimed to be doing, was retarding agricultural diversification and industry in the east. "The Railroad monopoly comes in and says in thunder tones, sir, you must plant cotton, nothing else that you can raise will be carried on our road except at such ruinous rates that you cannot afford to pay it." As early as 1868 the representative of a group of Columbus merchants called (unsuccessfully) on the state government to rescue the people from "the rapacity of [the] insatiable vampyres" who controlled the road in the interest of Mobile and for their own aggrandizement.[124] Embittered by the mistreatment that farmers and merchants had received along the Mobile and Ohio, another east Mississippian warned against the dangers of the railroad craze that was sweeping most of the state during the early 1870s. He observed: "This Railroad mania is a kind of valve through which the public mind relieves itself of the present oppression. The wickedness of the Legislature was conspicuous in its Railroad enactments, and the Railroad jobbers of the State and country are undoubtedly the most corrupt and unpatriotic of all the characters who figure in current events."[125]

The hostility toward the Mobile and Ohio led to the first significant demand for railroad regulation in the history of Mississippi. In 1871, while the fever for railroad development was high elsewhere

123. Harris, *Presidential Reconstruction in Mississippi*, 211; Forest *Register*, September 29, 1869; C. A. Johnston to Alcorn, March 25, 1871, in Governors' Correspondence, Vol. 73.
124. "East Mississippi" to the Jackson *Weekly Clarion*, April 13, 1871; W. H. Worthington to Benjamin G. Humphreys, April 18, 1868, in Governors' Correspondence, Vol. 69.
125. "William" to the Jackson *Weekly Clarion*, June 15, 1871.

in the state, legislators from east Mississippi, encouraged by the success of the Granger laws in Illinois, pressed for the passage of a bill that would regulate passenger and freight rates and would specifically eliminate the long-short haul differential. Under the provisions of the bill those companies that did not comply with the rates set by the state would lose their charters. The measure, introduced by Z. P. Landrum, a Bourbon leader from Columbus, received the approval of the house committee on railroads, but it was not called up for consideration by the full body.[126] In the same session carpetbagger Charles A. Foster introduced a bill to create a board of railroad commissioners that would have broad supervisory authority over the roads. This proposal, however, failed even to receive the endorsement of the committee on railroads.[127] Confronted by lobbyists who warned that capital for railroad development would dry up if the state attempted to regulate the roads, most legislators backed away from any serious consideration of the Landrum and Foster proposals.

A new round of demands for railroad regulation developed in 1873–1874, inspired partly by Granger attacks on "moneyed monopolists," partly by national revelations of railroad corruption, and even more so by McComb's flouting of the public interest. Charles E. Hooker, the main speaker at the state Grange convention of 1873, devoted most of his address to the alarming rise of the "Railroad power" and the need for regulating the monopolists. The next year the Grange convention memorialized the companies to cut their freight charges, warning that if they failed to do so the organization would lobby for a law fixing maximum rates.[128]

Other railroad critics took their cue from Hooker and began a vigorous attack on the roads. In lauding Hooker's speech, "Voter" in the Vicksburg *Times and Republican* called for the exposure of legislators and government officials who served railroad corporations rather than the public interest. "We are living in the days of investigation and reform," this observer declared. "Credit mobilier

126. *Ibid.*, February 9, 12, April 13, 1871; Jackson *Pilot*, February 12, 1871; Johnston to Alcorn, March 25, 1871, in Governors' Correspondence, Vol. 73; *House Journal, 1871,* pp. 112, 391, 675, 1015.

127. *House Journal, 1871,* pp. 297, 343; Natchez *Weekly Democrat*, March 8, 1871.

128. Vicksburg *Times and Republican*, September 15, 1873; Jackson *Weekly Clarion,* September 24, 1874.

and back salary jobs have awakened the people to a keen sense of public injuries, and they not only demand immediate redress for the wrongs they may suffer, but repudiate, with indignity, the men who betray them."[129]

Even Barksdale and fellow conservative editors turned momentarily from their attacks on the "carpetbag malignants" to campaign against railroad abuses. They specifically urged the legislature to pass a law regulating freight rates. "The Farmers' movement, which started in the West and is now spreading all over the Union," Barksdale revealed in a general attack on the railroads, "was inspired by a conviction that it was absolutely needed to resist the extortion and discrimination of Railroads. The Railroad interest at one time feeble, and dependent upon the fostering hand of Government, has become a monopoly which overrides and rules all others by means of the money which it commands, and with which it buys up Legislatures and corrupts whatever department of the civil service it has sought to control." The farmers, whose toil had built up this gigantic power, Barksdale declared, "have become the victims of this grasping spirit, and have found it necessary to organize to resist its encroachments. This they can do through the lawmaking power only, and the agency of an enlightened and incorruptible judiciary." Ultimately the farmers would succeed in their war against the railroad monopolists, Barksdale assured his readers, since "revolutions never turn backward. The people whose cause is represented by the Farmers will be triumphant in the end."[130] On the other hand, a few conservative spokesmen like Lamar, Robert Lowry, and Edward C. Walthall remained silent on the railroad issue, probably because they held legal retainers from various state railroads.

The upshot of the antirailroad agitation was the introduction in the 1873 house of representatives of a bill "to prevent unjust discrimination and extortion" in freight rates. Sponsored by conservative M. A. Metts, a merchant-legislator of a nonrailroad county, the bill received the endorsement of two committees, both dominated by Republicans. As in 1871, the regulatory bill failed to pass

129. Vicksburg *Times and Republican*, September 15, 1873.
130. Jackson *Weekly Clarion*, November 27, 1873. See also the issues of April 24, May 29, June 12, 1873, and the Pascagoula *Star*, May 22, 1875.

the house. In 1874 a similar measure was considered by the senate, only to die on the floor at the end of the session, victim of skillful parliamentary maneuvering by railroad senators. After this attempt at regulation, heightened political tensions in the state relegated the issue to the back burner of public interest. The Redeemer legislature of 1876 revived the controversy when it formed a committee to study the matter of regulating freight rates.[131] This investigation did not lead to a regulatory law, although a number of bills were introduced during the late 1870s that were designed to impose maximum rates.

The only fruit of the antirailroad movement was the decision of the Republican regime to end the tax-exempt status of the roads. Designed to encourage their construction, the state policy of exempting railroads from taxes began during the antebellum period. The privilege, as set forth in the antebellum laws, would expire in 1874, except for the Mobile and Ohio which received an additional and conflicting exemption that, according to its lawyers, guaranteed the road a tax-free status until it realized an 8 percent annual profit—a rather farfetched prospect during the postwar period.[132] Railroads chartered after the war demanded and usually received the same tax-exempt privilege as the older roads. But these charters had hardly been approved when the whole issue of railroad privileges erupted in the state. Since the recently chartered lines had failed at construction, with the exception of the short Ripley road, the issue of tax exemption for these companies was largely academic. Nevertheless, considerable excitement flared in 1873 when a proviso to an innocuous chartering bill passed the legislature extending a tax-exempt privilege to all railroads for a period of ten years. Finus H. Little, chairman of the senate railroad committee and the new president of the Vicksburg and Nashville, expressed shock at the inclusion of the proviso and claimed that it had been surreptitiously placed in the bill after the measure was reported to the floor of the senate.[133] Whatever its origins, the

131. *House Journal, 1873*, pp. 1489, 1673, 1757; *Senate Journal, 1874*, pp. 50, 487, 543; *House Journal, 1876*, pp. 245–46.
132. Charles H. Brough, "History of Taxation in Mississippi," *Publications of the Mississippi Historical Society*, II (1899), 119; *Mobile and Ohio Railroad Co. v. R. J. Mosely, Sheriff*, 52 Miss. 127 (1876).
133. Vicksburg *Times and Republican*, July 2, 8, October 31, 1873.

proviso spawned a welter of railroad claims to immunity from state taxation, especially from the established trunk lines whose charter exemptions would soon expire.

The railroads, however, did not count on the strong opposition of carpetbag Governors Powers and Ames to their efforts to avoid the tax collector. Powers not only refused to recognize the underhanded exemption proviso, he also asked the legislature of 1874 to levy a tax on the trunk lines in order to give some relief to hardpressed landowners who had shouldered most of the tax burden since the beginning of the Republican era. Since, according to a contemporary study, the railroads held one sixth of the property in Mississippi, all of which was tax exempt, the revenue from an equitable and enforceable tax on these companies would be substantial.[134] The legislature, nevertheless, failed to act on Powers' recommendation.

Ames, when he succeeded Powers as governor in 1874, secured the state board of tax equalization's approval to an assessment of railroad property at a rate of five thousand dollars per mile and directed that county officials begin collecting the taxes based on this evaluation. Moreover, and despite a vigorous lobbying effort by the companies, the legislature of 1875 imposed a privilege tax of seventy-five dollars per mile on the roads—the first such tax on railroads in the history of the state.[135] Only the Mobile and Ohio, claiming its charter rights, failed to pay taxes which in 1875 amounted to about eighteen thousand dollars. When sheriffs along the route of the road began seizing railroad property for the delinquent taxes, company lawyers hurried to court. The state supreme court ruled that only the company property actually used in operating the railroad was still exempt from taxes, whereas the land held by the road, which in Wayne County constituted a large proportion of its area, was subject to state levies.[136]

Disillusionment with the railroads extended into the early Re-

---

134. *Ibid.*, September 15, October 22, 1873; *House Journal, 1874*, p. 17.

135. Entry for May 28, 1874, in Minutes of the State Board of Equalization, Missisipi Department of Archives and History; *Laws of Mississippi, 1875*, pp. 66–67.

136. List of railroads that did not pay the privilege tax of 1875, and a list of lands in Kemper County, assessed to the Mobile and Ohio Railroad and sold by the tax collector of the county, both in Mississippi Railroad Papers; J. S. Hamm to John M. Stone, June 23, 1877, in Governors' Correspondence, Vol. 112; *Mobile and Ohio Railroad Co.* v. *R. J. Mosely, Sheriff*, 52 Miss. 127–37 (1876).

demption period. In fact, the Redeemers passed laws to hold railroads to a strict accountability for their charter privileges and to protect the property rights of customers and citizens along the roads. Periodic attempts during the late 1870s to enact freight rate legislation kept railroad executives in a constant state of anxiety. Not until the early 1880s, when a new mania for railroad expansion gripped the state, were these officials able to breathe easily again.[137]

The hard economic lessons of the early Reconstruction period also inspired an incipient "New South" movement designed to balance the state's agricultural economy with industry. Evangelists of industrialization had existed during the antebellum period, but their promotional activities were submerged in a flood of rhetoric proclaiming the virtues of slavery, land, and cotton. After the war there were few editors, either conservative or Republican, who did not at least occasionally preach the gospel of industrial progress and note with enthusiasm local attempts to establish manufactories. Promoters of industrial development constantly denounced the economic system by which the South generally and Mississippi specifically were almost entirely dependent on outside sources for agricultural implements, furniture, and wearing apparel. "Why is it," William H. Hardy, one of the leading promoters of the new faith asked, "that with boundless forests of Magnolia, Oak, Poplar, Cherry and Walnut, we send to other portions of the country for every piece of furniture manufactured from these woods? Why is it that every bucket, tub and broom, every ax, plow, hoe, chain, nail and stove is manufactured in some other portion of the country, and we deprived of untold millions of treasure afforded by these and other productions?" It was, Hardy answered, because of the practice of cultivating cotton to the exclusion of other economic enterprises, and until these goods were manufactured in the state the people would remain impoverished.[138] "We must produce

137. *Laws of Mississippi, 1876,* pp. 34, 264–65; *Journal of the House of Representatives of the State of Mississippi, 1878* (Jackson, 1878), 42–43, 110; Port Gibson (Miss.) *Southern Reveille,* August 18, 1877.

138. *Southern Field and Factory,* III (March, 1873), 98. For early expressions of the new faith in industrial progress, see the Aberdeen *Sunny South,* as reported in the New Orleans *Picayune,* November 25, 1865; Jackson *Clarion,* August 17, 1866, March 25, 1869; the Natchez *Courier,* as reported in the Forest *Register,* February 6, 1869; and the Vicksburg *Herald,* November 14, 21, December 1, 3, 1868.

everything we consume," carpetbagger Archie C. Fisk wrote, "and there will never be any money in the country nor any prosperity till we do."[139]

Governor Ames in his inaugural address expressed a similar concern, couching his remarks in a language remarkably similar to that of Henry W. Grady during the next decade. "With unlimited supplies of raw materials at our doors," he declared, "we send abroad for our farming implements, our household furniture, and the thousand and one articles used in daily life. The cotton we raised is returned to us as manufactured goods for which we pay, in addition to the cost of manufacture, the transportation to and fro, and the charges of the many agents through whose hands it passes. Mississippi might become an important manufacturing state if the people willed it. Capital and skill are necessary and will come if properly encouraged."[140]

A flurry of activity to give practical effect to the appeals for industrial establishments occurred in 1867 and again in 1870–1871. Throughout the state hopeful businessmen, politicians, and other prominent men formed associations and applied for charters for their enterprises. Most of these undertakings were designed to manufacture coarse cotton, woolen fabrics, or agricultural implements, such as plows, harnesses, and wagons. A Reconstruction innovation that later became significant was the establishment of five cottonseed oil mills, three of which owed their existence to the capital and energy of the northern colony in Vicksburg.[141]

In fact, transplanted Northerners, whether politician or businessman (or both like Alexander Warner), were active in many of the enterprises. In the case of the Canton Cotton Mill the local carpetbag hierarchy joined with a former secessionist congressman to make this textile enterprise one of the few successful ones in Mississippi.[142] Although some money to begin operations in the cotton mills was obtained locally, most of it was borrowed in New Orleans, Mobile, St. Louis, and Memphis. The depressed condi-

139. Vicksburg *Times and Republican*, February 19, 1873.

140. *Inaugural Address of Gov. Adelbert Ames to the Mississippi Legislature, Thursday, January 22, 1874* (Jackson, 1874), 7–8. For a similar analogy by another carpetbagger see the Jackson *Pilot*, May 26, 1871.

141. *Southern Field and Factory*, I (January, 1871), 28; I (February, 1871), 72–73; Vicksburg *Times and Republican*, November 18, 1871; Jackson *Pilot*, May 26, 1871.

142. *Southern Field and Factory*, I (February, 1871), 72–73; *Laws of Mississippi, 1870*, p. 189; Jackson *Pilot*, September 2, 1871.

tion of the regional economy and the tightness of the money and credit marts created high rates of interest (normally 18 percent on the loans). When economic conditions became especially severe, as during the winters of 1867–1868 and 1873–1874, credit could not be found on any terms for most of the enterprises and they consequently failed.

Henry B. Whitfield, the president of an ill-fated textile mill at Artesia, has left a woeful account of the difficulties of securing operating funds during the hard times of 1867–1868. "We are making as much, or more, money in proportion to quantity of yarns made than we ever have done since we commenced business," he wrote in December, 1867. "As cotton is low, and taxes may be taken off, we will not require much money to keep in supplies of raw material. In every department of our business we are doing well, but in order to continue, and do at all, it is evident we must have *working capital*. As to raising money in this country, that is out of the question. . . . Times are such that people who have money on hand seem fearful to invest it, though they may be satisfied [that] the business is paying well."[143] Whitfield, the scalawag son of an antebellum governor of Mississippi, attempted unsuccessfully to secure short-term loans in St. Louis and New Orleans. In March, 1868, he was forced to close the mill and seek a buyer for the machinery.[144]

Under the circumstances only a few of the proposed ventures materialized, and none prospered. Of the more than twenty textile companies chartered during Reconstruction only nine remained in business in 1880, producing goods valued at $691,415 annually.[145]

143. Henry B. Whitfield to "Cousin James," December 2, 1867, and Whitfield to S. L. Hahn, December 13, 1867, both in Whitfield and Company Papers.

144. Whitfield to James Hamilton, December 14, 1867, January 13, 14, 1868, and Whitfield to M. G. Perkins, March 5, 1868, *ibid*.

145. U.S. Bureau of the Census, *Tenth Census of the United States: 1880, Manufactures*, 141. Of the southern states, Mississippi was not alone in its efforts during Reconstruction to bring the cotton mills to the cotton fields. All of the southern states that attempted to develop a textile industry experienced difficulty in obtaining operating capital. Only in the South Atlantic states, where conditions were most conducive to the development of the industry, was this problem partly overcome and the foundations laid for the future expansion of the mills. E. Merton Coulter, *The South During Reconstruction, 1865–1877* (Baton Rouge, 1947), 268; Francis B. Simkins and Robert H. Woody, *South Carolina During Reconstruction* (Chapel Hill, 1932), 299; Richard L. Zuber, *North Carolina During Reconstruction* (Raleigh, 1969), 55.

The most successful, but still by no means prosperous, was Mississippi Mills, located at Wesson on the New Orleans railroad. Established by James M. Wesson immediately after the war, Mississippi Mills possessed more than one half of the spindles used in textile plants of the state during the period. By 1870 the company, now capitalized at $300,000, was employing 250 operatives and producing coarse textile and woolen fabrics valued at $153,401. Almost all of the goods were sold in the state, although a few shipments were made annually to the Midwest and New York.[146]

The problem of securing sufficient operating funds plagued Wesson from the beginning, and finally, in 1871, he was forced to sell the plant to a New Orleans firm. When the main buildings were destroyed by fire in 1873, the New Orleans company relinquished its control to a consortium of businessmen, most of whom were old citizens of the state. As the largest stockholder, Edmund Richardson, a merchant-planter and erstwhile lessee of the state penitentiary who was one of the few Mississippians to accumulate wealth during Reconstruction, became president of the company. With a source of working capital, Richardson quickly restored the productivity of the plant; by 1876 it had doubled its original capacity and was employing five hundred operatives. Mississippi Mills under Richardson's direction settled into the typical paternalistic pattern of southern textile plants during the New South era. Following the practice begun by Wesson, Richardson provided rent-free cottages for the workers, and he also employed children (above eleven years of age) and women to handle most of the tasks, compensating them at a rate of thirty to seventy-five cents per day.[147]

As in the case of the railroads, the financial difficulties involved in launching manufactory enterprises in Mississippi inspired efforts to obtain state encouragement and even direct assistance for such ventures. "There is no legislation that would benefit us so much as some action encouraging manufacturing interests," the Vicksburg *Times and Republican* announced. "They should be relieved for a

---

146. *Southern Field and Factory*, I (February, 1871), 72; Hazlehurst *Copiahan*, October 16, 1875; William Oliver to L. P. Reynolds, February 24, 1875, in Reynolds Papers; U.S. Bureau of the Census, *Ninth Census of the United States: 1870, Wealth and Industry*, 685.

147. *Southern Field and Factory*, I (April, 1871), 167; *Laws of Mississippi, 1871*, pp. 770–75; Beauregard and Wesson (Miss.) *Times*, March 19, 1874; Hazlehurst *Copiahan*, October 16, 1875; Jackson *Weekly Clarion*, May 16, 1883.

certain period from all taxation, and such other inducements should be offered, both public and private, as would induce their establishment here." This newspaper suggested a complicated method for granting tax exemptions for industries—one that would flank the constitutional provision requiring that all taxes be equal and uniform. Some conservatives also asked the legislature to grant a tax-exempt privilege to manufactories, and the Vicksburg *Evening News* even proposed that a state subsidy be given to new industries.[148]

With the blessing of Governor Powers, the legislature of 1872 ignored the constitutional prohibition against unequal taxation and approved a bill exempting from taxes for ten years all new cotton and woolen industries whose capitalization exceeded ten thousand dollars. Enacted by a Republican majority with only one conservative in the senate favoring it, the bill provided one safeguard for the state: whenever a company declared a 4 percent or more dividend it could no longer receive the exemption.[149] Since the law applied only to textile and woolen plants, promoters of industrial enterprise were not satisfied and continued their efforts to have other industries exempted. But not until 1882 did the legislature respond favorably to their entreaties by granting the ten-year tax exemption to all new manufactories.[150] Lacking mineral wealth, capital sources, and skilled personnel, in addition to being wedded to a colonial, agrarian way of life, Mississippi during the decades immediately following the war had little chance of developing the kind of balanced economy that would place it in the mainstream of the new industrial-commercial age in America.

---

148. Vicksburg *Times and Republican*, November 16 (quote), December 24, 1871, February 16, 1872. See also the issues of September 21, 1871, February 10, 11, 1872, and the Nåtchez *Weekly Democrat*, March 20, 1872.

149. Vicksburg *Times and Republican*, March 15, 1872; *Laws of Mississippi*, 1872, pp. 65–67.

150. Vicksburg *Times and Republican*, March 12, 1872; Albert D. Kirwan, *Revolt of the Rednecks, Mississippi Politics: 1876–1925* (New York, 1965), 43.

17

Country and Town
Life

The impact of the Civil War on Mississippi was shattering, but the everyday habits and patterns of living did not change dramatically during the decade that followed the surrender. People, however, had to adjust to having less of everything. For many the adjustment was painful; for some it was both painful and slow, and they frequently blamed their plight on the political changes produced by Republican reconstruction. An east Mississippian expressed the bitterness of those who refused to accommodate to postwar changes produced by defeat when he wrote in 1872: "Our people have lost their property, lost their government, lost their prestige, are aliens and strangers in the land of their fathers. They live under the government of those who hate them."[1]

Most old citizens, however, could not afford to remain bitter or repine for the past. Survival depended on planning for the future and working hard to obtain a meager return from the soil. The immediate past to these people was "the late unpleasantness," and during the first decade after the war they seemed willing to forget the disastrous events of secession and Civil War. The cult of the Lost Cause, if it ever possessed a controlling influence on southern behavior, certainly had not taken root in the minds of Mississippians during Reconstruction. Only an occasional appeal was made for the people to preserve the memory of the Confederacy. When the past was recalled, it was usually that of the early nineteenth century when such giants as David Holmes, George Poindexter, and Seargent S. Prentiss walked the land. Paeans on the territorial and early statehood periods, when life appeared simple and heroic, had greater appeal in postwar Mississippi than accounts of the rash events of the late antebellum era that terminated in the Civil War debacle.[2]

1. As reported in the Jackson *Weekly Clarion*, January 11, 1872.
2. John F. H. Claiborne's work during the 1870s on the early history of Mississippi, accompanied by an appeal to a number of survivors of that era for information and documents, contributed to the popularity of accounts of the golden age in the state's development. See the Claiborne Papers, University of North Carolina Library. In 1875–76 a

Diaries, correspondence, and private journals are replete with evidence of the difficulties of everyday life. Nevertheless, self-pitying complaints were infrequent, perhaps because most of these problems—the omnipresence of sickness and death, the vicissitudes of the agricultural economy, and the harshness of living in a semifrontier region where nature conspired against success—had existed before the war.[3] For most people life had traditionally been a struggle, and the difficulties of postwar adjustment seemed only a more severe form of the same. To be sure, the war-related losses that Mississippians had sustained were great, but a lifetime's experience in coping with the southern wilderness and climate and with the problems of race and security had conditioned them to uncertainty and hardship. The following expression of a river planter trapped in the devastating flood of 1874 typifies the fortitude and quiet determination of postwar Mississippians to overcome all obstacles. "I have been informed," he casually wrote a kinsman, "that we [are] about to be washed away. If so, it is certainly news to us. It will take 5 feet to stop us from planting, and 8 feet to make us pen the stock. Should we have 8 feet more water, we can get Mattingly Steam Tug and Coal Barge [Company] to move us for $50. . . . We fear no water, but rain."[4] Nonetheless, in contrast to their exuberant spirit before the war, Mississippians by the 1870s saw little hope for an early improvement in their status.

Despite the radical implications of the postwar political changes, the problems between landowners and blacks that created the greatest everyday difficulty were those associated with the labor system. Planters constantly expressed frustration with free labor, whereas blacks feared that they would be cheated in their labor contracts or placed in a work situation similar to slavery. Planter-labor relations had improved considerably by the 1870s, especially

---

series of articles, written by Claiborne, Albert Gallatin Brown, and scalawag G. S. Mc-Millan, appeared in the Jackson *Weekly Clarion* and other state newspapers recalling in a romantic fashion the careers of such distinguished early Mississippians as David Holmes, David O. Shattuck, and Hiram G. Runnels.

3. See especially the Agnew Diary, the Darden Diary, the voluminous Whitehurst Papers, the Pinson Family Papers, the John L. Power Papers in Mississippi Department of Archives and History, the Swanson and Yates Family Papers, the McWillie Family Papers, and Beaumont, *A Business Woman's Journal*.

4. Joe Swanson to Obedience Yates, April 9, 1874, in Swanson and Yates Family Papers.

in plantation districts where most blacks lived, but the daily vexation and disquietude of racial adjustment continued.[5] The fact that labor was at a premium in the plantation areas gave blacks a bargaining power with planters that they did not have elsewhere, and they fared better than Negro laborers in the nonplantation districts.

This higher standard of living, of course, existed only in a relative sense. Sometimes it meant little more for plantation blacks than having a steady diet of "fat-back," cornmeal, and molasses, whereas improvident Negroes of the hill and pine country were forced to "grub" and even steal to maintain an existence. But many plantation Negroes during relatively good years, as in 1869 and 1873, were able to improve their status, although in most cases the improvement was only temporary. In the Delta energetic black renters reportedly cleared two hundred dollars in years when spring floodings did not destroy the young plants and when the cotton market was good. The rental payment for land, which was usually ten dollars an acre, also entitled the black tenant to the use of a house, the wood on the land, hunting rights, and grazing for his stock in the nearby forest. A few Mississippi blacks after marketing a good crop were able to purchase a small homestead from demoralized white planters or farmers.[6] This condition, combined with their acquisition of political privileges, for a time provided Negroes with a measure of success suggesting to some sympathetic observers that blacks were indeed making progress under the umbrella of Republican political control. By the end of Reconstruction, however, all hopes of this kind had vanished, as the position of the former slave deteriorated into a condition of virtual peonage on the land.

As in slavery, blacks during Reconstruction experienced few of the amenities of white civilization, despite their general political and educational gains and the economic improvement realized by

5. Paramount concern with labor relations is clear in the following sources: Darden Diary, W. B. Jones and B. H. Smith Plantation Journal, in Mississippi Department of Archives and History, and Nicholson Diary-Journal. Though balanced with other matters, this concern is also evident in *Southern Field and Factory*, volumes I and II (1871–72).

6. *Southern Field and Factory*, III (February, 1873), 137; Charles Nordhoff, *The Cotton States in the Spring and Summer of 1875* (New York, 1965), 84; Somers, *Southern States Since the War*, 256–57 and Chap. IX.

some Negro farmers. They continued to occupy the lowest strata in society. Nevertheless, their freedom was real, and many of them were determined to exercise it in what they considered a meaningful fashion. The imposition of congressional reconstruction, as well as the growing planter awareness of the realities of free labor, provided blacks the necessary leverage to end the compulsory system of gang labor under the watchful eye of a white overseer or black driver, a system that had survived the war, particularly in the Delta. On large plantations black field laborers might still work in squads, but it was voluntary, usually under a leader of their own choice, and free of the coercive feature of the old method.[7] Agricultural productivity evidently declined after the system of direct white supervision was abandoned, but probably not nearly as much as planters claimed.

In an equally significant demonstration of freedom, which in many cases accompanied the end of coerced field labor, blacks moved away from the slave quarters near the big house and occupied distant cabins on the plantation or elsewhere in the community. This "segregation of quarters," as it was called, also gained the support of landlords who believed that the dispersal of cabins would encourage tenants to give more attention to their homes, thereby reducing the vice and immorality that appeared to whites to prevail in the close, unsupervised atmosphere of the old slave street.[8]

The impoverishment of most blacks dictated the kind of diversions they took from the monotony of everyday life. For Negro men and older boys, hunting became popular not only as a pastime but also as a necessary means to provide meat for the family table. Fishing, as during slavery days, continued to appeal to blacks of both sexes. Freed from compulsory labor in the fields, black women in their leisure activities sought to emulate their white counterparts, which meant spending a great deal of time "visiting" and attending church functions. The most excitement was generated by lavish picnics and barbecues. School commence-

7. Whitelaw Reid, *After the War: A Tour of the Southern States, 1865–1866* (New York, 1965), 485, 488, 500–501, 504, 572; Morgan, *Yazoo*, 98; Edward King, *The Great South*, ed. W. Magruder Drake and Robert R. Jones (Baton Rouge, 1972), 273.
8. Wharton, *The Negro in Mississippi*, 71; King, *The Great South*, 273.

ment exercises, "all-day" church services, and political rallies provided convenient settings for the picnics and barbecues that were
attended by hundreds and occasionally thousands of blacks.[9] It was
not unusual for a large number of whites to attend these affairs.
At one "grand barbecue" held in Rankin County in 1869 some
three hundred whites mixed with about twelve hundred blacks to
partake of the food and hear both Negro and conservative orators
proclaim the virtues of education and racial harmony. The speakers
avoided political topics. Blacks made the arrangements for the
Rankin barbecue, and apparently the only bow to the emerging
practice of racial segregation was the formation of separate serving
lines.[10]

As Reconstruction progressed town blacks turned increasingly to
social organizations for their diversions and also for mutual assistance in case of need. The Union Leagues provided a social and
political outlet for many, but these secret organizations declined
rapidly when the Republicans came to power in 1870. Introduced
at Vicksburg in 1867 by Thomas W. Stringer, Negro Masonry rapidly spread into the major towns of the state, and, though accused
of clandestine political activity, lodges remained remarkably free
of Reconstruction politics. Various benevolent societies, virtually
indistinguishable from the Masonic orders in their functions, became popular during the 1870s, providing fraternity as well as assistance to members during periods of personal tragedy. Volunteer
fire companies, which also emerged during the 1870s, functioned
more as social organizations than as a fire-fighting units, sponsoring
picnics, parades, dances, and train excursions to other towns.[11] All
of these organizations developed from white models; however, the
black emphasis on mutual aid in the benevolent and Masonic societies seemed stronger than that of their white counterparts and
reflected the stringent, but by no means demoralized, position of
black town dwellers.

Traditionally, church life has provided a major source of diversion for blacks, and the Reconstruction era was no exception. In

9. Wharton, *The Negro in Mississippi*, 269; Jackson *Weekly Pilot*, May 21, 1870;
Meridian *Semi-Weekly Gazette*, July 4, 16, 1867; Washington *New National Era*, July
31, 1873.
10. Jackson *Weekly Clarion*, September 2, 1869.
11. Wharton, *The Negro in Mississippi*, 270–71; Harris, "James Lynch," 43.

fact, the postwar period witnessed a resurgence of Negro interest in religion, accompanied by significant changes in black church practices. Almost immediately after the war freedmen began the familiar movement out of the white churches.[12] Blacks in the plantation districts seemed more anxious than those in predominantly white counties to break their ties with the old churches and form congregations of their own. The concentration of black minister-missionaries in the plantation counties (principally the river district) contributed significantly to this movement.

Once Negroes had established their own congregation, the church became an important center of family life. With only a hard existence to look forward to in this life, blacks, as they had done in slavery, flocked to hear ministers proclaim the glories of an afterlife when worldly troubles would be over. Primitive in every way, church congregations frequently assembled in open fields, under trees, or in improvised sheds. Before, during, and after the services—and more so than their white neighbors—black church-goers mingled in festive fellowship with one another. Protracted meetings often ran from three weeks to three months, much to the dismay of local planters who complained that such happenings disturbed labor conditions.[13]

Competition among the various denominations, including predominantly white ones, for black membership multiplied the roll of new churches and the list of communicants. "Every where in this State the people are ready to come to us," Presiding Elder James Lynch of the Northern Methodist Episcopal Church confidently wrote his superior in 1868. "Now is the time to plant our church in every county of the State." The Southern Methodist Church, Lynch complained, was already on the scene employing "the vilest democrat negroes in the state as their instruments" to establish black churches. At the same time the African Methodist Episcopal Church, though "professing to be radical in politics," was cooperating with the southern church in its efforts to exclude

12. Some blacks continued to attend white churches, and in other cases black and white congregations as late as 1870 shared the same white minister and the same building, although at a different time on Sundays. Entries for June 6, 1869, April 10, July 31, 1870, in Agnew Diary; Jesse Thomas Wallace, *A History of the Negroes of Mississippi from 1865 to 1890* (Clinton, Miss., 1927), 108–109.

13. Wharton, *The Negro in Mississippi*, 256, 263–64.

Lynch's organization from the Mississippi field.[14] When membership in the two black Methodist churches increased, mainly because of the activities of missionaries like Lynch and Stringer, the white leadership of the Southern church agreed in 1870 to sever its control of the Negro churches and permit the organization of a separate conference for blacks.[15]

While the Methodists were fighting among themselves for control of the black churches, the Baptists obtained the lion's share of the communicants. Independent of the white associations almost from the beginning, black Baptist churches sprang up like mushrooms during the postwar period. In Washington County alone, by 1870 one hundred Baptist churches had been established to serve plantation Negroes. Blacks were attracted to the Baptist denomination by its autonomous, congregational principle of government. By the end of Reconstruction most Negro adults proudly claimed membership in the Baptist church or in one of the Methodist denominations; only a scattering could be found in other Protestant denominations.[16] The moral and religious effect of black church membership and attendance, as with whites, fell short of the admonitions of Negro ministers, but it obviously provided freedmen with some relief from life's drudgery and semioppression.

Whites on the other hand found major sources of diversion from Reconstruction labors and uncertainties outside of the churches. Indeed, twentieth-century observers of Bible Belt religiosity would scarcely recognize postwar Mississippi society. Reports of "moral depravity" and "loose living" emanated from all areas of the state.[17] The Delta especially was reputed to be "a veritable Sodom" where "whiskey drinking, gambling and Sabbath-breaking were the common and prevailing sins of the country."[18]

The greatest cause for complaint was the easy availability and liberal consumption of alcoholic beverages by men of both races.

14. James Lynch to Matthew Simpson, December 3, 1868, in Simpson Papers.

15. Wharton, *The Negro in Mississippi*, 260–61.

16. *Ibid.*, 263; Jackson *Weekly Pilot*, November 12, 1870.

17. Jackson *Weekly Pilot*, June 25, September 24, 1870; Adelbert Ames to his wife, August 10, 1875, in Ames Blanche Butler (comp.), *Chronicles*, I, 131; Armistead Burwell, *Dramshops, Industry, and Taxes: An Address to the People of Mississippi* (New York, 1875), 1–2.

18. Moore, "Social and Economic Conditions in Mississippi During Reconstruction," 258–59.

Dramshops dotted the state after the war, and they were amply supplied by wholesale liquor dealers operating out of Vicksburg, New Orleans, and other commercial centers. In Vicksburg even merchants who dealt in plantation provisions advertised the availability in their stores of the best brands of liquor.[19] An east Mississippian attributed the pervasiveness of drinking in his area to an attempt by the people to drown their wartime and Reconstruction sorrows. "Parties who before the war never touched a drop are now quietly, surely gliding into drunkards' graves," he said.[20] The partaking of spirituous drink was so popular in Vicksburg that the *Herald* could openly recommend the soothing power of alcohol at Christmastide. "Christmas and frigid weather," the *Herald* announced, "makes one think of something warm, and fine old Jamaica rum, Scotch or Irish Whisky [are] an excellent antidote for all the complaints of the season."[21] Many evidently took the *Herald's* advice and indulged yearlong. State Attorney General Morris, a temperance advocate, estimated that in 1871 alone 600,000 gallons of liquor, valued at $2,700,000, were sold in the state through licensed establishments. He claimed that nine tenths of the cases that came before the state courts during the year resulted from the consumption of alcoholic beverages.[22]

Antiliquor forces did not permit this condition of affairs to continue without challenge. The financial distress of the people provided a certain urgency for imposing restraints on the purchase of alcohol with the hard-earned money available for each household. Numerous temperance societies were formed in Mississippi during the early 1870s to counter the evils of drink and specifically to work for local and state liquor regulation. Many Republicans sympathized with the antiliquor crusade, and several prominent members of the party joined with conservatives like George L. Potter and the Reverend Charles B. Galloway, the state's leading Southern Methodist, to agitate for temperance legislation.[23] In Vicks-

19. Natchez *Weekly Democrat*, November 30, 1870; Vicksburg *Herald*, November 4, 5, 1868.
20. Jackson *Weekly Clarion*, January 11, 1872.
21. Vicksburg *Herald*, December 19, 1868.
22. Vicksburg *Times and Republican*, February 8, 1872.
23. *Ibid.*, January 7, 1872; Vicksburg *Times*, March 29, April 1, 1874; Jackson *Weekly Pilot*, October 22, 1870; Natchez *Weekly Democrat*, May 3, 1871; entry for July 24, 1871, in Agnew Diary. An antiliquor monthly, the *Temperance Banner*, began publication at Jackson in 1874 with Galloway as editor.

burg the enthusiastic support for temperance reform by some Republicans damaged the party's standing among the "foreign" element of the town.[24]

The crusade for legislation regulating the sale of liquor bore no significant fruit until Ames became governor in 1874. A native of Maine, the first state to adopt a strong temperance law, this much-maligned carpetbagger actually preferred an outright prohibition of the sale and consumption of alcoholic spirits.[25] Although naïve in some matters, Ames recognized the will-o'-the-wisp character of prohibition sentiment; instead, as a practical alternative he pressed for and secured the passage of a local option law regulating the sale of beverages. This measure, which the conservative Aberdeen *Examiner* hailed as "the best enactment of the kind that is to be found upon the statute books of any State in the Union," provided that a liquor dealer must secure a petition signed by a majority of both the women and the local voters before he could obtain a license to do business.[26] In the senate, conservatives provided the temperance forces with the margin of victory for the bill. Nine of the eleven conservatives in that body joined with ten Republicans to pass the measure, whereas thirteen members of Ames's party voted against it.[27]

The role of women in the regulation of alcohol was not missed by aroused liquor dealers whose propaganda efforts to secure the law's repeal consisted mainly of ridiculing the assertiveness of the fair sex on this and other public issues. Himself an opponent of political rights for women, Governor Ames nonetheless refused to be intimidated by the sexist campaign against the law. Indeed, he declared that "one of the finest features of the law is its recognition of the voice of the women of the State. It recognizes their equal ability with male counterparts." The local option bill, he reminded

24. Vicksburg *Times and Republican*, March 13, 1872.
25. R. B. Avery to Ames, April 3, 1874, in Governors' Correspondence, Vol. 92; *House Journal, 1874*, p. 764. Ames was not alone in desiring an end to the sale of alcoholic beverages. The Vicksburg scalawag Armistead Burwell worked for a law that would prohibit the sale of liquor in the state. Burwell, *Dramshops, Industry, and Taxes*, 24.
26. The quote and the substance of the law are given in the Vicksburg *Times*, May 2, 1874. Ames also banned all alcoholic beverages, including wine, from the governor's mansion, initiating perhaps the first dry period in the mansion's history. *Ibid.*, April 9, 1874. Actually, the temperance movement had antebellum antecedents. The legislature of 1854, in response to a growing demand, passed a local option measure, which, however, proved ineffective. McLemore (ed.), *History of Mississippi*, I, 438–39.
27. *Senate Journal, 1874*, pp. 502–503.

the people, was enacted "to meet a gigantic evil which overshadowed the land, and incited violence and crime." Alcoholism had "filled our jails and Penitentiary with its deluded victims; entailed upon the State burdens and taxation, to an incredible amount, to meet the expenses of Courts and prisons; and carried desolation and grief, sorrow and want to thousands of households."[28]

The effects of the local option law were mixed. A number of small towns and villages in the interior acted immediately to deprive dramshop operators of their licenses until they could meet the requirements of the new law—which appeared unlikely in view of the hostility of most women to the sale of hard liquor. In the river counties and along the Gulf Coast the sale of spirits continued as if the law had not been passed and despite increasing pressure from local temperance societies for authorities to close the dramshops. A concerned Ames asked the legislature for a more stringent measure to ban the alcohol trade where it was not wanted. The Republican legislature ignored his appeal and, instead, succumbed to the pressure of the liquor lobby and the antifeminists in the state and repealed the local option law. The governor, however, vetoed the repeal bill, an action that was narrowly sustained by the legislature.[29] In defending their support of repeal, several legislators of moderate antiliquor sentiments insisted that they had done so only because local option could not be enforced. To demonstrate their good faith to the temperance cause, these lawmakers joined with antiliquor stalwarts in the legislature to impose a 2 percent tax on all whiskey sales and to increase the annual license fee for dramshops.[30]

The roll-call vote in the house of representatives on the repeal of local option indicated clearly that despite the implacable political divisions existing in the state, the issue of hard liquor was not viewed as a party matter. Republicans and conservatives in the legislature were about evenly divided on the repeal question.[31] Although Ames had become the bête noire to Democrats, the Carrollton *Conservative* even in the year of revolution against Repub-

28. *House Journal, 1875*, pp. 321–22.
29. Burwell, *Dramshops, Industry, and Taxes*, 12; *Annual Message of Governor Ames, 1875*, p. 7; *House Journal, 1875*, pp. 322–23.
30. Jackson *Weekly Pilot*, February 20, 1875.
31. *House Journal, 1875*, pp. 322–23. See also H. J. Harris to Ames, April 9, 1874, and R. B. Hussey to Ames, April 24, 1874, both in Governors' Correspondence, Vol. 97.

lican authority could still applaud his antiliquor efforts, declaring, "The governor deserves the hearty and sincere thanks of the people for forwarding the cause of Temperance in our State."[32]

The Redeemer legislature of 1876 repealed the local option law, although bills continued to be enacted banning alcohol in communities that petitioned for such action. These requests, however, were few until the revival of the temperance movement during the 1880s. Even Ames, during the last weeks of his administration, admitted the failure of local option and the quixotic nature of the effort to restrict by statute the sale of hard liquor. Nevertheless, the temperance crusade that had begun during the early 1870s, partly as a result of the reformist zeal of Republicans like Ames, brought public opinion to bear on the problem and caused a noticeable decline in the consumption of ardent spirits in Mississippi.[33] Furthermore, the temperance crusade served as a forerunner for the more successful prohibition movement of the last two decades of the century.

Although many Mississippians demonstrated a special fondness for the bottle, most people during Reconstruction found less troubling forms of diversion. Frontier customs such as logrollings (in which neighbors assisted in clearing land for cultivation), house-raisings, cornhuskings, and quilting parties continued into the postwar period. These practices, however, faded rapidly under the force of social change, the penetration of the interior by the railroad, and the renewed emphasis on familial cooperation instead of community-inspired activities. The popular equestrian sports of the antebellum period, principally horseracing and medieval style tournaments, also faded in significance during Reconstruction, mainly because of the wartime destruction of horses and the gentry's straitened circumstances.[34] Tournaments evidently ceased to be held after 1868, and only rarely during the postwar period did horses race before enthusiastic spectators.[35]

32. As reported in the Jackson *Weekly Pilot*, February 27, 1875.

33. *Laws of Mississippi, 1876*, pp. 38, 369–84; Travis Rhodes to C. A. Sullivan, February 8, 1876, in Combined Letterbook of Governors Ames and Stone; Natchez *Democrat*, October 3, 1875, April 25, 1876; William M. Compton, *The Influence of Alcohol* (N. p., 1877), 29–30.

34. Natchez *Democrat*, December 25, 1874.

35. Moore, "Social and Economic Conditions in Mississippi During Reconstruction," 300–301.

In a land where panthers, wolves, wildcats, and deer still roamed extensively, particularly in the Delta and the piney woods, the traditional sport of hunting remained popular. Reminiscences by old-timers of past encounters with panthers and catamounts (wildcats or lynx) furnished a thrilling and sometimes frightening subject for numerous nighttime tales on the porches of Mississippi homes during Reconstruction and after. The appearance in 1876 of a "tiger" (probably a jaguar) near Handsboro spawned a whole series of critter stories, exciting the imagination of boys and scaring the womenfolk.[36]

Like blacks, white farmers and planters enjoyed barbecues and picnics, which were frequently sponsored by political parties, churches, and volunteer fire departments in the towns. Picnics became standard fare for Grange rallies after the introduction of the order in 1871. The political strife of the Reconstruction era did nothing to dampen the enthusiasm for such social gatherings. On the eve of the revolutionary political campaign of 1875 a large railroad excursion of Grangers to the picnic grounds at Magnolia attracted three thousand people from a ten-county area.[37] Organizers of a temperance barbecue at Guntown in 1871 laid a table of food and drink (of the soft variety, of course) that extended for one quarter of a mile. At most of these gatherings fellowship and food were usually spiced with lengthy speeches—the topics varying according to the sponsoring organization—baseball games, and watermelon cuttings when in season.[38]

Baseball emerged during Reconstruction as the most popular sport in Mississippi, a distinction it would hold until the advent of the football mania in the mid-twentieth century. Introduced by Union troops during the war, baseball suited the competitive, outdoor spirit of the people. It also suited their straitened financial condition, since the game was inexpensive to play. The sport enjoyed its initial success in the Natchez-Jackson-Vicksburg triangle. Although there is no evidence that federal soldiers played with

36. Jackson *Weekly Clarion,* April 1, 1869; Natchez *Democrat,* February 16, March 31, 1876.

37. Vicksburg *Times,* August 26, 1869; Jackson *Weekly Pilot,* May 7, 1870; Jackson *Weekly Clarion,* August 11, 1875.

38. Entries for June 24, July 24, 1871, in Agnew Diary; Jackson *Weekly Clarion,* August 11, 1875.

civilians during the war, in 1867, when more than two thousand troops were sent to Mississippi to enforce the reconstruction laws, teams from military posts contested local clubs consisting of many Confederate veterans. An excursion to another town on a palatial steamboat like the *Natchez* was enough to inspire interest in baseball for many prospective ballplayers and fans. In 1870 the Hope Club of Vicksburg won the first state baseball championship when it defeated the Osyka team by a score of 78 to 41. But championships could be quickly lost in those days; another team could snatch the honor simply by defeating the champions in a single game. Immediately after the Hope Club players had won their victory, the carpetbag editor of the Jackson *Pilot* urged the men and boys of his town "to rub up their armor, or their bats, and give them a trial."[39]

By twentieth-century standards town life in Reconstruction Mississippi was lackluster. A variety of activities, however, provided important and frequently uplifting diversions for townsmen and their country neighbors. This was especially true in the two largest towns, Vicksburg and Natchez, whose locations on the Mississippi made them easily accessible to theatrical troupes and other traveling performers. The war had scarcely ended when the theater in Vicksburg was reportedly "in full blast," presenting both Shakespearean and contemporary plays.[40] The expansion and renovation of Apollo Hall in 1868 was designed to take advantage of the growing popularity of the theater in the Mississippi Valley as well as to attract first-rate troupes to the town. In addition to theater, an opera company of "world-renowned" performers visited Vicksburg in December, 1868, and played to full houses in Apollo Hall. During the same month "Emma," a black teenage pianist, performed before a large audience in the hall. Minstrels, European gymnasts, and circuses also visited Vicksburg during the late 1860s and attracted impressive crowds.[41]

The golden age of entertainment in Vicksburg, however, was

39. Vicksburg *Herald*, August 27, 1868; Natchez *Weekly Democrat*, July 12, September 27, 1871; Jackson *Weekly Pilot*, August 5, 1870.

40. Moore, "Social and Economic Conditions in Mississippi During Reconstruction," 291–92.

41. Vicksburg *Herald*, September 9, October 27, November 19, December 1, 2, 6, 17, 20, 23, 31, 1868.

short-lived. The commercial decline of the town, the continuation
of hard times in the valley, and to some extent the town's growing
reputation for violence and corruption virtually closed the doors of
Apollo Hall and other entertainment houses during the early
1870s. Unable to obtain adequate financial guarantees for performances in the town, circuses and minstrel shows now rarely appeared in Vicksburg, although in 1875 troupes showed a renewed
interest. While theatrical interest in Vicksburg was declining,
Natchez, Columbus, Aberdeen, and Jackson, which had not experienced an early postwar success with theater, were able to attract traveling companies.[42]

Because of the hard times, townsmen increasingly turned to
local talent for theatrical productions and other forms of entertainment. In addition to Vicksburg, dramatic associations were formed
in Natchez, Jackson, and even small towns like Port Gibson, Pascagoula, and McComb City. Concerts, using local musicians, became popular during the 1870s, although in normally sedate
Natchez the newspaper complained that "this is the only city in the
civilized world where men and boys are allowed to whistle and yell
indiscriminately, and without discretion, at public concerts."[43] A
mania for tableaux, usually accompanied by music and sometimes
dancing, swept the state during Reconstruction, providing still another alternative to expensive forms of entertainment for town
dwellers; even in small northeastern communities like Gunston,
where public amusements were almost nonexistent, tableau performances were held. After expenses were paid, revenues from the
modest charges for tickets to the various performances usually
went to local charities.[44]

Both town dwellers and country folk on the Mississippi were
frequently treated to the excitement of a steamboat race. These
sporting events, which could easily end in disaster for the passengers and crew, often occurred on the spur of the moment when
captains of rival packets, docked at the same landing, challenged

42. Natchez *Democrat*, December 3, 1874, June 13, 1875; Jackson *Weekly Pilot*, January
30, April 10, 1875.
43. Jackson *Clarion*, December 5, 1867; Pascagoula *Star*, issues of May, 1875; Natchez *Weekly Democrat*, February 8, 1871 (quote); Natchez *Democrat*, January 18, 1876.
44. Pascagoula *Star*, January 25, 1874; Natchez *Democrat*, January 29, 1876; entry for
August 29, 1868, in Agnew Diary; Vicksburg *Herald*, December 29, 1868.

each other to a race. Well-publicized in advance, the famous race from New Orleans to St. Louis between the *Natchez* and the *Robert E. Lee* in July, 1870, attracted thousands of Mississippians to the riverbank to cheer their favorite to victory. At Vicksburg the excitement of the race was punctuated by the firing of cannons when the steamboats passed the bluffs; at other places bonfires lit up the sky at night to herald the passing of the river giants.[45]

The most popular form of amusement for town dwellers was the festival. These affairs took a variety of forms, but they usually included a parade, featuring the various religious, benevolent, and social societies in the town, speeches of a nonpolitical nature, and a grand ball at night. Volunteer fire departments frequently sponsored the festivals, and companies would normally invite firemen from other towns, including New Orleans, to join in the festivities and compete in fire-fighting contests. A festival in Jackson in 1870 concluded with friendly speeches by Governor Alcorn, Lieutenant Governor Powers, Edward Stafford of the *Pilot*, and conservatives Amos R. Johnston and Charles E. Hooker.

In February, 1875, Natchez town fathers introduced Mardi Gras into Mississippi. Admittedly designed to attract customers to the languishing stores of the town, the Mardi Gras celebration became an immediate success, although not of the magnitude of the all-week New Orleans gala. An elaborate parade on Mardi Gras Day followed the arrival of Rex on "the Royal Steamer," and the festivities continued into the night with dancing and the popping of champagne corks at a ball sponsored by the Italian Society of Natchez. The festival attracted an even larger crowd in 1876, establishing Mardi Gras as a regular event in Natchez. Not to be outdone by its rival to the south, Vicksburg initiated plans for a Mardi Gras celebration as the Reconstruction era came to an end.[46]

Residents of most towns found few amusements outside of ordinary social intercourse. The economic doldrums that settled over these communities during Reconstruction, broken only occasionally by a mild upturn in the commerce of agriculture, predetermined a relatively dull existence. Despite the sanguine pronouncements

---

45. Jackson *Weekly Clarion*, July 7, 1870; Coulter, *The South During Reconstruction*, 302–303. The *Robert E. Lee* won the race.

46. Natchez *Democrat*, February 10, 1875, February 1, 24, March 1, 2, 1876.

of local promoters, few towns, including those with excellent railroad connections, prospered during the 1870s. Even Meridian, which soon after the war appeared destined to become the leading railroad center in the state, experienced a slowdown in its rate of growth, increasing only from a population of 2,709 in 1870 to 4,008 in 1880. A black visitor to Meridian in 1875 reported that although he found the people cheerful, "every thing seems dull, dusty and dry. Merchants are lounging around their doors in shirtsleeves, seemingly too indifferent to invite a customer in. . . . There are no signs of a revival of trade, and it seems that every body, who can, is anxious to get away." He blamed this sad state of affairs on the 1871 racial riot which had "placed a death-like hand upon this once promising town."[47] Probably a more important reason for the failure of Meridian to realize its potential was the continuing agricultural depression in its hinterland and the failure to complete a railroad connection with New Orleans.

The emergence of the new political order did not make the state capital into a thriving governmental center. No new public buildings were constructed in Jackson during Reconstruction, and the facilities of the town were hard-pressed to accommodate lawmakers and lobbyists when the legislature was in session. Jackson boasted of two small, second-rate hotels, both of which were near the railroad and a long walking distance from the capitol. The problem of distance was partially relieved during the early 1870s by the establishment of a horse-drawn street railway, which followed a route from the railroad depot to the capitol. The managers of this company, the first streetcar line in Jackson, included prominent carpetbaggers as well as businessmen of the town. As with most Mississippi towns of any size, Jackson was lighted by gas during Reconstruction. But improved lighting did not appreciably affect nighttime social life. Visiting the town in the spring of 1874, journalist Edward King found Jackson a pretty, "quiet, unambitious village of five or six thousand inhabitants." He reported that the evenings in town were "wonderfully beautiful, silent, impressive. Reaching Jackson from Vicksburg at dark, I strolled along the half-mile of street between the hotel and the business centre of the

47. As reported in the Vicksburg *Plain Dealer*, June 11, 1875.

town; there was no stir—no sound; one might as well have been in a wood." King also discovered "many charming drives in the town; a little beyond it, the roads are rough and the country is wild."[48]

Corinth, the leading center in northeast Mississippi, also presented a sluggish appearance to travelers. L. J. Dupree, a visitor in 1873, found Corinth the "perfect picture of a southern village and country life." Here on Saturdays, he reported, "we find the countryman in . . . homespun, fresh from the plow-handles, sunburnt, yellow haired and hard handed, indulging in his one-a-week sugar and whiskey." On the Saturday he visited Corinth he observed that the streets were crowded, and there were "ten negroes to one white man sauntering in the hot sunbeams and loitering about the dramshops." Dupree reported that the people of the town "move about lazily. They drag their feet and drawl out their words and stare listlessly at a stranger." The horses even appeared listless as they stood "with heads swinging below their knees and with one hind foot lifted, their lazy bodies rest[ing] upon the other three. Laziness is in the very air one breathes. . . . The town grows, but lazily. There are houses begun and never finished. The owners are too lazy."[49]

The great exception that travelers found to inertia-ridden Mississippi towns like Meridian, Jackson, and Corinth was Natchez. A Virginian temporarily employed on a nearby Louisiana plantation found life in Natchez in 1867 "quite a relief from the general oppression and doubt that renders every respectable person in this region unhappy and troubled about the future." Specifically, he reported, "Natchez has been quite gay in weddings and parties, the most of which I have attended and enjoyed very much." A party given at the Marshall's "reminded every one of former times," although in the faces of the guests "there was a tinge of gloom [and] those inexpressible traces of bereavement, loss, and mute suffering which will never be known to the world."[50]

48. Jackson *Weekly Clarion*, May 6, 1869; Jackson *Weekly Pilot*, January 29, February 12, 1870; Natchez *Weekly Democrat*, May 24, 1871; *Laws of Mississippi, 1870*, pp. 588–60; King, *The Great South*, 314, 316.

49. Cited in Moore, "Economic and Social Conditions in Mississippi During Reconstruction," 331–32.

50. John F. King to Lin Caperton, May 7, 24, 1867, in Thomas B. King Papers, Southern Historical Collection, University of North Carolina Library, Chapel Hill.

Even Blanche Butler Ames, the young wife of Adelbert Ames and the daughter of Benjamin F. Butler, who was usually contemptuous of Mississippi society, reluctantly admitted on a visit to Natchez that "this place redeemed the South in my eyes. Not that it is so beautiful, but it shows me that this state possesses more capabilities than I had given it credit for. Here the roadside is edged with turf, and the streets are shaded with graceful china trees. . . . The houses in and about the city are large ungainly structures, but betoken former prosperity and care."[51]

Other visitors to Natchez, a town of nine thousand people, expressed unqualified praise for the air of quiet beauty that it exuded. A Jewish visitor enthusiastically reported in 1871:

> I have traveled considerably through the South, and I may safely assert that Natchez is the handsomest city of its size in the Southern States. The streets are laid out with beautiful regularity, and are bordered with shady trees, which give a delightful appearance to the city. There are numerous splendid residences, each house having a considerable piece of ground attached, which is generally laid out as a garden and planted with sweet-smelling shrubs and flowers. . . . A large and extensive business is annually transacted here, and the stores and warehouses are truly fine structures.

He also found that Jewish-managed commercial houses were "among the most reliable and enterprising firms in the city."[52]

An English woman, en route to Woodville to assume control of her deceased husband's business, also believed that Natchez was "one of the most beautiful of Southern cities." She was especially attracted to the bluff area of the town, which was laid out as a public park for the enjoyment of the citizens. The view from the park, she wrote, was "exceedingly fine and extensive—the busy life at the foot of the bluffs, the great Mississippi rolling on in silent majesty, and, on the opposite shore, the green Parish of Concordia, with its beautiful lake gleaming like a sheet of silver in the distance."[53] None of these visitors, including Blanche Ames, described the Negro shanties in Natchez which, as in most Mis-

51. Entry for November 20, 1870, Journal of Blanche Butler Ames, in Blanche Butler Ames (comp.), *Chronicles*, I, 217.
52. Natchez *Weekly Democrat*, September 20, 1871, quoting the *Israelite*.
53. Beaumont, *A Business Woman's Journal*, 258–59.

sissippi communities, ringed the town, nor did they report the difficulties that black residents experienced in competing with whites for the few available jobs.

Sojourners also failed to describe the fear of disease that lurked in the minds of many townsmen, especially those in river communities like Natchez. Although sickness seemed omnipresent on the farms and plantations, it was an even greater threat in the towns where tropical fevers, cholera, and smallpox spread rapidly once the disease had struck. Black ghettoes were especially susceptible to smallpox and cholera. Cholera outbreaks reached epidemic proportions in 1866–1867 and again in 1873; otherwise the periodic visits of the disease created only mild distress in the Negro communities during Reconstruction.[54] The scourge for both races, however, was "Yellow Jack," or yellow fever, although whites believed that Negroes were largely immune to it. Memories of the deadly attack of 1853 when 750 died in the Natchez area were enough to cause consternation along the Mississippi at the first report of an outbreak. Fear quickly turned to panic when the death toll began to mount. Interior settlements did not normally suffer from yellow fever; however, people in the regions adjacent to the lowlands constantly worried that epidemics would spill over into their communities.[55]

During Reconstruction two yellow fever epidemics afflicted the state. In the early fall of 1871 the scourge struck Natchez and Vicksburg, claiming 148 lives before it had run its course. For two months, while the fever raged in Natchez, the harder hit of the two towns, life virtually stood still and businessmen lost heavily, since planters and farmers refused to bring their cotton crops to town to "settle up" their accounts. Then, in 1875, the yellow terror enveloped the Gulf Coast, killing an undetermined number of people. The epidemics of the Reconstruction period were mild, however, compared to the one of 1878 which struck hard in the interior as

54. Moore, "Social and Economic Conditions in Mississippi During Reconstruction," 345–46.

55. D. Clayton James, *Antebellum Natchez* (Baton Rouge, 1968), 267; *Report of the Mississippi State Board of Health, for the Years 1878–79* (Jackson, 1879), 77; Natchez *Weekly Democrat*, October and November issues, 1871; A. L. Hardeman to Bettie Stuart, October 13, 1867, in Dimitry Papers.

well as along the Mississippi and on the Gulf Coast, claiming more than 3,000 lives and leaving a number of towns in social and economic disarray.[56]

The fear of epidemic diseases like Yellow Jack and smallpox increased interest during Reconstruction in the formation of a professional state medical association and public medical boards with regulatory authority. A Mississippi State Medical Association had been organized before the war, but it did not begin to meet on a regular basis until 1869. Under the leadership of Dr. William M. Compton, superintendent of the state insane asylum and erstwhile scalawag, crusaders for improved health care lobbied the legislature during the 1870s for the creation of a state board of health. Their efforts did not bear fruit until the Redeemers assumed control of Mississippi. An advisory body in the beginning, the board of health after the deadly epidemic of 1878 was granted broad authority to study and take measures to prevent the spread of communicable diseases in the state.[57]

Following antebellum precedents, community boards of health were established in Natchez and Vicksburg during Reconstruction. Their activities mainly involved immunizing the citizenry against smallpox and formulating and maintaining sanitary standards. Vicksburg provided free smallpox vaccinations for its residents, but less than one in twenty blacks, who experienced a far higher incidence rate than whites, took advantage of the service even when the threat of an epidemic occurred in 1873.[58] Dominated by carpetbagger George St. Clair Hussey, the Natchez board was reasonably successful in maintaining sanitary conditions. The Vicksburg board on the other hand achieved very little, and the members charged that city officials, including the health officer, had refused to cooperate with them. As a result of this negligence "the city was allowed to lapse back into the same unwholesome condition in which we found it," the board reported in 1875. These conditions

56. Natchez *Weekly Democrat*, November 29, 1871; Pascagoula *Star*, September 11, 1875; Ernest Hartenstein, *The Epidemic of 1878 and Its Homeopathic Treatment: A General History of the Origins, Progress, and End of the Plague in the Mississippi Valley* (New Orleans, 1879), 31–34; *Report of the State Board of Health*, 4–5.

57. Newspaper sketch of the life of Dr. William M. Compton, in Craig Papers; Natchez *Weekly Democrat*, October 23, 1871; McLemore (ed.), *History of Mississippi*, II, 516–17.

58. Vicksburg *Times and Republican*, January 28, February 19, 1873.

included "imperfect sewerage, gutters and ditches clogged with filth and debris, decaying animal and vegetable matter, thrown upon the streets to laden the air with its putrescence; [and] stagnant pools of water to be found in many portions of the city, converted into hogwallows by swine which roam at large."[59]

The predominantly agrarian nature of the state, the semifrontier condition of much of the interior, and the impecunious lot of the people discouraged the development of intellectual and literary activities in Mississippi after the war. To some degree, political debates, church and school programs, Grange meetings, and theatrical performances stimulated intellectual interests. But for those persons who wanted greater breadth, there were few libraries worthy of the name that could supply them with reading materials. Of the 537 "public" libraries listed by the census takers of 1870, 523 were Sunday school and church reading rooms, bare of everything but church and biblical materials. Only two towns could boast of a public library, with combined holdings of 1,000 volumes. In addition, the state operated a small 7,000-volume library in the capitol. Although not easily accessible, there were 2,251 private libraries, containing 400,106 volumes, in the state. Only Vicksburg appears to have had a bookstore where a variety of reading materials could be purchased.[60] The society of enlightenment and knowledge that carpetbaggers and other Republicans hoped to create could hardly be developed with the dearth of sources for study and intellectual growth that existed in Mississippi during Reconstruction.

But intellectual activity in postwar Mississippi was by no means nonexistent. Interest in poetry, mostly of a melancholy kind, was particularly strong. Aspiring poets flooded local newspapers with poor and middling poetry, much of which was accepted uncritically for publication. The postwar period, however, produced four poets of some distinction. William Ward, a transplanted New Englander who has been judged by critics to be the best Mississippi poet of the nineteenth century, wrote most of his poetry during Recon-

59. Natchez *Weekly Democrat*, March 3, 1870; *Laws of Mississippi, 1870*, p. 354; Vicksburg *Vicksburger*, September 8, 1874 (quote).
60. *Compendium of the Ninth Census*, 506; Vicksburg *Herald*, October 25, 1868.

struction while serving as the editor of the Macon *Beacon*.[61] In 1878 S. Newton Berryhill, a Bourbon activist in Reconstruction politics, published *Backwood Poems*, a collection composed over a period of two decades. His verses breathed the spirit of the rugged interior and expressed the aspirations and prejudices of the area's yeoman whites. One of his most significant poems was a diatribe against Radical rule.[62]

Few young poets in the Reconstruction South possessed the talent and promise of Irwin Russell of Port Gibson. A master of Negro dialect, he contributed regularly to *Scribner's Monthly* and other northern magazines. Russell's best-known poem, "Christmas Night in the Quarter," was published in *Scribner's* in 1878, one year before his death at the age of twenty-five.[63] Another young postwar poet of considerable talent was Eliza Nicholson, who wrote under the name of Pearl Rivers. Raised in the lonely pine country of south Mississippi, Pearl Rivers began to write poetry at the age of fourteen, during the Civil War. A pensive and sensitive girl, she contributed poems regularly to the New Orleans *Picayune*, beginning in 1870. She soon moved to the Crescent City and in 1872 married the proprietor of the *Picayune*. A collection of her poems published the following year, the best of them dealing with her piney woods experience, drew praise from a host of critics, including the poet Paul Hamilton Hayne who reputedly was the leading literary critic in the South after the war.[64]

Perhaps Mississippi's most outstanding writer of fiction until the emergence of William Faulkner was Sherwood Bonner of Holly Springs. Born in 1849, the daughter of a physician of considerable refinement, Bonner published her first story in the *Boston Ploughman* during the war. This was followed by other contributions to northern literary journals, most of the stories treating southern themes. During the early 1870s she went to Boston to further her writing career and to provide a source of income for her hard-

61. Dabney Lipscomb, "William Ward," *Publications of the Mississippi Historical Society*, II (1899), 23–42.

62. S. Newton Berryhill, *Backwoods Poems* (Columbus, Miss., 1878). See pages 99–100 for his bitter anti-Republican poem.

63. McLemore (ed.), *History of Mississippi*, I, 636–37; Coulter, *The South During Reconstruction*, 280.

64. *Dictionary of American Biography*, XIII, 499; Coulter, *The South During Reconstruction*, 282, 283.

pressed family. In Boston she met Henry Wadsworth Longfellow and soon became his secretary and collaborator in his "Poems of Places, Southern States." A warm friendship developed between the two, and Longfellow encouraged her to pursue a literary career. The great poet on one occasion referred to her as the "American writer of the future." In 1878 her most outstanding work —and her only novel—was published by Harper and Brothers. Entitled *Like Unto Like*, the novel is set in the Reconstruction South and abounds in dialect and local color. The book received high praise from both northern and southern critics, and the demand for her future writings soared. But before she could achieve the literary greatness that Longfellow and others had predicted for her, Sherwood Bonner was struck down by cancer, dying at Holly Springs in 1883 at the age of thirty-four.[65]

After the war the historian John F. H. Claiborne, who had previously published two books, continued his labor on behalf of Clio. A man of some wealth even during Reconstruction (as a Unionist, he had profited during the war by selling cotton in Federally occupied New Orleans), Claiborne in 1871 arranged his plantation affairs so he could devote the remainder of his life to collecting documents and writing a history of Mississippi.[66] In 1880 he published the first volume, which told the story of the settlement and early history of the state.[67] Claiborne's second volume, dealing with the sectional conflict, Civil War, and Reconstruction, was in manuscript form when on March 2, 1884, fire swept his plantation home, "Dunbarton," near Natchez, destroying the work and most of the documents he had collected for it, including several valuable journals and diaries of Alcorn.[68] Two months after this devastating fire, Claiborne died.

The destruction of the part of Claiborne's manuscript dealing

65. Edwin A. Alderman, *et al.* (eds.), *Library of Southern Literature* (16 vols.; Atlanta, 1907–13), I, 439–45; McLemore (ed.), *History of Mississippi*, I, 636.

66. John F. H. Claiborne to William N. Whitehurst, November 15, 1866, January 7, 1871, in Whitehurst Papers.

67. John F. H. Claiborne, *Mississippi, as a Province, Territory and State, with Biographical Notices of Eminent Citizens* (Jackson, 1880). This book was reprinted in 1964.

68. James Lusk Alcorn to William H. McCardle, November 17, 1890, in McCardle Papers. Claiborne also had a home near Bay St. Louis, where he spent most of his time after the war. From here he contributed numerous articles to Gulf Coast newspapers during Reconstruction. Natchez *Weekly Democrat*, November 8, 1871, July 31, 1872; Jackson *Weekly Clarion*, July 24, 1873.

with Reconstruction was a tragic loss for historians. Because of his sympathy for the Republican program of equal rights and political tolerance in the South, it is reasonable to assume that his unpublished account drastically departed from the orthodox view of the Reconstruction period, a distorted view that by the 1880s had already become an article of faith, even in the North. If so, Claiborne's interpretation of the postwar era predated by more than four decades the twentieth-century revisionist accounts of the period.

The written word in postwar Mississippi received its most popular expression in the local newspapers. Because of the general impoverishment of the people, cheap local newspapers were more important than ever as sources of news and molders of public opinion. On the eve of the Civil War approximately 41 newspapers were published in the state, and they competed in circulation with national publications.[69] After the war subscriptions to outside newspapers and periodicals declined, and the burden of keeping Mississippians informed, or frequently misinformed, fell almost exclusively to local journals. For an annual fee of three hundred dollars, the Associated Press, a northern news-gathering agency, supplied the larger state papers with dispatches. In addition, local newspapers often copied articles and editorials from national papers that reflected their own editorial policies. The number of local journals increased substantially during Reconstruction, especially during the first five years after the war. From a low of 14 at the end of the conflict, the ranks of these journals grew to 111 in 1870, with a circulation of 71,868, and 118 in 1880.[70]

There were few towns of any size that did not have at least one weekly newspaper. Many of them operated on a shoestring, and many soon vanished. Neither literary nor journalistic standards were raised by these sheets, although some were reasonably well edited. A number of villages with populations of less than five hundred could claim newspapers whose permanence and influence reached beyond their boundaries. The Carrollton *Conservative*, the Pascagoula *Star*, the Fayette *Chronicle*, and the Raymond *Hinds*

69. McLemore (ed.), *History of Mississippi*, I, 419.
70. *Ibid.*, 539; Moore, "Economic and Social Conditions in Mississippi During Reconstruction," 365, 368; *Compendium of the Tenth Census*, 1628.

County Gazette, all published in rural hamlets of less than five hundred people, were reasonably well-edited journals of considerable prestige in the state. Since almost all of the newspapers served a political purpose, during the early 1870s most county seats where the parties were competitive possessed a Republican and a Democratic journal. The larger towns, notably Natchez, Vicksburg, and Jackson, frequently sustained more than two newspapers, and at one time, in 1875, six journals were published in Jackson alone. In such cases, the newspapers usually reflected the viewpoints of divergent wings of the two parties. In Jackson, for example, the *True Democrat*, a Bourbon paper, arose to contest the New Departure views of the *Clarion*, whereas the *Times*, a moderate Republican journal, moved from Vicksburg in 1875 to challenge the Radical *Pilot*. The other two Jackson newspapers in 1875, the *Farmers' Vindicator* (Grange) and the *Sunburst* (Irish-American), both claimed to be politically independent, but actually they expressed strong conservative sentiments.[71]

Although few newspapers prospered, Republican sheets found survival especially difficult. The major barriers to their success were the high illiteracy rate among blacks and the inability of many who could read to pay the subscription price. As a means of promoting the party locally, proprietors of Republican newspapers adopted the policy of distributing hundreds of free copies to blacks. And though financially disastrous, this practice had a remarkable effect in rallying blacks to the Republican standard. In 1872 carpetbagger John B. Raymond, the proprietor of two Republican journals, wrote that experience had taught him that not one in two hundred blacks would see a party newspaper if they had to pay for it, but "if they can get the paper free they will read or have read every word in it." Blacks "consider every word published in a republican paper almost law, and every paper taken on a plantation is better than a dozen speakers."[72]

The financial problems of the Republican press were compounded by the reluctance of merchants to advertise in the journals. Businessmen avoided Republican newspapers not so much because

71. Jackson *Weekly Pilot*, April 10, 1875.
72. John B. Raymond to O. C. French, August 3, 1872, in William E. Chandler Papers. See also O. J. Lee and J. F. Jordan to William E. Chandler, August 18, 1872, *ibid*.

they feared a white boycott of their establishments, but mainly because advertisements in these journals reached fewer potential customers than those in the conservative press. Nevertheless, the Vicksburg *Times and Republican* and the Jackson *Pilot*, the two leading Republican sheets in Mississippi, attained a circulation in the western part of the state in 1870–1871 that impelled many merchants to advertise their wares in these newspapers.[73]

In the final analysis, the survival of most Republican journals depended upon their success in obtaining the fairly lucrative privilege of printing legal advertisements. When the Republicans came to power in 1870 public printing flowed to the party newspapers, increasing their number from four in early 1868 to twenty in 1871 (only one of which was edited by a black Republican). But Governor Alcorn's successful veto of the bill requiring that legal advertisements be printed in "loyal" newspapers shattered Republican dreams for a strong press in the state. By 1872 the number of party sheets had dwindled to ten.[74] A renewal of hope occurred in 1874 when the legislature, with the approval of Governor Ames, passed a printing bill similar to the one that Alcorn had vetoed. The hour was late, however, for the establishment of a viable Republican press. The fast approaching conservative revolution would wash away all but one of the Republican newspapers.[75]

Whatever the party, editors held a position in Mississippi society that made them the constant focus of public attention. In the antebellum tradition, they felt a special responsibility to attack their opponents and exaggerate the virtues of their friends, distinctions that usually followed party lines. Ridicule and derision were the common literary weapons of these editors, some of whom were hardly skilled in the use of the English language, much less in the tools of clever political satire. Carpetbaggers, who virtually

73. Jackson *Weekly Pilot*, June 18, 1870; Vicksburg *Times and Republican*, July 24, 1870, September 24, October 28, 1871. In fact, the editors of the *Times and Republican*, one of three dailies in Mississippi at the time, claimed that their newspaper had a larger circulation than any other journal in the state and that in the river counties its circulation was twice that of its nearest competitor. Issue of March 31, 1872.

74. Friar's Point *Weekly Delta*, January 19, 1870; Natchez *Weekly Democrat*, August 7, 1872. Requests for financial assistance from the national Republican party fell on deaf ears. O. C. French to William E. Chandler, August 6, 1872, in William E. Chandler Papers.

75. *Laws of Mississippi, 1874*, pp. 65–67.

monopolized the Republican press in the state, fell into the same journalistic pits as their conservative opponents. While serving briefly as the editor of the Jackson *Pilot*, carpetbagger A. W. Webber went so far as to justify publicly the use of rumor and falsehood to discredit an adversary. In political matters, he declared, it is "justifiable to use any piece of scandal against a public man as though it were a portion of God's truth—and even to use it when known to be utterly false."[76]

Because of their penchant for excess, editors lived dangerously. A holdover from the antebellum period, "pugilistic journalism," or the resort to the knife or pistol to settle delicate editorial disputes, continued after the war. Nevertheless—and despite the editorial bombast and invective that appeared stronger during Reconstruction than before the war—fewer postwar "misunderstandings" actually resulted in physical violence. Numerous challenges were issued, and sparring between opponents short of engagement occurred. On one occasion, for example, A. J. Frantz of the conservative Brandon *Republican* and the editor of the Jackson *Pilot* agreed to meet on the main street of the capital, but purposely at different corners. Only two armed encounters during Reconstruction ended in the death of an editor, both of these occurring in March, 1875. At West Point, Democratic editor D. L. Love of the *Citizen* killed Republican L. H. Middleton of the *Times*, after Middleton accused him of climbing the flagpole at the courthouse to observe the ladies of the D'Este theatrical troupe in their dressing room. The second fatality was also related to the appearance of the D'Este company. A few days after the West Point affair the troupe's performance in Aberdeen elicited some disparaging remarks from editor M. R. Scullen of the *True Republican*. An aggrieved actor immediately sought out Scullen and shot him in the streets. The incidents, however, produced some good. Shocked by the killings over such petty matters, editors throughout the state denounced the resort to "pugilistic journalism" and called on their colleagues to exercise self-restraint in their columns as well as in the streets. Even Barksdale, who had earlier unsuccessfully challenged State Attorney General Morris to a duel, decried the violent deaths of the two

76. Jackson *Weekly Pilot*, December 10, 1870.

editors and indicated his support for a campaign to end the "vicious custom" of encounters between antagonistic editors.[77]

Ironically, in daily social intercourse some of the most invective editors were mild-mannered and amiable to friends and adversaries alike. Both Frantz and McCardle, the most vitriolic Bourbon editors in the state, were noted for their good humor and civility in public, even when meeting and conversing with Republicans. The hero of the "Mighty East" before the war, the diminutive Frantz seemed always to retain a smiling disposition and also a well-stocked cellar, which reputedly contained the best vintage of France.[78] But his editorials rarely reflected any concern for common social amenities or for the truth concerning his political opponents, who included conservatives as well as "the horde of carpet-bag thieves and ignorant negroes who have plundered and taxed the people" without mercy.[79] Like other editors whose careers spanned the turbulent decades of sectional conflict, Frantz and McCardle usually avoided the frequent challenges to confrontations in the streets, which often were accompanied by considerable abuse since their foes took advantage of their known reluctance to fight.[80]

Conservative newspaper editors filled the leadership vacuum that existed when the politicians became divided and disorganized by the course of Reconstruction events and the Republican hegemony. Several, like George W. Harper and Hernando D. Money, entered the political lists and became successful candidates for

77. *Ibid.*, March 27, April 17, 1875; Pascagoula *Star*, April 10, June 5, 1875; Jackson *Weekly Clarion*, March 31, 1875.

78. Henry, *Editors I Have Known*, 33–34.

79. As quoted in the Vicksburg *Times and Republican*, September 25, 1873.

80. For example, the following challenge, which McCardle ignored, appeared in the Vicksburg *Times and Republican* (as reported in the Jackson *Pilot*, June 21, 1871).

CARD.

To the Hon. Mayor and Aldermen of the City of Vicksburg:

Gentlemen—I ask for information as to what time will the lunatic asylum be in operation, for we have some lunatics running at large and we don't feel safe. Among the dangerous ones is W. H. McCardle, the grand old woman of the age, whom no one fears, but don't like to hear the cry of old age, and as he is running at large I feel it my duty to inform the citizens that he will hurt no one—but his noise is horrible, and the place for such a thing must soon be prepared. God send the time when he may look through the checkered gates of a lunatic asylum or jail.

Ben Allen.

P.S. I can be found any hour on Washington street.

office. Most editors preferred, however, to stay on the sidelines and use the columns of their newspaper to influence the masses and control party conventions. They also appeared at political rallies and made their influence felt. Heading this category of journalists was Barksdale who at this time earned the epithet "the Warwick of Mississippi politics."[81] Some editors became quite arrogant in the exercise of their influence and impatient with politicians who stood in their way. Alexander G. Horn, the Bourbon editor of the Meridian *Mercury*, expressed this attitude clearly when he wrote during the late Reconstruction period that newspapers "should be the masters, not the bootlicks of politicians. Let newspapers boldly cry aloud and spare not, and turn the whore of Expediency out of doors. Let us have no fornicating with the Radical Party, under the idea of begetting a 'new South,' but let us nail our colors to the mast, and stand by them like men. Nothing else will save us."[82]

It was Bourbon editors like Horn, Frantz, and McCardle who kept white Mississippians alive to the supposed villainies of Republican rule and who led the fight to unite conservatives under a militant white-line banner. Their efforts to arouse the white masses intensified in 1874 and climaxed in the bitter political campaign and election of 1875 that shook the social order to its roots and overthrew Republican rule in Mississippi. The influence of the newspapers, which included the full spectrum of conservatism, was at no time during the postwar era more powerful than in the struggle to "redeem" the state from Radical rule.

81. For an appraisal of Barksdale's influence by a contemporary editor see Henry, *Editors I Have Known*, 92–93.
82. As quoted in Hodding Carter, *Their Words Were Bullets: The Southern Press in War, Reconstruction, and Peace* (Athens, 1969), 43–44.

18

The Radical
Ascendancy

Thirty-eight-year-old Adelbert Ames took the oath of office as Mississippi's third Republican governor on January 22, 1874, two days after the legislature, dominated by his supporters, convened. In his inaugural address Ames sought to allay fears that his administration would, as many conservatives believed, institute a reign of radicalism for the benefit of blacks and carpetbag adventurers. He denied that he would act mainly for the Negroes of the state and announced that one of the highest goals of his administration would be to remove "all causes of distrust, real or imaginary, which may exist between the different classes of our citizens." The new governor admitted that blacks as a class "are uneducated and poor; but this is their misfortune rather than their fault." He reminded whites that the former slaves had been "as quiet, orderly and law-abiding as the same number of any class of people in other states." He declared that blacks in the legislature though "greatly influencing if not controlling legislation . . . have never forgotten, in securing their own rights, to guard with jealous care the rights of others."[1]

He specifically denigrated the Bourbon charge that the Radical ascendancy would trigger a war between the blacks and whites. "I speak the sentiment of the Republican party when I say it would deplore any and all controversies based upon race or color. . . . A war of the races is as improbable as it would be wicked." Ames asserted that "in all things save politics the two races are as closely united as are people of the same surroundings elsewhere. In business relations and the intercourse of daily life there is mutual confidence and friendship. There should be no cause for division, much less for war, if the same freedom of thought and action claimed by the one race for itself be accorded to the other. The colored people ask nothing in charity—they demand but their

1. *Inaugural Address of Governor Ames*, 4.

rights."[2] He revealed no plan, however, for guaranteeing the enjoyment of these rights or the enforcement of the ineffectual civil rights law of 1873. Moreover, he ignored the plank in the state Republican platform of 1873 calling for the integration of the public schools. Actually, Ames and his white associates in the legislature had lost much of their radical idealism in the fiery furnace of Reconstruction politics and intraparty squabbles. Their radicalism was now more directed toward preserving the new order and placing the state firmly in the hands of their faction rather than advancing any new program for the elevation of the black race. Conservatives evidently recognized this fact about the Ames administration, since during the next two years they rarely charged the Radicals with promoting "social equality" in the state.

On an issue that was becoming increasingly important to many people, the burden of heavy taxation, Ames promised in his inaugural address to institute a "rigid economy and a strict accountability" in the expenditure of public funds. The carpetbag governor, sensitive to constant charges that his party had tolerated corruptionists in office, declared that where malfeasance was suspected he would see that it was "mercilessly investigated, let the consequences of exposure fall upon whom they may." In closing, he invited "all good citizens to join" him in his efforts to establish "an economical, impartial and liberal administration of the laws."[3]

On February 7 Ames sent a financial message to the legislature outlining a program for curtailing the burgeoning expenses of the government. He recommended an immediate end to the pernicious warrant system and the institution of the cash (currency) system for meeting state obligations. "By a return to a cash basis at least twenty-five per cent in the cost of government can be saved, which would be equivalent to the reduction of our present expenses of some $300,000," he confidently informed the legislature.[4] To ad-

2. *Ibid.*, 4–5.

3. *Ibid.*, 8. Privately, the new governor promised "to lift my administration above suspicion, that even my late opponents shall be obliged to admit that Mississippi is far more fortunate under my rule than South Carolina or Louisiana." As reported in the New York *Times*, March 23, 1874.

4. *Special Message of Gov. Adelbert Ames, to the Legislature of the State of Mississippi, on the Subject of Finance, Session of 1874* (Jackson, 1874), 2.

vance the cause of retrenchment he called for a brief legislative session and also reductions in appropriations for Alcorn University —though not for the all-white University of Mississippi—and in the expenses of county superintendents of education. Finally, Ames asked for a law that would equalize property assessments, since under the locally controlled Reconstruction system "the same classes of property are returned at widely different valuations, even from contiguous counties, where there is actually no difference in their values." Such a reform, he said, would substantially increase public revenues.[5]

Widespread praise for the new governor greeted his expressions of support for financial reform and his promise to work for racial peace and honest government. Although his messages ignored the rising demand for curtailment in judiciary and public printing expenses, which outgoing State Auditor Henry Musgrove declared a fiscal necessity, conservatives breathed a sigh of relief and concluded that the governor would protect the people from "the iniquities of Radical legislation" and the ascendancy of "hungry political cormorants whose only idea is a division of the spoils of office." The Pascagoula *Star* said, "We don't expect Gov. Ames to turn Democrat, but we do hope to see him put down corrupt rings and to refuse to reward vice and ignorance with office merely because they have the assurance to claim it as Republicans."[6] Albert Gallatin Brown announced that he viewed "with great satisfaction" the retrenchment course that Ames had staked out for his administration, and he advised Mississippians to cooperate fully with the governor in his policies to bring the state out of "the mire of financial ruin and social despondence."[7] Even some Bourbons admitted that Ames had launched his administration on a good note. Horn of the Meridian *Mercury* believed that the carpetbag governor's messages represented a "declaration of war against corruption and extravagance."[8]

5. *Ibid.*, 3–4.
6. Pascagoula *Star*, February 1, 1874.
7. Jackson *Weekly Clarion*, February 12, 1874.
8. As reported in *ibid.* See also the Vicksburg *Times and Republican*, January 24, 1874, J. D. Barton to Adelbert Ames, February 27, 1874, in Governors' Correspondence, Vol. 91, and Blanche Butler Ames to her mother, February 13, 1874, in Blanche Butler Ames (comp.), *Chronicles*, I, 651.

Conservative expressions of friendliness toward the new administration were not merely a facade of goodwill toward a despised government that could not be ignored. A new economic crisis gripped Mississippi in early 1874, and the Ames administration offered the only immediate hope for relief. Although the difficulty was not fundamentally political, governmental policies, especially in the realm of taxation and finance, had a direct effect on the people's ability to cope with the hard times. The price of cotton dropped to fifteen cents a pound on the New Orleans exchange, almost exactly the market price of the staple during earlier winters of distress. In addition, the nationwide Panic of 1873 accentuated the difficulties Mississippians encountered in obtaining credit for the necessities of life. As an indicator of the financial pinch, the total capital of the eleven small banks in the state in 1874 fell to less than one million dollars, and none of these banks held a privileged national banking charter.[9]

Reports of distress emanated from all parts of the state. According to an east Mississippian, money and credit in his section were "almost obsolete" and property was reduced to one fourth of its normal value because of the depression. Suffering in the area was great, he said, and the future appeared bleak.[10] Another resident of the east recorded in his diary the somber situation faced by his neighbors: "Mrs. Ellen Nelson is out of meat and can get none for love or money. The Nelson renters are all out, Mrs. Goven on Uncle Joe's place has none. There is great distress in the county: many have no money to pay taxes or debts. [They have] no provisions to support and no credit to help them, and few friends willing or able to aid. I never saw such a time, and the worst I fear is not yet come."[11]

The river counties fared no better in the crisis of early 1874. Journalist Edward King reported from the Natchez area in March that stories of trouble and affliction on plantations were rife.[12] From Vicksburg, the *Times* observed that all groups and occupa-

9. Boyle, *Cotton and the New Orleans Cotton Exchange*, 180–81; Pascagoula *Star*, January 11, 1874; Jackson *Weekly Clarion*, November 6, 20, 1873; *Appleton's Annual Cyclopaedia*, 1874, p. 575.
10. Pascagoula *Star*, January 11, 1874.
11. Entry for January 22, 1874, in Agnew Diary.
12. King, *The Great South*, 302.

tions felt the financial pinch, and all had lost confidence in their ability to recover soon. And from Jackson, lawyer James Z. George, who would lead the conservatives in the campaign of 1875, told Lamar that he did not have time to write lengthy letters, since he was kept busy eking out a meager income for the support of his family. At the same time, he complained, he had "to meet the inexorable demands of the taxation" imposed by "the meanest and most corrupt government that ever existed in a civilized country!"[13] Even efficient Delta planters like Civil War Governor Charles Clark were hard pressed to secure credit and provisions for the year.[14] When recovery did not occur in the alluvial bottoms, a planter reported: "Bankruptcy and ruin seems inevitable, and only those who can get away have any chance to repair their losses."[15] This planter revealed that he had every intention of abandoning the lowlands, but the man who had promised to buy his land could not secure the money to purchase it.

At the bottom of the economic structure, blacks suffered worst when financial crises occurred during Reconstruction—and the one of 1874 was no exception. Unable to obtain provisions on credit, many interior blacks, like their counterparts in Alabama and Georgia, were forced to move to the inhospitable river counties in search of work and accommodations for the year.[16] A new wave of crime, characterized mainly by petty thievery, cotton stealing, and arson, swept the state as the hard times lingered and many of the lower classes became desperate in their efforts to make ends meet. Incidents of rape against white women were widely reported, creating the greatest consternation among whites. By late 1874 these reports and rumors probably owed as much to the intensification of political and racial tensions as they did to the distress created by the economic crisis. The vicious justice of Judge Lynch was revived for suspected rapists.[17] After one

13. Vicksburg *Times*, May 25, 1874; James Z. George to L. Q. C. Lamar, April 15, 1874, in Lamar-Mayes Papers.
14. Franklin A. Montgomery to Charles Clark, May 12, 1874, in Clark Papers.
15. C. L. Hardeman to John C. Burrus, December 11, 1875, in Burrus Papers.
16. Vicksburg *Times and Republican*, November 16, 1873; J. D. Penn to Ames, January 30, 1874, in Governors' Correspondence, Vol. 91.
17. Greenville *Times*, September 5, 1874; Pascagoula *Star*, August 29, November 21, 1874; Natchez *Democrat*, November 29, 1874, September 30, 1875; Jackson *Weekly Clarion*, October 1, 8, 1874, January 26, May 31, 1876; Jackson *Pilot*, July 29, 1875.

incident of rape the influential Jackson *Clarion* revengefully cried out in approval of the quick resort to vigilante justice, "Let the common law of this hideous crime be hanging, shooting, burning, drawing, or quartering after a ten minutes' trial before Judge Lynch."[18]

As before, the worst effects of the economic crisis were overcome with the harvesting of vegetable gardens during the late spring and summer and the increased yields from grains in the fall. But the winter of 1874–1875, though not as severe as the previous one, again strained the ability of the people to secure adequate provisions and promises of credit for the coming year.[19] In contrast to their reaction to earlier Reconstruction recessions, conservatives—and many Republicans—by this time had virtually ceased to speculate on the economic reasons for their chronic difficulties and were focusing their criticism on the Radical regime's failure to provide tax relief and financial reform. The chorus of criticism was also inspired by increasing reports of looseness and corruption in the handling of public funds by local officials.

Reform Republicans, many of whom had opposed Ames in the election of 1873, viewed affairs at this time with a special sense of political urgency. Surveying the tragic decline of the party in other southern states, these Republicans warned the Radical leadership that their state would go the way of the others unless economy in government was "fearlessly applied." The race issue, they claimed, was no longer the central issue dividing the parties in Mississippi; it had been superceded by the need for an honest, competent, and economical administration of the state and local governments. These Republicans argued that a strong commitment to reform and retrenchment by Mississippi Republicans would not only preserve the party's power, but it also would rally white support to the organization. The hour was not too late, they said, to achieve a true and lasting biracial party in Mississippi. They pointed out that even Ames had marveled at the number of whites who had supported him in the last campaign, despite his radical image. Furthermore, a conservative editor had admitted that "Democrats, hitherto recognized as rigid partisans, are every

18. Jackson *Weekly Clarion*, July 14, 1875.
19. *Annual Message of Governor Ames, 1875*, p. 9.

day being seen venturing out on territory of Republican acquisition."[20] The accession to the party of Harris Barksdale, the son of Ethelbert, was hailed by hopeful moderates as a major triumph for their strategy to build a reform, white-based party in the state. Even if a large number of white converts to the party did not materialize, a Republican policy of retrenchment and reform, these Republicans insisted, would lessen political tensions and keep the conservatives divided, thus continuing their incapacity to do harm.[21]

When the new legislature met in early 1874, it seemed willing to act on the plea of Governor Ames and reform Republicans for improvements in the system of state finance and property assessment. The legislature quickly approved Ames's recommendation for an end to the warrant system of meeting state obligations. Since the old warrants, along with Alcorn's certificates of indebtedness, required funding in order to retire them, the new policy added to the state debt of $1,614,332. Even so, the experiment did not last long enough to prove or disprove Ames's contention that a return to the currency system of finance would reduce the ordinary expenses of the government by 25 percent. In 1875 the legislature, short of cash and desperate to find a means to meet the operating expenses of the government, overrode the Ames veto of a bill restoring the warrant system.[22]

Ames hoped to increase state revenues—and thereby reduce the need for warrants—simply by equalizing property assessments for tax purposes. He proposed the creation of a state board of equalization to undertake the task, a recommendation that the legislature of 1874 approved. The creation of the board, which consisted of the seven elected state officers, immediately raised a storm of protest. The conservative press referred to it as "the crowning iniquity" of the Republican regime, since it would centralize an important function of government in the hands of a

20. Water Valley *Mississippi Central*, July 4, 1874.

21. The columns of the Vicksburg *Times* for January-March, 1874, are full of reform appeals and political suggestions of this kind, contributed by the carpetbag editors of the newspaper as well as by Republican correspondents. For specific comments on the importance of Harris Barksdale's affiliation with the party, see *ibid.*, April 1, 2, 1874.

22. *Laws of Mississippi, 1874*, pp. 7–13; *Annual Message of Governor Ames, 1875*, p. 6; *House Journal, 1875*, p. 447.

few Radical leaders at the capital. "Why should such power be vested in State officers," George W. Harper rhetorically asked, "when they are particularly interested in a high rate of taxation, and would profit by wholesale confiscation?" The carpetbag editor of the Vicksburg *Times* also expressed alarm that the act of the legislature conferred upon the board of equalization "a power of a most extra-ordinary if not dangerous character." Furthermore, he complained, the law in effect repealed the ceiling on local tax levies imposed by the legislature during the Powers period.[23]

Despite these forebodings, the state board of equalization refrained from making radical changes in county assessments. Only two changes involved an increase of more than 15 percent in the local assessments, and several of the board's decisions provided for reduced property evaluations. Significantly, the board did not tackle the tangled skein of real estate assessments; it limited its actions to personalty, although the legislature had given it the authority to rule on both kinds of property. After 1874 the board seldom met, and when the Redeemers came to power in 1876 it was abolished.[24]

However faulty the system of assessments might have been, including reports that in many cases assessments exceeded the market value of the property, the real difficulty in increasing state revenues was not in the evaluation of property for tax purposes.[25] The fundamental problem was the failure of land generally to produce the necessary income to pay the taxes imposed by the legislature and local authorities. When property holders failed to meet these levies, their lands were forfeited to the state and taxes suspended on the property. This in turn reduced tax revenues and put additional pressure on the property that had not been seized for taxes. The amount of tax-forfeited property increased substantially during Reconstruction. By the end of 1874 about one fifth of the entire land area of Mississippi was in the hands of public

23. *Hinds County Gazette*, April 8, 1874; Vicksburg *Times*, March 24, 1874. See also the Pascagoula *Star*, March 28, 1874, and the protest of conservative and moderate Republican members of the senate in *Senate Journal, 1874*, pp. 360–61.

24. Minutes of the State Board of Equalization, 1874–75, especially the minutes for October 2, 10, 1874; *Laws of Mississippi, 1876*, p. 37.

25. "Petition and Appeal of the Tax-payers to the Legislature," printed in the Jackson *Weekly Clarion*, January 7, 1875.

authorities, and the proportion rose during 1875.[26] Many of these lands were the most productive in the state during normal times. Despite appeals from both Republicans and conservatives for legislation to abate delinquent taxes and return forfeited lands to their owners, and thus to the tax rolls, the Ames administration made no move in this direction in 1874.

Ames and the Radical legislature also ignored appeals for substantial reductions in state expenditures. Radicals in the legislature specifically rejected bills designed to reduce the excessive costs of the judiciary, which at approximately $250,000 per year was by far the largest item of expense in the state budget. The legislature not only refused to cut the expense of public printing, as a number of reform Republicans had urged, it increased these costs by establishing an elaborate system of legal publishing for the chancery court districts of the state.[27] In view of the straitened circumstances of the taxpayers, reform Republicans proposed a reduction in public salaries, especially for judicial officers, and also a cut in the appropriations for the state institutions. A bill reducing the salaries of circuit judges, chancellors, and district attorneys passed the legislature, only to be vetoed by Ames because it was too searing. Finally, an attempt to cut appropriations to the state institutions met a silent death.[28]

At the same time the carpetbag governor acted vigorously to recapture for the state the college land-grant fund from the Vicksburg and Nashville Railroad, but neither the legislature nor the Republican state supreme court would sustain him.[29] On the other hand Ames provided little encouragement to an investigation of the shady Pearl River Improvement and Navigation Company, which was in the process of defrauding the state of thousands of acres of swamplands along the Pearl River. Chartered in 1871 ostensibly "to render the stream navigable for ordinary steam craft," the Pearl River enterprise was actually another postwar

26. State auditor's report for 1874 in *House Journal, 1875*, Appendix, 40; *Annual Report of the Auditor, 1875*, p. vi; Jackson *Weekly Clarion*, January 19, 1876.
27. Vicksburg *Times*, February 15, 20, 22, March 28, April 19, 1874; *Laws of Mississippi, 1874*, pp. 65–67. The chancery districts were conterminous with the counties.
28. *House Journal, 1874*, pp. 694–95; Vicksburg *Times*, February 15, 1874.
29. See Chap. 16 herein.

land-grab scheme.[30] This one was concocted by midwestern speculators who were interested in securing valuable timberlands in the piney woods in exchange for a promise to make navigation improvements on the Pearl River.

The Pearl River group shrewdly selected O. C. French and Alexander Warner, the two most powerful carpetbaggers in the legislature, as their Mississippi connections. At first Warner was persuaded that the company fully intended to invest in deepening and widening the channel of the river, and he believed that the virtual donation of state lands to the entrepreneurs was a small price to pay for improvements that would benefit the public interest. The company, however, failed to comply with the terms of its charter, and in 1873 it sold 130,000 acres of the land to a Michigan lumber syndicate without paying the state the twenty-five cents per acre that the agreement required. When the legislature met in 1874, reform Republicans, as well as conservatives, demanded an investigation of the whole enterprise. Now alive to the fraud involved and fearful of an investigation that might reveal his role in the scheme, Senator Warner introduced a bill to secure the immediate repeal of the charter. Legislators who had not been involved insisted on an investigation, which, however, was aborted when the legislature adjourned.[31] While the issue raged, Governor Ames seemed indifferent to it all, probably because he was reluctant to encourage conservative charges of wrongdoing against Warner and French, both of whom were members of his inner circle of friends. Although they received no more state lands from the Republicans, it was not until the Redeemers took the reins of government that the Pearl River speculators lost their charter.[32]

As the economic and social crisis of 1874 closed in on the state, Ames, although evidently sympathetic to the plight of the poor, rejected an active role in aiding the victims of the hard times. Like many Americans of the nineteenth century, he believed that governmental authority to provide material aid for the sufferers of an economic depression was limited. On constitutional grounds

30. *Laws of Mississippi, 1871*, pp. 482–86; *Laws of Mississippi, 1873*, pp. 120–23.
31. *Mississippi in 1875*, I, 326; Vicksburg *Times*, March 13, 14, 15, 26, 1874.
32. Natchez *Democrat*, January 20, 1876; *Laws of Mississippi, 1878*, p. 447.

he successfully vetoed a proposal postponing the payment of debts until a more propitious time, a solution advanced by a number of leading conservatives and Republicans. He also rejected a bipartisan measure passed by the legislature that would repeal the controversial crop lien act of 1867, which provided legal protection to merchants who furnished supplies to impecunious farmers. The carpetbag governor's objection to the repeal bill was more practical than constitutional; he believed that because of the hard times poor laborers would not be able to obtain provisions for the year unless the state continued to protect merchant liens on ungrown crops.[33]

Despite this negative view of the role of government in economic crises, Ames made a vigorous effort to aid the victims of a ravaging flood that swept the river counties in the spring of 1874. When the flood appeared suddenly in April, breaking the makeshift levees at several places in the Delta, reports reached Jackson of great distress in many of the counties, compounding the difficulties that already existed there because of the general economic depression. Blacks in the Delta especially suffered, although most of the victims were able to find refuge in nonflooded areas or in the hill country.[34] "Along the river counties of this State there exists a state of destitution that is fearful to contemplate," a group of Vicksburg citizens reported to Ames. "The waters are increasing, and provisions becoming scarce. Already hundreds are flocking to [Vicksburg] for relief, and thousands of others have not the means to extricate themselves from their perilous situations, being huddled together on the highest eminences, with their stock drowned and provisions exhausted. Immediate starvation is inevitable if speedy help is not rendered."[35]

From Beulah, Charles Clark reported that at the height of the flood more than two thirds of the plantations of Bolivar County were flooded and food was unavailable, since "the merchants are refusing to advance supplies even to those who have been punctual

33. *Senate Journal, Called Session, 1874*, p. 20; Jackson *Weekly Clarion*, November 20, 1873, March 19, April 9, 1874.

34. Vicksburg *Times*, May 21, 1874; George F. Brown to Ames, April 28, 1874, and Fred Barrett to Ames, April 29, 1874, both in Governors' Correspondence, Vol. 92.

35. Minutes of a citizens' meeting in Vicksburg, April 28, 1874, in Governors' Correspondence, Vol. 92.

customers." From Natchez, black leader William H. Lynch informed Ames that at Dead Man's Bend one thousand Negroes were "in a destitute and starving condition on account of the overflow."[36] Another correspondent revealed that "parched corn is the only food on several of the places, & it is a common sight to see a whole family feeding on it. . . . Private property in cows and hogs has ceased to be, and many are subsisting upon such stock as they can find regardless of ownership. [If] this state of affairs exists much longer it is sad to contemplate what the starving 'swampers' might be driven to do." In Jefferson County some black tenants in order to survive slaughtered the planters' livestock, then notified them of their action.[37] These correspondents, as well as others, beseeched the governor to organize an emergency relief campaign for the river counties.

Since the legislature was not in session to appropriate state funds for relief, Ames had to find other sources of aid. He obtained some rations and clothing from the state Grange and outside relief committees, which were also involved in providing aid for flooded areas in other states. His main hope for assistance, however, rested with the federal government.[38] The governor early wired the Mississippi delegation in Congress, informing them of the seriousness of the situation and requesting federal aid for 25,000 uprooted people.[39] But when a bill providing $160,000 for flood victims reached the floor of the Senate, Alcorn attacked it as extravagant and unnecessary. The scalawag senator, whose own plantations had escaped serious flooding, claimed that Ames had exaggerated the situation for political reasons. Alcorn's opposition to federal aid for the flood-stricken area seems to have been primarily motivated by his belief that the political position of his rival and the Radical wing of the party would be strengthened by the success of the governor's efforts to obtain shipments of rations and clothing for the predominantly black river counties. Alcorn also took the op-

36. Clark to A. K. Davis, May 20, 1874, *ibid.*, Vol. 93; William H. Lynch to Ames, May 1, 1874, *ibid.*, Vol. 92.
37. George E. Hasie to Ames, May 6, 1874 (quote), and Merriman Howard to Ames, May 1, 1874, *ibid.*
38. Benjamin A. Lee to Ames, May 9, 1874, *ibid.*; Monticello (Miss.) *Advocate*, June 18, 1874; Vicksburg *Times*, May, 1874.
39. Ames to Henry R. Pease, May 2, 1874, in Governors' Correspondence, Vol. 92.

portunity to chide Congress for its failure to assume responsibility for the construction of the levees. "The proper way, the economical way," he declared, "to render the relief that will be permanent would be for the Government to at once resolve to take charge of the levees, and when the flood subsides to provide labor for the people who will be left in the overflowed districts without employment." In spite of his initial opposition to federal relief, Alcorn indicated his willingness to support a smaller aid bill if the War Department rather than agents of Governor Ames were authorized to distribute the supplies.[40]

After some delay, due to Alcorn's objections, a revised bill passed Congress extending $100,000 in military rations for the relief of Mississippi and Louisiana flood victims. Despite the senator's opposition, the tasks of transporting from New Orleans and distributing the provisions were placed in the hands of agents selected by Ames. The governor immediately appointed a relief committee for each river county to handle the distribution, and he dispatched friends to New Orleans to arrange for the shipments.[41] Most of the aid officials tapped by Ames were local carpetbag leaders, which inevitably led to the conservative charge that the relief operation was designed "for election purposes," with rations going to black supporters who were not in need of assistance. Actually, relief officials, including former Governor Clark and a few other conservatives, tried to avoid such a charge by keeping careful records of their activities and, at Ames's insistence, by discontinuing the distribution as soon as the flood waters receded. In fact, the need for supplies, though probably not critical, continued long after Ames shut off the flow of rations to the affected area.[42] The waters fortunately receded sooner than expected and in time for a "fair crop" to be planted in most of the river counties.[43]

Ames, whose constitutional scruples were as sound as those of

40. Vicksburg *Times*, May 21, 1874.

41. Pease to Ames, May 5, 8, 1874, William W. Belknap to Albert R. Howe, May 9, 1874, A. K. Davis to Ames, May 9, 1874, all in Governors' Correspondence, Vol. 92.

42. George N. Raymond to Ames, May 21, 1874, Clark to Ames, May 20, 1874, Albert Morgan to Ames, May 4, 1874, all in *ibid*. Because of the necessity for the rapid distribution of the provisions, some rations, Ames admitted, fell into the hands of undeserving people. *Annual Message of Governor Ames, 1875*, p. 4.

43. H. T. Martin to Ames, May 14, 1874, M. B. Sullivan to Ames, May 24, 1874, both in Governors' Correspondence, Vol. 93.

any conservative despite an aversion to the states' rights dogma, later asked the legislature to refund the relief contribution of the federal government on the ground that "justice to ourselves, as well as to the United States," demanded it. The legislature did not see its responsibility in the same light; it thus rejected the governor's request.[44]

In spite of Ames's demonstration of concern for the public interest in the flood crisis, his administration became increasingly focused on intraparty politics to the neglect and detriment of state affairs. The governor's preoccupation with party matters can be traced to a large extent to the bitter election of 1873 when Alcorn had bolted the regular ticket. Almost all of the bolters, however, had made their peace with the party, if not with Ames himself. Nonetheless, even those moderates, like outgoing Governor Powers, who had technically remained loyal to the regular organization found their influence in eclipse after the Radical victory, and in order to continue as Republicans they had no choice but to submit as gracefully as possible to Ames's leadership. On the eve of the inaugural, Powers held a love feast at the governor's mansion for the leaders of all factions of the party. Ames made an appearance and seemed to give his blessings to the return of the prodigals to the regular party.[45] A ray of hope for party unity followed when the proud Alcorn, although refusing to come before his rival in sackcloth and ashes, reaffirmed his devotion to Republican principles and, in an attempt to repair his tarnished reputation with the Republican masses, spoke out in the Senate for Charles Sumner's radical civil rights bill, which in emasculated form became law in 1875.[46]

But the spirit of liberality that Ames manifested toward old foes at the time of his inaugural soon vanished. The carpetbag governor could not forget his past conflict with "sorehead" Republicans, as he dubbed all of his opponents in the party. Not only had they cooperated with former rebels to defeat the Radicals, but Ames believed that their leaders, Alcorn, Powers, and Musgrove, were corrupt. Much to his dismay, however, the gov-

---

44. *Annual Message of Governor Ames, 1875*, p. 4; *Senate Journal, 1875*, p. 306.
45. Vicksburg *Times and Republican*, January 23, November 15, 1874.
46. *Speech of Alcorn in the Senate, 1874.*

ernor discovered that not all who had supported him in the fall favored nailing his Republican antagonists to the wall. An Ames-inspired resolution censuring Alcorn and calling on him to resign from the United States Senate passed the state house of representatives but failed in the senate where several Radicals defied the wishes of their leader.[47] State Senator John J. Smith, a carpetbag friend of Ames, could not understand the vote of his colleagues. "I am against everything Alcorn says or does," he exclaimed. "Show me that he is in favor of anything, and I am immediately and inveterately opposed to it."[48]

From the beginning of his administration Ames surrounded himself with carpetbag partisans like Smith. Prominent also in this coterie of northerners, which included fewer than a dozen men, were the shady O. C. French, the highly partisan John B. Raymond of the Jackson *Pilot*, and the vacillating Alexander Warner, the administration's leader in the legislature and chairman of the Republican state executive committee.[49] Few scalawags or blacks enjoyed the confidence of Ames, and he shunned the fellowship of several of the state's more able and perceptive carpetbaggers. His reliance on carpetbag cronies for counsel almost immediately opened old wounds and created new divisions in the party.

Although Ames maintained a tight carpetbag circle around him, his appointments to local offices included all elements of the party. In making these selections Ames almost invariably followed the wishes of local men who had supported him in the 1873 campaign.[50] This meant that dissident or moderate Republicans, who represented an important source of talent for the party, were usually

47. *Congressional Globe*, 42nd Cong., 2nd Sess., Appendix, 395; Ames to his wife, August 20, October 15, 1874, in Blanche Butler Ames (comp.), *Chronicles*, II, 9–10, 28; *House Journal, 1874*, pp. 182–83; Vicksburg *Times*, February 18, 1874; Pascagoula *Star*, February 21, 1874.

48. Vicksburg *Times*, February 19, 1874.

49. A survey of the voluminous correspondence between Ames and his wife in Blanche Butler Ames (comp.), *Chronicles*, makes clear the cliquishness of the governor's administration.

50. For the governor's patronage policy see Barrett to Hugh McLeod, June 9, 1874, in Letterbook A of Governor Ames; Ames to Ira McDowell, October 22, 1874, in Letterbook B of Governor Ames.

ignored in the appointments. Ames, however, permitted all of Alcorn's excellent corps of circuit court judges to serve out their six-year terms. On the other hand he replaced the chancellors of the Alcorn-Powers period with stalwarts of his wing of the party; the new group, however, included a few more scalawags than carpetbaggers.[51] Despite his aversion to "rebels," he appointed four former Confederate officers, now Ames Republicans, to the chancery courts. In contrast to his policy as military governor in 1869, Ames in 1874–1875 chose local residents for office, including carpetbaggers who in most cases had resided in their districts for several years.

Under the circumstances local Republican talent was spread thin. Although not an unusual practice during the Alcorn-Powers years, a number of party faithfuls held two or three offices by virtue of Ames's appointment. Charges of mismanagement and malfeasance against local officers became rife. The most frequent complaints, as before, were against the county supervisors, who were elected officials and in many cases had been in office since 1871. Most of these charges had a partisan ring to them and therefore were exaggerated or completely false. But even Republicans admitted that an unusually large number of tax collectors and county treasurers, whether for corrupt reasons or not, were defaulters, and in most cases they were still holding office. Furthermore, county supervisors, reform Republicans reported, were acting in a more irresponsible way than ever before.[52] In one case, O. S. Lee, a carpetbag associate of Ames and deputy treasurer of Holmes County, absconded with $57,000 in public funds after killing two blacks in a local factional dispute. Lee was last seen in the Black Hills of Dakota where he reportedly was distributing reli-

---

51. A convenient list of Reconstruction chancellors, including dates of appointment, is found in Rowland, *Courts, Judges, and Lawyers*, 249–50.

52. F. Heiderhoff to Ames, September 14, 1874, and Wilson Hood to Ames, December 19, 1874, both in Governors' Correspondence, Vol. 99; Macon (Miss.) *Beacon*, October 23, 1875, giving report of grand jury investigation; Natchez *Democrat*, August 24, 1874; Kinlock Falconer to George E. Harris, May 20, 1876, in Combined Letterbook of Governors Ames and Stone; George E. Harris to U. S. Grant, November 24, 1875, printed in *Issues of the Canvass of 1876* (Jackson, 1876), 5–6. Not all of the defaulters were Republicans. Murray Quin to William N. Whitehurst, August 8, 1875, in Whitehurst Papers.

gious tracts to Indians.[53] The situation in the counties became so bad that Ames obtained legislative approval for the appointment of nine special revenue commissioners, at least six of whom were carpetbag friends, to investigate charges of defalcation and attempt to recover as much of the taxpayers' money as possible.[54]

The poison of division reached into the Radical leadership itself only four months after Ames took office. Tempers flared when the governor attempted to secure the defeat of G. Wiley Wells for reappointment as United States district attorney for north Mississippi. In turning on Wells, the conqueror of the Ku Klux Klan in the area, Ames acted on a charge brought by French that the district attorney's brother-in-law had offered him a bribe in exchange for supporting Wells for the Senate seat that Blanche K. Bruce subsequently won.[55] French's accusation came precisely at the time when Wells was being considered for reappointment, a fact that should have alerted Ames to an underlying political motive. Pell-mell, however, the governor dispatched a message to Senator Henry R. Pease in Washington demanding that he block the reappointment of the "dishonest" Wells.[56] When the Radical Pease refused and Wells was reappointed by President Grant, Ames became furious and denounced the senator as "a tricky double dealing fellow."[57] French later admitted to Wells, in a remarkable confession of wrongdoing, that "the pressure of circumstances which threatened [his] interest" had caused him to charge the district attorney with bribery. "My financial misfortunes in connection with my official position with the Government," he explained, "had been so much used against me for political purposes that I had been driven to desperation. I was threatened on so many various occasions that if I did not act in conformity with the wishes of different persons, I would be proceeded against, that I came to regard my difficulties as a commodity of political merchandise."

53. Ames to his wife, August 5, September 11, 1875, in Blanche Butler Ames (comp.), *Chronicles*, II, 125–26, 175; Yazoo City *Herald*, April 28, 1876; Jackson *Weekly Clarion*, May 3, 1876. Lee had also served as Ames's aide-de-camp in the new state militia.

54. Newspaper clipping from Vicksburg *Herald*, May 7, 1875, in Whitehurst Papers; *Laws of Mississippi, 1875*, p. 30.

55. O. C. French to Ames, May 13, 1874, in Governors' Correspondence, Vol. 92.

56. Ames to Pease, May 15, 1874, in Letterbook D of Governor Ames.

57. Ames to A. R. Howe, June 1, 1874, *ibid*.

The "different persons" in this case were the Republican foes of Wells in north Mississippi who plotted to destroy his influence and replace him with their candidate for district attorney.[58] Although Ames evidently knew of French's confession, he did nothing to repair the breach with Wells and Pease; to make matters worse, French continued in his confidence.

At the same time Governor Ames refused to take action against State Superintendent of Education Thomas W. Cardozo who soon after taking office found himself "shingled all over with indictments for embezzlement and fraud" that he had accumulated while serving as circuit clerk of Warren County. When informed of the indictments, Ames wrote privately: "I am mortified and chagrined at the event, but can do nothing."[59] He maintained an indiscreet public silence in the case, but he removed from office Cardozo's deputy clerk, who had also been indicted. By 1875 the governor's newspaper organ, the Jackson *Pilot*, was expressing doubt regarding Cardozo's guilt, despite the notoriety of Warren County affairs and the fact that members of the black superintendent's own race constituted a majority of the grand jury that had indicted him. The *Pilot* charged that the indictments were a political move to harass Cardozo and, by implication, the Ames administration. Circuit court officials in Warren County, all of whom were Ames appointees, delayed bringing Cardozo to trial. The trial was not placed on the court docket until 1876, and by this time Cardozo had left Mississippi for good, having been impeached and removed as state superintendent of education by the Redeemer legislature.[60]

The governor's cliquishness, his tolerance of men like French and Cardozo, and his policy of permitting local supporters to choose carte blanche the numerous officeholders who fell under his patronage widened the Republican split to serious proportions by the summer of 1874. Ames complained in June that Lieutenant Gov-

58. O. C. French to Wells, October 20, 1874, in Governors' Correspondence, Vol. 95. French's "financial misfortunes" refer to a claim of $6,640 the federal government pressed against him for shortages that had occurred during his stint as an agent of the Freedmen's Bureau in the late 1860s. Jackson *Weekly Clarion*, July 16, 1874.

59. Nordhoff, *Cotton States*, 75, 82; Ames to his wife, August 25, 1874, in Blanche Butler Ames (comp.), *Chronicles*, II, 14.

60. Jackson *Pilot*, July 28, 1875; New York *Times*, November 26, 1874; Jackson *Weekly Clarion*, July 19, 1876.

ernor Davis and Ham Carter, both influential black Republicans, Morris, Furlong, and Musgrove, in addition to Pease and Wells, had gone over to the "soreheads" and had received "an entire Democratic backing."[61] Soon Attorney General George E. Harris, whom Ames had ignored on controversial legal matters, Congressman George C. McKee, and Jason Niles had abandoned the Ames ship. Despite the governor's quickness to write them off as allies of the Democrats, few of the dissidents renounced their allegiance to the Republican party, and even at the time of the revolution of 1875 they retained their identity with the organization.

Ames could well afford to lose Lieutenant Governor Davis to the "soreheads." Believed by anti-Radicals to be dishonest and opportunistic before he was placed on the Ames ticket, Davis in office wasted little time demonstrating the correctness of this view. When Ames left the state in May, 1874, for a visit to New Orleans, Davis assumed control of the governor's office, an action provided for by the constitution. He immediately went to work removing Ames officeholders and appointing his friends to office. He also commenced pardoning state convicts, including some felons who were serving long terms in the penitentiary. Davis actually ordered the release of seventeen accused offenders who had been indicted but not tried.[62] Davis himself was later indicted for accepting a bribe in exchange for the release of a convict.[63]

Ames supporters frantically summoned him home before too much damage could be done by the energetic Davis. When he returned Ames immediately revoked Davis' appointments, but the pardoned convicts remained free. The tug of war between the carpetbag governor and the black lieutenant governor further injured the Republican party and deepened internal divisions at a time

---

61. Ames to Howe, June 1, 1874, in Letterbook D of Governor Ames. Cardozo, however, was never a member of the Ames clique, though he was an officer in his administration. Although popular, President Revels of Alcorn University felt the heavy hand of Governor Ames simply because he was associated politically with Alcorn. Revels was removed from office and replaced by an outsider who subsequently brought bitter disappointment to the party. Ames to J. F. Boulden, May 29, 1874, in Letterbook A of Governor Ames; Ames to C. F. Harris, August 4, 1874, Letterbook D of Governor Ames.

62. Ames to A. K. Davis, May 11, 1874, in Letterbook D of Governor Ames; report to the senate and house of representatives, January 11, 1875, in Letterbook C of Governor Ames; Blanche Ames to her mother, May 9, 1874, in Blanche Butler Ames (comp.), *Chronicles,* I, 677.

63. Jackson *Weekly Clarion,* July 14, 1875; Ames to his wife, August 1, 27, 1875, in Blanche Butler Ames (comp.), *Chronicles,* II, 119, 148.

when the conservatives were preparing a vigorous campaign to overthrow the Radical regime. Ames recognized the seriousness of the conflict with Davis when he wrote a Republican friend: "We will have all we can do to fight a common foe at the next election, and Davis' war only works to the injury of his own race."[64] In fact, anti-Radicals momentarily perceived Davis as the wedge that could finally be driven between "the carpetbag adventurers" and the black electorate. Although he later recanted, Barksdale referred to Davis at this time as "one of the best representatives of the colored race" in Mississippi.[65] One carpetbag foe of Ames even told Davis that "all Hell can't keep you from being elected Governor at the next election" and that Senator Alcorn would extend his support. "My opinion is that [Alcorn] is the rising Star of the Republican party and that Gov Ames is, or will be, a dead cock in the Pot!"[66] Support for Davis, however, disappeared when it became clear that he was corrupt. Nevertheless, the Radical legislature took no action against the lieutenant governor, despite his indictment for bribery. When the Redeemers came to power, the old charges against Davis were revived and he was removed from office.[67]

In 1874 Ames lost rather than gained friends as a result of his efforts to check the ambitions of the opportunistic lieutenant governor. On subsequent occasions when Ames left the state for visits in New Orleans and the North, he was forced to return in haste to prevent, as one supporter put it, "a state of anarchy" with Davis as acting governor.[68] Governor Ames's concern in the Davis affair arose more from his apprehension of the havoc that Davis might wreak on his friends who held office than from any genuine concern for the public interest.[69] Already, as evidenced by his

64. Ames to William M. Hancock, August 17, 1874, Letterbook A of Governor Ames.
65. Jackson *Weekly Clarion*, August 6, October 1, 1874.
66. J. H. Pierce to A. K. Davis, July 16, 1874, in Governors' Correspondence, Vol. 94.
67. *Senate Journal, Called Session, 1875*, p. 21; Ames to his wife, August 27, 1875, in Blanche Butler Ames (comp.), *Chronicles*, II, 148.
68. John T. Mosely to Ames, August 3, 1874, and H. C. Powers, *et al.* to Ames, September 14, 1874, both in Governors' Correspondence, Vol. 94; Water Valley *Mississippi Central*, July 4, 1874.
69. This is clear from the general tone of the correspondence, both incoming and outgoing, concerning the controversy. The outgoing correspondence, written by Ames or his secretary, appears in the Letterbooks of Governor Ames for 1874; incoming letters are from Ames's political friends and are contained in the Governors' Correspondence for the same year.

private correspondence, Ames was losing interest in Mississippi affairs. Although he was still intent on preserving the new order, he was easily persuaded that the people were not worth his efforts to come to grips with the problems of the state. "Mississippi, which has commanded my thoughts and time for the last six years," Ames wrote his wife in August, 1874, "has lost its power over me forever. . . . I have no cause to grieve over any fate, however adverse, to my political preferment. . . . We can say quits at any time, and [the state] will be my debtor."[70] His trips outside of Mississippi reflected his effort to escape the responsibilities of governing a society that he disdained.

Under attack from all sides by late 1874, Ames turned even more to his carpetbag cronies at the capital. Attorney General Harris, a scalawag, later informed President Grant that Ames at this time "seemed to contract his views and narrow his circle of friends to a few confidential advisers, [who] were a close corporation of mercenary men."[71] The governor's basis for making decisions had become tragically limited. Consequently, when confronted with a political crisis, as he soon would be, Ames was unable to assess properly the complexities involved and act realistically to control the situation. Equally significant, his decisions no longer carried the full weight of the Republican party in the state. With the Radical regime severely weakened internally, a successful conservative challenge appeared, for the first time since the Republican triumph in 1869, to be a distinct possibility. It remained to be seen, however, if the conservatives, whose demoralization and divisions were accentuated by the abandonment of the Democratic party in 1873, could take advantage of Republican troubles and unite on a common platform for the "redemption" of the state from Radical rule.

70. Ames to his wife, August 12, 1874, in Blanche Butler Ames (comp.), *Chronicles*, I, 707–708. See also Ames to his wife, October 18, November 14, *ibid.*, II, 32, 63.
71. C. F. Harris to Grant, November 24, 1875, printed in *Issues of the Canvass of 1876*, p. 5.

19

The Conservative
Resurgence

The conservative wait-and-see policy toward the Radical administration fell apart in April, 1874, when the legislature adjourned
without enacting the sweeping reform program that Ames had
seemingly promised when he became governor. In view of the
decline of Republican authority in other southern states and the
fact that the masses of Mississippi whites had only acquiesced
in the New Departure of their leaders—they had never really
embraced the principles embodied in congressional reconstruction
—probably nothing that Ames and the Republican lawmakers
could have done in 1874 would have appeased conservatives indefinitely. On the other hand, the failure of the Ames Radicals to
meet the broad demands for relief and reform, in addition to their
narrow partisanship and tolerance of corruptionists, ensured an
early revival of the Bourbon spirit of belligerence and intolerance.

All along Bourbons had railed out at the moderate tactic of
compromise with the "desperate plunderers" of the state, and in
early 1874 they had warned sanguine whites that Ames's promises
of retrenchment and reform were "merely thrown out to make a
great pretence, when in fact nothing [was] to be done."[1] When
the reforms did not materialize many moderates joined the Bourbons in denouncing the Ames regime, though the Bourbon goal
of rallying whites to a militant, color-line standard fell short of
success in 1874.

As in the past, when the Republican hegemony was secure behind its black ballots and federal might, self-appointed conservative spokesmen seemed to be talking to themselves in arguing the
old issue of whether or not to court black support in their efforts
to defeat the Radicals. Most conservative leaders still rejected outright the Bourbon demand for a direct assault on the bastion of
Republican power in the state—the black vote. Led by former
Democrat Albert Gallatin Brown in the south and old Whig John

1. Vicksburg *Vicksburger*, February 15, 1874.

W. C. Watson in the north, moderates continued to insist that the New Departure offered the only mode for overcoming the Republican majority at the polls and ridding the state of Radical misrule.[2] Bourbons countered by denouncing any accommodation with blacks as futile as well as degrading, although few would publicly admit any intention of subverting the Fourteenth or Fifteenth amendments. Throughout most of 1874 the sparring among conservative spokesmen made little difference to the apathetic white masses who had become demoralized by the past manipulations of their old leaders and by their failures to devise a plan for overcoming Republican rule.

With no immediate hope for political victory, conservatives, as well as a number of reform Republicans, organized taxpayers' leagues in order to obtain relief from their main source of complaint—oppressive taxes. These leagues, first suggested in 1873 by reform Republicans in Vicksburg, were designed as nonpartisan associations that would have an influence with the Radical administration.[3] By late 1874 local taxpayers' leagues had appeared throughout the state. "The great cardinal principle of the movement is this," the Natchez *Democrat* informed its readers, "that the State and county taxation to which our people have been and are now subjected is enormously excessive, unequal, unjust, oppressive, and incompatible with good government and the natural rights of men."[4] People simply could not pay their taxes, the *Democrat* announced, and the list of tax-forfeited property was growing by leaps and bounds. In explaining the local need for the tax reform movement, the moderate Greenville *Times* revealed that in 1874 Delta plantations assessed at $20,000 had to pay taxes (including the levee duty) that ranged between $3,000 and $4,000, despite the meager income realized after debts for supplies had been settled. As a result "over two-thirds of the most valuable plantations in Washington county were sold [recently] for taxes . . . and not a bid was made for one."[5] The numerous resolutions adopted by local taxpayers' leagues also graphically expressed the prob-

---

2. Jackson *Weekly Clarion*, August 27, September 3, 10, 24, 1874; Greenville *Weekly Times*, September 26, 1874; New York *Times*, September 15, 1874.
3. Vicksburg *Times and Republican*, February 20, March 12, 1873.
4. Natchez *Democrat*, December 2, 1874.
5. Greenville *Weekly Times*, November 7, 1874, March 27, 1875 (quote).

lems that taxpayers experienced as the time for paying new taxes approached in early 1875.

For a time the taxpayers' leagues were able to maintain their nonpartisan facade. A correspondent for the New York *Times* reported in December, 1874, at the height of the movement, that in the "manifestoes" of the leagues he saw "none of the old twaddle about white men's governments and the interests of the Caucasian. On the contrary, an effort has been made to bring such colored citizens as have property, and are of consequence in the State, into the movement for tax reform; and there are evidences that it will succeed."[6] By this time several prominent Republicans and four party journals, though not the stalwart Jackson *Pilot*, had endorsed the taxpayers' movement. Perhaps reflecting as much their dissatisfaction with Ames's leadership of the party as their desire for tax relief, carpetbaggers Henry Musgrove, Edward J. Castello, and George C. McKee and scalawags Joshua S. Morris, John L. Morphis, and Fleet T. Cooper actively participated in the taxpayers' leagues.[7] But the most significant convert to the cause of sweeping tax reform was Flournoy, "the John Brown of the Mississippi Radicals."

Soon after the legislature of 1874 adjourned without enacting a program of retrenchment and tax reform, Flournoy announced his support of the taxpayers' leagues. In an open letter "To the People of Mississippi," this Pontotoc scalawag asserted that despite the claims of Ames Republicans, the people of the state "are taxed beyond endurance." He thundered: "It is a fallacious and contemptible subterfuge to attempt to palliate a great wrong," as Ames partisans had when they compared the rate of taxation in Mississippi with that of other states, which in most cases had greater wealth than the Magnolia state. Mississippi, he pointed out, had the third highest tax rate in the nation, but was the seventh poorest in per capita wealth. Furthermore, Flournoy said, the tax rate in the state continued to rise; it had almost doubled during the past year, and no relief appeared in sight for oppressed taxpayers unless the legislature of 1875 could be persuaded to make drastic cuts in expenditures. He specifically called for the

6. New York *Times*, December 19, 1874.
7. Jackson *Weekly Clarion*, November 19, 26, 1874.

abolition of the chancery court system, the adoption of biennial legislative sessions, and the end of the registration requirement for voting, which, he asserted, in addition to reducing the state expenses would increase the number who voted.[8]

The enthusiasm of Flournoy and other reform Republicans for the taxpayers' movement waned considerably when the crusade lost its elevated tone and became largely a diatribe against Republican profligacy. In the Delta, the Greenville *Times*, a moderate journal in politics but a militant advocate of retrenchment and efficiency in government, averred that "in this State the fact that the cloak and machinery of taxation has been diverted to purposes of confiscation is undeniable." Claiming that "the present system of taxation is a robbery which the people are morally and religiously justified in resisting, short of revolution," Barksdale encouraged the taxpayers' leagues to pursue an aggressive policy to rid the state of the "Republican corruptionists."[9] The Natchez *Democrat* exclaimed, "The wrongs for which our English ancestry brought the head of Charles the First to the block are trivial compared to these we now suffer." Nevertheless, the *Democrat* cautioned against using violent methods to obtain relief. "Let the people present their grievances to the Legislature, and ask that they be redressed."[10]

Revisionist historians of southern Reconstruction have contended that conservative complaints of tax extortion at the hands of the Republicans were exaggerated, and no doubt there is much truth in this assessment. In Mississippi the state and county tax rates, which together rarely exceeded fifty dollars on the one thousand dollars of assessed property, were not very high by modern standards nor did they depart drastically from those then prevailing in the North.[11] But when other factors are considered—the heavy indebtedness of the people, the high rates of interest re-

8. As reported in *ibid.*, July 16, 1874, and the Vicksburg *Times*, July 18, 1874.

9. Greenville *Weekly Times*, March 27, 1875; Jackson *Weekly Clarion*, November 9, 1874.

10. Natchez *Democrat*, December 8, 1874. See also the Greenville *Weekly Times*, November 7, 1874.

11. It is difficult to determine precisely the tax burden on property, even though the state tax rate was the same for all areas, which in 1873 was fourteen dollars on the one thousand dollars of assessed property, and county taxes, according to an 1873 law, were

quired to obtain essential provisions, the dearth of income from the land, and the absence of a diversified economy in the state—it is clear that the taxes imposed by the Republicans were burdensome and added to the hardships that the people experienced during Reconstruction. Largely impecunious planters and farmers could not afford to pay even the relatively moderate levies required to sustain the expanded public programs of the postwar period. The Republicans' fiscal and tax policies obviously did not create the hard times of the 1870s, but the failure of the new political order to act realistically on the complaints of taxpayers and others contributed to the continuation of the agricultural depression and ultimately to the undoing of Republican authority in the state.

The climax of the taxpayers' movement occurred in January, 1875, when a state convention of protesters met in Jackson. Although it was hailed as a nonpartisan affair, few Republicans attended. The gathering contained many political leaders of the past; in fact, the register of delegates appeared to be a roll call of the most prominent Whig and Democratic survivors of the late antebellum period.[12] Of the surviving leaders of the 1850s only Jefferson Davis and Lamar were missing. Present also were a group of ambitious young men, who as junior and field-grade officers

not to exceed twenty-five dollars on the same amount of property. The tax information that local officials forwarded to the state auditor did not normally include levies for bond issues (*e.g.*, railroad bonds) nor did it accurately report the rate in all counties, since a few local governments attempted to hide the fact that they had exceeded the rate imposed by the 1873 law. In addition, the rates levied by incorporated towns were left out of the reports. Nevertheless, other sources indicate that the total rate, but not the effect, for most property owners was not exorbitant. *Laws of Mississippi, 1873*, p. 85; *Annual Report of the Auditor of Public Accounts to the legislature of Mississippi, for the Year 1873* (Jackson, 1874), 9; Griggs (comp.), *Guide to Mississippi*, 27; Vicksburg *Times and Republican*, February 18, 1873; Natchez *Weekly Democrat*, May 8, June 12, August 21, 1872; Greenville *Weekly Times*, March 6, 1875. The above analysis does not include a consideration of the tax on personalty, which in 1873 constituted 30 percent of the tax revenues of the state government. *Annual Report of the Auditor, 1873*, pp. 330–33.

12. The membership and proceedings of the state taxpayers' convention may be found in the Jackson *Weekly Clarion*, January 7, 1875. Republicans were by no means without representation in the convention; in attendance were Musgrove, A. J. Jamison, the Radical candidate for lieutenant governor in 1868, editors Fleet T. Cooper and John B. Deason, Reuben W. Millsaps, Benjamin D. Nabors, George M. Buchanan, who would soon be the Republican candidate for state treasurer, former congressman John L. Morphis, and Castello, the Radical "wheel-horse" of 1868.

in the Confederate army had shown potential for leadership and since the war had been impatient to demonstrate their talents in the public arena. The taxpayers' convention, which appeared to them to be the initial phase in a general rising of whites that would inevitably be followed by a thorough reorganization of the Democratic party, provided these upstarts with their first real opportunity for political glory. In the convention, however, it was soon clear that the old leadership controlled matters, and it intended to approve a set of conciliatory resolutions based on the assumption that a moderate policy might yet persuade Republican legislators to adopt a program of tax reform. Farther down the road in the thinking of moderate conservatives was the election of 1875 and the belief that the support of a significant bloc of Republican voters was necessary for their success. This aid, they believed, could only be attained through a policy of conciliation.

Old secessionist Brown, in the convention's main address, vigorously presented the position of the moderates, perhaps even embarrassing some of his supporters with his advanced doctrine of political cooperation with blacks and acceptance of their rights. "The man of color," Brown declared, "has the same right to vote and hold office that you or I have, and it ought to be admitted in theory, and faithfully carried out in practice." If whites would cease deluding blacks and honestly treat them as equals in politics, he told his audience, a majority of them would throw off the Radical Republicans and join conservatives of both parties in restoring economy and efficiency in the government. "We must not talk with two tongues, one dipped in oil and honey for the negro when we are talking to him, and another in gall and wormwood when we are talking about him; you would never get the confidence of a white man in that way, and it is folly to try it on the negro." [13]

The tone having been set by Brown's speech, moderate leaders such as Watson, Harvey W. Walter, and Winfield Scott Featherston secured the convention's approval of a conciliatory document entitled the "Petition and Appeal of the Tax-Payers to the Legislature." The address refrained from the usual conservative polemics against Republicans. It mainly beseeched the legislature to carry

13. Brown's address is printed in the Jackson *Weekly Clarion*, January 21, 1875.

out the frequent Republican pledges of governmental retrenchment and reform—specifically the adoption of a policy of biennial
legislative sessions, the abatement of past taxes (except for 1874),
and reductions in public printing, school expenses, and public salaries. The delegates also urged the legislature to bridle the authority of the county boards of supervisors, which, they charged, were
largely composed of men who "are totally unfit to discharge their
duties and are without respectability or accountability."[14]

The petition insisted that the only reason for the taxpayers' convention was "the benumbing influence of despair and threatened
ruin" in Mississippi. "If all the crops raised in the State this year
were sold at present market value," the delegates claimed, "the
proceeds of the sales would not . . . pay the cost of production and
the taxes. . . . These afflictions fall heaviest at present on the very
large class of our poor citizens; but all classes suffer more or less
from this common calamity."

The reaction of Governor Ames and his Republican associates to
the petition and appeal was mixed. Reform Republicans, though
skeptical at first of the motives behind the taxpayers' convention,
applauded the address and made still another appeal to Ames and
the legislature to enact sweeping reforms. State Attorney General Harris in strongly endorsing the taxpayers' cause declared that
"the people are in a state of exasperation, and in their poverty and
desperation they are in arms against the burden of taxes that is
annually levied and collected on the value of property that is un-
productive." Harris reminded Republicans in the legislature that
"there has been a steady increase of taxes for the last four years,
during which period the value of property has been gradually di-
minishing, thereby rendering it more difficult to pay the taxes; and
it is an appalling fact that only about one-third of the land in the
State is now paying taxes; and year after year, as the lands are forfeited to the State for the non-payment of taxes, the amount to be
taxed is growing 'beautifully less,' and this imposes a heavier tax on
the remaining portion to be taxed, and necessitates a higher per
centum on the valuation to raise the same amount of revenue."
This scalawag from Hernando made a special appeal to Alexander

14. *Ibid.*, January 7, 1875; Pascagoula *Star*, January 16, 1875.

Warner, the Republican floor manager in the state senate, to lead "our party friends" away from "their wild extravagance" and onto the road of reform as outlined in the taxpayers' petition.[15]

At the same time Congressman McKee, a Vicksburg carpetbagger, termed the petition and appeal "the ablest paper I have seen in Mississippi for years. . . . I hope our legislators will not allow themselves to be scared off from what is right" on the matter of reform and retrenchment "by any outcry of partisanship" charged against the taxpayers' convention.[16] The Vicksburg *Times* admonished Republican legislators not to be trapped by the dead issues of early Reconstruction and thus ignore the living issues of the middle 1870s as outlined in the petition. During the early period, this Republican newspaper said, the significant issues were those "of freedom, of the ballot, and of personal rights. Now, they are questions of administration. . . . Hence, the present, pressing, practical, overruling consideration is, whether the Republicans, when weighed in the balance, will be found wanting or not? On the result, depends, not only the fate of the party in the South, but in the Nation—for if we of the South are wanting in an honest and just administration of public affairs, we shall be deserted by our friends in the North, and our friends there will be overthrown in the Nation."[17] The hour was already late to save the Republican regimes in the South; all but four, including Mississippi's, had collapsed by 1875. The conclusion of the Vicksburg *Times* that the tarnished reputations of these governments in northern eyes would ultimately be their achilles heel proved an accurate assessment.

Ames again, as in early 1874, appeared willing to support the cause of financial reform. On the day the state taxpayers' convention convened, he sent a message to the legislature recommending that it institute "the most stringent economy in appropriations for the support of the government during the ensuing year, and that every possible step be taken in the direction of retrenchment and

---

15. George E. Harris to Alexander Warner, February 10, 1875, printed copy in James Z. George Scrapbook, Mississippi Department of Archives and History.

16. As reported in the Vicksburg *Times*, January 28, 1875. See also the lengthy retrenchment and reform speech of carpetbagger Hiram T. Fisher to the Republican club of Jackson, also reported in the *Times*, March 13, 1875.

17. *Ibid.*, March 13, 1875.

reform." He now accepted the need for biennial sessions of the legislature, a reduction in public printing, and a decrease in the number of chancellors from twenty to ten or twelve. An important concession to the demand for tax relief was his recommendation that all forfeited lands be restored to their owners simply upon the payment of the delinquent taxes for 1873 and 1874. But even more remarkable in view of his Radical Republican background, Ames called for a reduction in taxes on land and a "partial return to a system which formerly prevailed—that of taxes on privileges and so forth." On the pressing matter of judiciary expenses, which he admitted were unusually large, Ames merely asked the legislature to transfer to the counties the main tax burden for law enforcement.[18]

Dominant Radicals in the legislature, however, viewed the cause of retrenchment and tax relief with less enthusiasm than did Governor Ames or reform Republicans. Buffeted by an increasing torrent of abuse from Bourbons and outraged by the racial disorders that convulsed Vicksburg in December, 1874, Radical legislators rejected outright the petition and appeal of the taxpayers' convention as well as most of Ames's modest recommendations. They glibly dismissed the convention as merely the stalking horse for the revival of the "Ku Klux Democracy" in Mississippi. In fact, the editors of the Jackson *Pilot*, the organ of the Radical Republicans, found reason to gloat over the misfortunes of the old citizens who were behind the taxpayers' movement. For the first time in the history of the state, these carpetbag editors gleefully announced, the landowner had felt the heavy hand of taxation—and he bitterly resented it. "Let him squirm. We mistake the tendency of affairs [greatly] if real estate will ever get back to the happy condition it experienced in the good old Democratic days, when the 'mud-sills' and 'poor white trash' staggered under burdens of taxation that the ruling class might wallow in inglorious ease and increase in unearned wealth."[19]

Despite the *Pilot*'s admonition to let the landowner squirm, the legislature adopted the most significant of Ames's recommendations—a tax abatement law and a reduction of the tax rate on land.

18. *Annual Message of Governor Ames, 1875*, pp. 9–13.
19. Jackson *Weekly Pilot*, February 13, 1875. See also the issue of February 20.

Designed to restore the approximately six million acres of forfeited lands to the tax rolls, the abatement act provided that former owners could repossess their land by paying just the taxes for 1874, rather than for the two-year period that Ames had proposed.[20] Although forfeiture would be reversed and "dead hand" lands would again produce tax revenues, the immediate effect of the law was disappointing. In most cases the former owners of the forfeited properties simply did not have the money to pay the 1874 tax and thereby redeem their lands. Furthermore, some of the lands were no longer available for redemption, since speculators, despite the shaky titles to tax-forfeited properties, had already purchased them from the state.[21] In fact, only in a few cases did the former owners recover their lands, and during the post-Reconstruction period more and more of these properties passed into the hands of speculators and railroad corporations.[22] The abatement law was accompanied by an act of the legislature reducing the tax rate on land from fourteen dollars per one thousand dollars of assessed value to a little more than nine dollars. This reduction, however, provided little relief, since the counties had to raise their rates on property to pay for the judiciary expenses that were transferred to them from the state.[23]

When the legislature adjourned without taking significant action on the state's pressing financial problems, a number of Republicans, mostly those removed from the cauldron of capital politics, excoriated it for its failures. The Vicksburg *Times*, reflecting the demoralization of reform Republicans as they found themselves isolated and helpless to counter what now was an almost complete polarization of political attitudes in Mississippi, charged that instead of honoring the critical appeals for retrenchment, the legislature had actually increased appropriations. To be sure, state taxes had been reduced, but only by shifting the burden to the counties. This device and others that were employed by the legislature to obtain revenue and "conceal the heavy expenses of the govern-

20. *Laws of Mississippi, 1875*, pp. 11–22.

21. *Annual Report of the Auditor, 1875*, pp. v–vi; *Annual Report of the Auditor, 1876*, p. vii; Jackson *Weekly Clarion*, January 19, 1876.

22. For a discussion of the post-Reconstruction fate of the state lands, especially in the Delta, see Brandfon, *Cotton Kingdom*, Chaps. III–IV.

23. Wharton, *The Negro in Mississippi*, 178; *Laws of Mississippi, 1875*, pp. 40–43.

ment are very unworthy of a great party and will not bear investigation." It was because of this kind of deceit and dishonesty that "the party has been brought to its present lamentable condition," the editor concluded.[24]

Blacks, who held a large plurality of the seats in the legislature, but not a majority, came in for some criticism at the hands of their friends for their opposition to specific retrenchment and tax proposals. The Vicksburg *Plain Dealer*, a Negro Radical journal, particularly censured the black legislators for meeting in caucus and agreeing to oppose the proposal for biennial legislative sessions. Even Flournoy, after some hesitation, expressed regret that the black members had drawn the color line in voting against the reform measures.[25] All but three or four of the black legislators had indeed voted against retrenchment recommendations, but the extent of their opposition to financial reform was exaggerated. Evidently only on two occasions—the roll calls on biennial sessions and a reduction in the pay of legislators—did Negroes vote almost as a unit against bills advanced by their white leadership.[26] Black support for the abatement law was essential for its passage. But the belief, reinforced by the criticism of some Republicans, that Negro lawmakers had opposed the whole reform program became standard fare among conservatives, leading Bourbons to claim that the drawing of the color line by whites was a perfectly legitimate policy because blacks had already set the precedent. The white-line militancy of the fall campaign owed something to the perception that whites had of black performance in the legislature of 1875.

24. Vicksburg *Times*, March 21, 1875. Joshua S. Morris, a former Radical, did not wait for the legislature to adjourn before passing judgment. He characterized the Ames administration and the legislature as "the vilest and most infamous coalition of black thieves and white, native and imported, Radicals and Democrats, that ever had possession of any portion" of the United States. As quoted in the Natchez *Democrat*, January 7, 1875.

25. Natchez *Democrat*, March 7, October 8, 1875; *Hinds County Gazette*, March 3, 1875.

26. By indirection, Barksdale admitted (Jackson *Weekly Clarion*, April 28, 1875) that the blacks had voted against only two retrenchment measures. This, of course, did not include other "reform" bills, introduced by conservatives and moderate Republicans like Joseph Bennett, that did not come to a vote in the legislature. Perhaps blacks as a bloc opposed these measures, but so did most white Radicals and Governor Ames. Supported by blacks, the state police bill, or "Standing Army Gatling gun atrocity," as the conservatives dubbed it, was usually lumped with the retrenchment measures to demonstrate that blacks pursued color-line policies in the legislature.

By the spring of 1875 aroused conservatives in Mississippi needed no further proof of Republican perfidy and failure. Conservative unity under the banner of white supremacy, designed especially for the upcoming fall campaign, was rapidly becoming a reality. But the Bourbon emergence as the dominant force in the anti-Radical movement had not been easy and had been contested at every turn by Brown-Watson moderates. Actually, the state taxpayers' convention, although not quite the Democratic assemblage in disguise that the Radicals imagined, was a major attempt by the old leadership to keep the conservative movement focused on concrete issues, avert the social disruption that accompanied racial violence, and prevent the federal intervention that many believed would follow the employment of white-line tactics. But events and developments in late 1874 and early 1875 were ineluctably working against continuing moderate control of the anti-Republican movement and for the ascendancy of the "Radical Democrats," as Brown labeled the Bourbons.

What Bourbons needed to convince wary and still apathetic whites of the soundness of their strategy for redemption was an early and striking demonstration of its success in a Republican controlled county. Such a demonstration occurred in Vicksburg in late 1874. Here, in the largest town in the state, a clique of cynical and scampish Republicans, supported by black ballots, had controlled affairs since the late 1860s. Early reform movements, consisting of both Republicans and conservatives, had floundered on the shoals of white apathy and Republican solidarity when the chips were down. But the hard times of 1874, accompanied by soaring property taxes and a city and county debt that reportedly had risen to one million dollars, jolted the white people from their lethargy. When Ames refused to intervene and use his extensive removal authority or his influence with the local party to rectify matters, transplanted northern and native businessmen, who had earlier shunned an active role in politics lest their trade suffer, joined in the movement to redeem Vicksburg. With a municipal election set for August 4, conservatives abandoned all pretense of seeking black votes and organized a straight out white-line campaign. The Republican machine made matters worse for its side by selecting for municipal office candidates (mainly black) who possessed little abil-

ity, and for the nominee for mayor they chose a "notoriously corrupt white man" who had been the beneficiary of lucrative contracts from the "Ring."[27] Although remaining loyal to the ticket,
the black editor of the Vicksburg *Plain Dealer* admitted that
corruption existed in the management of the local Republican
party. "Our caucuses have been too much under the control of
demagogues and the mob," he lamented, "and our conventions too
much in the hands of corrupt rings."[28]

Inflamed by the anti-Republican tirades of the young editors of
the *Vicksburger* and old-pro McCardle of the *Herald*, the "People's" or "White Man's" party instituted a campaign of intimidation, martial display, and economic coercion to carry the election.
Armed militia units of both races, but with whites having a decided
edge in weapons and aggressiveness, appeared on the streets of
Vicksburg. White liners converted the machine shops of the Vicksburg and Meridian Railroad into an armory, producing artillery
pieces and sabers. The president of the road discovered the activity and he "put a stop to any further work, as the railroad company
has not yet decided to add an Ordnance Department to their business."[29] When Governor Ames demanded that the ragtag militiamen turn in their weapons, they refused, claiming that they needed them for self-defense.

Tension mounted as the election approached, and rumors of an
assault upon the town by country blacks swept the white community, expanding the conservative program of intimidation. On July
20 acting Governor A. K. Davis frantically wired President Grant
that he considered it "absolutely necessary that troops be at the
earliest possible moment stationed in the City of Vicksburg to prevent impending riot and bloodshed." Secretary of War William W.
Belknap received Davis' telegram in place of the absent Grant, and
he immediately agreed to send troops. Before the order was exe-

27. Adelbert Ames to Benjamin A. Lee, May 26, 1874, in Letterbook A of Governor
Ames; Vicksburg *Vicksburger*, March 7, August 1, 1874; Natchez *Democrat*, July 30, 1874;
John S. McNeily, "Climax and Collapse of Reconstruction in Mississippi, 1874–1876,"
Publications of the Mississippi Historical Society, XII (1912), 296; Nordhoff, *Cotton States*,
75.

28. As reported in the Jackson *Weekly Clarion*, August 13, 1874.

29. A. K. Davis to U. S. Grant, July 20, 1874 (telegram), in Letterbook A of Governor
Ames; Vicksburg *Times*, July 23, 29, 31 (quote), 1874.

cuted, however, Belknap changed his mind, evidently fearful that in consenting to dispatch troops he had exceeded his authority.[30] A few days later Ames, upon his return from Massachusetts, renewed the request for federal intervention. Prominent northerners in Vicksburg, including State Senator Charles E. Furlong who had lost out in his struggle to control the Ring, quickly wired Washington, denouncing the carpetbag governor's action as unwarranted and pleading with Grant not to send the troops. With national elections imminent and the Republican party hard pressed to retain control of the House of Representatives, the president accepted their advice and notified Ames that the federal government would not intervene.[31] The chagrined Ames suspected another reason for Grant's refusal, gruffly concluding that "He wants the support of the Southern Democrats for a third term."[32]

Although conservatives were buoyed by the president's decision, the prospect of racial warfare had a salutary effect upon both sides in the Vicksburg crisis, and no actual confrontation between the races occurred. The election passed off quietly, with blacks voting in substantial numbers for Republican candidates. Victory, however, went to the White Man's party by a margin of 350 votes. Some black voters had decided not to test the white-liners' threats and therefore had remained at home on election day. Equally significant to the conservative success was the fact that whites voted in larger numbers than before, casting their ballots solidly for the party's ticket. Reportedly, as few as four whites voted Republican.[33]

Bourbons throughout the state hailed the triumph of the Vicksburg People's party as the start of a revolution against Ames and his "carpetbag malignants." By a unified, white-line display of power conservatives had overthrown the "thieves and adventurers" in the heartland of Radical domination. A number of conservative newspapers now announced their support of white-line politics. George W. Harper, who had frequently wavered between

30. A. K. Davis to Grant, July 20, 1874, William W. Belknap to A. K. Davis, July 21, 1874, and A. K. Davis to Belknap, July 23, 1874 (telegram), all in Letterbook A of Governor Ames.

31. Ames to Grant, July 29, 1874, *ibid.*; Vicksburg *Vicksburger*, August 1, 1874.

32. Ames to his wife, July 31, 1874, in Blanche Butler Ames (comp.), *Chronicles*, I, 693.

33. New York *Times*, August 4, 5, 1874; Vicksburg *Times*, July 31, August 10, 1874.

moderation and bourbonism, declared his support of white militancy after the Vicksburg election. Harper explained that he had earlier "given the blacks credit for an honest desire to bring the country from its wretched condition to the paths of peace and prosperity, and argued that they were simply misled by white plunderers on whom they rely for advice and whose slaves mentally they are." But "recent events" had changed his mind. His belief now was that "the colored people have earnestly sought just the condition of things in Mississippi that we see here at every hand— an impoverished and plundered State, with public offices rolling in wealth, a people in poverty and ruin, and a tax list that no agricultural people on earth can pay and retain their property."[34]

A much more dramatic conversion to the Bourbon position was that of L. O. Bridewell, a state Grange leader and the editor of the Beauregard and Wesson *Times*. In March, 1874, before the Vicksburg election and at a time when moderates were expressing hope that Ames would cast his lot with the reformers, Bridewell proclaimed his faith in the "New South," as he labeled the political developments that had taken place since 1867. "The past belongs to the dead," he wrote; "that which has happened to us is an accomplished fact, and there is an end of it. . . . Let Southern Bourbonism die—it is the sham of the age." Bridewell continued: "We are for justice to the freedmen—and justice means a faithful observance of the laws without evasion or avoidance. Let the great fact which has been stamped upon this generation [*i.e.* black political and legal equality] have room and opportunity for full development."[35] But after the Vicksburg election Bridewell announced his support of the white-line party. Nevertheless, he denied that his new party desired to disfranchise blacks or "to build up a party of caste." He also refuted moderate criticism that the drawing of the color line would result in violent racial clashes; instead it would eliminate the source of racial conflict in the state—the control of the government by ignorant and corrupt men. He declared that the

> People's Party desires to unite the white people in a solid body as the only alternative left us against the unbroken black line fastened upon

34. *Hinds County Gazette*, September 23, 1874.
35. Beauregard and Wesson *Times*, March 19, 1874.

us by the endeavors and falsehoods of a few thousand white vampires; it denounces all compromises with the enemy; it asserts, as its fundamental principle, that ignorance in the shape of uneducated negroes, and corrupt white men shall be banished from the seats of official power; it demands representation for the intelligence and tax-paying interest of the State; it says to the negro, you are by the fundamental law of the land a political entity, but in the hands of a few white men for their own selfish ends, you have become, and likely to remain, only a political chattle [*sic*].

White Mississippians, Bridewell announced, "will no longer submit" to being "the bond servants and menials of five thousand political chattles [*sic*]."[36]

Bridewell was not the only Grange leader to promote the Bourbon cause. In fact, the Grange, though denying any direct political involvement, played a significant role in awakening whites from their political stupor and organizing them into a campaign to oust the Radicals. Following the example of their brethren in the Midwest, when they first organized Mississippi Grangers were content to hurl their angry missiles at outside capitalists and economic interest groups whom they charged with suppressing the right of farmers to gain a just return for their labor. In late 1874, however, Grangers, now some thirty thousand strong and overwhelmingly of the yeoman class, turned their attention to the absorbing political issues of oppressive taxation and profligacy in public office, which they perceived as a more immediate threat to the well-being of Mississippi farmers than were bloated "monopolists." The Pascagoula *Star*, the seacoast journal of the Grange, which also served as the Bourbon newspaper organ for the district, declared that before the status of farmers could be improved "we must have relief from the political evils which are reducing us to a state of abject poverty, and our fair country to a barren wilderness."[37] An early advocate of the white-line movement, the *Star* frequently reported Grange activities with exhortations for all whites to unite in a militant campaign to overthrow the carpetbaggers and their black minions.[38] The Jackson *Farmers' Vindicator* and the combative Corinth *Sub-Soiler*, both influential Grange newspapers, also

36. *Ibid.*, September 3, 1874.
37. Pascagoula *Star*, August 15, 22 (quote), 1874.
38. *Ibid.*, especially the issues for August-October, 1874.

joined in the crusade to put an end to Republican "misrule" as the first step in improving the position of farmers.[39] In early 1875, the *Farmers' Vindicator*, which reportedly was read by most farmers in the state, went on the warpath against the Radicals. Declaring that "resistance to tyrants is obedience to God," editor E. G. Wall called on farmers to refuse to pay taxes for the support of the "lazy horde of hireling soldiery" that Ames was authorized to raise by the militia law of 1875.[40]

When the whites achieved union in the dramatic political campaign of 1875, it was by no means a coincidence that several prominent Grangers received Democratic-Conservative nominations for important positions, including the office of the state treasurer, the only state position to be filled in the election. Furthermore, the Democratic-Conservative platform of 1875 contained nine of the twelve reform proposals advanced by the state Grange.[41]

Despite the growing support in 1874 and early 1875 for the militant, color-line movement, conservative leaders who sought to avoid political extremism and racial conflict retained the upper hand in the anti-Republican movement. This was clear when a Bourbon call for a convention in January, 1875, to reorganize the Democratic party on a white-line basis failed to materialize.[42] Especially in the predominantly black counties the white fear of racial strife continued, as at the time of the Ku Klux rising, to work in favor of moderation and against the Bourbons. If the "intolerant utterances" of the Bourbons "were of any weight," John S. McNeily of the Greenville *Times* commented, perhaps wistfully, "they would constitute quite a dilemma for the white people of communities like [ours] where the very opposite of this 'color line' policy has been beneficially and successfully practiced for several years past." The "mistaken and desperate policy" of the Bourbons, McNeily reiterated, was "pregnant with evil and misery" for Mississippi.[43] The Port Gibson *Standard*, also published in a predominantly black county, attacked the white-line movement on the

39. Corinth (Miss.) *Sub-Soiler*, August 29, September 12, 19, 1874.
40. As reported in the Pascagoula *Star*, March 13, 1875. See also the Jackson *Weekly Pilot*, February 27, 1875.
41. Ferguson, "Granger Movement in Mississippi," 128.
42. Pascagoula *Star*, November 29, 1874, January 2, 1875.
43. Greenville *Weekly Times*, September 12, 26, 1874.

grounds that it would precipitate racial conflict. "The color line bids fair to be a line of battle, and battle is not the thing we want," the *Standard* announced.[44] "There is but one thing for us to expect in communities where the negroes are largely in the ascendant if this movement becomes general among the whites," Brown declared, "and that is negro domination in its most galling and revolting form."[45] Taking his cue from Brown, the editor of the Holly Springs *Reporter* wrote that "it is difficult for us to believe that any sane, intelligent white man can hope to accomplish any good for his race or party by the advocacy of [the color-line] doctrine." Such a policy, he said, would inevitably lead to a war of the races.[46]

A racial disturbance in Tunica County in August, 1874, provided a poignant reminder to whites in the river counties of what might happen if relations between the races were further exacerbated. The death of a Negro girl who was accidentally shot by a white man in a fight with a black antagonist led to a Negro uprising in the county and the threat of an armed assault on Austin, the small county seat.[47] When the trouble erupted, local Republican officials sent out an urgent appeal for help. "Intense excitement here, the town is to be destroyed," they frantically wired the state capital. "The colored men are armed all through the county. The officers powerless. There is [*sic*] about seventy-five white men and twenty-five colored men in the town to protect. The mob is advancing about four hundred strong and increasing from everywhere. Some shooting—a fight expected every minute. For God's sake send us soldiers immediately or our town and county is destroyed."[48] As usual in times of racial crisis, these black-belt whites exaggerated the situation.

Actually, the Tunica insurrection quickly became a comic-opera affair. White women and children fled by steamboat to Memphis as white irregulars from the "hills" flooded into Austin to fight black insurgents who were rendezvousing two miles from this Delta

44. As reported in the Vicksburg *Vicksburger*, August 7, 1874.
45. Jackson *Weekly Clarion*, September 10, 1874.
46. As reported in *ibid.*, September 24, 1874.
47. New York *Times*, August 13, 1874.
48. As reported by A. G. Packer to Ames, August 10, 1874, in Letterbook A of Governor Ames.

hamlet.[49] Then, when the white troops discovered there were no civilians to defend, many went home, leaving about 100 men to repulse the blacks. An assault on the courthouse by the dusky warriors ended in a rapid retreat with only two wounded. White scouts were now sent out to reconnoiter the enemy lines, and they reported that more than 900 Negroes had surrounded the town in preparation for a major attack. Shocked by this intelligence, white leaders asked for and received peace terms. In the "treaty" the white forces agreed to abandon the town, permitting the black legions to enter peacefully. The Negro captains agreed to put out guards in Austin to prevent looting and damage to property. When the insurgents marched into town, it was discovered that instead of a force of 900 or more the black army consisted of only about 250 ragtag and poorly armed men. The terms of the treaty were largely honored; pillage was limited to one store whose owner refused the occupiers' request for tobacco.

Their anger spent, the insurgents disappeared into the cotton fields surrounding Austin, after occupying the village for only a few hours. When a white expeditionary force from Memphis arrived the next day, they found the town deserted except for eight black pickets guarding the houses. The return of Sheriff M. M. Manning, a carpetbagger who had the confidence of both races, calmed the troubled racial waters of the county. No attempt was made to track down and punish the insurgents, since planters believed that a program of reprisals would trigger a renewal of the fighting. The local Republican newspaper reported that only one death (a black) had occurred in the "Tunica War." Since it had erupted in a remote area of the state and had quickly subsided, the Tunica County disturbance did not attract so much attention as the Vicksburg troubles, but it did intensify white fears in the river counties regarding the consequences of intense racial polarization.

In addition to appealing to the traditional white fears of Negro insurrection, political moderates argued, as they had before, that the adoption of the Bourbon color-line strategy for winning the

49. The following account is based on a report, written after the collapse of the insurrection, that appeared in the Austin *Cotton Plant*, the local Republican newspaper. This report is found in the Jackson *Weekly Clarion*, August 20, 1874. See also Packer to Ames, August 11, 1874, and Ames to Marion Campbell, August 12, 1874, both in Letterbook A of Governor Ames.

state would end all hope of attracting black voters to the anti-Radical cause. Since Negroes constituted a majority of the registered voters in Mississippi, it was imperative that conservatives obtain the support of some of them in the campaign to redeem the state. Short of using intimidation, which they dismissed as foolhardy in view of the likelihood of federal intervention to protect a free ballot, these moderates believed that blacks would never cooperate politically with whites if the conservative party endorsed bourbonism. Nevertheless, they admitted that only in Natchez had blacks by late 1874 shown any disposition to vote with the conservatives.[50] Brown blamed this state of affairs on the fact that too many whites still were not "willing to admit the negro's clearly defined and well-understood constitutional rights. . . . I have an abiding confidence that the negro can yet be made to understand that his interests are identical with that of the Southern white man, and when he comes to understand that he will think with the white men of the South, act with them, and vote with them."[51] Watson was not as confident as Brown that Negroes would soon see the error of their ways and support conservative candidates. But he agreed that "as grave as are the evils that afflict the body politic [I] feel assured that they will be aggravated rather than diminished by the organization of parties on the color line."[52]

Other moderates insisted that an end of federal intervention to prop up Radical regimes in the South depended on the continued growth of accommodationist sentiment. Deliverance from Republican rule will come soon, the Jackson *Clarion* assured its readers, "if the Northern mind is not disturbed by apprehension of a 'new rebellion,' which Southern whites can prevent if they exercise patience and forbearance." Southerners should do nothing to give a new lease on life to northern Republican "demagogues whose stock in trade is the manufacture of outrages."[53]

Lamar's famous eulogy in Congress for Charles Sumner in April,

50. Natchez *Democrat*, November 5, 7, 1874.
51. As reported in the New York *Times*, September 15, 1874.
52. Jackson *Weekly Clarion*, August 27, 1874, quoting the Water Valley *Central Star*. See also Robert E. Richardson to William N. Whitehurst, September 9, 1874, in Whitehurst Papers, and excerpts from several moderate newspapers in the Jackson *Weekly Clarion*, September 24, 1874.
53. Jackson *Weekly Clarion*, October 22, 29, 1874.

1874, was designed, he admitted, to encourage the development of northern sympathy for the southern conservative position in the struggle against the Radicals. Delivered before the Vicksburg election and subsequent incidents had intensified political and racial feeling in the state, the eulogy reflected at the time the prevailing sentiment of the conservative leadership. However, Lamar, the only Mississippi conservative in Congress, cultivated the northern impression that the Sumner eulogy was a bold, innovative stroke of high statesmanship on his part. Actually, the policy of national conciliation and political moderation expressed in the speech had deeper roots and more vigorous champions than Lamar among the conservatives of the state. Indeed, one month before Lamar's eulogy conservative members of the legislature had joined Republicans in a tribute to Sumner. Only a handful of Bourbon newspapers found reason to denounce Lamar and these conservatives for their action.[54]

A prominent north Mississippi conservative succinctly summarized all of the moderate objections to the color line when he wrote: "A white man's party . . . would be fore-doomed to certain and overwhelming defeat, and its results would be to check the rising sentiment in our favor at the North and [produce] countless riots and murders in our midst."[55] The porportion of whites who resisted the white-line policy is difficult to determine. But it is clear that their numbers varied with the emotionalism of the moment, the racial composition of the local population, the current political situation as whites perceived it, and the reputation of the local Republican leadership. Moreover, an important influence on conservative politics and tactics was the prospect of federal intervention, either with federal troops or through the judicial mechanism of the Enforcement acts. When federal interference appeared remote, converts to the white-line strategy became more numerous, and, conversely, when the threat of national action seemed imminent, the ranks of the white extremists became thin. The refusal of federal authorities to intervene in the summer crisis in Vicksburg

54. Murphy, *L. Q. C. Lamar*, 119; James Z. George to L. Q. C. Lamar, May 3, 1874, in Lamar-Mayes Papers; *House Journal, 1874*, pp. 402–13; *Senate Journal, 1874*, pp. 334–35; Mayes, *Lucius Q. C. Lamar*, 188, 200.
55. Jackson *Weekly Clarion*, September 10, 1874.

gave encouragement to those who pursued white-line policies. But at the same time conservatives could not be sure about President Grant's reaction to subsequent events and to appeals for troops by Governor Ames. His continued willingness to intervene in other southern states, especially neighboring Louisiana, to protect Republican regimes caused many Mississippians to believe that Grant would not hesitate to send troops to support Ames, the son-in-law of Benjamin F. Butler. Even during the revolutionary days of late 1875 the possibility of Grant's intervention to save the tottering Republican government still loomed large in the minds of conservatives. But by then the dikes holding back the white-line torrent had broken, and trepidation about federal intervention was no longer of decisive importance in the political behavior of whites.[56]

The stunning Democratic success in winning control of the United States House of Representatives in the fall, 1874, elections was hailed by Mississippi moderates as an affirmation of their policy of sectional conciliation and accommodation to the changes produced by the war. To moderates the elections had sealed "the bloody chasm between the two sections" and had inaugurated "an era of good policy between the races." The end of federal interference in southern affairs was imminent, they jubilantly predicted. In the postelection exuberance, the Natchez *Democrat* admonished Mississippians to prove to Republicans by fair treatment of blacks and political tolerance "that we are [as good] Americans as they are; that we have the same interest in the country and seek only the good of the Republic, whose glory is ours, and whose still glorious future we must share."[57] Announcing that black votes had aided conservatives in winning other southern states, both the *Democrat* and the Jackson *Clarion* asserted that the elections had obliterated

56. Planters and merchants also could not ignore the fact that white-line politics shook the delicate labor system that had been carefully reconstructed since the war. As indicated in Chapter 12 herein, they had earlier resisted the Ku Klux Klan mainly for this reason, and in 1874–75 they made a similar effort against "color politics." Their commitment to moderation weakened, however, in the face of heavy debts and burdensome taxes. See the Greenville *Weekly Times*, September 12, 26, 1874, and the Port Gibson *Standard*, as reported in the Vicksburg *Vicksburger*, August 7, 1874.

57. Natchez *Democrat*, November 10, 1874. For reasons of economy, the scheduled 1874 congressional elections in Mississippi were postponed until 1875 when local elections were to be held. The change had no effect on the terms in Congress of old and new members, since the new Congress did not convene until December, 1875.

the color line in the South. "The victors are everywhere extending to [blacks] the right hand of political friendship and giving them the most solemn assurances that all their rights will be respected and protected," the *Democrat* declared. The *Clarion* also expressed the view that the federal government because of the national Democratic victory would "withdraw its countenance and support from those who have abused and misused their ill-gotten power in the reconstruction States."[58]

Any advantage that moderates might have gained over the Bourbons in the national elections was shattered in December when racial tension exploded in Vicksburg, sending shock waves throughout the state. The racial violence that wracked the town and the surrounding area also demonstrated the ineptness of the Ames administration in dealing with a major racial confrontation, and it raised a fundamental question: could the Radical regime be counted on to protect blacks and Republicans in subsequent encounters with armed whites, or white leagues as they were soon called?

Since the August election Vicksburg had been seething with racial and political discord. Although white conservatives controlled city hall, Republicans held sway in the Warren County courthouse. The difficulties posed by the duality of local authority were increased by the fact that the sheriff and four of the five members of the county board of supervisors were blacks. Conservatives and many white Republicans felt that the county authorities continued to levy heavy taxes on burdened property holders for the benefit of blacks or the propertyless class. "This is the rule of the proletariat," a St. Louis journalist declared of Warren County affairs; "it is naked communism—and a negro communism at that."[59] The Natchez *Democrat* claimed: "No community in the United States would [bear] as long and patiently as the people of Vicksburg . . . the continuity of outrage and plunder to which they have been for years subjected."[60] And the feeling among Vicksburg whites was that matters were getting worse rather than better. On the other hand blacks in the county correctly believed that

58. *Ibid.*; Jackson *Weekly Clarion*, November 12 (quote), 26, 1874.
59. As reported in the Natchez *Democrat*, January 17, 1875.
60. *Ibid.*, December 20, 1874. See also the issue of November 27, 1874, and the New York *Times*, December 25, 1874.

white league activity threatened their fundamental rights and liberty. Nevertheless, blacks played into the hands of their enemies by continuing to support corrupt and incompetent local officials, in some cases simply because Bourbons denounced them and sought their removal from office.

Events leading directly to racial violence in the Hill City began in late 1874 when Sheriff Peter Crosby, who served also as the county tax collector, refused to make a new bond when his old securities became worthless. Crosby also had recently been accused of withholding evidence against three black officials whom a racially mixed grand jury had indicted on charges of fraud (they were later found guilty). Unwilling to await the action of the courts on the matter of Crosby's bond, an aggressive crowd of five hundred "tax-payers" marched on the courthouse on December 2 and demanded the sheriff's resignation. Under these threatening circumstances, Crosby complied.[61]

The next day, however, Crosby hurried to Jackson, repudiated the forced resignation, and met with Ames and a number of leading Republicans at the governor's mansion. Although sharply divided on the method to be used, almost all of those present at the meeting agreed that an effort should be made to restore Crosby to office. Attorney General Harris, with the strong support of Justice Jonathan Tarbell, argued that the Republican-controlled state courts should be given a chance to settle the matter. Most of the other participants in the council believed that the militia, though imperfectly organized, should be dispatched to Vicksburg to aid the fallen sheriff. A few expressed the opinion that events in Vicksburg gave the governor ample reason to request federal troops for the task at hand—a request that appeared likely to be honored, since the national elections had been held and President Grant, instead of being subdued by the Democratic victories, seemed determined to intervene again in Louisiana to suppress the latest threat to Republican authority.

But Ames rejected all of these recommendations. He sent Crosby home with vague instructions to organize a *posse comitatus* con-

---

61. *Appleton's Annual Cyclopaedia*, 1874, pp. 568–69. An extensive collection of source materials on the disturbance in Vicksburg may be found in *House Report*, 43rd Cong., 2nd Sess., No. 265.

sisting of plantation blacks for the purpose of restoring his authority in Vicksburg. Admitting that such action would probably result in the death of a number of Negroes, Ames shrugged it off with the comment that "the blood of martyrs was the seed of the church," and in this case perhaps black sacrifices were necessary in order to sustain the freedom of the race.[62] The governor promised Crosby state assistance, but the dispatch of two militia officers to Vicksburg was the extent of his aid.

Upon his return to Warren County, Crosby issued a printed appeal for blacks to assist him in regaining the sheriff's office. He spent Sunday, December 6, in the country rallying his followers and making specific plans for a march on the courthouse. Hundreds of whites, many from the adjacent Louisiana lowlands, made frenzied military preparations to resist the black advance on Vicksburg.

Early on Monday morning the ringing of bells throughout the city signaled the first sighting of Crosby's ragtag legions as they approached along three roads leading into Vicksburg. When the black captains (Crosby early fell into the hands of the whites) saw that Vicksburg defenders were well prepared for a fight, they met with the white leaders and agreed to withdraw their forces. But as the blacks began to fall back along the Baldwin road, a mob spirit seized the white irregulars and they began to fire into the ranks of the frightened and retreating Negroes. Fighting soon became general on the outskirts of the town—ironically where the heaviest action of the siege of 1863 had occurred—only this time the battle was along racial lines and most of the federal soldiers who had settled in Vicksburg after the war were now fighting on the side of their former enemies.[63] Commanding a cavalry unit in the second battle of Vicksburg was none other than Charles E. Furlong, a

62. *Testimony in the Impeachment of Governor Ames,* 119–22 (testimony of Jonathan Tarbell), 123–25 (Captain A. W. Allyn), 148–51 (James Hill, the black secretary of state); statement of W. W. Dedrick, February 16, 1876, in Governors' Correspondence, Vol. 101.

63. Perhaps the most objective and informed account of the Vicksburg violence is that of a correspondent to the Cincinnati *Commercial* which appeared soon after the event. The Vicksburg *Times,* January 8, 1875, carried this account. A balanced account of the riot's causes, including a statement of the difficulties involved in arriving at the truth in the affair, is found in the New York *Times,* December 25, 1874. The writer of this account, who spent several days in Vicksburg immediately after the riot, could not find one black man, except for political leaders, who would comment on the "massacre," though he made a strenuous effort to obtain Negro descriptions of it.

member of General Sherman's staff in the siege of 1863 and until recently the head of the Republican machine in Warren County. Furlong's conversion to the conservative cause, though he was still nominally a Republican, occurred after emerging black leaders had deposed him as the leader of the "Ring."

Having routed the blacks in Vicksburg, armed whites vengefully swept the county, attacking suspected insurgents. When the racial excitement had run its course perhaps as many as three hundred blacks lay dead, whereas only two whites were killed. Planters, however, in a deliberate attempt to conceal the number of black casualties from their tenants lest labor relations suffer, reported to the press that only twenty-five had died.[64]

Shaken by the violence in Warren County, Ames called the legislature into an emergency session. The county, he told sober legislators, was in a state of anarchy, and under existing laws he was powerless to deal with the crisis. Ames warned that if the Vicksburg insurgents succeeded in their lawless designs such tactics would soon be employed throughout the state, to the ruin of liberty, constituted authority, and the material interests of the people.[65] The legislature responded immediately and, with ten conservatives in the house of representatives voting with the majority, appealed to President Grant to dispatch troops to Vicksburg to restore racial peace and citizens' rights.[66] After a brief period of hesitation while he tested opinion in Congress and in the North, Grant on January 5, 1875, dispatched a company of troops to Vicksburg to assist civil authorities in reestablishing order and security. Only a formal demonstration of military power was needed to reinstall Crosby in the courthouse, reopen the courts, and dissolve the armed bands of whites in the county.[67]

64. *Message of Gov. Adelbert Ames, to the Legislature of the State of Mississippi, Convened in Extra Session, December 17, 1874* (Jackson, 1874), 2–4; J. M. Gibson, *Memoirs of J. M. Gibson: Terrors of the Civil War and Reconstruction Days* (N.p., 1966), 81.

65. *Ibid.*, 5–7.

66. *House Journal, Called Session, 1874*, p. 14; resolution of the Mississippi legislature, December 19, 1874, in Blanche Butler Ames (comp.), *Chronicles*, II, 76–77.

67. Vicksburg *Times*, January 5, 13, 28, 1874; Ames to Grant, January 4[?], 1875 (telegram), in Letterbook C of Governor Ames; Philip H. Sheridan to Ames, January 5, 1875 (telegram), in Governors' Correspondence, Vol. 96. Actually, the army unit sent to Vicksburg deposed the usurping sheriff, making possible court action regarding the office. The

For a time peace returned to turbulent Warren County. Sheriff Crosby, however, did not remain long in Mississippi; he left in July after suffering a severe wound in a saloon brawl with a white deputy. Soon after this incident an affray between a white Republican and Thomas W. Cardozo, the black state superintendent of education who faced embezzlement charges in the county, precipitated a brief flurry of white-league violence that left three blacks dead and threatened a renewal of racial warfare.[68] But despite its recent history and its reputation as the center of white militancy in the state, Vicksburg escaped serious white-league activity in the climactic fall campaign. Although the conservatives carried the county by a comfortable margin, more than 2,000 of the approximately 4,500 registered black voters braved white threats to vote for Republican candidates in the 1875 election. The white leagues of Warren County, however, had no reason to feel that their contribution to the "redemption" of Mississippi was minor; their activities in late 1874 and early 1875 had inspired the cause of white-line militancy and had set an ominous stage for the campaign and election of 1875.

---

carpetbag chancellor, a close associate of Ames, appointed one of Crosby's white deputies as sheriff until Crosby could raise the required bond, which he did in a few days. Blanche Ames to her mother, January 25, 1875, in Blanche Butler Ames (comp.), *Chronicles*, II, 96–97; Vicksburg *Times*, January 28, 1875.

68. Vicksburg *Times*, June 8, July 7, 10, 27, 1875.

20

Revolution

Conservative preparations for the crucial fall election began early and with an intensity seldom seen in American political contests. The outrage that followed the legislature's rejection of the taxpayers' petition and appeal and the heightened racial excitement that began with the "Vicksburg Troubles" seemed at last to give the Bourbons the upper hand in the movement to overcome radicalism. In an editorial entitled "The Dirtiest Despotism on Earth," George W. Harper exclaimed that "Radicalism in the hands of Ames and his negroes has swept away every vestige of republican government in Mississippi." Ames through his vast appointive and removal power had prostituted the public service, Harper declared. "The people, once supreme in such things, are now powerless—have been robbed of their birthright through the rascality of the adventurer and the ignorance of the freedmen. . . . If our fathers threw off the British yoke (which was less humiliating and barbarous than the yoke which has been placed on our necks by Ames and his negroes), should we not make a powerful effort to throw off the yoke which now bears us to the earth?"[1]

The Bourbon editor of the Meridian *Mercury* expressed a similar feeling toward the Ames government and also excoriated the Brown-Barksdale conservatives who, he said, had misled Mississippi whites into believing that the black voters could be "conciliated." Radical adventurers "have brought the State to the verge of ruin, trampling order, thrift, decency, property, feeling, religion, morality and all that constitutes good government and refined society, under foot of their herded cattle," this east Mississippian thundered. It was now time to try the color line against the Radical demagogues. "The aggressive instincts of the white people, so long restrained by motives of policy which they could appreciate, and of leaders, which they could not, would jump with it [the color line],

1. *Hinds County Gazette*, March 31, 1875.

and we should have the first political campaign in the State since the war with the hearts of the people in it."[2]

Bourbons, like the *Mercury* editor, never publicly proclaimed their intention to rob the black man of the ballot, but by an exercise of the "aggressive instincts of the white people" he would be persuaded to support the conservative party. Prior to the revolutionary events of the fall campaign, the prospect of federal intervention caused Bourbons, despite their bravado, to cover up their design to destroy black political rights.

Moderate spokesmen, whose numbers thinned as the political and racial excitement increased, in 1875 began to manifest a shrillness and militancy that belied their professions of moderation and concern for black rights and political cooperation. Moderates especially focused their attacks on the failure of the Ames administration to provide tax relief and on the new militia law that gave the governor an appropriation of $65,000 to create a militia force, including the purchase of several dreaded Gatling guns. The conservatives naturally expected Ames to raise a black militia. Writing in an uncharacteristically truncated style, Lamar expressed the somber belief that "the future of Mississippi is very dark. Ames has it dead. There can be no escape from his rule. His negro regiments are nothing. He will get them killed up, and then Grant will take possession for him. May God help us!" The normally moderate Natchez *Democrat* asserted that the "standing army" measure, whose author was a madman, was "concocted to produce disorder and precipitate a race war for political effect."[3] Some conservative leaders raised the possibility of a taxpayers' revolt directed specifically against the organization of Ames's militia, but when the governor hesitated in forming militia units they dropped the idea.[4]

While the iron was hot, but well before the fall election, conservatives took steps to reorganize the anti-Radical party in the state. "There is no time to be lost," the Bourbon Columbus *Democrat* ex-

2. As reported in the Jackson *Times*, June 8, 1875. See also comments from the Edwards *Courier* in the Jackson *Times*, June 12, 1875.
3. L. Q. C. Lamar to his wife, February 15, 1875, in Mayes, *Lucius Q. C. Lamar*, 211; Natchez *Democrat*, February 11, 1875. See also the Vicksburg *Herald*, January 27, 1875, and the Jackson *Weekly Clarion*, April 7, 1875.
4. *Hinds County Gazette*, March 10, 31, April 28, 1875; Pascagoula *Star*, April 3, 1875.

claimed: "The task before us is a herculean one, and requires the earnest, unceasing labor and effort of every citizen who loves his State, for its accomplishment. Every man must do his duty, his whole duty, or our deliverance from the yoke of bondage is impossible."[5] Responding to the demand for immediate action, conservative members of the legislature selected a committee of forty prominent men of both conservative factions, as well as both traditional parties (Whig and Democrat), to meet in Jackson in May to put the organizational wheels into motion.[6]

When the committee met a dispute immediately arose over the name for the revived conservative party. John W. C. Watson and Amos R. Johnston, both past Whig leaders and opponents of white-line tactics during Reconstruction, insisted that the committee reject a proposal to reorganize the Democratic party. Such an action, they argued, would revive old animosities among whites and destroy all hopes of obtaining black support for the conservative cause in the coming election. Watson and Johnston preferred the name "Conservative" or simply "Reform" for the anti-Radical party. Their attempt failed, however, when Bourbon Whigs in the meeting announced that they had no objection to the name "Democratic" as long as the party adopted a white-line platform. The result was a compromise by which the party would be referred to as the "Democratic-Conservative" party; no mention was made of its relationship to the national Democratic organization. Much to the dismay of expectant Bourbons, the reorganization committee refused to endorse the color line, leaving the decision on the issue to the state convention which was scheduled for August 3.[7]

Confidence and enthusiasm abounded in the county meetings to select delegates to the state Democratic-Conservative convention. Although the influence of race-conscious yeomen was most pronounced at this level, no clear-cut position on the color-line program of white militancy for the campaign emerged from these meetings.[8] The delegations sent to the state convention represented a mixture of young former Confederates, who generally sup-

5. As reported in the Pascagoula *Star*, March 27, 1875.
6. Jackson *Weekly Clarion*, March 11, April 14, 1875.
7. *Ibid.*, May 19, 1875; Jackson *Times*, May 17, 1875.
8. Columbus (Miss.) *Weekly Index*, July 16, 1875; Jackson *Weekly Clarion*, July 7, 21, 28, August 4, 1875.

ported the color line, and the old leadership of both antebellum parties, who as a rule favored moderation. Perhaps the whites of the state in this time of crisis, as they obviously perceived it, took a page from the American Revolutionary past and selected as representatives their most experienced men, albeit with some concessions to the vigor of youth and the heroism of war. The August convention clearly brought together some of the most distinguished Mississippians of the nineteenth century.

Delegates Brown, Lamar, Barksdale, Winfield Scott Featherston, Wiley P. Harris, Josiah A. P. Campbell, and Thomas J. Wharton had all been leaders in the "secession and ruin" movement of the 1850s, and all now advocated reason and moderation.[9] Union-Whig leaders of the past were also very much in evidence in the convention. The presence of George L. Potter, former Governors Humphreys and Clark, George W. Harper, William T. Martin, Benjamin King, Amos R. Johnston, and former Confederate Senator Watson ensured that the word "Conservative" would be retained in the title of the new party and that old Whigs would not be ignored in its councils. Despite their party's heritage of moderation and compromise, several former Whigs in the convention were Bourbon, white-line extremists, notably Humphreys, Harper, McCardle, and Frantz. In fact, one commentator in referring to this group remarked, "Strange to say, the most impracticable among the Democracy of the present day are the late 'old line Whigs' who have crept into the party, and seek to rule it with their same old ideas of ostracizing all who do not agree with them."[10] The rising generation of Mississippi leaders was well represented by future governors John M. Stone, Robert Lowry, and Anselm J. McLaurin, as well as by Edward C. Walthall, James Z. George, J. B. Morgan, Charles E. Hooker (also a farm leader), Hernando D. Money, and Pat Henry, all of whom would serve for many years in Congress. Reflecting the role of the Grange in the anti-Radical crusade, in addition to Hooker, such farm leaders as C. M. Vaiden, William L. Hemingway, and L. O. Bridewell were also present.

The selection of former Governor Clark as president of the

9. The membership and proceedings of the state Democratic-Conservative convention can be found in the Jackson *Weekly Clarion*, August 4, 1875.

10. Jackson *Times*, August 5, 1875.

Democratic-Conservative convention appeared to be an important victory for the moderates. This feeling was reinforced when Clark appointed Watson to chair the important committee on resolutions. Lamar, whose rise to a position of influence in the conservative movement occurred late during Reconstruction, delivered the main address to the delegates. He spent most of the speech, which reportedly kept the delegates spellbound for two and one-half hours, excoriating the Ames and Grant administrations for their abuse of power, but he also included an emphatic warning against the adoption of a white-line platform. "The color line would be ruinous to its victors if victory could be won in that way," he declared. "It is not right. It is not Republican. One of the principles of Democratic Government is that all parts of the body politic should contribute to its support and control. Any race organization which seeks to assert the exclusive management of a country may have good government, but cannot have liberty. It is tyranny unmixed, and is fraught with disaster."[11]

The platform drawn up by the Watson committee and approved by the convention gave a surface indication that Mississippi Democrats had followed Lamar's advice and adopted the basic tenets of the moderate New Departure. The document affirmed "the civil and political equality of all men as established by the Constitution of the United States and the amendments thereto."[12] It also pledged the party to a continued support of "the education of all children of the State in public schools" but with a proper regard for economy in the administration of the system. As had the taxpayers' leagues, the convention emphasized its support for retrenchment in government and tax reform. White-line insurgents, however, blocked an attempt by Lamar-Brown moderates to place the state party on record as diametrically opposed to drawing the color line in the forthcoming campaign. The convention left the matter for the county meetings to determine, at the same time appealing to the voters of both races "to unite vigorously" with the

11. As reported in the Natchez *Democrat*, August 17, 1875. Disappointed that he did not endorse the color line, very few Bourbon newspapers in the state reported Lamar's speech; those that did omitted the part denouncing the white line. Jackson *Times*, August 7, 1875; Adelbert Ames to James G. Blaine, February 15, 1876, in Letterbook D of Governor Ames.

12. See *Appleton's Annual Cyclopaedia*, 1875, p. 514, for the platform.

party in the contest. As the Democratic candidate for state treasurer, the only state office to be filled by the fall election, the delegates nominated William L. Hemingway, master of the Grange in Mississippi. The selection of the Grange leader to head the Democratic-Conservative ticket took into account the farm organization's role in awakening the white masses to a militant opposition to Radical rule and also the emerging political influence, especially at the grass roots, of a number of its more active members.[13]

Some moderates in the convention perhaps genuinely believed that the mild platform would be honored by the party during the weeks ahead. It is clear, however, that the majority of the delegates did not take the document very seriously. Most of them had already succumbed to white-line fervor and did not believe that the adoption of a moderate platform would deter local conservatives from employing militant anti-Negro tactics to win the election. A number of the Democratic delegates went along with the platform in order to placate such important moderates as Watson and Brown, knowing full well that the counties would be controlled by aggressive Bourbons. The nomination of Hemingway was a victory for the white liners, since Democratic militancy was strongest in those areas—the small-farmer counties—where the Grange was strongest.

Governor Ames had no doubts about the Democratic convention's lack of commitment to the cause of racial and political peace. He reported to his wife after the convention, "The true sentiment of the assembly was 'color-line' though the platform says nothing about it. The understanding evidently is that each locality can act as it chooses, but the state convention put forth a platform for Northern consumption."[14]

Nevertheless, almost all of the local Democratic organizations at least formally refrained from a direct appeal to the racial passions of whites. Throughout the state resolutions were adopted calling on blacks to support Democratic-Conservative candidates and promising in return that Negro rights would be protected and the

13. In addition to Hemingway, numerous Grangers ran for local office and the legislature; Charles E. Hooker, a popular Grange speaker, won nomination and election to Congress on the Democratic-Conservative ticket.
14. Ames to his wife, August 4, 1875, in Blanche Butler Ames (comp.), *Chronicles*, II, 124. See also the Pascagoula *Star*, August 7, 1875.

biracial school system preserved if the party triumphed in the fall. Even in many predominantly white counties, where black support in a free election was not necessary to conservative success in winning the local offices, resolutions were adopted that sought to snare black voters. But these resolutions ignored the fact, perhaps deliberately in many counties, that conservatives expected to negate the black vote regardless of what tactics were required.[15]

As the campaign intensified, a number of influential conservatives who had earlier resisted the racial appeals of the Bourbon faction reluctantly arrived at a support for the white line on the grounds, as they insisted, that blacks had already drawn the color line. Preferring to forget, among other things, the conservative-sponsored Black Code of 1865, which was an unadulterated exercise in white supremacy, conservatives singled out blacks in the ill-starred legislature of 1875 as the instigators of color-line politics. By September the influential Jackson *Clarion* had cast its lot with the white liners, claiming that black members as a unit had voted against all of the reform proposals of the 1875 legislature while supporting the iniquitous Metropolitan Police Bill for Vicksburg (which did not pass) and the "Gatling Gun Law."[16] Nonetheless, the *Clarion* and a number of conservative spokesmen, including state Democratic campaign manager James George, continued to appeal to black voters and to express the view that many could be persuaded to vote the conservative ticket in the election.[17]

By the end of August Lamar, who was rapidly becoming the epitome of the New Departure statesman of the South, privately conceded that his sympathies lay with the Bourbons, although he found the color line inexpedient at this time. He explained to a friend:

> I have just emerged from a struggle to keep our people from a race conflict. I am not sure that we are yet safe, for the *black* line is still maintained by the agents of the Federal Government. The negro race, which has no idea of a principle of government or of society beyond

15. The proceedings of many of these meetings can be found in the August-September, 1875, issues of the Jackson *Weekly Clarion* and the *Hinds County Gazette*.

16. For Barksdale and the Jackson *Weekly Clarion's* conversion to the color-line policy, see the issues of August 11, 18, 1875.

17. *Ibid.*, September 15, 1875.

that of obedience to the mandate of a master, sees in these agents the only embodiment of authority (mastership) in the country, and their obedience to them is not a whit less slavish than it was formerly to their masters. We could, by forming the "color line," and bringing to bear those agencies which intellect, pluck, and will always give, overcome the stolid, inert, and illiterate majority; but such a victory will bring about conflicts and race passions and collisions with Federal power. Our only deliverance is in a change of Federal policy toward us.[18]

Euphemisms abounded in the Democratic effort to avoid the hard fact that racial passions had assumed the dominant role in the struggle against Republican rule. As Harper, the party leader in Hinds County, put it: "The negroes are all right—it is only the thieving white men that the people are after." Again, this Bourbon-Whig editor declared that the campaign of 1875 "will be an uprising of the tax-paying people to assert their rights as American citizens, and to indict before the world the illegal acts of Adelbert Ames and his party of imbeciles, corruptionists and plunderers." Or as the editor of a newspaper in Macon, where a severe racial confrontation had been narrowly averted, wrote: "The forces arrayed in this contest are the party of intelligence, economy and virtue, against that of ignorance, plunder and vice."[19] The line the Bourbons proposed to draw, according to another writer, was one "so rigid . . . between [them] and the party of ignorance and vice that no man of self respect, no good citizen of intelligence dare cross it without incurring the odium of treason."[20]

At the same time an increasing number of Democratic editors and spokesmen abandoned all pretext regarding the racialist purpose in the election. During the campaign the Forest *Register* of the "Mighty East" carried at its masthead the slogan: "A white man in a white man's place. A black man in a black man's place. Each according to the eternal fitness of things."[21] The Columbus *Index* declared that "the negro has proven a dangerous experiment in politics" and was "unfit for the privileges of a citizen" but admitted that the black man's exercise of the privilege of suffrage was un-

18. Lamar to Charles Reemelin, August 25, 1875, in Mayes, *Lucius Q. C. Lamar*, 258–59.

19. *Hinds County Gazette*, August 18, 1875; Macon *Beacon*, October 23, 1875.

20. Greenville *Weekly Times*, August 21, 1875.

21. As quoted in Wharton, *The Negro in Mississippi*, 184.

avoidable at this time.[22] This editor defined the color line as "a plain and open declaration by the white people that they will no longer . . . submit to the oppression and spoliation of the negro representatives."[23] From Vicksburg, former Governor Humphreys announced that "the color line as now held here by white men is simply the protest of nature against race degradation. It may lead to a war of the races. We all hope not. . . . We need the muscle and desire the friendship of the negro, but we cannot consent to race degradation."[24] Underlying the Bourbons' campaign strategy, although they never admitted it, was the determination to carry the election by intimidation and force if necessary.

Mississippi Republicans entered the critical contest of 1875 in sad disarray. With a registered majority of about 20,000 black voters, not including the few hundred whites that perhaps could still be counted on to vote the Republican ticket, the state party was convulsed by factionalism and by dissatisfaction with Governor Ames. Earlier, the Vicksburg troubles had motivated many Republicans to subdue their differences and close ranks behind Ames.[25] But this spirit of harmony was short-lived and never very deep. The governor's support of Sheriff Crosby, his continued dependence upon carpetbag cronies at the capital, his toleration of disreputable officeholders on the local level, and his failure to move the legislature of 1875 along the path of retrenchment and tax reform resulted in a quick revival of the bitter divisions in the party, which inevitably produced new additions to the anti-Ames faction. The Jackson *Pilot*, the Ames newspaper organ at the state capital, fueled the fires of the dispute by lashing out at those Republicans who criticized the administration, describing them as "miserable, malignant mongrels who snarl and snap at everybody and everything." The "baneful and negative effects" of the "sore-head" critics gave "strength and courage to the Democracy" in its war against the Republican order, the editors of this journal announced.[26] The Jackson *Times* and the *Pilot*, both edited by car-

22. As reported in the Jackson *Pilot*, October 5, 1875.
23. Columbus *Weekly Index*, July 16, 1875.
24. Benjamin G. Humphreys to Lamar, January 3, 1875, in Lamar-Mayes Papers.
25. Blanche Ames to her mother, December 30, 1874, in Blanche Butler Ames (comp.), *Chronicles*, II, 81.
26. Jackson *Weekly Pilot*, March 27, April 17 (quote), 1875.

petbaggers, carried on a running battle in their columns and seemed to gain greater satisfaction in attacking each other than in denouncing white-league activities. While the fate of republicanism hung in the balance, Ames spent a great deal of time assailing his opponents in the party and seeking the political destruction of Senator Pease, State Attorney General Harris, and United States District Attorney Wells, whom the *Pilot* dubbed the "trinity of demagogues."[27] He also, of course, continued to make war on his old rival Alcorn. The verbose scalawag senator responded in kind during the fall campaign with a flood of denunciatory letters in northern and southern newspapers, blaming Ames for the tragedy that was unfolding in the state.[28]

On the local level Republican factionalism was also rampant— even before the Democrats had a chance to apply their repetoire of pressure tactics designed partly to divide and weaken the grassroots' Radical leadership. Despite Republican professions that theirs was still the party of progress and freedom, cynicism and opportunism had replaced the early Reconstruction idealism of many local party functionaries, and their desire for position and influence spawned bitter intraparty struggles in almost all of the counties. Black leaders also got into the act. They vied with white Republicans for control of the local black community, and when the 1875 campaign was launched they brushed aside white Republicans in several counties and nominated a full slate of black candidates. In Holmes County a Negro challenge to carpetbag dominance resulted in the death of two black politicians. In Warren white Republicans regained control of the party; but their victory was a hollow one, since many blacks in the county, already intimidated by white-league activity, refused to risk their lives on election day in order to vote the ticket of their carpetbag adversaries.[29]

Divisions along racial lines had little to do with Republican factionalism in some counties. In Lowndes County moderate Republi-

27. Ames to O. E. Babcock, September 2, 1875, Ames to Edwards Pierrepont, September 27, 1875, both in Letterbook D of Governor Ames; Ames to his wife, August 18, 19, 1875, in Blanche Butler Ames (comp.), *Chronicles*, II, 140, 141; Jackson *Pilot*, October 13, 17, 1875.

28. Jackson *Weekly Clarion*, September 22, 1875; Pascagoula *Star*, October 2, 1875.

29. Ames to his wife, August 5, 1875, in Blanche Butler Ames (comp.), *Chronicles*, II, 125–26; Kyle, "Reconstruction in Panola County," 72; Jackson *Times*, June 23, October 18, 1875; Jackson *Weekly Pilot*, September 4, 1875.

cans ran Robert Gleed, an early black Radical, for sheriff in an effort to defeat a rival faction that had fused their strength with local conservatives. In Issaquena and Washington counties powerful black leaders struggled among themselves for control of the party, dividing Negro voters as the campaign of 1875 got underway.[30] "Like a nest of vipers, girdled with fire," the unsympathetic Water Valley *Courier* reported, "the Mississippi Radicals are striking their poisonous fangs into each other in a way that portends the destruction of the whole brood. At every gathering of their motley hordes, from a beat meeting to a district convention, there is a fierce and bitter strife."[31] Governor Ames, on the eve of the campaign that would decide the fate of his party in Mississippi, lamented, "Never before has the strife among our friends been so bitter."[32]

On August 25 the Republican party, primarily the Ames part of it, went through the motions of a state convention. For chairman, the predominantly black convention selected Albert T. Morgan, a Yazoo Radical and carpetbagger who had brought the party to grief in his county. Then in a perfunctory fashion it adopted the usual platform on equal rights, free speech, honesty and economy in government, and free schools. The delegates also congratulated themselves "on the success and economic administration of Governor Ames." In perhaps its wisest action, and despite the opposition of a powerful member of the Ames clique, the convention selected the able scalawag George M. Buchanan, a twice-wounded Confederate officer and Holly Springs businessman, as its nominee for state treasurer.[33] The difficult task of selecting candidates for Congress and the legislature was left for local Republicans.

The serious part of the campaign began on September 4 with a race riot at Clinton, a small town fifteen miles west of Jackson.

30. Jackson *Weekly Pilot*, September 4, 1875; Natchez *Democrat*, September 7, 1875; Jackson *Weekly Clarion*, September 8, 1875; Jackson *Times*, September 30, 1875.

31. As reported in the Jackson *Weekly Pilot*, September 11, 1875.

32. Ames to his wife, August 5, 1875, in Blanche Butler Ames (comp.), *Chronicles*, II, 126. As conservatives had repeatedly charged, Ames believed that the main source of conflict in the party was the desire for office. Ames to his wife, July 29, 1875, *ibid.*, 115.

33. Ames to his wife, August 26, 1875, *ibid.*, 146; New York *Times*, August 26, 1875; *Appleton's Annual Cyclopaedia*, 1875, pp. 514–15. For a biographical sketch of Buchanan see the Vicksburg *Plain Dealer*, June 11, 1875.

Fighting erupted spontaneously at a large Republican rally, in which Democrats had been invited to attend and share the speaking. Who fired the first shot remains a mystery, but it probably could be traced to an armed, drunken group of white youths on the fringe of the crowd.[34] In the rage that followed the first crackling of gunfire, several people of both races were killed or wounded. A report quickly spread that the three white men who were killed had been brutally murdered and mutilated by enraged blacks. When night fell, a special train arrived at Clinton with armed men from Vicksburg and other communities to the west. The next morning the slaughter began. Vicksburgers, who had had experience in such matters, moved out of Clinton and began a virtually indiscriminate assault on blacks. During the next two days between twenty and thirty blacks were killed before the armed bands returned to their homes. Terrified Negroes fled to Jackson and took refuge around the United States courthouse and the governor's mansion. Despite the advantage that the Vicksburgers had given them, whites in the Clinton area, fearing the worst, slept with their weapons and rarely took them off during the day. At night Negro bummers did their work, although not on the scale that whites later claimed.[35]

Meanwhile, Yazoo County had fallen to a white vigilante force. Trouble had been brewing for some time in this large, predominantly Delta county. Conservatives and dissident Republicans had long chaffed under the domination of Morgan, a Radical carpetbagger who in 1874 had killed his northern rival in a struggle for the sheriff's office. Tension mounted during the summer of 1875 as a result of the racial conflict in nearby Warren County and the approach of the fall election. Anticipating trouble, Morgan organized irregular military companies composed exclusively of blacks. He reportedly armed his ragtag legion with 1,600 surplus army

34. Report of (Biracial) Grand Jury to Investigate the Clinton Riot, Delivered to Judge Robert F. Brown, February 7, 1876, in Governors' Correspondence, Vol. 101; Jackson *Times*, October 2, 1875; Natchez *Democrat*, September 10, 1875.

35. Sarah Chilton to Mrs. L. N. Brown, September 17, 25, 1875, in Charles M. Norton, John H. Chilton, and William H. Dameron Family Papers, Southern Historical Collection, University of North Carolina Library, Chapel Hill; *Annual Message of Governor Ames, 1876*, pp. 3–6; New York *Times*, September 8, 1875; testimony of George T. Swann in *Mississippi in 1875*, I, 302–308.

guns and began drilling them at night.[36] With these inflammatory ingredients present, an outbreak of racial violence was almost inevitable. Fighting erupted at a Republican meeting in Yazoo County, while Morgan was speaking, when a Democratic intruder opened fire on a black man who had called for his expulsion from the hall. A skirmish between armed companies of blacks and whites near the village of Satartia soon followed. Few were killed in this encounter, but during the next few days "a hastily organized citizen force" of more than eight hundred men, designed ostensibly to "repel an invasion which was threatened from surrounding plantations," literally overthrew Republican rule in Yazoo County. Ames raised two companies of black militia to reinstate Republican officials in the county and disperse the rebels, but when Morgan perhaps wisely refused to leave Jackson, the governor abandoned the military operation.[37]

These and other steps by Ames to organize black militia units brought the state to the brink of warfare between the races. Only reluctantly, however, and then against the advice of leading Republicans, did Ames raise a force to preserve order. Several of his associates warned that such action, taken at a time when white passions were high and when armed white leagues were in the field, would inevitably bring bloody racial strife and general social disorders. Even General Christopher C. Augur, commander of the Department of the Gulf, though sympathizing with Ames in his plight advised him against arming blacks, warning that such a step would precipitate "a war of the races and one to be felt over the entire South."[38]

Actually, the governor had waited until it was too late to act under the militia law passed in early 1875 giving him authority to

36. Oscar J. E. Stuart to J. A. Mitchell, September, 1875, in Dimitry Papers; Pascagoula *Star*, January 18, 1874.

37. Jackson *Pilot*, September 4, 11, 1875; Jackson *Times*, October 22, 1875; Ames to his wife, September 3, October 14, 1875, in Blanche Butler Ames (comp.), *Chronicles*, II, 159–60, 217; Garnet Andrews *et al.* to J. Z. George, October, 1875, in Governors' Correspondence, Vol. 99. Morgan wrote an extensive account of the insurrection in Yazoo County; this account was published in the Jackson *Pilot*, September 22–25, 1875.

38. Ames to Pierrepont, September 11, 1875 (telegram), Governors' Correspondence, Vol. 99; Ames to his wife, September 7, 1875, in Blanche Butler Ames (comp.), *Chronicles*, II, 166–67; Christopher C. Augur to Ames, September 5, 1875 (telegram), in Governors' Correspondence, Vol. 99.

organize units to maintain order during the fall campaign.[39] Ames hesitated to form military companies partly because he believed that few reliable whites could be found who would accept commissions to lead black militiamen. Ever suspicious of former rebels and those northerners in the state who had succumbed to conservative influences, he rejected out of hand any attempt to obtain their services for the militia. Therefore, to Ames the implementation of the militia act would of necessity mean creating a predominantly Negro force with only a sprinkling of white Radical officers.[40] This step, which he knew would inflame white prejudices, he refused to take until confronted with revolution in the fall.

Another important reason for Ames's inaction was his faith that federal authorities would intervene to suppress the lawless and ensure a free election in the fall. Earlier in the year President Grant had given the carpetbag governor a clear indication that in an emergency he would intervene with federal troops. The resurgence of northern outrage against white-league violence in Vicksburg and New Orleans and Grant's dispatch of troops to Vicksburg in January demonstrated to Ames that, despite the national Democratic victories of 1874, the federal government would sustain his regime. In March Ames received what appeared to be a definite commitment of national assistance when Benjamin F. Butler, his father-in-law and an influential confidant of Grant, wrote him on behalf of the president that if the need arose the full force of the federal government would be used to put down revolutionary groups in the state.[41] With this in mind, it is little wonder that Ames at first refrained from organizing the militia.

When the Clinton and Yazoo troubles occurred, accompanied by other reports of racial violence, Ames put Grant's promises to the test. Declaring that "domestic violence prevails in various parts of

39. Ames preferred the organization of an elite, swift-striking state police force, similar to the "picked cavalry" unit that Governor Alcorn had earlier proposed. But when a state police bill failed to pass the legislature, Ames pressed for the militia authorization. Ames to Merriman Howard, August 18, 1874, in Letterbook A of Governor Ames; *Annual Message of Governor Ames, 1875*, p. 14; *Laws of Mississippi, 1875*, p. 30.

40. Jackson *Pilot*, October 8, 1875; Ames to his wife, September 5, 1875, in Blanche Butler Ames (comp.), *Chronicles*, II, 163; Ames to Pierrepont, September 11, 1875, in Governors' Correspondence, Vol. 99.

41. Vicksburg *Times*, January 5, 1875, quoting the Cleveland *Leader*; Benjamin F. Butler to Ames, March 3, 1875, in Blanche Butler Ames (comp.), *Chronicles*, II, 98.

this State, beyond the power of the State authorities to suppress," he applied on September 8 for federal troops to rescue Mississippi from the lawless.[42] Several federal officials in the state, including Judge Robert A. Hill, quickly endorsed the governor's appeal. Hill believed that the recent ruling of Justice Joseph P. Bradley in the Grant Parish case, which appeared certain to be sustained by the full Supreme Court, had destroyed the federal court's jurisdiction in instances of domestic violence.[43] With local federal officials helpless to avert disaster, the only way to prevent further violence and widespread intimidation by white leagues was to dispatch federal troops to the state, this scalawag judge declared. George T. Swann, the clerk of Judge Hill's court and a prominent antebellum lawyer, advanced a similar remedy to save the state from massive disorders. He wrote Justice Bradley: "My private opinion is that nothing short of an immediate display of a strong U.S. Military force, under cool men, at different points through the central part of this State, can give us quiet, or any possibility of a free ballot in our fall elections." Carpetbag District Attorney William W. Dedrick, who was associated with the moderate wing of the party, informed Attorney General Edwards Pierrepont that "the white people are so thoroughly armed, and so terribly bent upon pushing their advantage in this that the Elections in very many counties will be practically controlled by violence in spite of all that could be done" short of federal military intervention. Dedrick warned that "any lukewarm support or halfway measures" by the federal government to provide security would be disastrous, since such action would delude Republicans into conducting an active campaign which would backfire and jeopardize the lives of unprotected blacks.[44]

42. Ames to U. S. Grant, September 8, 1875 (telegram), September 8, 1875, in Combined Letterbook of Governors Ames and Stone. A printed copy of this dispatch can be found in *Appleton's Annual Cyclopaedia*, 1875, p. 516.

43. Hill was correct in his analysis of the effect of the Grant Parish case, which the Supreme Court later ruled on as *United States* v. *Cruikshank* (1876). Along with other Supreme Court pronouncements, the Cruikshank decision removed civil rights violations from federal jurisdiction to the state courts.

44. Robert A. Hill to William W. Dedrick, September 10, 1875, George T. Swann to Joseph P. Bradley, September 9, 1875, and Dedrick to Pierrepont, September 10, 1875, all in Records of the Department of Justice, Files for Mississippi, RG 60, NA. The Hill and Swann appeals for military intervention were forwarded to Pierrepont by Dedrick.

On September 10 Attorney General Pierrepont, in place of the absent president, wired Ames for more information on the crisis in Mississippi and specifically asked what action the state had taken to suppress the disorders. At the same time he indicated that "forces had been put in readiness" if the governor could demonstrate that an insurrection actually existed. In his reply Ames added little specific information to his earlier message; instead he stressed that the intensity of white-line sentiment in the state made it impossible to organize a white militia force to protect the rights of blacks in the campaign and election. Conceding that northerners were becoming increasingly critical of federal interference in southern affairs, Ames announced that he was prepared to accept full political responsibility for intervention in the Mississippi crisis. "As the Governor of a State, I made a demand which cannot well be refused," he told Pierrepont. "Let the odium, in all its magnitude, descend upon me. I cannot escape the conscientious discharge of my duty towards a class of American citizens whose only crime consists in their color." Under the circumstances, he said, President Grant and the Republican party would be absolved of blame for the intervention.[45]

Alarmed by the threat of federal intervention, Democratic leaders and a few anti-Ames Republicans, notably Pease and State Attorney General Harris, rushed dispatches to Washington in an effort to convince federal authorities that peace prevailed in Mississippi. From Vicksburg, Pease informed Pierrepont on September 11 that the "excitement arising from recent riots at Yazoo City and Clinton has in a great measure subsided. A civil posse, composed of good citizens of all political parties, and of sufficient force to protect life and property, can be had in any county in the State. No effort has yet been made by the State authorities in this direction. Until all legal measures have been exhausted, I am of the opinion that Federal intervention is unwise, impolitic, and will only tend to aggravate existing difficulties."[46] George, chairman of the state Democratic party, told Pierrepont, "The employment of

45. Pierrepont to Ames, September 10, 1875 (telegram), printed in the New York *Times*, September 13, 1875; Ames to Pierrepont, September 11, 1875 (telegram), in Combined Letterbook of Governors Ames and Stone.
46. As reported in the Jackson *Times*, September 11, 1875.

United States troops would but increase the distrust of the people in the good faith of the present State government." As a demonstration of their sincerity—and thus hoping to head off federal intervention—"the most responsible citizens in Mississippi" had offered to fill the governor's militia ranks with dependable white troops, George reported.[47] Ames summarily declined their offers.

When Pierrepont received these documents, including Ames's reply of September 11, he dispatched them to President Grant at Long Branch, his summer home in New Jersey. He also "made a full report" to Grant which evidently contained a recommendation of the policy the president would soon adopt.[48] The force of the materials that Grant saw was clearly on the side of those seeking to prevent federal interference. The case for intervention was also injured by two conflicting dispatches to Washington from black Sheriff William H. Harney of Hinds County. One message declared that perfect peace prevailed in his county, the scene of the recent Clinton tumult; the other, immediately following the first, claimed the reverse, emphasizing that no protection for blacks existed in the area.[49]

Meanwhile, the northern press, including the New York *Times*, the Chicago *Tribune*, and other influential Republican newspapers, denounced Ames's call for troops as unwarranted and urged the Grant administration to deny his request. "The administration of Gov. Ames, a carpetbagger and political adventurer, has done much to disorganize society and teach general contempt for all authority in Mississippi," the Republican Philadelphia *Press* announced. The disorder that Ames complained of, this newspaper averred, "is palpably the result of a corrupt and powerless government, that had taught its ignorant negro dependents that they were above the law in a struggle with the whites, and they have made the common mistake of taking the leaders at their word."[50] The powerful New York *Tribune* declared: "There is no evidence except in Governor Ames's excited imagination that [whites] have interfered or intend to interfere with the people whom he is so

---

47. Natchez *Democrat*, October 10, 1875.
48. New York *Times*, September 13, 1875.
49. Jackson *Times*, September 11, 1875; *Appleton's Annual Cyclopaedia*, 1875, p. 516.
50. As reported in the Jackson *Weekly Clarion*, September 29, 1875.

anxious to protect. The belief is coming to be quite general that except for the constant interference of such men as Gov. Ames between the two races there would be not only no occasion for troops but no disturbance whatever of their friendly relations."[51]

Attorney General Pierrepont's suggestion to Ames, prior to receiving the president's decision on the matter, that Republicans in the state should first look to their own organizations for security struck a responsive cord in the minds of the New York *Times* editors. Since Mississippi Republicans were a majority and controlled the state government, the *Times* pontifically proclaimed, they should be able "to organize and protect themselves against the violence to which they are exposed from the minority. . . . If they have not the pluck of [or?] capacity to do this, they will unquestionably go to the wall. No amount of outside aid from the United States authorities can prevent it. . . . The most that the United States Government can do is to help those who help themselves."[52] With such antiinterventionist pronouncements being broadcast in the North by Republican newspapers, Mississippi conservatives hardly needed the support, which they received anyway, of their northern Democratic friends in the campaign to discredit Ames's appeal for troops.

In opposing intervention, northern Republicans were more concerned with the fall elections in the North, and especially in Ohio, than with security and good government in Mississippi. Ames had implied as much in his September 11 dispatch to Pierrepont, and in private he wrote, "I am fully alive to the fact that my action [the call for troops] will be like an exploding shell in the political canvass at the North."[53] This point was driven home to President Grant in confidential contacts with northern Republicans. A delegation of Ohio Republicans told him that the employment of troops in Mississippi would bring defeat to Rutherford B. Hayes, the party's candidate for governor, in the fall election. In Washington, Pierrepont surveyed members of the cabinet and reported to

51. New York *Tribune*, September 21, 1875.
52. New York *Times*, September 16, 1875. See also the issue of September 13, 1875. For comments by other northern newspapers on the issue of intervention, see the Jackson *Weekly Clarion*, September 15, 22, 1875.
53. Ames to his wife, September 9, 1875, in Blanche Butler Ames (comp.), *Chronicles*, II, 169.

Grant at Long Branch that they opposed intervention; the emergency, they preferred to believe, was not such to justify the dispatch of federal forces to the state at this time. Years later, black leader John R. Lynch recalled that Grant told him soon after the election that the political situation in Ohio was the determining factor in his decision not to send troops.[54] And, in fact, Grant in justifying his decision not to intervene alluded to the changing climate of opinion in the nation regarding the employment of troops in southern states. "The whole public are tired out with these annual autumnal outbreaks in the South, and the great majority are ready now to condemn any interference on the part of the Government," he declared.[55]

Nevertheless, it is clear from his actions in Louisiana, where he shocked northerners by permitting General Philip Sheridan in early 1875 to purge the legislature of its Democratic members, that Grant was prepared to flout political opinion. In fact, the barrage of criticism that greeted his action in Louisiana was probably far more severe than any he would have received had he dispatched troops to preserve order in the Magnolia state election.[56] The president obviously agonized over his Mississippi decision; when he finally decided not to send troops he left the door open for a subsequent intervention if he felt the situation was further deteriorating. First, however, he wanted Ames to exhaust "his own resources before he receives Government aid." If intervention must come, he assured Mississippians, "I shall instruct the commander of the forces to have *no child's play*."[57]

54. John A. Carpenter, *Ulysses S. Grant* (New York, 1970), 144; John Lynch, *Facts of Reconstruction*, 150–51.

55. The president's statement was forwarded to Ames by the attorney general. Pierrepont to Ames, September 14, 1875, in Governors' Correspondence, Vol. 99. Although containing a few insignificant printing errors, a copy of this message may be found in *Appleton's Annual Cyclopaedia*, 1875, p. 516.

56. The Natchez *Democrat*, in its January, 1875, issues carried numerous excerpts from northern newspapers denouncing Grant and Sheridan for their intervention in Louisiana affairs. See also Carpenter, *Ulysses S. Grant*, 139. In an August letter in which he analyzed the prospects for Republican success in the Ohio election, Grant found only one issue in the contest—the financial policies of the government. He made no mention of affairs in the South as a factor in the election, suggesting that political considerations were not as great a cause for his action in the Mississippi crisis of 1875 as historians have supposed. James Grant Wilson (ed.), *General Grant's Letters to a Friend, 1861–1880* (New York, 1973), 74–76.

57. Pierrepont to Ames, September 14, 1875, in Governors' Correspondence, Vol. 99.

On September 14 Pierrepont informed Ames of the president's decision not to send troops, and at the same time he took the occasion to lecture the governor on his failure to provide state protection for Republicans. The administration, Pierrepont scolded Ames, "cannot understand why you do not strengthen yourself" by accepting the assistance of reliable whites in suppressing unruly citizens, "nor do we see why you do not call the Legislature together and obtain from them whatever power, and money, and arms you need. . . . I suggest that you take all lawful means and all needed measures to preserve the peace by the forces in your own State, and let the country see that citizens of Miss. who are largely favorable to good order, and who are largely Republican, have the courage and the manhood to fight for their rights, and to destroy the bloody ruffians who murder the innocent and unoffending freedmen."[58]

The finality of this decision was not as apparent during the days that followed as it would prove to be. Anticipating the president's negative response, Ames had rushed a delegation of leading Radicals to Washington to explain to Pierrepont, who was the fulcrum of the administration's southern policy, why state authorities could not control the tumult that was sweeping the state. The delegation met with the attorney general two days after Grant had revealed his policy, and he sent them home empty handed.[59] A few days later Butler reportedly persuaded Pierrepont to place the troops that were in camp in Mississippi at the governor's disposal for use in an emergency.[60] When it appeared in early October, one month before the election, that the Grant administration might capitulate to Radical demands for intervention, an anti-Ames delegation of Republicans dashed to Washington to counter the move. Consisting of Pease, State Attorney General Harris, and Wells, the delegation met with Pierrepont and assured him that conditions in Mississippi would be worse if troops were sent. The majority of the whites, they insisted, deprecated the violence that had been committed by the white leagues and were ready to suppress it. The

58. *Ibid.*
59. New York *Times,* September 16, 1875.
60. Blanche Ames to her husband Adelbert Ames, September 22, 1875, in Blanche Butler Ames (comp.), *Chronicles,* II, 190.

extreme partisanship and executive weakness of Governor Ames and the corruption of those around him, these Republicans told Pierrepont, were the fundamental reasons for the violent antagonism between the races and the organization of militant white leagues. Only a policy of conciliation, by both national and state authorities, could reverse the trend toward bloody revolution. Pierrepont agreed.[61] If the Grant administration had entertained any second thoughts about its nonintervention policy, this conference ended all such thinking.

Left to his own devices, Ames took the only course that he believed remained open to him in the struggle to protect his followers and to maintain order in the state. He began to organize predominantly black militia units, a step he had tried for months to avoid. To accomplish this purpose he sent dispatches to local Republican leaders in a number of threatened counties, asking them to raise militia companies. The response of these Republicans was mixed. In some areas, especially in the interior of the state, Republicans summarily rejected the governor's appeal for troops, whereas in several western plantation counties Ames supporters reluctantly answered the call and formed ragtag units, only two of which ever performed active service under the governor's command. These two companies had been directed to march into Yazoo County and suppress the white insurrection there; but before contact was made with the white leagues they were ordered back to Jackson.[62] Actually, Adjutant General A. G. Parker enrolled an all-white militia company in Jackson, but Ames ignored it, believing despite the contrary opinion of many Republicans, and the hope of the Grant administration, that whites could not be trusted to put down the white leagues.[63]

The conservative reaction to the Radical governor's action in raising a black militia was instantaneous and predictable. The state executive committee of the Democratic-Conservative party issued

61. This interview was reported by the Washington *Star* and was copied by several Mississippi newspapers, including the Hazlehurst *Copiahan*, October 16, 1875, and the Jackson *Times*, October 11, 1875.

62. Ames to J. P. Matthews, September 24, 1875, in Combined Letterbook of Governors Ames and Stone; Ames to his wife, September 24, October 14, 1875, in Blanche Butler Ames (comp.), *Chronicles*, II, 95, 217.

63. Jackson *Pilot*, September 24, 1875; Jackson *Times*, September 23, 1875.

an address denouncing the governor's maneuver "as a deliberate attempt to incite disturbances, so that there may be an imaginary insurrection, which he may suppress in blood." It called on whites to be calm in the face of impending racial conflict. "Ames is organizing murder, civil war, rapine, a war of races, in our otherwise peaceful State," the Jackson *Clarion* thundered. Visions of black insurrections of the kind that had engulfed Santo Domingo and Haiti swirled through the heads of many whites. During the night, as one Republican reported, "they nervously clutch at their Winchester rifle at the head of the bed. The day-time is spent mainly in cursing Ames."[64] Living in an area of Hinds County that had been disrupted by the Clinton disorders, Harper declared that he had never heard a public official so fiercely denounced as Ames since he began the organization of the Negro militia. "He is regarded as the most wicked and infamous man that ever lived in the State, at once unworthy of the association or the recognition of good citizens, and unworthy of the protection of the laws; a hyena in human form, unfit to live and wholly unfit to die."[65] Many conservatives seemed convinced that Ames's purpose in organizing the militia was to precipitate armed encounters between the races that would result in federal intervention and a Radical victory in the election.[66]

The militia policy of the governor intensified the efforts of whites to organize irregular companies for "self-defense." Ames himself observed that "they really fear the militia will disturb their families in case of a disturbance."[67] The organization of armed associations by whites called for a similar response by equally frightened blacks.

With racial passions heightened, a skirmish occurred in Coahoma County between one hundred white defenders of Friar's Point, the county seat, and several hundred blacks who were incited by Sheriff John Brown, a mulatto from Ohio, to launch an assault

64. Jackson *Weekly Clarion*, September 29, October 13, 1875; Jackson *Pilot*, October 6, 1875. See also the Greenville *Weekly Times*, October 16, 1875.
65. *Hinds County Gazette*, October 13, 1875.
66. See for example the Pascagoula *Star*, October 9, 1875, the Jackson *Weekly Clarion*, October 6, 1875, and Susan Dabney Smedes, *Memorials of a Southern Planter*, ed. Fletcher M. Green (New York, 1965), 252.
67. Ames to his wife, October 12, 1875, in Blanche Butler Ames (comp.), *Chronicles*, II, 216.

upon the town. Brown's call for an attack on the Delta village followed a heated debate that he had had with Senator Alcorn at a Republican meeting. Although no white league existed in the county, in fact there was no organized opposition to Republican rule there, whites under the leadership of Alcorn and former Confederate General James R. Chalmers quickly rendezvoused at the courthouse as Brown's force appeared on the outskirts of town. At this point a number of blacks, who had been told by Brown that their rights were endangered by the whites of the county, questioned the sheriff's authority to command. Unable to maintain unity in the ranks, Brown ordered his force to fall back a short distance from town where they could set up their battle lines. The white forces moved out of town to contest the ground, and a fight occurred which, according to Alcorn, miraculously left no one dead or wounded. Brown fled the county and later appeared in Memphis explaining that he had been "detached from his friends early in the trouble."[68]

Bloody clashes between armed forces of the two races were also narrowly averted in Tallahatchie and Hinds counties. In several areas of the state both blacks and whites, a Republican observed, "feel that they are slumbering upon a volcano, which may burst forth at any time and engulf them all in ruin."[69] The Mobile *Register* called for the organization of "bands of minute men in every county" in Mississippi and promised that in a conflict with Ames's minions Alabama would send "men, money and arms trooping across our border to defend our kinsmen and our trade."[70]

Faced with this explosive situation, Governor Ames agreed to hold "a peace conference" with James Z. George and a few prominent Jackson Democrats. Out of this remarkable meeting on October 13 came a "treaty of peace," which produced a degree of racial quiet for the remainder of the election campaign. The meeting and agreement were largely arranged through the influence of George K. Chase who had been sent to Mississippi by Attorney

68. This account of the fray is based mainly on Alcorn's report, which may be found in the Jackson *Weekly Clarion*, October 13, 1875. See also the Jackson *Times*, October 8, 1875. One report indicated that eight blacks were killed in the fighting. Otis A. Singletary, *Negro Militia and Reconstruction* (Austin, 1957), 95.

69. Jackson *Pilot*, October 7, 1875; Jackson *Weekly Clarion*, October 13, 1875.

70. As reported in the Jackson *Pilot*, October 6, 1875.

General Pierrepont to investigate and report on conditions there. In the treaty the governor agreed to send home the two militia units on active duty in the Jackson area and to encase their arms. No additional companies were to be mustered; however, those already organized, including the two units in Hinds County, could still be called out in case of an emergency. On their part, the Democrats agreed to preserve the peace and permit a fair election in November.[71]

As a result of the peace agreement a feeling of relief swept across Mississippi, followed by an eerie racial calm broken only by scattered instances of violence and physical threats. On the day following the agreement the Jackson *Times*, a Republican newspaper, proclaimed "The Dawn of Peace" and reported that "talks of insurrections and riots and murders have given place to congratulations, which are frequently exchanged in view of the fact that [disturbances], with their attendant horrors, are no longer anticipated or dreaded." Even Ames expressed confidence that the agreement would be observed by George and his political associates. "Consequently I believe that we will have peace, order and a fair election," he reported to Pierrepont.[72]

Nevertheless, even before the signing of the peace agreement white leaguers had accomplished their objective of virtually paralyzing the Republican party in a number of counties and communities. The chilling reports of white depredations near Clinton and in Yazoo County, along with the news that Governor Ames was unable to provide security for Republicans, spread rapidly through the black communities of Mississippi creating alarm and causing blacks to fear for their lives at the first appearance of the white league in their area.[73] Still, the many incidents of violence and intimidation did not significantly affect every community or even

71. Ames to his wife, October 14, 1875, in Blanche Butler Ames (comp.), *Chronicles*, II, 217; Ames to Pierrepont, October 16, 1875, in Governors' Correspondence, Vol. 99; Jackson *Times*, October 13, 14, 1875. James W. Garner is inaccurate when he writes that Ames agreed to disband his militia. Garner, *Reconstruction in Mississippi*, 388.

72. Jackson *Times*, October 15, 1875; Ames to Pierrepont, October 16, 1875, in Governors' Correspondence, Vol. 99.

73. Testimony of scalawag Thomas Walton in *Mississippi in 1875*, I, 56; Ames to his wife, October 12, 1875, in Blanche Butler Ames (comp.), *Chronicles*, II, 216; Jackson *Pilot*, October 15, 1875.

every county of the state.[74] Indeed, in most counties white leagues or similar militant groups were never organized, either because they were unnecessary for conservative political and social dominance, as in the overwhelmingly white counties whose affairs the conservatives already controlled, or because the local Democratic leadership feared the disruptive consequences of racial conflict, as in several of the river counties where major efforts had been made from the beginning of Reconstruction to forestall violence. (Significant exceptions to this pattern in the river country were Warren, Hinds, and Yazoo counties.) Although incidents of intimidation, both subtle and overt, and violence occurred in these areas, armed white leagues did not roam the counties employing their repertoire of coercive tactics against blacks and white Republicans.

Racial passion and conflict only partly explains the outburst of white enthusiasm and militancy during the campaign of 1875. In a dramatic fashion the campaign witnessed a white democratic uprising against the perceived existence of Republican corruption, tax oppression, and governmental mismanagement. In an October editorial Barksdale marveled at the spirit of the revolution that was sweeping the state and also attempted to explain its source. He wrote:

> When a government is oppressed with very bad rulers, and national affairs are tending toward corruption, the people (being patient and forebearing), as a general rule, bear these grievances for a long time, hoping that a reformation may come, through a returning sense of justice on the part of their oppressors. Finally, when hope begins to fade, by the constant increase of wrongs, a few bold and vigilant lovers of liberty become leaders in the work of reformation; and, as soon as the standard of resistance is raised, the masses . . . rise up in irresistible multitudes and rally under the revolutionary standard. . . .
>
> In monarchical and despotic governments, these reformatory revolutions are usually effected by physical force. In republican governments, where the masses are sovereign, through the exercise of the

74. Although he arrived at a different conclusion regarding the pervasiveness of campaign violence and intimidation, even Governor Ames in his account of white-league bulldozing suggested that all areas of the state were not affected by "Winchester rifle" operations. *Annual Message of Governor Ames, 1876*, pp. 6–8. The Radical Jackson *Pilot*, October 29, 1875, on the eve of the election questioned whether the balloting would be free, but specified only seven counties as areas of militant white-line activity.

ballot, reform and good government are realized by exerting the popular will through more peaceful remedies.[75]

Mississippi, Barksdale claimed, "had inaugurated a peaceful revolution" that was "deep-seated and wide-spread. The spirit of this revolution is resistance to corruption and misrule. . . . Such revolutions never go backwards!" This surge of white democratic enthusiasm required little in the way of direction from the conservative leadership; it was spontaneous and usually intolerant. Leaders like George served more to check the excesses of the crusade—and thereby avoid a bloodbath or federal intervention—than to rally whites to the Democratic standard. "It is evident," the Natchez *Democrat* announced, "that the political waters have been stirred to their very depths and that a storm has been aroused that will sweep over the State, carrying with it destruction to whatever opposes its course."[76] The candidacy of Grange leader William L. Hemingway for state treasurer, the only state office except for members of the legislature to be filled by the election, reflected the ground swell nature of the Democratic campaign. "The fatfaced Granger candidate," as one Republican described him, campaigned with "hay-seed in his hair and cotton-lint on his coat." Another observer reported, "He carries specimens of improved peas in his pockets, and promises a pair of Berkshire pigs for every vote in the district."[77]

The populist thrust of the conservative campaign was also evident in the introduction of the "primary election" device for nominating local Democratic candidates. In primary elections party candidates were voted on in a large meeting of all interested conservatives in the county, instead of in a convention of party functionaries. No one was excluded from these meetings, and excitement was reportedly high in those counties that employed this democratic method of selection. Barksdale and other self-proclaimed spokesmen of the conservative cause admitted their dislike for the primary, a system that would take away some of

75. Jackson *Weekly Clarion*, October 13, 1875.
76. Natchez *Democrat*, August 5, 1875.
77. Jackson *Pilot*, October 23, 1875.

their influence in the party. However, they soft-pedaled their opposition to it in view of the critical nature of the campaign and the need to secure a large turnout of white voters. In a few counties conservatives temporarily named their party the "People's party" as an indication of the grass-roots spontaneity of their campaign to overthrow Radical rule.[78]

Perhaps too much can be made of the democratic impulse in the election, since precisely the same white classes most affected by such appeals were also the most hostile to Negro rights. But, as George M. Fredrickson has demonstrated for Jacksonian Democracy, these two attitudes can exist side by side.[79] They did in the Mississippi contest of 1875, though it is impossible to determine where the concern for democracy and freedom from "Radical tyranny" left off and unadulterated racism took over. No doubt the expressed concern for political democracy and the restoration of "home rule" was a feeble attempt by many whites to hide a racialist outrage at Reconstruction developments, a feeling that was intensified in 1875 by armed confrontations between the races and the belief that Ames was encouraging "a war of races." But at the same time, moderates, however much they may have bent to the winds of racial passion, still saw the campaign as one of democratic reform to redeem the state from the depredations of adventurers and restore the rule of the people. They professed to believe, though in retrospect the notion might appear chimerical if not hypocritical, that this democratic crusade would not violate the rights of blacks and, in fact, would include them in the movement and in the benefits of redemption.[80]

White-league methods of obtaining Negro support or, more accurately, of reducing the Republican vote, appeared to George and associates to be a weak foundation for electoral success. Even if it were desirable, Democratic leaders could not be sure that a

78. Entries for September 30, October 3, 1875, in Agnew Diary; Jackson *Weekly Clarion*, August 11, December 1, 1875; Pascagoula *Star*, September 11, October 9, 1875; Greenville *Weekly Times*, September 25, 1875.

79. George M. Fredrickson, *The Black Image in the White Mind: The Debate on Afro-American Character and Destiny, 1817–1914* (New York, 1971), 61–62, 66, 84.

80. See for example the Natchez *Democrat*, October 7, 10, November 5, 1875; Greenville *Weekly Times*, August 28, 1875; speech of Absalom M. West, as reported in the Jackson *Weekly Clarion*, October 27, 1875; and Jackson *Weekly Clarion*, November 3, 1875.

program of intimidation would be able to overcome a twenty-to-thirty-thousand Republican majority in the state. Federal intervention remained a real possibility if coercion and violence became too prevalent. In addition, early white-league activities and racial clashes had created a somber economic situation in the plantation country—the main area of agricultural production in Mississippi. As the election approached, reports emanated from the river counties of the damaging effect that white-league forays in Warren, Hinds, and Yazoo counties had had on labor relations. In a trip along the Tallahatchie River in the Delta at the height of the campaign, a conservative lamented that he had observed only fifty hands in the fields picking cotton where there should have been thousands. Merchants and planters "are very much distressed at the state of affairs, as ruin stares them in the face, if the matured crop is left to rot in the fields; and the suffering that laborers must endure another year . . . is perfectly appalling, and calls for the most energetic efforts to avert the impending calamity."[81] A southern Republican reported that along the railroad between Jackson and Edwards, where white-league activity had been intense after the Clinton disorder, the fields were white with cotton, but no pickers could be found. "They have fled, and we all know why," this old citizen wrote. "Capital and land owners . . . will find by bitter experience, what common sense must teach every man, that capital and labor must live in peace if they want plenty."[82] Numerous planters understood this lesson, and when permitted to weigh the uncertain political benefits of white-league coercion against the economic and social realities of the time, they chose to be guided by the latter.

George and the Democratic leadership concluded that conservatives needed some black votes to win the election, and they believed these could best be obtained through regular campaign methods of persuasion. Consequently, Democrats staged large and impressive demonstrations for the benefit of blacks as well as whites. Hundreds of parades, barbecues, and rallies were held

81. "Obadiah" to the Jackson *Weekly Clarion*, October 20, 1875.
82. "A Worker" to the Jackson *Times*, October 29, 1875. One report estimated that one fifth of the cotton crop of 1875, worth about five million dollars, was lost as a result of the political excitement of the fall. *Ibid.*, November 6, 1875.

from the Gulf Coast to the Tennessee border as the campaign climaxed in October. In the larger towns immense torchlight processions highlighted the festivities. A prominent feature of the parades, which included women and children and some blacks, was the "transparencies." These luminous displays were built on frame wagons with white sheets providing the canvas for crude and satirical cartoons of Republican politicians; inside the wagons lanterns and lamps illuminated the images. Democrats and "faithful negroes" frequently wore a uniformed shirt, usually red, and shouted catchy political phrases as they marched down the main streets to the cheers of hundreds of onlookers. For the first time during Reconstruction the conservative party could boast of a campaign treasury, though modest by northern standards. In one county more than five thousand dollars was raised for campaign purposes, and a contribution of fifteen hundred dollars by planter-merchant Edmund Richardson to the party coffers was so generous that Republicans charged a corrupt bargain.[83]

In the hotbeds of white-league activity the campaign processions assumed a martial, menacing air. The conservatives, according to one local leader, "go in clubs, each club with its band of music, flags, and regalia, and a cannon in many instances," which boomed from a nearby hilltop. The women "worked by day and night on the uniforms" for the men, including blacks who joined the clubs.[84] Another local Democratic leader wrote years later: "Our purpose was to overawe the negroes and exhibit to them the ocular proof of our power and to present it to them in the most spectacular way." Rarely, however, did blacks constitute a majority of the participants in a Democratic rally. A notable exception was a conservative barbecue at Dobyn's Ferry in Jefferson County where hundreds of Negroes, wearing Democratic badges and waving Democratic banners, heard their old antagonist McCardle tell them why they should vote for his party.[85]

---

83. Fred M. Witty, "Reconstruction in Carroll and Montgomery Counties," *Publications of the Mississippi Historical Society*, X (1909), 127; Natchez *Democrat*, October 1, 1875; Jackson *Times*, October 29, 1875.

84. Smedes, *Memorials of a Southern Planter*, 249, 251–52.

85. Kyle, "Reconstruction in Panola County," 73–74 (quote); Natchez *Democrat*, October 6, 1875.

At Holly Springs on October 21 "the Conservatives had the grandest and most imposing demonstration ever witnessed in Mississippi," according to a report in the Natchez *Democrat*.

> Thousands of men, organized in clubs of fifties and hundreds, marched into town that morning with bands playing, banners waving, and raising such shouts of patriotic enthusiasm as were never heard in this part of the world. After parading the streets, the immense crowd of men dismounted and were addressed by Major H. H. Chalmers in one of the most telling and eloquent speeches. At night the torchlight procession and pyrotechnic display took place. Two thousand illuminated cartoons and three thousand torchlights were being carried, besides the illuminated wagons, carriages, etc., counted by the hundreds. Seven thousand men were in the procession.[86]

Most of these affairs, even in small villages, could attract such luminaries as Lamar, Barksdale, George, McCardle, Watson, Walthall, Lowry, and various congressional candidates. In areas where intimidation had not been tried or had not succeeded, joint debates with Republicans were held. The famed Kentucky abolitionist Cassius M. Clay, now an outspoken conservative, was brought to the Delta to persuade blacks to overthrow "the carpetbag despotism" in their area. Cheer after cheer greeted Clay when he spoke to an audience of blacks and whites in Greenville, and after he had left the local editor wrote: "His presence amongst us was an inspiration to the whites, and his voice was like an oracle to the black people."[87]

As a prerequisite for obtaining the confidence of blacks and therefore their votes, George encouraged local Democratic leaders to make a special effort to pacify Negroes regarding their rights under a conservative government. He wrote a lengthy letter, which took five columns to print in the conservative journals, providing arguments for local leaders to use in refuting the usual Republican charge that the Democratic party was the party of the Black Code of 1865 and would reimpose these discriminatory laws if restored to power. The Democratic party, he claimed, had

---

86. Natchez *Democrat*, October 26, 1875.
87. David M. Smiley, "Cassius M. Clay and the Mississippi Election of 1875," *Journal of Mississippi History*, XIX (October, 1957), 259–61; Natchez *Democrat*, October 26, 1875.

not controlled the legislature that had passed the code and therefore should not be held responsible for it.[88] In response to the
Republican assertion that a Democratic victory would result in the
disbandment of the public school system, George, Barksdale, and
other conservative spokesmen reminded blacks of the party's platform promise to maintain a sound, though economical, school system for both races. In addition, Barksdale, perhaps with his fingers
crossed, promised that if successful in the election the Democrats
would extend the school year to ten months.[89]

On several occasions George intervened to block white leaguers
from applying their full repertoire of intimidating tactics. He took
this action not only to prevent incidents of violence that might
invite federal intervention but also to reassure blacks in areas unaffected by menacing white-line activities that the Democratic party was sincerely concerned about their rights.[90] Although the
Bourbons rejected any appeal to Negro voters, moderate leaders
on the eve of the election uniformly encouraged whites to persuade at least one black man to go to the polls and vote the Democratic ticket. These spokesmen did not always indicate what form
the persuasion should take, leaving the door especially open for
the application of economic coercion by merchants and planters.[91]

The policy of fusion was a more common Democratic tactic for
obtaining black votes in the plantation counties than was persuasion or intimidation. Fearing the worst if white-league activities
spilled over into their communities, demoralized and divided Republican leaders in these counties entered into an arrangement
with conservatives by which they would deliver the black votes
they controlled to a fusion ticket, normally dominated by Democrats, in exchange for an end of white-line agitation and a free
election. River country conservatives justified the compromise arrangement with their political antagonists on the grounds that,

88. Jackson *Weekly Clarion*, September 15, 1875. Technically, George was correct. Old-
line Whigs controlled the legislature of 1865, but members of both old parties supported
the Black Code.

89. *Ibid.*, October 13, 1875.

90. George and Ethelbert Barksdale to Committee of Citizens, October, 1875 (telegram),
and J. D. Vertner to George, October 29, 1875 (telegram), both in Governors' Correspondence, Vol. 99; Jackson *Pilot*, October 13, 26, 1875; "A Worker" to the Vicksburg *Times*,
October 29, 1875.

91. Natchez *Democrat*, October 31, 1875; Jackson *Weekly Clarion*, November 3, 1875.

as the Adams County executive committee put it, "only by co-operation with intelligent, independent and fair-minded Republicans can the citizens of our county prevent fraud and incapacity in office and secure a representation in the Legislature and elsewhere in proportion to our voting strength."[92] In Adams County, where Republicans received the lion's share of the offices in the fusion arrangement, including a black man for sheriff, the conservatives' claim that they only merged with the "decent" wing of the party had some substance. But in most cases the distinction was not clear. In Washington County conservatives joined forces with a disreputable group of bolting Republicans who prior to fusion had been denounced by the planters as the "d——dest scoundrels and vagabonds in the county."[93] Despite their apparent sellout to the conservatives, most Republican fusionists insisted that they were Republicans and that cooperation with the Democrats was only a temporary expedient.

Except for the fusionists, local Republican leaders in the face of adversity in the fall campaign demonstrated a remarkable degree of steadfastness and loyalty to the party. Democrats, in fact, strained themselves searching for apostate Republican functionaries who would publicly denounce the "political robbers and vultures" who still held sway in the state. In the end they could claim only a handful of local Republican leaders who were willing to affiliate with the Democratic party and influence blacks to vote for the ticket. Many former Republican stalwarts campaigned half-heartedly or not at all; but they resisted impressment into the service of the party of George and Lamar. Demoralization rather than surrender or apostasy characterized the efforts of most Republican politicians in the campaign of 1875.[94]

92. As reported in the Natchez *Democrat*, October 10, 1875. See also the issues of October 6, 23, 1875.

93. Jackson *Times*, October 5, 1875 (quote); Jackson *Pilot*, October 2, 1875. The objectives of Republicans in the fusionist arrangement are outlined by Madison County chairman Henry R. Smith to the Republicans of his county, November 2, 1875, in Governors' Correspondence, Vol. 100, and in *Mississippi in 1875*, I, 826–33.

94. A number of the Republicans who were inactive in the campaign played prominent roles in the reorganization of the Republican party after the election debacle. Included among this group were Alcorn, Musgrove, and George Harris, all anti-Ames Republicans. Jackson *Times*, December 1, 1875. For a modest accounting of Republicans who cast their lots with the Democrats in the contest, see the Jackson *Weekly Clarion*, August 11, September 8, 22, 1875.

Remarkably, in view of the steamroller tactics of the Democrats, a number of Republican leaders canvassed for the party and attempted to leave the impression wherever they went that the new order was still strong and would not be intimidated. Former Governor Powers, who was running for Congress, was especially active on the stump. He and other Republican campaigners challenged conservatives to joint debates, and frequently they were accommodated. Outside of the few white-league counties, where threats were common, Republican participation in joint rallies with Democrats was usually peaceful and free of intimidation, though not of recrimination. Congressman Jason Niles, a scalawag, was cursed by a group of whites at Meridian, yet even at this site of earlier Ku Klux Klan terror Republicans revealed that no effort was made by the Democrats to break up their meetings. From other places in the east and in north Mississippi, Republican campaigners reported courteous treatment at the hands of whites when they spoke.[95]

At a Republican rally in the piney woods town of Summit, which was attended by Democrats and addressed by black Congressman John R. Lynch, "perfect order and decorum was preserved" despite fears that rowdy elements planned to disrupt the meeting. The intrepid scalawag Judge William M. Hancock not only campaigned vigorously for the party in southeast Mississippi but he also introduced a new element into the canvass. On one occasion during the heat of the campaign he refused to adjourn his court at Enterprise until the jury and audience had listened to speeches by Republican campaigners. Conservatives thought that such conduct from the bench smacked of Czarist Russia.[96]

Stalwart black leaders, though unable to campaign extensively, pleaded with their followers to persevere in the face of white-line methods, reject cooperation with the conservatives, and go to the polls and vote Republican on election day. Fourteen of them, including United States Senator Blanche K. Bruce, State

95. Jackson *Pilot*, October 8, 12, 15, 1875; Jackson *Times*, October 8, 19–22, 29, 1875; Natchez *Democrat*, October 22, 1875; entries for October 22, 24, 1875, in Niles Diary. Although a number of white Republicans found themselves ostracised from "decent society" during the course of the campaign, the practice was not universal. On a visit to Vicksburg a few days before the election, one old Unionist and scalawag received a "cordial hand-shaking," followed by a friendly conversation, from Jefferson Davis. "A Worker" to the Jackson *Times*, October 29, 1875.

96. Jackson *Pilot*, October 3, 1875; Pascagoula *Star*, August 21, 1875.

Senator Charles Caldwell, and Secretary of State James Hill, issued a printed address to "colored voters" prophetically warning them that their "civil rights and privileges as freemen" were at stake in the fall election. "The success of the Democratic party . . . frenzied as it is with hate and rancor," the address declared, "will, to all intents and purposes, sound the death knell of all the hopes that the colored man has indulged of educating, elevating and improving his race in this State. Once under the iron heel of Democracy, the colored man will at once sink back to the status he held in 1865—free in name, but not in fact—poor, ignorant and helpless, hedged in by unfriendly laws, which he will have no power to circumvent, a 'hewer of wood and a drawer of water' forever." Although blacks might retain a formal right to vote under Democratic rule, these Negro leaders predicted that "practical disfranchisement" would occur, since the ballot would be controlled by the conservatives. Obviously disturbed by local Republican divisions, the framers of this address implored blacks "not to fritter away your strength upon a divided ticket. . . . Have but one ticket in the field, and let that be composed of your best and worthiest men." The new order in the state, they concluded, could still be preserved if every black voter "without a single exception, with a prayer to God on his lips, made a firm resolve that he will prove himself worthy of all his rights by going to the ballot-box and casting his vote."[97]

Despite Republican electioneering efforts, their campaign was overwhelmed by the white Democratic masses as they paraded, shouted, and demonstrated for the cause of redemption. In white-league areas the intimidating presence of mounted riflemen and the firing of cannon accented the determination of the Democrats to carry the election by force if necessary.[98] No doubt many con-

97. This address was circulated in most of the state's Republican newspapers. It can be found in the Jackson *Pilot*, October 4, 1875, and the Jackson *Times*, October 4, 1875.

98. "Colored People" of Noxubee County to Ames, November 3, 1875, in Governors' Correspondence, Vol. 100; Jackson *Pilot* and Jackson *Times*, October, 1875, issues. Well before the election, the Republican party leadership at Jackson had become reconciled to defeat. Three days before the election Ames, who did not campaign, succinctly reported the depressed mood of the Republican leaders. "The election ceases to have any interest for us," he wrote his wife Blanche. "It is lost." Ames to his wife, October 30, 1875, in Blanche Butler Ames (comp.), *Chronicles*, II, 245. The Ames newspaper organ, however, insisted to the bitter end that the Republican ticket would prevail. Jackson *Pilot*, October 31, 1875.

servatives disapproved of such tactics, but caught up in the passion of the campaign and believing that their very liberties, not to mention their livelihoods, were at stake in the election, they looked the other way when incidents of intimidation and violence were brought to their attention. In fact, many professed to believe that such reports were part of a desperate Republican plot to secure federal intervention before the party went down to defeat.[99] In view of this attitude and the prevalence of armed Democratic irregulars in a number of counties it is remarkable that so few Republicans lost their lives during the campaign. The evidence contained in the testimony of Republicans before the United States Senate committee investigating the election indicates that after the Clinton riot of early September no more than ten or twelve blacks were killed. Four of them died in a riot at Columbus on the eve of the election, and four, including a legislator, were killed as a result of the Yazoo troubles. Only one white Republican, a carpetbagger, seems to have been murdered for political reasons during the fall contest, and this act occurred in a district of Hinds County that had been wracked by the Clinton disorders.[100]

Election day, November 2, passed with only a few incidents of violence and blatant intimidation. The night before the election a racial disturbance occurred in Columbus that left four blacks dead and several buildings in ashes. The election in the town was held without incident or overt intimidation, but several hundred Negroes in the county, fearing white-league activity, did not go to the polls. At Aberdeen white leaguers, many of whom had crossed the border from Alabama, appeared on the streets of this black-belt town before the polls opened on election day. Backed by a cannon loaded with scrap iron (which they did not fire), the armed whites during the day drove about seven hundred blacks from the polls. When scalawag Sheriff James W. Lee, a former officer in the Confederate army, attempted to intervene, the indig-

99. *Hinds County Gazette*, October 13, 20, 1875.
100. *Mississippi in 1875*, passim. The murder of carpetbagger Charles E. Fawn of Yazoo County is usually included in the list of Republican deaths caused by the white leagues. Actually, Fawn was a member of the moderate Republican faction that opposed the local Radical wing of the party led by Sheriff Morgan. Fawn was killed by the son of a Morgan deputy whose job he had taken. Jackson *Pilot*, October 27, 1875.

nant leaguers chased him into his jail.[101] In Kemper, where a bitter feud between conservatives and Sheriff William W. Chisholm, also a former Confederate officer, had raged for several years, armed Democrats on election day took up positions at all of the crossroads in the county. Despite their presence, one third of the county's Republicans braved the threats and voted the party ticket. In nearby Noxubee County, though the Republicans carried the county, one half of their voters remained at home after a white-league demonstration in Macon on the eve of the election left one black man dead.[102] In most areas a political and racial calm prevailed at the polls, which surprised many observers who had feared that widespread disorders would occur on the day ending the most turbulent political contest in Mississippi history.[103]

In spite of the general appearance of peace on election day, the campaign tactics and efforts of the Democrats had produced the desired results. Democratic-Conservatives won the state treasurer's office by a margin of 31,544 votes, captured four of the six seats in Congress, "redeemed" all but a handful of the plantation counties, and, most significantly insofar as the "redemption" of the state government was concerned, gained a comfortable majority in the legislature. The Democratic program of intimidation still fell short of keeping most Republicans from the polls in a majority of the counties. Indeed, based on a comparison of the county returns of 1875 with those of 1873, it seems that this coercion policy had only a marginal effect on the Republican vote in fifty of the seventy-two counties in the state, and in thirty-five of these counties the Republican vote was actually larger than in 1873.[104] Since the candidacy of the insurgent Republican Alcorn in 1873 complicates an analysis of the election returns of that

101. Jackson *Weekly Pilot*, November 13, 1875; Henry B. Whitfield to Ames, November 4, 1875, W. F. Connell to Ames, November 7, 1875, John E. Meek to Ames, November 2, 1875, James W. Lee to Ames, November 2, 1875, all in Governors' Correspondence, Vol. 100.

102. W. W. Chisholm to Ames, November 3, 1875, affidavit of O. A. Espinal, November 1, 1875, "Colored People" of Noxubee County to Ames, November 3, 1875, W. M. Connor to Ames, November 3, 1875, all in Governors' Correspondence, Vol. 100.

103. Jackson *Pilot*, November 4, 1875; Natchez *Democrat*, November 3, 4, 1875; Jackson *Times*, November 2, 1875; entry for November 2, 1875, in Jones-Smith Plantation Journal.

104. Returns for both elections are conveniently found in *Mississippi in 1875*, II, Documentary Evidence, 144–45.

year, a comparison with the results of the 1871 contest in which
no important Republican division occurred perhaps gives a better
indication of the effect on Republicans of white-line methods.
From this analysis it is clear that in 1875 twenty-one counties
experienced a major loss in Republican strength. Obviously, Democratic intimidation and Republican demoralization were the main
reasons for this decline. At the same time in twenty-three counties Republicans in 1875 actually increased their vote over that
of 1871, although by small margins in almost all cases.

The Democratic-Conservative victory of 1875 turned on the outpouring of white voters throughout the state and on the revolutionary campaign tactics of white leaguers in a handful of such
key black counties as Yazoo, Claiborne, Noxubee, and Hinds. In
these counties, which previously had been safely Republican,
thousands of Negroes remained at home on election day rather
than risk the wrath of local white extremists. Yet only in Yazoo,
as the election returns demonstrate, was there a countywide pattern of intimidation and terror that kept blacks from the polls
completely. In that turbulent county not only did the "shot-gun"
policy of fear prevail, but also the white-league tactic of confiscating Republican election tickets as they entered the county contributed to the Democratic success. Out of a black registration
of more than three thousand in Yazoo, only a handful were permitted to cast Republican ballots on election day.[105] In three large
black counties, Madison, Washington, and Lowndes, a policy of
Republican fusion with Democrats kept white threats to a minimum. But the effect was to disfranchise Republicans in the election, since the conservatives, with the assistance of fused Negro
votes, took all of the important offices in these counties and most
of the legislative seats, leaving only minor positions for cooperating Republicans. The reverse was true only in Adams County
where a fusion policy resulted in Republicans winning control of
the main offices, as well as carrying the county for Congressman

105. For Democratic methods in Yazoo County, see Hiram Johnson to Ames, November
3, 1875, Thomas H. Winston to Ames, November 3, 1875, and W. M. Colcote to Ames,
November 5, 1875, all in Governors' Correspondence, Vol. 100. Although Hinds County
went Democratic, interestingly, the Republicans won a majority at Clinton, the scene of
the bloodiest racial encounter of the campaign. Jackson *Pilot*, November 4, 1875.

Lynch and George M. Buchanan, the party's candidate for state treasurer.[106]

Whites turned out in large numbers to cast Democratic ballots. Hundreds who had not registered during Reconstruction enrolled their names and voted. Although registration statistics for 1875 are not available, it is clear from a review of earlier figures and the election returns that more than 90 percent of the white male population voted in the contest.[107] Of the 98,715 votes captured by the Democratic candidate for state treasurer perhaps as many as 85,000 were cast by whites. This estimated white vote, if accurate, was 22,000 votes more than the total Democratic poll in the stirring election of 1868, the next highest conservative turnout of the Reconstruction era.

In view of the emotionalism that characterized the campaign of 1875, the determination of outraged whites to overcome Radical rule, and Grant's refusal to intervene with federal power, the amazing thing about the election is not that violence occurred but that there was so little of it after the September riots. Furthermore, the fact that threatened and demoralized Republicans still went to the polls in substantial numbers in many counties was a remarkable demonstration of the courage and determination of thousands of blacks and their white allies who fully understood the significance of the campaign to their future.

This fact was small comfort to disconsolate Republicans who reacted with chagrin and outrage at the methods employed to bring about the end of their political dominance in Mississippi. Before abandoning the state for another visit in the North, Governor Ames pronounced the election "a farce—worse than a farce," and was surprised that "the murderous white leaguers" did not carry all of the counties. An embittered Aberdeen scalawag, even before the votes had been counted, charged that "J. Z. George and Co. [had] hoodwinked the President of [the] U.S. about peace in Miss. Election. . . . Armed rebellion has been tolerated by

---

106. Natchez *Democrat*, October 29, 1875.

107. This analysis assumes that the Democratic returns were not altered by election officials in counties already controlled by the conservatives. The practice of stuffing ballot boxes or falsifying returns apparently did not develop until the Redeemers were entrenched in power.

Genl. George and his co-workers to carry the election in this county & state." Even the usually mild-mannered Powers excitedly
wrote James A. Garfield that in Mississippi "the ballot box has
been overthrown and lawless violence that would shame savages
has been enacted by the white line Democracy in many counties
of the state."[108]

Blacks had even greater cause for alarm than carpetbaggers like
Ames and Powers. Not only were Negroes the objects of intimidation and violence in a number of places during the campaign,
their leaders in white-league strongholds became the targets of
Democratic retaliation after the election. The most brutal reprisal
occurred at Clinton in early December when the able Charles
Caldwell was shot down in the streets by a group of revengeful
whites. As he lay dying from fifteen bullet wounds, Caldwell struggled to tell his attackers, "You may fire as many shots as you
please, but you shall not say I did not die like a brave man."[109]
Numerous blacks who did not choose to die for a lost cause asked
Ames about the possibility of colonization in the West or in another country. Nothing came of their inquiries at this time.[110] Carpetbagger T. J. Reed, living in a county that had been engulfed
by white-league activity, wondered aloud: "Will the government
let these colored people go back into a worse condition than slavery
and let the lives and money lost go for nothing? If it does, then
I hope that my brother who sleeps at Andersonville will come
back and stand by the beds of those in power."[111] By the new
year and the meeting of the "Redeemer" legislature the white
terror had largely run its course.

Intraparty recrimination boiled over as Republicans in their
agony of defeat searched for scapegoats. Harris, Alcorn, Pease,
Revels, and Morris lashed out at Ames for his many failures and

108. Ames to his wife, November 4, 1875, in Blanche Butler Ames (comp.), *Chronicles*,
II, 249; Meek to Ames, November 2, 1875, in Governors' Correspondence, Vol. 100;
Ridgley C. Powers to James A. Garfield, November 15, 1876 [1875?], in Garfield Papers.

109. P. H. Green to Ames, November 22, 1875, Albert T. Morgan to Ames, January
6, 1876, Monk Joseph to Ames, January 6, 1876, all in Governors' Correspondence, Vol.
100; Blanche Ames to her mother, December 8, 1875, in Blanche Butler Ames (comp.),
Chronicles, II, 257–58.

110. Connor (on behalf of Noxubee County blacks) to Ames, November 5, 1875, E.
Lindsey (on behalf of Montgomery County blacks) to Ames, December 6, 1875, both
in Governors' Correspondence, Vol. 100.

111. T. J. Reed to Ames, November 6, 1875, *ibid.*

claimed that his ineptness and narrowness had given rise to the bitter strife of the campaign, making Republican defeat inevitable.[112] In addition to pointing the condemning finger at Ames, the Jackson *Times*, edited by two carpetbag founders of the state party, claimed that the Republican failure to reform the party had been its undoing. "Many of the laws and measures of the party are utterly inexcusable and indefensible. And many of our candidates have been men who deserved only ignoble defeat," this newspaper declared. Furthermore, "from the character of those who have controlled the primary caucusses of the party, and thence the leadership and policy and destiny of the Republican organization, defeat was only a question of time."[113] Revels, the first black man to sit in the United States Senate, affirmed the *Times*'s analysis of the Republican defeat and asserted that the overthrow of the "malignant demagogues [who] have devised to perpetuate the intellectual bondage of my people" was brought about by men of both races.[114]

On the other hand, friends of Ames waxed hot in denouncing President Grant and Attorney General Pierrepont for the decision not to intervene in the contest. Even before the election defeat, Ames had attempted to absolve himself from any blame for the disaster. He wrote his wife Blanche on October 12: "Yes, a Revolution has taken place—by force of arms—and a race are disfranchised—they are to be returned to a condition of serfdom—an era of second slavery. It is their fault (not mine, personally) that this fate is before them. They refused to prepare for war when in time of peace, when they could have done so. Now it is too late. The nation should have acted but *it* was 'tired of the annual autumnal outbreaks in the South.' . . . The political death of the Negro will forever release the nation from the weariness from such 'political outbreaks.'"[115]

Although state conventions were held in December and again

---

112. George E. Harris to Grant, November 24, 1875, in *Issues of the Canvass of 1876*; Jackson *Times*, November 30, December 1, 1875; Natchez *Democrat*, January 18, 1876.

113. Jackson *Times*, November 3, 1875.

114. Jackson *Weekly Clarion*, December 22, 1875; *Mississippi in 1875*, I, 1020–21.

115. Ames to his wife, October 12, November 4, 1875, in Blanche Butler Ames (comp.), *Chronicles*, II, 216, 250; Jackson *Times*, November 30, 1875.

in April to attempt a resuscitation of the party under anti-Ames auspices, the Republican organization lay in ruins, unable to pose a serious threat to Democratic control until 1875.

All was jubilation in the Democratic-Conservative camp. "We have met the enemy and they are routed," read the caption of the Pascagoula *Star*. The victory of the Democrats, Barksdale exclaimed, was "a more complete triumph than even the most sanguine of us had anticipated." According to Barksdale, the success was accomplished by the unified effort of whites, joined by thousands of blacks who resisted the lash of Radical demagogues and voted the Democratic ticket.[116] In overwhelmingly black Washington County John S. McNeily insisted, "We accomplished our redemption by honest hard work; no intimidation, no lost ballot boxes." McNeily reported that he traveled throughout his county on election day and found that not one merchant or planter failed to attend the polls "and do his whole duty! It was this spirit, this resolution to win which has enlisted all the energies of our people during the past month, that has achieved this signal victory." Expressing the belief that racial conciliation and black support had produced the conservative victory, Paul A. Botto of the Natchez *Democrat* declared that the "late battle was fought on the broad ground of opposition to corruption" and not on the issues that had been settled by the war and the postwar amendments. "We take it for granted," Botto confidently concluded, "that Bourbonism is dead and that the members of the next Legislature are men who fully comprehend that the world moves and that we have gone through a revolution that is real and that destroyed entirely and forever" the forces once governing the region. The legislature specifically should "act with that calm prudence which will soon reconcile all classes of the people of the State, and convince particularly the colored people that their rights and interests are safer in the hands of intelligent legislators than in those of ignorant colored men and corrupt carpet-baggers."[117] The state and nation would not have to wait long to see which postwar force in Mississippi conservatism—moderation or bourbonism—would prevail in the redemption settlement.

116. Pascagoula *Star*, November 6, 1875; Jackson *Weekly Clarion*, November 3, 1875.

117. Greenville *Weekly Times*, November 6, 1875; Natchez *Democrat*, November 4, 5, 11, 1875.

21

Redemption

The work of consolidating the Democratic victory and arranging a redemption settlement for the state began when the new legislature convened on January 4, 1876. The nine Republicans in the senate and twenty in the house of representatives offered no real opposition to the majority. Furthermore, with a two-thirds majority, Democrats in the legislature had little reason to fear an Ames veto. Far from being an assembly of planter-lawyers, as had normally been the case before Reconstruction, the legislature of 1876 contained a large agrarian contingent, which reflected the important role of the Grange and the white yeoman class in the defeat of the Radicals.[1] In the house of representatives there were forty-four farmers alone, not including several planters who identified with the yeoman interest. Except for the Republicans, few of the members of the lower house had had legislative experience. On the other hand most of the state senators had served in the legislature at some time during Reconstruction. The only "old fossils," or representatives of the antebellum gentry, that could be found in the new legislature were Winfield Scott Featherston, a former Democratic congressman, and Union Whigs Amos R. Johnston, C. M. Vaiden, Robert S. Hudson, and George W. Harper; all would play prominent, though by no means dominant, roles in the Redeemer legislature. As in the state Democratic convention of 1875, a number of young Confederates appeared in the new legislature and earned their political spurs in the formulation of the redemption settlement. Some of these aspiring politicians, notably John M. Stone, Hugh H. Street, Henry L. Muldrow, Robert H. Taylor, John W. Fewell, and James B. Morgan, would exercise considerable influence in Mississippi affairs throughout the age of the Redeemers.

Even before the legislature met, public opinion had willed that

1. A list of the membership in each house, including information on party affiliation and occupation, may be found in *Senate Journal, 1876*, pp. 690–91, and *House Journal, 1876*, pp. 678–82.

the first order of business should be to determine the fate of Governor Ames and other Radical state officers, whose terms had two years to run. More than any other element of Republican control, the continued presence of Ames in the governor's mansion gnawed at the Redeemers, creating an overpowering demand for his removal. The polls had hardly closed on election day when the debate on Ames's impeachment began. "His entire course," the Enterprise *Courier* declared, "has been marked only by a desire to humiliate and oppress our people. . . . He must be impeached and sent from the State, covered with the disgrace which his ignominious course has brought about."[2] The Water Valley *Mississippi Central* echoed this sentiment and insisted that the carpetbag governor's "recent attempts to corrupt the Judiciary, incite riot and bloodshed by sending out his brutal negro soldiery to murder our people and fire their dwellings," and retain corrupt men in office were sufficient grounds for removal.[3] "It is a political necessity to impeach Ames," Roderick Seal, a Democratic leader in south Mississippi, wrote. "If he remains in the State, he will fill it full of Federal troops next fall in order to carry the State for the Republican party."[4] Claiming that Ames was the equal of Richard III in "a morbid instinct for guilty ambition," the Okalona *Southern States* believed that his removal from office would be an excellent way "to open the grand centennial of American Liberty in 1876." National reconciliation would be advanced by ending all vestiges of carpetbag rule in the state and in the South, conservatives insisted.[5]

Despite the growing sentiment for impeachment, many conservatives urged the legislature to move with caution. Some were concerned that Ames might be impeached before the legislature had a chance to remove Lieutenant Governor A. K. Davis from office. Even Ames in the governor's mansion was preferable to having the corrupt Davis there. When the dispirited Ames threatened to resign soon after the election, a group of alarmed conservatives, including Barksdale and George, intrigued to keep him in office. Although only preliminary soundings were made, these

2. As reported in the Jackson *Weekly Clarion*, December 10, 1875.
3. As reported in *ibid.*
4. Roderick Seal to William N. Whitehurst, January 30, 1876, in Whitehurst Papers.
5. As reported in the Jackson *Weekly Clarion*, January 5, 1876.

Democrats in order to forestall Ames's resignation and Davis' elevation to the office evidently were prepared to promise Ames immunity from impeachment, provided only that he agree to the appointment, or reappointment in some cases, of moderate Republicans to the judiciary.[6] Both sides were embarrassed when the news of the negotiations leaked out, and the effort to arrange a compromise was abandoned before the legislature met in January.

The prospect of federal intervention also caused Democrats to pause in their haste to get rid of Ames. Although the Democrats controlled the new United States House of Representatives, the Republican Senate and President Grant sympathized with Ames. Many conservatives believed that unless they were careful in their treatment of the governor the federal government might yet, as Lamar put it, wage "a relentless, incessant, indefatigable war of detraction and infamy" against Mississippi.[7] Soon after the 1875 election Grant had sent an agent to investigate political conditions in the state. He followed this action with the garrisoning of troops in Claiborne, Amite, and Pike counties, making them available for immediate use in case he decided to intervene.[8]

Some conservatives also believed that Democratic chances in the presidential election of 1876 could be seriously jeopardized by a revival of the "outrage spirit" in the North, a development that Mississippi would contribute to if the legislature acted improperly in the Ames case. Already, on December 15, Senator Oliver Morton had issued a clarion call for a Senate investigation of the fall election, charging that Mississippi Republicans had been defeated by a system of fraud, intimidation, and violence unparalleled in American history. The resolution remained dormant and threatening while Mississippi conservatives debated the governor's fate.[9]

Generally, those Democrats who favored a cautious policy on impeachment had been aligned with the moderate faction during

6. Adelbert Ames to his wife, November 4, 1875, in Blanche Butler Ames (comp.), *Chronicles*, II, 250; *Mississippi in 1875*, II, 1801–19.

7. L. Q. C. Lamar to E. C. Walthall, March 7, 1876, in Mayes, *Lucius Q. C. Lamar*, 313.

8. Natchez *Democrat*, January 19, February 10, 1876; *House Journal, 1876*, pp. 410–11; Benjamin F. Butler to Ames, February 25, 1876, in Blanche Butler Ames (comp.), *Chronicles*, I, 304–305.

9. Garner, *Reconstruction in Mississippi*, 408–409.

the Republican era. As before, they viewed Mississippi affairs in the context of national developments, and they especially sought to placate northern opinion on the white South's acceptance of the results of the Civil War. Moderates wisely believed that if this could be achieved federal interference and threats would cease and the redemption of the southern states would be permanently secured.

On the other hand, Bourbons argued that federal threats, and specifically the Morton resolution, should have no bearing in the case against Ames. They refused to admit that external considerations, no matter how menacing, should enter into the decision on Ames's expulsion from office. Furthermore, Bourbons insisted that the president would not dare to intervene regardless of what happened to Ames and his cohorts or how loud Radical senators howled about affairs in the state, since opinion in the North had already swung decidedly against federal interference in the South —a fact that Grant and his Republican advisers would not ignore in this, a presidential election year.[10]

Despite Bourbon impatience, moderates controlled proceedings in the legislature, and they exercised delay and caution in drafting charges against Ames. First, they acted to remove Lieutenant Governor Davis before the governor's office became vacant. The impeachment of Davis, whom most Republicans as well as conservatives believed was unfit for office, created no controversy. Five charges of misconduct, including a strong bribery charge, were brought against him, and several Republicans, including Ames, testified to his guilt. While the senate deliberated his case, Davis made an effort to escape the odium attached to impeachment by tendering his resignation, but Ames refused to accept it. A few days later, on March 13, the senate voted overwhelmingly to remove him from office.[11]

While most attention was focused on the Ames and Davis investigations, committees of the house of representatives also

10. See excerpts from the Woodville *Republican* (a Democratic journal) and the Aberdeen *Examiner* in the Jackson *Weekly Clarion*, February 9, 1876. See also the *Hinds County Gazette*, February 2, 16, 1876.

11. Thomas J. Durant to Butler, March 15, 1876, in Jeremiah S. Black Papers, Manuscript Division, Library of Congress; *Impeachment Trial of Alexander K. Davis, Lieutenant Governor of Mississippi* (Jackson, 1876), 2–4, 23; Jackson *Weekly Clarion*, March 22, 1876.

launched inquiries into the conduct of Superintendent of Education Thomas W. Cardozo, Secretary of State James Hill, and State Auditor William H. Gibbs. The fates of carpetbagger Gibbs and Hill, a black man, were quickly decided—and in their favor. Moderates' insistence that only misconduct in office, and not mere partisanship, should constitute an impeachable offense saved these two Radical officers from house charges. In fact, a preliminary investigation led to their complete exoneration of any wrongdoing, and both were permitted without harassment to serve out their terms of office.[12]

Although Cardozo's administration of the superintendent's office was free of malfeasance, the house drew up impeachment charges based on his disreputable record as an official in Warren County. Unsure of the legal grounds for impeachment and removal, the legislature permitted Cardozo to resign before his case was considered by the senate.[13]

Considerable criticism from the conservative press greeted the decision to allow the "notorious" Cardozo to escape without an official airing of the charges against him. The Natchez *Democrat*, which consistently expressed concern for outside opinion regarding affairs in Mississippi, was especially dismayed that the legislature in permitting Cardozo to resign had lost an opportunity to publicize the kind of rascality that Mississippians had been forced to live under during the Radical period. "The publication of the evidence against this man," the *Democrat* declared, "would have gone far to vindicate the people of the State in the minds of the people abroad against the charges trumped up by men of the Morton school, and would have been a justification for much more extreme measures than have been resorted to to free the State from control of thieves" like Cardozo.[14]

The case against Ames was weaker and filled with political uncertainties. Despite the constant public clamor for his removal, by February impeachment sentiment in the legislature had declined. As Ames himself reported, the Democrats "really have no just grounds, and I think they are beginning to find out as

12. *House Journal, 1876*, pp. 138, 506–507.
13. *Ibid.*, 249, 486, 493, 497–98.
14. Natchez *Democrat*, March 25, 1876.

the[y] get before them reliable witnesses rather than newspaper articles or stump speeches."[15] But the momentum for impeachment regained its strength in late February when such powerful moderate journals as the Natchez *Democrat* and the Jackson *Clarion* increased their attacks on the carpetbag governor and joined the Bourbons in calling for his removal immediately after the expulsion of Lieutenant Governor Davis. Consequently, on March 2 the house of representatives, with most of the Republican members abstaining, overwhelmingly approved twenty-one articles of impeachment against the governor (two articles were later added). The charges, as Ames and his attorneys insisted, were political and constituted an assortment of unsubstantiated claims that he had neglected his duties as governor, pardoned criminals, degraded the judiciary, and attempted through his militia policy to stir up racial strife for political purposes.[16]

Still, moderate Democrats took pains to demonstrate that the charges against the governor went beyond political considerations. They asserted that Ames's presence in the governor's mansion was a standing menace to the rights of the people, a constant source of racial discord, and an invitation for acts of corruption by appointees of the governor. "Ames' tyrannical misdeeds," the Natchez *Democrat* announced, "would in any of the Northern States be characterized as high crimes and misdemeanors, and the Governor who had dared to commit them would be hurled from his position and treated with universal detestation."[17] Barksdale echoed these sentiments, declaring, "If our people want peace and the enforcement of the laws, they must impeach and remove from office the Governor who habitually violates the Constitution and laws, foments strife and encourages riots that he may 'quence them in blood.'"[18]

15. Ames to Robert W. Flournoy, January 21, 1876, in Letterbook D of Governor Ames. See also the Natchez *Democrat*, February 16, 1876, the Yazoo City *Herald*, January 21, 1876, and the Jackson *Weekly Clarion*, February 23, 1876, which indicate, by implication in the latter, that the movement for impeachment was losing ground.

16. *House Journal, 1876*, p. 449. The articles of impeachment are found in the *Impeachment Trial of Adelbert Ames, Governor of the State of Mississippi* (Jackson, 1876), 3–27, 52–53. The articles are also printed in Blanche Butler Ames (comp.), *Chronicles*, II, 312–47, 348–50.

17. Natchez *Democrat*, January 9, 1876.

18. Jackson *Weekly Clarion*, March 1, 1876.

Meanwhile, Benjamin F. Butler had obtained the services of Thomas J. Durant and Roger A. Pryor, two prominent southern attorneys then practicing law in the North, to defend his son-in-law. Both arrived in Jackson only a few days before the trial was to begin and with little time to prepare a defense. After a quick survey of the situation, Durant recommended that Ames employ either the prominent John W. C. Watson or Edward C. Walthall, a close friend of Lamar, to assist in the defense since their influence with the Democratic senators could be decisive. Ames, who claimed that the conservative object in the impeachment was "to restore the Confederacy," rejected the advice, preferring not to be compromised by the services of men who had been his bitter enemies.[19]

Without a conservative influence in his corner, Ames had little chance of winning his case before the Democratic senate. Even before the impeachment proceedings commenced on March 16 with Republican Justice Horatio F. Simrall presiding in place of the infirm chief justice, the governor realized that the vote on the articles "will be in harmony with the revolution which began last November."[20] In order to avoid the rigors and controversy of a futile trial, Ames at the suggestion of his wife Blanche notified Pryor a few days after the proceedings began that he would be amenable to an agreement with the Democrats permitting him to resign without the "imputation of any charge" affecting his "honor or integrity." On the night of March 27 Pryor met with conservative leaders in Barksdale's office at the *Clarion* building to work out such an arrangement. The "compromise," which Ames agreed to the next day, provided that the impeachment charges would be dropped in exchange for the governor's resignation. On the same day the compromise was hurriedly implemented, and John M. Stone, president pro tempore of the senate, became governor, thereby ending six years of Republican control of the Magnolia

19. Butler to Ames, December 23, 1875, February 2, March 25, 1876, in Blanche Butler Ames (comp.), *Chronicles*, II, 263, 281, 347; Ames to Charles A. Carleton, March 7, 1876, in Letterbook D of Governor Ames; Durant to Butler, March 15, 1876, in Black Papers. Durant was a prominent Unionist and Republican of Louisiana who had served as attorney general of the state during the antebellum period. Pryor, a Virginia conservative, had served in the Confederate army during the war, rising to the rank of brigadier general.

20. Ames to William H. Garland, March 7, 1876, in Letterbook D of Governor Ames.

state.[21] A few days later Adelbert Ames, surely the most vilified governor in Mississippi history, left the state, never to return during the remaining half century of his life.

As a member of the state senate since 1870, John M. Stone had earned his elevation to the governorship by providing steady and moderate opposition to the Republican majority. Except for a distinguished record as a Confederate officer, he had no ties with the antebellum gentry. Born in Milan, Tennessee, and raised in poverty, Stone moved to the hills of Tishomingo County, Mississippi, a few years before the war and became a clerk in a country store. Just before the war he was employed as depot agent at Iuka for the Memphis and Charleston Railroad. When the conflict began he entered the army as a private, and by the end of the war he had risen to the rank of colonel in Lee's army. After the surrender Stone returned to his job as depot agent but soon entered Reconstruction politics.[22] Educated in the field-house schools of Tennessee and a product of the yeoman society of northeast Mississippi, Stone was an excellent representative of the emergent democratic agrarian spirit that made possible the conservative victory in 1875.

Governor Stone immediately went to work to revamp the state's judiciary. On the supreme court he replaced carpetbagger Jonathan Tarbell and the aging Chief Justice Ephraim G. Peyton, a scalawag, with Hamilton H. Chalmers and Josiah A. P. Campbell, both political moderates; Campbell was a coauthor of the *Revised Code of 1871*, which had been commissioned and approved by a Republican legislature. Somewhat surprisingly, Chalmers and Campbell chose the Republican Simrall as the new chief justice, a position that he held until the end of his term in 1879.[23] Although several Republican circuit court judges and chancellors were men who possessed the confidence of many conservatives in their districts,

21. Durant and Roger A. Pryor to Ames, March 28, 1876, and Ames to Durant and Pryor, March 28, 1876, both in Garner, *Reconstruction in Mississippi*, 405–406; Blanche Ames to her mother, April 2, 1876, in Blanche Butler Ames (comp.), *Chronicles*, II, 355; Natchez *Democrat*, April 5, 1876.

22. For a biographical sketch of Stone see Clayton Rand, *Men of Spine in Mississippi* (Gulfport, 1940), 199–201.

23. Horatio F. Simrall to James W. Garner, December 9, 1899, in Anselm J. McLaurin Papers, Mississippi Department of Archives and History; Jackson *Weekly Clarion*, June 28, 1876.

Stone succumbed to the clamor for the wholesale removal of these men. The case of Circuit Judge Jehu A. Orr of Columbus, how-ever, proved especially vexatious for the new governor.

Even before Stone became governor, Orr's conservative and moderate Republican friends began a campaign to have him re-tained on the court. The Starkville *East Mississippi Times*, a Dem-ocratic newspaper, declared that Orr, who had served in both the United States and Confederate congresses and had publicly advocated black suffrage as early as 1865, was "one of the very best judges Mississippi has ever had."[24] Other residents of his district bombarded the Redeemers at the state capital with pleas for the retention of the judge. The Columbus *Press* claimed that Orr's popularity in the district was evidenced by the fact that "he has received almost the unanimous endorsement of every bar in the District, of a majority of the papers of all parties, and that the grand juries of every county in the District . . . have recom-mended him for reappointment."[25] But after agonizing over the fate of Orr, Governor Stone went against the wishes of the judge's constituents and replaced him with a Democrat.

Despite this decision, Stone's appointments to the circuit and chancery courts were excellent. The selection of such competent and moderate men as Watson, James M. Smiley, and former Gov-ernor Clark suggested that justice in the Redeemer courts would be administered in an evenhanded way and would include blacks.[26]

Having rubbed elbows with Republicans for six years in the legislature, Stone realized that all were not adventurers or plun-derers. Consequently, he retained five Republicans, including three carpetbaggers, on the board of trustees of the University of Mississippi. Although in a minority now, the Republican trustees continued to exercise an influence on the university's management and development. Stone also reappointed Revels as president of Alcorn University, which was not unexpected in view of this black

24. "Reminiscences of J. A. Orr" (MS in Jehu A. Orr Papers, Mississippi Department of Archives and History); clipping from the Starkville *East Mississippi Times*, January 15, 1876, in Jehu A. Orr Papers, Southern Historical Collection, University of North Carolina Library, Chapel Hill.
25. Clipping from the Columbus *Press*, January 1, 1876, in Orr Papers, University of North Carolina Library.
26. Natchez *Democrat*, April 9, 1876.

leader's opposition to Ames. On the other hand, his selection of Furlong, now a professed conservative, to command the state militia created rumblings of discontent among Democrats who remembered this carpetbagger's role in organizing the Vicksburg "Ring." But Redeemers in the heavily black river counties had already planned to use Furlong as a stalking-horse to capture Negro votes and defeat John R. Lynch in his bid for reelection to Congress from the district.[27] Furlong's appointment as militia commander was designed to give him credentials and promote his candidacy against Lynch.

The Redeemer legislature and governor also acted to reduce further Republican strength at the polls. Congressional districts were changed to ensure that the Republicans, despite a majority of registered black voters, had an advantage in only one district. The formation of this district, a grotesquely apportioned one running the length of the Mississippi River, actually followed the Republican precedent of malapportioning congressional constituencies. One Republican district, for example, extended like a wedge from Vicksburg in the western plantation region to Meridian in the eastern yeoman-white country.[28] Although conservatives during Reconstruction had frequently complained of the inequitable distribution of seats in the state senate, which gave an advantage to the Republican plantation counties, a bipartisan bloc of representatives from these favored districts were able to prevent reapportionment in 1876. And the redistribution act passed the following year contained few changes from the Reconstruction arrangement.[29]

The Redeemers of 1876 had little trouble in agreeing to a new voter registration law that would place Republicans at a disadvantage. Under the provisions of this statute a state board of registration, headed by the governor, was authorized to appoint three-member boards for each county. These registrars were to establish election districts and in registering voters were to administer to each applicant a complicated oath indicating in "what election district of the county he resides . . . and in what portion of said district; and, if resident in any incorporated city or town, in what

27. *Ibid.*, April 19, May 9, 1876; Jackson *Weekly Clarion*, July 26, 1876.
28. *Senate Journal, 1876*, p. 338; Jackson *Weekly Clarion*, March 1, 1876.
29. *Laws of the State of Mississippi, 1877* (Jackson, 1877), 40–41.

ward of said city or town; and his occupation . . . and if, in the employ of any one, whom, where, and the nature of such employment." Unlike the Reconstruction system, in which a simple registration certificate entitled a voter to cast his ballot at any precinct in the county, the Redeemer law provided that the names of those who passed the local board's inspection must be entered into a registration ledger and made available only at the assigned polling place.[30] Many legislators in approving the new law were motivated not so much by an intent to restrict Negro voting as by a desire to reform and tighten the loose system of registration and voting that had prevailed during the Republican era. In fact, the legislature rejected a Bourbon proposal that would require a poll tax receipt in lieu of registration; this proposal was rejected, according to one source, because many legislators believed that such a requirement, obviously directed at poor blacks, would drive Negroes away from the Democratic party. Despite the reform purpose of many Redeemers, the new registration law provided an excellent means for local Democrats to reduce Negro voters to a manageable proportion—an opportunity many seized upon immediately.[31] This form of electoral subterfuge provided an entering wedge for the more blatant methods of fraud that were later used to maintain Democratic hegemony in the face of white independent and dissident challenges.[32]

Even before the political settlement had taken shape, conservatives in the legislature plunged into the work of curtailing public expenses and reducing taxes at all levels. It was the taxpayers' outrage, the influential Jackson *Weekly Clarion* reminded the legislature, that was "the true secret of the tremendous uprising of last autumn." Agreeing with this interpretation, a "Granger" correspondent warned the new assembly not to drag its feet on the tax question lest the people quickly become disillusioned with the

30. *Laws of Mississippi, 1876*, pp. 66–67. Republicans had also used for partisan purposes the authority to locate polling places.

31. Natchez *Democrat*, May 4, 1876; Flournoy to John M. Stone, August 3, 1876, and J. L. Lake to State Board of Registration, August 7, 1876, both in Governors' Correspondence, Vol. 109.

32. Kirwan, *Revolt of the Rednecks*, 36, 58–59. Ironically, the leading dissident in the party during the late Redemption period was Barksdale, who had failed to win control of the Democratic organization for the agrarian cause that he championed mainly because of the illegal tactics used by the Lamar-George wing of the party.

revolution and repudiate Democratic leadership. Barksdale feared that the Republican party, which now appeared on the road to an early rejuvenation under the leadership of moderates like Alcorn and Musgrove, would regain power in the state if the Redeemers did not provide immediate and sweeping relief for taxpayers as well as for those people who had lost their property at sheriff's sales.[33]

The pruning knife sharpened by the large and clamorous agrarian contingent in the house of representatives, the Democratic legislature proceeded with a vengeance to cut deep into state appropriations. Salaries were slashed in all departments of the government, and one position, "the ornamental office of Commissioner of Immigration," was for all practical purposes abolished. The largest reduction in appropriations occurred in the state judiciary where $134,000 was eliminated from the 1875 expenses by consolidating districts, reducing the salaries of those court officials who were retained, and repealing the expensive district printing bill of 1874.[34] In their haste to reform the financial structure of the public school system, whose funds well-intentioned Republicans had slightly mismanaged, conservatives cut expenses so drastically that the program was relegated to a mere facade of a state educational system. Teachers' salaries were reduced sharply, the pay of county superintendents was cut to one fifth of the former rate, and school officials were prohibited from using either state or county funds for construction or physical improvements.[35] Republicans and moderate conservatives like the editor of the Natchez *Democrat* rebuked the legislature for its stringent treatment of the schools. "Nothing is more essential than a good system of common schools," editor Botto wrote, "and particularly is this the case in the States where slavery prevented the education of so large a part of the population." But he preferred to believe that despite the economy measures of 1876 the Redeemers would

33. Jackson *Weekly Clarion*, April 5, 1876. See also the Natchez *Democrat*, January-February, 1876, issues.

34. *Annual Message of Governor Stone, 1877*, pp. 6–7; *Hinds County Gazette*, April 5, 1876. In reducing the office of the Commissioner of Immigration to a shell, conservatives, however, insisted that they still favored immigration; indeed, in 1878 they revitalized the office. Jackson *Weekly Clarion*, January 19, 1876; *Laws of Mississippi, 1878*, pp. 125–29.

35. *Laws of Mississippi, 1876*, pp. 206–10.

honor their commitment to provide blacks with a good school system.[36]

James Z. George, whose numerous statements on Democratic policies and performance contained a large dose of hypocrisy, in a public letter defended the educational changes made by the Redeemers and smugly announced that "the Legislature of 1876 seems to have retrenched in everything except public schools."[37] Then George went into some detail explaining how the schools would prosper under the new system. Much of this prosperity, he admitted, would come from the sharp reductions in teachers' salaries, but this was desirable. George's argument for lower teacher salaries reflected an attitude toward public schools that was common in Redemption Mississippi. "The maximum salary of the present law (of 1876) is $40 per month, being $2 per day [for] 5 or 6 hours" of work, he pointed out. "I feel safe in saying there is no other employment in Mississippi, in the present depressed condition of affairs, which is so well paid, taking into consideration the labor performed and the qualifications required of the employee." He concluded in a statement that some found incredulous in view of the legislature's action.

> If there be any one thing which the Democrats and Conservatives of this State are more determined to carry out than another, it is to provide the means of educating every child in the State of whatever race or color. The people of Mississippi have suffered enough already from ignorance and its consequences, blind prejudice, in governmental affairs, and they will not refuse to use any means in their power to remove them. But what they mean by levying taxes for common schools is not to advance the fortunes of superintendents and others, but to give the children of the State the means and opportunity of being educated.

In terms of enrollment, George's promise that education would not be slighted under the Redeemers was generally fulfilled. School

36. Natchez *Democrat*, March 5, April 26, 1876. In his first annual report, State Superintendent of Education Joseph Bardwell, a Stone appointee, chastised the legislature for its searing reductions in salaries and reminded the conservatives that good government, a Redeemer trademark, depended on an educated electorate. *Annual Report of the State Superintendent of Public Education, to the Legislature of Mississippi [for the Year 1876]* (Jackson, 1877), 13–15.

37. James Z. George to Kinlock Falconer, September 22, 1876, in George Scrapbook.

enrollments for both races remained at Reconstruction levels, although a temporary decline in the number of black students occurred in 1877.[38] Qualitatively, however, the system of mass, free education that the Republicans had begun with such high hopes in 1870 would require a long time to recover from the Redeemer policy of financial retrenchment.

The Redeemers of 1876 also acted vigorously to pay Reconstruction debts—a policy designed to restore confidence in Mississippi's financial structure, both public and private. Excluding several hundred thousand dollars in trust funds held by public authorities since before the war, the state debt inherited from the Ames administration was $931,850. This amount did not include $185,000 in state warrants which were still outstanding and were being hawked in the streets for eighty to eighty-five cents on the dollar. Although figures for the Reconstruction debts of southern states are uncertain and have been inflated by conservative sources, making an accurate comparison difficult, it seems probable that the debt the Republican regime left Mississippi was, with the possible exception of the Texas one, the smallest of any state in the South.[39] Certainly the state portion of the public debt was a manageable one, and because of the reputedly blighting effect of past repudiation policies, even the farmers' representatives in the legislature followed Governor Stone's leadership in opposing "any proposition to defer the payment of maturing bonds."[40] In 1879 alone, the Redeemer government reduced the state debt by $301,728 and brought state warrants to virtual parity with greenbacks.

An energetic policy of debt payment did not interfere with the conservative promise to lower state taxes. The tax rate on property for 1876 was reduced by 30 percent from that of the previous year. Although privilege taxes were not substantially cut, the system for collecting these revenues was tightened, and receipts during the

38. Statistical table in Noble, Forty Years of the Public Schools in Mississippi, 139.

39. Republicans and conservatives, as well as historians, have disputed the size of the state debt. The amount arrived at in this study was the result of an analysis of the reports and messages of Governors Ames (Republican) and Stone (conservative), State Auditor William H. Gibbs (Republican), and State Treasurer William L. Hemingway (conservative). For the debts of the southern states, see B. U. Ratchford, American State Debts (Durham, N.C., 1941), 183. Based on 1880 figures, Ratchford reports that twenty states in the Union had a smaller debt than Mississippi (p. 254).

40. Stone to Lamar, April 1, 1876, in Lamar-Mayes Papers.

first year of the redemption increased by $64,218 over those of 1875. The Redeemer legislature of 1876 in large measure retained the Republican levy on personalty, including a one dollar poll tax for school purposes, but it declined to take action against local officials who failed to collect the tax from the poor.[41] As a result of Redeemer reforms, the state treasury showed a surplus of $160,944 at the end of 1876.[42]

The financial disarray existing in a number of counties posed a greater problem for the Redeemers than did the state debt. During the early 1870s irresponsible officials in several counties, especially in the river district, had increased public obligations far beyond the local means to amortize the debts. In the case of Warren County the jumbled public debt reportedly had risen to $1,790,943, which, if true, exceeded that of the state.[43] The Redeemer legislatures of 1876 and 1877 acted to restore the financial stability of hard-pressed counties and towns. It imposed principles of strict accounting on the issuance of local warrants, placed restrictions on the taxing authority of county officials, and provided for the funding of the legitimate portion of local debts. Despite these reforms, many counties were encumbered with large railroad and school obligations and continued to experience severe financial difficulty. Then, too, in the Delta where approximately one half of the land was under public control, no immediate relief resulted from Redeemer efforts to reduce the crushing burdens of old levee debts and restore the value of the land, at least for tax purposes.[44]

The vaunted conservative commitment to honesty and capacity in government was only partly realized. In addition to their failure to maintain an untrammeled ballot in the state, the Redeemers proved unequal to the task of reforming the local governments that had been mismanaged during the Republican era. The re-

41. This form of tax relief had become widespread by the end of the Republican era. Auditor Gibbs reported in 1876 that the public schools annually lost between $75,000 and $90,000 in revenues because of poll-tax evasion, which occurred with the blessings of local officials and collectors. *Annual Report of the Auditor, 1876*, p. 9.

42. *Ibid.*, 5.

43. Natchez *Democrat*, May 9, 1876.

44. *Laws of Mississippi, 1876*, pp. 31–32, 342–44; *Laws of Mississippi, 1877*, pp. 121–25, 130–31; *Appleton's Annual Cyclopaedia*, 1877, p. 526; *Annual Message and Inaugural Address of Governor J. M. Stone, to the Legislature of Mississippi, Session of 1878* (Jackson, 1878), 16; *Annual Report of the Auditor, 1876*, pp. vi–vii.

placement of many unlettered Republican officials with conservatives in the river district brought some improvements in the administration of most of the counties. But in others, after an initial salute to probity in government Democrats fell victims to the legacy of Reconstruction mismanagement.[45] This was especially true of Warren County, the epitome of Reconstruction excess and corruption in the state. An old resident of Vicksburg has left a revealing description of affairs in the county under the early Redeemers. He wrote:

> From my standpoint I am forced to say that the administration of impartial justice and the punishment of crime in this county, since the accession of the Democratic party to power in the state has been a failure and a disgrace to our civilization.
> The press is muzzled so that the crookedness of officials is not made public. Of course, there must be and is a head Devil whose agents are sufficiently numerous and venal to control not only our board of Supervisors but the grand and petit juries in many cases. To be brief it seems to work about this way—Each member of the Board of Supervisors seems to be supreme in all matters in his district, and when a bill is presented for allowance and approved by the member in whose district the work is done, as a matter of courtesy to that member, all or nearly all the members vote for the allowance without any enquiry as to its legality or reasonableness. In this way the County Treasury is with commendable and systematic regularity robbed and plundered and that too with impunity for the Board in its selection of Grand Jurors, having all necessary knowledge upon this subject, select a Grand Jury usually that . . . refuse to indict any county official. . . .
> If any official should be indicted as has been the case, the Judge, and I say it with shame and sorrow, finds some mode, entirely unknown to the law of getting rid of the indictment without bringing the offender to justice.[46]

On the state level Democratic rule was reasonably honest during the Redemption era. Although frequently cited by historians to demonstrate the existence of corruption in the Redeemer state government, the conviction of State Treasurer William L. Hem-

45. This is not to deny the existence of local mismanagement before the Republicans came to power, but it is the conclusion of this study that maladministration in the counties and towns was more prevalent during the Republican period than earlier.

46. H. Shannon to Robert Lowry, November 19, 1881, in Governors' Correspondence, Vol. 132.

ingway for the embezzlement of $315,612 in public funds actually
constituted a miscarriage of justice. While Hemingway was serving a five-year sentence for the crime, evidence was uncovered
that completely exonerated him and brought his immediate release
from prison.[47]

Other changes made by the early Redeemer leadership fell short
of the counterrevolutionary implications contained in the Democratic-Conservative rhetoric and promises of 1875–1876. Revision
of the Republican constitution of 1868 went no further than the
approval of two amendments, only one of which, the adoption
of a measure for biennial sessions of the legislature, was significant. Writing in 1880, Redeemer State Supreme Court Justice
Josiah A. P. Campbell admitted that despite the fiery promises,
conservative control had resulted in very little change in the fundamental laws of the state.[48]

With a United States Senate investigation of Mississippi affairs
imminent, the conservative legislature of 1876 made no move to
repeal the civil rights guarantees for blacks that had been enacted
by Republicans. Even the civil rights act of 1873, the most radical of these laws in that it provided for the equal treatment of
blacks in public places, remained on the books. But the law had
been a virtual nullity since its passage, and dominant conservatives
of the late 1870s permitted it to die a silent death. A formal respect
by the Redeemers for the rights of blacks did not bring racial
peace to Mississippi, as conservatives of the George-Lamar faction
had promised, nor did it prevent their rapid relegation to a status
of serfdom. Now at the mercy of whites, so-called black "desperadoes" and "fiends" met a summary justice at the hands of Judge
Lynch, despite the mild efforts of Governor Stone and the state
judiciary to prevent the practice.[49] One "negro scoundrel" was
lynched in 1876 at Port Gibson within two hundred yards of a

47. Report of Hinds County Grand Jury, term of January, 1893, to Stone; clipping
from the Memphis *Appeal-Avalanche*, n.d., and the Jackson *Clarion-Ledger*, June 27,
1890, all in William L. Hemingway Papers, Mississippi Department of Archives and
History.

48. *Senate Journal, 1880*, pp. 40–41.

49. Summit (Miss.) *Conservative Times*, March 29, 1878; Jackson *Weekly Clarion*, January 26, 1876; Stone to J. S. Hoskins, August 21, 1876; officers of "Aberdeen Guards"
to Stone, August 23, 1876, and Franklin A. Montgomery to Stone, August 18, 1876, all
in Governors' Correspondence, Vol. 113.

United States army post. Other blacks, who were accused of stealing, often were "bulldozed" into submission by white vigilantes.[50]

Blacks did not always react passively to such fierce treatment, but the consequences of their aggressiveness were usually the same—the further suppression of their rights. The most violent challenge to the iron vise of white supremacy occurred in May, 1876, in Wilkinson County, one of the few Republican counties to survive, at least nominally. Wilkinson County witnessed the rise of "Honest Men's Clubs" in early 1876, which were ostensibly designed to suppress a wave of petty thievery that threatened the county. The May disturbance in this river county began when a local club whipped a Negro who was accused of stealing and killing a beef, which reportedly belonged to another black man. A Jewish merchant, who lived below the state line in Louisiana, was one of the three-member "committee" of the club that actually administered the punishment. The following night a band of thirty blacks visited the merchant at his store and killed him. Immediately, a group of whites pursued the blacks, captured several of the band after a brief skirmish, and lynched two of them upon their "confession of guilt."[51]

News of the lynchings spread quickly throughout the western part of Wilkinson County, and within two days about 150 outraged blacks had raised the standard of revolt. Panic gripped both the black and white communities, whites fearing the murder of their women and children by the rebels and noncombatant blacks fearing the inevitable white reaction to the uprising. Seeking safety, white families fled to Woodville, the small county seat, and blacks hid out in the woods and swamps until the terror had passed. Meanwhile, Sheriff William H. Noble, a scalawag and a former Confederate officer, had organized a military force of whites, some of whom had come from Louisiana and adjacent Mississippi counties, to march against the insurgents. The two forces met near

---

50. Natchez *Democrat*, May 30, 1876, June 30, 1877; *Laws of Mississippi, 1878*, pp. 259–60. The legislature indirectly gave encouragement to the practice of "bulldozing," or vigilante activity against blacks, by passing an act, known as the Hog Law, that classified as grand larceny the theft of ten dollars or more in property or in stock animals worth one dollar or more. Natchez *Democrat*, April 15, 1876.

51. Louis F. Griffin to Stone, May 18, 1876, in Governors' Correspondence, Vol. 107; Natchez *Democrat*, May 19, 1876.

Fort Adams on the river, and after prominent black leaders of the county failed to persuade the rebels to lay down their arms, fighting broke out. The battle and subsequent pursuit was one-sided. Approximately fifty black insurgents died in the fighting; there were no white fatalities.[52]

The disturbance did not end with the battle of Fort Adams. Believing that they would soon feel the wrath of the whites, about three hundred blacks in the northern part of the county and in Adams County organized a force, seized arms and supplies, and barricaded themselves on an island in the backwaters of the Mississippi. Sheriff Noble, who was flooded with offers of help from Baton Rouge, Natchez, and other communities, went to "Old River Island" and persuaded the blacks there to lay down their arms and return home. With the insurrection suppressed, Wilkinson County planters met at Woodville and assured apprehensive blacks that their rights would be protected in the future. By the end of May race relations had returned to normal, but with the major difference that black subordination to white control was even more complete than before the insurrection.[53] Nevertheless, the Wilkinson uprising reminded river county whites of the explosiveness of racial emotions and of the need to exercise care in their treatment of blacks. In Redemption as in Reconstruction, the concern for social order and labor stability frequently surmounted any desire by planters of these counties to maintain a rigid subordination of blacks; a system of control and suppression, they knew, contained latent racial strife and must be avoided. As a result, bulldozing practices affected only a few alluvial areas, and compared to the tyranny existing in the interior, in most river counties blacks continued to exercise a surprising degree of freedom and political action.[54]

In economic matters the Redeemers of 1876–1877 left many Reconstruction policies standing, albeit with modifications in most

52. Griffin to Stone, May 18, 1876, in Governors' Correspondence, Vol. 107; Beaumont, *A Business Woman's Journal*, 355–57; Natchez *Democrat*, May 26, 1876.

53. William H. Noble to Stone, May 19, 1876, and William T. Martin to Stone, May 18, 1876, both in Governors' Correspondence, Vol. 107; Natchez *Democrat*, May 20, 26, 1876; Beaumont, *A Business Woman's Journal*, 358–59.

54. Charles W. Clarke to Jonathan Tarbell, April 30, 1877, in Rutherford B. Hayes Papers, Rutherford B. Hayes Memorial Library, Fremont, Ohio; John Lynch, *Reminiscences of an Active Life*, 229–30.

cases. For example, they retained and later enlarged upon the practice of leasing penitentiary prisoners to a handful of favored businessmen and planters. The conservative legislature also continued the debilitating crop lien (or cotton mortgage) law, despite a growing demand for its repeal. The lawmakers did revise the act to provide some protection for the tenant farmer in his arrangements with the merchant.[55] Except for the prison concession, which was perceived more as a benefit to the state than to business interests, the early Redeemers displayed no disposition to provide public aid for private enterprise. In fact, Governor Stone, a product of the yeoman class of northeast Mississippi who was supported by a large bloc of agrarian legislators, expressed outright hostility toward the granting of privileges and assistance to special economic groups.[56]

Reflecting the general antirailroad sentiment that was sweeping the Mississippi Valley at this time, the new regime continued the efforts begun by Governor Ames to make the railroads more responsive to the public interest. The Redeemers specifically recaptured for public use the large state trust funds (the Chickasaw School Fund and the college land-grant endowment) that had been carelessly loaned to railroad corporations by earlier conservative and Republican administrations. Furthermore, dominant conservatives compelled defiant companies to honor the railroad tax measure of 1875, the first significant levy on railroad property in the history of the state, and they also threatened to regulate freight rates if the railroads continued to ignore the public interest.[57] But conservative efforts in the direction of railroad regulation were short-lived; by the 1880s even early reformers like Governor Stone had succumbed to the forces seeking a privileged status for railroads.

The conservative coalition that had "redeemed" the state from Radical rule showed signs of division after the presidential elec-

55. *Laws of Mississippi, 1876*, pp. 109–15; Yazoo City *Herald*, January 28, 1876; Newton (Miss.) *Reporter*, January 18, 1878.

56. *House Journal, 1876*, pp. 645–46; *Laws of Mississippi, 1876*, pp. 15–16; *Laws of Mississippi, 1877*, pp. 72–73.

57. *Laws of Mississippi, 1876*, pp. 34, 64–65, 275–76; *House Journal, 1876*, pp. 245–46.

tion of 1876, when the threat of a Republican restoration appeared remote. In addition to the political rivalries that normally develop in a party that is secure in power, a major cause for the disintegration of the coalition was the failure of its leaders to sustain the white democratic tendencies of the 1875 uprising. Local cliques gained control of county politics, abandoned the emerging system of primary elections, and revived the county convention method of selecting party nominees. "In almost every instance," the Vicksburg *Herald* reported in 1877, "the men who have the majority— the support of the people, and who would get that support in a Primary Election, are defeated by the tricks of a convention," controlled by a few politicians.[58] Throughout Mississippi dissident conservatives, some calling themselves "Independents," arose in 1877 to denounce the Democratic party for not honoring its 1875 promises and for "yield[ing] itself up to the management of rings and cliques so that honest and sensible men by straight ways can have no influence in it for the public good."[59]

Yeoman farmers, who had rallied to the Democratic standard by the thousands in 1875, had an additional reason to be disgruntled with the Redeemer leadership after the euphoria of success against the Radicals had vanished. Conservative campaign orators and editors in 1875 had constantly preached that material conditions would improve once redemption had occurred and good government was restored. But economic conditions did not improve and farmers continued to experience the blighting effects of the agricultural depression that had begun soon after the war.[60] When yeomen protested their plight and criticized such laws as the crop lien act (which was more of a scapegoat for their troubles than a barrier to recovery), the Democratic leadership ignored their pleas.[61] Then, when dissidents threatened to bolt the party and

58. Vicksburg *Herald*, July 4, 1877. See also unsigned letter from Corinth correspondent in Jackson *Weekly Clarion*, October 10, 1877.

59. Port Gibson *Southern Reveille*, August 18, 1877 (quote); E. J. Williams to Stone, October 31, 1877, and Charles A. Stovall to Stone, September 18, 1877, both in Governors' Correspondence, Vol. 113; Edwards (Miss.) *Citizen*, July 28, 1877.

60. *Annual Message of Governor Stone, 1878*, 3–4; Jackson *Clarion*, January 18, 1878; J. B. Ellis to Stone, October 7, 1877, in Governors' Correspondence, Vol. 113.

61. Port Gibson *Southern Reveille*, August 18, 1877; Yazoo City (Miss.) *Sentinel*, November 26, December 31, 1878; Newton *Reporter*, January 18, 1878; James S. Ferguson, "Agrarianism in Mississippi, 1871–1900: A Study in Non-Conformity" (Ph.D. dissertation, University of North Carolina, Chapel Hill, 1952), 360.

join the Independents in 1877 and the Greenbackers in 1878, even farm leader and editor E. G. Wall warned them that such action risked "losing the fruits of the glorious victories of 1875 and '76."[62] If whites divided, the conservative litany proclaimed, Radicals would enter the breach, regain power, and reenact the bitter scenes of Reconstruction. Put in this light, most white yeomen suppressed their grievances against the hardening Democratic oligarchy and continued to support the party of white supremacy.[63] Nevertheless, despite the conservative tactics of recalling the horrors of Reconstruction, appealing to white racial prejudices, and employing fraud at the polls to reduce the dissident vote of both whites and blacks, Mississippi during the age of the Redeemers was never solidly Democratic.[64] But these methods had the desired effect of consolidating Democratic rule. By the turn of the century the Democratic party, although no longer in the hands of men like George and Lamar, had successfully suppressed all challenges to its authority, and Mississippi had indeed become a one-party state, ready for the likes of James K. Vardaman and Theodore G. Bilbo. The legend of the "Tragic Era" played no small part in the fastening of the Democratic vise on the state and its continuance for many years.

62. Jackson *Farmers' Vindicator*, October 5, 1877.
63. Ferguson, "Agrarianism in Mississippi," 400, 409–10.
64. Kirwan, *Revolt of the Rednecks*, 309.

Epilogue

The denouement of the new order in Mississippi was sudden, but many Republicans continued into the 1880s to express hope that as a result either of federal intervention or an alliance with independents they might yet regain power.[1] Immediately after the debacle of 1875, moderate Republicans, the most prominent of whom had supported Alcorn in 1873, seized control of the state organization from demoralized Ames men and clothed the party in the garb of reform. Their success reduced the influence of blacks in party councils and alienated Negro leaders John R. Lynch and James Hill, who ultimately brought their followers into a fusion with Lamar Democrats.[2] White Republicans, however, made no serious effort to drive blacks from the party, as occurred in the twentieth century.

The moderate Republican strategy to make the party "respectable" in the eyes of whites did not work. Only in 1881, when Republicans temporarily muffled their differences and fused with the Greenbackers to win 40 percent of the vote in the gubernatorial election, did they seriously threaten the Redeemer hegemony.[3] Increasingly as the years passed, the control of federal patronage became of major importance to Republican politicians who found themselves excluded at the polls from the perquisites of local and state office. The struggle for the few available offices accentuated the factionalism that had plagued the party almost from its origin in 1867, further reducing the chances of Republican unity against the Democrats. By the twentieth century the Republican party in Mississippi existed almost solely for the emoluments of federal

1. Charles W. Clarke to James A. Garfield, January 26, 1876, in Garfield Papers; Thomas Y. Berry to John M. Stone, September 4, 1876, in Governors' Correspondence, Vol. 109; Willie D. Halsell (ed.), "Republican Factionalism in Mississippi, 1882–1884," *Journal of Southern History*, VIII (February, 1941), 91–92, 97.

2. Jackson *Times*, December 7, 1875; Natchez *Democrat*, January 30, April 5, 1876; Jackson *Weekly Clarion*, February 16, 1876; John Lynch, *Facts of Reconstruction*, xlvii–xlviii.

3. John Lynch, *Facts of Reconstruction*, xlvi.

office. Those few Republicans, including a handful of survivors of the Reconstruction era, who still hoped for a strong party organization in the state had no illusions that their party could soon overcome its baleful reputation and again challenge the Democrats.

The fate of individual Republicans was frequently a great deal better than that of their party. Even many black leaders of the Reconstruction period suffered no dramatic eclipse in their fortunes. A few like Blanche K. Bruce and John R. Lynch eventually were impelled by circumstances to look to national Republican administrations for positions in Washington, but several like James Hill, George W. Gayles, Thomas W. Stringer, and Hiram R. Revels stayed in the state and managed to retain a measure of their Reconstruction influence as leaders of their race in politics (in the case of Hill and Gayles) and religion (Stringer and Revels). As late as 1882, twelve blacks were serving in the legislature. Most Negro leaders of the Reconstruction era, however, either remained in the state pursuing such mundane occupations as blacksmith, carpenter, or farmer, or left Mississippi never to be heard of again. One notable expatriate was William H. Gray, whose indictment for grand larceny and embezzlement by a Kentucky grand jury soon after he left the state confirmed in the minds of conservatives their long-held belief that this Radical legislative leader was corrupt.[4]

After the collapse of their political influence a number of carpetbaggers and scalawags refused to be relegated to the obscurity and ignominy that conservative contemporaries, as well as later historians, had assigned to them. As relatively young men of talent and energy, some became successful and prominent citizens in their communities during the years that followed Reconstruction. Very few scalawags left the state to seek opportunities in places more congenial to their political views, and a surprising number maintained the esteem of their neighbors while continuing to support the Republican party.[5] A tragic exception was William W.

4. Port Gibson *Southern Reveille*, August 18, 1877; *Journal of the Senate of the State of Mississippi, 1877* (Jackson, 1877), 251–55.

5. Local accounts of Reconstruction, written soon after the turn of the century and reflecting a conservative bias, are replete with examples of former scalawags who, instead of being ostracized as historians have concluded, became "respectable" citizens of their communities and were mourned by many when they died. See Ruth Watkins, "Reconstruction in Newton County," *Publications of the Mississippi Historical Society*, XI (1910), 213; Irby C. Nichols, "Reconstruction in DeSoto County," *ibid.*, XI (1910), 298; M. G.

Chisolm, sheriff of Kemper County, who paid with his life for his republicanism and support for Negro rights. In 1877 Chisolm and two of his children died in a shoot-out with a mob of whites who had come to lynch him for the alleged murder of a local Democratic chief.[6]

The most prominent scalawag, Alcorn, found the rule of the Redeemers no barrier to his presiding over a Delta domain in a style befitting a prince. His home at Eagle's Nest became, according to his biographer, "a symbol of what the South liked to think the earlier period had been."[7] Joshua S. Morris and George E. Harris, the state attorney generals during the Republican period, enjoyed prosperous law practices after Reconstruction. During the 1880s Harris moved to Washington where, in addition to his practice of law, he obtained a measure of distinction for his authorship of several legal treatises.[8] Although continuing to be active in the Republican party, "Old Osawatomie" Flournoy joined in the prohibition movement of the 1880s, and when he died in 1894 the early radicalism he had often expressed in the columns of the Pontotoc *Equal Rights* had been forgotten by the citizens of his county. Flournoy was now remembered as the local Republican leader who had saved the county from the rule of the carpetbag adventurers and ignorant blacks and had established the county's "magnificent public school system."[9]

Some former scalawags achieved considerable success in business during the Redemption era. George M. Buchanan, the great hope of the Republican party in the 1875 election, became a prosperous planter, merchant, and banker in north Mississippi,

Abney, "Reconstruction in Pontotoc County," *ibid.*, XI (1910), 235; Ernest F. Puckett, "Reconstruction in Monroe County," 122; Hattie Magee, "Reconstruction in Lawrence and Jeff Davis Counties," *ibid.*, XI (1910), 172; Edward Clarke Coleman, "Reconstruction in Attala County," *ibid.*, X (1909), 154; J. H. Jones, "Reconstruction in Wilkinson County," *ibid.*, VIII (1904), 170; Luke W. Conerly, *Pike County, Mississippi, 1798–1876* (Nashville, 1909), 256, 264–65.

6. James M. Wells, *The Chisolm Massacre: A Picture of "Home Rule" in Mississippi* (Chicago, 1878), 307–308.

7. Pereyra, *James Lusk Alcorn*, 185.

8. Joshua S. Morris to Marie Swanson, July 16, 1879, in Swanson and Yates Family Papers; *Biographical Directory of the American Congress, 1774–1961* (Washington, D.C.: 1971), 1074; *The National Union Catalog: Pre-1956 Imprints* (329 vols. completed; London, 1968—), Vol. 232, p. 8.

9. E. T. Winston, *Story of Pontotoc County, Mississippi* (Pontotoc, 1931), 312–13.

and lived into the second decade of the twentieth century.[10] Judge Orlando Davis spent the two decades after his forced retirement from the bench as a prominent banker in Holly Springs.[11] Probably no former scalawag achieved the distinction of Reuben W. Millsaps, a minor Republican functionary in Reconstruction, who accumulated considerable wealth in commerce and banking during the late nineteenth century and used some of it to establish an outstanding institution of higher learning in the state—Millsaps College.[12] Despite these examples of success, most scalawags, like their conservative contemporaries, spent the remainder of their lives in modest or poor circumstances.

Two scalawags, Dr. William M. Compton, a leading Alcorn Republican, and Thomas Walton, Radical Republican judge and Lamar's successor as professor of law in the state university, died heroically in the catastrophic yellow fever epidemic of 1878. Compton contracted the fever and died while administering to the sick in Holly Springs, and Walton met a similar fate after taking charge of affairs in Grenada and bringing order out of chaos at the height of the epidemic. Of Walton's heroism, the Grenada *Sentinel* reported that he was "the most intrepid man in the hour of danger we ever knew. Whatever may have been the mistakes of his past life (if such they were), there are none so unforgiving that would not freely place them under the martyr's crown he so richly deserves."[13] The examples of Compton and Walton, along with the deaths in the epidemic of several other Republican activists, did a great deal to reduce the antagonism that most whites had long felt toward the leaders of the party of Negro rights.

Most carpetbaggers also attempted to make the adjustment from the cauldron of Reconstruction politics to the peaceful pursuits of private life without leaving Mississippi. In most cases they failed,

10. Dunbar Rowland (ed.), *Mississippi: Comprising Sketches of Counties, Towns, Events, Institutions, and Persons, Arranged in Cyclopedic Form* (3 vols.; Atlanta, 1907), III, 94.

11. Sketch of Orlando Davis in William H. McRaven, "Mississippi Profiles," Mississippi Department of Archives and History.

12. *Biographical and Historical Memoirs of Mississippi* (2 vols.; Chicago, 1891), II, 442–43.

13. John L. Power, *The Epidemic of 1878*, in *Mississippi: Report of the Yellow Fever Relief Work Through J. L. Power, Grand Secretary of Masons and Grand Treasurer of Odd Fellows* (Jackson, 1879), 131 (quote), 196–200.

and a gradual migration of carpetbaggers from the state occurred during the decade after 1875, usually prompted by appointments to minor federal positions in Washington and in the western territories. G. Wiley Wells, the conqueror of the Ku Klux Klan, left in 1877 to become the United States consul general in China. Jonathan Tarbell, Albert T. Morgan, and J. L. Lake, proprietor of the Vicksburg (later Jackson) *Times and Republican*, accepted appointments to clerkships in Washington during the early Redemption period.[14]

The West held the greatest attraction for fallen carpetbaggers. In 1879 Ridgley C. Powers sold his plantations in east Mississippi and moved to Prescott, Arizona Territory. With a background in civil engineering he became prominent in the development of Arizona's rich mineral wealth and also took time to serve as president of the Good Government League, a nonpartisan organization formed to rid the territory of outlaws. At the turn of the century this former carpetbag governor moved to Los Angeles and spent his remaining days (until 1912) commuting between the city and his ranch in the Imperial Valley.[15]

Several carpetbaggers migrated to Kansas where they used their talents to gain enviable reputations in the development of the state. Beroth B. Eggleston, the chairman of the Black and Tan Convention and the Radical candidate for governor in 1868, migrated to Wichita in 1878. Before his death in 1891 he had served as superintendent of the city's water works and chief of the police department, in addition to being a local leader in the Republican party.[16] The powerful carpetbagger Alexander Warner also settled in Kansas, after serving for two terms as the state treasurer of his native state of Connecticut. A banker by occupation, he sat in the state legislature during the turbulent 1890s and made use of his six years of experience as a leader in the Mississippi assembly to play a vital role in Republican opposition to the Populists in Kansas. When Warner died in 1914 at the age of eighty-eight, he could

14. Edwards *Citizen*, August 4, 1877; *Hinds County Gazette*, April 14, 1883; Albert T. Morgan to James W. Garner, January 13, 1900, in Garner Papers.

15. Powers, "Biographical Memoranda of Powers"; Los Angeles *Times*, November 12, 1912; Phoenix *Arizona Gazette*, November 14, 1912.

16. *Portrait and Biographical Album of Sedgwick County, Kansas* (Chicago, 1888), 469–71.

claim the distinction of having been influential in the public affairs of three states.[17]

Lesser carpetbaggers Charles S. Jobes and Hiram W. Lewis, a former Mississippi sheriff and editor of the Columbus *Press*, also became leading citizens of Kansas. During the 1890s Jobes emerged as "one of the main spokes" in the Republican machine in that state. After he moved to Kansas City and entered banking, he gained a reputation even in the East for his financial ability.[18] Lewis also achieved success as a banker, and with the wealth he accumulated from the profits of several Kansas banks that he controlled, this former Radical founded Lewis Academy, a prestigious private school in Wichita. Like Eggleston, Lewis played an important role in the civic development of this growing Kansas town.[19]

Colorado also became a mecca for dispossessed carpetbaggers of the Magnolia state. A "Mississippi colony" had developed in Denver even before the end of Reconstruction, and it grew to perhaps a dozen expatriates by the 1880s. None evidently achieved prominence in the affairs of the state, although Eugene P. Jacobson served in the Colorado senate and John Corcoran became the United States postmaster in Denver.[20] Chicago also became the home of several former carpetbaggers, including former Congressman Legrand W. Perce who lived out his years as a prominent lawyer in the city and E. K. Bliss, a Columbus editor during Reconstruction, who attained the office of district attorney in Cook County.[21] No transplanted carpetbagger exceeded the professional distinction of J. N. Bishop, a celebrated physician and lecturer from New York who treated the epilepsy of Mrs. William McKin-

17. *Directory of the State Government of Kansas, For the Years 1877 and 1878* (N. p., 1878), 122; Kansas City *Times*, September 9, 1914; Hiram W. Lewis to Garner, January 10, 1900, in Garner Papers.

18. Kansas City *Journal*, April 15, 1904; Wichita *Morning Eagle*, April 24, 1904; Topeka *Daily Capital*, September 28, 1929.

19. Wichita *Morning Eagle*, February 15, 1912; *Portrait and Biographical Album of Sedgwick County*, 206–207.

20. Vicksburg *Times*, March 12, 1874; Jackson *Weekly Pilot*, March 13, 1875; John Corcoran to Garner, December 20, 1899, in Garner Papers; Jackson *Weekly Clarion*, April 21, 1881.

21. New York *Times*, March 18, 1911; Hiram W. Lewis to Garner, January 18, 1900, in Garner Papers.

ley when she lived in the White House. Bishop's postwar activities in Mississippi centered largely around his position as superintendent of education in Lowndes County.[22]

The most amazing career of a Mississippi carpetbagger after Reconstruction belonged to Charles E. Furlong. The organizer of the Vicksburg Republican "Ring" and the Talleyrand of postwar politics in the state, Furlong remained in Mississippi for several years after Reconstruction, gaining Democratic praise for his work as "a zealous and efficient champion" of reform in the legislature.[23] The crusty George W. Harper even suggested that he would be an excellent candidate for governor on the Democratic ticket. But his hopes for political preferment at the hands of his former adversaries turned topsy-turvy in 1881 when an enterprising district attorney hauled him into court to make restitution for public funds that he had allegedly misused while sheriff of Warren County during the early 1870s. Although he was never indicted, his civil trial before the state supreme court reminded conservatives of his disreputable past.[24] Under the circumstances, Furlong, now a wealthy man, decided to follow other carpetbaggers into exile, but in characteristic fashion he donated several thousand dollars to a Vicksburg church before he left the state. He moved to New York where he established a base for the series of world tours he made during the remaining quarter century of his life. He also maintained an intimate association with the family of General Grant, on whose staff he had served for a time during the war. When Furlong died in 1907, the New York *Times* wrote that despite the fact that his name could not be found in any biographical directories he "was one of the best-known Americans in foreign cities." He had "a wide acquaintance among diplomats and rulers of every nation in the world."[25]

22. Hiram Lewis to Garner, January 18, 1900, in Garner Papers; Margaret Leech, *In the Days of McKinley* (New York, 1959), 27. Bishop also wrote and published accounts of his travels in South Africa and the Hawaiian Islands. *National Union Catalog*, Vol. 58, p. 697.

23. Jackson *Weekly Clarion*, October 10, 1877.

24. *Hinds County Gazette*, May 2, 1877; *State of Mississippi* v. *Charles E. Furlong*, 60 Miss. 839–46 (1883).

25. Interview with Lucius Bryan Dabney, August 8, 1966; New York *Times*, September 26, 1907.

Many carpetbaggers, however, did not succeed after their political power had faded. Indeed, many died in obscurity. Henry R. Pease followed a minor federal position to the windswept plains of South Dakota where he died in 1907 with no one to recall that he had once been a United States senator and had been the architect of Mississippi's public school system.[26] Driven from a clerkship in Washington when Grover Cleveland became president, an embittered Albert T. Morgan settled in Durango, Colorado, in a fruitless effort to regain a semblance of his early affluence. O. C. French and John B. Raymond, the influential proprietor of the Jackson *Pilot*, also died in obscurity in the West.[27]

Those northern Republicans who remained in Mississippi, though generally forgiven for their Reconstruction sins, struggled as did their conservative neighbors to make ends meet during the age of the Redeemers and after. Surprisingly, the list of carpetbaggers who stayed contained a number of the more prominent ones; few of them, however, had had reputations as Radicals when Reconstruction ended. Edward J. Castello, the wheel-horse of the party in the constitutional convention of 1868, Edward Stafford, Charles W. Clarke, Henry Musgrove, George C. McKee, and William H. Gibbs adjusted reasonably well to their powerless roles in Mississippi society. Although they had been castigated collectively as "mongrel adventurers" or worse during Reconstruction, these carpetbaggers had rarely been exposed to insults in private, everyday life. At some point during Reconstruction a number of the prominent carpetbaggers, including some who later left Mississippi, had lost their early feeling of alienation toward the white community and, despite their politics, had at least in their own minds become identified with their adopted state and their local communities. During the Redemption era a few carpetbaggers who remained in the state held federal positions until the Democrats came to power in Washington in 1885, but evidently most of them, numbering probably no more than twenty-five, pursued the tradi-

26. Jackson *Weekly Clarion*, March 31, 1881; *Biographical Directory of Congress*, 1522–23.

27. Charles S. Jobes to Garner, December 31, 1899; Morgan to Garner, January 13, 1900, in Garner Papers.

tional Mississippi occupations of law and planting.[28] Gibbs, whose
adjustment to conservative dominance in the state was fairly easy,
had the sad distinction of being the only important carpetbagger in
Mississippi to be tried and convicted for a felony. During the late
1880s he was sentenced to five years in federal prison for embezzling funds while postmaster at Jackson. He was soon pardoned by
President Benjamin Harrison and returned to Jackson where he
died in obscurity in 1909.[29]

It was perhaps fitting that Adelbert Ames, the most prominent
and most vilified northerner in postwar Mississippi, should be the
last carpetbag survivor and should also be the object of a final
Reconstruction controversy in the state. When he left Mississippi
in 1876 he joined his father in the flour-milling business in North-
field, Minnesota. In 1879 he moved to New Jersey, across the river
from New York, where he served as the eastern agent for the
Minnesota mill. He also acquired an interest in textile mills at
Lowell, Massachusetts, and patented a number of inventions, a
hobby he had cultivated while in Mississippi.[30] Ames took time out
from accumulating his fortune to serve as a brigadier general of
volunteers in the Spanish-American War. His pleasant association
in Cuba with General Joseph Wheeler and other former Confederate soldiers finally mellowed Ames's view of white southerners,
and he remarked that "this war with Spain in many and devious
ways is obliterating Civil War animosities."[31] Although for two
decades he had vigorously defended the performance of the Republicans in Reconstruction and denounced the conservatives'
methods of overthrowing his regime in Mississippi,[32] the fight
went out of him after the Spanish-American War. When a newspaper reporter asked him whether the Reconstruction policy of en-

28. Jackson *Weekly Clarion*, March 31, July 7, September 8, October 22, 1881; *Biographical Directory of Congress*, 1380–81; *Hinds County Gazette*, March 28, 1885.

29. New York *Times*, August 18, 1909.

30. Richard N. Current, *Three Carpetbag Governors* (Baton Rouge, 1967), 92; Blanche
Ames Ames, *Adelbert Ames*, 495. He later moved to Tewksbury, Massachusetts, near
Lowell.

31. Ames to his wife, November 5, 1898, in Blanche Butler Ames (comp.), *Chronicles*, II,
662.

32. See for example Adelbert Ames to the historian E. Benjamin Andrews, May 24,
1895, February 29, March 11, 1896, in Ames Papers.

franchising blacks had been wise, he answered by evading his own partisan role in it. The issue of Negro suffrage, he informed the reporter, "is still a mooted question. Aside from the right or wrong of that policy I was [in Mississippi] to execute the laws of Congress which took unto itself the task of reconstruction. As a soldier, it was not for me to reason why, but to carry out the will of those to whom I was responsible. It was only natural for the white Southerners to look upon me as an enemy. I was a damn Yankee, an abolitionist and a Black Republican."[33] A wealthy man in his old age, Ames hobnobbed with John D. Rockefeller, Sr., and other millionaires of his generation. A measure of fame came his way during the 1920s when he became the last surviving Union general of the Civil War, and newspapers announced each of his birthdays. On April 13, 1933, at the age of ninety-eight, Adelbert Ames died.[34]

But he was not permitted to rest in peace for long. During the 1950s Mississippi officials asked Ames's daughter for a portrait of her father to hang in the hall of governors in the state capitol. She complied with an oil portrait, not of her father in civilian attire but in the dress uniform of a Union general.[35] Controversy immediately swirled when the picture was hung in "a place of distinction in the very shadow of the bronze statue of Theo. G. Bilbo and shown side-by-side with others among Mississippi's great leaders."[36] Henry M. Faser, who had cut down the state flag from the balcony railing in the national Democratic convention of 1948, announced that he was "shocked beyond words" at the spectacle of Ames's portrait in the capitol. The controversy, however, soon subsided, due in no small part to Governor James P. Coleman's opposition to the removal of the picture.[37]

And there Ames's portrait hangs today, symbolic of an era that was tragic not because of the suppression and humiliation of a proud people (which really never occurred), but because victorious northerners and southerners of goodwill failed to take advantage of

33. As reported in Blanche Ames Ames, *Adelbert Ames*, 535.
34. *Ibid.*, 540; Richard N. Current, *Three Carpetbag Governors*, 93.
35. Blanche Ames Ames, *Adelbert Ames*, 515.
36. Clipping from the Jackson *Daily News*, January 20, 1958, in Adelbert Ames Folder, Subject File, Mississippi Department of Archives and History.
37. *Ibid.*; clipping from the Jackson *State Times*, January 20, 1958, in Ames Folder.

the federal-Republican ascendancy in the South, the inchoate state of society there, and the opportunities, however tentative, for racial rapprochement to lay a solid foundation for equal rights, political tolerance and diversity, and the material rehabilitation of the region. The failure to act wisely along these lines during Reconstruction extended the agony of southern history for another seventy-five years—an agony that had begun in the travail of slavery, intensified as a result of the Civil War, and became the common heritage of southerners of both races during the long decades that followed.

Bibliography

PRIMARY SOURCES

PRIVATE MANUSCRIPTS

Duke University Library, Durham, North Carolina

Bryant, John E. Papers.
Dimitry, John B. S. Papers.
Reynolds, Lafayette P. Papers.

Rutherford B. Hayes Memorial Library, Fremont, Ohio

Hayes, Rutherford B. Papers.

Louisiana State University, Department of Archives, Baton Rouge

Pinson, Hamet. Family Papers.

Manuscript Division, Library of Congress, Washington, D.C.

Black, Jeremiah S. Papers.
Butler, Benjamin F. Papers.
Chandler, William E. Papers.
Chandler, Zachariah. Papers.
Claiborne, John F. H. Papers.
Covode, John. Papers.
Garfield, James A. Papers.
Grant, Ulysses S. Papers.
Holt, Joseph. Papers.
Johnson, Andrew. Papers (on microfilm).
McPherson, Edward. Papers.
Sherman, John. Papers.
Sherman, William Tecumseh. Papers.
Simpson, Matthew. Papers.
Stevens, Thaddeus. Papers.
Washburne, Elihu B. Papers.

Mississippi Department of Archives and History, Jackson

Alcorn, James Lusk. Papers.
Ames, Adelbert. Papers, and Folder in Subject File Collection.
Burrus, John C. Papers.

Clark, Charles. Papers.
Craig, Elizabeth. Papers.
Darden, Susan Sillers. Diary.
Davis, Joel R. and George H. Appel. Papers.
Davis, R. A. Papers.
Foster, Anthony. Papers.
Garner, James W. Papers.
George, James Z. Scrapbook.
Hemingway, William L. Papers.
Jones, W. B. and B. H. Smith. Plantation Journal.
Lamar, L. Q. C. and Edward Mayes. Papers.
McCardle, William H. Papers.
McLaurin, Anselm J. Papers.
McRaven, William H. "Mississippi Profiles" (typescript).
McWillie, William. Family Papers.
Matthews, James E. and Samuel. Papers.
Nicholson, Flavellus G. Diary-Journal.
Orr, Jehu A. Papers.
Power, John L. Papers.
Powers, Ridgley C. Folder, Subject File Collection.
Revels, Hiram R. Folder, Subject File Collection.
Reynolds, Lafayette P. Papers.
Shannon, Marmaduke, and Mrs. William O. Crutcher. Family Papers.
Sharkey, H. Clay. Papers.
Stuart, Oscar J. E. Papers.
Swanson, Alexander B., and Mrs. Obedience Yates. Family Papers.
Whitehurst, William N. Papers.
Whitfield, Henry B., and Company. Papers.

Southern Historical Collection, University of North Carolina Library, Chapel Hill

Agnew, Samuel A. Diary.
Alcorn, James Lusk. Papers.
Campbell, Josiah A. P. Papers.
Claiborne, John F. H. Papers.
Fowler, Joseph S. Papers.
King, Thomas B. Papers.
Niles, Jason. Diary and Scrapbook.
Norton, Charles M., John H. Chilton, and William H. Dameron. Family Papers.
Orr, Jehu A. Papers.

University of Tennessee Library, Knoxville

Eaton, John. Papers.

OFFICIAL PAPERS

Mississippi Department of Archives and History, Jackson
Many of the records in the archives are being converted from the old series-volume numbers to a record-group file designation. This process has been completed for the voluminous Governors' Correspondence or Records. See Preliminary Conversion Chart, April 19, 1974, Mississippi Department of Archives and History.

Combined Letterbook of Governors Adelbert Ames and John M. Stone, 1876.

Election Returns, 1871–1900, Records of the Secretary of State of Mississippi.

Governors' Correspondence, Record Group 27, Vols. 68–110.

Letterbook of the Auditor of the State of Mississippi for April 20– September 9, 1868.

Letterbook of the State Treasurer of Mississippi, April 2, 1874– December 16, 1874.

Letterbooks of Governor Adelbert Ames, 1874–76.

Minutes of the State Board of Equalization, 1874–75.

Papers Relating to Railroads in Mississippi, File N-19.

Report of the Levee Commissioners, 1871–75, File N-18.

National Archives, Washington, D.C.

Papers of the United States House of Representatives' Select Committee on Reconstruction, 40th and 41st Congresses, Dealing Primarily with Conditions in the Former States of the Confederacy: Mississippi. Legislative Records, Record Group 233.

Petitions for the Removal of the Legal and Political Disabilities Imposed by the Fourteenth Amendment: Mississippi. Legislative Records, Record Group 233.

Records of the Bureau of Refugees, Freedmen, and Abandoned Lands. Record Group 105.

Records of the Department of Justice, Files for Mississippi. Record Group 60.

Records of the Office of the Inspector General of the Army. Record Group 159.

Records of the United States Army Commands, Fourth Military District, Civil Affairs, 1867–69; Letters Received and Sent in 1867; and Special Orders, 1867. Record Group 98.

Records of the War Department, United States Army Commands, Fourth Military District, Orders, 1867–70. Record Group 98 (microfilm available at the Mississippi Department of Archives and History).

Source-Chronological File, Northern Mississippi, January, 1871–December, 1875, General Records of the Department of Justice. Record Group 60, Microcopy Roll 1.

PRINTED GOVERNMENT DOCUMENTS

United States

Biographical Directory of the American Congress, 1774–1961. Washington, D.C.: Government Printing Office, 1971.

Compendium of the Ninth Census (June 1, 1870) Compiled Pursuant to a Concurrent Resolution of Congress and Under the Direction of the Secretary of the Interior. Washington, D.C.: Government Printing Office, 1872.

Compendium of the Tenth Census (June 1, 1880), Compiled Pursuant to an Act of Congress Approved August 7, 1882. Washington, D.C.: Government Printing Office, 1888.

Congressional Globe, 40th to 42nd Cong., 1869–72.

General Court Martial Orders, from the Headquarters, Fourth Military District, 1868. Vicksburg: Government Printing Office, 1869.

Hilgard, Eugene W. *Report on Cotton Production in the United States*. 2 parts. Washington, D.C.: Government Printing Office, 1884.

Mississippi in 1875: Report of the Select Committee to Inquire into the Mississippi Election of 1875, with the Testimony and Documentary Evidence. 2 vols. Washington, D.C.: Government Printing Office, 1876.

Report of the Commissioner of Agriculture for the Year 1867. Washington, D.C.: Government Printing Office, 1868.

Report of the Commissioner of Agriculture for the Year 1868. Washington, D.C.: Government Printing Office, 1869.

Report of the Commissioner of Agriculture for the Year 1869. Washington, D.C.: Government Printing Office, 1870.

Report of the Commissioner of Education for the Year 1870. Washington, D.C.: Government Printing Office, 1870.

Report of the Commissioner of Education for the Year 1871. Washington, D.C.: Government Printing Office, 1872.

Report of the Commissioner of Education for the Year 1873. Washington, D.C.: Government Printing Office, 1875.

Report of the Commissioner of Education for the Year 1874. Washington, D.C.: Government Printing Office, 1875.

Report of the Commissioner of Education for the Year 1875. Washington, D.C.: Government Printing Office, 1875.

U.S. Bureau of the Census. *Ninth Census of the United States: 1870. Population.* Washington, D.C.: Government Printing Office, 1872.

———. *Ninth Census of the United States: 1870. Wealth and Industry.* Washington, D.C.: Government Printing Office, 1872.

———. *Tenth Census of the United States: 1880. Manufactures.* Washington, D.C.: Government Printing Office, 1883.

———. *Tenth Census of the United States: 1880. Population.* Washington, D.C.: Government Printing Office, 1883.

U.S. Congress. *House Executive Documents.* 40th Cong., 1st Sess., No. 14.

———. *House Executive Documents.* 40th Cong., 1st Sess., No. 34.

———. *House Executive Documents.* 40th Cong., 2nd Sess., No. 342.

———. *House Executive Documents.* 41st Cong., 2nd Sess., No. 1.

———. *House Miscellaneous Documents.* 40th Cong., 3rd Sess., No. 53.

———. *House Reports.* 42nd Cong., 2nd Sess., No. 22, Vols. XI–XII. 2 parts, cited as *Ku Klux Klan Report, Mississippi.*

———. *House Reports.* 43rd Cong., 2nd Sess., No 265.

———. *Senate Executive Documents.* 39th Cong., 2nd Sess., No. 6.

———. *Senate Executive Documents.* 40th Cong., 1st Sess., No. 14.

———. *Senate Executive Documents.* 42nd Cong., 3rd Sess., No. 32.

U.S. *Statutes at Large.* Vols. XIV–XV.

Mississippi

Annual Message of Governor Jas. L. Alcorn to the Mississippi Legislature, Session of 1871. Jackson: Kimball, Raymond, and Co., 1871.

Annual Message of Governor R. C. Powers to the Legislature of Mississippi, Session of 1872. Jackson: Alcorn and Fisher, 1872.

Annual Message of Governor Adelbert Ames, to the Legislature of Mississippi, Session 1875. Jackson: Pilot Publishing, 1875.

Annual Message of Governor Adelbert Ames, to the Legislature of Mississippi, Session 1876. Jackson: Pilot Publishing, 1876.

Annual Message of Governor J. M. Stone, to the Legislature of Mississippi, Session of 1877. Jackson: Power and Barksdale, 1877.

Annual Message and Inaugural Address of Governor J. M. Stone, to the Legislature of Mississippi, Session of 1878. Jackson: Power and Barksdale, 1878.

Annual Report of the Auditor of Public Accounts to the Legislature of Mississippi, for the Year 1872. Jackson: Kimball, Raymond, and Co., 1873.

Annual Report of the Auditor of Public Accounts to the Legislature of Mississippi, for the Year 1873. Jackson: Kimball, Raymond, and Co., 1874.

Annual Report of the Auditor of Public Accounts to the Legislature of Mississippi, for the Year 1875. Jackson: Pilot Publishing, 1876.

Annual Report of the Auditor of Public Accounts to the Legislature of Mississippi, for the Year 1876. Jackson: Power and Barksdale, 1877.

Annual Report of the State Superintendent of Public Education to the Legislature of Mississippi for the Scholastic Year 1874. Jackson: Power and Barksdale, 1877.

Annual Report of the State Superintendent of Public Education, to the Legislature of Mississippi [for the Year 1876]. Jackson: Power and Barksdale, 1875.

Annual Report of the State Superintendent of Public Education to the Legislature of Mississippi for the Scholastic Year 1874. Jackson: Pilot Publishing, 1875.

Annual Report of the State Treasurer for the Year 1875. Jackson: Power and Barksdale, 1876.

Biennial Message of Governor J. M. Stone to the Legislature of Mississippi, Session of 1880. Jackson: Power and Barksdale, 1880.

Biennial Report of the State Superintendent of Public Education to the Legislature of Mississippi, for the Years 1880–81. Jackson: J. L. Power, 1882.

Biennial Report of the State Superintendent of Public Education to the Legislature of Mississippi, for the Scholastic Years 1889–90 and 1890–91. Jackson: Power and McNeily, 1892.

Griggs, Richard, comp. *Guide to Mississippi.* Jackson: Pilot Publishing, 1874.

Impeachment Trial of Adelbert Ames, Governor of the State of Mississippi. Jackson: Power and Barksdale, 1876.

Impeachment Trial of Alexander K. Davis, Lieutenant Governor of Mississippi. Jackson: Power and Barksdale, 1876.

Inaugural Address of Gov. Adelbert Ames to the Mississippi Legislature, Thursday, January 22, 1874. Jackson: Kimball, Raymond, and Co., 1874.

Journal of the Proceedings in the Constitutional Convention of the State of Mississippi, 1868. Jackson: E. Stafford, 1871.

Journals of the Senate and House of Representatives of the State of Mississippi, 1865, 1870–78, 1880. Jackson.

Laws of the State of Mississippi, 1865–67, 1870–78, 1880. Jackson.

Message of Governor Adelbert Ames to the Legislature of the State of Mississippi, Convened in Extra Session, December 17, 1874. Jackson, 1874.

The Revised Code of the Statute Laws of the State of Mississippi [1857]. Jackson: E. Barksdale, 1857.

The Revised Code of the Statute Laws of the State of Mississippi, As Adopted at January Session, A.D. 1871, and Published by Authority of the Legislature. Jackson: Alcorn and Fisher, 1871.

Report of the Levee Commissioner of the State of Mississippi, January, 1872. Jackson: Kimball, Raymond, and Co., 1872.

Report of the Mississippi State Board of Health, for the Years 1878–79. Jackson: Power and Barksdale, 1879.

Special Message of Gov. James L. Alcorn, on the Subject of the Establishment of a University for the Colored People, Etc. Jackson: Kimball, Raymond, and Co., 1871.

Special Message of Gov. Adelbert Ames, to the Legislature of the State of Mississippi, on the Subject of Finance, Session of 1874. Jackson: Kimball, Raymond, and Co., 1874.

The Testimony in the Impeachment of Adelbert Ames, as Governor of Mississippi. Jackson: Power and Barksdale, 1877.

Judicial Decisions: United States Supreme Court

Ex parte McCardle, 6 Wallace 320 (1867).
Ex parte McCardle, 7 Wallace 515 (1868).
Ex parte Yerger, 8 Wallace 75 (1869).

Judicial Decisions: Mississippi State Supreme Court

Frank Hawkins et al. v. *Board of Supervisors of Carroll County,* 50 Miss. 735–66 (1874).
George Donnell v. *State of Mississippi,* 48 Miss. 661–82 (1873).
Mississippi Central Railroad v. *State of Mississippi,* 46 Miss. 157–222 (1871).
Mobile and Ohio Railroad Co. v. *R. J. Mosely, Sheriff,* 52 Miss. 127–37 (1876).
State of Mississippi v. *Charles E. Furlong,* 60 Miss. 839–46 (1883).
The State v. *Vicksburg and Nashville Railroad Company,* 51 Miss. 361–75 (1875).
W. H. Gibbs, Auditor, et al. v. *Joshua Green,* 54 Miss. 592–612 (1877).

PRINTED LETTERS, SPEECHES, REMINISCENCES, DIARIES, AND OTHER CONTEMPORARY SOURCES

Address of J. L. Alcorn to the People of Mississippi. Friar's Point, Miss.: N.p., 1869.

Address to the Reconstruction Committee in Relation to Mississippi. N.p., 1869.

Alcorn, James Lusk. *Views of the Honorable J. L. Alcorn on the Political Situation of Mississippi.* Friar's Point, Miss.: N.p., 1867.

Alvord, John W. *Semi-Annual Report on Schools for Freedmen.* Washington, D.C.: Government Printing Office, 1868.

Ames, Blanche Butler, comp. *Chronicles from the Nineteenth Century: Family Letters of Blanche Butler and Adelbert Ames.* 2 vols. Clinton, Mass.: Colonial Press, 1957.

Appleton's Annual Cyclopaedia and Register of Important Events. 15 vols. New York: D. Appleton, 1861–75.

Beaumont, Betty. *A Business Woman's Journal: A Sequel to "Twelve Years of My Life".* Philadelphia: T. B. Peterson and Brothers, 1888.

Berryhill, S. Newton. *Backwoods Poems.* Columbus, Miss.: Charles C. Martin, 1878.

Biddle, Ellen McGowan. *Reminiscences of a Soldier's Wife.* Philadelphia: J. B. Lippincott, 1907.

Brown, Albert Gallatin. *Statement on Mississippi Affairs, Filed by Permission with the Reconstruction Committee.* Washington, D.C.: N.p., 1869.

Browning, Orville H. *The Diary of Orville Hickman Browning.* 2 vols. Springfield: Illinois State Historical Library, 1933.

Burwell, Armistead. *Dramshops, Industry, and Taxes: An Address to the People of Mississippi.* New York: National Temperance Society, 1875.

Claiborne, John F. H. *The Pine District of Mississippi.* N.p., 1881.

Compton, William M. *The Influence of Alcohol.* N.p., 1877.

Directory of the State Government of Kansas, For the Years 1877 and 1878. N.p., 1878.

Freeman, John D. *Petition of the New Orleans, Jackson, and G. N. Railroad Company to the Governor and Legislature of Mississippi.* Jackson: Clarion Book and Job Printing, 1870.

Furlong, Charles E. *Origin of the Outrages at Vicksburg: Speech of Hon. Chas. E. Furlong, Senator from Warren County, in the Senate of Mississippi, December 18, 1874.* Vicksburg: Vicksburg Herald Print, 1874.

Gibson, J. M. *Memoirs of J. M. Gibson: Terrors of the Civil War and Reconstruction Days.* N.p., 1966.

Hardy, William H. "Recollections of Reconstruction in East and Southeast Mississippi." *Publications of the Mississippi Historical Society,* IV (1901), 105–32, and VIII (1904), 137–51.

Henry, R. H. *Editors I Have Known Since the Civil War.* New Orleans: E. S. Upton Printing, 1922.

Hillyard, M. B., comp. *Letters Descriptive of the Climate, Soil and Resources of Central Mississippi and of the Country Adjacent to the New Orleans, St. Louis & Chicago Railroad.* McComb City, Miss.: Intelligencer Publishing, 1876.

Issues of the Canvass of 1876. Jackson: State Executive Committee of the Democratic-Conservative Party, 1876.

King, Edward. *The Great South.* Edited by W. Magruder Drake and Robert R. Jones. Baton Rouge: Louisiana State University Press, 1972.

Lee, Benjamin A. *Inaugural Message of Hon. Benj. A. Lee, Mayor of the City of Vicksburg, to the Board of Aldermen, September 3, 1872.* Vicksburg: Vicksburg Times, 1872.

Loring, Francis W., and C. F. Atkinson, eds. *Cotton Culture and the South, Considered with Reference to Emigration.* Boston: A. Williams, 1869.

Lynch, John Roy. *Reminiscences of an Active Life: The Autobiography of John Roy Lynch.* Edited with an introduction by John Hope Franklin. Chicago: University of Chicago Press, 1970.

McPherson, Edward. *The Political History of the United States [1865–70].* New York: Negro Universities Press, 1969.

The Mobile and North-Western Railroad. New York: S. W. Green, 1871.

Montgomery, Franklin A. *Reminiscences of a Mississippian in Peace and War.* Cincinnati: Robert Clark Press, 1901.

Morgan, Albert T. *Yazoo, or on the Picket Line of Freedom in the South.* Washington, D.C.: published by the author, 1884.

Nordhoff, Charles. *The Cotton States in the Spring and Summer of 1875.* Originally published in 1875. New York: Burt Franklin, 1965.

Power, John L. *The Epidemic of 1878, in Mississippi: Report of the Yellow Fever Relief Work Through J. L. Power, Grand Secretary of Masons and Grand Treasurer of Odd Fellows.* Jackson: Clarion Steam Publishing, 1879.

Rainwater, Percy L., ed. "The Autobiography of Benjamin Grubb Humphreys, August 26, 1808–December 20, 1882." *Mississippi Valley Historical Review*, XXI (September, 1934), 231–55.

Reid, Whitelaw. *After the War: A Tour of the Southern States, 1865–1866.* Originally published in 1866. New York: Harper and Row, 1965.

Report of Mississippi State Board of Centennial Managers, Including Historical Address of Gen. A. M. West, and Letter from Hon. J. F. H. Claiborne, Descriptive of the Pine Region of Mississippi. Jackson: Clarion Steam Printing, 1877.

Richardson, James D., comp. *A Compilation of the Papers of the*

Presidents. 11 vols. New York: Bureau of National Literature and Art, 1896–1908.

Simrall, Horatio F. *Statement Made Before the Reconstruction Committee on the State of Affairs in Mississippi, February 6, 1869*. N.p., 1869.

Smedes, Susan Dabney. *Memorials of a Southern Planter*. Edited with an Introduction and Notes by Fletcher M. Green. New York: Alfred A. Knopf, 1965.

Somers, Robert. *The Southern States Since the War, 1870–71*. Originally published in 1871. Tuscaloosa: University of Alabama Press, 1965.

The Southern Railroad Association: Lease of the Mississippi Central Railroad; Agreement for Milan Extension; and Articles of Agreement Between the Trustees, June 25, 1868. Wilmington, Del.: Jenkins and Atkinson, 1868.

Speech of Hon. Henry W. Barry, of Mississippi, Delivered in the House of Repres., April 5, 1871, on the Ku Klux Klan Democracy. N.p., 1871.

Speech of Hon. James L. Alcorn of Mississippi, in the United States Senate, May 22, 1874. Washington, D.C.: Government Printing Office, 1874.

Speech of Hon. Henry W. Barry, of Mississippi, Delivered in the House of Repres., April 5, 1871, on the Ku Klux Klan Democracy. N.p., 1871.

Speech of Hon. Geo. J. Mortimer at the Great Mass Meeting of the Republicans at Crystal Springs. N.p., 1869.

Waddel, John N. *Memorials of Academic Life: Being an Historical Sketch of the Waddel Family*. Richmond: Presbyterian Committee of Publication, 1891.

Wall, E. G., comp. *The State of Mississippi: Resources, Condition, and Wants*. Jackson: Clarion Steam Printing, 1879.

Warren, Henry W. *Reminiscences of a Mississippi Carpetbagger*. Holden, Mass.: Davis Press, 1914.

Wells, James M. *The Chisolm Massacre: A Picture of "Home Rule" in Mississippi*. Chicago: Agency for Chisolm Monumental Fund, 1878.

Wilkinson, W. S. M. *Trial of E. M. Yerger Before a Military Commission for the Killing of Bv't-Col. Joseph G. Crane, at Jackson, Miss., June 8, 1869*. Jackson: Clarion Book and Job Printing, 1869.

Wilson, James Grant, ed. *General Grant's Letters to a Friend, 1861–1880*. New York: T. Y. Crowell, 1973.

CONTEMPORARY PERIODICALS

Commercial and Financial Chronicle: Banker's Gazette, Commercial Times, Railway Monitor, and Insurance Journal, 1874.
De Bow's Review, After the War Series, 1867.
Harper's Weekly, 1870.
Merchant's Magazine and Commercial Review, 1869.
Mississippi Educational Journal, 1871–72.
Nation: A Weekly Journal Devoted to Politics, Literature, Science, and Art, 1869–70.
Southern Field and Factory: A Monthly Magazine Devoted to Agriculture, Horticulture, Manufactures, and Mechanic Arts, 1871–73.

NEWSPAPERS

Mississippi

Beauregard and Wesson *Times*, 1874.
Beulah *Bolivar Times*, 1870.
Brandon *Republican*, 1872, 1876–77.
Carrollton *Mississippi Conservative*, 1874.
Columbus *Democrat*, 1872.
Columbus *Press*, 1872–73.
Columbus *Southern Sentinel*, 1867, 1869.
Columbus *Weekly Index*, 1875.
Corinth *Sub-Soiler*, 1874.
Corinth *Weekly News*, 1868.
Crystal Springs *Monitor*, 1873.
Edwards *Citizen*, 1877.
Forest *Ku-Klux*, 1871.
Forest *Register*, 1868–70.
Friar's Point *Weekly Delta*, 1869–70.
Greenville *Weekly Times*, 1874–75.
Greenwood *Times*, 1873.
Greenwood *Yazoo Valley Flag*, 1878.
Hazlehurst *Copiahan*, 1869, 1875.
Hernando *Weekly Press*, 1869–70.
Hernando *Weekly Press and Times*, 1872.
Hinds County Gazette (Raymond), 1867–77, 1882–83, 1885.
Jackson *Clarion*, 1866–69.
Jackson *Farmers' Vindicator*, 1877.
Jackson *Pilot*, 1871, 1873, 1875.
Jackson *Semi-Weekly Pilot*, 1871.
Jackson *State Leader*, 1872.
Jackson *Times*, 1875.

Jackson *Weekly Clarion*, 1867, 1869–78, 1881, 1883.
Jackson *Weekly Mississippian*, 1858.
Jackson *Weekly Pilot*, 1869–71, 1875.
Liberty *Advocate*, 1866.
Macon *Beacon*, 1875.
Meridian *Chronicle*, 1868.
Meridian *Semi-Weekly Gazette*, 1867.
Meridian *Weekly Gazette*, 1867.
Monticello *Advocate*, 1874.
Natchez *Courier*, 1863.
Natchez *Democrat*, 1867, 1874–77.
Natchez *Tri-Weekly Courier*, 1868.
Natchez *Tri-Weekly Democrat*, 1867.
Natchez *Weekly Democrat*, 1867–72, 1874–75.
Natchez *Weekly Courier*, 1868.
Newton *Reporter*, 1878.
Pascagoula *Star*, 1874–75, 1877–78.
Port Gibson *Southern Reveille*, 1877.
Summit *Conservative Times*, 1878.
Vicksburg *Herald*, 1867–68, 1870, 1875.
Vicksburg *Journal*, 1865.
Vicksburg *Plain Dealer*, 1875.
Vicksburg *Times*, 1867–71, 1874–75.
Vicksburg *Times and Republican*, 1869–74.
Vicksburg *Vicksburger*, 1874.
Vicksburg *Weekly Herald*, 1868.
Vicksburg *Weekly Republican*, 1868.
Water Valley *Mississippi Central*, 1874.
Yazoo City *Herald*, 1876.
Yazoo City *Mississippi Democrat*, 1868.
Yazoo City *Sentinel*, 1878.

Other

Kansas City *Journal*, 1904.
Kansas City *Times*, 1914.
Los Angeles *Times*, 1912.
Memphis *Avalanche*, 1871.
Mobile *Register*, 1868, 1871.
New Orleans *Picayune*, 1865, 1868.
New York *Times*, 1867–75, 1907, 1909, 1911, 1920.
New York *Tribune*, 1865, 1868–69, 1875.
Phoenix *Arizona Gazette*, 1912.
Topeka *Daily Capital*, 1929.

Washington (D.C.) *New Era*, 1870.
Washington (D.C.) *New National Era*, 1870–74.
Wichita *Morning Eagle*, 1904, 1912.

SECONDARY SOURCES

BOOKS

Alderman, Edwin A., *et al.*, eds. *Library of Southern Literature.* 16 vols. Atlanta: Martin and Hoyt, 1907–13.

Alexander, Thomas B. *Political Reconstruction in Tennessee.* Nashville: Vanderbilt University Press, 1950.

Ames, Blanche Ames. *Adelbert Ames, 1835–1933: General, Senator, Governor.* New York: Argosy-Antiquarian, 1964.

Beale, Howard K. *The Critical Year: A Study of Andrew Johnson and Reconstruction.* New York: Harcourt, Brace, 1930.

Biographical and Historical Memoirs of Mississippi. 2 vols. Chicago: Goodspeed Publishing, 1891.

Boyle, James E. *Cotton and the New Orleans Cotton Exchange: A Century of Commercial Evolution.* Garden City, N.Y.: Country Life Press, 1934.

Brandfon, Robert L. *Cotton Kingdom of the New South: A History of the Yazoo Mississippi Delta from Reconstruction to the Twentieth Century.* Cambridge: Harvard University Press, 1967.

Cabaniss, James A. *A History of the University of Mississippi.* Oxford: University of Mississippi, 1949.

Carpenter, John A. *Ulysses S. Grant.* New York: Twayne Publishers, 1970.

Carroll, Thomas B. *Historical Sketches of Oktibbeha County (Mississippi).* Gulfport: Dixie Press, 1931.

Carter, Hodding. *Their Words Were Bullets: The Southern Press in War, Reconstruction, and Peace.* Athens: University of Georgia Press, 1969.

Claiborne, John F. H. *Mississippi, as a Province, Territory and State, with Biographical Notices of Eminent Citizens.* Jackson: Power and Barksdale, 1880. Reprinted in 1964.

Conerly, Luke W. *Pike County, Mississippi, 1798–1876.* Nashville: Brandon Printing, 1909.

Coulter, E. Merton. *The South During Reconstruction, 1865–1877.* Baton Rouge: Louisiana State University Press, 1947.

Cox, LaWanda, and John H. Cox, eds. *Reconstruction, the Negro, and the New South.* New York: Harper and Row, 1973.

Current, Richard N. *Three Carpetbag Governors.* Baton Rouge: Louisiana State University Press, 1967.

Fairman, Charles. *Reconstruction and Reunion, 1864–1888.* Vol. VI of *History of the Supreme Court of the United States*. New York: Macmillan, 1971.

Fleming, Walter L. *The Freedmen's Savings Bank: A Chapter in the Economic History of the Negro Race*. Chapel Hill: University of North Carolina, 1927.

Fredrickson, George M. *The Black Image in the White Mind: The Debate on Afro-American Character and Destiny, 1817–1914*. New York: Harper and Row, 1971.

Garner, James W. *Reconstruction in Mississippi*. Originally published in 1901. Gloucester, Mass.: Peter Smith, 1964.

Gillette, William. *The Right to Vote: Politics and the Passage of the Fifteenth Amendment*. Baltimore: Johns Hopkins Press, 1965.

Hardy, William H., and Toney A. Hardy. *No Compromise with Principle: Autobiography and Biography of William Harris Hardy*. New York: Stratford Press, 1946.

Harris, William C. *Presidential Reconstruction in Mississippi*. Baton Rouge: Louisiana State University Press, 1967.

Harrison, Robert W. *Levee Districts and Levee Building in Mississippi: A Study of State and Local Efforts to Control Mississippi River Floods*. Stoneville, Miss.: Delta Council, 1951.

Hartenstein, Ernest. *The Epidemic of 1878 and Its Homeopathic Treatment: A General History of the Origins, Progress, and End of the Plague in the Mississippi Valley*. New Orleans: J. S. Rivers, 1879.

Hickman, Nollie. *Mississippi Harvest: Lumbering in the Longleaf Pine Belt, 1840–1915*. Oxford: University of Mississippi Press, 1962.

Horn, Stanley F. *Invisible Empire: The Story of the Ku Klux Klan, 1866–1871*. Boston: Houghton Mifflin, 1939.

James, D. Clayton. *Antebellum Natchez*. Baton Rouge: Louisiana State University Press, 1968.

Kirwan, Albert D. *Revolt of the Rednecks, Mississippi Politics: 1876–1925*. New York: Harper and Row, 1965.

Klingberg, Frank W. *The Southern Claims Commission*. Berkeley: University of California Press, 1955.

Lang, John H. *History of Harrison County, Mississippi*. Gulfport: Dixie Press, 1936.

Leech, Margaret. *In the Days of McKinley*. New York: Harper and Brothers, 1959.

Lynch, James D. *The Bench and Bar of Mississippi*. New York: E. J. Hale and Son, 1881.

Lynch, John R. *The Facts of Reconstruction*. Edited with an introduction by William C. Harris. Indianapolis: Bobbs-Merrill, 1970.

————. *Some Historical Errors of James Ford Rhodes*. Boston: Cornhill, 1922.

McGrane, Reginald C. *Foreign Bondholders and American State Debts*. New York: Macmillan, 1935.

McLemore, Richard A., ed. *A History of Mississippi*. 2 vols. Hattiesburg: University and College Press of Mississippi, 1973.

Maddex, Jack P., Jr. *The Virginia Conservatives, 1867–1879*. Chapel Hill: University of North Carolina Press, 1970.

Mantell, Martin E. *Johnson, Grant, and the Politics of Reconstruction*. New York: Columbia University Press, 1973.

Mayes, Edward. *Lucius Q. C. Lamar: His Life, Times, and Speeches, 1825–1893*. Nashville: Methodist Episcopal Church, South, 1896.

Murphy, James B. *L. Q. C. Lamar: Pragmatic Patriot*. Baton Rouge: Louisiana State University Press, 1973.

National Union Catalog: Pre-1956 Imprints. 329 vols. completed. London: Mansell Information Publishing, 1968—.

Noble, Stuart G. *Forty Years of the Public Schools in Mississippi, with Special Reference to the Negro*. New York: Columbia University Teachers College, 1918.

Nordin, D. Sven. *Rich Harvest: A History of the Grange, 1867–1900*. Jackson: University Press of Mississippi, 1974.

Pereyra, Lillian A. *James Lusk Alcorn: Persistent Whig*. Baton Rouge: Louisiana State University Press, 1966.

Portrait and Biographical Album of Sedgwick County, Kansas. Chicago: Chapman Brothers, 1888.

Ramsdell, Charles W. *Reconstruction in Texas*. Gloucester, Mass.: Peter Smith, 1964.

Rand, Clayton. *Men of Spine in Mississippi*. Gulfport: Dixie Press, 1940.

Randall, James G., and David Donald. *The Civil War and Reconstruction*. Boston: D. C. Heath, 1969.

Ratchford, B. U. *American State Debts*. Durham: Duke University Press, 1941.

Roark, James L. *Masters Without Slaves: Southern Planters in the Civil War and Reconstruction*. New York: W. W. Norton, 1977.

Rowland, Dunbar. *Courts, Judges, and Lawyers of Mississippi, 1798–1935*. Jackson: Hederman Bros., 1935.

————, ed. *Mississippi: Comprising Sketches of Counties, Towns, Events, Institutions, and Persons, Arranged in Cyclopedic Form*. 3 vols. Atlanta: Southern Historical Publishing Association, 1907.

Sefton, James E. *The United States Army and Reconstruction, 1865–1877*. Baton Rouge: Louisiana State University Press, 1967.

Simkins, Francis B., and Robert H. Woody, *South Carolina During*

Reconstruction. Chapel Hill: University of North Carolina Press, 1932.

Singletary, Otis A. *Negro Militia and Reconstruction*. Austin: University of Texas Press, 1957.

Stampp, Kenneth M. *The Era of Reconstruction, 1865–1877*. New York: Alfred A. Knopf, 1965.

Stover, John F. *The Railroads of the South, 1865–1900*. Chapel Hill: University of North Carolina Press, 1955.

Taylor, Joe Gray. *Louisiana Reconstructed, 1863–1877*. Baton Rouge: Louisiana State University Press, 1974.

Thigpen, Samuel G. *Pearl River: Highway to Glory Land*. Kingsport, Tenn.: Kingsport Press, 1965.

Trefousse, Hans L. *The Radical Republicans: Lincoln's Vanguard for Racial Justice*. New York: Alfred A. Knopf, 1969.

Trelease, Allen W. *Reconstruction: The Great Experiment*. New York: Harper and Row, 1972.

———. *White Terror: The Ku Klux Klan Conspiracy and Southern Reconstruction*. New York: Harper and Row, 1971.

Vaughn, William P. *Schools for All: The Blacks & Public Education in the South, 1865–1877*. Lexington: University Press of Kentucky, 1974.

Wallace, Jesse Thomas. *A History of Negroes of Mississippi from 1865 to 1890*. Clinton, Miss.: n.p., 1927.

Watkins, James L. *King Cotton: A Historical and Statistical Review, 1790 to 1908*. New York: James L. Watkins and Sons, 1908.

Wharton, Vernon Lane. *The Negro in Mississippi, 1865–1890*. Chapel Hill: University of North Carolina Press, 1947.

Winston, E. T. *Story of Pontotoc County, Mississippi*. Pontotoc: Pontotoc Progressive Print, 1931.

Woodman, Harold D. *King Cotton and His Retainers: Financing and Marketing the Cotton Crop of the South, 1800–1925*. Lexington: University of Kentucky Press, 1968.

Woodward, C. Vann. *Reunion and Reaction: The Compromise of 1877 and the End of Reconstruction*. Boston: Little Brown, 1951.

Wooster, Ralph A. *The People in Power: Courthouse and Statehouse in the Lower South, 1850–1860*. Knoxville: University of Tennessee Press, 1969.

Zuber, Richard L. *North Carolina During Reconstruction*. Raleigh: North Carolina State Department of Archives and History, 1969.

ARTICLES

Abney, M. G. "Reconstruction in Pontotoc County." *Publications of the Mississippi Historical Society*, XI (1910), 229–69.

Alexander, Thomas B. "Persistent Whiggery in Mississippi: The Hinds County Gazette." *Journal of Mississippi History*, XXIII (April, 1961), 71–93.

Brough, Charles H. "History of Taxation in Mississippi." *Publications of the Mississippi Historical Society*, II (1899), 113–24.

Coleman, Edward Clarke, "Reconstruction in Attala County." *Publications of the Mississippi Historical Society*, X (1909), 147–61.

Current, Richard N. "Carpetbaggers Reconsidered," in David H. Pinkney and Theodore Ropp (eds.), *A Festschrift for Frederick B. Artz*. Durham: Duke University Press, 1964.

Ellem, Warren A. "Who Were the Mississippi Scalawags?" *Journal of Southern History*, XXXVIII (May, 1972), 217–40.

Gates, Paul W. "Federal Land Policy in the South, 1866–1888." *Journal of Southern History*, VI (August, 1940), 303–30.

Halsell, Willie D., ed. "Republican Factionalism in Mississippi, 1882–1884." *Journal of Southern History*, VIII (February, 1941), 84–101.

Harris, William C. "The Creed of the Carpetbaggers: The Case of Mississippi." *Journal of Southern History*, XL (May, 1974), 199–224.

———. "James Lynch: Black Leader in Southern Reconstruction." *Historian*, XXXIV (November, 1971), 40–61.

———. "A Reconsideration of the Mississippi Scalawag." *Journal of Mississippi History*, XXXII (February, 1970), 3–42.

Humphrey, George D. "Public Education for Whites in Mississippi." *Journal of Mississippi History*, III (January, 1941), 26–36.

Jones, J. H. "Reconstruction in Wilkinson County." *Publications of the Mississippi Historical Society*, VIII (1904), 153–75.

Kendel, Julia. "Reconstruction in Lafayette County." *Publications of the Mississippi Historical Society*, XIII (1913), 223–72.

Kutler, Stanley I. "Ex parte McCardle: Judicial Impotency? The Supreme Court and Reconstruction Reconsidered." *American Historical Review*, LXXII (April, 1967), 835–51.

Kyle, John W. "Reconstruction in Panola County." *Publications of the Mississippi Historical Society*, XIII (1913), 9–98.

Lang, Herbert H. "J. F. H. Claiborne at 'Laurel Wood' Plantation, 1853–1870." *Journal of Mississippi History*, XVIII (February, 1956), 1–17.

Lipscomb, Dabney. "William Ward." *Publications of the Mississippi Historical Society*, II (1899), 23–42.

McNeily, John S. "Climax and Collapse of Reconstruction in Mississippi, 1874–1876." *Publications of the Mississippi Historical Society*, XII (1912), 283–474.

——. "The Enforcement Act of 1871 and the Ku Klux Klan in Mississippi." *Publications of the Mississippi Historical Society,* IX (1906), 109–71.

——. "War and Reconstruction in Mississippi, 1863–1890." *Publications of the Mississippi Historical Society, Centenary Series,* II (1918), 165–535.

Magee, Hattie. "Reconstruction in Lawrence and Jeff Davis Counties." *Publications of the Mississippi Historical Society,* XI (1910), 163–204.

Nichols, Irby C. "Reconstruction in DeSoto County." *Publications of the Mississippi Historical Society,* XI (1910), 295–316.

Puckett, Ernest F. "Reconstruction in Monroe County." *Publications of the Mississippi Historical Society,* XI (1910), 103–61.

Smiley, David M. "Cassius M. Clay and the Mississippi Election of 1875." *Journal of Mississippi History,* XIX (October, 1957), 252–62.

Stover, John F. "Colonel Henry S. McComb, Mississippi Railroad Adventurer." *Journal of Mississippi History,* XVII (July, 1955), 177–90.

Timberlake, Elsie. "Did the Reconstruction Regime Give Mississippi Her Public Schools?" *Publications of the Mississippi Historical Society,* XII (1912), 72–93.

Wade, John W. "Lands of the Liquidating Levee Board Through Litigation and Legislation." *Publications of the Mississippi Historical Society,* IX (1906), 273–313.

Watkins, Ruth. "Reconstruction in Newton County." *Publications of the Mississippi Historical Society,* XI (1910), 205–25.

Witty, Fred M. "Reconstruction in Carroll and Montgomery Counties." *Publications of the Mississippi Historical Society,* X (1909), 115–34.

Theses and Dissertations

Binning, Francis Wayne. "Henry Clay Warmoth and Louisiana Reconstruction." Ph.D. dissertation, University of North Carolina, Chapel Hill, 1969.

Currie, James T. "Vicksburg, 1863–1870: The Promise and the Reality of Reconstruction on the Mississippi." Ph.D. dissertation, University of Virginia, 1975.

Ferguson, James S. "Agrarianism in Mississippi: 1871–1900: A Study in Non-Conformity." Ph.D. dissertation, University of North Carolina, Chapel Hill, 1952.

——. "The Granger Movement in Mississippi." M.A. thesis, Louisiana State University, 1940.

Ganus, Clifton L., Jr. "The Freedmen's Bureau in Mississippi."
Ph.D. dissertation, Tulane University, 1953.
Moore, Ross H. "Social and Economic Conditions in Mississippi During Reconstruction." Ph.D. dissertation, Duke University, 1938.
Swinney, Everette. "Suppressing the Ku Klux Klan: The Enforcement of the Reconstruction Amendments, 1870–1874." Ph.D. dissertation, University of Texas, Austin, 1966.

INTERVIEWS

Dabney, Lucius Bryan, August 8, 1966.

Index

745

Index

Mississippi Educational Journal, 318, 321n
Mississippi Mills, 571
Mississippi Planters, Manufacturers, and
  Mechanics' Association, 376–77, 485,
  493–94
Mississippi State Medical Association, 365n,
  592
Mississippi Supreme Court, 338, 374, 417,
  448–49, 480, 491–92, 553, 555–56, 567,
  610, 698
Mississippi Valley Company, 524–25
Mississippi Valley Navigation Company,
  503–504
Mobile, Ala., 46, 238n, 522, 531–32, 537,
  563
Mobile and Northwestern Railroad, 426,
  531–39 *passim*, 548, 550
Mobile and Ohio Railroad, 31,440, 500, 531,
  562–63, 566, 567
Mobile *Register*, 532, 537, 672
Money, Hernando D., 600, 653
Monroe County, 31, 172, 328, 329–30, 386
Montgomery, Benjamin T., 7
Montgomery, Isaiah, 278
Moore, B. F., 398
Moore, J. Aaron, 95–96, 397–98
Morgan, Albert T., 119–20, 130, 140, 144–
  46, 247, 312, 325, 425, 438, 475, 660,
  661–62, 684n, 717, 720
Morgan, Charles, 119, 120
Morgan, James B., 653, 691
Morphis, John L., 531, 625, 627n
Morris, Joshua S., 16, 17, 18, 94, 104n, 139,
  242n, 244, 251, 317, 448–49, 477, 536,
  580, 599, 620, 625, 633n, 688, 715
Morton, Oliver P., 215, 693, 694
Mosely, Robert J., 396–97
Muldrow, Henry L., 691
Murdock, Abram, 338–39
Murdock, John, 380
Musgrove, Henry, 244, 291–92, 302, 359,
  417, 434, 466, 468, 512, 523, 555, 604,
  615, 620, 625, 627n, 681, 702, 720
Myers, Cyrus, 210n
Mygatt, Alston, 70, 101–102, 104, 116, 129,
  130, 140–41, 144, 145, 228, 462, 478, 533,
  537, 550

Nabors, Benjamin D., 627n
Natchez, Jackson, and Columbus Railroad,
  49, 285–86, 535, 541–45, 548, 550, 554
Natchez, Miss., 15, 82, 122, 261, 266, 280–
  81, 284, 285–86, 299n, 421, 427, 445, 458,
530, 535, 541–42, 544, 547, 586, 587,
  589–91, 592, 642, and *passim*
Natchez (steamboat), 585, 587
Natchez and Jackson Railroad. *See* Natchez,
  Jackson, and Columbus Railroad
Natchez *Democrat*, 113–14, 165, 286, 287,
  289, 450, 480, 504, 624, 626, 644–45,
  651, 675, 679, 690, 695, 696, 702
Natchez *New South*, 475–76
Natchez *Weekly Democrat*, 54n, 74n
National Freedmen's Savings and Trust
  Bank, 279
National Union Republican party, 224–28,
  234–43 *passim*, 248–58 passim, 411
Negro: suffrage, 2, 4–5, 79, 89, 90, 96, 120,
  127, 128, 143–44, 162, 170, 197, 208,
  215–16, 249, 259, 268, 657–58, 721–22;
  rights, 18–19, 29, 56, 78, 96, 104, 128, 152,
  222–23, 246–47, 249, 268, 408, 414,
  437–52, 474, 602–603, 683, 707; emigration, 31–32, 510, 688; officeholding,
  55–56, 107, 249, 268, 427–28; leaders,
  82, 94–96, 460–61, 542, 682–83, 714;
  education, 128, 249, 316–33 *passim*, 343,
  347–50, 702–703; immigration, 506,
  508–10; religion, 577–79
Negroes: Freedmen's Bureau aid to, 19–24;
  as laborers, 22–25, 31–33, 78, 128, 274–
  75, 384, 483–84, 574–76; economic conditions of, 26, 135–36, 278–80, 575, 606,
  612–13; and Humphreys proclamation,
  29–30; registration of, as voters, 73–76;
  and cooperationists, 82–83; in Republican party formation, 94–96; voting by,
  109, 194–95, 256–60 *passim*, 649; in constitutional convention, 115, 146, 150; and
  support for conservatives, 175–76, 188,
  199–200, 219, 425, 470, 628, 642, 644–
  45, 655–56, 677–81 *passim*; intimidation
  of, 176, 191–94, 635, 636, 659, 677–86
  passim; National Union Republicans and,
  224, 225, 239–40, 242–43, 250, 258; in
  legislature, 264, 360, 428, 479, 633, 656;
  and Alcorn, 301, 307, 414–15, 418; and
  militia, 392–93, 462, 651, 662–63, 670–
  71; New Departure and, 410–12, 455, 470;
  political dominance by, 419–23, 427–28;
  and Powers, 460; on immigration, 505;
  and railroad promotion, 539, 542–43,
  549–50, 556; mentioned, *passim*
Neilson, C. P., 240
Nelson, Mrs. Ellen, 605
New, C. B., 409